Lecture Notes in Computer Science 12393

More information about this series at http://www.springer.com/series/7409

Min Song · Il-Yeol Song · Gabriele Kotsis ·
A Min Tjoa · Ismail Khalil (Eds.)

Big Data Analytics
and Knowledge Discovery

22nd International Conference, DaWaK 2020
Bratislava, Slovakia, September 14–17, 2020
Proceedings

Springer

Editors
Min Song
Department of Library
and Information
Yonsei University
Seoul, Korea (Republic of)

Gabriele Kotsis
Johannes Kepler University
of Linz
Linz, Austria

Ismail Khalil
Johannes Kepler University
of Linz
Linz, Oberösterreich, Austria

Il-Yeol Song
Drexel University
Philadelphia, PA, USA

A Min Tjoa
Software Competence
Center Hagenberg (Au)
Vienna, Wien, Austria

ISSN 0302-9743   ISSN 1611-3349   (electronic)
Lecture Notes in Computer Science
ISBN 978-3-030-59064-2   ISBN 978-3-030-59065-9   (eBook)
https://doi.org/10.1007/978-3-030-59065-9

LNCS Sublibrary: SL3 – Information Systems and Applications, incl. Internet/Web, and HCI

This Springer imprint is published by the registered company Springer Nature Switzerland AG
The registered company address is: Gewerbestrasse 11, 6330 Cham, Switzerland

Preface

During the past 21 years, the International Conference on Big Data Analytics and Knowledge Discovery (DaWaK) has been a prominent international forum in data warehousing, big data management, and analytics areas. DaWaK has brought researchers and practitioners together to exchange their experience and knowledge in developing and managing the systems, applications, and solutions for data warehousing, big data analytics, and knowledge discovery. With a track record of 22 editions, DaWaK has established itself as a high-quality forum for researchers, practitioners, and developers in the field of big data analytics.

This year's conference (DaWaK 2020) also builds on this tradition, facilitating the interdisciplinary exchange of ideas, theories, techniques, experiences, and future research directions. The DaWaK submission covered broad research areas on both theoretical and practical aspects of big data analytics and knowledge discovery. In the areas of big data analytics, the topics covered by submitted papers included data lakes, meta-data management, data engineering for data science, ETL processing, database encryption, text analytics, data integration, data-driven paradigms, NoSQL databases, and big data and cloud computing. In the areas of knowledge discovery, the topics covered by submitted papers included not only traditional data mining papers on classification, regression, clustering, anomaly detection, association rules, recommender systems, ensemble techniques, but also recent hot topics on machine learning algorithms and optimization, deep learning, graph analytics, stream data analytics, text analytics, and privacy-preserving data analysis. In the areas of application-oriented areas, the topics covered by submitted papers included energy-related data, smart meter stream data, financial time-series data, credit scoring, smart farming, tour data analysis, and biomedical data analysis. It was notable to see that some innovative papers covered emerging real-world applications such as smart farming, smart building, and stream data analytics. All these diverse papers show that DaWaK has become a key forum for innovative developments and real-world applications in the areas of big data analytics and knowledge discovery technologies.

Dawak 2020's call for papers attracted 77 papers from 25 countries, from which the Program Committee selected 15 full papers and 14 short papers, yielding an acceptance rate of 20% for full paper category and of 38% for both categories. Each paper was reviewed by at least three reviewers and in some cases up to four. Accepted papers cover a variety of research areas on both theoretical and practical aspects. Some trends found in accepted papers include data lakes, as a new generation of big data repository, data pre-processing, data mining, text mining, sequences, graph mining, and parallel processing. Thanks to the reputation of DaWaK, selected best papers of DaWaK 2020 will be invited for a special issue in *Data & Knowledge Engineering* (DKE, Elsevier) journal. We would like to thank the DKE Editor-in-Chief, Prof. Peter P. Chen, who approved the special issue.

Although COVID-19 struck all aspects of daily lives, and holding an international conference became extremely difficult, DaWak 2020 succeeded in terms of the number of submissions and the quality of submitted papers. We would like to thank all the authors who submitted their papers to DaWaK 2020, as their contributions formed the basis of an excellent program for DaWaK 2020. We would also like to express our sincere gratitude to all Program Committee members and the external reviewers who reviewed the papers profoundly and in a timely manner. Finally, we would like to thank the support and guidance from the DEXA conference organizers, especially, Prof. Ismail Khalil for having provided a great deal of assistance in planning and administering DaWaK 2020.

For virtual conference attendants, we hope they enjoy the technical program and interaction with colleagues from all over the world. For readers of these proceedings, we hope these papers are interesting and they provide insights and ideas for you to conduct future research.

September 2020   Min Song
                                                                      Il-Yeol Song

Organization

General Chair

Bernhard Moser   Software Competence Center Hagenberg (SCCH), Austria

Program Committee Chairs

Min Song   Yonsei University, South Korea
Il-Yeol Song   Drexel University, USA

Steering Committee

Gabriele Kotsis   Johannes Kepler University Linz, Austria
A Min Tjoa   Vienna University of Technology, Austria
Ismail Khalil   Johannes Kepler University Linz, Austria

Program Committee and Reviewer

Alberto Abello   Universitat Politècnica de Catalunya, Spain
Julien Aligon   Université de Toulouse, France
Toshiyuki Amagasa   University of Tsukuba, Japan
Amin Beheshti   Macquarie University, Australia
Ladjel Bellatreche   LIAS, ENSMA, France
Sadok Ben Yahia   Université de Tunis El Manar, Tunis
Fadila Bentayeb   ERIC, Université Lumière Lyon 2, France
Rafael Berlanga   Universitat Jaume I, Spain
Jorge Bernardino   ISEC, Polytechnic Institute of Coimbra, Portugal
Besim Bilalli   Universitat Politècnica de Catalunya, Spain
Sandro Bimonte   Irstea, France
Kamel Boukhalfa   University of Science and Technology Houari Boumediene, Algeria
Stephane Bressan   National University of Singapore, Singapore
Tania Cerquitelli   Politecnico di Torino, Italy
Sharma Chakravarthy   The University of Texas at Arlington, USA
Isabelle Comyn-Wattiau   ESSEC Business School, France
Alfredo Cuzzocrea   ICAR-CNR, University of Calabria, Italy
Laurent D'Orazio   University of Rennes, CNRS-IRISA, France
Jérôme Darmont   Université de Lyon, France
Karen Davis   Miami University, USA
Ibrahim Dellal   LIAS, ENSMA, France
Curtis Dyreson   Utah State University, USA

Markus Endres	University of Passau, Germany
Leonidas Fegaras	The University of Texas at Arlington, USA
Philippe Fournier-Viger	Harbin Institute of Technology, China
Filippo Furfaro	DIMES, University of Calabria, Italy
Pedro Furtado	Universidade de Coimbra, CISUC, Portugal
Carlos Garcia-Alvarado	Pivotal Inc., USA
Kazuo Goda	The University of Tokyo, Japan
Matteo Golfarelli	University of Bologna, Italy
Marcin Gorawski	Silesian University of Technology and Wroclaw University of Technology, Poland
Hyoil Han	Illinois State University, USA
Frank Höppner	Ostfalia University of Applied Sciences, Germany
Stephane Jean	LISI, ENSMA, University of Poitiers, France
Petar Jovanovic	Universitat Politècnica de Catalunya, Barcelona Tech, Spain
Vana Kalogeraki	Athens University of Economics and Business, Greece
Min-Soo Kim	DGIST, South Korea
Uday Kiran	The University of Tokyo, Japan
Nicolas Labroche	Université François-Rabelais Tours, France
Jens Lechtenbörger	University of Muenster, Germany
Young-Koo Lee	Kyung Hee University, South Korea
Jae-Gil Lee	Korea Advanced Institute of Science and Technology, South Korea
Mong Li Lee	National University of Singapore, Singapore
Wolfgang Lehner	TU Dresden, Germany
Daniel Lemire	LICEF Research Center, Université du Québec, Canada
Sebastian Link	The University of Auckland, New Zealand
Xiufeng Liu	Danish Technical University, Denmark
Sofian Maabout	LaBRI, University of Bordeaux, France
Sanjay Madria	Missouri S & T, USA
Patrick Marcel	Université François Rabelais Tours, France
Adriana Marotta	Universidad de la Republica, Uruguay
Alejandro Maté	University of Alicante, Spain
Jose-Norberto Mazon	University of Alicante, Spain
Amin Mesmoudi	LIAS, Université de Poitiers, France
Jun Miyazaki	Tokyo Institute of Technology, Japan
Anirban Mondal	The University of Tokyo, Japan
Yang-Sae Moon	Kangwon National University, South Korea
Yasuhiko Morimoto	Hiroshima University, Japan
Sergi Nadal	Universitat Politècnica de Catalunya, Spain
Bernd Neumayr	Johannes Kepler University Linz, Austria
Makoto Onizuka	Osaka University, Japan
Carlos Ordonez	University of Houston, USA
Torben Bach Pedersen	Aalborg University, Denmark
Verónika Peralta	University of Tours, France
Praveen Rao	University of Missouri, USA

Stefano Rizzi	University of Bologna, Italy
Oscar Romero	Universitat Politècnica de Catalunya, Spain
Keun Ho Ryu	Chungbuk National University, South Korea
Alkis Simitsis	HP Labs, USA
Benkrid Soumia	ESI, Algeria
Dimitri Theodoratos	New Jersey Institute of Technology, USA
Maik Thiele	TU Dresden, Germany
Christian Thomsen	Aalborg University, Denmark
Predrag Tosic	Washington State University, USA
Juan Trujillo	University of Alicante, Spain
Panos Vassiliadis	University of Ioannina, Greece
Robert Wrembel	Poznan University of Technology, Poland
Hwan-Seung Yong	Ewha Womans University, South Korea
Yongjun Zhu	Sungkyunkwan University, South Korea

Organizers

Contents

Machine Learning and Deep Learning

Supervised Learning

Unsupervised Learning

Position Paper

Analyzing the Research Landscape of DaWaK Papers from 1999 to 2019

Tatsawan Timakum[1,2] , Soobin Lee[1] , Il-Yeol Song[3], and Min Song[1(✉)]

[1] Department of Library and Information Science, Yonsei University, Seoul, Korea
{tatsawan_9,bini122,min.song}@yonsei.ac.kr
[2] Department of Information Sciences, Chiang Mai Rajabhat University, Chiang Mai, Thailand
[3] Drexel University, Philadelphia, PA, USA
songiy@drexel.edu

Abstract. The International Conference on Big Data Analytics and Knowledge Discovery (DaWaK) has become a key conduit to exchange experience and knowledge among researchers and practitioners in the field of data warehousing and knowledge discovery. This study has quantitatively analyzed the 775 papers published in DaWaK from 1999 to 2019. This study presents the knowledge structure of the DaWaK papers and identifies the evolution of research topics in this discipline. Several text mining techniques were applied to analyze the contents of the research fields and to structure the knowledge presented at DaWaK. Dirichlet Multinomial Regression (DMR) is used to examine the trend of the research topics. Research metrics were used to identify conference and paper performance in terms of citation counts, readers, and the number of downloads. The study shows that DaWaK research outcomes have been receiving consistent attention from the scholarly community in the past 21 years. The 775 papers were cited by 4,339 times, marking the average number of citations of each proceeding as 207 times, and the average number of citations per published paper as six times.

Keywords: Content analysis · Data warehousing knowledge mapping · Data warehousing research trends

1 Introduction

As the sheer volume of data available to the public has increased exponentially for past decades, data warehousing and knowledge discovery has produced many important research issues and technologies to support decision making and business intelligence. The big data analytics stand as the core components of various disciplines such as business intelligence, biological and health science, engineering, and social science to discover the knowledge from big data or multiple data sources.

During the past 21 years, the International Conference on Data Warehousing and Knowledge Discovery (DaWaK) has played a pivotal role in linking researchers and practitioners to exchange their experience and knowledge in developing and organizing the systems, applications, and solutions for data warehousing and knowledge discovery.

M. Song et al. (Eds.): DaWaK 2020, LNCS 12393, pp. 3–13, 2020.
https://doi.org/10.1007/978-3-030-59065-9_1

Since DaWAK 2015, the conference title has been changed into the International Conference on Big Data Analytics and Knowledge Discovery from the 17th in its series. The change reflects the needs of expanding the scope of the conference from data warehouses to big data and to emphasize big data analytics. Throughout two decades, various innovative researches and emerging information technologies have been presented in DaWaK. Subsequently, the proposals and findings published in DaWaK were disseminated as public knowledge to the scholarly community. DaWaK has become one of the most influential international conferences in the field of big data analytics, and the leading researchers were recognized as influential researchers in the field.

Despite the importance and the impact of DaWaK in the field, however, there was no prior research that quantitatively measured impact and importance of the conference. In order to investigate the growth and achievement of DaWaK for the last 21 years, the present study first maps out the knowledge structure as a knowledge graph out of DaWaK topics. We then present the evolution of topics in terms of increasing interests and decreasing interests. Finally, we identify several key research performance metrics in terms of citation counts, number of readers, and the number of downloads, and the most influential articles and authors in DaWaK.

This paper is organized as follows. Section 2 presents experimental design, covering data collection and employed analysis methods. Section 3 shows analysis results and Sect. 4 summarizes the paper.

2   Experiment Design

2.1   Data Collection

The datasets were collected from the DaWaK conference papers (PDF file format) over the past 21 years (1999–2019) and the research metrics information from Bookmetrix. We downloaded the dataset of papers from the Springer Link database (https://link.spr inger.com/conference/DaWaK) in a total of 21 copies, which comprises 775 full-text papers. The bibliometrics data was retrieved from the Bookmetrix (http://www.bookme trix.com). We collected three types of data counts, include citations, readers (readership data), and downloads. We gathered the DaWaK research metrics on January 11 in 2020.

2.2   Analysis Methods

We applied the co-words analysis to the knowledge structure of past DaWaK conferences and examined the research topics and trends using a Dirichlet Multinomial Regression (DMR) topic modeling method. Moreover, we analyzed the research performance by assessment of the research outcome of a particular scholar to the DaWaK community. The research metrics approach was used to examine the impact of the research fields, researchers, and their papers. Therefore, a result of this study should help understand the current state of the research and identify new research areas for the DaWaK conference. The overview of the processes of this study is shown in Fig. 1 as follows.

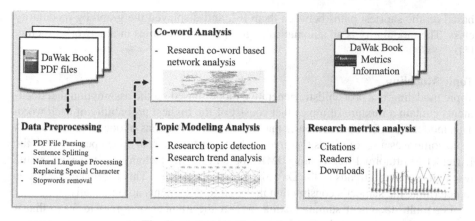

Fig. 1. Flowchart of research overview

Data Pre-processing

We used PDF parser in Apache PDFBox (https://pdfbox.apache.org/) to extract raw data from PDF documents. Once each article is converted to the text format, we partitioned the text into paragraphs. We treated each paragraph as a document for the proposed method. Next, we applied a list of stopwords removing the noise-words such as "a," "an," and "any." Moreover, we used the OpenNLP Sentence Detector [1] to split the sentences based on a punctuation character that finds the start and marks the end of a sentence, which is required for supporting the language processing functions while analyzing the text. We also employed the Stanford CoreNLP [2] for Part-of-Speech tagging (POS), which was used to identify a word in a dataset with a corresponding word type such as noun, verb, and adverb, based on a token and a context itself. Also, a lemmatization was applied to analyze the lemma of each word. This process evaluates the lemma of words to decrease inflection and linguistics related forms of words and returns the suffixes to the ordinary form of the words [3].

Co-word Map Analysis

A co-word analysis was used for identifying the relationship between concepts presented in the documents. It has been widely used in text mining to overview a knowledge structure in huge data. The input for computing co-occurrence of two words is a sentence splitter by OpenNLP sentence splitter. For efficient calculation of the co-occurrence of words in each sentence, we used CombinatoricsLib [4]. It is a Java-based library that can be employed to generate different permutations or combinations for a given set of items. The library can be employed to generate combinatorial objects, such as simple permutations, permutations with repetitions, simple combinations, combinations with repetitions, subsets, integer partitions, list partitions, and integer compositions. Later on, it was passed into a graphML format process to create a network of co-words, and this data was exported to Gephi [5] for visualization. In this study, we measured the network by betweenness centrality, which is a measuring of the influence of a node in a network based on the shortest paths between them [6], and displayed the graph by modularity class. The modularity is an automatically grouped communities in a network structure [5].

Topic Modeling

Topic modeling is a probabilistic generative model based on the assumption that documents contain a mixture of topics that consist of the highest probability of each word. This model identifies abstract topics that arise in the collections of documents, and each topic comprises a set of words that frequently occur together. In this paper, we used the Dirichlet-Multinomial Regression (DMR) topic modeling technique [7] to examine the research topics and trends of the DaWaK conference papers. This approach enables us to determine the subject's construction in the large documents automatically.

For multi-document summarization, we set the number of topics to 30 in that it represents the content of the DaWaK papers most vividly as well as most accurate in terms of perplexity t (a measurement score of a probability distribution of a topic). Moreover, for each topic, we set a parameter of the number of words as 20, which having higher probabilities under that topic.

Research Metrics Analysis

In order to analyze the metrics of papers, we retrieved bookmetrix data from www. bookmetrix.com, which is calculated from a variety of data sources and updated every week. CrossRef added the citation counts. The reader (readership data) counts came from Mendeley, and Springer provided download counts. We collected metrics into a spreadsheet and visualized the research information ranking and trends by bar chart and line chart.

3   Results

3.1   Co-words Map Analysis

We used the results of co-occurrences frequency to create a word network, which was imported into Gephi for visualization, to landscape the knowledge structure in DaWaK research in the past 21 years.

Figure 2 shows a DaWak research knowledge graph that consists of a total of 7798 of nodes and 7230 of edges. Each node refers to a word extracted from 775 papers, and the edge denotes the relationship between the nodes. The result shows the co-occurrence words such as a tree – structure (145951), swami – mining (35102), and query – reduction (31939), which has edges with the highest weight scores, respectively. In the graph, we displayed only modularity classes that contain the nodes with a high weight score of betweenness centrality (from 569 classes). The most significant component is a community of words that identified the "data," as a core of the nodes. This "data" component comprises the associated words such as preparation, expansion, composition, migration, and lymphography. The second most significant component is the community of *"mining,"* which connects with a set of terms such as swaml (Semantic Web Archive of Mailing Lists), marc (Machine-readable cataloging), implementation, purchase, and imaging.

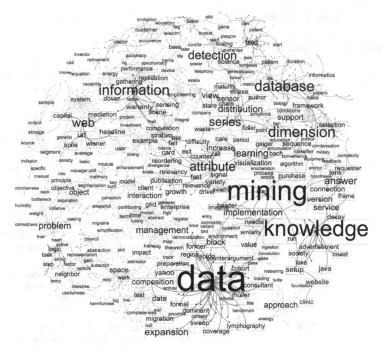

Fig. 2. Overview of the knowledge structure in DaWaK research papers

The co-words in a network give the meaning of various clusters in big data analytics fields such as data mining, data science, data/information management, database systems, programming language, query language, algorithms, and mining techniques.

3.2 Topic Analysis

Once the topics were generated by DMR, we manually labeled each topic based on the terms belonging to the topic. Moreover, we removed the groups of words that appeared as stand-alone words that did not offer any information about what the topic is, such as *end, case,* and *with.* And then, we replaced them with the next word, rank and showed the top-15 terms for each topic. Table 1 shows the top-10 topics of the central idea of DaWaK research topics. We provided the full result (30 topics) via a DOI link (https://doi.org/10.6084/m9.figshare.12593618).

In Table 1, we sorted the topics by probability weight scores, which labels how likely the topic occurs in the dataset. We briefly describe the top-10 topics as follows.

Table 1. DMR-based topic modeling result (Top-10 topics)

Weights (probability)	Topics	Top terms
0.04665	Data mining approach	Data, mining, paper, work, approach, problem, results, algorithms, patterns, method, techniques, research, model, framework, knowledge
0.03299	Algorithm performance	Number, time, size, data, results, dataset, performance, table, experiments, algorithm, memory, execution, method, algorithms, threshold
0.03217	Information systems	Data, warehouse, olap, information, systems, analysis, knowledge, model, business, process, sources, integration, approach, decision, mining
0.03117	Database design and implementation	Query, cost, data, processing, performance, views, time, number, execution, results, index, space, storage, algorithm, database
0.02757	Mining frequent patterns	Patterns, support, items, itemsets, algorithm, database, mining, transaction, set, candidate, number, table, example, apriori, sequence
0.02089	Multi-dimensional database	Dimension, level, data, cube, fact, schema, hierarchy, olap, aggregation, model, measure, hierarchies, values, analysis, xml
0.02047	Machine learning	Classification, data, class, accuracy, training, classifier, feature, learning, model, decision, prediction, selection, dataset, method, results
0.01939	Cluster analysis	Cluster, clustering, data, distance, algorithm, number, points, kmeans, method, objects, results, similarity, density, noise, groups
0.01727	Dimensions and attributes	Table, dimension, attribute, values, fact, key, column, data, number, schema, record, set, records, example, type
0.01645	Sequential pattern mining	Time, event, series, data, interval, sequence, window, detection, patterns, distance, intervals, sequences, example, period, types

The first ranked topic is the **Data mining approach** (0.04665), which represents the process of discovering knowledge patterns using various algorithms. The next ranked topic is **Algorithm performance** (0.03299), which intends to test the efficiency of the proposed algorithms to determine the usage of different resources and processes. The third ranked topic is **Information systems** (0.03217), which is related to supporting the decision-making process that applies business intelligence technology such as data warehouses and OLAP. The fourth topic is **Database design and implementation** (0.03117), which includes a data warehouse prototype such as system architecture, schema design, implementation, testing, and comparing the performance by running a query. The fifth topic is **Mining frequent patterns** (0.02757), which finds itemsets that frequently appear together from huge data by examining the relationships between items in a dataset.

The sixth topic is **Multi-dimensional database** (0.02089), which is about creating dimensions and cubes, a logical model, cube design, dimension hierarchies, and OLAP. The seventh topic is **Machine learning** (0.02047), which focuses on the development of computer algorithms that learn from data. Most machine learning papers in the DaWaK were on automatic classification algorithms and the performance of proposed algorithms. The eighth topic is **Cluster analysis** (0.01939), which studies techniques for automatically finding groups by density-based clustering algorithms such as K-Means. Also, the similarity and distance metrics were frequently mentioned in this subject. The ninth topic is **Dimensions and attributes** (0.01727), which extracts data from multiple data sources and the extracted data is categorized into dimensions and measures. And the last of the top-10 topic is **Sequential pattern mining** (0.01645), which is concerned with finding statistically relevant patterns between data examples whose values are distributed in a sequence of events.

In addition to the top-10 ranked topics, other related topics include healthcare database management, network analysis and visualization, and text analytics.

3.3 Topic Trends Analysis

We further analyzed the topic's relative distribution and observed the trends of 30 topics over time. We took the time of publication as a variable for DMR. We found the trends of 30 topics that show increasing, consistent, or decreasing patterns. Overall, the results show that each topic was constantly evolving. However, in this paper, we report only two types of predicted trends, which are shown by linear line, including the increasing (hot topic trends) and decreasing trends (falling topic trends). Readers can find the full results from the DOI link (https://doi.org/10.6084/m9.figshare.12199005).

Hot Topic Trends
The prediction of hot topic trends is presented in Fig. 3. The graph shows the rate of relative distribution ratio of each topic over 21 years from 1999 to 2019. We can see

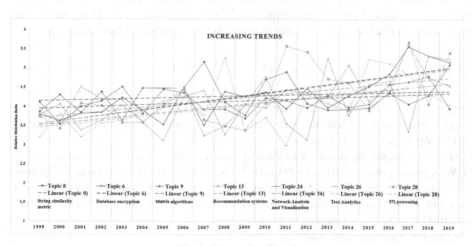

Fig. 3. Increasing Trends

that the topics related to **Database encryption** (Topic 6) and **ETL processing** (Topic 28) increased dramatically during this period, followed by **Recommendation systems** (Topic 13) and **Text Analytics** (Topic 26). And, the topics of **String similarity metric** (Topic 0) and **Matrix algorithms** (Topic 9) climbed up slowly.

Falling Topic Trends

In contrast, Fig. 4 displays the falling trends of seven topics. They comprise **Approximate query processing** (Topic 1), **Multi-dimensional database** (Topic 4), **Association rule mining algorithms** (Topic 8), **Data warehousing and OLAP technology** (Topic 14), **Database design and implementation** (Topic 15), **Database systems** (Topic 17), and **Information systems** (Topic 25). Most of the topics slightly declined.

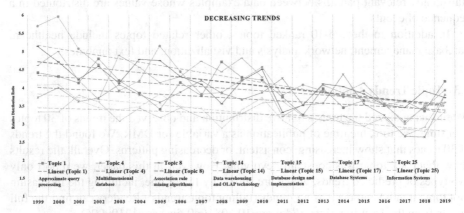

Fig. 4. Decreasing Trends

The downward trends of the topics shown in Fig. 4, which reflects the maturity of data warehousing and OLAP technology. The upward trends of the topics shown in Fig. 3, which reflects the evolution of DaWaK conferences toward more on data mining and analytical aspects, reflecting recent trends in big data analytics. This justifies the renaming of DaWaK conference from data warehousing into Big Data Analytics.

3.4 DaWaK Research Paper Metrics

We used the information from Bookmetrix for the research metrics presented in this section. Due to the lack of space, we highlight only key information. We provide all metrics information of DaWaK papers in the past 21 years via DOI link (https://doi.org/10.6084/m9.figshare.11912154).

Figure 5 shows the numbers of citations, readers, downloads performance of 775 DaWaK papers published from 1999 to 2019. The total number of citations of 775 papers reached 4339, readers 5781, and downloads 70230 times. In 2006, the conference articles were published 54 papers, which is the highest number of overtime, followed by 2005 and 2000 with 52 and 44 papers, respectively.

The top-3 ranked conference in terms of the citation counts are 1999 with 374 citations, followed by 2008 with 371 times, and 2002 with 353. The top counts of

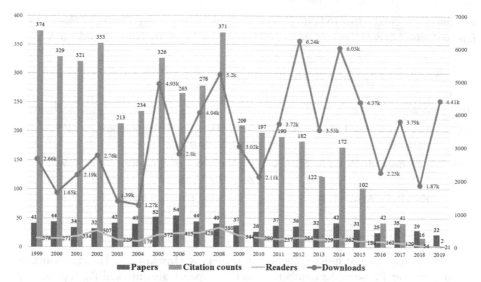

Fig. 5. Graph of twenty-one years DaWaK research paper metrics

readers are the years 2008, 2002, and 2007 with the numbers of 580, 506, and 428, respectively. The top-3 ranked conference in terms of number of downloads is the year 2012 with 6240 times, followed by 2014 with 6030 times, and 2008 with 5200 times.

From the metrics results, we found that the year 2008 performed well, being included in the top-3 rankings of every metrics counts. We looked back to the topic trends result and found that the hot topic trend in 2008 is related to **Text analytics**. We found that most of the papers in 2008 are interrelated in the subject of clustering, classification, and text mining. Furthermore, the Year 1999 brought up the highest citation that belongs to the year 1999 counts, which is inaugural version of the DaWaK conferences. The hot topic in 1999 is **Data warehousing and OLAP technology**.

Year 2002 is included in the top-3 rankings twice in terms of the citation counts and the reader counts. The hot topic in Year 2002 is **Web mining**. The first ranking of top download is in 2012, and the interesting topic is **Business process modeling**, which is also related to cloud computing and decision support. Also, the year 2007 got a high reader counts, and the topic trend is related to a **String similarity metric**. Additionally, at the top-3 level, the papers in the year 2014 were downloaded frequently, and the hot topic is the **Recommendation systems**.

To evaluate the performance of the authors among the scholars, we report the top-3 authors who have high performance in each category (Citations, Readers, and Downloads), as follows.

Table 2 shows the top-3 most cited papers published in the DaWaK Conference over the past 21 years. The paper with the highest number of citations (177 counts) is entitled *"Outlier Detection Using Replicator Neural Networks"* published in 2002 and co-authored by **Hawkins S., He H., Williams G., and Baxter R.** The second most cited paper (76 counts) is entitled *"The Evaluation of Sentence Similarity Measures,"* published in 2008 and co-authored by **Achananuparp P., Hu X., and Shen X.** And the third most cited paper (64 citations) is entitled *"Discovering Temporal Patterns for Interval-based Events,"* published in 2000 and co-authored by **Kam P. and Fu A.W.**

Table 2. The Top-3 papers by citation counts

Year	Authors	Title	Citations
2002	Hawkins S., He H., Williams G., Baxter R.	Outlier Detection Using Replicator Neural Networks	**177**
2008	Achananuparp P., Hu X., Shen X.	The Evaluation of Sentence Similarity Measures	**76**
2000	Kam P., Fu A.W.	Discovering Temporal Patterns for Interval-based Events	**64**

Table 3 displays the most influence on readers is **Hawkins S., He H., Williams G., and Baxter R.**, with the numbers at 311. The paper also marked the top ranking in the citation as presented above. Followed by 214 times of the reader's counts, is **Achananuparp P., Hu X., and Shen X.** who also recorded the second in the top citation ranking. And **Madria S.K., Bhowmick S.S., Ng W.K., and Lim E.P.**, are the third in the top ranking by 78 counts; their paper *"Research Issues in Web Data Mining"* was published in 1999.

Table 3. Top-3 authors by readership counts

Year	Authors	Chapter	Readers
2002	Hawkins S., He H., Williams G., Baxter R.	17	**311**
2008	Achananuparp P., Hu X., Shen X.	29	**214**
1999	Madria S.K., Bhowmick S.S., Ng W.K., Lim E.P.	32	**78**

4 Discussion and Conclusion

The study shows the landscape of DaWaK research in the past 21 years from 1999 to 2019. The analysis includes a total of 775 papers published during the period. This study allows us to understand the knowledge structure and detect the evolution of research topics in this discipline. The co-words analysis was performed to visualize the knowledge network structure. Dirichlet Multinomial Regression (DMR) topic modeling was used to identify the topics and trends over time. The achievement of research was examined using Bookmetrix to explore how DaWaK conference papers performed in the scholarly community. Through this analysis, we identified the DaWaK research specialty and the evolution of research topics over time. Also, we assessed the accomplishment of the researchers and the DaWaK performance in the field of big data analytics and knowledge discovery.

The top-10 major topics are data mining, algorithm performance, information systems, database design and implementation, mining frequent patterns, multi-dimensional database, machine learning, cluster analysis, dimensions and attributes, and sequential pattern mining. The six hot topics with increasing interests are database encryption, ETL processing, recommendation systems, text analytics, string similarity metric, and matrix algorithms. In contrast, the three topics with decreasing interests are data warehousing and OLAP technology, database systems, and association rule mining algorithms.

Lastly, the DaWaK research metrics confirm that DaWaK research outcomes have been receiving consistent attention from the scholarly community in the past 21 years. The 775 papers were cited by 4,339 times and were downloaded by 70,230 times. The average number of citations of each proceeding is 207 times, and the average number of citations per published paper is six times. Papers published in the year 1999 received the highest citations as the inaugural conference. The papers of DaWaK 2008 have been performed well in terms of the top-3 rankings in every metrics counts (citations, readers, and downloads), and the topic trends in 2008 were related to text analytics. The most cited paper was *"Outlier Detection Using Replicator Neural Networks,"* with the 177 citations, co-authored by Hawkins S., He H., Williams G., and Baxter R. and published in 2002.

Since this study focused on a content analysis based on text mining techniques, in the follow-up study, we plan to incorporate a bibliometric approach such as author co-citation analysis (ACA) into understanding the past DaWaK conferences more comprehensively.

Acknowledgment. This work was supported by the National Research Foundation of Korea (NRF) grant funded by the Korea government (MSIT) (No. NRF-2019R1A2C2002577).

References

1. Apache OpenNLP Development Community: Apache OpenNLP Developer Documentation.pdf. https://opennlp.apache.org/docs/1.9.0/manual/opennlp.html
2. Manning, C., Surdeanu, M., Bauer, J., Finkel, J., Bethard, S., McClosky, D.: The Stanford CoreNLP natural language processing toolkit. In: Proceedings of 52nd Annual Meeting of the Association for Computational Linguistics: System Demonstrations, pp. 55–60 (2014). https://doi.org/10.3115/v1/p14-5010
3. Song, M., Kim, W.C., Lee, D., Heo, G.E., Kang, K.Y.: PKDE4J: entity and relation extraction for public knowledge discovery. J. Biomed. Inform. **57**, 320–332 (2015). https://doi.org/10.1016/j.jbi.2015.08.008
4. CombinatoricsLib 2.0 Features: CombinatoricsLib - Very Simple Java Library to Generate Permutations, Combinations and Other Combinatorial Sequences. http://code.google.com/p/combinatoricslib/
5. Blondel, V.D., Guillaume, J.L., Lambiotte, R., Lefebvre, E.: Fast unfolding of communities in large networks. J. Stat. Mech: Theory Exp. (2008). https://doi.org/10.1088/1742-5468/2008/10/P10008
6. Wolfe, A.W.: Social network analysis: methods and applications. Am. Ethnol. (1997). https://doi.org/10.1525/ae.1997.24.1.219
7. Mimno, D., McCallum, A.: Topic models conditioned on arbitrary features with Dirichlet-multinomial regression. In: Proceedings of the 24th Conference on Uncertainty in Artificial Intelligence, UAI 2008 (2008)

Applications

DHE²: Distributed Hybrid Evolution Engine for Performance Optimizations of Computationally Intensive Applications

Oana Stroie, Elena-Simona Apostol$^{(\boxtimes)}$, and Ciprian-Octavian Truică

University Politehnica of Bucharest, Bucharest, Romania
`oana.stroie@cti.pub.ro`
`{elena.apostol,ciprian.truica}@cs.pub.ro`

Abstract. A large number of real-world optimization and search problems are too computationally intensive to be solved due to their large state space. Therefore, a mechanism for generating approximate solutions must be adopted. Genetic Algorithms, a subclass of Evolutionary Algorithms, represent one of the widely used methods of finding and approximating useful solutions to hard problems. Due to their population-based logic and iterative behaviour, Evolutionary Algorithms are very well suited for parallelization and distribution. Several distributed models have been proposed to meet the challenges of implementing parallel Evolutionary Algorithms. Among them, the MapReduce paradigm proved to be a proper abstraction of mapping the evolutionary process. In this paper, we propose a generic framework, i.e., DHE² (Distributed Hybrid Evolution Engine), that implements distributed Evolutionary Algorithms on top of the MapReduce open-source implementation in Apache Hadoop. Within DHE², we propose and implement two distributed hybrid evolution models, i.e., the MasterSlaveIslands and MicroMacroIslands models, alongside a real-world application that avoids the local optimum for clustering in an efficient and performant way. The experiments for the proposed application are used to demonstrate DHE² increased performance.

Keywords: Distributed Hybrid Evolution Engine · Hybrid evolution models · Distributed Genetic Algorithms · MapReduce

1 Introduction

Many optimization and search problems suffer from large irregular search space or local optimum solutions. These problems are either unsolvable by following an algorithm, or too computationally intensive to be accurately resolved. Therefore, a different mechanism needs to be used in order to generate optimal solutions.

O. Stroie, E.-S. Apostol and C.-O. Truică—These authors contributed equally to the work.

© Springer Nature Switzerland AG 2020
M. Song et al. (Eds.): DaWaK 2020, LNCS 12393, pp. 17–27, 2020.
https://doi.org/10.1007/978-3-030-59065-9_2

Genetic Algorithms, which are a sub-class of the Evolutionary Algorithms, are search procedures that model the natural selection and evolution mechanism. They use techniques inspired by nature, i.e., reproduction, gene crossover, gene mutation and natural selection, in order to evolve and generate optimal solutions to hard mathematical problems. Due to their population-based and iterative behaviour, Evolutionary Algorithms are easy to parallelize and distribute. This characteristic makes them well suited for efficiently resolving computationally intensive problems. Numerous parallel models have already been proposed and basic models using the MapReduce paradigm have exhibited improved performance in terms of scalability and fault tolerance. Even so, more complex parallel models are needed in order to increase performance. One of the possible approaches is by creating hybrid models. Thus, in this article we propose such a solution: DHE^2 (Distributed Hybrid Evolution Engine).

Motivation. Many of the current problems can be efficiently resolved by mapping them on Genetic Algorithms. For example, clustering algorithms are frequently used in different applications, that with technological growth have become more and more compute-intensive. As demonstrated further in this article, clustering problems can be efficiently resolved using distributed Genetic Algorithms. Moreover, the solutions are obtained faster and more accurate than by using a classic algorithm. Even though Genetic Algorithms successfully resolve many hard problems in a fast way, developers are hesitant to learn their basics steps and how to efficiently distribute their computation. This problem can be solved by developing an easy to use framework that would offer any user the possibility of implementing and executing with minimum effort any problem that can be mapped on Genetic Algorithms. Therefore, the only work that has to be done by the user is mapping the problem on a Genetic Algorithms' model and implementing the problem-specific components by following the existing interfaces.

Objectives. The main objective of this article is to present our framework that offers an easy way of implementing any kind of distributed Genetic Algorithm, i.e, DHE^2. DHE^2 contains a generic implementation for all the non-problem-specific components of Genetic Algorithm. Also, using DHE^2 the complexity of the evolutionary process and of the distribution model are hidden from the user. Moreover, DHE^2 is responsible for efficiently distributing the computation on the user's network. For distribution, we propose two hybrid models, Master-SlaveIslands and MicroMacroIslands model. A user may choose and determine which model gives better results for his/her problem. The distribution details are going to be hidden by using a well-documented solution, Apache Hadoop. To demonstrate the scalability, performance, and improved runtime of DHE^2, we implement an optimized K-Means clustering algorithm that uses our solution of Genetic Algorithms to avoid the local optimum in centroid selection.

Outline. This article is structured in seven sections. Section 2 establishes the research work and the already proposed solutions related to distributing Genetic Algorithms. Section 3 presents the concepts and technologies used in order to develop DHE^2. Section 4 describes DHE^2 architecture alongside a brief presentation of the developed application. Section 5 presents the experimental results obtained, offers a brief analysis, and a general discussion about DHE^2. Section 6 presents the conclusions and hints at future work.

2   Related Work

Genetic algorithms in distributed environments have been used for a variety of applications, e.g. unit testing [4], resource optimization [12], big data application [11], implementing Machine Learning algorithms [1,2], etc. The majority of distributed solutions that use Genetic Algorithms are designed to work on Apache Hadoop and implemented using the MapReduce model.

MapReduce for Parallelizing Genetic Algorithms (MRPGA) [8] is a solution for parallelizing Genetic Algorithms by extending the MapReduce model. Because Genetic Algorithms cannot be expressed directly by the MapReduce model, the proposed solution uses a modified MapReduce model which includes a second reduce phase for global selection, alongside an optimization on the merge phase for the added reduce step.

Genetic algorithms are also implemented using the MapReduce paradigm by transforming the algorithms into the map and reduce primitives [13]. This approach is build on top of Apache Hadoop MapReduce programming Framework. The initialization of the population (i.e., the serial component of the Genetic Algorithm) is parallelized by adding another MapReduce phase. The solution uses a chain of Map and Reduce functions for each generation of the algorithm and HDFS (Hadoop Distributed File System) as a data transfer medium between each generation. This approach is very I/O (Input/Output) intensive and decreases the performance significantly.

A new parallelized model for Genetic Algorithms that uses only one MapReduce phase was proposed to address the intensive I/O drawback [9]. The solution processes the data in the Map phase while storing the data in memory instead of using HDFS.

A generic framework that uses the island and neighborhood models is proposed for developing parallelized Genetic Algorithm in Cloud Computing [3]. The solution offers the island model, with isolated subpopulations, and the neighborhood model, with overlapping subpopulations, for solving different distributed Genetic Algorithms problems.

MapReduce Genetic Programming (MRGP) [1] is a parallelized method that employs the MapReduce model to decrease the execution time of classification problems solved with Genetic Algorithms. MRGP transforms the genetic programming process into the Map and Reduce operations and achieves faster convergence by being able to use large population sizes due to parallelized computation. The experimental evaluation proves that the solution is maintaining the speedup and scalability properties while improving the accuracy of classification problems. Sequential Genetic Algorithms are used succesfully to search for a suitable configuration of Support Vector Machines (SVMs) to predict for inter-release fault [6].

Parallel k-Means clustering algorithm (PKCA) [2] uses a hybrid data clustering approach that combines the search process of Genetic Algorithm to generate new data clusters with parallel K-Means to further speed up the quality of the search process during clusters formation. The implementation uses the MapReduce programming model from the Apache Hadoop framework.

3   Methodology

The basic idea behind distributing computation is to divide a task into chunks and solve them simultaneously on different machines. Due to their high level of independence between components, Genetic Algorithms have been demonstrated to be good candidates for parallelization. As of today, the literature contains several examples of successful parallel implementations and solutions for modelling Genetic Algorithms, most of them using the MapReduce Paradigm. Two main models of parallelizing Genetic Algorithms have been proposed in current solutions: master-slave and coarse-grained evolution models. The master-slave evolution model creates a single population and the evaluation of the fitness function is computed in parallel. This model is well suited for massively parallel computers. The coarse-grained evolution model consists of several subpopulations that evolve in parallel and migration is used to exchange individuals and increase the level of diversity. Both models have been successfully implemented using the Apache Hadoop framework.

In order to reduce the execution time and resolve some of the basic models' drawbacks, different complex models can be obtained by combining basic models and producing hierarchical parallel Genetic Algorithms. In this article, we propose two hybrid models for DHE^2, i.e., MasterSlaveIslands and Micro-MacroIslands, alongside with their implementation, in order to demonstrate the computational advantage that is obtained.

In the second part of this section, we present a Machine Learning application than is implemented on top of DHE^2. We use the proposed models to test and demonstrate their usability and scalability to improve the clustering problem by avoiding local optimum.

3.1   The Proposed Hybrid Evolutionary Algorithms

MasterSlaveIslands Model. MasterSlaveIslands model is one of DHE^2 proposed models for distributing Evolutionary Algorithms using MapReduce operations. The model produces a hierarchical parallel Genetic Algorithm by combining the master-slave basic model at the top level and the coarse-grained basic model at the bottom level. Briefly, the population is composed of multiple subpopulations that exchange individuals through migration. The operation that is executed in a distributed way is the fitness evaluation of each individual. In the following, we present the four steps of this model with their detailed description.

Step 1: The initial seed population is generated by the master node. Afterwards, the master node creates a specified number of subpopulations and assigns each individual to one of them.

Step 2: Every functional node in the network becomes a Mapper and receives a proportional number of individuals to evaluate. One map task is executed for each individual received as input. This map task will evaluate the candidate and pass it alongside its fitness score to the next step. Each individual is associated with a key equal to the subpopulation index it belongs to, thus individuals belonging to the same subpopulation will be sent to the same reducer.

Step 3: The evaluated individuals generated after step 2 are shuffled and grouped by their associated key, their subpopulation index. Each reducer receives a complete subpopulation and is in charge of evolving it. The parents' selection is computed, followed by recombination and mutation. The offsprings are then evaluated and a new subpopulation is selected. If migration is selected, a part of the individuals is associated to another subpopulation index. The new subpopulation is written to HDFS for the next iteration.

Step 4: The master node merges all evolved subpopulation creating the new population. It also checks if any termination condition is satisfied, thus evolution can stop, or else, a new iteration begins from Step 2, using the evolved subpopulations as input.

MicroMacroIslands Model. The second proposed hybrid model implemented in DHE^2 is MicroMacroIslands, which produces a hierarchical parallel Genetic Algorithm using the coarse-grained basic model at both the upper and the lower levels. Thus, the population is divided into micropopulations that are evolved separately. A group of micropopulations form a macropopulations. The idea is to force a high migration rate at the lower level while a low migration rate is used at a high level. This evolution model consists of 5 steps which are further detailed.

Step 1: This step is performed sequentially by the master node which generates the initial population. The population is then divided into a specific number of micropopulations proportional to the number of nodes. Micropopulations are then grouped and form macropopulations.

Step 2: Each Mapper receives one or more micropopulations depending on the number of functional nodes. Every micropopulation is evolved in a different map task for a specified number of generations. A subset of evolved individuals are chosen to migrate to a neighbour micropopulation (belonging to the same macropopulation) and another subset of migrators is sent to another macropopulation (external migrators).

Step 3: The micropopulations generated after step 2 are shuffled and grouped by their associated key, their macropopulation index. Each reducer receives a complete evolved macropopulations and additionally the set of individuals that migrate from another macropopulation. The responsibility of a reduce task is to perform the migrations. The internal migrators (that migrate to another micropopulation belonging to the same macropopulation) are added to the corresponding micropopulation while the external migrators are merged and equally distributed to the local micropopulations.

Step 4: The master node merges all micropopulations and checks if any termination condition is satisfied and if so, stops the evolution. Otherwise, a new iteration starts from Step 2, using the evolved micropopulations as input.

Discussions. It is important to emphasize that while some parallelization models do not affect the behaviour of the algorithm, the two proposed models change the way the Genetic Algorithm work. In both models of parallel Genetic Algorithms, selection and mating only consider a subset of individuals from the total population, different from the original Genetic Algorithms where selection and mating are operations that takes into account all the population.

Another aspect to discuss is the use of migration in DHE^2. The migration is used to maintain the level of diversity inside each subpopulation and to improve the performance of each subpopulation by exchanging information. The migration scheme used by DHE^2 is the ring topology (individuals are transferred between directionally adjacent subpopulations), a basic migration scheme, that is independent of the network topology.

Elitism is another feature that can have an important impact on the Genetic Algorithm performance. It can avoid wasting computational time for re-discovering previously generated partial solutions. A drawback of this feature is that elitism can cause the Genetic Algorithm to converge on local maximum instead of the global maximum. DHE^2 supports three different types of elitism that can be selected: copying all parents (ALL), keeping only a part of the best parents (PART) or choosing a random set of parents to be kept (RANDOM).

3.2   Algorithm. Avoiding Local Optimum for Clustering

Clustering algorithms are unsupervised Machine Learning algorithms used to group similar data together and discover underlying patterns. One technique is to group objects around a centroid. Initial centroids are usually selected at random which make the clustering algorithm prone to find local optimum. We propose a Genetic Algorithm approach to avoiding local optimum for clustering using K-Means.

K-Means is prone to find a local optimum [5], depending on the choice of the initial cluster centers. The DHE^2 K-Means implementation that avoids finding a local optimum works as follows. For an N-dimensional space, each *candidate* is encoded as a sequence of $N \times K$ real numbers, where each continuous subsequence of N numbers is one of the K cluster centers coordinates. The initial population is created by generating a number of candidates, each encoded as K randomly chosen points from the dataset. The *fitness* computation consists of two steps: i) the clusters are formed according to the centers encoded in the candidate that is evaluated and the centroids are computed as the mass-weight center of each cluster, and ii) the fitness is computed as the sum of Euclidean distances between a centroid and the cluster points. *Crossover* exchanges information between two parents using a modified version of Single Point Crossover with a fixed probability. The Crossover Point $c_p < K$ is randomly generated. The number of the candidates lying to the right of the $c_p \times N$ point is exchanged to produce two new offsprings that contain complete centroids, thus avoiding splitting the dimensions of a center. Each candidate undergoes a mutation on a fixed number of values: given v the initial value and number uniformly generated $d \in [0, 0.5]$, the new value becomes $v \pm d \cdot \max(0, v)$. The *parent selection* strategy uses the fitness proportionate approach which means that each individual has a chance of being selected as parent proportional to its fitness value. The *termination condition* stops the evolution process when a specified number of generations is reached.

4   Distributed Hybrid Evolution Engine Architecture

This section presents the DHE^2 (Distributed Hybrid Evolution Engine) architecture which implements two hybrid models for parallelizing Genetic Algorithms.

DHE^2 is implemented using as a starting point the Evolutionary Algorithm implementation from Apache Mahout and it distributes the computation using Apache Hadoop. Two models for parallelizing Genetic Algorithms have been implemented on top of the Mahout framework.

To efficiently distribute the computation of Genetic Algorithms, the MapReduce paradigm has been used, alongside its open-source implementation, Apache Hadoop, and HDFS, for storage. The MapReduce model offers superior performance due to its highly distributed processing, thus a transformation of Genetic Algorithms using map and reduce operations has been preferred. Apache Hadoop offered a suitable framework and a highly distributed, scalable, fault-tolerant environment for running jobs under the MapReduce paradigm.

Apache Mahout [10] is a Machine Learning library created with scalability in mind. This library offered a foundation for building our framework. In comparison with Mahout, DHE^2 supports two hybrid models of Evolutionary Algorithms, presented in Sect. 3. To test and to demonstrate the increased performance of the DHE^2, a Machine Learning application was developed on top of it. Thus, DHE^2 handles the entire distributed evolution process transparently and it offers two different models of transforming Genetic Algorithms using MapReduce.

5   Result Analysis

In this section, DHE^2 performance is evaluated based on experimental testing. In order to properly test DHE^2, a highly distributed environment was needed, i.e., Grid5000 [7], a large-scale testbed for experiment-driven research. For the experiments, we used the Lille site composed of three clusters. For the optimization of clustering, we collected a dataset from sensors located in multiple greenhouses. It contains 2500 records.

The *MasterSlaveIslands* model uses an initial population size of 200 and 20 generations. The elitism is set to ALL, thus the whole population is kept from one generation to another. For these experiments, the model uses 3 subpopulations (Islands).

The *MicroMacroIslands* Model uses an initial population size of 1500 and 50 generations. For these experiments, the model uses 9 micropopulations corresponding to 3 macropopulations and each epoch has 5 generations.

The fitness value is computed as the sum of Euclidean distances between the centroids and the points in the clusters for both models, thus a smaller value shows a better clustering result. Table 1 presents the performance of the two proposed models using different cluster configurations.

Table 1. Avoiding local optimum for clustering performance comparison

# Nodes	MasterSlaveIslands		MicroMacroIslands	
	Execution time (s)	Best fitness	Execution time (s)	Best fitness
2	2 677.64	8 015.85	6 254.81	8 482.57
4	1 316.58	8 021.06	2 893.85	8 462.86
6	1 234.77	8 015.26	1 677.22	8 527.39
8	1 117.05	8 027.48	1 650.24	8 484.98
10	1 105.91	8 008.64	1 087.39	8 466.76

We use the Apache Mahout implementation of K-Means as the baseline for comparing the clustering results obtained with DHE^2 Genetic Algorithms implementation of K-Means with local optimum optimization (Table 2). DHE^2 models achieve a fitness value of almost 20% smaller than the baseline. The evolutionary resolver provides optimal clustering due to evolving different starting combinations of centers in parallel, thus avoiding local optimum. This advantage is assured by combining the simplicity of the K-Means algorithm with the population-based behavior of Genetic Algorithms.

Table 2. Local optimum avoidance for clustering accuracy comparison

	Mahout	MasterSlaveIslands			MicroMacroIslands		
# Generations		10	10	16	10	10	30
Population dimension		300	600	300	300	600	300
Best fitness	841.88	800.40	805.58	812.67	812.67	804.23	798.01

Discussions. The first important aspect to be discussed is the granularity that each model implemented in DHE^2 has. The first model, MasterSlaveIslands, has a fine granularity, meaning that at each generation, the mappers are in charge of evaluating a set of candidates nearly equal to each mapper (with a maximum difference of 1 candidate). On the other hand, the second model, MicroMacroIslands, has a coarse granularity, meaning that at each generation, the population is divided into micropopulations that are evolved by the mappers, thus a difference of maximum 1 subpopulation between the sets of micropopulations to be evolved by a mapper. Therefore, the part that cannot be executed in parallel is represented by the evaluation of a candidate at the first model and the evolution of one micropopulation to the second model. This difference can become significant when the evolution of the micropopulation for one epoch implies a big number of generations while an evaluation of one candidate is radically less time-consuming. This difference depends also on the activity processed on the reducers, where the first model needs more computation for evolving the population while the second model only processes the migrations. Therefore, it can be assumed that this is the reason for the big computation time needed by the second model when using a small number of nodes (i.e., 2).

Another significant aspect of the two models implemented in DHE^2 that influences the scalability is the number of subpopulations of the first model and the number of micro and macro population of the second model. These values influence the number of reducers that are running in parallel (if the number of populations is less than the number of nodes, some nodes are inactive) or the granularity previously discussed (maximum one task difference between reducers).

The number of Hadoop jobs created and configured in each model also impacts the performance of DHE^2. While the first model creates and configures a new job at each generation, the second model computes this part only at each epoch. Therefore, by executing a new MapReduce job for each generation the first model, MasterSlaveIslands, can cause large overhead. However, if the fitness evaluation is significantly more time consuming than the creation of a new MapReduce process, the advantage of running the evaluation in parallel combined with the fine granularity can overcome the additional overhead.

Another difference between the two models is represented by the achieved accuracy. As observed in the experimental results, the first model obtains better fitness values than the second model. This can be due to the higher number of populations in the second model. The micropopulations are low in number of candidates which means that one individual can take over the island causing fast convergence in a local optimum. However, this problem is partially resolved using migration, and different migration count values can be tested to obtain better results. Also, by significantly increasing the size of the population the local optimum can be avoided and the second model can offer better results than the first one.

6   Conclusions and Future Work

The main objective of this article is to present a framework which enables users to easily and efficiently implement any kind of distributed Genetic Algorithm. We achieved our objective by developing the DHE^2 (Distributed Hybrid Evolution Engine), a generic framework that can distribute the computation of problems by mapping them on Genetic Algorithms. Generic implementations of many non-specific problem components are offered as part of DHE^2 and their complexity is hidden using generic interfaces. Thus, the user is responsible only for the problem-specific components. Moreover, DHE^2 offers two different hybrid models, MasterSlaveIslands and MicroMacroIslands model, that efficiently distribute the computation using a MapReduce implementation.

To demonstrate the applicability and performance of DHE^2, two Machine Learning applications have been developed and tested on a real cluster environment, Grid5000. Both of DHE^2 proposed model's scale and exhibit increased accuracy which concludes that performance optimizations is obtained for computationally intensive applications by using hybrid models of the Evolutionary Algorithms.

Different improvements can be added to DHE^2 as future work. While gathering the experimental results, it has been observed that the used memory increases dramatically when the size of the population or the size of the object used to encode a candidate grows, resulting in a significant limitation for large input data. Therefore, the algorithm would benefit from in-memory optimizations. More types of real-world problems can also be implemented and tested, and specific optimizations can be developed.

Acknowledgments. The publication of this paper is supported by the University Politehnica of Bucharest through the PubArt program.

References

1. Al-Madi, N., Ludwig, S.A.: Scaling genetic programming for data classification using MapReduce methodology. In: World Congress on Nature and Biologically Inspired Computing, pp. 132–139. IEEE (2013)
2. Alshammari, S., Zolkepli, M.B., Abdullah, R.B.: Genetic algorithm based parallel k-means data clustering algorithm using MapReduce programming paradigm on hadoop environment (GAPKCA). In: Recent Advances on Soft Computing and Data Mining. pp. 98–108. Springer, Cham (2019). https://doi.org/10.1007/978-3-030-36056-6_10
3. Apostol, E., Băluță, I., Gorgoi, A., Cristea, V.: A parallel genetic algorithm framework for cloud computing applications. In: Pop, F., Potop-Butucaru, M. (eds.) ARMS-CC 2014. LNCS, vol. 8907, pp. 113–127. Springer, Cham (2014). https://doi.org/10.1007/978-3-319-13464-2_9
4. Di Geronimo, L., Ferrucci, F., Murolo, A., Sarro, F.: A parallel genetic algorithm based on hadoop MapReduce for the automatic generation of JUnit test suites. In: International Conference on Software Testing, Verification and Validation. pp. 785–793. IEEE (2012)
5. Douzas, G., Bacao, F., Last, F.: Improving imbalanced learning through a heuristic oversampling method based on k-means and SMOTE. Inf. Sci. **465**, 1–20 (2018)
6. Ferrucci, F., Salza, P., Sarro, F.: Using hadoop MapReduce for parallel genetic algorithms: a comparison of the global, grid and island models. Evol. Computat. **26**(4), 535–567 (2018)
7. INRIA CNRS: Grid'5000, April 2020. http://www.grid5000.fr/w/Grid5000:Home
8. Jin, C., Vecchiola, C., Buyya, R.: MRPGA: an extension of MapReduce for parallelizing genetic algorithms. In: International Conference on eScience, pp. 214–221. IEEE (2008)

9. Keco, D., Subasi, A.: Parallelization of genetic algorithms using hadoop map/reduce. Southeast Europe J. Soft Comput. **1**(2), 56–59 (2012)
10. Lyubimov, D., Palumbo, A.: Apache Mahout: Beyond MapReduce. CreateSpace Independent Publishing Platform (2016)
11. López, S., Márquez, A.A., Márquez, F.A., Peregrín, A.: Evolutionary design of linguistic fuzzy regression systems with adaptive defuzzification in big data environments. Cogn. Computat. **11**(3), 388–399 (2019)
12. Rajeswari, D., Prakash, M., Suresh, J.: Computational grid scheduling architecture using MapReduce model-based non-dominated sorting geneticalgorithm. Soft Comput. **23**(18), 8335–8347 (2019)
13. Verma, A., Llorà, X., Goldberg, D.E., Campbell, R.H.: Scaling genetic algorithms using MapReduce. In: International Conference on Intelligent Systems Design and Applications, pp. 13–18. IEEE (2009)

Grand Reports: A Tool for Generalizing Association Rule Mining to Numeric Target Values

Sijo Arakkal Peious[1](✉)[ID], Rahul Sharma[1][ID], Minakshi Kaushik[1][ID],
Syed Attique Shah[2][ID], and Sadok Ben Yahia[3][ID]

[1] Information Systems Group, Tallinn University of Technology, Akadeemia tee 15a,
12618 Tallinn, Estonia
{sijo.arakkal,rahul.sharma,minakshi.kaushik}@taltech.ee
[2] Faculty of Information and Communication Technology BUITEMS,
Quetta, Pakistan
attique.shah@buitms.edu.pk
[3] Software Science Department, Tallinn University of Technology, Akadeemia tee
15a, 12618 Tallinn, Estonia
sadok.ben@taltech.ee

Abstract. Since its introduction in the 1990s, association rule mining(ARM) has been proven as one of the essential concepts in data mining; both in practice as well as in research. Discretization is the only means to deal with numeric target column in today's association rule mining tools. However, domain experts and decision-makers are used to argue in terms of mean values when it comes to numeric target values. In this paper, we provide a tool that reports mean values of a chosen numeric target column concerning all possible combinations of influencing factors – so-called grand reports. We give an in-depth explanation of the functionalities of the proposed tool. Furthermore, we compare the capabilities of the tool with one of the leading association rule mining tools, i.e., RapidMiner. Moreover, the study delves into the motivation of grand reports and offers some useful insight into their theoretical foundation.

Keywords: Grand report · Association rule mining · Relational algebra

1 Introduction

The continuous development of information technology created a massive amount of data [8]. Data mining can be defined, in general, as the process of finding rules and patterns from large data sets. Association rule mining (ARM) is one of the leading data mining techniques. ARM helps to find relationships between attributes and to create rules according to these relationships. In ARM, impractical rules are created along with important rules. The ARM algorithms compare association rules with ancestor association rules to eliminate redundant

© Springer Nature Switzerland AG 2020
M. Song et al. (Eds.): DaWaK 2020, LNCS 12393, pp. 28–37, 2020.
https://doi.org/10.1007/978-3-030-59065-9_3

and impractical rules [12]. The target column and its influencing factors are the heart of an association rule. Nevertheless, in RapidMiner, it is often called as a conclusion and premises. Support and confidence are the two essential measures of interestingness. Support and confidence calculate the strength of the association between itemsets.

The implementation of support and confidence with a minimum threshold could eliminate the association which are below than this minimum threshold. Some useful association rules might miss due to this method. The decision-makers need to observe all the valuable association and its measures in order to make productive decisions. The listing of all possible combinations and its measures called as a grand report [4]. A grand report contains the list of associations and their measures on every attribute in a data set. The ARM tools discretize the target numeric value columns for easy handling. The discretized values association rules give an idea of the association and its measures, however, decision-makers need to have a better picture. The mean value method could help decision-makers to overcome this situation.

This paper attempts to implement the grand report and the mean value method in ARM with the help of a new tool[1]. This tool generated a grand report for the data set and calculated the mean value for numeric target columns concerning the influencing factors. The tool also calculates the support, lift and conditional probability for the target columns. Grand report and mean value calculations are generated with the help of relational algebra functions. A comprehensive description of the grand report and its calculations is given in Sect. 2. Section 3 illustrates the details about ARM and discretization of the target numeric values. Whereas, development and comparison of the tool are described in Sect. 4.

2   Grand Reports

A *grand report* is the complete print-out of a generalized association rule. In the grand report, work with most minimal minimum supports (i.e., support threshold larger than zero but smaller than $1/N$, with N being the number of rows) and the minimal minimum confidences (i.e. zero). The grand report could produce all possible combinations of the influencing factors against the target columns. A grand report is the complete unfolding of the pivot table. The grand report will generate many rows as a report. This is because it does not have any constraints on support and confidence. It is generalized ARM through which analyst incorporate every line of the report in decision making [4]. The grand report generates 2n combinations of influencing factors by using the sum of the binomial coefficients, where n is the number of columns. Usually, a grand report is massive in size, so users might feel inconvenience to read the entire report. Let T be a table with columns C where $C = X_1 : T_1, \ldots, X_n : T_n, X_1 \ldots X_n$ are the column names and $T_1 \ldots T_n$ are the column types.
To generate the report for table T,

$$\forall 1 \leq \psi \leq n \tag{1}$$

---

[1] http://grandreport.me/.

$$\forall D = \{X_1' : D_1, \ldots, X_{\psi-1}' : D_{\psi-1}\} \subseteq C \qquad (D_i = d_1, \ldots, d_{ni}) \qquad (2)$$

$$\forall d_1' \in D_1, \ldots, d_{\psi-1}' \in D_{\psi-1} \qquad\qquad (3)$$

Here, D is the subset of C and the influencing factor.

$$\forall Y : \Re \in C \ or \ Y = X_{ij} : B, X_i : d_i \in C \qquad\qquad (4)$$

Y is the target column, $\Re$ is the real-valued numbers. One can use a select query with "where" condition in relation algebra, to generate the grand report. The select query returns the average value of the target column. In "where" conditions, it is necessary to specify the influencing factors:

$$\text{SELECT AVG}(Y) \text{ FROM } T \text{ WHERE } X_1' = d_1, \ldots, X_{\psi-1}' = d_{\psi-1} \qquad (5)$$

In SQL we can use "group by" instead of "where" conditions:

$$\text{SELECT AVG}(Y) \text{ FROM } T \text{ GROUP BY } X_1', \ldots, X_{\psi-1}' \qquad\qquad (6)$$

3   Association Rule Mining (ARM)

Association rule mining(ARM) is the process of finding the association of frequent itemsets in a large data set and generate rules according to the associations [2]. The ARM first introduced by a research team from Vancouver, British Columbia in 1993 [1]. There are numerous algorithms used in ARM; each of it has its advantages and disadvantages [10]. The 'Apriori' algorithm is the most popular and commonly used algorithm in the ARM [2]. Various types of constraints that can be applied to identify interesting association rules from a data set [7]. Sometimes, These constraints will generate different rules according to their property, and these rules might be conflicting [13]. The most popular constraints in association mining are support and confidence with a minimum threshold [9]. Support is the percentage of transactions which contain a particular itemset. For an itemset X, supp(X) is the percentages of transaction which contain X. Confidence defines how often itemset Y occurs during the transaction with itemset X.

$$\text{supp}(X) = \{t \in T \mid t \text{ satisfies } X\}/|T| \qquad\qquad (7)$$

$$\text{conf}(X \Rightarrow Y) = \text{supp}(X \cup Y)/\text{supp}(X) \qquad\qquad (8)$$

$$T = Transactions, \ X \subseteq T, \ Y \subseteq T, \ usually : X \cap Y = \theta, |Y| = 1$$

A sample binary representation of data is shown in Table 2. In the table, every row is corresponds to a transaction (T_1, T_2, T_3, T_4), and each column corresponds to a data item. If an item is present in a transaction, then its value is 1 else it is 0 in the table.

$$
\begin{aligned}
&T_1 : \{Milk, Bread, Diaper, Beer\} \\
&T_2 : \{Diaper, Beer\} \\
&T_3 : \{Milk, Bread, Diaper, Beer\} \\
&T_4 : \{Milk, Bread, Beer\}
\end{aligned} \qquad (9)
$$

Table 1. Binary data set.

TID	Milk	Bread	Diaper	Beer
1	1	1	0	0
2	0	0	1	1
2	1	1	1	1
2	1	1	0	1

In a database, let I be a set of M binary attributes $\{i_1, i_2, i_3, \ldots, i_m\}$ called database items. T be a set of n Transactions $\{t_1, t_2, t_3, \ldots, t_n\}$, each transaction t has a unique ID and is a subset of the Items in I, i.e. t $\subseteq I$. An Association Rule may be represented as an implication of the form

$$X \Rightarrow Y \tag{10}$$

where $X, Y \subseteq I$ (Item set) and $X \cap Y = \phi$. The left-hand side of the implication known as the antecedent and right hand side of the implication is known as consequent:

$$X \Rightarrow Y := X = \{x_1, \ldots, x_n\} \subseteq I \Rightarrow Y = \{y_1, \ldots, y_n\} \subseteq I \tag{11}$$

$$\{Bread, Butter\} \Rightarrow \{Milk, Butter\} \tag{12}$$

In this association rule example $\{Bread, Butter\}$ is antecedent and $\{Milk\}$ is consequent. Generally, an association rule may be represented as a production rule in the expert system, if statement in programming and implication in logic.

In ARM, the target cluster method is used to generate association rules for numeric target values [11]. Target clustering and discretization of the target column are equivalent. In association rule mining numeric target columns are generally discretized for easy mining [3]. Garćia et al. (2013) [6] and Fayyad and Irani (1993) [5] described well about the discretization of the target column. Once the discretization applied on a target column, then it will be easy to identify those columns as binary values. For example, the column age contains the value from 0 to 140, and column age discretized into different groups. Age 70, 140 group is considered as older people in this example [6]. Most of the interesting measures of ARM are only adaptive with binary target columns [7]. Sometimes misinterpretation of association rules or loss of information occurred by discretization of the target column. Determining the median of the target column, calculation of mean value and identifying the variance of target attributes are the different possible way to find the association rules on numeric target column. Determining the mean value of a numeric target column is much easier than discretization. This tool is using the generalized selection of relational algebra to find the mean value of a numeric target column. For example, 'SELECT' syntax with 'AVG' function.

4   The Proposed Tool

In this study, a web application created to generate a grand report and verify data set. As explained in the previous section, the grand report is complete print-out of a generalized association rule. The tool computes all possible combinations of influencing factors against the target column to generate generalized association rules. A data set of four columns has used to test the application. This data set creates seven combinations of influencing factors and calculates the aggregate value or conditional probability of the target column for each combination. This tool is capable of accessing data from the Oracle database and Excel file and is a combination of RapidMiner association mining and relational algebra functions.

4.1   Development and Functionalities

ASP.NET, an open-source framework, is used to develop this tool. The Ajax request method used to establish the communication between the server-side and client-side. For a smooth data transfer, JSON serialization and deserialization functions are used. As mentioned earlier, this tool is capable of accessing data from the Oracle database and Excel files. Furthermore, the Oracle Data provider and OLE DB methods used to access the Oracle database and Excel file.

Table 2. Technologies used for the development of the tool.

C#	Language
ASP.NET	Framework
Ajax	To send and retrieve data from a server asynchronously
Oracle Data Provider (ODP)	Data access to the Oracle database
OLE DB	Data access to the Excel file

Determining the support, lift and conditional probability or aggregate values are the main functionality of this tool. A few steps need to be carried out to find these results. At first, the user needs to select the input source. It can be either Oracle or Excel source. The user needs to provide host address, port number, sid, table name, username and password to connect the Oracle database. Whereas, the user needs to upload the file for Excel. If the uploaded Excel file contains more than one sheet, then the user needs to select the sheet name as well. After these steps, the tool will load each column head with a radio button and checkbox. The radio button is to set the column as the target column and checkbox is to set the column as an influencing factor. If a column is selected as a target column, then it can not be selected for influencing factor and vice versa. After selecting the target column and influencing factors, press the report button to generate the report. While generating the report, the tool will identify the target column type.

The aggregate function is used for the numeric value target column. In aggregate, the average value of the target column calculated against the influencing factors (select AVG(target column) from table group by influencing factors). If the target column type is categorical, the tool will calculate the conditional probability of the target column (select (conditional probability of target column under influencing factor) from table group by target column and influencing factors). For both functions, support and lift also calculated. The order of columns for numeric target column report is support, lift, the average value of the target column and the influencing factors. The column order for categorical target column report is support, lift, conditional probability, target column and the influencing factors. A sample pseudo-code for finding the combinations of influencing factors and retrieving data from the Oracle database is given in Listing 1.

Listing 1. Pseudo-code for finding the combinations of influencing factors and retrieving data from the Oracle database.

```
FUNCTION column_combination(
   influencingColumns:STRING[], numberofColumns:INTEGER,
   startPosition:INTEGER, columns:STRING[]
)
IF numberofColumns != 0 THEN
FOR i FROM startPosition TO lengthOf(influencingColumns)-1
    columns[lengthOf(columns)-numberofColumns] := influencingColumns[i]
    call: column_combination(
    influencingColumns, numberofColumns-1, i + 1, columns
    )
ENDFOR
ENDFUNCTION
FUNCTION generate_report (
   tableName:STRING, targetColumn:STRING,
   influencingColumns:STRING[], numberofColumns:INTEGER
)
columnCombination := call: column_combination(
                        influencingColumns, numberofColumns,
                        0, columns
                        )
orclQuery := "
   Select Count(*)/ (Select count(*) from  tableName ) AS SUPPORT,
   (Select Avg(targetColumn)from tableName) / Avg(targetColumn) AS LIFT,
   Avg(targetColumn) AS AVG_targetColumn, columnCombination
   from tableName group by columnCombination order by columnCombination";
ENDFUNCTION
```

There are three different colours used in the report. Red colour indicates influencing factors; green used for target/principle measures. Principle measures are the average value of the target column or conditional probability of the target column, and target means of the target column. Either conditional probability or the average value will be present in the report. Blue is used to further measures like support and lift. Support and lift showed in the first, in order to maintain the uniqueness. For numeric target columns, there is only one column in green because the average column is the representation of the target columns aggregate value. In categorical target column, there are two columns in green. The first column is the conditional probability of the target column, and the second one is the target column value.

In categorical target column, it shows the fibrillation mechanism. It means the tool will compute the conditional probability for all instances of the target column. For example, consider a target column called 'education' and its values are 'A, B, C, D, E'. The column name 'education' is the factor, and its values are the instances of the factor. In report generation, the tool will calculate the conditional probability for each instance.

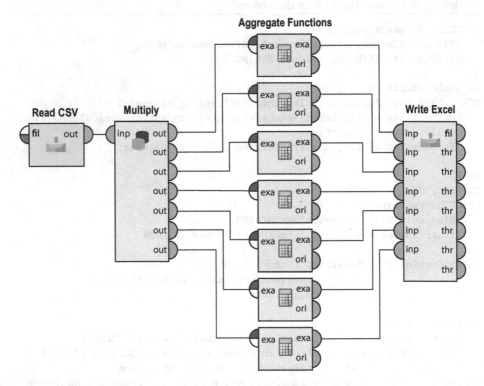

Fig. 1. A sample project for generating all possible combinations of influencing factors against target column in RapidMiner.

4.2   Comparison and Advantages

This tool is a combination of RapidMiner association rule mining and relational algebra. In RapidMiner average value of numeric target column against all possible combinations of influencing factors, the user needs to create different functions for different combinations (Fig. 1). Similarly, for different data set user needs to modify the columns and its combinations. That means users need to create a different project for different data sets. In this tool, the user needs to select the target column and select all from the list to generate all combinations of influencing factors. The tool will automatically identify the combination and generate the report (Fig. 2).

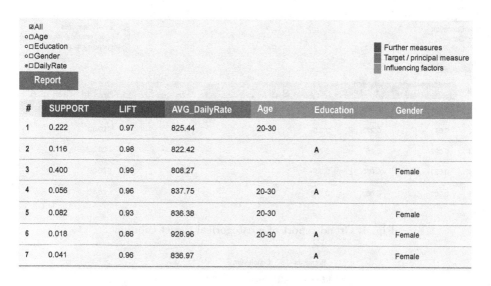

Fig. 2. First record of all combinations in grand report.

In RapidMiner categorical columns are converted into binominal columns (Fig. 3). The binominal columns are treated as separate columns, and a separate report generated for each column. RapidMiner shows influencing factors and its values in the column called 'conclusion'. Meanwhile, target columns and values in the column called 'premises' (Fig. 4). In conclusion and premises column, combinations are shown in the style of "factor=value, factor=value". It is hard for users to identify each factor and its instance. The grand report tool creates separated columns for each factor to avoid this. In this tool, all the measures are located on the left side of the table. It is beneficial for users to verify the output. In the next stage, the column will have the options for filtering the output (Fig. 5).

Education = A	Education = B	Education = C	Education = D	Education = E
true	false	false	false	false
false	true	false	false	false
true	false	true	false	false
false	false	true	true	false
false	true	false	false	true

Fig. 3. Binominal column conversion in RapidMiner.

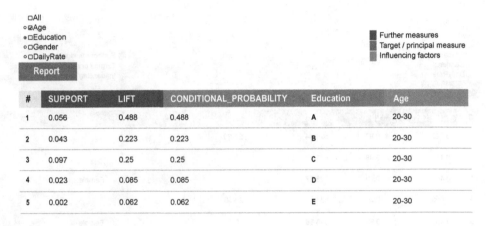

Fig. 4. Grand report of a categorical target column.

Premises	Conclusion
Education = D	Gender, Age = 30-40
Gender	Age = 30-40, Education = D

Fig. 5. Premises and conclusion in RapidMiner.

5   Conclusion

The outcome of the present study shows that the study could able to generate the grand report for a data set. The study tried to calculate the mean value for the numeric target columns. The grand report, which generated in this tool, is providing more association rules and giving a better understating of associations between the attributes. The discretization and mean value calculation creates different kinds of the association on numeric target columns. One of the attractions of the studied tool is that the decision-makers can quickly identify different measures and influencing factors with the help of different colours. It observed that the grand report generates numerous number of records. It is deemed that a filtering option must be needed in place to make the grand report more user friendly. The tool can be accessed publicly (http://grandreport.me/).

Acknowledgements. This work has been conducted in the project "ICT programme" which was supported by the European Union through the European Social Fund.

References

1. Agrawal, R., Imieliński, T., Swami, A.: Mining association rules between sets of items in large databases. In: Proceedings of the 1993 ACM SIGMOD International Conference on Management of Data, pp. 207–216 (1993)
2. Cox, M.T., Funk, P., Begum, S. (eds.): ICCBR 2018. LNCS (LNAI), vol. 11156. Springer, Cham (2018). https://doi.org/10.1007/978-3-030-01081-2
3. Draheim, D.: Generalized Jeffrey Conditionalization: A Frequentist Semantics of Partial Conditionalization. Springer, Cham (2017). https://doi.org/10.1007/978-3-319-69868-7
4. Hartmann, S., Josef, K., Chakravarthy, S., Anderst-Kotsis, G., Tjoa, A.M., Khalil, I. (eds.) DEXA 2019. LNCS, vol. 11706. Springer, Cham (2019). https://doi.org/10.1007/978-3-030-27615-7
5. Fayyad, U., Irani, K.: Multi-interval discretization of continuous-valued attributes for classification learning. In: Proceedings of the 13th International Joint Conference on Artificial Intelligence (IJCAI), pp. 1022–1027 (1993)
6. Garcia, S., Luengo, J., Sáez, J.A., Lopez, V., Herrera, F.: A survey of discretization techniques: taxonomy and empirical analysis in supervised learning. IEEE Trans. Knowl. Data Eng. **25**(4), 734–750 (2012)
7. Geng, L., Hamilton, H.J.: Interestingness measures for data mining: a survey. ACM Comput. Surv. (CSUR) **38**(3), 9-es (2006)
8. Han, J., Kamber, M.: Data Mining Concepts and Techniques, pp. 335–391. San Francisco (2001)
9. Hornik, K., Grün, B., Hahsler, M.: arules-a computational environment for mining association rules and frequent item sets. J. Stat. Softw. **14**(15), 1–25 (2005)
10. Kumbhare, T.A., Chobe, S.V.: An overview of association rule mining algorithms. Int. J. Comput. Sci. Inf. Technol. **5**(1), 927–930 (2014)
11. Moreland, K., Truemper, K.: Discretization of target attributes for subgroup discovery. In: Perner, P. (ed.) MLDM 2009. LNCS (LNAI), vol. 5632, pp. 44–52. Springer, Heidelberg (2009). https://doi.org/10.1007/978-3-642-03070-3_4
12. Srikant, R., Agrawal, R.: Mining generalized association rules. Future Generation Comput. Syst. **13**(2–3), 161–180 (1997)
13. Tan, P.N., Kumar, V., Srivastava, J.: Selecting the right objective measure for association analysis. Inf. Syst. **29**(4), 293–313 (2004)

Expected vs. Unexpected: Selecting Right Measures of Interestingness

Rahul Sharma[1]([⊠])[iD], Minakshi Kaushik[1][iD], Sijo Arakkal Peious[1][iD], Sadok Ben Yahia[2][iD], and Dirk Draheim[1][iD]

[1] Information Systems Group, Tallinn University of Technology, Akadeemia tee 15a, 12618 Tallinn, Estonia
{rahul.sharma,minakshi.kaushik,sijo.arakkal,dirk.draheim}@taltech.ee
[2] Software Science Department, Tallinn University of Technology, Akadeemia tee 15a, 12618 Tallinn, Estonia
sadok.ben@taltech.ee

Abstract. Measuring interestingness in between data items is one of the key steps in association rule mining. To assess interestingness, after the introduction of the classical measures (support, confidence and lift), over 40 different measures have been published in the literature. Out of the large variety of proposed measures, it is very difficult to select the appropriate measures in a concrete decision support scenario. In this paper, based on the diversity of measures proposed to date, we conduct a preliminary study to identify the most typical and useful roles of the measures of interestingness. The research on selecting useful measures of interestingness according to their roles will not only help to decide on optimal measures of interestingness, but can also be a key factor in proposing new measures of interestingness in association rule mining.

Keywords: Knowledge discovery in databases · Association rule mining · Measures of interestingness

1 Introduction

In knowledge discovery in data (KDD), association rule mining (ARM) is one of the most established data mining techniques. It is commonly used to find out interesting patterns between data items in large transactional data sets. In ARM, association rules are accompanied by measures of interestingness (support, confidence, lift etc.)[1]; all of these measures of interestingness use different methods (frequency, probability and counts) to calculate frequent itemsets in data sets. The frequency of items represents basic interestingness in association rules. A main origin of measures of interestingness is from common mathematical and information theories such as found in statistics, e.g., Yule's Q method, Yule's Y method, correlation coefficient and odds ratio. Out of the 40 different measures of interestingness available in the literature, no single measure of interestingness is perfect to calculate interestingness in every ARM task. In this paper, based on

© Springer Nature Switzerland AG 2020
M. Song et al. (Eds.): DaWaK 2020, LNCS 12393, pp. 38–47, 2020.
https://doi.org/10.1007/978-3-030-59065-9_4

the diversity of measures proposed to date, we are identifying their roles, classifying their usefulness from several perspectives to start an extended discussion on different properties of measures of interestingness.

Issues in Selecting Measures of Interestingness in ARM

(i) A large number of measures of interestingness are available to choose and many of these measures are not useful in each ARM task.

(ii) The classical measures of interestingness generate a lot of rules, most of these rules are irrelevant and redundant in many scenarios.

(iii) Based on the meaning of measure of interestingness, it's hard to decide on the appropriate measure in a concrete decision support scenario.

(iv) Various interestingness evaluation methods seem not to be rationalized. Some literature seems to simply combine several kinds of interestingness evaluations to new kinds of measures.

This paper is structured as follows. In Sect. 2, we describe expectedness and unexpectedness with respect to the roles of different measures in ARM. Section 3 focuses on the different properties for selecting the right measures of interestingness. Section 4 presents the conclusions and future work.

2 Expectedness and Unexpectedness in ARM

A simple ARM task using classical measures for a data set containing d items potentially generates $3^d - 2^d + 1$ possible association rules and most of these association rules are expected, obvious and duplicate. Take association rules for the data items {Milk, Bread, Butter} as an example. In the association rule in Eq. (1), it can be easily understood that the association of these three items is rather obvious. In ARM, obvious or common association rules can be referred to as *expected* association rules.

$$\{Milk, Bread\} \Rightarrow \{Butter\} \tag{1}$$

The main objective of ARM is to find the interesting association rules, hidden patterns and – most importantly – unexpected association rules in the data set. The association rules generated using the following combination of {Milk, Diaper, Beer} is not as obvious andy more and creates a rather novel pattern of items; in ARM, these types of association rules can be identified as unexpected association rules:

$$\{Milk, Diaper\} \Rightarrow \{Beer\} \tag{2}$$

Based on the variety of definitions of interestingness, the interestingness of an association rule can be categorized via the following nine properties [8]: (1) conciseness, (2) coverage, (3) reliability, (4) peculiarity, (5) diversity, (6) novelty, (7) surprisingness, (8) utility and (9) actionability. Descriptions of all of these properties are summarized in Table 1. Based on these nine definitions of interestingness, the measures of interestingness can be classified into three major

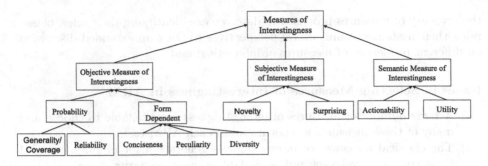

Fig. 1. Types of measures of interestingness.

categories: (1) objective measures of interestingness, (2) subjective measures of interestingness and (3) semantic measures of interestingness [14,18]. Figure 1 is showing all the different types of measures of interestingness.

2.1 Objective Measures of Interestingness for Expected Association Rules

Every transactional data set has some hidden patterns that can be easily identified by using predictive performance or statistical significance. In ARM, such kind of patterns may be referred to as expected patterns and can be computed using objective measures of interestingness. Objective measures mainly focus on the statistics and use statistical strength (probability, count etc.) to assess the degree of interest. As per the definition of interestingness, reliability, generality, conciseness, diversity and peculiarity are based only on data and patterns; therefore, these properties are the foundation of objective measures of interestingness [8]. Support, confidence, lift, conviction and improvement are some examples of objective measures of interestingness.

2.2 Subjective Measures of Interestingness for Unexpected Association Rules

Association rule mining based on common statistical approaches sometimes produces rather obvious or trivial rules. Therefore, the research of Padmanabhan and Tuzhilin [18] first explored the problem of interestingness through the notion of unexpectedness [18,19]. Subjective measures of interestingness usually determine the unexpected association rules in knowledge discovery. Unexpected patterns are opposite to the person's existing knowledge and contradict their expectations and existing knowledge [18].

Finding unexpected patterns in association rule mining is not an easy task, it needs a substantial amount of background information from domain experts [7]. For example, the association rule in Eq. (3) will rather not be considered interesting, even in cases where the rule has a particularly high support and high

Table 1. Interestingness properties in ARM, summarized and apobted from [2–6,9, 10,12,15,16,19,21,23,24,26–28].

Property	Description
Conciseness [4,19]	A small number of attribute-value pairs in a pattern represents the conciseness of the pattern and a set of small number of patterns refers to a concise pattern set
Generality/Coverage [2,27]	The generality/coverage property in ARM covers most of the general patterns in ARM
Reliability [16,24]	Association rules or patterns based on common and popular relationships can be identified as reliable association rules or patterns
Peculiarity [3,28]	Peculiarity refers to unexpected behaviour of patterns. A pattern is said to be peculiar if it is significantly different from all other discovered patterns
Diversity [9]	For a pattern, diversity refers to the degree of differences between its elements; for a pattern set, diversity refers to the degree of differences in between the patterns
Novelty [21]	Combinations of unexpected items which create a pattern unknown to a person are known as novel patterns in ARM. These types of patterns can be discovered but can not be identified easily
Surprisingness [5,10,23]	Patterns which are opposite to a person's existing knowledge or expectations or create contradictions are known as surprising patterns in ARM
Utility [6,15]	Patterns which contribute to reaching a goal are called patterns with utility. Patterns with utility allow the user to define utility functions to get particular information from data
Actionability/Applicability [12,26]	Patterns with actionability allow a person to do a specific task for their benefits. These types of patterns usually reflect the person's action to solve a domain problem [12]

confidence, because the relationship expressed by the rule might be rather obvious to the analyst. As opposed to this, the association rule between $Milk$ and $Shaving\ Blades$ in Eq. (4) might be much more interesting, because the relationship is rather unexpected and might offer a unique opportunity for selling to the retail store.

$$\{Bread\} \Rightarrow \{Milk\} \tag{3}$$

$$\{Milk\} \Rightarrow \{Shaving\ Blades\} \tag{4}$$

Unexpectedness in Association Rule Mining. Many different definitions of unexpectedness have been proposed in the literature. In [18], unexpectedness has been defined with respect to association rules and beliefs. An association rule $P \Rightarrow Q$ is unexpected in regards to the belief $X \Rightarrow Y$ on a data set D if it follows the following rules:

- (i) $Q \wedge Y \models FALSE$ (This property states that Q and Y logically contradict each other.)
- (ii) This property states that set $P \wedge X$ has a large subset of tuples in the data set D.
- (iii) Rule $P, X \Rightarrow Q$ holds. As per the property (i), Q and Y logically contradict each other, therefore it logically follows that $P, X \Rightarrow \neg Y$.

2.3   Semantic Measures of Interestingness

In ARM, semantic measures are a special kind of subjective measures of interestingness which include utility, application-specific semantics of patterns and domain knowledge of the person.

Utility: A utility function reflects the clear goal of the user. For example, to check the occurrence of a rare disease, a doctor might select association rules that correspond to low support rules over those with higher. A user with additional domain knowledge can use a utility-based approach. The domain knowledge of the user does not relate to his personal knowledge and expectations from data.

Actionability: In ARM, there is no widespread way to measure the actionability, i.e., it is up to the ability of an organization to do something useful with a discovered pattern; therefore, a pattern can be referred to as interesting if it is both actionable and unexpected. Generally, actionability is associated with a pattern selection strategy, whereas existing measures of interestingness are dependent on applications.

3   Properties for Selecting Objective Measures of Interestingness

It is important to care for applying consistent sets of measures of interestingness, as sometimes a wrong selection of measures may produce conflicting results. To select appropriate objective measures of interestingness, 15 key properties have been introduced in the literature [8,11,20,24]. Some of these properties are well known and some of the properties are not as popular. These properties are very useful to select appropriate measures for an ARM task.

Piatetsky-Shapiro [20] proposed three basic properties that need to be followed by every objective measure R

Property P1: "$R = 0$ if X, Y are two statistically independent data items, i.e., $P(XY) = P(X)P(Y)$". This property states that accidentally occurred patterns or association rules are not interesting.

Property P2: "R monotonically increases with $P(XY)$ when $P(X)$ and $P(Y)$ are same". *P2* states that if a rule $X \Rightarrow Y$ have more positive correlation then the rule is more interesting.

Property P3: "R monotonically decreases when other parameters $P(X)$, $P(Y)$, $P(X, Y)$ remain unchanged."

Tan et al. [24] based on 2×2 contingency tables, Tan et al. [24] proposed five more properties for probability-based objective measures.

Property O1: "A measure of interestingness R is *symmetric under variable permutation* if it is preserved under the transformation $\Rightarrow_p$ of variable permutation, where $\Rightarrow_p$ is defined as matrix transpose as usual."

$$
\begin{array}{c|c|c}
 & B & \neg B \\
\hline
A & x & y \\
\hline
\neg A & r & s
\end{array}
\Rightarrow_p
\begin{array}{c|c|c}
 & B & \neg B \\
\hline
A & x & r \\
\hline
\neg A & y & s
\end{array}
$$

Property O2: "R is same in row and column scaling. This property is known as the row-and-column scaling invariance."

$$
\begin{array}{c|c|c}
 & B & \neg B \\
\hline
A & x & y \\
\hline
\neg A & r & s
\end{array}
\Rightarrow
\begin{array}{c|c|c}
 & B & \neg B \\
\hline
A & k_3 k_1 x & k_4 k_1 y \\
\hline
\neg A & k_3 k_2 r & k_4 k_2 s
\end{array}
$$

Property O3: "R is anti-symmetric under row and column permutation."

$$
\begin{array}{c|c|c}
 & B & \neg B \\
\hline
A & x & y \\
\hline
\neg A & r & s
\end{array}
\Rightarrow
\begin{array}{c|c|c}
 & B & \neg B \\
\hline
A & r & s \\
\hline
\neg A & x & y
\end{array}
$$

Property O4: "R should remain same under both row and column permutation. This is inversion invariance which shows a special case of the row/column permutation where both rows and columns are swapped simultaneously."

$$
\begin{array}{c|c|c}
 & B & \neg B \\
\hline
A & x & y \\
\hline
\neg A & r & s
\end{array}
\Rightarrow
\begin{array}{c|c|c}
 & B & \neg B \\
\hline
A & s & r \\
\hline
\neg A & y & x
\end{array}
$$

Property O5: "This property represents the null invariance."

	B	$\neg B$
A	x	y
$\neg A$	r	s

$\Rightarrow$

	B	$\neg B$
A	x	y
$\neg A$	r	$s+k$

Lenca et al. [11] proposed five more properties to evaluate measures of interestingness. In these properties, Q1, Q4 and Q5 properties are preferred over the Q2, Q3 properties

Property Q1: "An interesting measure R is constant if there is no counterexample to the rule". As per this property all the association rules with confidence 1 should have same interestingness value.

Property Q2: "R decreases with $P(X \neg Y)$ in a linear, concave, or convex fashion around 0+." This property describes that the value of interestingness decreases with respect to the counterexamples.

Property Q3: "R increases as the total number of records increases."

Property Q4: "The threshold is easy to fix." This property focuses on selecting the easy threshold to separate the interesting association rules from uninteresting association rules.

Property Q5: "The semantics of the measures are easy to express." As per this property, semantics of the interestingness measures should be understandable.

Hamilton et al. [8] have also proposed two more properties to select the right measures of interestingness.

Property S1: "An interesting measure R should be an increasing function of support if the margins in the contingency table are fixed."

Property S2: "An Interesting measure R should be an increasing function of confidence if the margins in the contingency table are fixed."

3.1   Towards Selecting Optimal Measures of Interestingness

All three categories of measures (objective, subjective and semantic) consist of many different measures; therefore, it is very difficult to select appropriate measures for an ARM task. Table 2 might be a useful step in the selection of optimal measures of interestingness.

With respect to objective measures of interestingness, Tan et al. and Lenca et al. [11,24] proposed a ranking method to select measures. The ranking method is based on a specific data set that allows specific patterns having greatest standard deviations in all of the rankings. Lenca et al. [11] proposed also another approach to select measures; in this approach, a value and a weight is assigned to each important property in purpose of selecting measures. In the approach proposed by Vaillant et al. [25], objective measures of interestingness are grouped according to their properties and outcomes.

Table 2. Suggested approaches for selecting optimal measures of interestingness.

Objective Measures of Interestingness	Subjective Measures of Interestingness	Semantic Measures of Interestingness
Ranking method based on data sets [24]	Approaches based on formal specification of user knowledge [10, 13, 23]	Utility-based [22]
Ranking method based on properties of measures of interestingness [11]	Eliminating uninteresting patterns [21]	Actionable patterns [13]
Clustering method based on data sets [25]	Constraining the search space [17]	–
Clustering method based on properties of measures of interestingness [25]	–	–

In subjective measures of interestingness, user knowledge and data are the two crucial factors in deciding on optimal measures. Based on existing and vague knowledge of the user, Liu et al. [13] proposed different subjective measures. The approach proposed by Sahar et al. [21] is about eliminating uninteresting patterns; in this approach, there is no specific measure of interestingness. The method proposed by Padmanabhan et al. [17] is about constraining the search space , here, user belief is used as a constraint in mining association rules. In this method, a user's belief is mined as an association rules and if existing knowledge contradicts to the mined belief, it is referred to as a surprising pattern.

With respect to selecting optimal semantic measures of interestingness, [22] have proposed an approach that is about patterns with utility, here, "Interestingness (of a pattern) = probability + utility" [22]. In the actionability approach proposed by [13], a user provides some patterns in the form of fuzzy rules to represent both the possible actions and the situations in which they are likely to be taken.

4   Conclusion

In ARM, it is clear that no single measure of interestingness is suitable for all ARM tasks – a combination of subjective measures and objective measures seem to be the future in ARM. Selecting optimal measures of interestingness is still an open research problem. In this paper, we have conducted a preliminary study of properties that have been proposed to select optimal measures of interestingness.

We have summarized the role of expected and unexpected association rules in data mining and discussed the importance of the degree of user-involvement within the ARM process. Based on this preliminary work, we aim to design a user interface that supports the decision maker in selecting optimal measures of interestingness. The findings should also be helpful in efforts of designing new measures of interestingness in the future.

Acknowledgements. This work has been conducted in the project "ICT programme" which was supported by the European Union through the European Social Fund.

References

1. Agrawal, R., Imieliński, T., Swami, A.: Mining association rules between sets of items in large databases. ACM SIGMOD Record **22**(2), 207–216 (1993). https://doi.org/10.1145/170036.170072
2. Agrawal, R., Srikant, R.: Fast algorithms for mining association rules in large databases. In: Proceedings of VLDB'1994 - the 20th International Conference on Very Large Data Bases, p. 487–499. Morgan Kaufmann (1994)
3. Barnett, V., Lewis, T.: Outliers in Statistical Data. Wiley, 3rd edn (1994)
4. Bastide, Y., Pasquier, N., Taouil, R., Stumme, G., Lakhal, L.: Mining minimal non-redundant association rules using frequent closed itemsets. In: Lloyd, J., et al. (eds.) CL 2000. LNCS (LNAI), vol. 1861, pp. 972–986. Springer, Heidelberg (2000). https://doi.org/10.1007/3-540-44957-4_65
5. Bay, S.D., Pazzani, M.J.: Detecting change in categorical data: mining contrast sets. In: Proceedings of KDD 1999 - the 5th ACM International Conference on Knowledge Discovery and Data Mining, pp. 302–306. ACM (1999)
6. Chan, R., Yang, Q., Shen, Y.D.: Mining high utility itemsets. In: Proceedings of ICDM'2003-the 3rd IEEE International Conference on Data Mining, pp. 19–26. IEEE, USA (2003)
7. Hartmann, S., Küng, J., Chakravarthy, S., Anderst-Kotsis, G., Tjoa, A.M., Khalil, I. (eds.) DEXA 2019. LNCS, vol. 11706. Springer, Cham (2019). https://doi.org/10.1007/978-3-030-27615-7
8. Geng, L., Hamilton, H.J.: Interestingness measures for data mining: a survey. ACM Comput. Surv. **38**(3) 56–63 (2006). https://doi.org/10.1145/1132960.1132963
9. Hilderman, R.J., Hamilton, H.J.: Knowledge Discovery and Measures of Interest. Kluwer (2001)
10. Lee, Y.C., Hong, T.P., Lin, W.Y.: Mining association rules with multiple minimum supports using maximum constraints. Int. J. Approximate Reason. **40**(1–2), 44–54 (2005). https://doi.org/10.1016/j.ijar.2004.11.006
11. Lenca, P., Meyer, P., Vaillant, B., Lallich, S.: A multicriteria decision aid for interestingness measure selection. Technical report LUSSI-TR-2004-01-EN, École Nationale Supérieure des Télécommunications de Bretagne (2004)
12. Ling, C.X., Chen, T., Yang, Q., Cheng, J.: Mining optimal actions for profitable CRM. In: Proceedings of ICDM'2002 - the 2nd IEEE International Conference on Data Mining, pp. 767–770. IEEE (2002)
13. Liu, B., Hsu, W., Chen, S.: Using general impressions to analyze discovered classification rules. In: Proceedings of KDD 1997 - The 3rd International Conference on Knowledge Discovery and Data Mining, pp. 31–36. AAAI (1997)

14. Liu, B., Hsu, W., Chen, S., Ma, Y.: Analyzing the subjective interestingness of association rules. IEEE Intell. Syst. Appl. **15**(5), 47–55 (2000). https://doi.org/10.1109/5254.889106
15. Lu, S., Hu, H., Li, F.: Mining weighted association rules. Intell. Data Anal. **5**(3), 211–225 (2001)
16. Ohsaki, M., Kitaguchi, S., Okamoto, K., Yokoi, H., Yamaguchi, T.: Evaluation of rule interestingness measures with a clinical dataset on hepatitis. In: Boulicaut, J.-F., Esposito, F., Giannotti, F., Pedreschi, D. (eds.) PKDD 2004. LNCS (LNAI), vol. 3202, pp. 362–373. Springer, Heidelberg (2004). https://doi.org/10.1007/978-3-540-30116-5_34
17. Padmanabhan, B., Tuzhilin, A.: A belief-driven method for discovering unexpected patterns. In: Proceedings of KDD 1998 - The 4th International Conference on Knowledge Discovery and Data Mining, pp. 94–100. AAAI (1998)
18. Padmanabhan, B., Tuzhilin, A.: Unexpectedness as a measure of interestingness in knowledge discovery. Decision Support Syst. **27**(3), 303–318 (1999). https://doi.org/10.1016/S0167-9236(99)00053-6
19. Padmanabhan, B., Tuzhilin, A.: Small is beautiful: discovering the minimal set of unexpected patterns. In: Proceedings of KDD'2000 - The 6th ACM SIGKDD International Conference on Knowledge Discovery and Data Mining, pp. 54–63. AAAI (2000). http://doi.acm.org/10.1145/347090.347103
20. Piatetsky-Shapiro, G.: Discovery, analysis, and presentation of strong rules. In: Piatetsky-Shapiro, G., Frawley, W.J. (eds.) Knowledge Discovery in Databases, pp. 229–248. AAAI/MIT Press (1991)
21. Sahar, S.: Interestingness via what is not interesting. In: Proceedings of ACM SIGKDD'1999–The 5th ACM SIGKDD International Conference on Knowledge Discovery and Data Mining, pp. 332–336 (1999)
22. Shen, Y.D., Zhang, Z., Yang, Q.: Objective-oriented utility-based association mining. In: Proceedings of ICDM'2002–The 2nd IEEE International Conference on Data Mining, pp. 426–433. IEEE Computer Society (2002)
23. Silberschatz, A., Tuzhilin, A.: What makes patterns interesting in knowledge discovery systems. IEEE Trans. Knowl. Data Eng. **8**(6), 970–974 (1996). https://doi.org/10.1109/69.553165
24. Tan, P.N., Kumar, V., Srivastava, J.: Selecting the right interestingness measure for association patterns. In: Proceedings of ACM SIGKDD' 2002–The 8th ACM SIGKDD International Conference on Knowledge Discovery and Data Mining, vol. 2, pp. 32–41 (2002). https://doi.org/10.1145/775052.775053
25. Vaillant, B., Lenca, P., Lallich, S.: A Clustering of Interestingness Measures. In: Suzuki, E., Arikawa, S. (eds.) DS 2004. LNCS (LNAI), vol. 3245, pp. 290–297. Springer, Heidelberg (2004). https://doi.org/10.1007/978-3-540-30214-8_23
26. Jensen, C.S., et al. (eds.) EDBT 2002. LNCS, vol. 2287. Springer, Heidelberg (2002). https://doi.org/10.1007/3-540-45876-X
27. Webb, G.I., Brain, D.: Generality is predictive of prediction accuracy. In: Proceedings of PKAW'2002- Pacific Rim Knowledge Acquisition Workshop, pp. 117–130 (2002)
28. Zhong, N., Yao, Y.Y., Ohishima, M.: Peculiarity oriented multidatabase mining. IEEE Trans. Knowl. Data Eng. **15**(4), 952–960 (2003)

SONDER: A Data-Driven Methodology for Designing Net-Zero Energy Public Buildings

Ladjel Bellatreche[1]($\boxtimes$), Felix Garcia[2], Don Nguyen Pham[1],
and Pedro Quintero Jiménez[3]

[1] LIAS/ISAE-ENSMA, Poitiers, France
{bellatreche,don-nguyen.pham}@ensma.fr

[2] Centro Nacional del Hidrogeno, 13500 Puertollano, Ciudad Real, Spain
felix.garcia@cnh2.es

[3] Hospital de La Axarquía, Malaga, Spain
pedrom.quintero.sspa@juntadeandalucia.es

Abstract. The reduction of carbon emissions into the atmosphere has become an urgent health issue. The energy in buildings and their construction represents more than 1/3 of final global energy consumption and contributes to nearly 1/4 of greenhouse gas emissions worldwide. **H**eating, **V**entilation, and **A**ir-**C**onditioning (HVAC) systems are major energy consumers and responsible for about 18% of all building energy use. To reduce this huge amount of energy, the Net-Zero Energy Building (nZEB) concept has been imposed by energy authorities. They recommend a massive use of renewable energy technology. With the popularization of Smart Grid, Internet of Things devices, and the **M**achine **L**earning (ML), a couple of data-driven approaches emerged to reach this crucial objective. By analysing these approaches, we figure out that they lack a comprehensive methodology with a well-identified life cycle that favours collaboration between nZEB actors. In this paper, we share our vision for developing Energy Management Systems for nZEB as part of *IMPROVEMENT EU Interreg Sudoe programm*. First, we propose a comprehensive methodology (SONDER), associated with a well-identified life cycle for developing data-driven solutions. Secondly, an instantiation of this methodology is given by considering a case study for predicting the energy consumption of the domestic hot water system in the Regional Hospital of La Axarquia, Spain that includes gas and electricity sections. This prediction is conducted using four ML techniques: multivariate regression, XGBoost, Random Forest and ANN. Our obtained results show the effectiveness of SONDER by offering a fluid collaboration among project actors and the prediction efficiency of ANN.

L. Bellatreche—This work has been carried out with the financial support of the European Regional Development Fund (ERDF) under the program Interreg SUDOE SOE3/P3/E0901 (Project IMPROVEMENT).

© Springer Nature Switzerland AG 2020
M. Song et al. (Eds.): DaWaK 2020, LNCS 12393, pp. 48–59, 2020.
https://doi.org/10.1007/978-3-030-59065-9_5

Keywords: nZEB · HVAC · Methodology · ML · Microgrids ·
Prediction

1 Introduction

In the near-past years, several efforts have been deployed to consider Energy
Efficiency (*EE*) of buildings. Energy regulation authorities set up directives to
reach this goal, by proposing the Net-Zero Energy Building (nZeB) concept. The
completion of this objective has been facilitated by the development of **S**mart
Grids (SGs) [6]. In this context, any building will become a node of the SG.
Thanks to an Energy Management System (EMS), operators of SGs monitor,
control, and optimize the energy use of all energy-intensive-equipments of a
building [16].

These conditions are in favor of implementing the concept of nZEBs. The
buildings get a share of their energy from the grid and return the same amount
during the year when their production of renewable energy is higher than the
demand. Basically, this concept recommends the intensive usage of *renewable
energy technology* to produce a mix of renewable electricity and other *heat
resources* like biomass and solar to generate as much energy as they consume
[17]. Energy regulation institutions gave definitions of nZEBs and recommendations to be implemented by their respective countries. For instance, the directive
2010/31/EU of the European Parliament and of the council of 19 May 2010 on
the energy performance of buildings gave this definition:

> *nZEB means a building that has very good energy performance. The
> nearly zero or very low amount of energy required should be supplied
> to a very significant extent by energy from renewable sources, including
> energy from renewable sources, produced on-site or nearby.*

In terms of plans, this directive imposes all nZEB Member States to reach the
following objectives: **(I)** by 31/12/2020, all new buildings are nearly zero-energy
buildings, and **(II)** after 31/12/2018, new buildings occupied and owned by
public authorities are nearly nZEB. The Member States shall draw up national
plans for increasing the number of nearly zero-energy buildings. These national
plans may include targets differentiated according to the category of building.

Most of the initiatives for reaching nZEB are focused on existing buildings
that represent a large stock. They provide relevant recommendations, data,
infrastructures, intelligent IT programs, scenarios, expertise, services, etc. EU
projects such as ZenN[1] and Zebra[2] are examples materializing these efforts. The
achievement of NZeB passes through an audit of the whole building to identify
more energy-intensive components. HVAC systems are generally responsible for
a significant proportion of total building energy consumption. At the same time,
they are the most common to automate, control and predict.

---

[1] https://www.zenn-fp7.eu/.
[2] https://zebra2020.eu/.

Our EU project IMPROVEMENT aims at converting existing public buildings into nZEB by integrating combined cooling, heating, and power microgrids with neutral clamped inverters using hybrid Energy Storage Systems (ESSs). *We consider the Regional Hospital of La Axarquia, Spain (an existing building) as a case study.* This will guarantee the power quality and continuity of service of sensitive equipment while increasing the EE of that hospital, by managing the domestic hot water system that uses solar radiation, gas, and electricity to heat or cool water and distribute heated water throughout the building.

It should be noticed that Microgrid (MG) has been developed to integrate green and renewable energy on campuses and communities and provide reliable power with economic, environmental, and technical benefits [18]. Hybridization of solar and electric ESS technologies is required to achieve EE for the HVAC systems. To reach this objective, IMPROVEMENT project has to develop advanced EMS able to maximize the advantages of each ESS while avoiding the causes of degradation and/or limitations of each ESS at each sample instant. Control is one of the key disciplines for enabling MG applications. As discussed in [3], usually the control process in MGs is divided into three hierarchical-control layers. The optimization of the MG operation in the electrical market is carried out in the tertiary control where a long-term schedule of the energy exchange with the external grid and among the different units of the MG is executed [10]. Based on inputs such as generation and consumption forecast, operational costs, or energy prices, **the tertiary controller** deals with the long-term schedule for every component of the MG, which is communicated to the **secondary controller** which is responsible for its implementation in the short-term [7]. The power quality in the MG is managed in the **primary control** according to the references calculated by the secondary controller. Model Predictive Control (MPC) has been proposed to handle the different subsystems constraints while a cost function is optimized subjected to generation and demand forecast. As described in [3], MPC provides an intuitive approach to the optimal control of the system subject to constraints. The MPC strategy is based on the selection of the best among all feasible control sequences over a future horizon according to several optimization criteria formulated in a cost function to be minimized.

While the advantages in the results of the MPC controller are widely discussed in the literature, MPC controllers have also their drawbacks. One of the most important limitations is related to the accuracy of the predictive model of the plant to be optimized. With this limitation in mind, we propose in this paper a predictive model for the energy generation and consumption of the HVAC systems using collected data from sensors located in our hospital.

The rapid progress of AI-driven solutions is an asset for nZEBs. To assist designers of these solutions, the development of a comprehensive methodology that favours *collaboration among a multidisciplinary team* has become a necessity. One of the deliverable reports of AZEB (Affordable Zero Energy Buildings) EU project published in 2017 pointed the interdisciplinary barrier in the construction process of a nZEB and recommended the development of integrated methodologies for nZEBs, educational programs, and dissemination strategies[3].

Two main contributions of this paper are: (i) proposing a methodology with a well-identified life-cycle for developing data-driven solutions for nZEBs and (ii) instantiating it using a case study for predicting the energy consumption of the domestic hot water system in the Regional Hospital of La Axarquia.

The paper is organized as follows: Sect. 2 describes our life cycle for designing data-driven solutions for nZEBs. In Sect. 3, an instantiation of this life cycle is given, where four ML algorithms are presented. Section 4 concludes the paper.

2 SONDER Methodology for Designing nZeB Solutions

With the spectacular use of ML in various domains, the second class of data-driven methods has been proposed that exploit historical data to predict energy use.

Preliminary, data-driven approaches follow a 5-step methodology which includes the following steps [14]: **(1) Pre-processing** of raw data which is an essential step for any data-driven approach because any incorrect or inconsistent data may potentially cause errors in the final prediction model and consequently biases the analysis [9]. It includes other sub-steps such as data cleaning, data integration/fusion, data transformation, and/or data reduction. **(2) Feature selection** that consists in automatically or manually selecting features that contribute most to the prediction variable or output in which we are interested in. **(3) Prediction model development** using supervised/unsupervised ML algorithms such as SVM, ANN, decision trees, and/or other statistical algorithms. **(4) model validation** and error calculation to quantify the quality of the obtained models and (5) **prediction**.

This 5-steps methodology is too generic and often fails in putting all actors in the scope of the design. For instance, data preprocessing has to integrate the nature, infrastructures, and constraints issuing this data. Another important aspect in nZEDB concerns the communication/networking technologies used to vehicle data from the source side to the data processing layer, which is completely ignored by this methodology.

By making the parallel of the worldwide success of data management solutions, we realize that they were obtained thanks to the presence of popular and comprehensive methodologies associated with a well-known life cycle. For instance, the design methodologies of traditional databases follow the ANSI/SPARC architecture [2]. For each generation of databases, these methodologies have been extended to consider the specificities of this type of databases [8].

---

[3] https://azeb.eu/wp-content/uploads/2019/04/Potential-barriers-for-the-construction-of-nZEBs-and-energy-buildings.pdf.

> *We claim that the success of data-driven approaches in nZEBs passes through the presence of a comprehensive methodology with well-defined phases augmenting the collaboration among multidisciplinary actors. This issue is one of the main objectives of the IMPROVEMENT project.*

To do so, we exploit our great experience in **contributing** to different phases of data warehousing (*DW*) technology [11,12].

The scientific multidisciplinary of the partners of our IMPROVEMENT project triggers our reflection in leveraging the *DW* life cycle to fulfil the requirements nZEB. Figure 1 shows important layers of our methodology, called SONDER. It includes 5 layers related to <u>S</u>ources, <u>N</u>etworks, <u>D</u>ata, <u>E</u>xploitation, and <u>R</u>eporting.

1. Source Layer. The role of this layer is to describe in detail different producers of data such as sensors, IoT objects, social networks and external resources such as data lakes and weather information. Note that each sensor has its own trademark and constraints (e.g., size, price, etc.).

2. Network Layer. The huge amount of heterogeneous data (different formats and structures) generated by sources cannot be exploited directly. This is because it has to be transferred to the data layer via networks, where each type of data has to be handled by its favorite network itself has its own specificities.

3. Daya Layer. This data cannot be sent directly to exploitation because it is not cleaned and prepared due to the presence of noises, redundancies, malicious elements and interference. The data layer has for mission to pre-process it before being committed to storage repositories. This step increases the quality of data and consequently the taken decisions. This phase has been widely studied in *DW* under the ETL (Extract/Transform/Load) name. New programming paradigms such as Spark and distributed storage infrastructures represent an important asset to perform the preprocessing phases.

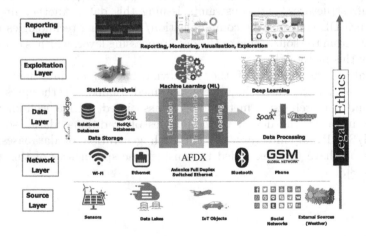

Fig. 1. Our Life Cycle of Designing NZeB Solutions

4. Exploitation Layer. Once the data is prepared it will be stored in appropriate stores or polystores [15] to be ready for the exploitation layer, where On-line Analytical Processing operations, Statistical analysis tools (e.g. R), ML Techniques (e.g., regression methods, neural networks) will be performed. Popular libraries about these techniques are Pytorch (Facebook), Tensorflow (Google), Keras and Caffe (UC/Berkeley, USA).

5. Reporting Layer. The obtained results will be visualized using tools in the reporting layer. The outputs of this phase facilitate data exploration, scientific insight, communication, education, and recommendation. Visualization techniques in this layer can be also used to assist actors of nZEB in their process of modeling and visualizing the transformations applied to the data (**in data layer**) before obtaining a dataset feeding the ML Models. ER4ML is an example of such a tool [13].

6. Legal and Ethic. Issues such as privacy, datafication, dataveillance and data uses are orthogonal to these layers. For instance, data collected by sensors could provide information about the occupancy of offices and could be potentially used to control the presence of people in their working place [4].

SONDER connects automatically each actor of the project to her layer(s) and everyone will have a great vision about the evolution of the nZEB project. SONDER can be used to convince stakeholders in adopting nZEB solutions.

3   SONDER and ML as a Service for nZEBs

In this section, we propose an example of the usage of SONDER to predict the energy consumption of the domestic hot water system of our hospital.

SONDER Layer Identification. This system is composed of three components representing our source layer: the boiler section, the solar energy section, and the domestic hot water distribution section.

Sensors are placed in the Boiler section to monitor pulse gas meter, energy meter (inlet and outlet temperature, flow, power, energy), collector temperature probe, two heating collector's temperature probes, buffer tank temperature probe, pressure probes, actuated valves, and boiler control communications. Regarding the solar energy, sensors are associated with: four energy meters for sub-circuits (which give inlet/outlet temperatures, flow, power, energy), solar radiation probe, outside temperature probe, solar primary inlet, and outlet temperature probes, three temperature probes in each solar energy storage tank, etc. Sensors placed in Domestic Hot Water Distribution (DHW) are related to an energy meter, DHW inlet/outlet temperature probe, the DHW tank, etc.

Note that the different sensors or register points of the system come from different controllers. Some of them are equipped with field elements such as temperature probes[4] whose manufacturing process gives us a range of values that are programmed in each controller according to their specifications. Most

---

[4] https://partners.trendcontrols.com/trendproducts/cd/en/ecatdata/pg_tbtx.html.

of these controllers with physical field elements are from the Trend Controls brand. The server that we use for data collection is also from Trend Controls 963.

Regarding the network layer, we have also integrated elements for communications with very different protocols, specifically the KAMSTRUP energy meters communicate through Modbus protocol and connected in Jace Tridium Niagara "Gateways"[5]. These devices do not belong to Trend components. They are integrated into the network passing data to other Trend components. This data is displayed on the 963-Trend-Control device that carried out their periodic collection in a SQL Database.

Multiple protocols that the Niagara systems support are bidirectional. This means that in addition to the memory capacity that they have, they also allow calculating and programming actions directly inside them. They can interact with the rest of the installation (TREND components and rest of devices) in an agile and secure way. Specifically, we are using several communication protocols such as Modbus, Modbus TCP, BACnet, BACnet IP, LonWorks, as well as TREND's proprietary protocol. All of these data records which are obtained directly from the different types of equipment are saved in the database through the *SCADA 963*.

At the end of all these programming and integration processes, all registration points are treated by the database as they were physical field elements. Their precision is conditioned by the measurement quality offered by the component manufacturer. This precision can be also affected by several issues related to communications or physical problems of the different components of the whole system. Nevertheless, this matter is not frequent. In addition, concerning the Trend Controls devices, we use the SET programming tool. It allows us to program as much as possible in the programmable controllers of this brand, including field elements, probes, etc.

Now the data is ready to be exploited. It is extracted in CSV files from the DBMS (*in Data Layer*). It is taken at different times depending on the sensor. Two-time intervals are considered: every 15 mins and every 24 h. We use "Pandas" is a data analysis and manipulation tool, which is used in this report to process, clean, combine and arrange data for the input of prediction models. Furthermore, missing values in the dataset are taken into account in order to secure the compatibility in size between variables.

Finally, the data is ready for the *exploitation process*. Its dataset is split into 80% and 20% of the data size for the training dataset and testing dataset respectively. We use the root mean squared error (RMSE) to evaluate the performance of the consumption prediction models. $RMSE = \frac{\sum_{i=1}^{n}(y_{predict,i} - y_{data,i})^2}{n}$.

From our dataset, two sets of variables are identified: *dependent variables*: gas consumption and electricity consumption and *independent variables*: heating or cooling degree days, daily enthalpy, and daily temperature. These variables will be used for predicting boiler gas and electricity consumption.

---

[5] https://www.tridium.com/en-mx/products-services/niagara4.

In this study, we choose four algorithms: multivariate regression, random forest, XGBoost, and Artificial Neural Networks (ANN). This choice is based on the recommendations given in [1]. These algorithms are tested and compared using the data set (527 days). Our development was conducted in the Spyder 3.7 software, with the Python programming language. The following libraries are used: Seaborn for data visualization, Keras and Scikit-learn for machine learning, where Keras for ANN and Scikit-learn enables other algorithms, including multivariate regression, random forests.

Boiler Gas Consumption Prediction. The gas consumption is measured by energy meters which are equipped for each boiler. First of all, we conduct the feature selection algorithm to choose the three most important regressors for gas consumption. The result is arranged in order of priority as: *heating degree days* x_1, *daily enthalpy* x_2, and *daily mean outdoor temperature* x_3 that are used for the training process.

Multivariate Regression: It performs through more variables compared to traditional linear regression. It is supposed to get more accurate results. Feature selection is conducted to choose the three features used to predict the total boiling gas consumption (y) which are: heating degrees (x_1), daily enthalpy (x_2) and medium outdoor degrees (x_3). The obtained multivariate equation is: $y = 1025.19 + 10.84 \times x_1 + (-1.47) \times x_2 + (-42.93) \times x_3$. Figure 2 summarizes its prediction model.

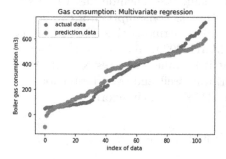 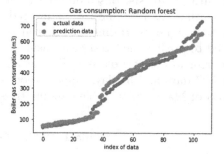

Fig. 2. Multivariate regression prediction model

Fig. 3. Random forest prediction model (Gas).

Random Forest Model: is a tree-based ensemble, where each tree depends on a collection of random variables. We implement this algorithm using 6 predictor variables (enthalpy, heating degrees, humidity, max temperature, min temperature, medium temperature). The obtained results are shown in Fig. 3.

XGBoost: is one of the most popular and efficient implementations of the Gradient Boosted Trees algorithm, a supervised learning technique. It is based on function approximation by optimizing specific loss functions as well as applying several regularization techniques [5]. It is an open-source library. The obtained results applying XGBoost on our 6 dataset variables are summarized in Fig. 4.

ANN: ANN models are used for deriving meaningful information from imprecise and complicated data. The model that we propose for 6 dataset variables has three hidden layers with Rectified Linear Unit as the activation function and the training phase is conducted with 500 epochs. The obtained results are described in Fig. 5.

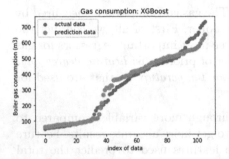

Fig. 4. XGBoost prediction model (Gas).

Fig. 5. ANN Prediction Model (Gas).

Result Analysis. Based on the experiment results, we conclude that the ANN algorithm has the lowest error in predicting the gas consumption of the boiler system and outperforms the other algorithms. Furthermore, this ANN model is used to predict the latest gas consumption (March 2020) to evaluate the change of error in the new dataset. This means that it is trained and tested with data in 527 days and 31 days respectively. It performs well and even better for the data of March 2020. Table 1 summarizes the RMSE of each algorithm.

Table 1. RMSE of different algorithms

Data size (days)	Algorithm	Error (RMSE)
527	Multivariate regression	105.26
527	Random forest	103.26
527	XGBoost	83.50
527	Neural networks	80.69

Electric Consumption Prediction. The electric is consumed by production and distribution of chilled water for air conditioning. To be more specific, these are the electrical consumption of the chillers that are in operation at any given time, and the electrical consumption of the secondary pumps for distribution to the different air conditioning circuits. We implement the same four above algorithms with electric datasets. Their results are illustrated in Figs. 6, 7, 8, 9. For multivariate regression the predicted consumption (y) is defined by the following equation: $y = -815.23 + 353.73 \times x_1 + (-49.15) \times x_2 + 174.03 \times x_3$, where x_1, x_2 and x_3 represent respectively cooling degrees-day, daily max temperature, and daily medium temperature.

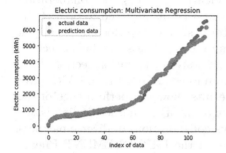

Fig. 6. Multivariate regression prediction model (Electric).

Fig. 7. Random forest prediction model (Electric).

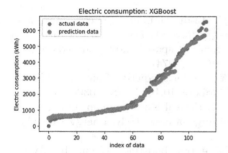

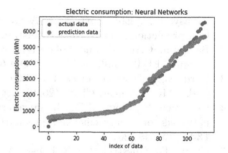

Fig. 8. XGBoost prediction model.

Fig. 9. ANN prediction model.

Table 2 summarizes the performance in terms of RMSE of our studied algorithms.

Table 2. RMSE of each studied algorithm

Data size (days)	Algorithm	Error (RMSE)
562	Multivariate regression	945.12
562	Random forest	1021.90
562	XGBoost	1114.67
562	ANN	927.51

4   Conclusion

In this paper, we present the first findings of our IMPROVEMENT project, carried out with the financial support of the European Regional Development Fund (ERDF) under the program Interreg SUDOE SOE3/P3/E0901. In this project, we propose a comprehensive methodology named *SONDER* to deal with any nZEB project. It includes five layers corresponding to sources, networks, data, exploitation, and reporting. This life cycle clearly enhances the collaboration between building actors. This methodology has been instantiated to predict the energy consumption of the domestic hot water system of the Hospital Axarquia of Velez-Malaga, Spain that includes three main components: the boiler section, the solar energy section, and the domestic hot water distribution section. Four ML algorithms: multivariate regression, random forest, XGBoost, and ANN have been used for this purpose. The obtained results show the performance of the ANN in the energy prediction in the context of nZEBs. Another finding is the effectiveness of our methodology which allows collaborations of diverse partners.

Currently, we are integrating our results in the IMPROVEMENT Energy Management System. Another direction concerns the standardization of SONDER methodology.

References

1. Amasyali, K., El-Gohary, N.M.: A review of data-driven building energy consumption prediction studies. Renew. Sustain. Energy Rev. **81**, 1192–1205 (2018)
2. Bachman, C.W.: Summary of current work - ansi/x3/sparc/study group - database systems. FDT - Bull. ACM SIGMOD **6**(3), 16–39 (1974)
3. Bordons, C., Garcia-Torres, F., Ridao, M.A.: Model Predictive Control of Microgrids. AIC. Springer, Cham (2020). https://doi.org/10.1007/978-3-030-24570-2
4. Casconea, Y., Luigi, M.F., GianlucaSerale, G.: Ethical issues of monitoring sensor networks for energy efficiency in smart buildings: a case study. Energy Procedia **134**, 337–345 (2017)
5. Chen, T., Guestrin, C.: Xgboost: A scalable tree boosting system. In: ACM SIGKDD, pp. 785–794 (2016)
6. El-hawary, M.E.: The smart grid: state-of-the-art and future trends. Electric Power Comp. Syst. **42**(3–4), 239–250 (2014)
7. Garcia-Torres, F., Bordons, L.V.C.: Optimal load sharing of hydrogen-based microgrids with hybrid storage using model predictive control. IEEE TIE **63**(8), 4919–4928 (2016)
8. Fankam, C., Jean, S., Bellatreche, L., Ameur, Y.A.: Extending the ANSI/SPARC architecture database with explicit data semantics: an ontology-based approach. In: ECSA, pp. 318–321 (2008)
9. García, S., Luengo, J., Herrera, F.: Tutorial on practical tips of the most influential data preprocessing algorithms in data mining. Knowl. Based Syst. **98**, 1–29 (2016)
10. Garcia-Torres, F., Bordons, C.: Optimal economical schedule of hydrogen-based microgrids with hybrid storage using model predictive control. IEEE TIE **62**(8), 5195–5207 (2015)
11. Golfarelli, M.: Data warehouse life cycle and design. In: Encyclopedia of Database Systems, Second Edition (2018)

12. Khouri, S., Semassel, K., Bellatreche, L.: Managing data warehouse traceability: a life-cycle driven approach. In: CAiSE, pp. 199–213 (2015)
13. Lanasri, D., Ordonez, C., Bellatreche, L., Khouri, S.: ER4ML: an ER modeling tool to represent data transformations in data science. In: ER Demos, pp. 123–127 (2019)
14. Liu, Z., Wu, D., Wei, H., Cao, G.: Machine learning for building energy and indoor environment: a perspective. ArXiv abs/1801.00779 (2018)
15. Meehan, J., Aslantas, C., Zdonik, S., Tatbul, N., Du, J.: Data ingestion for the connected world. In: CIDR (2017)
16. Saleh, M., Esa, Y., Mohamed, A.A.: Communication-based control for DC micro-grids. IEEE Trans. Smart Grid **10**(2), 2180–2195 (2019)
17. Sartori, I., Marszal, A., Napolitano, A., Pless, S., Torcellini, P., Voss, K.: Criteria for Definition of Net Zero Energy Buildings, pp. 25–36 (2010)
18. Wissner, M.: The smart grid - a saucerful of secrets? Appl. Energy **88**(7), 2509–2518 (2011)

Reverse Engineering Approach for NoSQL Databases

Fatma Abdelhedi[1,2], Amal Ait Brahim[1], Rabah Tighilt Ferhat[1(✉)], and Gilles Zurfluh[1]

[1] Toulouse Institute of Computer Science Research (IRIT), Toulouse Capitole University,
Toulouse, France
{amal.ait-brahim,rabah.tighilt-ferhat,
Gilles.Zurfluh}@ut-capitole.fr
[2] CBI2 – TRIMANE, Paris, France
Fatma.Abdelhedi@trimane.fr

Abstract. In recent years, the need to use NoSQL systems to store and exploit big data has been steadily increasing. Most of these systems are characterized by the property "schema less" which means absence of the data model when creating a database. This property offers an undeniable flexibility allowing the user to add new data without making any changes on the data model. However, the lack of an explicit data model makes it difficult to express queries on the database. Therefore, users (developers and decision-makers) still need the database data model to know how data are stored and related, and then to write their queries. In previous works, we have proposed a process to extract the physical model of a document-oriented NoSQL database. In this paper, we aim to extend this work to achieve a reverse engineering of NoSQL databases in order to provide an element of semantic knowledge close to human understanding. The reverse engineering process is ensured by a set of transformation algorithms. We provide experiments of our approach using a case study taken from the medical field.

Keywords: Reverse engineering · NoSQL · Big data · Schema-less · Conceptual model

1 Introduction

Big Data have attracted a great deal of attention in recent years thanks to the huge amount of data managed, the types of data supported and the speed at which this data is collected and analyzed. This has definitely impacted the tools required to store Big Data, and new kinds of data management tools i.e. NoSQL systems have arisen [7]. Compared to existing DBMSs, NoSQL systems are generally accepted to support greater data volume and to ensure faster data access, undeniable flexibility and scalability [1].

One of the NoSQL key features is that databases can be schema-less. This means, in a table, meanwhile the row is inserted, the attributes names and types are specified. This property offers an undeniable flexibility that facilitates the data model evolution and allows end-users to add new information without the need of database administrator; but, at the same time, it makes the database manipulation more difficult. Indeed, even

© Springer Nature Switzerland AG 2020
M. Song et al. (Eds.): DaWaK 2020, LNCS 12393, pp. 60–69, 2020.
https://doi.org/10.1007/978-3-030-59065-9_6

in Big Data context, the user still needs a data model that offers a visibility of how data is structured in the database (tables name, attributes names and types, relationships, etc.). In practice, the developer that has created the database, is also in charge of writing queries. Thus, he already knows how data is stored and related in the database; so, he can easily express his requests. However, this solution cannot be applied to all cases; for instance, the developer who is asked for doing the application maintenance, does not know the data model. It is the same for a decision maker who needs to query a database while he was not involved in its creation.

On the one hand, NoSQL systems have proven their efficiency to handle Big Data. On the other hand, the needs of a NoSQL database model remain up-to-date. Therefore, we are convinced that it's important to provide to users (developers and decision-makers) two data models describing the database: (1) a physical model that describes the internal organization of data and allows to express queries and (2) a conceptual model that provides a high level of abstraction and a semantic knowledge element close to human comprehension, which guarantees efficient data management [15].

In a previous works, we have proposed a process for extracting a physical model starting from a NoSQL database [5]. In this paper, we aim to propose an extension of this work by transforming the physical model (already obtained) into a conceptual model; a reverse engineering process will be used for this.

The remainder of the paper is structured as follows. Section 2 reviews previous work. Section 3 describes our reverse engineering process. Section 4 details our experiments and compare our solution against those presented in Sect. 2. Finally, Sect. 5 concludes the paper and announces future work.

2 Related Work

The problem of extracting the data model from schema-less NoSQL databases has been the subject of several research works. Most of these works focus on the physical level [2, 3, 9, 11–14]. In this context, we have proposed a process to extract a document-oriented database physical model [5]. This process applies a sequence of transformations formalized with the QVT standard proposed by the Object Management Group[1] (OMG). Which is original in our solution is that it takes into account the links between different collections.

However, we should highlight that only few works, [8, 11, 15], have addressed the extraction of a NoSQL database conceptual model. In [8], the authors propose an extraction process of a conceptual model for a graph-oriented NoSQL database (Neo4J). In this particular type of NoSQL databases, the database contains nodes (objects) and binary links between them. The proposed process takes as input the insertion requests of objects and links; and then returns an Entity/Association model. This process is based on an MDA architecture and successively applies two transformations. The first is to build a graph (Nodes + Edges) from the Neo4j query code. The second consists of extracting an Entity/Association model from this graph by transforming the nodes with the same label into entities and the edges into associations. These works are specific to graph-oriented NoSQL databases generally used to manage strongly linked data such as those

---

[1] https://www.omg.org/.

from social networks. Authors in [11] propose a process to extract a conceptual model (UML class diagram) from a JSON document. This process consists of 2 steps. The first step extracts a physical model in JSON format. The second step generates the UML class diagram by transforming the physical model into a root class RC, the primitive fields (Number, String and Boolean) into attributes of RC and the structured fields into component classes linked to RC by composition links. Thus, this work only considers the composition links and ignores other kinds of links (association and aggregation links for example). The process proposed in [15] deals with the mapping of a document-oriented database into a conceptual model. It consists of a set of entities with one or more versions. This work considers the two types of links: binary-association and composition. Binary-association and composition links are respectively extracted using the reference and structured fields. This solution does not consider other links that are usually used like n-ary, generalization and aggregation links.

Regarding the state of the art, the existing solutions have the advantage to start from the conceptual level, but they do not consider all the UML class diagram features that we need for our medical use case. Indeed, the process in [8] concern only graph-oriented systems that, unlike document-oriented databases, do not allow to express structured attributes and composition links. On the other hand, the solution of [11] starts from a document-oriented database but do not consider aggregation, generalization and association links that are used to link data in our case study. As [11], authors in [15] use a document-oriented database, but do not consider the generalization and aggregation links, association classes and also n-ary association links that are the most used in the medical application.

3   Reverse Engineering Process

Our work aims to provide users with models to manipulate NoSQL databases. Two models are proposed: (1) the physical model to write queries on this database and application code and (2) the conceptual model to give the meaning of the data contained in the database. When data structures are complex, these two models are essential to enable users (usually, developers and decision-makers) to understand and manipulate data independently.

As part of this work, we proposed mechanisms for discovering a physical model from a NoSQL database in a previous paper [5]. The current paper completes the latter and focuses on the transformation of the physical model into a conceptual model represented by using a UML class diagrams (red frame in Fig. 1) and which provides users with the semantics of the data.

Note that we limit our study to document-oriented NoSQL databases that are the most complete to express links between objects (use of referenced and nested data). We propose the *ToConceptualModel* process which applies a set of transformations ensuring the passage of a NoSQL physical model towards a UML class diagram.

In the following sections, we detail the components of the *ToConceptualModel* process by specifying the three elements: (a) the source, (b) the target and (c) the transformation algorithms.

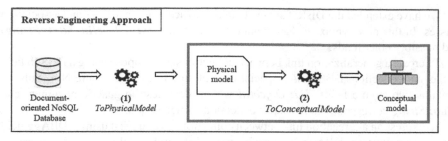

Fig. 1. Overview of *ToConceptualModel* process (Color figure online)

3.1 Source: Physical Model

The physical model is produced by the *ToPhysicalModel* process (shown in Fig. 1). In this paper, it is the source of the *ToConceptualModel* process that we will study here. The physical model is defined as a pair (N, CL), where:

- N is the physical model name,
- $CL = \{cl_1, \ldots, cl_n\}$ is a set of collections.
  $\forall$ i $\in$ [1...n], a collection $cl_i \in CL$ is defined as a pair (N, F), where:

  - $cl_i.N$ is the collection name,
  - $cl_i.F = AF \cup SF$ is a set of fields, where:

    - $AF = \{af_1, \ldots, af_m\}$ is a set of atomic fields. $\forall$ j $\in$ [1...m], an atomic field af_j $\in AF$ is defined as a tuple (N, T, M), where:
    - af_j.N is the af_j name,
    - af_j.T is the af_j type; it is one of the standard data types such as Integer, String, Boolean, ...,
    - af_j.M is a boolean which indicates whether af_j is multivalued or not.

    - $SF = \{sf_1, \ldots, sf_l\}$ is a set of structured fields. $\forall$ k $\in$ [1...l], a structured field sf_k $\in SF$ is defined as a tuple (N, F', M), where:

      - sf_k.N is the sf_k name,
      - $sf_k.F' = AF' \cup SF'$ is a set of fields that compose the structured field sf_k (see above),
      - sf_k.M is a boolean which indicates whether sf_k is multivalued or not.

To express a link between two collections, we used a field called DBRef, which is un standard proposed by MongoDB[2]. A DBRef field is a special case of a structured field (N, F', M), where: N is the link name; F' contains two atomic fields: *$id: ObjectId* which corresponds to the identifier of the referenced document and *$Ref: String* which corresponds to the name of the collection that contains the referenced document; M indicates whether the link is monovalued or multivalued.

---

[2] https://www.mongodb.com/.

We have extended the DBRef syntax to take into account n-ary links and association classes. In this new syntax, F' can contain several pairs *($id: ObjectId, $Ref: String)* and possibly other fields.

To create a generalization link between collections, we propose using a DBSub field in the sub-collection. DBSub is a special case of structured field where N = Sub; F' contains two atomic fields: *$id: ObjectId* which identifies the generic document and *$Sub: String* corresponds to the super-collection name; M = 0.

To express an aggregation link between collections, we suggest using a DBAgg field in the part collection. DBAgg is a special case of structured field (N, F', M) where N = Agg; F' contains two atomic fields: *$id: ObjectId* which identifies the part document (aggregated) and *$Agg: String* corresponds to the name of the part collection.

3.2 Target: Conceptual Model

A UML Class Diagram (CD) is defined as a tuple *(N, C, L)*, where:

- N is the CD name,
- $C = \{c_1, \ldots, c_n\}$ is a set of classes,
- $L = AL \cup CL \cup AGL \cup GL$ is a set of links.

Classes:
$\forall\, i \in [1\ldots n]$, a class $c_i \in C$ is defined as a pair (N, A), where:
- $c_i.N$ is the class name,
- $c_i.A = AA \cup SA$ is a set of attributes, where:

  - $AA = \{aa_1, \ldots, aa_m\}$ is a set of atomic attributes. $\forall\, j \in [1\ldots m]$, an atomic attribute $aa_j \in AA$ is defined as a tuple (N, T, M), where:

    - $aa_j.N$ is the aa_j name,
    - $aa_j.T$ is the aa_j type; T can have the value: String, Integer, Boolean …,
    - $aa_j.M$ is a boolean which indicates whether aa_j is multivalued or not.

  - $SA = \{sa_1, \ldots, sa_l\}$ is a set of structured attributes. $\forall\, k \in [1\ldots l]$, a structured attribute $sa_k \in SA$ is defined as a tuple (N, A', M), where:

    - $sa_k.N$ is the sa_k name,
    - $sa_k.A' = AA' \cup SA'$ is a set of attributes that compose sa_k (see above),
    - $sa_k.M$ is a boolean which indicates whether sa_k is multivalued or not.

Links:
- $AL = \{al_1, \ldots, al_m\}$ is a set of association links. $\forall\, i \in [1\ldots m]$, an association link $al_i \in AL$ is defined as a tuple (N, RC, A), where:

  - $la_i.N$ is the al_i name,

- $la_i.RC = \{rc_1, \ldots, rc_f\}$ a set of related collections with degree $f \geq 2$. $\forall\, j \in [1\ldots f]$, rc_j is defined as a pair (c, cr), where:

  - $rc_j.c$ is the related class name,
  - $rc_j.cr$ is the multiplicity corresponding to c.

- $la_i. A = AA \cup SA$ is a set of attributes of al_i (see above). Note that if $al_i. A \neq \emptyset$ then al_i is an association class.

- $CL = \{cl_1, \ldots, cl_m\}$ is a set of composition links. $\forall\, i \in [1\ldots m]$, a composition link $cl_i \in CL$ is defined as a pair $(rc^{composite}, rc^{component})$ où:

  - $cl_i.rc^{composite}$ is a pair defining the composite class; it is in the form of (c, cr), where:

    - $rc^{composite}.c$ is the composite class name.
    - $rc^{composite}.cr$ is the multiplicity corresponding to the composite class. This multiplicity generally contains the value $0\ldots1, 1\ldots1$ or 1 for the contracted form.

  - $cl_i.rc^{component}$ is a pair defining the component class; it is in the form of (c, cr), where:

    - $rc^{component}.c$ is the component class name.
    - $rc^{component}.cr$ is the multiplicity corresponding to the component class.

- $AGL = \{agl_1, \ldots, agl_m\}$ is a set of aggregation links. $\forall\, i \in [1\ldots m]$, an aggregation link $agl_i \in AGL$ is defined as a pair $(rc^{aggregate}, rc^{part})$, where:

  - $agl_i.rc^{aggregate}$ is a pair defining the aggregate class; it is in the form of (c, cr), where:

    - $rc^{aggregate}.c$ is the aggregate class name,
    - $rc^{aggregate}.cr$ is the multiplicity corresponding to the aggregate class,

  - $agl_i.rc^{part}$ is a pair defining the part class; it is in the form of (c, cr), where:

    - $rc^{part}.c$ is the part class name,
    - $rc^{part}.cr$ is the multiplicity corresponding to the part class,

- $GL = \{gl_1, \ldots, gl_m\}$ is a set of generalization links. $\forall\, i \in [1\ldots m]$, a generalization link $gl_i \in LH$ is defined as a pair (sc, SSC), where:

  - $gl_i.sc$ is the super-class name,
  - $gl_i.SBC = \{sbc_1, \ldots, sbc_k\}$, where: $\forall\, j \in [1\ldots k]$, with $k \geq 1$, ssc_j is a sub-class.

3.3 Transformation Algorithms

The mapping from the physical model to the conceptual model is ensured by applying six transformation algorithms: $TA_{Collection}$, $TA_{AtomicField}$, $TA_{StructuredField}$, TA_{DBRef}, TA_{DBSub} and TA_{DBAgg}.

- $TA_{Collection}$

This algorithm transforms a collection into a class. $TA_{Collection}$ possesses the following properties:

Input: $cl = (N, F)$: a collection defined by a name N and a set of fields $F = AF \cup SF$.
Output: $c = (N, A)$: a class defined by a name N and a set of attributes $A = AA \cup SA$.

- $TA_{AtomicField}$

This algorithm transforms an atomic field into an atomic attribute. $TA_{AtomicField}$ possesses the following properties:

Input: $af = (N, T, M)$: an atomic field defined by a name N, a type T and a boolean M.
Output: $aa = (N, T, M)$: an atomic attribute defined by a name N, a type T and a boolean M.

- $TA_{StructuredField}$

This algorithm transforms a structured field which is not a DBRef. The result of this transformation can be either a composition link if the structured field consists of at least one DBRef field or a structured attribute otherwise. $TA_{StructuredField}$ possesses the following properties:

Input: $sf = (N, F', M)$: a structured field defined by a name N, a set of fields $F' = AF' \cup SF'$ and a boolean M. sf is declared in the collection c_0.
Output:

- $cl = (rc^{composite}, rc^{component})$: a composition link defined by a composite class $rc^{composite}$ and a component class $rc^{component}$.
- Or $sa = (N, A', M)$: a structured attribute defined by a name N, a set of attributes A' and a boolean M.

- TA_{DBRef}

This algorithm transforms a DBRef field into an association link. TA_{DBRef} possesses the following properties:

Input: $dbref = (N, F', M)$: a DBRef field defined by a name N, a set of fields F'(composed of n pairs *($id: ObjectId, $Ref: C_i$)* with $i \in [1...n]$ and possibly, m atomic fields and l structured fields) and a boolean M. $dbref$ is declared in the collection c_0.
Output: $al = (N, RC, A)$: an association link defined by a name N, a set of related classes RC and a set of attributes $A = AA \cup SA$.

- TA_{DBSub}

This algorithm transforms a DBSub field into a generalization link. TA_{DBSub} possesses the following properties:

Input: $dbsub = (N, F', M)$: a DBSub field defined as a structured field whose N = Sub; F' consists of two atomic fields: *$id: ObjectId* and *$Sub: SCl*; the value of M is 0. *dbsub* is declared in the collection SbCl.
Output: $gl = (sc, SBC)$: a generalization link defined by a super-class sc and a set of sub-classes SBC.

- TA_{DBAgg}

This algorithm transforms a DBAgg field into an aggregation link. TA_{DBAgg} possesses the following properties:

Input: $dbagg = (N, F', M)$: a DBAgg field defined by N = Agg, a set of fields F' (consists of two atomic fields *$id: ObjectId* and *$Agg: c_1*) and a boolean M = 0. *dbagg* is declared in the part collection c_0.
Output: $agl = (rc^{aggregate}, rc^{part})$: an aggregation link defined by an aggregate class $rc^{aggregate}$ and a part class rc^{part}.

4   Experiments

4.1   Implantation of the *ToConceptualModel* Process

To implement the *ToConceptualModel* process, we used the Eclipse Modeling Framework EMF [6] which is a suitable environment for modeling, meta-modeling and model transformation. Our process is expressed as a sequence of elementary steps that build the resulting model (UML class diagram) step by step from the source model (physical model). **Step1:** we create a source and a target metamodel to represent the concepts handled by our process. **Step2:** we build an instance of the source metamodel. For this, we use the standard based XML Metadata Interchange (XMI) format. This instance is shown in Fig. 2. **Step3:** we implement the transformation algorithms by means of the QVT language provided within EMF. **Step4:** we test the transformation by running the QVT script created in step 3. This script takes as input the source model built in step 2 (physical model) and returns as output a UML class diagram. The result is provided in the form of XMI file as shown in Fig. 3.

4.2   Comparison

The aim of this section is to compare our solution with the three works [8, 11, 15] presented in Sect. 3 and which studied the process of extracting a NoSQL database conceptual model. To overcome the limits of these works, we have proposed a more complete solution which addresses different types of attributes and links: atomic and structured attributes, association (binary and n-ary), generalization, aggregation and composition links as well as association classes.

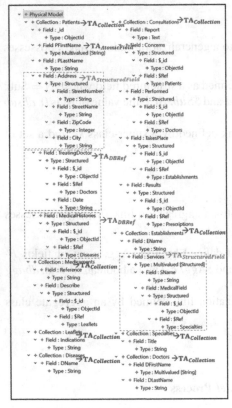

Fig. 2. Source model   **Fig. 3.** Target model

5 Conclusion and Future Work

Our works are dealing with the reverse engineering mechanisms of schema-less NoSQL databases to provide users with models to manipulate this type of database.

We have presented in this paper an automatic process for mapping a UML conceptual model starting from a NoSQL physical model. We note that we have proposed, in previous works, a process to extract a NoSQL physical model starting from a document-oriented NoSQL database. So, we use this physical model to generate a conceptual model that makes it easier for developers and decision-makers to (1) understand how data are stored and related in the database and (2) write their queries. The mapping between the two models, physical and conceptual, is ensured by a set of transformation algorithms.

Regarding the state of the art, which is original in our solution is that it addressed different types of attributes and links: atomic and structured attributes, association (binary and n-ary), generalization, aggregation and composition links as well as association classes.

As future work, we plan to complete our transformation process to have more semantics in the conceptual model by taking into account other types of links such as reference links.

References

1. Angadi, A.B., Gull, K.C.: Growth of new databases & analysis of NOSQL datastores. Int. J. Adv. Res. Comput. Sci. Softw. Eng. **3**, 1307–1319 (2013)
2. Baazizi, M.A., Lahmar, H.B., Colazzo, D., Ghelli, G., Sartiani, C.: Schema inference for massive JSON datasets. In: Extending Database Technology (EDBT) (March 2017)
3. Baazizi, M.-A., Colazzo, D., Ghelli, G., Sartiani, C.: Parametric schema inference for massive JSON datasets. VLDB J. **28**(4), 497–521 (2019). https://doi.org/10.1007/s00778-018-0532-7
4. Bondiombouy, C.: Query processing in cloud multistore systems. In: BDA: Bases de Données Avancées (2015)
5. Brahim, A., Ferhat, R., Zurfluh, G.: Model driven extraction of NoSQL databases schema: case of MongoDB. In: Proceedings of the 11th International Joint Conference on Knowledge Discovery, Knowledge Engineering and Knowledge Management, KDIR, vol. 1, pp. 145–154 (2019). ISBN 978-989-758-382-7
6. Budinsky, F., Steinberg, D., Ellersick, R., Grose, T.J., Merks, E.: Eclipse Modeling Framework: A Developer's Guide. Addison-Wesley Professional (2004)
7. Philip Chen, C.L., Zhang, C.Y.: Data-intensive applications, challenges, techniques and technologies: a survey on Big Data. Inf. Sci. **275**, 314–347 (2014)
8. Comyn-Wattiau, I., Akoka, J.: Model driven reverse engineering of NoSQL property graph databases: the case of Neo4j. In: 2017 IEEE International Conference on Big Data (Big Data), pp. 453–458. IEEE (December 2017)
9. Extract Mongo Schema, 5 October 2019. https://www.npmjs.com/package/extract-mongo-schema/v/0.2.9
10. Gallinucci, E., Golfarelli, M., Rizzi, S.: Schema profiling of document-oriented databases. Inf. Syst. **75**, 13–25 (2018)
11. Izquierdo, J.L.C., Cabot, J.: JSONDiscoverer: visualizing the schema lurking behind JSON documents. Knowl. Based Syst. **103**, 52–55 (2016)
12. Klettke, M., Störl, U., Scherzinger, S.: Schema extraction and structural outlier detection for JSON-based NoSQL data stores. In: Datenbanksysteme für Business, Technologie und Web, BTW 2015 (2015)
13. Maity, B., Acharya, A., Goto, T., Sen, S.: A framework to convert NoSQL to relational model. In: Proceedings of the 6th ACM/ACIS International Conference on Applied Computing and Information Technology, pp. 1–6. ACM (June 2018)
14. Sevilla Ruiz, D., Morales, S.F., García Molina, J.: Inferring versioned schemas from NoSQL databases and its applications. In: Johannesson, P., Lee, M.L., Liddle, Stephen W., Opdahl, Andreas L., López, Ó.P. (eds.) ER 2015. LNCS, vol. 9381, pp. 467–480. Springer, Cham (2015). https://doi.org/10.1007/978-3-319-25264-3_35
15. Chillón, A.H., Ruiz, D.S., Molina, J.G., Morales, S.F.: A model-driven approach to generate schemas for object-document mappers. IEEE Access 7, 59126–59142 (2019)

Big Data/Data Lake

HANDLE - A Generic Metadata Model
for Data Lakes

Rebecca Eichler[1(✉)], Corinna Giebler[1], Christoph Gröger[2], Holger Schwarz[1],
and Bernhard Mitschang[1]

[1] University of Stuttgart, Universitätsstraße 38, 70569 Stuttgart, Germany
{rebecca.eichler,corinna.giebler,
holger.schwarz,bernhard.mitschang}@ipvs.uni-stuttgart.de
[2] Robert Bosch GmbH, Borsigstraße 4, 70469 Stuttgart, Germany
christoph.groeger@de.bosch.com

Abstract. The substantial increase in generated data induced the development of new concepts such as the data lake. A data lake is a large storage repository designed to enable flexible extraction of the data's value. A key aspect of exploiting data value in data lakes is the collection and management of metadata. To store and handle the metadata, a generic metadata model is required that can reflect metadata of any potential metadata management use case, e.g., data versioning or data lineage. However, an evaluation of existent metadata models yields that none so far are sufficiently generic. In this work, we present HANDLE, a generic metadata model for data lakes, which supports the flexible integration of metadata, data lake zones, metadata on various granular levels, and any metadata categorization. With these capabilities HANDLE enables comprehensive metadata management in data lakes. We show HANDLE's feasibility through the application to an exemplary access-use-case and a prototypical implementation. A comparison with existent models yields that HANDLE can reflect the same information and provides additional capabilities needed for metadata management in data lakes.

Keywords: Metadata management · Metadata model · Data lake

1 Introduction

With the considerable increase in generated data, new concepts were developed for exploiting the value of this data, one of which is the data lake concept. In this concept an organization's data is incorporated in one big data repository [7]. It is a storage concept designed for data at scale, that integrates data of varying structure, from heterogeneous sources, in its raw format. The focus of the concept is to enable flexible extraction of the data's value for any potential use case.

In order to exploit the data's value, metadata is required [1]. Metadata can be used to document various aspects of the data such as the meaning of its content, information on data quality or security, data lifecycle aspects and so on. Just like any other data, metadata needs to be managed. Metadata management

© Springer Nature Switzerland AG 2020
M. Song et al. (Eds.): DaWaK 2020, LNCS 12393, pp. 73–88, 2020.
https://doi.org/10.1007/978-3-030-59065-9_7

constitutes activities which involve managing an organizations' knowledge on its data [1]. Without this knowledge, data may not be applicable for the intended purpose, e.g., due to a lack of quality or trust.

A central aspect of metadata management is the definition of a metadata model (e.g., [10,15,17]). By our definition a metadata model describes the relations between data and metadata elements and what metadata is collected, e.g., in the form of an explicit schema, a formal definition, or a textual description. In order to store all kinds of knowledge on the data to increase its value, a generic metadata model is required. To be generic, a metadata model must reflect any potential metadata management use case of a data lake. This includes standard use cases, e.g., the collection of lineage information, as well as organization-specific use cases, e.g., use cases for the manufacturing domain. It follows that the generic metadata model can represent all metadata regardless of its type.

However, existent metadata models, e.g., [2,16,18], are not sufficiently generic as they cannot support every potential metadata management use case. For instance, some of them were developed for only one specific metadata management use case [8,11,21]. The existent metadata models are based on metadata categorizations and/or lists of metadata management features. As our discussion reveals, both do not produce truly generic models. In this paper we address this gap by making the following contributions: (1) We introduce a new approach for constructing a generic metadata model by investigating existent models and their shortcomings. (2) Based on this approach, we developed a generic metadata model called HANDLE, short for Handling metAdata maNagement in Data LakEs. (3) We assess HANDLE by firstly, testing its applicability on a standard use case in the Industry 4.0 context, secondly, we prototypically implemented HANDLE based on this use case, and lastly, compare it to existing metadata models. The comparison yields that HANDLE can reflect the content of the existent metadata models as it is defined on a higher abstraction level which also makes it more generic and that it provides additional metadata management capabilities.

This paper is structured as follows. Related work is introduced and discussed in Sect. 2. Section 3 specifies the requirements for the new metadata model, which is presented in Sect. 4, followed by an assessment of it in Sect. 5. Lastly, the paper is concluded by Sect. 6.

2   Related Work: Discussion of Existent Metadata Models

A literature research was conducted to get an overview of the existent models. Metadata models presented in the scope of metadata management systems applicable to data lakes include the model for the Generic and Extensible Metadata Management System (GEMMS) [15], for Walker and Alrehamy's personal data lake solution [22], and lastly, the metadata model for the data context service Ground [10]. Many systems both in the research context as well as commercial metadata management systems do not disclose their metadata model and thus we cannot examine their generic extent, e.g., [7,9,12]. Other models exist which are not part of a specific system. However, many of these, also including that by Walker and Alrehamy, only focus on a specific topic and thus, only support a limited set of use cases which makes them non-generic, e.g., [8,11,17,20,21]. Thenceforth these models are not considered here. More general models also created for data lakes include those by Ravat and Zhao [16], Diamantini et al. [2], and lastly, Sawadogo et al.'s model MEtadata for DAta Lakes (MEDAL) [18].

The generic degree of the five models GEMMS, Ground, MEDAL, and those by Ravat and Zhao, and Diamantini et al. is examined and discussed in the following. Sect. 2.1 shows that the basis on which the existent models were constructed is insufficient for building a generic metadata model. A representative use case is presented in Sect. 2.2 and Sect. 2.3 shows that it cannot be realized by the existing models, thereby demonstrating that these are not sufficiently generic.

2.1 Assessing the Basis of Existent Models

An examination of the five selected metadata models yields that these were built with two general approaches. The first approach uses a *categorization of metadata*, the second, employs a *list of metadata management features* that must be supported.

The categorization-based approach differentiates types of metadata. As can be seen in Fig. 1, each categorization differentiates metadata through other qualities, thereby providing different perspectives on metadata. For example, the categories in MEDAL refer to how the metadata is modeled whereas Diamantini et al. categorize the metadata by its content. Building a metadata model based on only one of these perspectives makes it less generic. Furthermore, a categorization does not provide any guidance on modeling use cases and therefore does not contribute to building a generic metadata model.

The feature-based approach involves building the model to support a predefined list of features. Features are derived from metadata management use cases. If the list covers all relevant metadata management features, and if the metadata model supports all of these features, then the model would be complete. As can be seen in Fig. 2, some of the lists contain high-level and some detailed feature descriptions, making it impossible to combine them. Defining high-level features might not suffice to derive all necessary requirements for a metadata model.

MEDAL	GEMMS	GROUND	Ravat and Zhao	Diamantini et al.	Gröger and Hoos
INTRA	STRUCTURE	APPLICATION	INTRA	BUSINESS	API
INTER	SEMANTIC	BEHAVIORAL	INTER	BUSINESS-TECHNICAL	CORE
GLOBAL	METADATA-	VERSION		TECHNICAL	IOT
	PROPERTIES			TECHNICAL-OPERATIONAL	ANALYSIS RESULTS
				OPERATIONAL	
				OPERATIONAL-BUSINESS	

Fig. 1. Set of metadata categorizations, the first five belong to the selected metadata models [2,10,15,16,18]. The sixth, in dashes, does not belong to a metadata model [6].

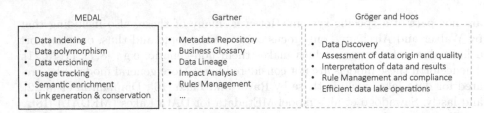

Fig. 2. This is a display of three lists of metadata management features. The first belongs with the model MEDAL [18], whereas the other two, in dashes, by Gartner [19], and Gröger and Hoos [6] are created independent of a metadata model.

However, defining one comprehensive list of detailed features is not realistic as each organization will have its own set of relevant metadata management use cases and a different thematic focus, also visible in Fig. 2.

In conclusion, neither the categorization-based nor the feature-based approach are an adequate foundation for building a generic metadata model.

2.2   Metadata Management Use Case for Model Evaluation

To evaluate the existent models by testing their limits and generic extent we use a representative metadata management use case, which is based on an Industry 4.0 scenario with an enterprise data lake. The data lake contains data on products, processes and customers including personal data (see [13] for data management in industrial enterprises and Industry 4.0).

Data lake projects which involve personal data on EU citizens, e.g., data on customers, are subject to legal requirements such as the General Data Protection Regulation (GDPR) [4]. Conformity to the GDPR requires the collection of information on the personal data's use and the users accessing it [3]. Therefore, we introduce the data-access-use-case, which involves collecting access information. It is a representative metadata management use case frequently implemented in the data lake context.

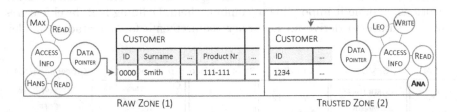

Fig. 3. The image displays access metadata collected on varying granular levels of the customer table. The customer table is stored twice, once in each data lake zone. The green circles are metadata objects with properties, e.g., a user object with the name "Max". They belong to the accordingly highlighted part of the table. The blue circles denote a pointer containing the data's storage location. (Colored figure online)

Within our Industry 4.0 scenario, access information is collected amongst other things on a table containing customer data, as depicted in Fig. 3. Data access information may include details on the user or application accessing it, and the type and time of the action. Hence, the model must support some form of metadata object with properties to reflect most varied information. For example, an object could be created for each user and action with properties such as name, id, or action time and type. Figure 3 illustrates metadata objects, in green, grouped by a metadata object called "Access Info". In order to allocate the metadata to a specific dataset some form of pointer or reference is required, depicted as the blue "Data Pointer" object.

Data within data lakes is often organized in so-called zones according to its processing degree [5], e.g., as standardized data in the trusted zone [23]. Therefore, the same dataset may be stored multiple times in different zones in varying processing degrees. The metadata collected on datasets throughout zones should be distinguishable according to the particular zone. Consequently, the access information must be collected per zone. Assuming the example data lake has two or more zones, such as a raw zone containing the data in its native format, and a trusted zone holding pseudonymised data. It should be recognizable who accessed a customer's personal information and who only saw the customer's pseudonym. For example, in Fig. 3 "Max" read personal data, but "Ana" only saw pseudonymised data.

Assuming it is desired to track the access to each customer's personal data, then the access information must be collected per customer. The pseudonymised version of the customer table does not yield any personal information and consequently does not require collecting the access info per customer. In this case, it is sufficient to collect the access information on the entire table as opposed to a single row. Therefore, our use case requires collecting metadata on varying granular levels.

The presented scenario imposes three requirements which we use to test the metadata models' limits. For this use case the metadata models must be flexible in creating *Metadata properties* for Metadata objects to reflect most varied information, the model must *support data lake zones* and it must support the collection of metadata on *various granular levels*.

2.3 Assessing the Generic Extent of the Existent Models

Within this section, the five models selected in the beginning of Sect. 2 are examined in respect to the three use case requirements: *metadata properties, data lake zones* and *granularity*.

As signified in Table 1, all models except that by Diamantini et al. support adding metadata properties in some way or another, and therefore fulfill the first requirement. Ravat and Zhao's model is partially checked as they support adding keywords describing their data elements, which does not however, suffice for modeling, e.g., an actor accessing the data. For this purpose, they have explicitly defined access properties, but they are missing the type of action performed.

Table 1. Coverage of Access-Use-Case Requirements by the Metadata Models. The √ represents a fulfilled requirement and the (√) a partially fulfilled requirement.

Requirements	GEMMS	Ravat and Zhao	Ground	Diamantini et al.	MEDAL
Metadata properties	√	(√)	√		√
Data lake zones		(√)		(√)	(√)
Granularity	(√)			(√)	

Of the five models, only that by Ravat and Zhao addresses the zone concept of data lakes. They use a specified zone architecture. However, their model description does not reveal how they allot their data and metadata to specific zones. Therefore, this quality is partially checked for their model. Diamantini et al.'s model and MEDAL both support data polymorphism, which denotes the ability to store multiple representations of the same data [2,18]. This is required for building zones. It does not however, enfold all the zone concept's characteristics, such as a clear specification of the data's processing degree within each zone. Therefore, they are partially checked in Table 1.

GEMMS and Diamantini et al.'s model define two levels of granularity, partially fulfilling requirement three. Ravat and Zhao mention dataset containment, but it is not clear whether this can be used to implement the granularity topic. Therefore, none of the models support adding multiple levels of granularity.

In conclusion, none of the five metadata models are flexible enough to support the presented access-use-case and thus, are not sufficiently generic.

3   Requirements for a Generic Metadata Model

Section 2 demonstrated the necessity for a new generic metadata model for data lakes. We acquired the knowledge that both a categorization- and feature-based approach do not yield a truly generic model. This was demonstrated with a set of use case specific requirements. Therefore, a different approach is proposed to define *a new set of more general requirements* for building a generic model which reflects a broader scope of use cases. This approach is flexibility-oriented, whereby the requirements are based on the existent models' strengths and limits, but mainly aim at providing a basis for a highly flexible model.

In order to support any metadata management use case, the model must be very flexible in its ability to assimilate metadata. Therefore, the first requirement is *(1) modeling the metadata as flexible as possible*. According to our analysis of the existent models, a high level of flexibility is achieved through the following six conditions: *(1.1)* Metadata can be stored in the form of metadata objects, properties and relationships; *(1.2)* The amount of metadata objects per use case is unlimited; *(1.3)* Each metadata object can have an arbitrary number of properties; *(1.4)* Metadata objects can exist with or without a corresponding data element; *(1.5)* Metadata objects can be interconnected and *(1.6)* Data elements can be interconnected.

The second requirement denotes the ability to collect metadata on *(2) multiple granular levels*, thus maintain flexibility with regard to the level of detail and allocation of metadata. Through granular levels the model supports heredity of metadata. For example, technical metadata added on a schema level also applies to more granular data elements such as tables, columns, rows and fields.

The metadata model is developed for metadata management in data lakes and should therefore support data lake characteristics. Most metadata is collected on specific data elements, which are organized in zones, thus the model must support *(3) the concept of data lake zones* [5]. This means, metadata should be distinguishable across zones, hereby gaining flexibility in allocating metadata.

Lastly, it should be flexible in the sense that it can *(4) integrate any categorization in the form of labels*, e.g., MEDAL's intra, inter and global labels or Gröger and Hoos' labels API, Core and so on (see Fig. 1). This helps to speedily identify the context of the data. It can also be used to check whether all types of metadata are being collected.

These four requirements constitute the new set of general requirements for a generic metadata model in the data lake context.

4   HANDLE - A Generic Metadata Model

We used the requirements given in Sect. 3 to develop a new model which we present in this section. The new model is called HANDLE, short for "Handling metAdata maNagement in Data LakEs". The new model's intent is to handle all metadata management use cases, thereby getting a handle on all metadata.

The conceptual metadata model consists of two parts, the core model, illustrated in Fig. 4, and three core model extensions, which need to be adapted for each data lake implementation. The core model is a metamodel defining all the elements and the relations required for modeling a metadata management use case. The core model extensions each address the zone, granularity and categorization topics in more detail, according to the requirements 2–4. All of the models are modeled according to the Crow's Foot Notation.

As depicted in Fig. 4, one of the core models main entities is the *data* entity, illustrated in blue. In order to avoid storing data redundantly, the data entity represents a pointer to the data in the data lake. The path to the data element is stored in the *storageLocation* attribute. According to requirement 1.6, data elements can be interconnected. For instance, a data element representing a table's row can be connected to the superior data element representing the overall table. The data element has two entities attached to it, the zoneIndicator and the granularityIndicator. They indicate the zone the data is stored in and the level of granularity on which the metadata is collected, as dictated by the requirements 2 and 3. The intended usage of both indicators is explained on the basis of model extensions in the subsequent paragraphs.

The second central entity of the core model is the *metadata* entity, depicted in green. It is the metadata object specified in requirement 1.1, by way of example it could represent a user who accessed data. The metadata entity is connected to

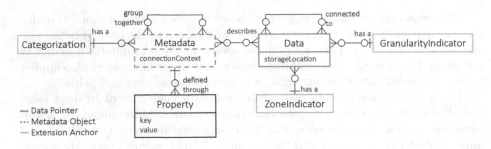

Fig. 4. HANDLE's Core Model (Colored figure online)

none, one, or many data elements and each data entity may have zero or many metadata entities connected to it, hereby fulfilling requirement 1.4. For instance, the user can access many data elements and data elements can be accessed by many users. An attribute called *connectionContext* describes what information the metadata element contains. For example, the user metadata element may have a connection context called "accessing user". In line with requirement 1.3, the metadata entity can have an arbitrary number of *properties* in the form of key-value pairs, e.g., "name: Hans Müller". According to requirement 1.5, the metadata entity's self-link enables to group zero or more metadata elements together, like the "Access Info" group, as illustrated in Fig. 3. Grouping the elements according to some context is helpful when a lot of metadata on the same topic is collected for a data element. As specified through requirement 4, the metadata entity is labeled according to any content-based categorization, represented by the *categorization* entity.

The Granularity Extension: The granularityIndicator enumerations have to be adapted according to the specific use, e.g., for relational structures, as depicted in Fig. 5. Thus, it is modeled as an extension to the core model. The granularityIndicator entity enables collecting metadata on different granular levels. These levels are closely tied to some kind of structure in the data. For example, the object, key, value, or key-value pair instances in a JSON Document may be used as granularity levels. The granularityIndicator is not, however, limited to "structured data." For instance, videos are categorized as "unstructured data" and yet, one may want to collect metadata on single frames of the video. In this

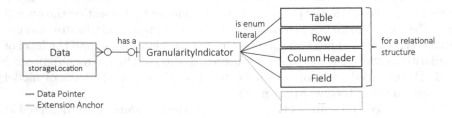

Fig. 5. The Granularity Extension to the Core Model (Colored figure online)

case, there would be a video level and a frame level. Domain knowledge can be helpful for selecting granularity levels, as often it is necessary to understand, e.g., if the metadata refers to the content of a single frame or an entire video.

Figure 5 lists a few enumerations, which can be used to indicate the granular levels of relational data. The "..." indicates that other enumerations may be added as needed. In order to collect metadata on different levels, a corresponding data element must be created that points to that granular instance. So, there may be a set of data elements all referring to the same data set, simply pointing to more or less specific granular levels. Demonstrating the granularityIndicators defined here, the "Data Pointer" in Fig. 3's raw zone would have a label called *Row* and the "Data Pointer" in the trusted zone would have a label called *Table*. There could be other "Data Pointers" in these zones, for instance another pointer to the overall table in the raw zone with the label *Table*.

The Zone Extension: Figure 6 illustrates the intended usage of the *zone-Indicator* entity, using the zone model by Zaloni [23]. The zoneIndicator entity is a label on the data entity supplying information on the location of the data element in the data lake's zone architecture. Depending on the zone definition, the data's transformation degree is immediately apparent through it. The different zones are modeled as enumerations for the zoneIndicator. In order to use another kind of architecture, the zone enumerations and their relationships need to be adjusted.

The model illustrates that every data element must have exactly one zone-Indicator. The *Raw Zone* entity is designed to be the central zoneIndicator, as data is stored in any of the other zones will have a corresponding data element in the raw zone, making the raw zone the most stable reference. The zones depicted on the right hand side have a *link* entity, connecting them to the corresponding data element in the raw zone. The information from where the data was imported into the zone as well as the corresponding *timestamp* is stored with the link. The *importedFrom* attribute may contain the name of a zone or the original source. The link and importedFrom attribute enables tracing the data's progress through the zones. By Zaloni's definition, the data may not be moved into the raw zone from the transient loading zone, therefore, this enumeration can exist without a link to the rawZone element [23]. If the data was moved into the raw zone, then it must have a link connecting them.

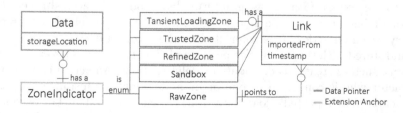

Fig. 6. The Zone Extension to the Core Model, Using Zaloni's Zones [23]. (Color figure online)

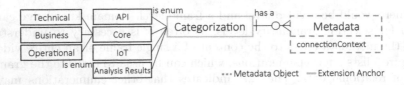

Fig. 7. Categorization Extension to Core Model, with the categorization by Gröger and Hoos [6] and subcategories they adopted from [1]. (Colored figure online)

The Categorization Extension: Figure 7 illustrates the intended usage of the *categorization* entity, exemplified using the metadata categorization by Gröger and Hoos [6]. Like the zone and granularityIndicator, the *categorization* entity is a label assigned according to the metadata element's context. For instance, access information is core metadata and therein operational metadata as defined by [1], and thus a metadata element storing any type of access information will have an operational label. This extension together with the granularity and zone extension as well as the core model add up to be HANDLE.

5   HANDLE Assessment

To asses HANDLE's suitability as a generic metadata model we assess its applicability to a metadata management use case and its implementation aspects. Furthermore, we examine whether it fulfills the requirements specified for a generic metadata model in Sect. 3 and we compare it to the five metadata models discussed in Sect. 2.

5.1   HANDLE Demonstration on Access-Use-Case

Figure 8 shows an example instantiation of HANDLE. The depicted model belongs to the access-use-case described in Sect. 2.2.

As defined through the core model, a *data* instance with zone and granularity-Indicator as well as three metadata instances, *action, actor* and *accessInfo*, with the categorization *operational*, are introduced in Fig. 8. A data entity has zero or exactly one accessInfo entity. In order to avoid the data element being overloaded by indefinitely increasing access information, all access related nodes are connected to the accessInfo entity as an intermediate node. The accessInfo entity is a way of adding structure. The model suggests that an action element is created for every executed action. It is connected to the involved data's accessInfo element and stored with the time it was performed. The term access covers a variety of actions, such as create, read, update or delete actions. An action is performed by an actor who is connected to one or many actions. For instance, a specific data scientist may repeatedly load data from the customer table. The accessInfo element for the customer table will have one actor element with the data scientist's name and id. This actor element will be connected to *read* actions, one for every time they loaded the data with the according time.

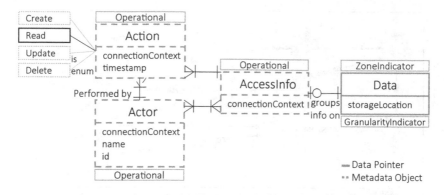

Fig. 8. Instance of HANDLE for Access-Use-Case (Colored figure online)

5.2   Prototypical Implementation

Apart from HANDLE's applicability, we assess its realizability, that is, whether it can be properly implemented. As previously emphasized, flexibility is one of the most important features of the new metadata model. This poses an additional challenge during the implementation as the system components must be able to reflect this flexibility. More specifically, the database of choice must support the aspects of the model which constitute its flexibility. This section shows by way of example that a graph database provides the necessary prerequisites for implementing HANDLE. As a graph database is a NoSQL database it does not require a predefined schema, which makes it more flexible than the traditional relational databases [14]. Also, it is well suited for storing strongly linked data, which is required for many metadata management use cases such as the access-use-case described above, lineage-use-case etc. In the following example, we use the graph database Neo4J[1].

Figure 9 illustrates an implementation of the access model and thus of the core model, as well as aspects of the zone, granularity and categorization extensions. It depicts an extract of a Neo4J graph database and therefore a set of nodes and edges each with labels. The three blue nodes are instantiations of the *data* entity and each have the property *storageLocation* containing the path to the according data element, here the customer table. The *granularityIndicators* introduced in Fig. 5 are implemented through labels on the data elements. For example, the highlighted data element on the top left hand side has the label "Table". The blue data element on the top right points to a row and thus has the label "Row". The *zoneIndicators* presented in Fig. 6 are also implemented through a label on the data elements. For instance, Fig. 9 lists the label "Raw" for the highlighted data element. The zone extension's *link* entity is implemented through an edge in the graph with the according properties. As can be seen in Fig. 9, the two blue nodes on the left are connected through an edge with the label "Link". The link connects the bottom data element to its according instance

---

[1] https://neo4j.com/.

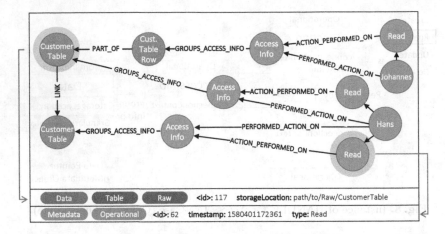

Fig. 9. Visualization of the HANDLE access-use-case implementation in Neo4J. The blue and green nodes represent data and metadata objects respectively. The two highlighted node's labels are depicted on the bottom left, e.g., Data, Table and Raw. The elements' properties are listed next to the labels. The text on the edges is the metadata entity's connectionContext attribute, e.g., actor "Johannes" performed an action and is connected to the data's accessInfo with the connectionContext "performed_action_on". (Colored figure online)

in the raw zone. The green nodes are instances of the core model's *metadata* entity. They are also instances of the access-use-case model's metadata entities: *accessInfo*, *actor* and *action*. The metadata object's *connectionContext* is realized as a label on their relations, e.g., the actor elements' "performed_action_on" and accessInfo elements' "groups_access_info" connectionContext describe the relation to the according data object. As can be seen, the actors "Hans" and "Johannes", on the far right in Fig. 9, have performed "Read" actions on data elements. "Johannes" read information on a particular customer stored in the raw zone. "Hans" read the entire customer table in both the raw zone in its unpseudonymised state and in another zone, in its pseudonymised state, as indicated by Fig. 3. The *categorization* entity is also implemented as a label, e.g., the highlighted "Read" action's "Operational" label can be seen in Fig. 9.

5.3   Fulfillment of Requirements

To begin with, Requirement (1), enabling flexible modeling, comprises the six sub-requirements (1.1)–(1.6). As prescribed by (1.1), the core model allows the creation of metadata objects with properties. It also allows to interconnect metadata objects and data objects, facilitating the wanted relationships in (1.1). As defined per (1.2), the core model does not restrict the amount of metadata objects created and thus, any use case can have an arbitrary number of metadata objects. Equally, metadata properties can be created freely for metadata objects, as required by (1.3). Metadata objects may or may not be connected to a data element, thereby fulfilling (1.4). The self-link of both the metadata and data objects enable the required interconnection of these objects, defined in (1.5) and (1.6). Requirement (2), denoting the support of multiple granular levels, is realized by creating multiple data objects, containing a path to more or less granular elements of a dataset, labeled through the granularityIndicator. Requirements (3) and (4), denoting the support of zones and any categorization, are supported through the zoneIndicator and categorization entities, as explained in Sect. 4. In conclusion, HANDLE supports all of the specified requirements.

5.4   Comparison to Existent Models

To further asses HANDLE's generic extent we also compare it to the five selected metadata models. HANDLE can represent the content of all five models through the core model because it is defined on a higher abstraction level. It addresses the use cases in a more general way and can represent any metadata through its abstract entities: *data, metadata* and *property*. This means that metadata stored according to one of the existent models can be transferred and mapped into HANDLE and possibly even combined with metadata stored through yet another model. Besides representing their content, HANDLE adds additional features such as the granularityIndicator, zonIndicator and categorization label.

We exemplary demonstrate how HANDLE can represent the content of other models, using GEMMS. Figure 10 exemplifies how GEMMS' model can be mapped onto HANDLE. GEMMS' model is depicted on the left hand side and an example instantiation of it through HANDLE on the right hand side. The colors indicate that the blue elements are an instance of the core model's data entity and the green ones instances of the metadata entity. All of GEMMS' entities can be represented through the core model's data, metadata and property

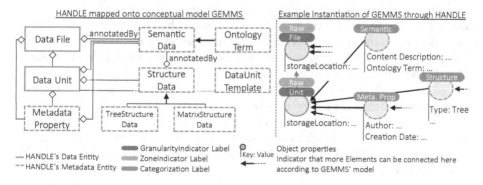

Fig. 10. The left side depicts the model of GEMMS [15]. The entities are color matched to the entities in HANDLE's core model. The right side shows an instantiation of GEMMS through HANDLE. The image shows that HANDLE can represent GEMMS content and adds features, e.g., the zoneIndicator, shown on the "File" entity in grey. (Color figure online)

entities. In contrast to GEMMS, HANDLE strictly separates data and metadata, therefore the metadata is not stored within the "Data File" or "Data Unit" entities but in the "Metadata Property" nodes. Furthermore, HANDLE's categorization and granularity topics can be integrated, hereby adding some of HANDLE's features to GEMMS. As can be seen on the right hand side, the "Data File" and "Data Unit" instantiations are labeled with the granularityIndicators "File" and "Unit". According to GEMMS' metadata types, the categorization labels are added to the metadata instantiations on the right hand side, "Semantic", "Structure" and "Metadata Property". Although GEMMS does not address the zone concept, HANDLE's zoneIndicator can be attached, as shown through the grey "Raw" label on the "File" entity. Thereby GEMMS is extended and becomes compatible with zones. The other four models' content can be represented through HANDLE in a similar fashion, by mapping their main entities onto HANDLE's data, metadata and property elements.

Having demonstrated that HANDLE fulfills the specified requirements, can represent the content of other metadata models, and extends these with features required for metadata management in data lakes, it can be said that HANDLE is more comprehensive and is a generic metadata model which can reflect any metadata management use case and consequently any metadata.

6 Conclusion

In order to exploit the value of data in data lakes, metadata is required, which in turn needs to be handled through metadata management. One central aspect of metadata management is the design of a metadata model. This metadata model should be generic, meaning it should be able to reflect any given metadata management use case and consequently all metadata.

We selected five comprehensive metadata models and pointed out that the two approaches on which they were built are not suited for creating a generic model. Therefore, the existent models do not fulfill the required generic extent, as also demonstrated through an exemplary use case in an Industry 4.0 scenario.

A new approach was used to develop a new metadata model for data lakes, called HANDLE. Our assessment shows that it is easily applicable to metadata management use cases, can be implemented through a graph database, can reflect the content of existent metadata models and offers additional metadata management features. As the research has demonstrated, it is the most generic metadata model for data lakes up to date. In future, we intend to investigate whether HANDLE is applicable beyond the scope of data lakes, e.g., in an enterprise-wide federation of data storage systems.

References

1. DAMA International: DAMA-DMBOK: Data Management Body of Knowledge. Technics Publications (2017)

2. Diamantini, C., et al.: A new metadata model to uniformly handle heterogeneous data lake sources. In: Proceedings of the 22nd European Conference on Advances in Databases and Information Systems ADBIS (2018)
3. GDPR.EU: Art. 15 GDPR - Right of access by the data subject. https://gdpr.eu/article-15-right-of-access/. Accessed 28 Feb 2020
4. GDPR.EU: What is GDPR, the EU's new data protection law?. https://gdpr.eu/what-is-gdpr/. Accessed 28 Feb 2020
5. Giebler, C., Gröger, C., Hoos, E., Schwarz, H., Mitschang, B.: Leveraging the data lake: current state and challenges. In: Ordonez, C., Song, I.-Y., Anderst-Kotsis, G., Tjoa, A.M., Khalil, I. (eds.) DaWaK 2019. LNCS, vol. 11708, pp. 179–188. Springer, Cham (2019). https://doi.org/10.1007/978-3-030-27520-4_13
6. Gröger, C., Hoos, E.: Ganzheitliches Metadatenmanagement im Data Lake: Anforderungen, IT-Werkzeuge und Herausforderungen in der Praxis. In: Proceedings of the 18. Fachtagung für Datenbanksysteme für Business, Technologie und Web BTW (2019)
7. Hai, R., et al.: Constance: an intelligent data lake system. In: Proceedings of the 2016 International Conference on Management of Data SIGMOD (2016)
8. Hai, R., Quix, C., Wang, D.: Relaxed functional dependency discovery in heterogeneous data lakes. In: Laender, A.H.F., Pernici, B., Lim, E.-P., de Oliveira, J.P.M. (eds.) ER 2019. LNCS, vol. 11788, pp. 225–239. Springer, Cham (2019). https://doi.org/10.1007/978-3-030-33223-5_19
9. Halevy, A., et al.: Managing Google's data lake: an overview of the Goods system. IEEE Data Eng. Bull. **39**, 5–14 (2016)
10. Hellerstein, J.M., et al.: Ground : a data context service. In: Proceedings of the 8th Biennial Conference on Innovative Data Systems Research CIDR (2017)
11. Suriarachchi, I., Plale, B.: Provenance as essential infrastructure for data lakes. In: Mattoso, M., Glavic, B. (eds.) IPAW 2016. LNCS, vol. 9672, pp. 178–182. Springer, Cham (2016). https://doi.org/10.1007/978-3-319-40593-3_16
12. Kandogan, E., et al.: LabBook: metadata-driven social collaborative data analysis. In: Proceedings of the IEEE International Conference on Big Data (2015)
13. Kassner, L., Gröger, C., Königsberger, J., Hoos, E., Kiefer, C., Weber, C., Silcher, S., Mitschang, B.: The stuttgart IT architecture for manufacturing. In: Hammoudi, S., Maciaszek, L.A., Missikoff, M.M., Camp, O., Cordeiro, J. (eds.) ICEIS 2016. LNBIP, vol. 291, pp. 53–80. Springer, Cham (2017). https://doi.org/10.1007/978-3-319-62386-3_3
14. Kaur, K., Rani, R.: Modeling and querying data in NoSQL databases. In: Proceedings of the IEEE International Conference on Big Data (2013)
15. Quix, C., et al.: Metadata extraction and management in data lakes with GEMMS. Complex Syst. Inform. Model. Quarterly **9**, 67–83 (2016)
16. Ravat, F., Zhao, Y.: Metadata management for data lakes. In: Welzer, T., et al. (eds.) ADBIS 2019. CCIS, vol. 1064, pp. 37–44. Springer, Cham (2019). https://doi.org/10.1007/978-3-030-30278-8_5
17. Sawadogo, P.N., et al.: Metadata management for textual documents in data lakes. In: Proceedings of the 21st International Conference on Enterprise Information Systems, ICEIS (2019)
18. Sawadogo, P.N., Scholly, É., Favre, C., Ferey, É., Loudcher, S., Darmont, J.: Metadata systems for data lakes: models and features. In: Welzer, T., et al. (eds.) ADBIS 2019. CCIS, vol. 1064, pp. 440–451. Springer, Cham (2019). https://doi.org/10.1007/978-3-030-30278-8_43
19. Simoni, G.D., et al.: Magic Quadrant for Metadata Management Solutions (2018)

20. Spiekermann, M., et al.: A metadata model for data goods. In: Proceedings of the Multikonferenz Wirtschaftsinformatik MKWI (2018)
21. Theodorou, V., Hai, R., Quix, C.: A metadata framework for data lagoons. In: Welzer, T., et al. (eds.) ADBIS 2019. CCIS, vol. 1064, pp. 452–462. Springer, Cham (2019). https://doi.org/10.1007/978-3-030-30278-8_44
22. Walker, C., Alrehamy, H.: Personal data lake with data gravity pull. In: Proceedings of the 5th International Conference on Big Data and Cloud Computing, BDCloud (2015)
23. Zaloni: The Data Lake Reference Architecture - Leveraging a Data Reference Architecture to Ensure Data Lake Success. Technical report (2018)

Data Mining

A SAT-Based Approach for Mining High Utility Itemsets from Transaction Databases

Amel Hidouri[1,2], Said Jabbour[2(✉)], Badran Raddaoui[3],
and Boutheina Ben Yaghlane[1]

[1] LARODEC, Univeristy of Tunis High Institut of Management,
Cite Bouchoucha, Tunisia
amelhidouri123@gmail.com, boutheina.byaghlane@gmail.com
[2] CRIL - CNRS UMR 8188, University of Artois, Arras, France
jabbour@cril.fr
[3] SAMOVAR, Télécom SudParis, Institut Polytechnique de Paris, Paris, France
badran.raddaoui@telecom-sudparis.eu

Abstract. Mining high utility itemsets is a keystone in several data analysis tasks. High Utility Itemset Mining generalizes the frequent itemset mining problem by considering item quantities and weights. A high utility itemset is a set of items that appears in the transadatabase and having a high importance to the user, measured by a utility function. The utility of a pattern can be quantified in terms of various objective criteria, e.g., profit, frequency, and weight. Constraint Programming (CP) and Propositional Satisfiability (SAT) based frameworks for modeling and solving pattern mining tasks have gained a considerable attention in recent few years. This paper introduces the first declarative framework for mining high utility itemsets from transaction databases. First, we model the problem of mining high utility itemsets from transaction databases as a propositional satifiability problem. Moreover, to facilitate the mining task, we add an additional constraint to the efficiency of our method by using weighted clique cover problem. Then, we exploit the efficient SAT solving techniques to output all the high utility itemsets in the data that satisfy a user-specified minimum support and minimum utility values. Experimental evaluations on real and synthetic datasets show that the performance of our proposed approach is close to that of the optimal case of state-of-the-art HUIM algorithms.

Keywords: Data mining · High utility · Constraint programming · Propositional satisfiabilty · Maximal clique

1 Introduction

Data mining is a key research field aiming at discovering novel, unexpected and useful patterns in databases. Mining High Utility itemsets (HUIM, for short) is a keystone in several data analysis and data mining tasks. HUIM generalizes

© Springer Nature Switzerland AG 2020
M. Song et al. (Eds.): DaWaK 2020, LNCS 12393, pp. 91–106, 2020.
https://doi.org/10.1007/978-3-030-59065-9_8

the problem of frequent itemsets by considering item quantities and weights. The concept of HUIM refers to finding the set of items that appear in a given transaction database and having a high importance to the user, measured by a utility function. Given a transaction T, the utility of items in T depends on the importance of distinct items, i.e., external utility, and the importance of the items in T, i.e., internal utility. The utility of an itemset is defined as the external utility multiplied by the internal utility. Then, an itemset is called a *high utility itemset* if its utility is no less than a user threshold; otherwise, the itemset is a low utility itemset [1]. Mining high utility itemset from transaction databases is an important task and it has a wide range of applications such as stream analysis, online e-commerce management, and biomedical field [2–5, 29].

The HUIM problem is not easy to solve because the property of downward closure [6, 29] in frequent itemset mining does not hold, i.e., a superset of a low utility itemset may be a high utility itemset. Various algorithms have been studied for HUIM (see [7] for a survey of the field). A popular approach to solve this problem is to enumerate the set of high utility itemsets in two phases. This method commonly adopts the Transaction-Weighted-Downward Closure model to prune the search space. First, this method generates the high-utility itemsets candidates by overestimating their utility. Next, this method performs an extra database scan to compute the exact utility of candidates and remove low-utility itemsets. The two phases based approach is adopted by Two-Phase [12], IHUP, Up-Growth [13], and Up-Growth+ [13]. However, this approach is inefficient because it not only generates too many candidates in the first phase, but it also needs to scan the database multiple times in phase 2, which can be computation demanding. To circumvent these limitations, many studies have been carried to develop efficient methods to discover high utility itemsets using a unique phase. Among these algorithms, we can mention, HUI-Miner [14], D2HUP [15], HUP-Miner [15], FHM [16], EFIM [17]. mHUIMiner [18], and ULB [19]. According to the comparisons given in [7] between these different HUIM algorithms, it has been shown that one phase algorithms are better than algorithms with candidate generation such as Two-Phases and Up-Growth, since they are impractical for discovering HUIs. In addition, the authors have shown that the most efficient algorithms are EFIM (in memory consumption) and D2HUP (in running time). The newest HUIM algorithms mHUIMiner and ULB-Miner usually fall between EFIM and d2HUP, but in a few cases, mHUIMiner has the best performance.

Generally speaking, the previous approaches are designed to address a particular mining problem in transaction databases. In other words, new additional constraints require new implementations in these specialized approaches, and they can not been easily integrated in the original framework. Recently, a new declarative data mining research trend has been initiated by Luc De Raedt et al. [9] by employing symbolic Artificial Intelligence techniques. More specifically, several constraint-based languages for modeling and solving data mining problems have been designed. For this kind of approaches, the data mining task is modeled as a constraint network or a propositional formula whose models correspond to the patterns of interest. Clearly, this allows data mining problems to benefit from several generic and efficient Artificial Intelligence solving techniques. In [9], the authors proposed a framework for classical itemset mining offering a declarative and flexible representation model and benefiting from several generic and efficient constraint programming solving techniques. Let us also mention the propositional satisfiability based approaches [8–11] that have been gained a considerable attention with the advent of a new generation of SAT solvers able to solve large instances encoding data mining problems, e.g. frequent itemsets [11], sequences [28], and association rules [24,25].

Encouraged by these promising results, in this work, we propose a declarative approach for utility mining by providing a SAT-based encoding for discovering high utility itemsets over transaction databases. Our encoding takes into account the different measures of interestingness that reflect the significance of an itemset beyond its frequency of occurrence. To the best of our knowledge, this paper presents the first attempt for a cross-fertilisation between HUIM and symbolic Artificial Intelligence.

This paper is organized as follows: The next section presents preliminaries in which we give some basic definitions about HUIM and Boolean satisfiability problem. Section 3 is devoted to our novel SAT-based framework for discovering itemsets with highest utilities. Section 4 presents and discusses the results of our experimental evaluation on real and synthetic datasets. Finally, we conclude our work in Sect. 5 with some further perspectives.

2 Preliminaries

This section presents the important preliminaries and formally defines the utility mining and the propositional satisfiability problems. Notice that all the notations used in the rest of paper are presented in Table 1.

2.1 High Utility Itemset Mining

In this subsection, we formally define the key terms of utility mining using the standard conventions followed in the literature.

Let Ω denote a universe of distinct items (or symbols), called alphabet. An itemset is a nonempty set that contains one or more items, denoted as $I = \{x_1, x_2, \ldots, x_n\}$ where $x_i \in \Omega$, $\forall i = 1, \ldots, n$. A transaction database is a set of m transactions $D = \{T_1, T_2, \ldots, T_m\}$ where for each transaction T_c, $T_c \subseteq \Omega$ and T_c has a unique identifier c called its transaction identifier (TID, for short). Each transaction T_c ($1 \leq c \leq m$) is denoted as a couple (c, I) s.t. $I \subseteq \Omega$. Each item $i \in \Omega$ is associated with a positive number $p(i)$, called its external utility (e.g. unit profit). For each transaction T_c s.t. $i \in T_c$, the positive number $q(i, T_c)$ is called the internal utility of the item i (e.g. purchase quantity). We define the cover of an itemset I as the set of transactions in D that contain I.

Definition 1 (Utility of an item/itemset in a transaction). Let $D = \{T_1, T_2, \ldots, T_m\}$ be a transaction database. Then, the utility of an item i in a

Table 1. Summary of notations

Notation	Meaning
Ω	A set of n items $\{i_1, \ldots, i_n\}$ s.t. each item i_j has a profit value p_j
D	An original quantitative database, $D = \{T_1, T_2, \ldots, T_m\}$
TID	An identifier of a transaction $T_c \in D$
I	A k-itemset containing k distinct items $\{i_1, i_2, \ldots, i_k\}$
$q(i_j, T_c)$	The purchase quantity of an item i_j in a transaction T_c
$p(i_j)$	The unit profit of an item i_j
$u(i_j, T_c)$	The utility of an item i_j in a transaction T_c
$u(I, T_c)$	The utility of an itemset I in a transaction T_c
$u(I)$	The utility of an itemset I in the whole database
$TU(T_c)$	The sum of the utilities of items in a transaction T_c
$TWU(I)$	The transaction-weighted utility of an item I in D
θ	A predefined minimum high-utility threshold
HUI	A high-utility itemset
Prop	A set of propositional variables
Form	A set of propositional formulas
$\mathscr{I}$	A Boolean interpretation

transaction $T_c \in D$, denoted by $u(i, T_c)$, is defined as $u(i, T_c) = p(i) \times q(i, T_c)$. In addition, the utility of an itemset I in a transaction $T_c \in D$, denoted by $u(I, T_c)$, is defined as:

$$u(I, T_c) = \sum_{i \in I} u(i, T_c) \tag{1}$$

Example 1. Let us use a transaction database, containing four transactions, given in Table 2, which will serve as a running example through the present paper. Each row in Table 2 represents a transaction, where each letter represents an item and has a purchase quantity (i.e., internal utility). For instance, the transaction T_2 indicates that items a, c, and e appear in this transaction with an internal utility of $2, 6$ and 2, respectively. Also, Table 3 indicates that the external utility of these items are respectively $4, 1$ and 3. Now, let us consider the unit profit table (see Table 3) given in Example 1. Then, the utility of the item a in T_2 is $u(a, T_2) = 4 \times 2 = 8$. Moreover, the utility of the itemset $\{a, c\}$ in T_2 is $u(\{a, c\}, T_2) = u(a, T_2) + u(c, T_2) = 4 \times 2 + 1 \times 6 = 14$.

The utility of an itemset I in a transaction database D is defined as the sum of the itemset utilities in all the transactions of D where I appears. More formally:

Definition 2 (Utility of an itemset in a transaction database). *Let $D = \{T_1, T_2, \ldots, T_m\}$ be a transaction database. Then, the utility of an itemset I in D, denoted by $u(I)$, and defined as:*

Table 2. Sample transaction database

TID	Items
T_1	(a, 1) (c, 1) (d, 1)
T_2	(a, 2) (c, 6) (e, 2)
T_3	(a, 1) (b, 2) (c, 1) (d, 6) (e, 1)
T_4	(b, 4) (c, 3) (d, 3) (e, 1)

Table 3. External utility

Item	Unit profit
a	4
b	2
c	1
d	2
e	3

$$u(I) = \sum_{T_c \in D \wedge I \subseteq T_c} u(I, T_c) \tag{2}$$

Example 2. Let us consider again the transaction database given in Example 1. Then, the utility of the itemset $\{a, c\}$ is $u(\{a, c\}) = u(\{a, c\}, T_1) + u(\{a, c\}, T_2) + u(\{a, c\}, T_3) = 5 + 14 + 5 = 24$.

Problem Definition

Given a transaction database D and a user-specified minimum utility threshold θ, the goal of mining high utility itemsets problem from D is to find the set of the itemsets with a utility no less than θ, i.e.,

$$HUI = \{I : u(I) \mid I \subseteq \Omega, u(I) \geq \theta\} \tag{3}$$

That is, identifying high utility itemsets is equivalent to finding the itemsets that cover the largest portion of the total database utility.

Example 3. Let us consider again the transaction database given in Example 1. If we set $\theta = 28$, then the high-utility itemsets with their utility in the database are $\{a, c, e\} : 28, \{c, d, e\} : 28, \{b, c, d, e\} : 40$.

The problem of HUIM is recognized as more difficult than the classical frequent itemset mining problem (FIM, for short). More precisely, the postulate of downward-closure in FIM states that the support of an itemset is anti-monotonic: that means that all the supersets of an infrequent itemset are not frequent and subsets of a frequent itemset are frequent [29]. Clearly, this property is very powerful to prune the search space. However, the utility of an itemset in HUIM is neither monotonic or anti-monotonic. In other words, a high utility itemset may have a subset or superset with higher, lower or equal utility [6]. Various HUIM algorithms avoid this problem by overestimating the utility of an itemset using the measure of *Transaction-Utilization* defined as follows.

Definition 3 (Transaction Utility). *Let* $D = \{T_1, T_2, \ldots, T_m\}$ *be a transaction database. The Transaction Utility of a transaction* T_c *in* D *is the sum of the utility of the items in* T_c, *i.e.,*

$$TU(T_c) = \sum_{x \in T_c} u(x, T_c) \tag{4}$$

Definition 4 (Transaction Weighted Utilization). *Let* $D = \{T_1, T_2, \ldots, T_m\}$ *be a transaction database. The Transaction Weighted Utilization of an itemset* I, *denoted by* $TWU(I)$, *is defined as the sum of the transaction utility of transactions containing* I, *i.e.,*

$$TWU(I) = \sum_{I \subseteq T_c | T_c \in D} TU(T_c) \tag{5}$$

Based on the above definition of TWU, the difference between $TWU(I)$ and $u(I)$ is that for $TWU(I)$, we sum the utilities of the whole transactions containing I, while $u(I)$ only computes the utilities of I in the transactions where I appears.

Example 4. Let us consider again Example 1. We have, $TWU(\{a, c, d\}) = TU(T_1) + TU(T_3) = 7 + 24 = 31$.

Notice that the transaction weighted utilization measure has three important properties that are exploited to prune the search space.

Overestimation. The TWU of an itemset I is always equal or higher than the utility of I, i.e., $TWU(I) \geq u(I)$.

Anti-monotonicity. Given two itemsets I and J, if $I \subseteq J$, then $TWU(I) \geq TWU(J)$.

Pruning. Let I be an itemset. If $TWU(I) < \theta$, then I is a low-utility itemset as well as all its supersets.

2.2   Propositional Logic and SAT Problem

In this subsection, we introduce the syntax and the semantics of classical propositional logic. Let *Prop* be a countably set of propositional variables. We use the letters p, q, r, etc. to range over *Prop*. The set of propositional formulas, denoted *Form*, is defined inductively started from *Prop*, the constant $\top$ denoting *true*, the constant $\bot$ denoting *false*, and using logical connectives $\neg, \wedge, \vee, \rightarrow$. It is worth noticing that we can restrict the language to the connectives $\neg$ and $\wedge$, since we have the equivalences: $A \vee B \equiv \neg(\neg A \wedge \neg B)$ and $A \rightarrow B \equiv \neg B \vee A$. We use $P(A)$ to denote the set of propositional variables appearing in the formula A. The equivalence connective $\leftrightarrow$ is defined by $A \leftrightarrow B \equiv (A \rightarrow B) \wedge (B \rightarrow A)$. A Boolean interpretation $\mathscr{I}$ of a formula A is defined as a function from $P(A)$ to $(0, 1)$ (0 corresponds to *false* and 1 to *true*). Given a formula A, a *model* of A is a Boolean interpretation $\mathscr{I}$ that satisfies A, i.e., $\mathscr{I}(A) = 1$. Moreover, A is *satisfiable* if there exists a model of A. A is valid or a theorem, if every Boolean interpretation is a model of A. We use $Mod(A)$ to denote the set of all models of A.

Let us now define the Conjunctive Normal Form (CNF, for short) to represent the propositional formulas. A CNF formula is a conjunction ($\wedge$) of clauses where a clause is a disjunction ($\vee$) of literals. A literal is a propositional variable (p) or its negation ($\neg p$). A CNF formula can also be seen as a set of clauses, and a clause as a set of literals. The size of the CNF formula A corresponds to the value $\sum_{c \in A} |c|$ where $|c|$ is the number of literals in the clause c. Notice that any propositional formula can be translated to a CNF formula equivalent w.r.t. satisfiability, using linear Tseitin's encoding [20].

SAT is the decision problem that aims to determine the satisfiability of a CNF formula, i.e., whether there exists a model of all clauses. This is known as NP-Complete problem. Interestingly, state-of the art SAT solvers have been shown of practical use solving real world instances encoding industrial problems up to million of clauses and variables. SAT technology has been applied in different new fields such as planning, bioinformatics, cryptography and more recently data mining. In most of these applications, we are usually interested in determining the satisfiability of a given CNF formula (i.e., decision problem), or in discovering an optimal solution such as in Maximum Satisfiability problem. However, in data mining, we mainly deal with the enumeration of all the models of a given propositional formula.

3   SAT-Based Approach for High Utility Itemset Mining

In this section, we introduce our proposed SAT-based formulation that enables us to specify in terms of constraints the task of enumeration high utility itemsets over transaction databases. Given a transaction database $D = \{(1, I_1), \ldots, (m, I_m)\}$ and a user specified threshold θ, the idea of our SAT based encoding consists of formalizing the items as well as the transactions identifiers in the transaction database D in terms of propositional variables and clauses.

To that end, we associate for each item a (resp. transaction identifier i), a propositional variable, denoted as p_a (resp. q_i). Intuitively, in a model of the SAT encoding, the propositional variables associated to the items represent a high utility itemset and those associated to the transaction identifiers represent its cover. These propositional variables will be used in 0/1 linear inequalities to find all possible candidates itemsets and their covers.

More formally, given a Boolean interpretation $\mathscr{I}$, the candidate itemset and its cover are expressed as $\{a \in \Omega \mid \mathscr{I}(p_a) = 1\}$ and $\{i \in \mathbb{N} \mid \mathscr{I}(q_i) = 1\}$, respectively. Now, we introduce our SAT-based encoding using the propositional variables described previously. The first propositional formula allows us to obtain the cover of the candidate itemset. Notice that this constraint is identical to the one introduced in [24].

$$\bigwedge_{i=1}^{m} (\neg q_i \leftrightarrow \bigvee_{a \in \Omega \setminus I} p_a) \tag{6}$$

This propositional formula expresses the fact that q_i is true if and only if the item a is supported by the transaction i. In other words, the candidate itemset is supported by the ith transaction (q_i is false), when there exists an item a (p_a is true) that does not belong to the transaction ($a \in \Omega \setminus I$).

The following propositional formula allows us to compute the utility of an itemset I in a transaction T_i:

$$u(I, T_i) = \sum_{a \in I} u(a, T_i) \tag{7}$$

We express the utility of an itemset I in the database as follows:

$$u(I) = \sum_{I \subseteq T_c \mid T_c \in D} u(I, T_i) \tag{8}$$

Let us now give the formula expressing that the utility of the candidate itemset has to be larger than the specified utility threshold θ:

$$\sum_{i=1}^{m} \sum_{a \in T_i} u(a, T_i) \times p_a \wedge q_i \geqslant \theta \tag{9}$$

Using additional variables, Constraint 9 can be rewritten using the following two formulas:

$$\sum_{i=1}^{m} \sum_{a \in T_i} u(a, T_i) \times r_{ai} \geqslant \theta \tag{10}$$

$$\bigwedge_{1 \leq i \leq m, a \in T_i} r_{ai} \leftrightarrow p_a \wedge q_i \tag{11}$$

In the sequel, we use Φ_{HUIM} to denote the CNF encoding corresponding to the conjunction of (6), (10) and (11).

Proposition 1. Φ_{HUIM} *encodes the problem of mining high utility itemsets.*

Proposition 1 specifies that enumerating the set of high utility itemsets is equivalent to have the models of Φ_{HUIM}.

Example 5. We consider the transaction database given in Example 1. Then, the formula that encodes the enumeration of all high utility itemsets in D with $\theta = 20$ can be written as follows:

$$\neg q_1 \leftrightarrow (p_b \vee p_e) \qquad \neg q_2 \leftrightarrow (p_b \vee p_d) \qquad \neg q_3 \leftrightarrow \perp \qquad \neg q_4 \leftrightarrow (p_a)$$

$$r_{a1} \leftrightarrow p_a \wedge q_1 \qquad r_{c1} \leftrightarrow p_c \wedge q_1 \qquad r_{d1} \leftrightarrow p_d \wedge q_1 \qquad r_{a2} \leftrightarrow p_a \wedge q_2$$

$$r_{c2} \leftrightarrow p_c \wedge q_2 \qquad r_{e2} \leftrightarrow p_e \wedge q_2 \qquad r_{a3} \leftrightarrow p_a \wedge q_3 \qquad r_{b3} \leftrightarrow p_b \wedge q_3$$

$$r_{c3} \leftrightarrow p_c \wedge q_3 \qquad r_{d3} \leftrightarrow p_d \wedge q_3 \qquad r_{e3} \leftrightarrow p_e \wedge q_3 \qquad r_{b4} \leftrightarrow p_b \wedge q_4$$

$$r_{c4} \leftrightarrow p_c \wedge q_4 \qquad r_{d4} \leftrightarrow p_d \wedge q_4 \qquad r_{e4} \leftrightarrow p_e \wedge q_4$$

$$4r_{a1} + r_{c1} + 2r_{d1} + 8r_{a2} + 6r_{c2} + 6r_{e2} + 4r_{a3} + 4r_{b3} + r_{c3} + 12r_{d3} + 3r_{e3} + 8r_{b4}$$
$$+ 3r_{c4} + 6r_{d4} + 3r_{e4} \geq 20$$

A DPLL based SAT procedure [30] can be used in order to enumerate all models of the obtained formula Φ_{HUIM} as described in Algorithm 1. Each found model of Φ_{HUIM} gives rise to a high utility itemset of the transaction database. More specifically, the algorithm proceeds by recursively assigning variables corresponding to items and performs unit propagation (line 5). If a conflict occurs (line 6) a backtrack is performed. Otherwise, Constraint (10) is checked during (line 14) to verify its consistency. Such checking can be easily performed by con-

---

Algorithm 1: SAT-Based models enumeration

Input: a CNF formula Σ
Output: S: the models of Φ_{HUIM}

1   $\mathscr{I} = \emptyset$;   /* interpretation */
2   $dl = 0$;   /* decision level */
3   **while** (true) **do**
4     $\gamma = \text{unitPropagation}(\Sigma, \mathscr{I})$;
5   **if** $(\gamma != \text{null})$ **then**
6       $btl = \text{decisionLevel}()$;
7   **if** $(btl == 0)$ **then return** UNSAT;
8       $dl = btl$;
9   **else**
10   **if** $(\mathscr{I} \models \Sigma)$ **then**
11        $S \leftarrow S \cup \{\mathscr{I}\}$;   /* new found model */
12        $\text{backtrack}()$;
13   **end**
14   **if** check_utility_candiate() is not valid **then**
15        $\text{backtrack}()$;
16   **end**
17      $\ell = \text{selectDecisionVariable}(\Sigma)$;
18      $dl = dl + 1$;
19      $\mathscr{I} = \mathscr{I} \cup \{selectPhase(\ell)\}$;
20   **end**
21 **end**
22 **return** S;

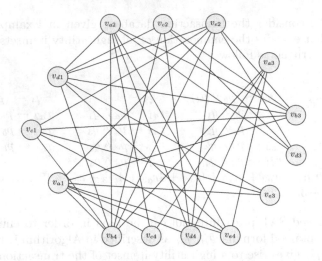

Fig. 1. The graph G_D associated to the transaction database 1

sidering the value $\sum_{i=1}^{m} \sum_{a \in T_i} u(a, T_i)$ and by subtracting $u(a, T_i)$ each time r_{ai} becomes *false*. A comparison to θ is then performed to continue the search or to backtrack.

This basic version of our algorithm performs a backtrack search similarly to the TWU measure in order to prune the search space. Now, a useful extension to perform better pruning in the search tree would be to add a new constraint to the previous encoding. Notice that this constraint will be derived from the inequation (10) using the weighted clique cover problem [21,22]. Our main idea is to identify the subsets of variables r_{ai} which can not be true simultaneously. Next, we show how this new constraint can be derived in a suitable way in order to make our pruning strategy more efficient. To do so, let us first introduce a graphical representation for the original transaction database as follows.

Definition 5. *Let D be a transaction database. Then, the graph of D is an undirected graph $G_D = (V, E)$ such that each item in each transaction represents a vertex in G_D, i.e., v_{ai} is the vertex associated to the item a in the transaction i. In addition, an edge $(v_{ai}, v_{a'j}) \in E$ iff the transaction i contains a but not a'.*

Example 6. Given the transaction database of Example 1. Then, the graph G_D associated to this base is depicted in Fig. 1.

Each edge of G_D connects two items of D that cannot be simultaneously in a high utility itemset. For instance, in database of Example 1, the item a of the transaction T_1 cannot be appear with b of transaction T_3.

In the sequel, we define the **clique cover** of a graph G as a partition of G into cliques.

Definition 6 (Clique Cover). *Let $G = (V, E)$ be an undirected graph and $C = \{C_1, \ldots, C_k\}$ where $V_i \subseteq V$ for $1 \leq i \leq k$. Then, S is a clique cover of G iff $\bigcup_{1 \leq i \leq k} C_i = V$ s.t. each sub-graph $G_i = (C_i, E_i)$ where $E_i = \{(a, b) \in E \mid a, b \in C_i\}$ is a clique.*

Clique cover is a fundamental problem in graph theory and has numerous applications in several areas such as social network analysis and bioinformatics. The problem of minimal clique cover has extensively studied in the literature [26,27].

Example 7. Let us consider the graph in Example 6. Clearly, the set of sets $S = \{\{v_{a1}, v_{b4}\}, \{v_{d1}, v_{e3}\}, \{v_{c1}\}, \{v_{a2}, v_{b4}\}, \{v_{c2}, v_{d4}\}, \{v_{c2}, v_{d3}\}, \{v_{a3}, v_{e4}\}\{v_{c3}\}, \{v_{c4}\}\}$ is a clique cover of the graph G_D.

Given the graph G_D, the cliques of G_D are a convenient way of conceptualizing the required constraint that we need to consider in our encoding. In fact, a clique of G_D corresponds to a subset of variables r_{ai} that among them at most one can be assigned to *true*. This allows us to introduce a new constraint that can be used to prune effectively the search space compared to the TWU measure. Consequently, our new constraint can be derived where the sum of weights of each subset is replaced with the maximum weight as stated in the following proposition.

Proposition 2. *Let $D = \{T_1, T_2, \ldots, T_m\}$ be a transaction database and G_D the graph associated to D. If $C = \{C_1, \ldots, C_k\}$ is a clique cover of G_D, then the following constraint holds*

$$\sum_{1 \leq i \leq k} \max_{v_{aj} \in C_i} u(a, T_j)(\bigvee_{v_{aj} \in C_i} r_{aj}) \geq \theta \tag{12}$$

Additional variables x_i can be used to simplify Constraint (12)

$$x_i \leftrightarrow \bigvee_{v_{aj} \in C_i} r_{aj} \quad \forall 1 \leq i \leq k$$

Note that the weighted clique cover problem is NP-hard and the number of solutions can be very large. Our aim here is to minimize the following gain $\sum_{i=1}^{m} \alpha_i$. The goal is then to obtain large cliques with maximum weights. To avoid the NP-Hardness of the related problem, we next consider a greedy approach to find a possible cover. To do this, we proceed by gathering first nodes with high utility together.

Example 8. Let us reconsider again Example 6. For the clique cover $S = \{\{v_{a1}, v_{b4}\}, \{v_{d1}, v_{e3}\}, \{v_{c1}\}, \{v_{a2}, v_{b4}\}, \{v_{c2}, v_{d4}\}, \{v_{c2}, v_{d3}\}, \{v_{a3}, v_{e4}\}\{v_{c3}\}, \{v_{c4}\}\}$, we can deduce the following constraint:

$$4x_1 + 3x_2 + r_{c_1} + 8x_3 + 6x_4 + 12x_5 + 4x_6 + r_{c3} + 3r_{c4} \geq 20$$

where

$$x_1 = (r_{a1} \lor r_{b4}) \qquad x_2 = (r_{d1} \lor r_{e3})$$
$$x_3 = (r_{a2} \lor r_{b4}) \qquad x_4 = (r_{c2} \lor r_{d4})$$
$$x_5 = (r_{e2} \lor r_{d3}) \qquad x_6 = (r_{a3} \lor r_{e4})$$

Using this new constraint, it is clear that if the minimum threshold exceeds 42, then we can trivially check that the set of high utility itemsets is empty which is not the case when considering only Constraint (9). More generally, by considering both the Constraint (9) and the new derived one allows us to prune the search space more efficiently.

The pseudo-code of our method is summarized in Algorithm 2. The algorithm has two input parameters: a transaction database D and a minimum utility threshold θ. It then outputs all high utility itemsets. At first, our algorithm encodes the high utility itemsets mining task into a graph G (line 1). Then, the minimum weighted clique cover method is called to find a clique cover (line 3). For that, we employ a greedy method as detailed in [21,22]. The keys step of our algorithm is to generate a CNF formulas that represent the task of HUIM by using the graph G and its cover C (line 4). Last, the SAT solver outputs the set of high utility itemset by enumerating all models of the CNF formula.

Algorithm 2: SAT based High Utility Itemset Enumeration (SATHUIM)

   Input: D: a transaction database, θ: a user-specified threshold
   Output: S: the set of all high-utility itemsets
1 $G \leftarrow SATEncodingTable(D)$;
2 $C \leftarrow \varnothing$;
3 $C \leftarrow Clique\_Cover(G)$;
4 $HUI \leftarrow enumModels(C, G, \theta)$;
5 **return** S;

---

4 Empirical Evaluation

This section presents an experimental assessment of the proposed approach to compute high utility itemsets over transaction databases. Experiments were performed to evaluate the performance of the proposed algorithm against other state-of-the-art algorithms. The baseline methods include one phase algorithms such as EFIM [17] and D2HUP [15] and the two phase based approach Up-Growth [13]. For the implementations of these algorithms, we used the SPMF (Sequential Pattern Mining Framework) open-source data mining library [23]. SPMF is a cross-platform and open-source data mining library written in Java, specialized in HUIM algorithms, has tools to generate utility transaction databases, and has been deployed in many research works [29].

All the experiments are performed on Intel Xeon quad-core machine with 32 GB of RAM running at 2.66 Ghz. Our algorithm is implemented in C++. For the enumeration of all models of the Boolean formula encoding the corresponding HUIM problem, we use MiniSAT [30] solver based on the DPLL procedure.

We compare our proposed approach, coined SATHUIM, against competing algorithms over real and synthetic datasets generated using the transaction database generator implemented in SPMF [23] in which the number of transactions and items in the database and the average or maximum length of transaction need to be specified. We imposed 1800 s time limit for all the methods.

In Table 4, for each instance, we mention the number of transactions (#Transactions), the number of items (#Items), the density of the dataset (Density(%)), the size of the formula encoding the whole problem in terms of number of variables (#Vars) and clauses (#Clauses). Notice that the number of variables and clauses depends on the size of the database. The larger the database, the larger the number of variables and clauses.

We ran SATHUIM without and with the additional constraint (12) (SATHUIM*) on each of the datasets for different values of minimum threshold θ. The latter is mentioned in percent as used in the literature. For each tested dataset, we recorded the running time (in seconds) as shown in Table 5.

Table 4. Datasets characteristics

Instance	#Transactions	#Items	Density(%)	#Vars	#Clauses
Mushroom	8124	119	9.33	1344997	1919723
Chess	3196	75	49.33	121486	354865
DS1	1000	500	15.82	11769	32411
DS2	500	50	30.2	8071	22789

Table 5. SAT-based methods vs (EFIM, DHUP, Up-Growth)

Dataset	θ value	EFIM	D2HUP	Up-Growth	SATHUIM	SATHUIM*
Mushroom	45%	87.55	130.25	901.74	801.74	103.74
Mushroom	35%	184.23	250.27	1500.12	317.74	222.15
Mushroom	25%	450.41	912.88	–	901.74	522.93
Chess	45%	34,41	98,12	643.56	345.61	77.38
Chess	35%	157,00	200,08	1000.77	208.06	819.68
Chess	25%	288,00	537,53	–	1769.34	375.55
DS1	45%	62,90	39,71	442.21.08	385.39	75.07
DS1	35%	147,78	101,57	754.33	801.02	186.34
DS1	25%	403,19	302,28	1159.12	1078.27	366.22
DS2	35%	0.126	0.186	92.07	65.23	0.93
DS2	25%	7.25	9.67	202.17	134.44	7.09
DS2	15%	21.43	37.186	543.23	234.66	29.89

Table 5 summarizes the obtained results. As we can remark, EFIM is the best on real data and D2HUP on synthetic data (i.e., DS1 and DS2). Up-Growth is the worst compared to EFIM and D2HUP. For all algorithms, the time needed increases when the minimum threshold decreases. Concerning our algorithm SATHUIM, it is clear that adding the additional constraint (12) improves considerably the performances of the algorithm. Interestingly, we notice that our SATHUIM* algorithm is the second-fastest method, next EFIM for Mushroom and Chess and D2HUP for synthetic datasets. This clearly demonstrates that our constraint-based approach can be competitive for mining high utility itemsets.

5   Conclusion and Future Work

In this paper, we presented a novel approach for discovering high utility itemsets from transaction databases. Our approach is based on an encoding into propositional logic and a SAT solver is used to enumerate high utility patterns. Moreover, in order to improve the approach efficiency, the weighted clique cover problem is used to derive a new constraint to to efficiently prune the search space. Preliminary results have shown interesting performance against the state-of-the-art algorithms. This work can be extended in different ways. First, we would like to perform more extensive experiments for a large comparison. Second, we plan to use decomposition as a mean to handle large transaction databases. Finally, we would like to extend our work to explore other kinds of patterns such as closed and maximal itemsets.

References

1. Erwin, A., Gopalan, R.P., Achuthan, N.R.: Efficient mining of high utility itemsets from large datasets. In: Washio, T., Suzuki, E., Ting, K.M., Inokuchi, A. (eds.) PAKDD 2008. LNCS (LNAI), vol. 5012, pp. 554–561. Springer, Heidelberg (2008). https://doi.org/10.1007/978-3-540-68125-0_50
2. Chan, R., Yang, Q., Shen, Y.: Mining high utility itemsets. In: Proceedings of the IEEE Third International Conference on Data Mining, pp. 19–26, November (2003)
3. Ahmed, C.F., Tanbeer, S.K., Jeong, B.-S., Lee, Y.-K.: Efficient tree structures for high utility pattern mining in incremental databases. IEEE Trans. Knowl. Data Eng. **21**, 1708–1721 (2009)
4. Shie, B.-E., Hsiao, H.-F., Tseng, V.S., Yu, P.S.: Mining high utility mobile sequential patterns in mobile commerce environments. In: Yu, J.X., Kim, M.H., Unland, R. (eds.) DASFAA 2011. LNCS, vol. 6587, pp. 224–238. Springer, Heidelberg (2011). https://doi.org/10.1007/978-3-642-20149-3_18
5. Yen, S.-J., Lee, Y.-S.: Mining high utility quantitative association rules. In: Song, I.Y., Eder, J., Nguyen, T.M. (eds.) DaWaK 2007. LNCS, vol. 4654, pp. 283–292. Springer, Heidelberg (2007). https://doi.org/10.1007/978-3-540-74553-2_26
6. Fournier-Viger, P., Lin, J.C.-W., Vo, B., Chi, T.T., Zhang, J., Le, H.B.: A Survey of Itemset Mining. WIREs Interdisciplinary reviews - Data Mining and Knowledge Discovery, Wiley (2017)

7. Chonsheng, Z., et al.: An empirical evaluation of high utility itemset mining algorithms. In: 101, pp. 91–115 (2018)
8. Guns, T., Nijssen, S., Raedt, L.D.: Itemset mining: a constraint programming perspective. Artif. Intell. **175**, 1951–1983 (2011)
9. Raedt, L.D., Guns, T., Nijssen, S.: Constraint programming for itemset mining. In: ACM SIGKDD, pp. 204–212 (2008)
10. Coquery, E., Jabbour, S., Sais, L., Salhi, Y.: A SAT-based approach for discovering frequent, closed and maximal patterns in a sequence. In: Proceedings of ECAI, pp. 258–263 (2012)
11. Jabbour, S., Sais, L., Salhi, Y.: The top-k frequent closed itemset mining using top-k SAT problem. In: Blockeel, H., Kersting, K., Nijssen, S., Železný, F. (eds.) ECML PKDD 2013. LNCS (LNAI), vol. 8190, pp. 403–418. Springer, Heidelberg (2013). https://doi.org/10.1007/978-3-642-40994-3_26
12. Liu, Y., Liao, W., Choudhary, A.: A two-phase algorithm for fast discovery of high utility itemsets. In: Ho, T.B., Cheung, D., Liu, H. (eds.) PAKDD 2005. LNCS (LNAI), vol. 3518, pp. 689–695. Springer, Heidelberg (2005). https://doi.org/10.1007/11430919_79
13. Tseng, V.S., Shie, B.-E., Wu, C.-W., Yu, P.S.: Efficient algorithms for mining high utility itemsets from transaction databases. IEEE Trans. Knowl. Data Eng. **25**(8), 1772–1786 (2013)
14. Liu, M., Qu, J.: Mining high utility itemsets without candidate generation. In: Proceedings of the 22nd ACM International Conference on Information and Knowledge Management, p. 5564 (2012)
15. Krishnamoorthy, S.: Pruning strategies for mining high utility itemsets. Expert Syst. Appl. **42**(5), 2371–2381 (2015)
16. Fournier-Viger, P., Wu, C.-W., Zida, S., Tseng, V.S.: FHM: faster high-utility itemset mining using estimated utility co-occurrence pruning. In: Proceedings of the 21st International Symposium on Methodologies for Intelligent System, p. 8392 (2014)
17. Zida, S., Fournier-Viger, P., Lin, J.C.W., Wu, C.W., V.S. Tseng: EFIM: A Highly Ecient Algorithm for High-Utility Itemset Mining
18. Peng, A.Y., Koh, Y.S., Riddle, P.: mHUIMiner: a fast high utility itemset mining algorithm for sparse datasets. In: Kim, J., Shim, K., Cao, L., Lee, J.-G., Lin, X., Moon, Y.-S. (eds.) PAKDD 2017. LNCS (LNAI), vol. 10235, pp. 196–207. Springer, Cham (2017). https://doi.org/10.1007/978-3-319-57529-2_16
19. Duong, Q.-H., Fournier-Viger, P., Ramampiaro, H., Nørvåg, K., Dam, T.-L.: Efficient high utility itemset mining using buffered utility-lists. Appl. Intell. **48**(7), 1859–1877 (2017). https://doi.org/10.1007/s10489-017-1057-2
20. Tseitin, G.: On the complexity of derivations in the propositional calculus. In: Structures in Constructives Mathematics and Mathematical Logic, Part II, pp. 115–125 (1968)
21. Hsu, W.-L., Nemhauser, G.L.: A polynomial algorithm for the minimum weighted clique cover problem on claw-free perfect graphs. Discrete Math. **38**(1), 65–71 (1982)
22. Golumbic, M.C., Stern, M., Levy, A., Morgenstern, G. (eds.): WG 2012. LNCS, vol. 7551. Springer, Heidelberg (2012). https://doi.org/10.1007/978-3-642-34611-8
23. Fournier-Viger, P.: SPMF: a Java open-source data mining library. www.philippe-fournier-viger.com/spmf/. Accessed 15 Aug 2018
24. Boudane, A., Jabbour, S., Sais, L., Salhi, Y.: A SAT-based approach for mining association rules. In: Proceedings of IJCAI, pp. 2472–2478 (2016)

25. Boudane, A., Jabbour, S., Sais, L., Salhi, Y.: Enumerating non-redundant association rules using satisfiability. In: Kim, J., Shim, K., Cao, L., Lee, J.-G., Lin, X., Moon, Y.-S. (eds.) PAKDD 2017. LNCS (LNAI), vol. 10234, pp. 824–836. Springer, Cham (2017). https://doi.org/10.1007/978-3-319-57454-7_64
26. Cheng, J., Ke, Y., Ada Wai-Chee, F., Yu, J.X., Zhu, L.: Finding maximal cliques in massive networks. ACM Trans. Database Syst. **36**, 4 (2011)
27. Eblen, J.D., Phillips, C.A., Rogers, G.L., et al.: The maximum clique enumeration problem: algorithms, applications, and implementations. BMC Bioinform. **13**, S5 (2012)
28. Jabbour, S., et al.: Boolean satisfiability for sequence mining. In: Proceedings of CIKM 2013, pp. 649–658 (2013)
29. Fournier-Viger, P., Chun-Wei Lin, J., Truong-Chi, T., Nkambou, R.: A survey of high utility itemset mining. In: Fournier-Viger, P., Lin, J.C.-W., Nkambou, R., Vo, B., Tseng, V.S. (eds.) High-Utility Pattern Mining. SBD, vol. 51, pp. 1–45. Springer, Cham (2019). https://doi.org/10.1007/978-3-030-04921-8_1
30. Sörensson, N.E.: An Extensible SAT-solver. In: Proceedings of SAT, pp. 502–518 (2003)

High-Utility Interval-Based Sequences

S. Mohammad Mirbagheri[(✉)] and Howard J. Hamilton

Department of Computer Science, University of Regina, Regina, Canada
{mirbaghs,Howard.Hamilton}@uregina.ca

Abstract. Sequential pattern mining is an interesting research area with broad range of applications. Most prior research on sequential pattern mining has considered point-based data where events occur instantaneously. However, in many application domains, events persist over intervals of time of varying lengths. Furthermore, traditional frameworks for sequential pattern mining assume all events have the same weight or utility. This simplifying assumption neglects the opportunity to find informative patterns in terms of utilities, such as cost. To address these issues, we incorporate the concept of utility into interval-based sequences and define a framework to mine high utility patterns in interval-based sequences i.e., patterns whose utility meets or exceeds a minimum threshold. In the proposed framework, the utility of events is considered while assuming multiple events can occur coincidentally and persist over varying periods of time. An algorithm named *High Utility Interval-based Pattern Miner* (*HUIPMiner*) is proposed and applied to real datasets. To achieve an efficient solution, HUIPMiner is augmented with a pruning strategy. Experimental results show that HUIPMiner is an effective solution to the problem of mining high utility interval-based sequences.

Keywords: High utility interval-based · Utility mining · Sequential mining · Temporal pattern · Event interval sequence

1 Introduction

Sequential pattern mining aims to find patterns from data recorded sequentially along with their time of occurrence. Depending on the application scenario, symbolic sequential data is categorized as either *point-based* or *interval-based*. Point-based data reflect scenarios in which events happen instantaneously or events are considered to have equal time intervals. Duration has no impact on extracting patterns for this type. Interval-based data reflect scenarios where events have unequal time intervals; here, duration plays an important role.

In many application domains, such as medicine [1,2], sensor technology [3], sign language [4], and motion capture [5], events persist over intervals of time of varying lengths, which results in complicated temporal relations among events. Thirteen possible temporal relations between a pair of event intervals were nicely categorized by Allen [6]. Some studies have been devoted to mining frequent

© Springer Nature Switzerland AG 2020
M. Song et al. (Eds.): DaWaK 2020, LNCS 12393, pp. 107–121, 2020.
https://doi.org/10.1007/978-3-030-59065-9_9

sequential patterns from interval-based data and describing the temporal relations among the event intervals. Wu and Chen [7] presented a nonambiguous representation of temporal data utilizing the beginning and ending time points of the events. By adapting the PrefixSpan [8], they proposed the TPrefixSpan algorithm to mine frequent temporal sequences. Chen et al. [9] proposed the coincidence representation to simplify the processing of complex relations among event intervals. They also proposed an algorithm named CTMiner to discover frequent time-interval based patterns in large databases.

The aforementioned work has focused on representations of temporal data and discovering frequent temporal patterns. However, *frequent pattern mining* (FPM) may not be the right solution to problems where the weight of patterns may be the major factor of interest and the frequency of patterns may be a minor factor. The weight of a pattern can be interpreted differently depending on the problem or scenario. For example, it may represent the profit or the cost that a business experiences when a particular pattern occurs. Some patterns of interest may have high weights but low frequencies. Thus, FPM may miss patterns that are infrequent but valuable. FPM may also extract too many frequent patterns that are low in weight. To address these problems, *high utility pattern mining* (HUPM) has emerged as an alternative to FPM. The goal of HUPM is to extract patterns from a dataset with utility no less than a user-specified minimum utility threshold.

Tackling the HUPM problem requires facing more challenges than FPM. The major FPM algorithms rely on the downward closure property (also known as the Apriori Property) [10] to perform efficiently. This property, which is utilized by most pruning strategies, states that if a pattern is frequent then all of its sub-patterns are frequent and if a pattern is infrequent all of its super-patterns are infrequent. However, this property does not hold in utility mining because the utilities of patterns are neither monotone nor anti-monotone [11]. As a result, the existing optimization approaches for FPM are not applicable to HUPM. To cope with this challenge, previous studies introduced several domain-dependent weighted downward closure properties, including the transaction-weighted downward closure property (TDCP) [12] for itemset pattern mining, the sequence-weighted downward closure property (SDCP) [13] for sequential pattern mining, and the episode-weighted downward closure property (EDCP) [14,15] for episode pattern mining.

Most prior studies on HUPM have been devoted to transactional data rather than sequential data. However, such studies do not address the problem of HUPM in interval-based sequences, which covers a wide range of applications mentioned above. Interval-based applications can be better described when the concept of utility is employed. For example, interval-based sequences commonly occur in businesses where different services or packages, which persist over time, are offered to customers. Providing informative patterns to policy makers is an essential task, especially in a competitive marketplace. Neglecting the fact that these services or packages have various utilities (or weights) results in misleading information. For instance, HUPM can be beneficial to telecommunication companies or insurance companies which sell products that last over varying periods of time at various costs.

To the best of our knowledge, Huang et al. [16] recently made the first attempt to mine interval-based sequence data for patterns based on utility. They suggested a method to discover the top-K high utility patterns (HUPs). Their approach consists of two main parts. It first discovers a set of frequent patterns, and then it extracts the top-K HUPs from the set. This indirect approach suffers from a major drawback. The set of frequent patterns may not contain all HUPs. Hence, the approach may miss some high utility but infrequent patterns and consequently, it may select low-ranked HUPs as the top-K HUPs.

For the above reasons, we formalize the problem of the mining of high utility interval-based patterns (HUIPs) from sequences and propose a new framework to solve this problem. The major contributions of this work are as follows: 1) We propose the *coincidence eventset representation* (*CER*) to represent interval-based events. 2) We incorporate both internal and external utilities into interval-based sequences and propose an algorithm called *HUIPMiner* to mine all high utility sequential patterns from interval-based sequences; 3) We introduce the *L-sequence-weighted downward closure property* (*LDCP*), which is used in our pruning strategy and utilize LDCP in HUIPMiner to reduce the search space and identify high utility sequential patterns efficiently; and 4) We report on experiments that show the proposed framework and algorithm are able to discover all high utility patterns from interval-based data even with a low minimum utility threshold.

The rest of the paper is organized as follows. Section 2 provides background and preliminaries. It then proposes a framework of interval-based sequence utility and finally it formulates the problem of mining high utility interval-based sequential patterns. Section 3 presents the details of the HUIPMiner algorithm and the pruning strategy. Experimental results on real datasets and evaluation are given in Sect. 4. Section 5 presents conclusions and future work.

2   Problem Statement

Let $\sum = \{A, B, \ldots\}$ denote a finite alphabet. A triple $e = (l, b, f)$, where $l \in \sum$ is the event label, $b \in \mathbb{N}$ is the beginning time, and $f \in \mathbb{N}$ is the finishing time ($b < f$), is called an *event-interval*. An event-interval sequence or *E-sequence* $s = \langle e_1, e_2, \ldots, e_n \rangle$ is a list of n event intervals ordered based on beginning time in ascending order. If event-intervals have equal beginning times, then they are ordered lexicographically by their labels. The size of E-sequence s, denoted as $|s| = n$, is the number of event-intervals in s. A database D that consists of set of tuples $\langle sid, s \rangle$, where sid is a unique identifier of s, is called an *E-sequence database*. Table 1 depicts an E-sequence database consisting of four E-sequences with identifiers 1 to 4.

Definition 1. Given an E-sequence $s = \langle (l_1, b_1, f_1), (l_2, b_2, f_2), \ldots, (l_n, b_n, f_n) \rangle$, the multiset $T = \{b_1, f_1, b_2, f_2, \ldots, b_n, f_n\}$ consists of all time points corresponding to sequence s. If we sort T in ascending order and eliminate redundant elements, we can derive a sequence $T_s = \langle t_1, t_2, \ldots, t_m \rangle$, where $t_k \in T, t_k < t_{k+1}$.

Table 1. Example of an E-sequence database

Sid	Event label	Beginning time	Finishing time	Event sequence			
1	A	8	16	A			
	B	18	21		B		
	C	24	28				C
	E	25	27				E
2	A	1	5	A			
	C	8	14			C	
	E	9	12			E	
	F	9	12			F	
3	B	6	12	B			
	A	7	14		A		
	C	14	20			C	
	E	16	18			E	
4	B	2	7	B			
	A	5	10		A		
	D	5	12		D		
	C	16	22				C
	E	18	20				E

T_s is called the *E-sequence unique time points* of s. We denote the number of elements in T_s by $|T_s|$, that is, $|T_s| = m$.

Definition 2. Let $s = \langle (l_1, b_1, f_1), \ldots, (l_j, b_j, f_j), \ldots, (l_n, b_n, f_n) \rangle$ be an E-sequence. A function $\Phi_s : \mathbb{N} \times \mathbb{N} \to 2^{\Sigma}$ is defined as:

$$\Phi_s(t_p, t_q) = \{l_j \mid (l_j, b_j, f_j) \in s \ \wedge \ (b_j \leq t_p) \wedge (t_q \leq f_j)\} \tag{1}$$

where $1 \leq j \leq n$ and $t_p < t_q$. Given an E-sequence s with corresponding E-sequence unique time points $T_s = \langle t_1, t_2, \ldots, t_m \rangle$, a *coincidence* c_k is defined as $\Phi_s(t_k, t_{k+1})$ where $t_k, t_{k+1} \in T_s$, $1 \leq k \leq m-1$, are two consecutive time points. The duration λ_k of coincidence c_k is $t_{k+1} - t_k$. The size of a coincidence is the number of event labels in the coincidence.

For example, the E-sequence unique time points of s_2 in Table 1 is $T_{s_2} = \{1, 5, 8, 9, 12, 14\}$. Coincidence $c_4 = \Phi_{s_2}(9, 12) = \{C, E, F\}$, $\lambda_4 = 3$ and $|c_4| = 3$.

Definition 3. A coincidence label sequence, or *L-sequence* $L = \langle c_1 c_2 \ldots c_g \rangle$ is an ordered list of g coincidences. An L-sequence is called a *K-L-sequence*, iff there are exactly K coincidences in the L-sequence. We define the size of an L-sequence, denoted Z, to be the maximum size of any coincidences in the L-sequence.

For example, $\langle \{B\}\{A, B\}\{A\} \rangle$ is a 3-L-sequence because it has 3 coincidences and its size is 2 because the maximum size of the coincidences in it is $max\{1, 2, 1\} = 2$.

Table 2. C-sequence database corresponding to the E-sequences in Table 1

Sid	C-sequence
1	$\langle(A,8)(\varnothing,2)(B,3)(\varnothing,3)(C,1)(\{C,E\},2)(C,1)\rangle$
2	$\langle(A,4)(\varnothing,3)(C,1)(\{C,E,F\},3)(C,2)\rangle$
3	$\langle(B,1)(\{A,B\},5)(A,2)(C,2)(\{C,E\},2)(C,2)\rangle$
4	$\langle(B,3)(\{A,B,D\},2)(\{A,D\},3)(D,2)(\varnothing,4)(C,2)(\{C,E\},2)(C,2)\rangle$

2.1 The Coincidence Eventset Representation (CER)

The representations proposed in previous studies, such as [7,9], do not store the durations of intervals. These approaches transform each event interval into a point-based representation encompassing only temporal relations. Although these formats are described as unambiguous, they actually leave an ambiguity with respect to duration. It is true that the temporal relations among intervals can be mapped one-to-one to the temporal sequence by these representations, but the duration for which these relations persist is ignored. Consequently, it is impossible to reverse the process and reconstruct the original E-sequence if we receive one of these representation. In this section, we address this limitation by incorporating the duration of intervals into a new representation called the *coincidence eventset representation* (CER).

Definition 4. Given a coincidence c_k in E-sequence s, a coincidence eventset, or *C-eventset*, is denoted σ_k and defined as an ordered pair consisting of the coincidence c_k and the corresponding coincidence duration λ_k, i.e.:

$$\sigma_k = (c_k, \lambda_k) \tag{2}$$

For brevity, the braces are omitted if c_k in C-eventset σ_k has only one event label, which we refer as a *C-event*. A coincidence eventset sequence, or *C-sequence*, is an ordered list of C-eventsets, which is defined as $C = \langle\sigma_1 \ldots \sigma_{m-1}\rangle$, where $m = |T_s|$. A *C-sequence database* δ consists of a set of tuples $\langle sid, C\rangle$, where sid is a unique identifier of C.

For example, the E-sequences in the database shown in Table 1 can be represented by the CER to give the C-sequences shown in Table 2. We denote the $sid = 1$ C-sequence as C_{s_1}; other C-sequences are numbered accordingly. The "$\varnothing$" symbol is used to distinguish disjoint event intervals. A "$\varnothing$" indicates a gap between two event intervals, whereas the lack of a "$\varnothing$" indicates that the two event intervals are adjacent. It can be seen that CER incorporates the durations of the event intervals into the representation.

Definition 5. Given two C-eventsets $\sigma_a = (c_a, \lambda_a)$ and $\sigma_b = (c_b, \lambda_b)$, σ_b contains σ_a, which is denoted $\sigma_a \subseteq \sigma_b$, iff $c_a \subseteq c_b \wedge \lambda_a = \lambda_b$. Given two C-sequences $C = \langle\sigma_1\sigma_2 \ldots \sigma_n\rangle$ and $C' = \langle\sigma'_1\sigma'_2 \ldots \sigma'_{n'}\rangle$, we say C is a *C-subsequence* of C', denoted $C \subseteq C'$, iff there exist integers $1 \leq j_1 \leq j_2 \leq \ldots \leq j_n \leq n'$ such that $\sigma_k \subseteq \sigma'_{j_k}$ for $1 \leq k \leq n$. Given a C-sequence $C = \langle\sigma_1\sigma_2 \ldots \sigma_n\rangle = \langle(c_1, \lambda_1)(c_2, \lambda_2) \ldots (c_n, \lambda_n)\rangle$ and an L-sequence $L = \langle c'_1 c'_2 \ldots c'_m\rangle$, C *matches* L, denoted as $C \sim L$, iff $n = m$ and $c_k = c'_k$ for $1 \leq k \leq n$.

For example, $\langle (A, 2) \rangle$, $\langle (A, 2)(A, 3) \rangle$, and $\langle (\{A, B, D\}, 2) \rangle$, are C-subsequences of C-sequence C_{s_4}, while $\langle (\{A, F\}, 2) \rangle$ and $\langle (A, 2)(D, 5) \rangle$ are not. It is possible that multiple C-subsequences of a C-sequence match a given L-sequence. For example, if we want to find all C-subsequences of C_{s_4} in Table 2 that match the L-sequence $\langle A \rangle$, we obtain $\langle (A, 2) \rangle$ in the second C-eventset and $\langle (A, 3) \rangle$ in the third C-eventset.

2.2   Utility

Let each event label $l \in \Sigma$, be associated with a value, called the *external utility*, which is denoted as $p(l)$, such that $p : \Sigma \to \mathbb{R}_{\geq 0}$. The external utility of an event label may correspond to any value of interest, such as the unit profit or cost, that is associated with the event label. The values shown in Table 3 are used in the following examples as the external utilities associated with the C-sequence database shown in Table 2.

Table 3. External utilities associated with the event labels

Event label	A	B	C	D	E	F	∅
External utility	1	2	1	3	2	1	0

Let the utility of a C-event (l, λ) be $u(l, \lambda) = p(l) \times \lambda$. The utility of a C-eventset $\sigma = (\{l_1, l_2, \ldots, l_n\}, \lambda)$ is defined as: $u_e(\sigma) = \sum_{i=1}^{n} u(l_i, \lambda)$. The utility of a C-sequence $C = \langle \sigma_1 \sigma_2 \ldots \sigma_m \rangle$ is defined as: $u_s(C) = \sum_{i=1}^{m} u_e(\sigma_i)$. Therefore, the utility of the C-sequence database $\delta = \{\langle sid_1, C_{s_1} \rangle, \langle sid_2, C_{s_2} \rangle, \ldots, \langle sid_r, C_{s_r} \rangle\}$ is defined as: $u_d(\delta) = \sum_{i=1}^{r} u_s(C_{s_i})$. For example, the utility of C-sequence $C_{s_3} = \langle (B, 1)(\{A, B\}, 5)(A, 2)(C, 2)(\{C, E\}, 2)(C, 2) \rangle$ is $u_s(C_{s_3}) = 1 \times 2 + 5 \times (1 + 2) + 2 \times 1 + 2 \times 1 + 2 \times (1 + 2) + 2 \times 1 = 29$, and the utility of the C-sequence database δ in Table 2 is $u_d(\delta) = u_s(C_{s_1}) + u_s(C_{s_2}) + u_s(C_{s_3}) + u_s(C_{s_4}) = 22 + 19 + 29 + 46 = 116$.

Definition 6. The *maximum utility of k C-eventsets in a C-sequence* is defined as: $u_{max_k}(C, k) = max\{u_s(C') \mid C' \subseteq C \land |C'| \leq k \}$. Note: In the name of the u_{max_k} function, the "k" is part of the name rather than a parameter.

For example, the maximum utility of 2 C-eventsets in C-sequence $C_{s_3} = \langle (B, 1) (\{A, B\}, 5)(A, 2)(C, 2)(\{C, E\}, 2)(C, 2) \rangle$ is $u_{max_k}(C_{s_3}, 2) = u_s(\langle (\{A, B\}, 5)(\{C, E\}, 2) \rangle) = 15 + 6 = 21$.

Definition 7. Given a C-sequence database δ and an L-sequence $L = \langle c_1 c_2 \ldots c_n \rangle$, the utility of L in C-sequence $C = \langle \sigma_1 \sigma_2 \ldots \sigma_m \rangle \in \delta$ is defined as a *utility set*:

$$u_l(L, C) = \bigcup_{C' \sim L \land C' \subseteq C} u_s(C') \tag{3}$$

The utility of L in δ is also a utility set:

$$u_l(L) = \bigcup_{C \in \delta} u_l(L, C) \tag{4}$$

For example, consider L-sequence $L = \langle\{B\}\{A\}\rangle$. The utility of L in C_{s_3} shown in Table 2 is $u_l(L, C_{s_3}) = \{u_s(\langle\langle(B,1)(A,5)\rangle\rangle), u_s(\langle\langle(B,1)(A,2)\rangle\rangle), u_s(\langle\langle(B,5)$ $(A,2)\rangle\rangle)\} = \{7, 4, 12\}$, and thus the utility of L in δ is $u_l(L) = \{u_l(L, C_{s_3}),$ $u_l(L, C_{s_4})\} = \{\{7, 4, 12\}, \{8, 9, 7\}\}$. From this example, one can see that an L-sequence may have multiple utility values associated with it, unlike a sequence in frequent sequential pattern mining.

2.3 High Utility Interval-Based Pattern Mining

Definition 8. The *maximum utility* of an L-sequence L in C-sequence database δ is defined as $u_{\max}(L)$:

$$u_{\max}(L) = \sum_{C \in \delta} \max(u_l(L, C)) \tag{5}$$

For example, the maximum utility of an L-sequence $L = \langle\{B\}\{A\}\rangle$ in C-sequence database δ shown in Table 2 is $u_{\max}(L) = 0 + 0 + 12 + 9 = 21$.

Definition 9. An L-sequence L is a *high utility interval-based pattern* iff its maximum utility is no less than a user-specified minimum utility threshold ξ. Formally: $u_{\max}(L) \geq \xi \iff L$ is a high utility interval-based pattern.

Problem I: Given a user-specified minimum utility threshold ξ, an E-sequence database D, and external utilities for event labels, the problem of high utility interval-based mining is to discover all L-sequences such that their utilities are at least ξ. By specifying the maximum length and size of the L-sequence, Problem I can be specialized to give **Problem II**, which is to discover all L-sequences with lengths and sizes of at most K and Z, respectively, such that their utilities are at least ξ.

3 The HUIPMiner Algorithm

In this section, we propose the *HUIPMiner* algorithm to mine high utility interval-based patterns. HUIPMiner is composed of two phases in which each iteration generates a special type of candidates of a certain length. We also obtain the L-sequence-weighted downward closure property (LDCP) (Theorem 1), which is similar to the sequence-weighted downward closure property (SDCP) [13]. LDCP is utilized in the proposed pruning strategy to avoid generating unpromising L-sequence candidates. LDCP has an advantage over SDCP since it reduces the size of the search space by using a tighter upper bound, which we present in Definition 10.

Definition 10. (LWU_k) The L-sequence-weighted utilization of an L-sequence w.r.t. a maximum length k is defined as:

$$LWU_k(L) = \sum_{C' \sim L \wedge C' \subseteq C \wedge C \in \delta} u_{\max_k}(C, k) \tag{6}$$

For example, the L-sequence-weighted utilization of $L = \langle\{B\}\{A\}\rangle$ w.r.t. the maximum length $k = 2$ in the C-sequence database shown in Table 2 is $\mathrm{LWU}_2(\langle\{B\}\{A\}\rangle) = 0 + 0 + 21 + 24 = 45$.

Theorem 1 (L-sequence-weighted downward closure property). *Given a C-sequence database δ and two L-sequences L and L', where $L \subseteq L'$ and $|L'| \leq k$, then*

$$\mathrm{LWU}_k(L') \leq \mathrm{LWU}_k(L) \tag{7}$$

Proof. Let α and β be two C-subsequences that match the L-sequences L and L', respectively. Since $L \subseteq L'$, then $\alpha \subseteq \beta$. Let $Q' \in \delta$ be the set of all C-sequences containing β and $Q \in \delta$ be the set of all C-sequences containing α. Since $\alpha \subseteq \beta$, then Q must be a superset of Q', that is, $Q \supseteq Q'$. Therefore, we infer

$$\sum_{\beta \sim L' \wedge \beta \subseteq C' \wedge C' \in Q'} \mathrm{u_{max_k}}(C', k) \leq \sum_{\alpha \sim L \wedge \alpha \subseteq C \wedge C \in Q} \mathrm{u_{max_k}}(C, k) \tag{8}$$

and equivalently we derive $\mathrm{LWU}_k(L') \leq \mathrm{LWU}_k(L)$.   □

Algorithm 1 shows the main procedure of the HUIPMiner algorithm. The inputs are: (1) a C-sequence database δ, (2) a minimum utility threshold ξ, (3) a maximum pattern length $K \geq 1$, and (4) a maximum pattern size $Z \geq 1$. The output includes all high utility interval-based patterns. The algorithm has two phases, a *coincident phase* to obtain high utility coincidence patterns (L-sequences with lengths equal to 1) and a *serial phase* to obtain high utility serial patterns (L-sequences with lengths greater than 1).

3.1   The Coincident Phase

The coincident phase, which is the first phase of HUIPMiner (Lines 1–13), generates coincidence candidates by concatenating event labels.

Definition 11. Let $c = \{l_1, l_2, \ldots, l_n\}$ and $c' = \{l'_1, l'_2, \ldots, l'_m\}$ be two coincidences. The *coincident concatenation* of c and c' is the ordinal sum of the coincidences and is defined as coincident-concat$(c, c') = (c \cup c', \leq) = c \oplus c'$.

For example, coincident-concat$(\{A, B\}, \{A, C\}) = \{A, B, C\}$.

In the first round of this phase, all event labels are considered as coincidence candidates with a size of 1 (Line 1). Then, the algorithm searches each C-sequence to find matches to these candidates. Next, it calculates the maximum utility $\mathrm{u_{max}}$ and L-sequence-weighted utilization LWU_k of each candidate. If $\mathrm{u_{max}}$ for a candidate is no less than the given threshold ξ, then the candidate is classified as a high utility coincident pattern and placed in set HUCP. For example, suppose we want to find all HUIPs of Table 2 when the threshold is 14, the maximum size of a coincidence Z is 2, and the maximum length of an L-sequence K is 2. For simplicity, suppose all event labels have equal external utilities of 1. Table 4 shows the coincidence candidates of size 1 and their maximum utilities and L-sequence-weighted utilizations, which are denoted LWU_2.

Table 4. HUIPMiner example - coincidence phase

Candidate	{A}	{B}	{C}	{D}	{E}	{F}
u_{max}	20	11	9	3	9	3
LWU_2	51	38	51	12	51	13

At the end of the first round, {A} is the only candidate that is added into HUCP because $u_{max}(\langle\{A\}\rangle) \geq 14$.

Before the next round is started, coincidence candidates of size 2 are generated. In order to avoid generating too many candidates, we present a pruning strategy, which is based on the following definition.

Definition 12. A coincidence candidate c is *promising* iff $LWU_k(c) \geq \xi$. Otherwise it is unpromising.

Property. Let a be an unpromising coincidence candidate and a' be a coincidence. Any superset produced by coincident-concat(a, a') is of low utility.

Rationale. Property 1 holds by the LDCP property (Theorem 1).

Pruning strategy. Discard all unpromising coincidence candidates.

If the LWU_k value of a candidate is less than ξ, the candidate will be discarded since it is unpromising. If the LWU_k value of a candidate is no less than ξ, the candidate is promising and thus it will be added to set P, the set of promising candidates for the current run. The HUIPMiner algorithm also extracts the unique elements of the promising candidates (Line 10). Before the algorithm performs the next round, P is added into WUCP, which is the set of all weighted utilization coincident patterns with sizes up to Z. WUCP is later used in the serial phase. In our example, the algorithm prunes (discards) {D} and {F} in the first round because their LWU_2 values are less than 14. Therefore, {D} and {F} will not be involved in generating candidates for the second round. {A}, {B}, {C} and {E} are identified as promising candidates and added into P. Then, coincidence candidates of size 2 are generated for the next round by calling the *Ccandidate* procedure and sending P and the unique elements as input arguments (Definition 11). The algorithm repeats this procedure until it reaches Z or no more candidates can be generated. At the end of this phase, the algorithm has found all high utility coincident patterns and stored them in HUCP; it has also found all weighted utilization coincident patterns of maximum size Z such that LWU_k is no less than ξ and stored them in WUCP. In the serial phase, WUCP is used to find the serial patterns.

3.2   The Serial Phase

In the serial phase, the second phase of HUIPMiner (Lines 14–27), serial candidates are generated by concatenating the weighted utilization coincident patterns found in the first phase.

Definition 13. Let $L = \langle c_1, c_2, \ldots, c_n \rangle$ and $L' = \langle c_1', c_2', \ldots, c_m' \rangle$ be two L-sequences. The *serial concatenation* of L and L' is defined as serial-concat$(L, L') = \langle c_1, c_2, \ldots, c_n, c_1', c_2', \ldots, c_m' \rangle$.

For example, the serial concatenation of two L-sequences $L = \langle \{A, B\}, \{A, C\} \rangle$ and $L' = \langle \{E\}, \{D, C, F\} \rangle$ is $L'' = \langle \{A, B\}, \{A, C\}, \{E\}, \{D, C, F\} \rangle$.

In the first round of this phase, all serial L-sequence candidates of length 2 are generated. For this purpose, each coincident pattern w in WUCP is used to generate serial L-sequence candidates that start with w as the first coincidence of the L-sequence. This is done by calling the *Scandidate* procedure and sending w and WUCP as input arguments (Definition 13). Then, the algorithm searches each C-sequence in the C-sequence database to find matches to serial L-sequence candidates. The search for matches in this phase is more challenging than the search in the coincidence phase. It requires that the order of the coincidences also be taken into account. Therefore, it adds more complexity as the length of the L-sequence increases. After matches are found, as in the coincidence phase, the algorithm calculates u_{max} and LWU_k of every serial candidate. If u_{max} for a candidate l is no less than the given threshold ξ, then l is classified as a high utility serial pattern (HUSP). If LWU_k for a serial candidate l is no less than threshold ξ, then l is added into the set of promising candidates P. In order to generate longer serial candidates, the algorithm extracts the unique coincidences located at the kth position of the candidate (last coincidence) and stores them in $NewL$. Next, Scandidate procedure generates serial candidates of length 3 for the next round by serially concatenating P and $NewL$. The algorithm repeats these steps until it reaches the maximum length of patterns K or no more candidates can be generated. At the end of this phase, the algorithm has found all high utility serial patterns with lengths up to K and stored them in HUSP. After the serial phase ends, the high utility coincident and serial patterns are sent to the output.

4   Experiments

The HUIPMiner algorithm was implemented in C++11 and tested on a desktop computer with a 3.2 GHz Intel Core 4 CPU and 32 GB memory. We used four real-world datasets from various application domains in our experiments to evaluate the performance of HUIPMiner. The datasets include three publicly available datasets, namely Blocks [3], Auslan2 [3], ASL-BU [4], and a private dataset, called DS, obtained from our industrial partner. DS includes event labels corresponding to various services offered to customers. An E-sequence in this dataset

---

Algorithm 1. HUIPMiner: High Utility Interval-based Pattern Miner

---

Input: A C-sequence database δ,
minimum utility threshold ξ,
maximum length $K \geq 1$,
maximum size $Z \geq 1$

Output: All high utility
interval-based patterns
$HUIP$

1 Initialize the set of high utility coincident patterns $HUCP = \varnothing$, the set of weighted utilization coincident patterns $WUCP = \varnothing$, $z = 1$, and $C^z =$ all event labels

2 **while** $z \leq Z$ and $C^z \neq \varnothing$ **do**

3    $P = \varnothing, NewL = \varnothing$

4   **for** each candidate c in C^z **do**

5   Find c in δ and Calculate $\text{LWU}_K(c)$

6   **if** $u_{\max}(c) \geq \xi$ **then**

7        $HUCP = HUCP \cup c$

8   **if** $\text{LWU}_K(c) \geq \xi$ **then**

9        $P = P \cup c$

10        $NewL = NewL \cup \{p \mid p \in c\}$

11    $WUCP = WUCP \cup P$

12    $z = z + 1$

13    $C^z = \text{Ccandidate}(P, NewL)$

14 Initialize the set of high utility serial patterns $HUSP = \varnothing$ and $k = 2$

15 **for** each weighted utilization pattern w in $WUCP$ **do**

16    $L^k = \text{Scandidate}(w, WUCP)$

17   **while** $k \leq K$ and $L^k \neq \varnothing$ **do**

18      $P = \varnothing, NewL = \varnothing$

19   **for** each candidate l in L^k **do**

20   Find l in δ and Calculate $\text{LWU}_K(l)$

21   **if** $u_{\max}(l) \geq \xi$ **then**

22          $HUSP = HUSP \cup l$

23   **if** $\text{LWU}_K(l) \geq \xi$ **then**

24          $P = P \cup l$

25          $NewL = NewL \cup \{k^{th} \text{ coincidence in } l\}$

26      $k = k + 1$

27      $L^k = \text{Scandidate}(P, NewL)$

28 $HUIP = HUCP \cup HUSP$

---

represents a customer receiving services. The minimum, maximum and average external utilities associated with the event labels in DS are 10, 28, and 18, respectively. There are no external utilities associated with the public datasets. Therefore, we assume every event label in these datasets have an external utility of 1. The statistics of the datasets are summarized in Table 5.

4.1 Performance Evaluation

We evaluate the performance of HUIPMiner on the four datasets in terms of their execution time and the number of extracted high utility patterns, while varying the minimum utility threshold ξ and the maximum length of patterns K. These two evaluations are shown on a log-10 scale in Fig. 1 and Fig. 2, respectively. The execution time of HUIPMiner in seconds is shown on the left and the number of patterns discovered by HUIPMiner is presented on the right of the two figures. The maximum size of patterns Z is set to 5 in all experiments.

Table 5. Statistical information about datasets

Dataset	# Event intervals	# E-sequences	E-sequence size			# Labels	Interval duration			
			min	max	avg		min	max	avg	stdv
Blocks	1207	210	3	12	6	8	1	57	17	12
Auslan2	2447	200	9	20	12	12	1	30	20	12
ASL-BU	18250	874	3	40	17	216	3	4468	594	590
DS	71416	10017	4	14	8	15	1	484	70	108

Figure 1 shows the evaluation of the HUIPMiner on the datasets while varying ξ and keeping K set to 4. The algorithm is able to discover a large number of HUIPs in a short time, especially for smaller datasets. For instance, the algorithm can extract more than 4500 HUIPs in about 60 s from Blocks under a low minimum utility. It is evident that as ξ increases, the execution time drops exponentially and fewer patterns are discovered. This is especially well supported for larger datasets like ASL-BU and DS. Apart from the way that event intervals are distributed, the large number of event labels in ASL-BU are the major factor that contributes to high computational costs for extracting patterns. Similarly, the large number of E-sequences in DS requires more execution time to extract patterns from this dataset. The results also show that HUIPMiner is effective at finding patterns for small thresholds.

Figure 2 shows the evaluation of the HUIPMiner on the four datasets when K is varied between 1 and 4. In these experiments, a small ξ corresponding to each dataset is used to benchmark the algorithm. As shown in Fig. 2, HUIPMiner discovers a high number of HUIPs from Blocks in a short time when ξ is set to 0.02. The algorithm performs similarly on Auslan2 when $\xi = 0.01$. When the algorithm is applied to ASL-BU and DS, patterns are discovered at lower speeds than from the two other datasets, when the minimum thresholds are set to 0.1 and 0.05, respectively. As expected, K plays an important role in determining both the execution time of the algorithm and the number of extracted patterns. As K increases, the execution time increases and more patterns are discovered.

In general, the performance of the algorithm depends on the dataset characteristics (mentioned in Table 5) as well as the parameters used in the experiments (Z, K, ξ). The experiments show that HUIPMiner can successfully extract high utility patterns from datasets with different characteristics under various parameters setups.

4.2   Effect of Pruning Strategies

The computational benefits of the proposed pruning strategy is also evaluated. We compare our pruning strategy, which is based on the LDCP property, against a pruning strategy based on the SDCP property and also against the execution of HUIPMiner when no pruning strategy is applied. Figure 3a shows the time

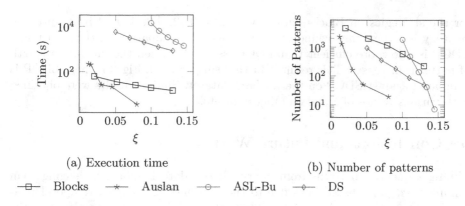

(a) Execution time

(b) Number of patterns

—◻— Blocks   —✳— Auslan   —◦— ASL-Bu   —◇— DS

Fig. 1. Execution time and number of patterns for different ξ values

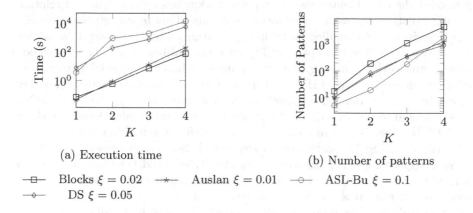

(a) Execution time

(b) Number of patterns

—◻— Blocks $\xi = 0.02$ —✳— Auslan $\xi = 0.01$ —◦— ASL-Bu $\xi = 0.1$
—◇— DS $\xi = 0.05$

Fig. 2. Execution time and number of patterns for different K values

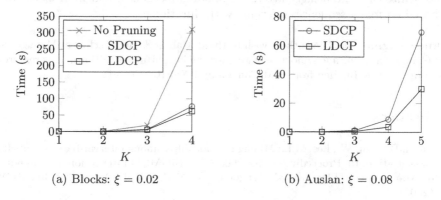

(a) Blocks: $\xi = 0.02$

(b) Auslan: $\xi = 0.08$

Fig. 3. Comparison of pruning strategies

for the strategies on Blocks dataset with $\xi = 0.02$. The LDCP based pruning strategy is a dominant winner on this dataset in comparison with no pruning. LDCP is also more efficient than SDCP, especially when the maximum length of patterns increases. This result is further supported in Fig. 3b where LDCP is compared against SDCP on the Auslan2 dataset. Similar results were obtained with various values of ξ and on other datasets.

5   Conclusions and Future Work

Mining sequential patterns from interval-based data is more challenging than mining from point-based data due to the existence of complex temporal relations among events. Seeking high utility patterns increases the complexity of the problem because the downward closure property does not hold. In this paper, we proposed the coincidence eventset representation to express temporal relations among events along with the duration of events. This representation simplifies the description of complicated temporal relations without losing information. We incorporated the concept of utility into interval-based data and provided a novel framework for mining high utility interval-based sequential patterns. An effective algorithm named HUIPMiner was proposed to mine patterns. Furthermore, in order to mine the dataset faster, a pruning strategy based on LDCP was proposed to decrease the search space. Experimental evaluations have shown that HUIPMiner is able to identify patterns with low minimum utility.

Utility mining in interval-based sequential data could provide benefits in diverse applications. For instance, more industries could take advantage of the utility concept to model their monetary or non-monetary considerations. In medicine, alternatives for courses of treatment over a long period may have different utilities. Our approach could be applied to find high utility alternatives from records of many patients with long-lasting diseases. Similarly, managers could utilize the high utility patterns in making decisions about increasing profits based on many sequences of events with durations.

Acknowledgments. The authors wish to thank Rahim Samei (Technical Manager at ISM Canada) and the anonymous reviewers for the insightful suggestions. This research was supported by funding from ISM Canada and NSERC Canada.

References

1. Patel, D., Hsu, W., Lee, M.L.: Mining relationships among interval-based events for classification. In: Proceedings of the 2008 ACM SIGMOD International Conference on Management of Data, SIGMOD 2008, New York, NY, USA, pp. 393–404. ACM (2008)
2. Sheetrit, E., Nissim, N., Klimov, D., Shahar, Y.: Temporal probabilistic profiles for sepsis prediction in the ICU. In: Proceedings of the 25th ACM SIGKDD International Conference on Knowledge Discovery & Data Mining, pp. 2961–2969. ACM (2019)

3. Mörchen, F., Fradkin, D.: Robust mining of time intervals with semi-interval partial order patterns. In: Proceedings of the 2010 SIAM International Conference on Data Mining, pp. 315–326. SIAM (2010)
4. Papapetrou, P., Kollios, G., Sclaroff, S., Gunopulos, D.: Mining frequent arrangements of temporal intervals. Knowl. Inf. Syst. **21**(2), 133 (2009)
5. Liu, Y., Nie, L., Liu, L., Rosenblum, D.S.: From action to activity: sensor-based activity recognition. Neurocomputing **181**, 108–115 (2016)
6. Allen, J.F.: Maintaining knowledge about temporal intervals. Commun. ACM **26**(11), 832–843 (1983)
7. Wu, S.Y., Chen, Y.L.: Mining nonambiguous temporal patterns for interval-based events. IEEE Trans. Knowl. Data Eng. **19**(6), 742–758 (2007)
8. Han, J., et al.: PrefixSpan: mining sequential patterns efficiently by prefix-projected pattern growth. In: Proceedings of the 17th International Conference on Data Engineering, pp. 215–224 (2001)
9. Chen, Y.C., Jiang, J.C., Peng, W.C., Lee, S.Y.: An efficient algorithm for mining time interval-based patterns in large database. In: Proceedings of the 19th ACM International Conference on Information and Knowledge Management, pp. 49–58. ACM (2010)
10. Srikant, R., Agrawal, R.: Mining sequential patterns: generalizations and performance improvements. In: Apers, P., Bouzeghoub, M., Gardarin, G. (eds.) EDBT 1996. LNCS, vol. 1057, pp. 1–17. Springer, Heidelberg (1996). https://doi.org/10.1007/BFb0014140
11. Yao, H., Hamilton, H.J.: Mining itemset utilities from transaction databases. Data Knowl. Eng. **59**(3), 603–626 (2006)
12. Ahmed, C.F., Tanbeer, S.K., Jeong, B.S.: A novel approach for mining high-utility sequential patterns in sequence databases. ETRI J. **32**(5), 676–686 (2010)
13. Yin, J., Zheng, Z., Cao, L.: USpan: an efficient algorithm for mining high utility sequential patterns. In: Proceedings of the 18th ACM SIGKDD International Conference on Knowledge Discovery and Data Mining, pp. 660–668. ACM (2012)
14. Wu, C.W., Lin, Y.F., Yu, P.S., Tseng, V.S.: Mining high utility episodes in complex event sequences. In: Proceedings of the 19th ACM SIGKDD International Conference on Knowledge Discovery and Data Mining, pp. 536–544. ACM (2013)
15. Fournier-Viger, P., Yang, P., Lin, J.C.-W., Yun, U.: HUE-Span: fast high utility episode mining. In: Li, J., Wang, S., Qin, S., Li, X., Wang, S. (eds.) ADMA 2019. LNCS (LNAI), vol. 11888, pp. 169–184. Springer, Cham (2019). https://doi.org/10.1007/978-3-030-35231-8_12
16. Huang, J.W., Jaysawal, B.P., Chen, K.Y., Wu, Y.B.: Mining frequent and top-k high utility time interval-based events with duration patterns. Knowl. Inf. Syst. **61**, 1331–1359 (2019)

Extreme-SAX: Extreme Points Based Symbolic Representation for Time Series Classification

Muhammad Marwan Muhammad Fuad[(⊠)]

Coventry University, Coventry CV1 5FB, UK
ad0263@coventry.ac.uk

Abstract. Time series classification is an important problem in data mining with several applications in different domains. Because time series data are usually high dimensional, dimensionality reduction techniques have been proposed as an efficient approach to lower their dimensionality. One of the most popular dimensionality reduction techniques of time series data is the Symbolic Aggregate Approximation (SAX), which is inspired by algorithms from text mining and bioinformatics. SAX is simple and efficient because it uses precomputed distances. The disadvantage of SAX is its inability to accurately represent important points in the time series. In this paper we present Extreme-SAX (E-SAX), which uses only the extreme points of each segment to represent the time series. E-SAX has exactly the same simplicity and efficiency of the original SAX, yet it gives better results in time series classification than the original SAX, as we show in extensive experiments on a variety of time series datasets.

Keywords: Extreme-SAX · Symbolic Aggregate Approximation (SAX) · Time series classification

1 Introduction

Time Series Classification (TSC) is encountered in several applications ranging from medicine (electrocardiogram, electroencephalogram), finance (stock market, currency exchange rates), to industry (sensor signals) and weather forecast. For this reason, TSC has gained increasing attention over the last decade [2, 6–8, 18].

Time series data are usually high dimensional, and may contain noise or outliers. Therefore, dimensionality reduction techniques have been proposed as an efficient approach to perform TSC.

Several time series dimensionality reduction techniques have been proposed, of these we mention Piecewise Aggregate Approximation (PAA) [9, 19], Adaptive Piecewise Constant Approximation (APCA) [10], and the Clipping Technique [17].

One of the powerful time series dimensionality reduction techniques is the Symbolic Aggregate Approximation (SAX) [11, 12], which first converts the time series into PAA and then transforms the data into symbols using discretization. Despite its efficiency and simplicity, SAX has a drawback, which is its inability to keep track of important points. Such points are of particular interest in many applications. This is due to the

© Springer Nature Switzerland AG 2020
M. Song et al. (Eds.): DaWaK 2020, LNCS 12393, pp. 122–130, 2020.
https://doi.org/10.1007/978-3-030-59065-9_10

fact that SAX actually applies two dimensionality reductions steps – the PAA and the discretization, without any mechanism to highlight these important points.

In this paper we present a very simple modification of SAX, yet this modification outperforms SAX in TSC task because it focusses on extreme points.

The rest of the paper is organized as follows; In Sect. 2 we present background on the topic. In Sect. 3 we present our new method, which we test in Sect. 4. We draw conclusions and discuss future work in Sect. 5.

2 Background

A univariate time series $T = (t_1, t_2, \ldots, t_n)$ is an ordered collection of n observations measured at, usually equally-spaced, timestamps t_n. Time series data are ubiquitous and appear in a wide variety of applications.

Classification is one of the main data mining tasks in which items are assigned predefined classes. There are a number of classification models, the most popular of which is *k-nearest-neighbor* (*k*NN). In this model the object is classified based on the *k* closest objects in its neighborhood. Performance of classification algorithms can be evaluated using different methods. One of the widely used ones is *leave-one-out cross-validation* (LOOCV) - also known by *N-fold cross-validation*, or *jack-knifing*, where the dataset is divided into as many parts as there are instances, each instance effectively forming a test set of one. N classifiers are generated, each from N − 1 instances, and each is used to classify a single test instance. The classification error is then the total number of misclassified instances divided by the total number of instances [3].

What makes TSC different from traditional classification tasks is the natural temporal ordering of the attributes [1]. This is why several classification methods have been developed to address TSC in particular.

Applying the Euclidean distance on raw data in TSC has been widely used as it is simple and efficient. But it is weak in terms of accuracy [16]. The use of DTW gives more accurate TSC results, but this comes at the expense of efficiency.

A large amount of research in time series mining has focused on time series representation methods, which lower time series dimensionality, making different time series tasks, such as classification, clustering, query-by-content, anomaly detection, and motif discovery, more efficient.

One of the first, and most simple, time series representation methods is PAA [9, 19], which divides a time series T of n-dimensions into m equal-sized segments and maps each segment to a point of a lower m-dimensional space, where each point in this space is the mean of values of the data points falling within this segment.

PAA gave rise to another very efficient time series representation method; the Symbolic Aggregate Approximation – SAX [11, 12]. SAX performs the discretization by dividing a time series T into w equal-sized segments (words). For each segment, the mean value for the points within that segment is computed. Aggregating these w coefficients forms the PAA representation of T. Each coefficient is then mapped to a symbol according to a set of breakpoints that divide the distribution space into *alphabetSize* equiprobable regions, where *alphabetSize* is the alphabet size specified by the user. Figure 1 shows an example of SAX for *alphabetSize* = 4

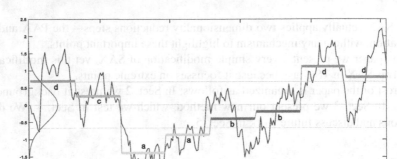

Fig. 1. Example of SAX for *alphabetSize* = 4, *w* = 8. In the first step the time series, whose length is 256, is discretized using PAA, and then each segment is mapped to the corresponding symbol. This results in the final SAX representation for this time series, which is *dcaabbdd*

The locations of the breakpoints are determined using a statistical lookup table for each value of *alphabetSize*. These lookup tables are based on the assumption that normalized time series subsequences have a highly Gaussian distribution [12].

It is worth mentioning that some researchers applied optimization, using genetic algorithms and differential evolution, to obtain the locations of the breakpoints [14, 15]. This gave better results than the original lookup tables based on the Gaussian assumption.

Table 1 shows the lookup table for *alphabetSize* = 3, ..., 10. Lookup tables for higher values of *alphabetSize* can be easily obtained.

Table 1. The lookup tables for *alphabetSize* = 3, ..., 10

	3	4	5	6	7	8	9	10
β_1	−0.43	−0.67	−0.84	−0.97	−1.07	−1.15	−1.22	−1.28
β_2	0.43	0	−0.25	−0.43	−0.57	−0.67	−0.76	−0.84
β_3		0.67	0.25	0	−0.18	−0.32	−0.43	−0.52
β_4			0.84	0.43	0.18	0	−0.14	−0.25
β_5				0.97	0.57	0.32	0.14	0
β_6					1.07	0.67	0.43	0.25
β_7						1.15	0.76	0.52
β_8							1.22	0.84
β_9								1.28

3   Extreme-SAX (E-SAX)

Despite its popularity and efficiency, SAX has a primary drawback, which is its inability to represent important points accurately. This is due to the loss of information during transformation, first during the PAA stage and second during the discretization stage.

In Fig. 2 we see how the two extreme points, represented by red circles in the figure, of the segment were represented by symbol c using SAX with *alphabetSize* $= 4$, which is clearly not an accurate approximation for these extreme points. This inaccurate representation aggravates in the cases where the accuracy of the representation is mainly based on such extreme points (as in financial time series data, for instance).

In [13] the authors extend SAX to improve its performance in handling financial data. This is done by adding two special new points, that is, max and min points of each segment, therefore each segment is represented by three values; the mean, the min, and max of each segment. Their method uses a modification of the similarity measure that the original SAX uses. The authors say they conducted preliminary experiments on financial time series (the experiments are very briefly discussed in their paper), and they say the results they obtained in a similarity search task is better than those of the original SAX.

The method presented in [13] has a few drawbacks; whereas the original SAX uses one symbol to represent each segment, the method presented in [13] uses three symbols to represent each segment. Using more symbols actually means more information, so it is not surprising that they get better results than the original SAX. Also the similarity measure they apply is slightly more costly than that of the original SAX. In addition, their experiments are quite preliminary, and are applied to financial time series only, so the performance of their method on a large scale of time series datasets of types other than financial is unknown.

In this paper, we present a very simple modification of the original SAX that does not add any additional complexity to it. It still uses one symbol only for each segment, and the similarity measure has the same computational cost as that of the original SAX (which we call *classic-SAX* hereafter). We call our method *Extreme-SAX* (E-SAX).

Let T be a time series in a n-dimensional space to be transformed by E-SAX into a m-dimensional space, where the size of the word is w, i.e. T is segmented into w equal-sized segments. After this first step T will be represented as:

$$T \rightarrow w_1 w_2 w_3 \ldots w_m \tag{1}$$

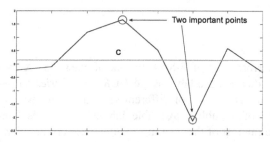

Fig. 2. SAX representation for the segment shown in blue, using *alphabetSize* $= 4$. As we can see, the two extreme points, shown in red circles, are approximated by c, which is not an accurate representation. (Color figure online)

Let p^i_{min}, p^i_{max} be the minimum (maximum) of the data points falling within segment w_i. We define:

$$p^i_{mean} = \frac{p^i_{min} + p^i_{max}}{2} \tag{2}$$

Using p^i_{mean} to represent w_i, Eq. (1) can be written as:

$$T \rightarrow p^1_{mean} p^2_{mean} p^3_{mean} \cdots p^m_{mean} \tag{3}$$

In the last step, each coefficient p^i_{mean} is mapped to its corresponding symbol using discretization, the same way as in classic-SAX, using *alphabetSize* symbols.

The distance measure we use in E-SAX is:

$$E - SAX\_DIST\left(\hat{S}, \hat{T}\right) = \sqrt{\frac{n}{m}} \sqrt{\sum_{i=1}^{m} \left(dist\left(\hat{s}_i, \hat{t}_i\right)\right)^2} \tag{4}$$

Where $\hat{S}$ and $\hat{T}$ are the E-SAX representations of the two time series S and T, respectively, and where the function *dist*() is implemented by using the appropriate lookup table. This lookup table is the same used in classic-SAX for the corresponding *alphabetSize*.

Unlike classic-SAX, the distance measure defined in Eq. (4) is not a lower bound of the original distance defined on the n-dimensional space. However, this is not important in TSC tasks.

As we can see, E-SAX is very simple. Its symbolic representation has the same length as that of classic-SAX, so it requires the same storage, it does not include any additional preprocessing or post-processing steps, and it uses the same lookup tables as those of classic-SAX.

We can also add that E-SAX clearly emphasizes important points more than classic-SAX. In fact, as we can see, E-SAX representation is completely based on the extreme points of each segment.

4   Experiments

We compared the performance of E-SAX to that of classic-SAX in a 1NN TSC task using 45 time series datasets available at the *UCR Time Series Classification Archive* [4]. This archive contains datasets of different sizes and dimensions and it makes up between 90 and 100% of all publicly available, labeled time series datasets in the world, and it represents the interest of the data mining/database community, and not just one group [5].

Each dataset in this archive is divided into two datasets; train and test. The length of the time series on which we conducted our experiments varies between 24 (ItalyPowerDemand) and 1882 (InlineSkate). The size of the train datasets varies between 16 instances (DiatomSizeReduction) and 560 instances (FaceAll). The size of the test datasets varies between 20 instances (BirdChicken), (BeetleFly) and 3840 instances (ChlorineConcentration). The number of classes varies between 2 (Gun-Point),

Table 2. Summary of the datasets on which we conducted our experiments

Dataset	Type	Train	Test	Classes	Length
synthetic_control	Simulated	300	300	6	60
Gun_Point	Motion	50	150	2	150
CBF	Simulated	30	900	3	128
FaceAll	Image	560	1690	14	131
OSULeaf	Image	200	242	6	427
SwedishLeaf	Image	500	625	15	128
Trace	Sensor	100	100	4	275
FaceFour	Image	24	88	4	350
Lighting2	Sensor	60	61	2	637
Lighting7	Sensor	70	73	7	319
ECG200	ECG	100	100	2	96
Adiac	Image	390	391	37	176
Yoga	Image	300	3000	2	426
Fish	Image	175	175	7	463
Plane	Sensor	105	105	7	144
Car	Sensor	60	60	4	577
Beef	Spectro	30	30	5	470
Coffee	Spectro	28	28	2	286
OliveOil	Spectro	30	30	4	570
CinCECGTorso	Sensor	40	1380	4	1639
ChlorineConcentration	Sensor	467	3840	3	166
DiatomSizeReduction	Image	16	306	4	345
ECGFiveDays	ECG	23	861	2	136
FacesUCR	Image	200	2050	14	131
Haptics	Motion	155	308	5	1092
InlineSkate	Motion	100	550	7	1882
ItalyPowerDemand	Sensor	67	1029	2	24
MedicalImages	Image	381	760	10	99
MoteStrain	Sensor	20	1252	2	84
SonyAIBORobotSurface1	Sensor	20	601	2	70
SonyAIBORobotSurface2	Sensor	27	953	2	65
Symbols	Image	25	995	6	398
TwoLeadECG	ECG	23	1139	2	82
InsectWingbeatSound	Sensor	220	1980	11	256
ArrowHead	Image	36	175	3	251
BeetleFly	Image	20	20	2	512
BirdChicken	Image	20	20	2	512
Herring	Image	64	64	2	512
ProximalPhalanxTW	Image	400	205	6	80
ToeSegmentation1	Motion	40	228	2	277
ToeSegmentation2	Motion	36	130	2	343
DistalPhalanxOutlineAgeGroup	Image	400	139	3	80
DistalPhalanxOutlineCorrect	Image	600	276	2	80
DistalPhalanxTW	Image	400	139	6	80
WordsSynonyms	Image	267	638	25	270

Table 3. The classification errors of classic-SAX and E-SAX. The best result for each dataset is shown in boldface printing, yellow-shaded cells

Dataset	Method	
	classic-SAX	E-SAX
synthetic_control	0.023	**0.003**
Gun_Point	0.147	**0.140**
CBF	**0.076**	0.081
FaceAll	0.305	**0.275**
OSULeaf	**0.475**	0.484
SwedishLeaf	0.253	**0.248**
Trace	0.370	**0.320**
FaceFour	0.227	**0.216**
Lighting2	0.197	**0.164**
Lighting7	0.425	**0.398**
ECG200	0.120	0.120
Adiac	0.867	**0.854**
Yoga	0.180	**0.179**
Fish	0.263	**0.246**
Plane	0.029	0.029
Car	0.267	0.267
Beef	0.433	**0.367**
Coffee	0.286	0.286
OliveOil	0.833	0.833
CinCECGTorso	0.073	0.073
ChlorineConcentration	0.582	**0.508**
DiatomSizeReduction	**0.082**	0.088
ECGFiveDays	**0.150**	0.235
FacesUCR	0.242	**0.206**
Haptics	**0.643**	0.662
InlineSkate	0.680	**0.670**
ItalyPowerDemand	0.192	**0.112**
MedicalImages	0.363	**0.358**
MoteStrain	0.212	**0.193**
SonyAIBORobotSurface1	**0.298**	0.306
SonyAIBORobotSurface2	**0.144**	0.146
Symbols	0.103	0.103
TwoLeadECG	0.310	**0.278**
InsectWingbeatSound	**0.447**	0.453
ArrowHead	0.246	**0.223**
BeetleFly	0.250	0.250
BirdChicken	0.350	0.350
Herring	0.406	0.406
ProximalPhalanxTW	0.370	**0.362**
ToeSegmentation1	0.364	**0.355**
ToeSegmentation2	**0.146**	0.192
DistalPhalanxOutlineAgeGroup	0.267	**0.250**
DistalPhalanxOutlineCorrect	**0.340**	0.398
DistalPhalanxTW	0.292	**0.272**
WordsSynonyms	0.371	0.371
	10	**24**

(ECG200), (Coffee), (ECGFiveDays), (ItalyPowerDemand), (MoteStrain), (TwoLead-ECG), (BeetleFly), (BirdChicken), and 37 (Adiac). They have a variety of types (simulated, motion, image, sensor, ECG, and spectro). Table 2 shows a summary of the datasets on which we conducted our experiments.

The experimental protocol is as follows; in the train stage each of classic-SAX and E-SAX is applied to each train dataset of the datasets presented in Table 2. The purpose of this stage is to obtain the optimal value of *alphabetSize*, i.e. the value that yields the minimum classification error in TSC for each of the datasets. In the test stage this value of *alphabetSize* is used in the corresponding test dataset. The final results of TSC on the test datasets for each of classic-SAX and E-SAX are shown in Table 3. The best result (the minimum classification error) for each dataset is shown in boldface printing, yellow-shaded cells.

There are several measures used to evaluate the performance of time series classification methods. In this paper we choose a simple and widely used one, which is to count how many datasets on which the method gave the best performance.

The results show that E-SAX clearly outperforms classic-SAX in TSC as it yielded a lower classification error in 24 datasets, whereas classic-SAX gave better results in 10 datasets only. The two methods gave the same classification error in 11 datasets.

5 Conclusion

Classic-SAX is popular time series representation method because of its simplicity and efficiency. It has been widely applied to perform time series tasks such as classification. However, one of its main drawbacks is that it is unable to represent important points accurately.

In this work we presented Extreme-SAX (E-SAX), which uses the extreme points of each segment to discretize the time series. E-SAX has exactly the same advantages of classic-SAX in terms of efficiency and simplicity, but it is better than classic-SAX at representing important points, as it is based completely on the extreme points of each segment to transform the time series into sequences.

We validated E-SAX through TSC experiments on a variety of datasets. Our experiments showed that E-SAX clearly outperforms classic-SAX as it yielded a lower classification error in 24 out of 45 datasets, whereas classic-SAX gave a lower classification error in only 10 datasets. The two methods gave the same classification error in 11 datasets.

For future work, it is worth studying this phenomenon further to know why a representation using less information, based only on the extreme points of segments, gives better results in TSC than a representation that uses more information resulting from all data points of the time series.

References

1. Bagnall, A., Lines, J., Bostrom, A., Large, J., Keogh, E.: The great time series classification bake off: a review and experimental evaluation of recent algorithmic advances. Data Min. Knowl. Disc. **31**, 606–660 (2017)

2. Baydogan, M., Runger, G., Tuv, E.: A bag-of-features framework to classify time series. IEEE Trans. Pattern Anal. Mach. Intell. **25**(11), 2796–2802 (2013)
3. Bramer, M.: Principles of Data Mining. Springer, London (2007). https://doi.org/10.1007/978-1-84628-766-4
4. Chen, Y., et al.: The UCR time series classification archive (2015). www.cs.ucr.edu/~eamonn/time_series_data
5. Ding, H., Trajcevski, G., Scheuermann, P., Wang, X., Keogh, E.: Querying and mining of time series. In: Proceedings of the 34th VLDB (2008)
6. Fawaz, H.I., Forestier, G., Weber, J., Idoumghar, L., Muller, P.A.: Adversarial attacks on deep neural networks for time series classification. In: Proceedings of the 2019 International Joint Conference on Neural Networks (IJCNN), Budapest, Hungary, 14–19 July (2019)
7. Hatami, N., Gavet, Y., Debayle, J.: Bag of recurrence patterns representation for time-series classification. Pattern Anal. Appl. **22**, 877–887 (2019)
8. Karim, F., Majumdar, S., Darabi, H., Chen, S.: LSTM fully convolutional networks for time series classification. IEEE Access 1–7 (2017)
9. Keogh, E., Chakrabarti, K., Pazzani, M. and Mehrotra: Dimensionality reduction for fast similarity search in large time series databases. J. Know. Inform. Sys. (2000)
10. Keogh, E., Chakrabarti, K., Pazzani, M., Mehrotra, S.: Locally adaptive dimensionality reduction for similarity search in large time series databases. In: SIGMOD, pp. 151–162 (2001)
11. Lin, J., Keogh, E., Lonardi, S., Chiu, B.Y.: A symbolic representation of time series, with implications for streaming algorithms. DMKD **2003**, 2–11 (2003)
12. Lin, J., Keogh, E., Wei, L., Lonardi, S.: Experiencing SAX: a novel symbolic representation of time series. Data Min. Knowl. Discov. **15**(2) (2007)
13. Lkhagava, B., Suzuki, Y., Kawagoe, K.: Extended SAX: extension of symbolic aggregate approximation for financial time series data representation. In: Proceedings of the Data Engineering Workshop 2006, 2006, 4A0-8 (2006)
14. Muhammad Fuad, M.M.: Differential evolution versus genetic algorithms: towards symbolic aggregate approximation of non-normalized time series. Sixteenth International Database Engineering & Applications Symposium– IDEAS'12, Prague, Czech Republic,8–10 August, 2012. Published by BytePress/ACM (2012)
15. Muhammad Fuad, M.M.: Genetic algorithms-based symbolic aggregate approximation. In: Cuzzocrea, A., Dayal, U. (eds.) DaWaK 2012. LNCS, vol. 7448, pp. 105–116. Springer, Heidelberg (2012). https://doi.org/10.1007/978-3-642-32584-7_9
16. Ratanamahatana, C., Keogh, E.: Making time-series classification more accurate using learned constraints. In: Proceedings of the SIAM International Conference on Data Mining, pp. 11–22 (2004)
17. Ratanamahatana, C., Keogh, E., Bagnall, A.J., Lonardi, S.: A novel bit level time series representation with implication of similarity search and clustering. In: Ho, T.B., Cheung, D., Liu, H. (eds.) PAKDD 2005. LNCS (LNAI), vol. 3518, pp. 771–777. Springer, Heidelberg (2005). https://doi.org/10.1007/11430919_90
18. Wang, Z., Yan, W., Oates, T.: Time series classification from scratch with deep neural networks: a strong baseline. In: Proceedings of the International Joint Conference on Neural Networking (IJCNN), May 2017, pp. 1578–1585 (2017)
19. Yi, B.K., Faloutsos, C.: Fast time sequence indexing for arbitrary Lp norms. In: Proceedings of the 26th International Conference on Very Large Databases, Cairo, Egypt (2000)

Framework to Optimize Data Processing Pipelines Using Performance Metrics

Syed Muhammad Fawad Ali$^{(\boxtimes)}$ and Robert Wrembel

Poznan University of Technology, Poznań, Poland
fawadali.ali@gmail.com, robert.wrembel@cs.put.poznan.pl

Abstract. Optimizing Data Processing Pipelines (DPPs) is challenging in the context of both, data warehouse architectures and data science architectures. Few approaches to this problem have been proposed so far. The most challenging issue is to build a cost model of the whole DPP, especially if user defined functions (UDFs) are used. In this paper we addressed the problem of the optimization of UDFs in data-intensive workflows and presented our approach to construct a cost model to determine the degree of parallelism for parallelizable UDFs.

Keywords: ETL workflow · ML workflow · Workflow optimization · Cost model · Parallelization

1 Introduction

A *data processing pipeline* (DPP) is referred to a workflow of tasks aiming at ingesting data from multiple (typically heterogeneous and distributed data sources), and then homogenizing, cleaning, integrating, and deduplicating these data. Two types of a DPP become a de facto standards in the industry. The first one, called Extract-Transform-Load (ETL) is applied in data warehouse architectures. The second one, called End-to-End Machine Learning Pipeline (MLP) is applied to pre-processing of data for a given ML algorithm. Both of these types of DPPs orchestrate multiple tasks. Building a DPPs is a time-expensive task and it accounts to almost 80% of time on building an analytical system [1]. Having in mind that DPPs process large amounts of data of heterogeneous structures, reducing execution time of these DPPs is of great importance, thus *DPP optimization* should come into play.

Ideally, a DPP optimization should be based on the principles of the cost-based query optimization. If so, a DPP designed by a user could be automatically re-designed based on an overall cost of the whole DPP, to produce a more efficient DPP. To this end, a cost model of each DPP task must be known, similarly as a cost model of each SQL operator is available. If DPP tasks were expressed by means of SQL their cost model would be available, however, in practice most ETL tools provide the functionality to write custom programs in multiple procedural programming languages, as the so-called User Defined Functions (UDFs).

© Springer Nature Switzerland AG 2020
M. Song et al. (Eds.): DaWaK 2020, LNCS 12393, pp. 131–140, 2020.
https://doi.org/10.1007/978-3-030-59065-9_11

UDFs are especially useful to process big data and to implement prediction models. Often, such programs are only available as black-box software snippets, which cannot be 'opened'. As a consequence, their cost models are unavailable, and conversely, a cost model of the whole DPP is unavailable. For this reason, a performance of a DPP depends on manually orchestrating its tasks by a designer.

Developing a cost model for a DPP is challenging and few approaches to solve this problem have been proposed so far [5,8]. The few existing and promising DPP optimization techniques are based on task reordering [11,12,16,20] or parallelization [3] (for an up-to-date overview the reader is referred to [22] and to Sect. 4).

This paper is the continuation of our previous works, where we proposed (1) *ETL Framework - cp-UDF* to address the challenges posed by UDFs in DPPs [2,4] and (2) a cost model in *cp-UDF* to optimize UDFs in an ETL Workflow, based on user-defined performance metrics [5] (cf. Section 2 for a brief overview).

In this paper we **extend the cost model of *cp-UDF* with the combination of Decision Optimization techniques and Machine Learning models**. The contribution of this paper is then twofold. First, we propose a method towards parallelization of UDF execution by generating an optimized distributed machine configuration using machine learning (c.f., Sect. 3.1). Second, we extend our cost model to enable data scientists to choose the best possible machine learning model based on user-defined performance metrics e.g., accuracy, precision, or recall of a model using decision optimization (c.f., Sect. 3.2).

2   ETL Framework: Overview

As the work presented in this paper extends our previous work on *ETL Framework - cp-UDF* [2,5], in this section we outline the main concepts of the *Framework*.

2.1   Extendable ETL Framework - *cp-UDF*

cp-UDF consists of four modules, namely: (1) an *UDFs Component*, (2) a *Cost Model*, (3) a *Recommender*, and (4) a *Monitoring Agent*, c.f., Fig. 1.

The *UDF Component* allows ETL developers to write parallelizable UDFs by separating parallelization concerns from the code. It contains a library of *Parallel Algorithmic Skeletons* (PASs), to be executed in a distributed environment like Map-Reduce or Spark. The *UDF Component* provides to the ETL developer: (1) the already parallelizable code of some commonly used big data operators (a.k.a *Case-based PASs*) including: sentiment analysis, de-duplication of rows, outlier detection and (2) a list of *Generic PASs* (e.g., worker-farm model, divide and conquer, branch and bound, systolic, MapReduce).

The *Cost Model* uses the *Recommender Module* and *Monitoring Agent* to generate optimized ETL workflows. It includes an extendible set of machine learning algorithms (e.g., classification, recommendation, prediction algorithms) and decision optimization techniques to generate an optimal configuration plan

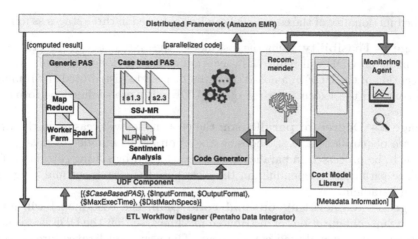

Fig. 1. The architecture of the *Extendible ETL Framework - cp-UDF*

to execute UDFs in an ETL workflow. To this end, it uses performance statistics (stored in a repository), collected during past ETL executions by a dedicated module, called *Monitoring Agent*.

2.2   Cost Model

The cost model leverages *Decision Optimization* and *Machine Learning techniques* in order to generate a (sub-)optimal configuration to optimize the execution of parallelizable UDFs in an ETL workflow, cf., Fig. 2. *Decision Optimization* is used to find an optimized configuration for *Case-based PAS*, fulfilling user-defined performance metrics: execution time and monetary costs. *Machine Learning techniques* or models are trained on historical data and fine-tuned. They are applied to finding the (sub-)optimized machine configuration to execute UDFs based on *Generic PAS*. The dotted line indicates that if the *Decision Optimization* fails to find the (sub-)optimal solution, then *Machine Learning techniques* are used to find the solution.

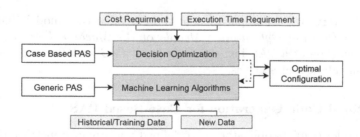

Fig. 2. High level design of the cost model

The functionality of the cost model can be explained in three stages as follows:

- **Stage 1 - Feasibility**: using the cost model, the system assesses whether parallelizing an UDF will reduce its execution cost. It is done by simulating the execution of the UDF in a non-distributed or pseudo-distributed environment to compare the execution time of the UDF with user-defined performance metrics.
- **Stage 2 - Degree of parallelism**: the cost model will reason on the right degree of parallelism, e.g., choosing the appropriate number of data partitions to be processed in parallel. It can be achieved by tuning certain performance parameters depending on the distributed environment and programming paradigm.
- **Stage 3 - Generating optimal code plan**: the cost model will guide setting up configurations of distributed machines, so that the UDF is executed optimally in a distributed environment. The cost model takes into account execution performance and monetary cost constraints, given by the developer as an input to the *UDF Component*.

In [5], we have presented techniques based on decision optimization to parallelize the *Case-based PAS*. We tested our technique in a case where a user selects a PAS for the de-duplication of data. The de-duplication algorithm run in three stages ($n = 3$) and for each stage there existed two possible semantically equivalent UDF implementations ($m = 2$) in the library of PASs. Finding the best possible solution for each stage is of complexity $O(n^m)$ and it corresponds to an NP-hard problem. We modeled the problem using Multiple Choice Knapsack Problem (MCKP), as a special case of a *Decision Optimization* problem.

3 Extension to the Cost Model

In this section we present the extension of our cost model to enable data scientists to choose the best possible machine learning model based on user-defined performance metrics e.g., accuracy of a model using decision optimization module of the cost model, therefore, contributing towards a framework to optimize ETL and machine learning pipelines that based on user-defined performance metrics.

Figure 3 overviews the application of the extended cost model that either executes the *Decision Optimization Module* or the *Machine Learning Module* based on the type of a PAS i.e., the *Case-based PAS* and *Generic PAS*. It is discussed in subsequent sections.

3.1 Optimal Code Generation for Case-Based PAS

The cost model requires obligatory user-defined performance metrics: (1) maximum execution time for an ETL workflow (T) and (2) maximum monetary budget for an ETL workflow to be executed in the distributed environment (B), as an input from the ETL developer. Optional parameters include: the size of a

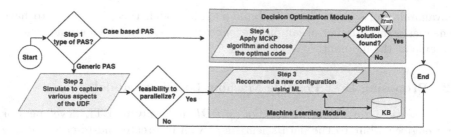

Fig. 3. The processing workflow of the extended cost model

dataset (R) in terms of the number of rows and a configuration of distributed machines (M).

When the ETL developer selects the *Generic PAS*, then an UDF provided by the ETL developer is first executed in a simulated environment to collect run-time execution statistics. At this point, the cost model is only interested in the execution time and estimated monetary cost. If both are within the user-defined performance metrics constraints, the processing is stopped. Otherwise, it continues to *Step 3*. This step generates the best possible machine configuration for an UDF based on *Machine Learning* techniques using input from *Step 2* and an integrated *Knowledge Base* (KB). The KB is built on past executions of the UDFs in a distributed environment within the *ETL Framework -cp-UDF* and is updated after every execution. This KB also serves for the training purposes of the machine learning model. The structure of KB is as follows:

```
ExecutionHistory(executionId, executionTime, rowsProcessed, bytesProcessed, sizeOfData,
rowsRead, rowsWrite, cpuUsage, machineId)
```

```
Machine(machineId, memory, numOfCPUs, operatingSystem, provider, price, costType,
otherCosts)
```

Attributes in table *ExecutionHistory* are the candidates for the feature set for machine learning models, except *machineId*, which serves as a class label.

Predicting *machineId*, i.e., a class, is essentially a classification problem. The configuration for the predicted value of *machineId* then can be obtained from the *Machine* table. A sample response from the machine learning model is shown below:

```
"machineId":"m5.xlarge",
"memory":16,
"numOfCPUs":6,
"operatingSystem":"Linux",
"provider":"AWS",
"price":0.192,
"costType":hourly,
"otherCosts":10
```

As of now, the implementation of the machine learning model to predict the best possible configuration is one of the future works mainly because of the unavailability of sample data. To build such a model, there is a need to have some reasonable number of samples per *machineId* (class), which are not readily available at the moment.

3.2   Proposing Best Possible Machine Learning Model

In this section, we extend the use of *cp-UDF* not only to ETL developers or data engineers but to the data scientists as well to create end-to-end Machine Learning Pipeline (MLP). The MLP may comprise multiple steps, such as data pre-processing, feature selection, and training & testing of a given ML algorithm. The user may select a MLP from the *cp-UDF* as a *Generic PAS*, which may consist of a number of stages (data preprocessing, feature selection, ML model), as shown in Fig. 4.

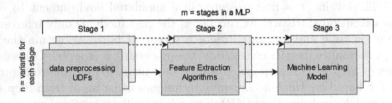

Fig. 4. An end-to-end machine learning pipeline

Besides providing the obligatory user-defined performance metrics i.e., (1) maximum execution time for an MLP (T) and (2) maximum monetary execution cost for the MLP(B), the user will need to provide the size of a dataset (S) and the performance metric for the ML model i.e., accuracy, precision, or recall (P). These parameters are used by the *Decision Optimization Module* to provide the best possible ML algorithm. The problem of finding this algorithm is modeled as the Multiple Choice Knapsack Problem that can be formulated as follows.

Let *maximize(Z)* be an optimal solution containing the best possible MLP, based on P (i.e., accuracy, precision, or recall), such that: execution time $E \leq T$ and execution cost $C \leq B$. Note that we want to provide the maximum value of accuracy, precision, or recall P_{ij} of an UDF or a ML model variant N_j from each stage m, such that the total cost $C_{ij} \leq B$ and execution time of the entire MLP $E_{ij} \leq T$.

Our problem is mapped to the MCKP as follows: (1) n classes in MCKP definition **to** m stages, (2) a weight constraint c **to**: B - budget constraint and E - execution time constraint, (3) a cost of item for a class w_{ij} **to** C_{ij} - a cost of variant j at stage i and E_{ij} - execution time of variant j at stage i, (4) a profit of each item p_i **to** P_i - a maximum performance metric. Then, we can find out the optimal solution as follows:

$$\text{Maximize(Z):} \quad \sum_{i=1}^{m} \sum_{j \in N_i} P_{i,j} \cdot x_{i,j}$$

$$\text{subject to:} \quad \sum_{i=1}^{m} \sum_{j \in N_i} C_{ij} \cdot x_{ij} \leq B$$

$$\sum_{i=1}^{m} \sum_{j \in N_i} E_{ij} \cdot x_{ij} \leq T$$

$$\sum_{j \in N_i} x_{ij} = 1; i = 1, \ldots, m; x_{ij} \in \{0,1\}; j \in N_i; i = 1, \ldots, m$$

3.3 Preliminary Experimental Results

In order to evaluate the correctness of our MCKP-based cost model, we mapped our problem on to the *Linear Integer Programming Model*. The cost model is implemented in Python using Google OR-Tools[1]. The implementation of the cost model is accessible via our online git repository[2].

As a preliminary evaluation of our approach to generate the best possible ML model, we used the experimental testbed and results on the sentiment analysis described in [13] that include: (1) three different sentiment analysis ML models, namely: *Bernoulli Naïve Bayes* (BNB), *Multinomial Naïve Bayes* (MNB), and *Support Vector Machine* (SVM), where each model has two variants, (2) accuracy of each ML model, (3) execution time of each variant of the model in seconds. To generate preliminary experimental results, we built an execution environment based on machines indicated in [21] (2,6 GHz 6-Core Intel Core i7, 16 GB RAM) and near equivalent configuration available in Amazon EC2 instances[3].

Table 1. Experimental results on finding the best possible ML Model. The shaded row (MNB-1) indicates the model predicted by our extended cost model, with execution time of 0.05 s and an accuracy of 81.34%

ML Model	Execution Time [s]	Accuracy [%]	Cost/hour [$]
BNB-1	0.24	75.21	1.6
BNB-2	0.61	65.18	2.0
MNB-1	0.05	81.34	1.6
MNB-2	0.11	72.14	2.0
SVM-1	4.22	77.16	1.6
SVM-2	12.95	69.95	2.0

Table 1 presents the obtained results, which we used as an input to our extended cost model. Column *ML Model* represents the variants of the aforementioned ML models i.e., {*BNB-1, BNB-2, MNB-1, MNB-2, SVM-1, SVM-2*}, *Execution Time [s]* is the execution time of each variant in seconds, *Accuracy [%]* represents the accuracy of the ML algorithm, and *Cost/hour [$]* represents

---

[1] https://developers.google.com/optimization/mip/mip.
[2] https://github.com/fawadali/MCKPCostModel/blob/master/ML-CostModel/.
[3] https://calculator.s3.amazonaws.com/index.html.

execution cost in \$ per hour, for each sentiment analysis ML model. The average execution time of the cost model to predict the best possible ML was **4 ms**. The shaded row in Table 1 indicates the obtained result from the cost model as the best possible ML model for a given input performance metric parameters:

$$\text{Execution Time} \leq 1.0 \text{ s; Cost per hour} \leq \$2.0$$

At this point in time, the experiments were carried out on part of the machine learning pipeline dedicated to finding an optimal ML model. In the future, we will conduct experiments with different use cases and will also include the entire MPL, i.e., data pre-processing, feature selection, and training & testing of a given ML algorithm, in order to fine-tune the MCKP algorithm.

4   Related Work

Industrial approaches to increasing performance of ETL (DPP) processes apply: (1) horizontal or vertical scaling of ETL servers and (2) parallel processing of individual tasks. Informatica and IBM DataStage additionally support task reordering. Informatica implements the *push down* optimization, where the most selective tasks are moved towards or even into a data source, to reduce a data volume as soon as possible [12]. IBM DataStage implements the *balanced* optimization, where some tasks can be moved towards either a data source or a data warehouse [11].

Research approaches propose two basic techniques, namely: (1) task reordering, supported by simple cost functions and reordering heuristics and (2) parallel processing. In the first case, an ETL process is assigned an estimated execution cost [8], and next, by using task reordering, alternative processes are produced with their estimated costs [14,20]. As the reordering problem is NP-complete, [15,16,20] propose some reordering heuristics. Parallel processing of ETL was proposed in [17], where first, an ETL process is partitioned into linear sub-processes. Next, data parallelization is applied to each of the sub-processes. At the end, tasks of heavy load are executed with multi-threading. Finally, [18] researches a solution for constructing an optimal DPP for data science, i.e., a DPP is composed of data pre-processing tasks and model building tasks. DPP is defined as a directed acyclic graph. The optimization problem extends the CASH problem with time constraints. Nonetheless, the aforementioned approaches do not support ETL processes with UDFs.

Optimizing workflows with UDFs received so far little attention. The few proposed solutions use manual annotations of UDFs [7,9,10]. The annotations instruct an workflow engine how to re-order a workflow or instruct how to execute it in parallel. [6] proposes a Map-Reduce-based framework, which enables parallelization of UDFs in a massively-parallel shared-nothing database. However, UDFs are implemented from scratch for this environment. In [19] an ETL engine re-orders a workflow based a set of rewriting rules and on inferring the semantics of an UDF. This inferring is based on explicit code annotations and some automatically detectable UDF properties, e.g., read/write behavior.

The approaches outlined here require from the developer to follow certain code-based keywords or parallelism hints to enable parallelism and they do not treat an UDF as a black-box. Moreover, the approaches tend to use all the hardware resources to achieve parallelism and do not cater whether the parallelism is required at the first place or not, or do not take into account the required degree of parallelism.

In contrast, our approach first assesses if the performance of an UDF may increase by applying parallelization. If so, the optimizer, based on the cost model proposes the optimal configuration by using simulation, recommendation, and prediction algorithms for an UDF to be executed in the distributed framework. A positive feature of our approach is that it does not require code annotations, which make the development of an UDF independent on an execution environment, programming language, and cost model.

5   Conclusion

This paper is the continuation of our work [2–5], where we presented an *Extendible ETL Framework - cp-UDF* to allow the ETL developer to efficiently write parallelizable UDFs treated as black-boxes.

In this paper, we extended the cost model towards: (1) applying Machine Learning techniques in order to execute *Generic PAS* optimally in a distributed environment and (2) proposing users (specifically data scientists) an optimal end-to-end MLP, based on input performance parameters such as accuracy, precision, and recall, using the Decision Optimization module of the cost model. We evaluated experimentally our Decision Optimization module with the final goal to find the best possible ML model. The problem of finding the model was mapped into the MCKP and implemented in Python using Google OR-tools.

In the next steps, we will bring our vision of the Machine Learning Module to reality by pre-processing required datasets for the classification model in order to generate optimal configuration plan to execute *Generic PAS* in a distributed environment. Furthermore, we will extend our evaluation of the Decision Optimization module with different use cases to propose the best possible end-to-end ML pipeline, based on user performance metrics.

We believe that *cp-UDF* is another step towards the next generation DPP framework, which supports the end-to-end development of data and machine learning pipelines from a collection and organization of data to the optimal machine learning model development.

References

1. Data Engineering, Preparation, and Labeling for AI 2019. Technical report, Cognilytica Research (2019)
2. Ali, S.M.F.: Next-generation ETL framework to address the challenges posed by big data. In: DOLAP (2018)

3. Ali, S.M.F., Mey, J., Thiele, M.: Parallelizing user-defined functions in the ETL workflow using orchestration style sheets. AMCS J. **29**, 69–79 (2019)
4. Ali, S.M.F., Wrembel, R.: From conceptual design to performance optimization of ETL workflows: current state of research and open problems. VLDB J. **26**(6), 777–801 (2017). https://doi.org/10.1007/s00778-017-0477-2
5. Ali, S.M.F., Wrembel, R.: Towards a cost model to optimize user-defined functions in an ETL workflow based on user-defined performance metrics. In: Welzer, T., Eder, J., Podgorelec, V., Kamišalić Latifić, A. (eds.) ADBIS 2019. LNCS, vol. 11695, pp. 441–456. Springer, Cham (2019). https://doi.org/10.1007/978-3-030-28730-6_27
6. Friedman, E., Pawlowski, P., Cieslewicz, J.: SQL/MapReduce: A practical approach to self-describing, polymorphic, and parallelizable user-defined functions. VLDB Endown. **2**(2), 1402–1413 (2009)
7. Große, P., May, N., Lehner, W.: A study of partitioning and parallel UDF execution with the SAP HANA database. In: SSDBM, p. 36 (2014)
8. Halasipuram, R., Deshpande, P.M., Padmanabhan S.: Determining essential statistics for cost based optimization of an ETL workflow. In: EDBT, pp. 307–318 (2014)
9. Hueske, F., Peters, M., Krettek, A., Ringwald, M., Tzoumas, K., Markl, V., Freytag, J.-C.: Peeking into the optimization of data flow programs with MapReduce-style UDFs. In: ICDE, pp. 1292–1295 (2013)
10. Hueske, F., Peters, M., Sax, M.J., Rheinländer, A., Bergmann, R., Krettek, A., Tzoumas, K.: Opening the black boxes in data flow optimization. VLDB Endown. **5**(11), 1256–1267 (2012)
11. IBM. IBM InfoSphere DataStage Balanced Optimization. Whitepaper
12. Informatica. How to Achieve Flexible, Cost-effective Scalability and Performance through Pushdown Processing. Whitepaper
13. Ismail, H., Harous, S., Belkhouche, B.: A comparative analysis of machine learning classifiers for twitter sentiment analysis. Res. Comput. Sci. **110**, 71–83 (2016)
14. Jovanovic, P., Romero, O., Simitsis, A., Abelló, A.: Incremental consolidation of data-intensive multi-flows. IEEE TKDE **28**(5), 1203–1216 (2016)
15. Karagiannis, A., Vassiliadis, P., Simitsis, A.: Scheduling strategies for efficient etl execution. Inf. Syst. **38**(6), 927–945 (2013)
16. Kumar, N., Kumar, P.S.: An efficient heuristic for logical optimization of ETL workflows. In: Castellanos, M., Dayal, U., Markl, V. (eds.) BIRTE 2010. LNBIP, vol. 84, pp. 68–83. Springer, Heidelberg (2011). https://doi.org/10.1007/978-3-642-22970-1_6
17. Liu , X., Iftikhar, N.: An ETL optimization framework using partitioning and parallelization. In: ACM SAC, pp. 1015–1022 (2015)
18. Quemy, A.: Binary classification in unstructured space with hypergraph case-based reasoning. Inf. Syst. **85**, 92–113 (2019)
19. Rheinländer, A., Heise, A., Hueske, F., Leser, U., Naumann, F.: Sofa: An extensible logical optimizer for udf-heavy data flows. Inf. Syst. **52**, 96–125 (2015)
20. Simitsis, A., Vassiliadis, P., Sellis, T.K.: State-space optimization of ETL workflows. IEEE TKDE **17**(10), 1404–1419 (2005)
21. Vernica, R., Carey, M.J., Li, C.: Efficient parallel set-similarity joins using mapreduce. In: SIGMOD (2010)
22. Wrembel, R.: Still open issues in ETL design and optimization (2019). www.cs.put.poznan.pl/rwrembel/ETL-open-issues.pdf. Res. seminar, BarcelonaTech

A Scalable Randomized Algorithm for Triangle Enumeration on Graphs Based on SQL Queries

Abir Farouzi[1,3]($\boxtimes$), Ladjel Bellatreche[1], Carlos Ordonez[2],
Gopal Pandurangan[2], and Mimoun Malki[3]

[1] ISAE/ENMSA, Poitiers, France
{abir.farouzi,bellatreche}@ensma.fr
[2] University of Houston, Texas, USA
carlos@central.uh.edu, gopal@cs.uh.edu
[3] ESI-SBA, Sidi Bel Abbès, Algeria
m.malki@esi-sba.dz

Abstract. Triangle enumeration is a fundamental problem in large-scale graph analysis. For instance, triangles are used to solve practical problems like community detection and spam filtering. On the other hand, there is a large amount of data stored on database management systems (DBMSs), which can be modeled and analyzed as graphs. Alternatively, graph data can be quickly loaded into a DBMS. Our paper shows how to adapt and optimize a randomized distributed triangle enumeration algorithm with SQL queries, which is a significantly different approach from programming graph algorithms in traditional languages such as Python or C++. We choose a parallel columnar DBMS given its fast query processing, but our solution should work for a row DBMS as well. Our randomized solution provides a balanced workload for parallel query processing, being robust to the existence of skewed degree vertices. We experimentally prove our solution ensures a balanced data distribution, and hence workload, among machines. The key idea behind the algorithm is to evenly partition all possible triplets of vertices among machines, sending edges that may form a triangle to a proxy machine; this edge redistribution eliminates shuffling edges during join computation and therefore triangle enumeration becomes local and fully parallel. In summary, our algorithm exhibits linear speedup with large graphs, including graphs that have high skewness in vertex degree distributions.

Keywords: Inside DBMS solution · Parallel triangle enumeration · Graph · Columnar DBMS

1 Introduction

Large graphs are becoming pervasive as the world is more interconnected than before. Examples include real-world networks such as social, transportation,

G. Pandurangan—He was supported, in part, by NSF grants IIS-1633720. CCF-1717075, and CCF-1540512.

© Springer Nature Switzerland AG 2020
M. Song et al. (Eds.): DaWaK 2020, LNCS 12393, pp. 141–156, 2020.
https://doi.org/10.1007/978-3-030-59065-9_12

Web, and biological networks. One of the fundamental graph problems is triangle enumeration, which has attracted much interest because of its numerous practical applications, including the analysis of social processes in networks [26], dense subgraph mining [25], joins in databases [16], etc. The interested reader may refer to [5,7] for additional applications. Triangle detection and triangle counting are also well-studied problems, and potentially significantly easier than triangle enumeration. However, we emphasize that for many applications, including all the aforementioned ones, triangle detection, and triangle counting are not enough, and a complete enumeration of all the triangles is required.

Graphs can be modeled in terms of a database perspective. DBMSs provide a different angle of graph processing since they offer an easily load/import data into them. Nonetheless, processing large graphs in DBMSs did not receive much interest as long as DBMSs did not define graph concepts. Some recent studies offer support for the vertex-centric query interface to express graph queries like Pregel and its open-source successor Giraph [15]. Other works such as [6,18] study and compare different graph problems on row, array and columnar DBMSs with Spark GraphX. These works showed that DBMSs are faster.

In our work, we present an adaption of a parallel randomized algorithm [19] to solve the triangle enumeration problem. We prove that our approach guarantees the load balancing between the processors. We study how to express this algorithm using *standard* SQL queries that can be executed on any DBMS. We discuss various possible optimizations in order to obtain the optimum execution time while using columnar DBMS to execute the algorithm.

Our paper is organized as follows. Section 2 states an overview of related works. Preliminary concepts and notations including graph, triangle enumeration problem, columnar DBMS and parallel computational model are described in Sect. 3. In Sect. 4, we present the standard algorithm and its limitations; then we detailed our proposed randomized algorithm while discussing its complexity and load balancing. We introduce our experimental findings in Sect. 5 and we conclude in Sect. 6 with general remarks and potential future works.

2   Related Work

In this section, we summarize the most relevant, state of the art, triangle enumeration works. We start by highlighting numerous applications related to graph processing using relation queries on DBMSs. Then, we present an overview of triangle enumeration with a brief description of recent studies.

Processing graphs in DBMSs have been studied in recent years. The work of [28] revisited graph processing support in the RDBMS at SQL level. [18] studied the optimization of recursive queries on two complementary graph problems: transitive closure and adjacency matrix multiplication. The authors experimentally proved that the columnar DBMS is the fastest with tuned query optimization. [6] studied how to solve four important graph problems: reachability, single-source shortest path, weakly connected components and page rank using relational queries on columnar DBMS, array DBMS and spark's GraphX on share-nothing architecture. Other works like [10,23] stored graphs in relational tables with schema optimized for graph queries by adding a specific layer supporting graph processing on RDBMS. Other interesting work of processing graph in DBMSs can be found at [2,9,17]. Moreover, there exist powerful parallel graph engines in the Hadoop big data ecosystem like Neo4j and Spark GraphX, but they require significant effort to link and integrate information about the graph and, in general, they provide query languages inferior as compared to SQL. In contrast, our system can readily exploit diverse relational tables, which can be easily loaded and integrated with the graph edge table. Our SQL solution provides good time performance, but it does not intend to be the fastest compared to Hadoop systems. On the other hand, our goal is to provide perfect load balancing, which ensures scalability as more parallel processing nodes are available. A detailed benchmark comparison is left as future work.

The foundational algorithms for enumerating triangles are the node iterator [21] and the edge iterator [12] suitable for one host execution. Nonetheless, with the expansion of graph size, they become less efficient, and one host processing on the main memory is infeasible. Some works like MGT [11] and Trigon [8] use one host processing but with better I/O techniques which reduce the overhead caused by the I/O access. Other works focus on paralleling the processing and present multi-core solutions like [14,22]; the first presented a load balance guarantee and the second proposed a cache-friendly algorithm supporting dynamic parallelism without tuning parameters. Many distributed works have been also introduced, [4] proposed MPI-based distributed memory parallel algorithm based on node iterator for counting triangles in massive networks that can be easily adapted for triangle enumeration.[27] is another approach based on distributing the processing over a cluster while reducing messages during run-time. On the other hand, many solutions have been explicitly addressed in the MapReduce framework by [1,20,24,29]. These solutions paralleled the processing through two rounds of MapReduce where the first focuses on finding all the wedges and the second checks whether there is an edge connecting each wedge endpoints. However, those solutions are time-costly because of the large amount of intermediate data exchanged between the hosts during processing.

The work of [19] presented a randomized distributed algorithm for triangle enumeration and counting in the k-machine model, a popular theoretical model for large-scale distributed graph computation [13]. In this model, $k \geq 2$ machines jointly perform computations on graphs with n nodes (typically, $n \gg k$). The input graph is assumed to be initially partitioned among the k machines in a balanced fashion. Communication is point-to-point by message passing (no shared memory), and the goal is to minimize the number of communication *rounds* of the computation. The work of [19] presented a distributed algorithm that enumerates all the triangles of a graph in $\tilde{O}(m/k^{5/3} + n/k^{4/3})$ rounds (the $\tilde{O}$ notation hides a *polylog(n)* multiplicative and additive factor), where n and m are the number of nodes and edges of the input graph respectively. It also showed that this algorithm is essentially optimal with respect to the number of communication rounds by presenting a lower bound that showed that there exist graphs with m edges where any distributed algorithm requires $\tilde{\Omega}(m/k^{5/3})$

rounds. The current work builds on the algorithm of [19] and shows how to modify and efficiently implement this algorithm on a DBMS with queries which is significantly different from a fairly straightforward MPI implementation of the algorithm in a traditional language such as C++ or Python.

3 Preliminaries

This is a reference section that introduces definitions of a graph from mathematics and database perspectives, our problem definition, an overview of distributed processing using columnar DBMS, and a description of the computational model.

3.1 Graph

Let $G = (V, E)$ be an undirected unweighted graph with V non-empty set of vertices (nodes) and E a possibly empty set of edges. We denote $n = |V|$ and $m = |E|$. Each edge $e \in E$ links between two vertices u, v and defines a direction (from u to v and v to u). We denote for each $u \in V$, $N(u) = \{v \in V : (u, v) \in E\}$ the set of neighbors of a vertex u. Thereby, the degree of u is defined as $deg(u) = |N(u)|$.

By this definition, we allow the presence of cliques and cycles. A clique defines a complete sub-graph of G. A cycle is a path that starts and ends on the same vertex. A cycle of length l is called l-cycle; hence a 3-cycle refers to a triangle.

Mathematically, a graph G can be represented by an adjacency matrix of $n \times n$ (see Fig. 1 (b)), where the cell i, j holds 1 if there is an edge combining vertex i to vertex j. In database perspective, a graph G is stored as adjacency list in an edge table $E(i, j)$ with primary key (i, j) representing source vertex i and destination vertex j (see Fig. 1 (c)). An entry in table E defines existence of an edge. Figure 1 (a) depicts an undirected graph, (b) shows its adjacency matrix representation and (c) its adjacency list representation.

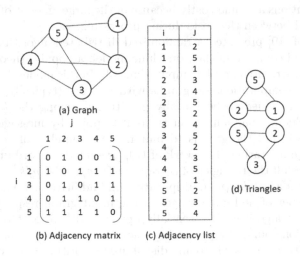

Fig. 1. Graph representations

3.2   Triangles Properties

Definition 1. *Given a graph, a connected triple* (u, v, w) *at vertex* v *is a path of length 2 for which* v *is at the center. If* $(w, u) \in E : (u, v, w)$ *is a closed triple called triangle otherwise it is open triple named wedge or open triad. A triangle contains three closed triples:* $(u, v, w), (v, w, u)$ *and* (w, u, v).

By Definition 1, we allow the enumeration of triangles on both directed and undirected graph as triangle is a cycle of 3 edges.

Besides triangle enumeration problem, the problem of finding *open triads* has many applications, e.g., in social networks, where vertices represent people, edges represent a friendship relation, and open triads can be used to recommend friends.

Definition 2. *A triangle denoted as* $\Delta_{(u,v,w)}$, *is the smallest clique in graph* G *composed of three distinct vertices* u, v *and* w. *The triangle formed by these vertices include the existence of three edges* (u, v), (v, w) *and* (w, u). *The set* $\Delta(G)$ *includes all the triangles* $\Delta_{(u,v,w)}$ *of the graph* G. *Figure 1 (d) represents an example of triangles in an undirected graph (Fig. 1. (a)). Notice that the two examples of produced triangles are in lexicographical order. This eliminates the listing of the triangle multiple times.*

Definition 3. *Two triangles* Δ_1 *and* Δ_2 *may belong to the same clique. Figure 1 (d) shows that both enumerated triangles* $\Delta_{(1,2,5)}$ *and* $\Delta_{(2,3,5)}$ *belong to the same clique formed of vertices* $\{2,3,4,5\}$.

For a given graph G, triangle enumeration problem is to list all the unique triangles present in the set $\Delta(G)$ which is expensive compared to counting because enumeration tests the possibility of each triplet of edges to form a triangle. Therefore, using the results of the enumeration task, one can easily obtain the count of triangles in the graph. In contrast, just counting does not necessarily give the list of resulting triangles [3].

Notably, in practice, most graphs are sparse and therefore $m = O(n)$. However, detecting embedded triangles is computationally hard with time $O(n^3)$.

3.3   DBMS Storage

In order to enumerate triangles, standard SQL queries can be employed based on SPJ operations (selection, projection and join). These operations can be useful in simplifying and understanding the problem by formulating the solution using relational algebra (σ, π and $\bowtie$) then translating it into SQL queries that can be executed in parallel on any distributed DBMS. To handle a graph in a database system, the best storage definition is a list of edges as edge table $E(i, j)$ where it is assumed the edge goes from i to j. If the graph is undirected, we include two edges for each pair of connected vertices. Otherwise, only the directed edge is inserted. In this manner, we can always get a triangle vertices in order $\{u, v, w\}$ instead of $\{v, w, u\}$ or $\{w, u, v\}$ with $u < v < w$.

Figure 2 depicts physical schema for a graph in DBMS, where the table E_s represents the adjacency list of the graph, it holds all the edges. While, the table 'User' stocks all the information related to vertices (i and j) of table E_s.

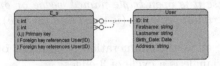

Fig. 2. A physical database model for the graph representation

We opted for columnar DBMSs such as Vertica or MonetDB to execute our queries, since they present better efficiency of writing and reading data to and from disk comparing to row DBMSs. Thus, speeding up the required time to perform a query [18]. In fact, physical storage between the two types of DBMSs varies significantly. The row DBMSs use indexes that hold the *rowid* of the physical data location. Whereas, the columnar DBMSs rely on projections, optimized collections of table columns that provide physical storage for data. They can contain some or all of the columns of one or more tables. For instance, Vertica allows storing data by projections in a format that optimizes query execution, and it compresses data and/or encodes projection data, allowing optimization of access and storage.

3.4 Parallel Computation Architecture

We assume a k-machines cluster (k represents the count of the hosts in the cluster) built over share-nothing architecture. Each machine can communicate directly with others. All the machines define a homogeneous setup configuration providing at least the minimum hardware and software requirements for the best performance of the columnar DBMS. Following the guidelines presented by the DBMS, each machine should provide at least 8 cores processor, 8 GB RAM and 1 TB of storage.

The number of machines k must be chosen as: $k = p^3$ with $p \in \mathbb{N}$. This is important for our algorithm to achieve a perfect load balancing.

4   Triangle Enumeration

In this section, we present our contribution to solve the triangle enumeration problem in parallel using SQL queries. Most of the queries bellow are specific to Vertica, particullary, CREATE TABLE/PROJECTION and COPY queries. For other DBMSs including row DBMSs like Oracle and SQL Server, a DBA can easily adapt them depending on their data loading and retrieval strategies.

4.1   Standard Algorithm

Enumerating triangle in a given graph G can be done in two main iterations, the first aims to identify all the directed wedges in the input graph while the second focuses on finding whether there exists an edge connecting the endpoints of each wedge.

Basically, listing triangles using standard algorithm is performed by three nested loops, which can be translated in SQL by three self-join of table E ($E1 \bowtie E2 \bowtie E3 \bowtie E1$) on $E1.j = E2.i$, $E2.j = E3.i$ and $E3.j = E1.i$ respectively with $E1 = E, E2 = E$ and $E3 = E$ ($E1,E2$ and $E3$ are alias table of E). However, since only triangles defining lexicographical order ($v_1 < v_2 < v_3$) are output (see Sect. 3.3), we can eliminate the third self-join by taking both $E2.j = E3.i$ and $E3.j = E1.i$ within the second self-join. As a result, the above-mentioned process can be formulated using only two self-joins on table E ($E \bowtie E \bowtie E$). In SQL queries bellow, we use E_dup which is a duplicate table of E used to speed up the local join processing. Indeed, partitioning the first table by i and the duplicate one by j divides the two corresponding tables into small pieces based on the aforementioned columns which will make local joining on $E.j = E.i$ faster.

```
SELECT E1.i As v1,E1.j AS v2,E2.j As v3
    FROM
        E E1 JOIN E_dup E2 ON E1.j=E2.i
        JOIN E E3 ON E2.j=E3.i AND E3.j=E1.i
        WHERE E1.i<E1.j AND E2.i<E2.j;
```

One problem can occur with this query executed in parallel. If the clique size is too large, there would be a redundancy in listed triangles caused by assigning each vertex and its neighbors to different machines to speed up local joins.

4.2 Randomized Triangle Enumeration

The high-level idea behind the randomized triangle enumeration algorithm of [19] is to randomly partition vertices into subsets of certain size and then compute the triangles within each subset in parallel. Specifically, the vertex set is partitioned into $k^{1/3}$ random subsets (thus each subset will have $n/k^{1/3}$ vertices), where k is the number of machines. Then each triplet of subsets of vertices (there are a total of $(k^{1/3})^3 = k$ triplets, including repetitions) and the edges between the vertices in the subset are assigned to each one of the k machines. Each machine then computes the triangles in the subgraph induced by the subset assigned to that machine locally. Since every possible triplet is taken into account, every triangle will be counted (it is easy to remove duplicate counting, by using lexicographic order among the vertices, as described later). Hence correctness is easy to establish. The main intuition behind the randomized algorithm is that a random partition of the vertex set into equal sized subsets also essentially *balances* the number of edges assigned to a machine. This crucially reduces communication, but also the amount of work done per machine. While this is balancing is easy to see under expectation (an easy calculation using linearity of expectation shows that on average, the number of edges are balanced); however there can be a significant variance. It is shown in [19] via a probabilistic analysis, that the number of edges assigned per machine is bounded by $\tilde{O}(\max\{m/k^{2/3}, n/k^{1/3}\})$. We note that the randomized algorithm is always correct (i.e., of Las Vegas type), while the randomization is helpful to improve the performance.

The Fig. 3 illustrates the overview of the randomized triangle enumeration algorithm. To distinguish each partition of vertices, a color from $k^{1/3}$ colors is assigned to it. The communication between machines is needed when creating sub-graphs or collecting edges from proxies. Otherwise, the processing is local.

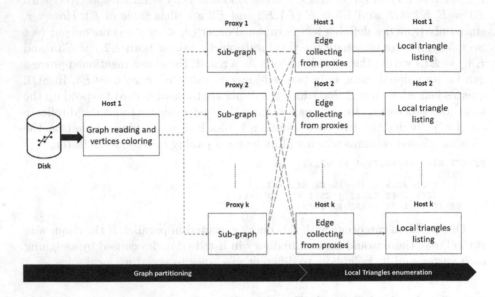

Fig. 3. Random triangle enumeration process

4.3   Graph Reading

The first step to enumerate triangles is to read the input graph on one host. If the graph is directed, the edge table E_s is built as adjacency list into the database system. Otherwise, for each tuple *(i,j)* inserted in the edge table E_s, *(j,i)* is also inserted. The following queries are used to read the input graph:

```
CREATE TABLE E_s(i int,j int);
COPY E_s FROM "link/to/graph_data_set";
/*if the input graph is undirected*/
INSERT INTO E_s SELECT j,i FROM E_s;
```

4.4   Graph Partitioning

We assume k-machine model as presented in Sect. 3.4. The input graph G is partitioned over the k machines using the random vertex partition model that is based on assigning each vertex and its neighbors to a random machine among the k machines [19]. Notably, for a graph $G = (V, E)$, a machine k hosts $G_k = (V_k, E_k)$ a sub-graph of G, where $V_k \subset V$ and $\cup_k V_k = V$, G_k needs to be formed in a manner that for each $v \in V_k$ and $u \in N(v)/(u,v) \in E_k$.

As explained previously, our partitioning strategy (proposed in [19]) aims to partition the set V of vertices of G in $k^{1/3}$ subsets of $n/k^{1/3}$ vertex each. Initially, the table "V_s" in the query bellow ensures that each vertex $v \in V$ picks independently and uniformly at random one color from a set of $k^{1/3}$ distinct colors using the function randomint of vertica. To be noted that 1 and 2 in the query bellow refer to subsets of colors of k-machine model ($k = 8$). A deterministic assignment of triplets of colors through the table "Triplet" in the following queries assigns each of the k possible triplets of colors formed by $k^{1/3}$ distinct colors to one distinct machine. This can be translated by the following queries:

```
/*Each vertex picks a random color of qr=k^(1/3), for k=8, qr=2 */
CREATE TABLE V_s(i int,color int);
INSERT INTO V_s
    SELECT i,randomint(qr)+1
    FROM
        (SELECT DISTINCT i FROM E_s
        UNION
        SELECT DISTINCT j FROM E_s)V;
/*triplet_file values for k=8: (1,1,1,1)(2,1,1,2)
(3,1,2,1)(4,1,2,2)(5,2,1,1)(6,2,1,2)(7,2,2,1)(8,2,2,2)*/
CREATE TABLE Triplet(machine int,color1 int,color2 int,color3 int)
    UNSEGMENTED ALL NODES;
COPY Triplet FROM "link/to/triplet_file";
```

Then for each edge it holds, each machine designates one random machine as edge proxy for that edge and sends all its edges to the respective edge proxies, the table "E_s_proxy" holds all the edges with their respective edge proxies. This table is formed by coloring edge table "E_s" end-vertices with the vertex table "V_s" having for each vertex its picked color by using double join between the two tables. Building "E_s_proxy" is the most important step because all the partitioning depends on it. Using this table, we can identify the edges end-vertices picked colors which help the next query of "E_s_local" building to decide which host will hold which edge according to the deterministic triplet assignment to each machine. In other words, each host collects its required edges from edge proxies to process the next step.

```
/*Sending edges to proxies*/
CREATE TABLE E_s_proxy(i_color int,j_color int,i int,j int);
INSERT INTO E_s_proxy
    SELECT Vi.color, Vj.color,E.i,E.j
    FROM
        E_s E JOIN V_s Vi ON E.i=Vi.i
        JOIN V_s Vj ON E.j=Vj.i;
/*Collecting edges from proxies*/
CREATE TABLE E_s_local(machine int,i int,j int,i_color int,j_color int);
INSERT INTO E_s_local
    SELECT machine, i, j, i_color, j_color
        FROM
            E_s_proxy E JOIN triplet edge1 ON E.i_color=edge1.color1
                AND E.j_color=edge1.color2 WHERE E.i<E.j
    UNION
    SELECT machine, i, j, i_color, j_color
        FROM
            E_s_proxy E JOIN triplet edge2 ON E.i_color=edge2.color2
                AND E.j_color=edge2.color3 WHERE E.i<E.j
    UNION
    SELECT machine, i, j, i_color, j_color
        FROM
            E_s_proxy E JOIN triplet edge3 ON E.i_color=edge3.color3
                AND E.j_color=edge3.color1 WHERE E.i>E.j;
```

Having $E.i < E.j$ and $E.i > E.j$ in last query guarantee the output of each triangle on a unique machine. For instance, a triangle (u, v, w) picking colors (c, b, c) is output on a unique machine m having triplet (c, b, c) assigned to it with $u < v < w$, hence triangles like (w, u, v) and (v, w, u) where $w > u < v$ and $v < w > u$ won't be taken in account which eliminates redundancy of enumerated triangles.

4.5 Local Triangle Enumeration

To enumerate triangles locally on each host and in parallel, each machine examines its edges whose endpoints are in two distinct subsets among the three subsets assigned to it. This happens in two steps:

1. Each machine lists all the possible wedges that vertices have identical color and order as its triplet
2. To output triangles, each host checks whether there is an edge connecting the end-vertices of each listed wedge

The aforementioned steps are ensured through a local double self-join on table E ($E \bowtie E \bowtie E$) on columns $E.j = E.i$ on each host locally and in parallel. The queries are presented in the following:

```
SELECT E1.machine, E1.i AS v1, E1.j AS v2, E2.j AS v3
    FROM
            E_s_local E1 JOIN E_s_local E2 ON E1.machine=E2.machine AND E1.j=E2.i
            JOIN E_s_local E3 ON E2.machine=E3.machine AND E2.j=E3.i
            JOIN Triplet T on T.machine = E3.machine
    WHERE E1.i<E1.j AND E2.i<E2.j AND E1.i=E3.j
            AND E1.i_color=T.color_1 AND E1.j_color=T.color_2
            AND E2.j_color=T.color_3 AND local_node_name()='node_name'
    ORDER BY v1,v2,v3;
```

As explained in previous section, having $E1.i < E1.j$ and $E2.i < E2.j$ in the query eliminates redundancy. The last join with the table "Triplet" eliminates having triangles with vertex having same colors to be output by other machines then theirs. Figure 4 illustrates the random partitioning and triangle enumeration in a cluster of eight machines.

Furthermore, to check similarity between triangles output by randomized algorithm and those with standard algorithm, a set difference between the results of the two algorithms can be employed. The following queries are executed in Sect. 5 to prove the similarity of the output of both algorithms (notice that Triangle is a table containing the list of triangles resulting from randomized algorithm execution):

```
SELECT u, v, w FROM Triangle
EXCEPT
    (SELECT E1.i As v1,E1.j AS v2,E2.j As v3
        FROM E E1 JOIN E E2 ON E1.j=E2.i
            JOIN E E3 ON E2.j=E3.i AND E3.j=E1.i
        WHERE E1.i<E1.j AND E2.i<E2.j);
```

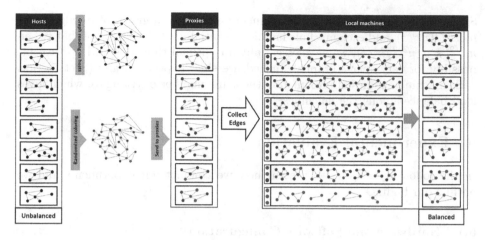

Fig. 4. Randomized triangle enumeration on 8 machines.

4.6 Load Balancing

Parallel computing is considered complete when all the hosts complete their processing and output the results. Therefore, reducing running time requires that all processors finish their tasks at almost the same time [4]. This is possible if all hosts acquire an equitable amount of data that they can process on.

We mentioned in data partitioning section that each vertex of the set V pick randomly and independently a color c from $k^{1/3}$ distinct colors. This gives rise to a partition of the vertices set V into $k^{1/3}$ subsets s_c of $O(n/k^{1/3})$ vertex each. Each machine then receives a sub-graph $G_k = (V_k, E_k)$ of G. As mentioned at the beginning of Sect. 4.2, the analysis of [19] shows that the number of edges among the subgraphs $G_k = (V_k, E_k)$ is relatively balanced with high probability. Hence each machine processes essentially the same number of edges which leads to a load balance. The endpoints of each $e \in E_k$ are in two subsets s_c. This means that each triangle (u, v, w) satisfying $u < v < w$ will be output.

4.7 Time Complexity of Randomized Algorithm

The time complexity taken by a machine is proportional to the number of edges and triangles it handles. Each machine handles a particular triplet of colors (c_x, c_y, c_z) so it handles $O(n/k^{1/3})$ random sized subset of vertices. The worst-case number of triangles in this subset is $O(n^3/k)$; however the number of edges is much lower. Indeed, as mentioned in Sect. 4.2 the key idea of the random-ized algorithm as shown in [19], is that a random subset of the above-mentioned size (i.e., $O(n/k^{1/3})$) will have no more than $\max\{\tilde{O}(m/k^{2/3}, n/k^{1/3})\}$ edges with high probability. Hence each machine handles only so many edges with high probability. Since it is known that the number of triangles that can be listed using a set of ℓ edges is $\Omega(\ell^{3/2})$ (see e.g., [19]) the number of trian-gles that each machine has to handle is at most $\max\{\tilde{O}(m^{3/2}/k, n^{3/2}/k^{1/2})\}$.

Since, the maximum number of (distinct) triangles in a graph of m edges is at most $O(m^{3/2})$, and each machine handles essentially a $1/k$ fraction of that (when $m^{3/2}/k > n^{3/2}/k^{1/2}$), we have essentially an optimal (linear) speed up (except, possibly for very sparse graphs). Indeed, we show experimentally (Sect. 5) that each machine handles approximately the same number of triangles, which gives load balance among the machines.

5   Experimental Evaluation

In the following section, we present how we conduct our experiments and we outline our findings.

5.1   Hardware and Software Configuration

The experiments were conducted on 8 nodes cluster ($k = 8$) each with 4 virtual cores CPU of type GeniuneIntel running at 2.4 Ghz, 48 GB of main memory, 1 TB of storage, 32 KB L1 cache, 4 MB L2 cache and Linux Ubuntu server 18.04 operating system. The total of RAM on the cluster is 384 GB and total of disk storage is 8 TB and 32 cores for processing. We used Vertica, a distributed columnar DBMS to execute our SQL queries and Python as the host language to generate and submit them to the database for its fastness comparing to JDBC.

5.2   Data Set

Table 1 summarizes the data sets used in our experiments. We used seven real and synthetic (both directed and undirected) graph data sets. These data sets represent different sizes and structures. The aforementioned table exhibits for each data set, its nodes, edge, and expected triangle count with its type, format, and source.

Table 1. Data sets

Data set	n	m	Triangle count	Type	Format	Skewness	Source
LiveJournal	3,997k	34,681k	177,820k	Real	Undirected	Low	SNAP
as-Skitter	1,696k	11,095k	28,769k	Real	Undirected	Low	SNAP
flickr-link	105k	2,316k	548,174k	Real	Undirected	High	KONECT
hyves	1,402k	2,777k	752k	Real	Undirected	High	KONECT
Graph500_s19	335k	15,459k	186,288k	Synthetic	Directed	High	Generated
Linear	141k	49,907k	3,300,095k	Synthetic	Directed	High	Generated
Geometric	8k	22,361k	13,078,242k	Synthetic	Directed	High	Generated

5.3   Edge Table Partitioning

For the triangle enumeration problem, the input graph is mostly partitioned locally by source vertex i or destination vertex j to speedup the local join as explained in Sect. 4.1. Whereas the segmentation of the Vertices set V accross the hosts is done randomly using the random vertex partition model mentioned in Sect. 4.4. In Vertica DBMS, this process is performed in the DDL step through the segmentation clause definition in the projection creation query:

```
CREATE PROJECTION E_s_local_super(machine ENCODING RLE, i, j,
        i_color ENCODING RLE, j_color ENCODING RLE)
    AS
    SELECT machine, i,j, i_color,j_color
        FROM E_s_local
    ORDER BY i,j
    SEGMENTED BY (machine*4294967295//k) ALL NODES OFFSET 0 KSAFE 1;
```

In fact, Vertica attributes for each machine a segment between 0 and 4 bytes that represents its hash values interval. Initially, the hash value of each tuple is calculated using the segmentation clause then according to the resulting value, the tuple is sent to the corresponding machine owning that hash value within its segment. We exploited this property to send each edge to its corresponding machine. This allowed us to perform joins locally on each machine independently from other hosts by specifying the name of the host in the WHERE clause of the triangle enumeration SQL query.

5.4   Triangle Enumeration

Here we analyze the performance of the randomized triangle enumeration algorithm output and compare it to the standard algorithm results.

We start by discussing our randomized algorithm results in terms of load balancing between processors and time execution on each machine. Our main purpose is to experimentally prove that the count of output triangles is almost even on all hosts. Thus, we present Fig. 5 and Fig.6 pie charts of examples of triangles count (TC) on two data sets on each host. The count of triangles output on each host is 1/8 of the total count which confirms our theoretical statement.

Figure 7 represents the triangles count output on each machine for the remaining data sets. It is obvious that the distribution of output triangles is balanced over machines. Moreover, Fig. 8 presents the execution time of the randomized algorithm on each host. The lines chart reveals that all the processors finish their tasks at almost the same time on all the data sets with small-time shifts due to data movement in the preprocessing phase or the presence of skewness. For instance, data sets present a small overhead on machine 1 responsible for data read and shuffling which explains this additional processing time. Experimenting on high skewed graphs data sets, we can notice that there is some machines that take less time than the other hosts and finish first for the same data set, these machines may have fewer cliques compared to other machines.

We compare now the results between the standard algorithm and the randomized algorithm, summarized in Table 2. We notice that the triangle count is

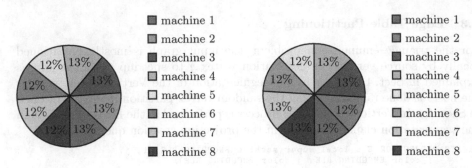

Fig. 5. as-Skitter TC by machine   **Fig. 6.** Geometric TC by machine

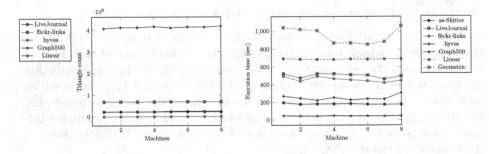

Fig. 7. Triangle count (TC)   **Fig. 8.** Execution time

the same as the expected triangle count defined in Table 1. The load balancing is not ensured and a lot of data movement is performed to complete the join task using the standard algorithm. Thus, we added the preprocessing step as we want to ensure the load balancing in the standard algorithm, however this costs a significant overhead in execution time. The column "Rebalanced" in Table 2 exhibits the cost of such approach.

The column "Randomized" give the average time execution of randomized algorithm on the different data sets. As the data set size grows or presents high skewness, the performance of the randomized algorithm becomes better than standard algorithm such as the case for directed graph Graph500_s19 and undirected graph flickr-link or hyves respectively. Moreover, when the skewed graph data set is becoming significantly large like Linear and Geometric, standard algorithm fails because of the data movement during the join processing causing memory issues while randomized algorithm succeeds to finish the task because the triangle listing is done locally on the subgraph stored on each machine and no data exchange is performed.

Columns TC_{stand} and TC_{rand} summarize the resulting triangle count using both algorithms, we notice that both algorithms give the same triangle count. We experimentally executed the set difference SQL query presented in Sect. 4.5 between the two results that returns an empty set for each data set, hence, the similarity of results from both algorithms is confirmed.

Table 2. Triangle count (in millions) and execution time (secs) results

Data set	TC_{stand}	TC_{rand}	Standard	Rebalanced	Randomized
com-LiveJournal	177,820k	177,820k	480	Stop	503
as-Skitter	28,769k	28,769k	90	1988	180
flickr-link	na	548,174k	Stop	Stop	485
hyves	752k	752k	49	604	47
Graph500_s19	186,288k	186,288k	610	Stop	250
Linear	na	3,300,095k	Stop	Stop	365
Geometric	na	13,078,242k	Stop	Stop	954

6   Conclusions

We presented a parallel randomized algorithm for triangle enumeration on large graphs using SQL queries. Our approach using SQL queries provides elegant, shorter and abstract solution compared to traditional languages like C++ or Python. We proved that our approach scales well with the size of the graph and its complexity especially with skewed graph. Our partitioning strategy ensures balanced load distribution of data between the hosts. The experimental findings were promising. They were compatible with our theoretical statements.

For our future work, we are planning to perform a deeper study of the randomized algorithm with dense and complex graphs. As well as, running further experiments to compare the randomized algorithm with graph engine solutions for triangle enumeration. Finally, we are opting for expanding our algorithm to detect larger cliques which is another computationally challenging problem.

References

1. Afrati, F.N., Sarma, A.D., Salihoglu, S., Ullman, J.D.: Upper and lower bounds on the cost of a MapReduce computation. PVLDB **6**(4), 277–288 (2013)
2. Al-Amin, S.T., Ordonez, C., Bellatreche, L.: Big data analytics: exploring graphs with optimized SQL queries. In: Elloumi, M., et al. (eds.) DEXA 2018. CCIS, vol. 903, pp. 88–100. Springer, Cham (2018). https://doi.org/10.1007/978-3-319-99133-7_7
3. Al Hasan, M., Dave, V.S.: Triangle counting in large networks: a review. Wiley Interdisc. Rev. Data Min. Knowl. Discov. **8**(2), e1226 (2018)
4. Arifuzzaman, S., Khan, M., Marathe, M.: A space-efficient parallel algorithm for counting exact triangles in massive networks. In: HPCC, pp. 527–534 (2015)
5. Berry, J.W., Fostvedt, L.A., Nordman, D.J., Phillips, C.A., Seshadhri, C., Wilson, A.G.: Why do simple algorithms for triangle enumeration work in the real world? Internet Math. **11**(6), 555–571 (2015)
6. Cabrera, W., Ordonez, C.: Scalable parallel graph algorithms with matrix-vector multiplication evaluated with queries. DAPD J. **35**(3–4), 335–362 (2017). https://doi.org/10.1007/s10619-017-7200-6

7. Chu, S., Cheng, J.: Triangle listing in massive networks. ACM Trans. Knowl. Discov. Data **6**(4), 17 (2012)
8. Cui, Y., Xiao, D., Cline, D.B., Loguinov, D.: Improving I/O complexity of triangle enumeration. In: IEEE ICDM, pp. 61–70 (2017)
9. Das, S., Santra, A., Bodra, J., Chakravarthy, S.: Query processing on large graphs: approaches to scalability and response time trade offs. Data Knowl. Eng. **126**, 101736 (2020). https://doi.org/10.1016/j.datak.2019.101736
10. Fan, J., Raj, A.G.S., Patel, J.M.: The case against specialized graph analytics engines. In: CIDR (2015)
11. Hu, X., Tao, Y., Chung, C.W.: Massive graph triangulation. In: ACM SIGMOD, pp. 325–336 (2013)
12. Itai, A., Rodeh, M.: Finding a minimum circuit in a graph. SIAM J. Comput. **7**(4), 413–423 (1978)
13. Klauck, H., Nanongkai, D., Pandurangan, G., Robinson, P.: Distributed computation of large-scale graph problems. In: ACM-SIAM SODA, pp. 391–410 (2015)
14. Latapy, M.: Main-memory triangle computations for very large (sparse (power-law)) graphs. Theor. Comput. Sci. **407**(1–3), 458–473 (2008)
15. Malewicz, G., et al.: Pregel: a system for large-scale graph processing. In: ACM SIGMOD, pp. 135–146 (2010)
16. Ngo, H.Q., Ré, C., Rudra, A.: Skew strikes back: new developments in the theory of join algorithms. SIGMOD Rec. **42**(4), 5–16 (2013)
17. Ordonez, C.: Optimization of linear recursive queries in SQL. IEEE Trans. Knowl. Data Eng. **22**(2), 264–277 (2010)
18. Ordonez, C., Cabrera, W., Gurram, A.: Comparing columnar, row and array DBMSs to process recursive queries on graphs. Inf. Syst. **63**, 66–79 (2017)
19. Pandurangan, G., Robinson, P., Scquizzato, M.: On the distributed complexity of large-scale graph computations. In: SPAA, pp. 405–414 (2018)
20. Park, H.M., Chung, C.W.: An efficient MapReduce algorithm for counting triangles in a very large graph. In: ACM CIKM, pp. 539–548 (2013)
21. Schank, T.: Algorithmic aspects of triangle-based network analysis (2007)
22. Shun, J., Tangwongsan, K.: Multicore triangle computations without tuning. In: ICDE, pp. 149–160 (2015)
23. Sun, W., Fokoue, A., Srinivas, K., Kementsietsidis, A., Hu, G., Xie, G.: SQLGraph: an efficient relational-based property graph store. In: ACM SIGMOD, pp. 1887–1901 (2015)
24. Suri, S., Vassilvitskii, S.: Counting triangles and the curse of the last reducer. In: WWW, pp. 607–614 (2011)
25. Wang, N., Zhang, J., Tan, K.L., Tung, A.K.H.: On triangulation-based dense neighborhood graph discovery. Proc. VLDB Endow. **4**(2), 58–68 (2010)
26. Watts, D.J., Strogatz, S.H.: Collective dynamics of 'small-world' networks. Nature **393**, 440–442 (1998)
27. Zhang, Y., Jiang, H., Wang, F., Hua, Y., Feng, D., Xu, X.: LiteTE: lightweight, communication-efficient distributed-memory triangle enumerating. IEEE Access **7**, 26294–26306 (2019)
28. Zhao, K., Yu, J.X.: All-in-one: graph processing in RDBMSs revisited. In: SIGMOD, pp. 1165–1180 (2017)
29. Zhu, Y., Zhang, H., Qin, L., Cheng, H.: Efficient MapReduce algorithms for triangle listing in billion-scale graphs. Distrib. Parallel Databases **35**(2), 149–176 (2017). https://doi.org/10.1007/s10619-017-7193-1

Data Engineering for Data Science: Two Sides of the Same Coin

Oscar Romero[1] and Robert Wrembel[2]

[1] Universitat Politècnica de Catalunya, Catalunya, Spain
oromero@essi.upc.edu
[2] Poznan University of Technology, Poznań, Poland
robert.wrembel@cs.put.poznan.pl

Abstract. A de facto technological standard of data science is based on notebooks (e.g., Jupyter), which provide an integrated environment to execute data workflows in different languages. However, from a data engineering point of view, this approach is typically inefficient and unsafe, as most of the data science languages process data locally, i.e., in workstations with limited memory, and store data in files. Thus, this approach neglects the benefits brought by over 40 years of R&D in the area of data engineering, i.e., advanced database technologies and data management techniques. In this paper, we advocate for a standardized data engineering approach for data science and we present a layered architecture for a data processing pipeline (DPP). This architecture provides a comprehensive conceptual view of DPPs, which next enables the semi-automation of the logical and physical designs of such DPPs.

Keywords: Data science · Data analytics · Data engineering · Data management · Data processing pipeline

1 Introduction

Within the last years *data science*, whose main goal is to extract business value from massive data, has become the most popular research and technological topic as well as the most wanted IT profession, e.g., [12].

Extracting value from data requires deploying a *data processing pipeline* (DPP), which typically includes the following major tasks: (1) integrating heterogeneous and distributed data, (2) cleaning and standardizing data, (3) eliminating duplicates, and (4) storing cleaned data in a centralized repository. Tasks (1)–(4) represent the common backbone to ingest, model, and standardize relevant data, for the final goal to make them ready for analysis. Note that these tasks are generic and therefore, not tailored to a specific data analysis task. Once data are cleaned and stored in a repository, they can be analyzed by the following tasks: (5) extracting a data view from the centralized repository (and potentially persisting it in another repository), (6) specific pre-processing for a given analytical task at hand, (7) creating test and validation data sets (which

© Springer Nature Switzerland AG 2020
M. Song et al. (Eds.): DaWaK 2020, LNCS 12393, pp. 157–166, 2020.
https://doi.org/10.1007/978-3-030-59065-9_13

also include labeling data for supervised machine learning), (8) and analyzing the data by means of descriptive statistical analysis (e.g., reporting or OLAP) or by advanced data analysis: predictive approaches (e.g., machine learning) or graph analytics. This step also includes the deployment in run-time environments of the model created. The design of the DPP requires multiple iterations throughout the aforementioned tasks before deploying a final model. These tasks are based on both data engineering and data analysis technologies.

Data engineering primarily refers to data management, i.e., data ingestion, storage, modeling, processing, and querying, cf. [16], but also embraces system building aspects, e.g., service creation and orchestration. As reported by experts in the field [1,2], up to 80% of time devoted to build a DPP is spent on *pre-processing data* (i.e., tasks (1)–(3) and (6)). This is because such tasks have not been standardized yet and practitioners are approaching them in a case-by-case manner. However, these tasks can benefit from data engineering solutions that could help standardizing them. Indeed, standardization is inevitable in order to achieve the semi-automatization of the most time-consuming and error-prone DPP tasks [14].

A USA job market analysis [17] highlights the relevance of data engineering for data science. Out of the 364,000 estimated data scientist jobs openings in 2020, only 62,000 require analytical skills, and the rest require blended engineering and analytical skills. Similarly, [12] highlights the shortage of 400,000 data workers in Europe blending data engineering and data analysis skills.

A successful application of standardizing DPPs has happened in the domain of Business Intelligence (BI), where for over two decades the industry is applying a reference architecture for data management and On-Line Analytical Processing (OLAP). In this architecture, called the *data warehouse architecture* (DWA), heterogeneous and distributed data sources are integrated by means of a layer called *extract-transform-load* (ETL) or its *extract-load-transform* (ELT) variant. This layer is composed of standardized, i.e., **pre-defined and orchestrated** data processing tasks, which are responsible for a **systematic** preparation of data for further analysis. Then, the data are represented by a multidimensional model that eases the analysis. Note that, for us, standardization does not mean full automation but structuring and orchestrating the DPP in such a way that the system is able to *understand* how data are processed. Indeed, this is the case of ETL DPP pipelines, whose design can hardly be automated, but there are multiple powerful tools that standardize these pipelines as well as facilitate their creation, maintenance (including optimization), and deployment (e.g., IBM Data Stage, Informatica PowerCenter, Ab Initio).

Unfortunately, a standardized approach for data science has not been proposed yet. As a consequence, many companies deploy independent fragments of the whole DPP using multiple technologies and often choose an inadequate technology for a task at hand (e.g., using analytical tools such as R, SAS, or Python scripts for typical data engineering tasks such as integrating heterogeneous and distributed data). This results in non-optimal scenarios, as highlighted in the Beckman Report [3], which advocates for more comprehensive and automatable

DPPs. In the same spirit, [6] calls for adapting data management techniques to the new analytical settings. [4] recommends new solutions for developing an 'end-to-end data-to-insights pipeline', which would encompass among others: metadata management, data provenance, declarative way for defining a data pipeline and its optimization with the support of machine learning techniques. Finally, [19] discusses challenges related to DPPs, w.r.t. data organization, data quality, and feature engineering for analytics, based on real-world use cases.

To sum up, in the current data science approaches, data engineering solutions are mostly neglected. Typically, data engineering and analytical tasks, are conducted by independent teams, resulting in multiple independent DPPs. For this reason, a standardized single end-to-end design of a DPP is needed for the system to understand how data are processed through the whole pipeline and to open the door for semi-automatic optimization of the DPP.

In this paper we propose a **complete** *rethinking* **of DPPs, such that they are orchestrated and unified into one solution**. Accordingly, we discuss how DPPs can benefit from data engineering solutions to standardize, semi-automate, and facilitate data management. Finally, we present an augmented architecture that unifies data engineering and analytical tasks, offering an integrated development, optimization, and execution environment. Section 2 motivates our work with real use cases. Section 3 presents our vision on the augmented architecture.

2   Motivation: Real Cases

In this section we outline two real projects, we currently run, which apply DPPs in a typical way. These particular projects were selected for being representative of practices conducted in several organizations with which the authors collaborate. We especially focus on the bad practices from the data engineering point of view. The practices were identified when these projects started.

- **Development of a data-driven culture in a company.** This project is run at Universitat Politècnica de Catalunya in collaboration with an international company that has several departments developing advanced predictive models for decision making. Each department had a different goal and they focused on different domains. However, most of the data they used were in common, but each department created their own processes to build models. Yet, there was no common data backbone and they independently built their DPPs from data copies stored locally in each department. These copies were in the form of relational database dumps or CSV files, in most of the cases. Importantly, most of the employees were advanced data analysts (with a strong statistical background) but had not been trained in data management techniques. Thus, they did not know where to find relevant data variables for their day-by-day tasks. Simply, they used the datasets at hand within the department and each of them, even inside the same department, created their own DPPs. As the result, even if they were able to share their DPPs in the form of notebooks, each of them executed an independent DPP.

The company identified this lack of data governance as a main drawback since: DPPs were not optimized, data analysts did not have access to relevant variables and data were replicated all over the company without control. Going back to the main tasks described in Sect. 1, this solution neglected the following data engineering solutions:

- Tasks (1)–(4) were not considered at all. They were embedded inside specific analytical DPPs dispersed within the company.
- Task (5) was not implemented. Data were not selected from a common repository but extracted from partial copies. Thus, analysts did not have a clear view on available variables.
- Tasks (6)–(8) were typically conducted in notebooks, on local workstations. Thus, code snippets were executed from scratch each time, without the possibility to share intermediate common results with other DPPs, causing data redundancy.

- **Predicting consumption of thermal energy.** This project is run at Poznan University of Technology for a Polish company that builds co-generating energy grids. The company collects measurements on thermal energy consumption of their customers (a measurement is taken every hour). Monthly measurement data are stored in separate files. The initial set of data includes over 160 csv files with measurements and weather parameters (for years 2016–2020). The goal of this project is to build separate statistical models and ML models for predicting thermal energy consumption. Within the project only one DPP is used, but it is essential to the whole decision support system. All the steps used in the DPP are implemented in Python. With respect to the main tasks described in Sect. 1, this solution neglected the following data engineering solutions:

- Tasks (1)–(3) were implemented as Python scripts and run in a Jupyter notebook on a local workstation. As a consequence, a private cleaned dataset was created each time the script was run.
- Task (4) was implemented as csv files.
- Task (5) was not implemented at all, as data were stored locally in OS files. As a consequence, data were not shared and access to data was non-optimal.
- Tasks (6)–(8) were executed in a Jupyter notebook on a local workstation. For this reason, pre-processing, intermediate results, and model building were executed from scratch each time, without the capability to share the results.

To sum up, from the aforementioned projects we can draw the following observations. First, omitting tasks (1)–(4) in a DPP compromises **data governance, persistence, concurrency, safety, security**, and **performance** [16]. Second, conducting tasks (6)–(8) independently leads to the same problems. Third, omitting task (5) compromises **data sharing**, since there is no single source of truth. The observations from the aforementioned projects and other similar we participated in, result in the augmented data processing architecture that we propose in this paper.

3   Augmented Data Processing Architecture

In this section **we discuss how to overcome the main disadvantages of a data science approach** to building DPPs and **propose an architecture that promotes the benefits of using data engineering solutions**. In particular, this section highlights four essential challenges to advance in the architecture. The architecture we propose is composed of three layers, as shown in Fig. 1. We exemplify it by means of the DPP from the project discussed in Sect. 2.

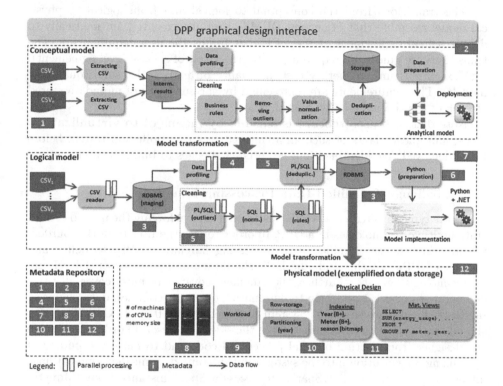

Fig. 1. The augmented data processing architecture

The top layer represents the *conceptual model* of a DPP. The model is designed by means of a unified processing language (cf. Sect. 3.1). The common data engineering and data analysis tasks (cf. Sect. 1) are standardized, i.e., available from a pre-defined palette of tasks. Additionally, the DPP designer can implement UDFs. This model abstracts from an implementation, i.e., from particular technologies and optimization techniques of the DPP. At the conceptual layer we envision user-friendly interfaces in the line of Swan - the data mining service [20] and, to a minor extent - JupyterLab.

The *logical model* instantiates the conceptual one and chooses the appropriate technologies. The logical model leverages workflow optimization techniques (cf. Sect. 3.3) and applies specific data engineering and data analysis solutions per task (e.g., streaming, batch processing, in-memory), including: (1) the **type** of DBMS, e.g., relational, key-value, graph and (2) the most suitable implementation language for each task.

The *physical model* defines physical components, and their parameters, for the logical model. It includes among others: (1) memory size of workstations, (2) the number of CPUs and threads, (3) physical data layout (e.g., column store or row store), (4) physical data structures in a database, (5) if applicable, the size of a hardware cluster.

The transitions from the conceptual to logical and from logical to physical model resemble that of current DBMSs, and are executed automatically to deliver a final deployment of the DPP that fulfills the user requirements. The transitions are guided by requirements (in the spirit of service level agreement), e.g., execution time, monetary cost, or quality of analytical results (quality of models). The requirements are represented by various types of metadata stored at each of the three levels (cf. Sect. 3.2).

Note that such **architecture is feasible by means of to virtualization**. Thus, multiple variants of such an architecture can be built and tested, before being deployed. We identified four essential challenges to build the architecture.

3.1   Challenge 1: Unified Data Processing Language

DPPs are typically created at the logical/physical level forcing the user to orchestrate multiple technologies in a DPP. In order to free the user from this burden, we advocate to use a unified data processing language (DPL) to define and maintain DPPs. To this end, the DPL should sit at the conceptual level and be technology agnostic. Further, the language constructs must cover all tasks enumerated in Sect. 1 and help to automatize the most common data engineering tasks. Ideally, we envision a system equipped with a friendly GUI. The DPL should have a declarative counterpart at the side of the user, in order to alleviate the designer from writing optimal procedural code and to move the burden of optimizing its execution into the system. In this context, some development have already been made, e.g., PySpark - to access a Spark instance from a Jupyter notebook, SparkR - to run R on Spark, KSQL - to execute declarative queries on a Kafka stream, and nipyapi - to access NiFi from Python, but they still does not offer a homogeneous declarative programming environments.

The DPL should include the required information to automate as much as possible the other layers (cf. Fig. 1). The minimum set of features supported by the DPL should include: (1) task orchestration (similar to that of ETL tools), including off-the-shelf operations, (2) notebook-style coding for writing tailored code, i.e., a user-defined function (UDF), and (3) on-line recommendations. The recommendations must include the use of machine learning algorithms to learn the most suitable tasks for a given type of processing. A few approaches have already been proposed for on-line recommendations of DPP tasks, e.g., [10] - where we proposed ML techniques for data pre-processing for classification, or [21] - that addresses hyper-parameter tuning of ML models.

3.2 Challenge 2: Metadata Management

Metadata are essential to: (1) enable data governance, (2) automate different tasks within a DPP, (3) transform one model into another, (4) optimize execution of a DPP, and (5) self-tune the system. Data governance refers to the capability that enables an organization to ensure that high quality data exist throughout the complete data life-cycle. Data governance encompasses characteristics of data sources, data themselves, and data transformations. In the architecture shown in Fig. 1, the following *metadata categories* are needed, in the spirit of [23] (metadata artifacts are depicted in Fig. 1 as rectangles enumerated from |1| to |12|):

- *Data source description* |1|: describing a content and structure of each source.
- *DPP conceptual design* |2|: describing technology-agnostic tasks and their orchestration, represented by conceptual workflow models, such as BPMN.
- *Capabilities of data storage models* |3|: describing a type of data model and its fundamental features: data representation alternatives and data access plans (i.e., full scan, range scan, random access). For example, the metadata may describe relational databases, their row-oriented data storage, and their wide range of indexing capabilities (B+, hashing, bitmap). These metadata is used to select a type of technology and not a specific DBMS.
- *Data characteristics* |4|: describing the set of data characteristics that are required to automate the transformation from the logical to the physical model, obtained by traditional data profiling techniques [5].
- *Rules for data cleaning and deduplication* |5|: describing domain rules for data cleaning and removing duplicates. Such rules must be described in a computer processable manner.
- *Data preparation rules* |6|: describing the rules preparing data for the analytical task at hand, e.g., discretization of values or value imputation [10].
- *DPP logical design* |7|: describing tasks and their orchestration, including the type of technologies chosen, based on the previously mentioned metadata artifacts; e.g., as a data storage a relational DBMS may be selected with a column store and a particular partitioning scheme.
- *Hardware characteristics* |8|: describing the physical parameters needed for cost-based data access optimization (DAO) [11] of the system (e.g., a size of a computer cluster, the number of available CPUs and memory size, disk block size, disk and network bandwidth).
- *Workload description* |9|: describing the analytical workload. Specifically, the characteristics of queries (e.g., the number of tables accessed, functions used) retrieving the needed data for the analytical tasks and frequencies of the queries. These metadata are required by cost-based DAO.
- *Physical data characteristics* |10|: describing the characteristics of stored data (e.g., data cardinality, average record size, number of blocks occupied by a table or any other structure), which are required for cost-based DAO.
- *Characteristics of physical data structures* |11|: describing physical structures created as part of the self-tuning process, e.g.., partitioning schemes or indexes.

– *Run-time monitoring* |12|: describing error logging and execution statistics of the DPP (e.g.., query execution time as well as elapsed processing time, CPU time, and I/O of the whole DPP). These statistics are essential for self-tuning capabilities.

All the components of the architecture must be able to generate and consume inter-operable metadata. To this end, we envision a dedicated subsystem, called a *metadata repository* that systematically gathers metadata from all layers and enables metadata exploitation for diverse tasks, i.e., either data governance or automation [18]. Even though multiple metadata representation and metadata management techniques have been have been proposed, a metadata standard for such a complex architecture has not been developed yet.

3.3   Challenge 3: Workflow Optimization

The whole DPP needs to be optimized using solutions from the cost-based query optimization [11]. The problem of DPP optimization is similar to ETL optimization, which a very difficult and still open problem (c.f., [8] for the state of the art). DPP optimization is becoming more difficult in the presence of UDFs, as they are typically treated as black boxes, i.e., their performance characteristics are not known in advance and their semantics cannot be inferred automatically. To attack this problem, [22] propose to infer a UDF behaviour by means of experiments. [13] proposes to include formalized annotations when deploying an UDF, so that the system can learn basic behavioral aspects of the UDF from the annotations. Finally, we proposed an architecture and method for executing UDFs in a parallel environment [9]. The optimization of a DPP in the architecture presented in Fig. 1 should draw upon these solutions.

The overall optimization idea that we envisage in the architecture is the following. First, a designer creates a DPP in the design interface, using the combination of predefined tasks and UDFs. Second, based on the cost-based optimization techniques the system builds an optimal (in reality sub-optimal) execution model and executes it. Next, from each execution, statistics are collected for the optimizer to learn and evolve the execution model for future use.

3.4   Challenge 4: Self-tuning Capabilities

The system that we propose must support the following self-tuning features:

– From the available data models (e.g., relational, object, semi-structured, NoSQL, graph), identify the most suitable for a common data pipeline.
– Identify the most suitable database type. To this end, each database can be identified by its capabilities and therefore, it should be possible to select the most adequate to a given problem [15].
– Identify the best physical data layout (i.e., row-store, column-store, and pointer-based), taking into account their features [7].

- Identify the best physical data structures to be deployed in the chosen database, i.e., indexes (bitmap, join, B-tree like, hash, spatial), clusters, partitions, materialized views - all of them offer different performance characteristics.
- Identify relevant intermediate results to be materialized to optimize the DPP execution.
- Decide the physical architecture - single node vs. cluster, and types of machines (e.g., disk-based vs. main memory, number of CPUs, RAM size, disk type) and their number.

All of the aforementioned features need to be described by metadata and a cost model of the whole system must be developed. To the best of our knowledge, neither a metadata standard nor a cost model for such complex systems has been developed yet.

4   Conclusions

In this paper we claim that data processing pipelines used by data scientists and by data engineers are immature and do not fully exploit the advantages of the existing data engineering technologies. Current approaches (i.e., *data analytics* and *data engineering*) have their own advantages and disadvantages and they can be substantially improved to increase: development productivity, processing performance, and self-tuning capabilities. Following our claim, we propose an architecture for a modern data processing pipeline with augmented functionalities: (1) a unified data processing language, (2) metadata management, (3) workflow optimization, and (4) self-tuning capabilities. Building and testing such architectures is feasible by means of the virtualization technologies.

The approach that we propose not only aims at improving a DPP design, performance, and maintenance, but also opens numerous new research and technological directions, including:

- the development of a unified data processing language for designing DPPs at the conceptual level;
- a metadata standard for sharing and exchanging metadata by all the DPP components at the conceptual, logical, and physical level;
- cost-based and dynamic optimization of DPPs, including multi-flow optimization;
- optimization of DPPs with user-defined functions;
- the development of a cost model for a complex, multi-layered system;
- self-tuning technologies, e.g., based on machine learning, to optimize DPPs at the logical and physical levels.

Such extensions should open the door to reach DPP-as-a-service.

References

1. Data Warehouse Trends Report. Technical report, Panoply (2018)
2. Data Engineering, Preparation, and Labeling for AI 2019. Technical report, Cognilytica Research (2019)
3. Abadi, D., Agrawal, R., Ailamaki, A., et al.: The Beckman report on database research. Commun. ACM **59**(2), 92–99 (2016)
4. Abadi, D., Ailamaki, A., Andersen, D., et al.: The Seattle report on database research. SIGMOD Rec. **48**(4), 44–53 (2020)
5. Abedjan, Z., Golab, L., Naumann, F., Papenbrock, T.: Data Profiling. Synthesis Lectures on Data Management. Morgan & Claypool, San Rafael (2018)
6. Abiteboul, S., Manolescu, I., Rigaux, P., Rousset, M., Senellart, P.: Web Data Management. Cambridge University Press, Cambridge (2011)
7. Alagiannis, I., Idreos, S., Ailamaki, A.: H2O: a hands-free adaptive store. In: Proceedings of SIGMOD, pp. 1103–1114 (2014)
8. Ali, S.M.F., Wrembel, R.: From conceptual design to performance optimization of ETL workflows: current state of research and open problems. VLDB J. **26**(6), 777–801 (2017). https://doi.org/10.1007/s00778-017-0477-2
9. Ali, S.M.F., Wrembel, R.: Towards a cost model to optimize user-defined functions in an ETL workflow based on user-defined performance metrics. In: Welzer, T., Eder, J., Podgorelec, V., Kamišalić Latifić, A. (eds.) ADBIS 2019. LNCS, vol. 11695, pp. 441–456. Springer, Cham (2019). https://doi.org/10.1007/978-3-030-28730-6_27
10. Bilalli, B., Abelló, A., Aluja-Banet, T., Wrembel, R.: Intelligent assistance for data pre-processing. Comput. Stand. Interf. **57**, 101–109 (2018)
11. Chaudhuri, S.: An overview of query optimization in relational systems. In: Proceedings of PODS, pp. 34–43 (1998)
12. European Commission: Towards a Thriving Data-driven Economy (2018)
13. Ewen, S., Schelter, S., Tzoumas, K., Warneke, D., Markl, V.: Iterative parallel data processing with stratosphere: an inside look. In: Proceedings of SIGMOD, pp. 1053–1056 (2013)
14. Forrester Consulting: Digital Businesses Demand Agile Integration (2019)
15. Gadepally, V., et al.: The BigDAWG polystore system and architecture. In: Proceedings of IEEE HPEC, pp. 1–6 (2016)
16. Garcia-Molina, H., Ullman, J.D., Widom, J.: Database Systems - The Complete Book. Pearson Education, London (2009)
17. IBM: The Quant Crunch Report (2017)
18. Nadal, S., et al.: A software reference architecture for semantic-aware big data systems. Inf. Softw. Technol. **90**, 75–92 (2017)
19. Nazábal, A., Williams, C.K.I., Colavizza, G., Smith, C.R., Williams, A.: Data engineering for data analytics: a classification of the issues, and case studies. CoRR, abs/2004.12929 (2020)
20. Piparo, D., Tejedor, E., Mato, P., Mascetti, L., Moscicki, J.T., Lamanna, M.: SWAN: a service for interactive analysis in the cloud. Future Gener. Comput. Syst. **78**, 1071–1078 (2018)
21. Quemy, A.: Data pipeline selection and optimization. In: Proceedings of DOLAP (2019)
22. Vaandrager, F.: Model learning. Commun. ACM **60**(2), 86–95 (2017)
23. Varga, J., Romero, O., Pedersen, T.B., Thomsen, C.: Analytical metadata modeling for next generation BI systems. J. Syst. Softw. **144**, 240–254 (2018)

Mining Attribute Evolution Rules in Dynamic Attributed Graphs

Philippe Fournier-Viger[1](✉), Ganghuan He[1], Jerry Chun-Wei Lin[2], and Heitor Murilo Gomes[3]

[1] Harbin Institute of Technology (Shenzhen), Shenzhen, China
philfv@hit.edu.cn, heganghuan@gmail.com
[2] Western Norway University of Applied Sciences (HVL), Bergen, Norway
jerrylin@ieee.org
[3] University of Waikato, Waikato, New Zealand
heitor.gomes@waikato.ac.nz

Abstract. A dynamic attributed graph is a graph that changes over time and where each vertex is described using multiple continuous attributes. Such graphs are found in numerous domains, e.g., social network analysis. Several studies have been done on discovering patterns in dynamic attributed graphs to reveal how attribute(s) change over time. However, many algorithms restrict all attribute values in a pattern to follow the same trend (e.g. increase) and the set of vertices in a pattern to be fixed, while others consider that a single vertex may influence its neighbors. As a result, these algorithms are unable to find complex patterns that show the influence of multiple vertices on many other vertices in terms of several attributes and different trends. This paper addresses this issue by proposing to discover a novel type of patterns called *attribute evolution rules* (AER). These rules indicate how changes of attribute values of multiple vertices may influence those of others with a high confidence. An efficient algorithm named AER-Miner is proposed to find these rules. Experiments on real data show AER-Miner is efficient and that AERs can provide interesting insights about dynamic attributed graphs.

Keywords: Dynamic graphs · Attributed graphs · Pattern mining · Attribute evolution rules

1 Introduction

In the last decades, more and more data has been collected and stored in databases. In that context, graphs are playing an increasingly important role because they can model complex structures such as chemical molecules, social networks, computer networks, and links between web pages [5–7,10,15]. To discover interesting knowledge in graphs, algorithms have been proposed to mine various types of patterns such as frequent subgraphs, trees, paths, periodic patterns and motifs [9,15]. However, many studies consider that graphs are static.

© Springer Nature Switzerland AG 2020
M. Song et al. (Eds.): DaWaK 2020, LNCS 12393, pp. 167–182, 2020.
https://doi.org/10.1007/978-3-030-59065-9_14

However, in real life, graphs often evolve, and studying these changes can provide crucial information. Graph data can be encoded as *dynamic graphs* to consider temporal information, i.e., graphs observed at different timestamps, where edges, vertices, and labels may change. Several traditional pattern mining tasks have been extended to cope with dynamic graphs [3, 8]. However, most algorithms can only handle graphs where each edge or vertex is described using one label. But for many applications such as social network mining, it is desirable to describe graph vertices using multiple attributes (e.g. each person may have attributes such as age, gender, location and musical tastes).

To address this issue, a generalization of dynamic graphs has been studied, called *dynamic attributed graphs*, where vertices are described using multiple continuous attributes [5, 6]. This representation allows to store rich information about vertices. Several algorithms have been designed to mine patterns in dynamic attributed graphs to reveal interesting attribute changes over time [5–7, 10]. Although those algorithms have several useful applications, patterns have a simple structure and the algorithms impose many restrictions. For example, Desmier et al. [6] proposed to discover sets of vertices in a dynamic graph, where attributes change in the same way over consecutive timestamps. Hence, patterns involving different types of changes (trends) cannot be found. Cheng et al. [5] partly solved that problem by proposing to find sequences of vertex sets that can contain different trends and attributes. However, a pattern is not allowed to match with more than a vertex set and no measure of confidence is used. Hence, spurious patterns may be found, containing uncorrelated changes. Algorithms by Kaytoue et al. [10] and Fournier-Viger et al. [7] find patterns involving various trends but focus on the influence of single vertices on their neighbors. In other words, these algorithms cannot find complex patterns that show the influence of multiple vertices on other vertices.

This paper addresses these issues by proposing to discover a novel type of patterns called *Attribute Evolution Rules* (AER) which indicate how changes of attribute values of multiple vertices may influence those of others with a high confidence. The contributions of this study are as follows. The problem of mining the novel pattern type of AERs is defined and its properties are studied. The algorithm relies on frequency and confidence measures inspired by association rule mining [1] to ensure that changes in patterns have a strong correlation. AERs are easy to interpret. They indicate likely attribute changes for a subgraph following some attribute changes. Such rule can be useful to predict the future status of a subgraph or to compress a subgraph. An efficient algorithm named AER-miner is proposed to extract these pattern from a dynamic attributed graph. An experimental evaluation was done on two real datasets (airport flight and research collaboration graphs), which shows that the algorithm is efficient and that insightful patterns are found that could not be revealed by previous algorithms. Moreover, two synthetic datasets are generated for experiments.

The rest of this paper is organized as follows. Section 2 reviews related work. Section 3 introduces preliminaries and defines the proposed problem of mining attribute evolution rules. Then, Section 4 describes the designed AER-Miner algorithm, Sect. 5 presents the experimental evaluation, and Sect. 6 draws a conclusion and discusses future work.

2   Related Work

Recently, a large and growing body of work aimed at mining patterns in dynamic attributed graphs, where vertices are annotated with one or more continuous attributes. The first work in this direction was done by Jin et al. [9]. They proposed an algorithm, which first transforms a dynamic attributed graph into a trend graph. A trend graph is a representation of a dynamic attributed graph where attribute values are replaced by trends indicating whether an attribute value has increased, decreased or stayed the same for two consecutive timestamps. Then, the algorithm mines a type of patterns called *trend motif* from the trend graph, which is a connected subgraph where all vertices display the same attribute change (e.g. an increase). An important limitation of that algorithm is that it can only process graphs having a single attribute (called a weighted dynamic graph), and all vertices of a pattern must follow the same trend.

Then, several studies proposed to mine other types of patterns in dynamic attributed graphs using the trend graph representation. To consider multiple attributes, Desmier et al. [6] proposed to mine *cohesive co-evolution patterns* in dynamic attributed graphs. A cohesive co-evolution pattern is a set of vertices that show a same trend during a time interval for one or more attributes, and appear frequently over time. Limitations of this work are that vertices may not be connected and these patterns do not allow to see how a change may influence another change since patterns describe a single time interval.

To study how some changes may influence the structure of a graph, Kaytoue et al. [10] proposed to mine *triggering patterns*. A *triggering pattern* is a rule of the form $L \rightarrow R$, where L is a sequence of attribute variations followed by a single topological change, R. An important limitation of this work is that each pattern consider changes for a single node. Thus, these patterns cannot explain how the attributes of one or more nodes may influence each other. Moreover, a strong restriction is that all rules have a fixed consequent.

Then, Cheng et al. [5] addressed some of these limitations with a novel pattern type named *recurrent patterns*. A recurrent pattern indicates how attribute values have evolved for a set of vertices over more than one time interval. However, a major limitation of this study is that the set of vertices is fixed for a pattern. Thus, this approach does not allow finding general patterns occurring for several sets of vertices having the same topological structure. Moreover, there is no measure of confidence that a change will likely be followed by another change. Hence, spurious patterns may be found containing changes that are uncorrelated to the following changes.

Recently, Fournier-Viger et al. [7] addressed this latter issue by proposing a pattern named *significant trend sequence* indicating a strong correlation between some attribute changes. But this study only considers the very specific case where a node's attributes influence its neighbors' attributes. Thus, it ignores the case where multiple nodes may influence other node's attributes.

In summary, most of the above studies have one or more of the following important limitations: to consider a single attribute [9], to consider a single time interval [6,9], to mine a set of vertices that may not be connected [5,6], to consider that all vertices must follow the same trend(s) [6,9], to consider only the influence of a single node on its neighbors [7], and to not assess whether a change is correlated with a following change [5].

This paper address these issues by proposing a new type of patterns named *attribute evolution rules*. It is a type of rules of the form $A \rightarrow C$ where the antecedent and consequent describe how some attributes have changed for a connected subgraph at two consecutive time intervals. This type of rules is designed to reveal the influence of attribute changes from multiple nodes on those of multiple other nodes, a type of relationship that could not be revealed by prior work. To ensure that strong rules are found, a confidence measure and a lift measure are used inspired by studies on association rule mining [1].

The work that is the closest to the current work is that of Berlingerio et al. [2], which developed an algorithm to mine rules called *graph evolution rules* (GER) in dynamic graphs. A GER indicates that a subgraph having a given topological structure may evolve into another structure thereafter. Another similar concept is that of *link formation rules* (LFR) [12], proposed to study the conditions that result in edges addition in a dynamic graph. A related study also proposed to find correlation and contrast link formation rules [13]. However, a limitation of these studies is that they only handle simple dynamic graphs for the case of edge addition, and do not consider edge or node deletion and relabeling. To address this problem, Scharwachter et al. [14] designed an algorithm named *EvoMiner* to mine rules with both topology and label evolution. But most work on rule mining in dynamic graphs only consider topological evolution rather than label evolution, and are restricted to dynamic graphs containing one attribute. This is unsuitable for real-life applications where graphs have many attributes and studying how they influence each other may reveal useful information.

3   Preliminaries and Problem Definition

This section first introduces preliminaries related to dynamic attributed graphs and then defines the proposed problem.

Definition 1 (Graph). *A graph is a tuple $G = (V, E)$ where V is a vertex set, and $E \subseteq V \times V$ is an edge set.*

Definition 2 (Dynamic attributed graph). *A dynamic attributed graph is a sequence of attributed graphs $\mathcal{G} = \langle G_{t1}, G_{t2}, \ldots, G_{t_{max}} \rangle$ observed at some timestamps $t_1, t_2, \ldots t_{max}$. An attribute graph G_t is a tuple $G_t = (\mathcal{V}_t, \mathcal{A}_t, E_t, \lambda_t)$, where $\mathcal{V}_t$ is a set of vertices, $\mathcal{A}_t$ is a set of attributes, $E_t \subseteq \mathcal{V}_t \times \mathcal{V}_t$ is a set of edges, and $\lambda_t : \mathcal{V}_t \times \mathcal{A}_t \rightarrow \mathbb{R}$ is a function that associates a real value to each vertex-attribute pair, for the timestamp t.*

For instance, Fig. 1 A) shows a dynamic attributed graph observed at timestamps $t_1, t_2 \ldots t_4$, containing two vertices denoted as 1 and 2, connected by a

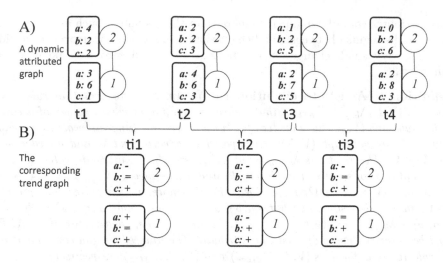

Fig. 1. A) a dynamic attributed graph, B) a trend graph

single edge, and where vertices are described using three numerical attributes a, b and c. It is to be noted that the topological structure is not required to stay the same for different timestamps.

To analyze how attribute values change over time in a dynamic attributed graph, a popular approach is to convert it into a trend graph [5–7,9]. This transformation consists of calculating trends for each time interval (two consecutive timestamps). A trend indicates whether an attribute value has increased, decreased or stayed the same $\{+, -, =\}$ during a time interval.

Definition 3 (Trend graph). *Let there be a dynamic attributed graph $\mathcal{G} = \langle G_{t1}, G_{t2}, \ldots, G_{t_{max}} \rangle$ observed at some timestamps $t1, t2, \ldots t_{max}$. Let there be a set of trends Ω which are set of discrete value indicating attributes status. The trend graph corresponding to $\mathcal{G}$ is a dynamic attributed graph $\mathcal{G}' = \langle G'_1, G'_2, \ldots, G'_{max-1} \rangle$, where $G'_k = (\mathcal{V}'_k, \mathcal{A}'_k, E'_k, \lambda'_k)$ for $1 \leq k \leq max-1$ is an attributed graph where $\lambda'_k : \mathcal{V}'_k \times \mathcal{A}'_k \to \Omega$ is a function that associates a symbol to each vertex-attribute pair and such that (1) $V'_k = V_k$, (2) $E'_k = E_k$, (3) $\mathcal{A}'_k = \mathcal{A}_k$, (4) $\exists (v, a, +) \in \lambda'_k$ iff $\lambda_{k+1}(v, a) - \lambda_k(v, a) > 0$, $\exists (v, a, -) \in \lambda'_k$ iff $\lambda_{k+1}(v, a) - \lambda_k(v, a) < 0$, and $\exists (v, a, =) \in \lambda'_k$ iff $\lambda_{k+1}(v, a) = \lambda_k(v, a)$. In other words, the k-th graph G'_k of a trend graph indicates how attribute values have changed in the **time interval** from timestamp k to $k+1$.*

For instance, Fig. 1 B) shows the trend graph corresponding to the dynamic attributed graph of Fig. 1 A). The trend graph has three time intervals $ti1$, $ti2$ and $ti3$, representing timestamps $t1$ to $t2$, $t2$ to $t3$, and $t3$ to $t4$, respectively. At $ti1$, the attribute a of vertex 2 has a $-$ value because its value decreased from timestamps $t1$ to $t2$.

In this project, $\Omega = \{+, -, =\}$ indicating that an attribute value has increased, decreased or stayed the same. But without loss of generality, contin-

uous attributes could be mapped to more than three symbols such as $++, +, =,$
$-, --$ to distinguish between small changes and larger ones. Moreover, to avoid
detecting very small changes, a constant greater than zero may be used in
Definition 3.

Definition 4 (Attribute evolution rule). *An attribute evolution rule is a
tuple $R : (V, E, \lambda_{before}, \lambda_{after})$ that indicates how the attribute values of a connected subgraph (V, E) have evolved for two consecutive time intervals in a trend
graph $\mathcal{G}'$. The subgraph (V, E) is composed of a vertex set V and an edge set
$E \subseteq V \times V$. The relations λ_{before} and λ_{after} specify the attribute values of the
vertices at two consecutive time intervals, and are defined as $\lambda_{before} : V \times \mathcal{A} \rightarrow \Omega$
and $\lambda_{after} : V \times \mathcal{A} \rightarrow \Omega$, respectively. Furthermore, it is required that for all
$v \in V$, there exists some attributes $a, b \in \mathcal{A}$ and some values $\omega, \gamma \in \Omega$ such that
$(v, a, \omega) \in \lambda_{before}$ and $(v, b, \gamma) \in \lambda_{after}$. In other words, each vertex of an AER
must be described using at least one attribute. The antecedent and consequent of
the rule R are defined as (V, E, λ_{before}) and (V, E, λ_{after}), respectively.*

For instance, consider the four attributes $A = \{a, b, c, d\}$ of the trend graph of
Fig. 1 B). Figure 2 shows an attribute evolution rule consisting of three vertices
$V = \{x, y, z\}$ and two edges $E = \{(x, y), (y, z)\}$ indicating how attributes values
have changed for two successive time intervals. For instance, it indicates that
the attribute a of vertex x has increased $(a+)$ and the attribute b of vertex z
has decreased $(b-)$, which then caused vertex y's attribute c to increase and
attribute d to decrease at the next timestamp.

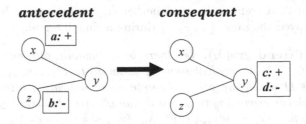

Fig. 2. An attribute evolution rule

An attribute evolution rule R may have multiple occurrences in a trend
graph, called *matches*. A match of a rule R is an injective mapping between the
vertices of the rule and a set of vertices of two consecutive time intervals of a
trend graph. It is formally defined as follows.

Definition 5 (Matches of an attribute evolution rule). *Let there be a
trend graph $\mathcal{G}'$ and a rule $R : (V, E, \lambda_{before}, \lambda_{after})$. The rule R is said to have
an match ϕ from time interval j to $j+1$ iff there exists a subgraph (V_S, E_S) such
that $V_S \subseteq \mathcal{V}'_j \cap \mathcal{V}'_{j+1}. E_S \subseteq \mathcal{E}'_j \cap \mathcal{E}'_{j+1}$, and ϕ is a bijective mapping $\phi \subseteq V \times V_S$
such that $\exists (v_x, v_y) \in E \Leftrightarrow \exists (\phi(v_x), \phi(v_y)) \in E_S$. Moreover, it is required that
$\forall (v, a) \in \lambda_{before} \Rightarrow \exists (\phi(v), a) \in \lambda'_j$ and $\forall (v, a) \in \lambda_{after} \Rightarrow \exists (\phi(v), a) \in \lambda'_{j+1}$.*

Based on the concept of match, the support (occurrence frequency) of an AER in a trend graph can be defined. However, one needs to be careful about how to define the support because a subgraph may have many matches and some of them may overlap [4]. If one simply defines the support of a subgraph as its number of matches, then the support measure is neither monotonic nor anti-monotonic, and thus would not allow to reduce the search space, but this is important for developing an efficient pattern mining algorithm. To obtain an anti-monotonic support measure for attribute evolution rules, this paper defines the support as follows, inspired by the concept of minimum image based support used in frequent subgraph mining in a single graph [4].

Definition 6 (C-support of a rule). *Let $matches_{j,j+1}(R, \mathcal{G}')$ be all matches of an attribute evolution rule R in a trend graph $\mathcal{G}'$ for time interval j to $j+1$. The c-support of R in $\mathcal{G}'$ is defined as $support(R, \mathcal{G}') = \sum_{j=1...max-2} min_{v \in V} | \{\phi(v) : \phi \in matches_{j,j+1}(R, \mathcal{G}')\} |$. In other words, the c-support of R for two consecutive time intervals is the least number of distinct consequent nodes (from $\mathcal{G}'$) that a vertex from R is mapped to. And the c-support of R in the whole trend graph $\mathcal{G}'$ is the sum of R's support for all consecutive time intervals.*

For example, consider the small trend graph of Fig. 3 (left), where some irrelevant attribute values have been omitted. Figure 3 (right) shows the c-support of three AERs, having 3, 2, and 3 matches, respectively, and a c-support of 2. A proof that the c-support measure is anti-monotonic is given below.

Lemma 1 (Anti-monotonicity of the c-support). *If an AER R_2 is an attribute extension of another rule R_1, then $support(R_1) \geq support(R_2)$.*

Proof. Let γ be the c-support of a rule R_1, and R_2 be an attribute extension of R_1. Since the c-support is the least number of distinct *consequent* nodes, the total number of different consequent of R_1 is γ. To obtain R_2, an attribute is added to R_1, and each mapping of R_1 can either be extended (+1) with the attribute or not (+0) to obtain a mapping for R_2. Hence, $support(R_2) \leq \gamma \leq support(R_1)$.

Though the c-support measure is useful to filter infrequent patterns, it is desirable to also assess how correlated the attributes of a rule are to filter out spurious rules. In pattern mining, some popular measures to assess the correlation between the consequent (C) and antecedent (A) of a rule $A \rightarrow C$ that do not consider time are the confidence and lift [1,11]. The confidence of a rule is the ratio of its support to that of its antecedent, that is $conf(A \rightarrow C) = sup(A \cap C)/sup(A)$, which is an estimation of $P(C|A) = P(A \cap C)/P(A)$. But a drawback of the confidence is that it does not consider $P(C)$. The lift addresses this problem. For this reason, we use the *lift* as main measure to select interesting rules. The lift is defined as $lift(A \rightarrow C) = P(A \cap C)/[P(A) \times P(C)] = conf(A \rightarrow C)/P(C)$. The confidence can be rewritten as $P(C|A) = [P(A|C) \times P(C)]/P(A)$ by the Bayes's theorem. Based on this observation and because $P(C)$ for AERs is constant while $P(A)$ can contain many vertices and change, we redefine the confidence as $P(A|C)$, which we call the *confidence based on consequent (c-confidence)*. This measure can also find strongly correlated patterns but is easier to calculate than the original confidence. Then, the lift can be rewritten as $P(A|C)/P(A)$. The proposed AER-Miner algorithm checks both the c-confidence and lift of rules to filter spurious rules.

Definition 7 (C-confidence of a rule). *The c-confidence of an AER R :* $(V, E, \lambda_{before}, \lambda_{after})$ *in a trend graph* $\mathcal{G}'$ *is defined as* $conf(R, \mathcal{G}') = Support(R,$ $\mathcal{G}')/Support(Consequent, \mathcal{G}')$.

Definition 8 (Expected confidence of an antecedent attribute). *The Expected confidence of an antecedent attribute a in a trend graph* $\mathcal{G}'$ *is defined as* $expectedConf(a) = P(a)$ *if there is no rule consequent and as* $expectedConf(a)$ $= P(a|c)$ *if there is a consequent attribute c.*

Definition 9 (Lift of a rule). *The lift of an AER R in a trend graph* $\mathcal{G}'$ *is defined as* $lift(R, \mathcal{G}') = conf(R, \mathcal{G}')/expectedConf(antecedent, \mathcal{G}')$. *The expected confidence of the antecedent attribute is the probability that its attributes will appear without other conditional influence. The lift is the ratio of the real probability to the expected probability and it can measure the effect of adding an attribute to the antecedent of a smaller pattern. The lift can thus assess if the consequent and antecedent are correlated. A lift less than, equal to, and greater than 1, indicates a negative correlation, no correlation and a positive correlation, respectively.*

For instance, consider the trend graph of Fig. 3 (left), and that each trend $\{-, =, +\}$ has a uniform occurrence probability (each attribute's expected confidence is $1/3$). Figure 3 (right) shows the c-support and c-confidence of three rules. The lift of rule $< (a+) > \to < (c+) >$ is $(3/5)/(1/3) = 9/5$. The lift of $< (b-) > \to < (c+) >$ is $(2/5)/(1/3) = 6/5$. The c-confidence of $< (a+), (b-) > \to < (c+) >$ can be calculated when adding attribute $b-$ to rule $< (a+) > \to < (c+) >$, as $conf = P(b - | < (a+) > \to < (c+) >) = 2/3$. Thus, its lift is $5/3$.

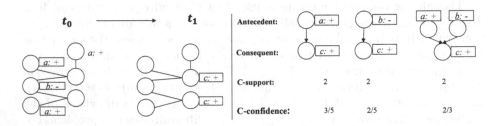

Fig. 3. The c-support and c-confidence of three AERs

Definition 10 (Problem setting). *Given a dynamic attributed graph* $\mathcal{G}$, *a minimum support threshold minsup, a minimum confidence threshold minconf,* *and a minimum lift threshold minlift, the problem of AER mining is to output all valid AERs. A rule R is **frequent** if support$(R, \mathcal{G}') \geq$ minsup. A rule is said to be **valid** if it is frequent, conf$(R, \mathcal{G}') \geq$ minconf and lift$(R, \mathcal{G}') \geq$ minlift.*

The traditional problem of mining frequent patterns in a graph is a hard problem because the number of patterns is very large and it requires to do subgraph isomorphism checking, which is an NP-complete problem [4]. The problem of AER mining is more difficult for two reasons. First, the graph is dynamic and thus finding matches of each rule must be done for many time intervals. Second, considering many attributes greatly increases the number of potential patterns. Let there be a trend graph containing v distinct vertices and e distinct edges transformed into a trend graph using a set of trends Ω. The number of possible attribute value combinations for each vertex is $(2^{|a|} - 1) \times |\Omega|$. The number of edges combinations to create a subgraph is $(2^{|e|} - 1)$ if we ignore the requirements that subgraphs must be connected[1]. And since a rule has an antecedent and consequent and there are v vertices, the search space is in the worst case roughly $2 \times (2^{|e|} - 1) \times v \times (2^{|a|} - 1) \times 3$, so a pruning strategy must be used.

4 The AER-Miner Algorithm

This section introduces the proposed AER-Miner algorithm to efficiently find all AERs in a dynamic attributed graph (or trend graph). An attribute evolution rule R is a tuple of the form $R : (V, E, \lambda_{before}, \lambda_{after})$, where V_{before} and V_{after} are relations mapping nodes of the rule's antecedent and consequent to attribute values (for two consecutive timestamps), and where each node may be described using multiple attributes. Hence, the structure of an AER is relatively complex. Thus, rather than trying to enumerate all AERs directly, the proposed algorithm first finds core patterns, which are a simplified form of AERs. AER-Miner performs a breadth-first search using a generate-candidate-and-test strategy to explore the search space of core patterns. Then, core patterns are merged to obtain the AERs. The benefit of using this approach is that part of the AER mining problem can be solved using a modified frequent subgraph mining algorithm. The following paragraphs describe the main steps of AER-Miner and how it reduces the search space. Then, the pseudo-code is presented.

Step 1: Generating 1-Size Core Patterns. The algorithm first considers each attribute from the dynamic attributed graph to generate core patterns having that attribute as consequent.

Definition 11 (Core Pattern). *A core pattern is an AER composed of a consequent node and several antecedent nodes, where each consequent-antecedent node pair is connected. Moreover, each node is described using a single attribute. We define a k-size pattern as a core pattern whose total vertice count is k. A core pattern of size $k >= 2$, can be considered as an attribute evolution rule.*

---

[1] It was observed using computer simulations that the number of connected labeled graphs with $v = 2, 3, 4, 5, 6, 7$, and 8 nodes is 1, 4, 38, 728, 26,704, 1,866,256, and 251,548,592, respectively (https://oeis.org/A001187).

AER-Miner calculates the expected confidence of each attribute, that is without considering the impact of other attributes.

Step 2: Extending Core Patterns. Then, AER-Miner extends the initial core patterns to generate larger core patterns. A generate-candidate-and-test approach is utilized where a core pattern is extended by adding a new node with an attribute to the antecedent node list of a pattern to obtain a novel core pattern. This is done iteratively following a breadth-first search. During an iteration, k-1 size patterns are combined to generate k-size patterns, and this process ends when no new pattern can be generated. To avoid generating a same pattern more than once, attributes are sorted according to the lexicographical order, and an attribute is used to extend a core pattern only if it is larger than the last attribute in the pattern's antecedent node list. To reduce the search space and filter many uninteresting patterns, attributes that have no changes for an attribute (=) are not used for extending core patterns.

Moreover, the support measure is used for reducing the search space. While some other studies have defined the support of a pattern as the number of its instances (called matches), this measure is not anti-monotonic. In other words, an extension of a core pattern may have more, the same number, or less matches. To be able to reduce the search space, the redefined support measure (Definition 6) is used, which is anti-monotonic. Thus, if a core patterns has a support less than $minsup$, it can be safely ignored as well as all its extensions. This search space pruning property can considerably reduce the search space.

Besides, the lift measure (Definition 9) is also used to reduce the search space. If the lift of a core pattern is less than $minlift$, it is discarded and all its extensions are ignored. The proof that the lift is anti-monotonic w.r.t core pattern extensions is omitted due to the page limitation.

Step 3: Filtering and Merging Core Patterns to Obtain AERs. After obtaining all core patterns, AER-Miner filters core patterns based on their confidence. The reason for filtering patterns at Step 3 rather than Step 2 is that the confidence is not anti-monotonic. In other words, extending a rule antecedent with more attributes may result in a rule having a greater, smaller or equal confidence. For example, the confidence of a rule $(A) \rightarrow (C)$ may be larger than that of a rule $(A, B) \rightarrow (C)$, where A and B are two attributes of different nodes. The reason is that A and B may each have a positive correlation with C.

Thereafter, the remaining core patterns are merged to obtain the AERs that respect the pattern selection conditions. A pair of core patterns is merged to generate an AER if (1) they have the same antecedent attributes and (2) they have the same consequent. A merge operation is considered successful if more than 90% of the support is retained.

The Pseudocode. AER-Miner (Algorithm 1) takes as input a dynamic attributed graph $\mathcal{G}$ or trend graph $\mathcal{G}'$, and the $minsup$, $minlift$ and $minconf$ thresholds. The algorithm first initializes a map structure for storing candidate core patterns. All patterns having a single consequent attribute are added to that map (Line 1). Then, all possible core patterns are generated and stored in a list (Line 2). Then a loop is performed to iteratively generate larger core patterns (Line 3 to 21). Finally, uninteresting patterns are filtered using $minconf$, and others are merged to obtain the set of AERs.

Algorithm 1: The AER-Miner algorithm

---

input : a dynamic attributed graph $\mathcal{G}$ or trend graph $\mathcal{G}'$, the $minsup$, $minlift$ and $minconf$ thresholds

output: all the valid attribute evolution rules

1 Initialize a core pattern Map $map_{candidates}$ <core pattern,instances> for growing patterns. Initially, each pattern contains one consequent attribute.

2 Initialize a list $list_{patterns}$ for storing all possible core patterns.

3 **while** $map_{candidates} \neq \emptyset$ **do**

4      $map_{k+1sizecandidate} \Leftarrow \emptyset$

5   **foreach** $candidate \in map_{candidates}$ **do**

6          $pattern \leftarrow candidate.key$

7          $instances \leftarrow candidate.value$

8   **foreach** $attr \in attributelist$ **do**

9   **if** $attr \geq$ the last attribute of pattern and $attr \neq '='$ **then**

10                $newPattern \leftarrow pattern \cup attr$

11                $newInstances \leftarrow extendInstances(pattern, attr, instaces)$

12                $support \Leftarrow sizeofnewInstance$

13                $lift, confidence \leftarrow calLiftAndConfi(pattern, attr, instaces)$

14   **if** $support \geq minsup$ and $lift \geq minlift$ **then**

15                    $put < newPattern, newInstance > \in map_{k+1sizecandidate}$

16   **end**

17   **end**

18   **end**

19   **end**

20     $list_{patterns} \leftarrow list_{patterns} \cup map_{k+1sizecandidate}$

21 **end**

22 $list_{patterns} \leftarrow filterPatterns(list_{patterns}, minconf)$

23 Return $AERs = list_{patterns} \cup mergePatterns(list_{patterns})$

---

5 Experimental Evaluation

Experiments were performed to evaluate the performance of AER-Miner and its ability to discover interesting patterns in real data. AER-Miner was implemented in Java and experiments were carried out on a 3.6 GHz Intel Xeon PC with 32 GB of main memory, running Windows 10. Two real world datasets were used in the experiments and two synthetic datasets were generated to assess the statistical validity of AERs. The source code of AER-Miner and datasets can be downloaded from the open-source SPMF data mining library http://www.philippe-fournier-viger.com/spmf/. The following datasets were used:

DBLP [6] is a co-authorship dataset containing data from the DBLP online bibliographic service. There are 2,723 vertices, each representing an author having published at least 10 papers in data mining and/or database conferences/journals between 1990 to 2010. This time period is divided into nine timestamps: ([1990–1994][1992–1996]...[2004–2008][2006–2010]). An edge indicates a co-authorship relation between two authors, while an attribute value indicates the number of papers published by an author in a conference/journal.

US Fight [10] contains data about US air traffic during the Katrina hurricane period (from 01/08/2005 to 25/09/2005). Vertices stand for US airports. Two vertices are connected by an edge if there was a flight connecting them during the time period.

Moreover, we randomly generated two datasets, named *synthetic-DBLP* and *synthetic-USFlight*. They have the same vertex, average edge, timestamp and attribute count as the DBLP and US Flight datasets, respectively. But attribute values of each vertex were generated following a Gaussian distribution. Characteristics of the datasets are as follows. The number of vertices, average edges per timestamps, timestamps and attribute count for DBLP and synthetic DBLP is 2,723, 10,737, 9 and 43, while for the US Flight and synthetic-USFlight, it is 280, 1,206, 8 and 8.

Statistical Validation Experiment. The first experiment was designed to check if AER-Miner can find statistically valid rules and determine an appropriate range of *minlift* values to obtain valid rules. For this purpose, AER-Miner was run on each real dataset and the corresponding synthetic dataset while varying the *minlift* parameter. Because an AER describes the correlation between the attributes of a rule's antecedent and consequent, and that synthetic datasets have the same structure as real datasets except for the randomly generated attribute values, no AER should be found in the synthetic datasets for high enough *minlift* values. The *minlift* threshold was increased from 1.05 (weak positive correlation) to 1.4 (strong positive correlation) while noting the number of patterns found. The *minsup* threshold was set to a fixed value (0.004 for DBLP and 0.004 for US Flight) that is high enough to find patterns, but *minsup* was not varied because it has a small influence on correlation.

Figure 4 shows results for the (a) DBLP and (b) US Flight datasets. It can be observed that no AER was found in synthetic datasets in most cases, while some were found in real data. This is reasonable as synthetic datasets contain random values that are weakly correlated. Because AERs were found in synthetic data for *minlift* < 1.1, it can be concluded that this parameter should be set to a value of at least 1.1 to find valid rules. Otherwise, random AERs may be found.

Quantitative Experiments. Three additional experiments were done to evaluate the influence of dataset characteristics and parameters values on the performance of AER-Miner in terms of runtime and peak memory usage.

First, the influence of a dynamic attributed graph's properties on performance was assessed. Attribute count was first varied, while parameter values where fixed (*minsup* = 0.04, *minlift* = 1.3 and *minconf* = 0.3). Figure 5 (a) shows the influence of attribute count on runtime and memory for the DBLP

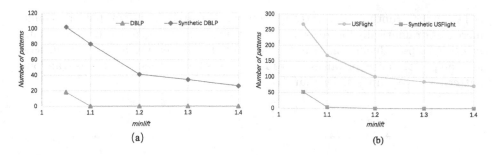

Fig. 4. Statistical validation with real and synthetic datasets.

dataset. As attribute count increased, execution times and memory consumption increased. But there is a difference between the growth rate of execution time and memory. At first, when attribute count is small, execution time increases slowly. Then, when the attribute count becomes quite large, its grows more quickly and then remains stable. For memory, it is the opposite. This is because when the attribute count is small, no attribute correlations are found. Thus, most of the memory is spent for storing the dynamic attributed graph, while as the attribute count increases, much memory is spent to store (candidate) patterns in memory.

Second, the influence of a dynamic attributed graph's graph count (number of timestamps) on performance was evaluated. Figure 5 (b) shows results for the US Flight dataset when the algorithm's parameters are fixed ($minsup = 0.04$, $minlift = 1.3$ and $minconf = 0.3$). It is found that execution time linearly increases and memory also increases as graph count increases. This shows that AER-Miner has excellent scalability for processing numerous time periods.

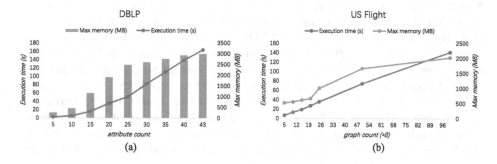

Fig. 5. Influence of attribute count and graph count on performance.

Third, an experiment was done on DBLP to evaluate the influence of the $minsup$ and $minlift$ thresholds on runtime and pattern count. Figure 6 (a) shows results when $minsup$ is varied while $minlift = 1.3$ and $minconf = 0.3$ are fixed. Figure 6 (b) presents results when $minlift$ is increased while $minsup = 0.004$ and $minconf = 0.2$ are fixed. It is found in Fig. 6 (a) that as the $minsup$ constraint is less strict, runtime and pattern count are greater, and that pattern count increases dramatically for $minsup = 0$. It is observed in Fig. 6 (b) that increasing $minlift$ helps reducing the search space and that increasing $minlift$ influences less the performance for values above 1.4. This is because most spurious (random patterns) have a lift smaller than 1.4.

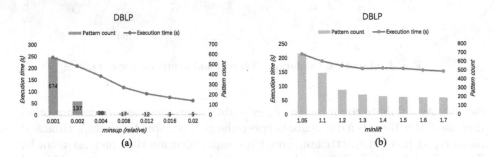

Fig. 6. Influence of $minsup$ and $minlift$ on runtime and pattern count.

Qualitative Assessment. An additional evaluation was performed on the DBLP and US Flight datasets to assess the usefulness of patterns found. First, rules were extracted from DBLP using $minsup = 0.004$, $minlift = 1.5$ and $minconf = 0.3$. An example pattern found is $< (PVLDB+), (PVLDB+), (PVLDB+) > \rightarrow < (VLDB-) >$. It indicates that co-authors of an author who published more papers in PVLDB then published less papers in VLDB at the next timestamp. This is reasonable since there is a correlation between VLDB and PVLDB and a person is likely to follow trends of his co-authors. Another pattern is $< (ICDE+) > \rightarrow < (PVLDB+, EDBT+) >$, which indicates that if an author published more ICDE papers, his co-authors are more likely to publish more in PVLDB and EDBT. Second, rules were extracted using $minsup = 0.004$, $minlift = 1.24$ and $minconf = 0.3$ from US Flight to discover rules related to the impact of Hurricane Katrina on flights. The pattern $< (NbDeparture-) > \rightarrow < (NbCancelation+) >$ was found to have many occurrences. It indicates that departure cancellations caused by the hurricane are strongly correlated with a flight cancellation increase at the next timestamp. Another interesting pattern is $< (NbDeparture+), (NbDeparture+), (NbDeparture+) > \rightarrow < (NbDeparture+) >$, which indicates that flights are returning to normal after a hurricane.

6   Conclusion

This paper has proposed a novel type of patterns called attribute evolution rules, indicating how changes of attribute values of multiple vertices may influence those of others with a high confidence. An efficient algorithm named AER-Miner was proposed to find these rules. Moreover, experiments on real data have shown that the proposed algorithm is efficient and that AERs can provide interesting insights about real-life dynamic attributed graphs. In future work, we plan to extend AER-Miner to let the user specify temporal constraints on AERs and discover concise representations of AERs.

References

1. Agrawal, R., Srikant, R., et al.: Fast algorithms for mining association rules. In: Proceedings of 20th International Conference Very Large Data Bases, VLDB, vol. 1215, pp. 487–499 (1994)
2. Berlingerio, M., Bonchi, F., Bringmann, B., Gionis, A.: Mining graph evolution rules. In: Buntine, W., Grobelnik, M., Mladenić, D., Shawe-Taylor, J. (eds.) ECML PKDD 2009. LNCS (LNAI), vol. 5781, pp. 115–130. Springer, Heidelberg (2009). https://doi.org/10.1007/978-3-642-04180-8_25
3. Borgwardt, K., Kriegel, H., Wackersreuther, P.: Pattern mining in frequent dynamic subgraphs. In: Proceedings of the 6th IEEE International Conference on Data Mining, pp. 1818–822 (2006)
4. Bringmann, B., Nijssen, S.: What is frequent in a single graph? In: Washio, T., Suzuki, E., Ting, K.M., Inokuchi, A. (eds.) PAKDD 2008. LNCS (LNAI), vol. 5012, pp. 858–863. Springer, Heidelberg (2008). https://doi.org/10.1007/978-3-540-68125-0_84
5. Cheng, Z., Flouvat, F., Selmaoui-Folcher, N.: Mining recurrent patterns in a dynamic attributed graph. In: Kim, J., Shim, K., Cao, L., Lee, J.-G., Lin, X., Moon, Y.-S. (eds.) PAKDD 2017. LNCS (LNAI), vol. 10235, pp. 631–643. Springer, Cham (2017). https://doi.org/10.1007/978-3-319-57529-2_49
6. Desmier, E., Plantevit, M., Robardet, C., Boulicaut, J.-F.: Cohesive co-evolution patterns in dynamic attributed graphs. In: Ganascia, J.-G., Lenca, P., Petit, J.-M. (eds.) DS 2012. LNCS (LNAI), vol. 7569, pp. 110–124. Springer, Heidelberg (2012). https://doi.org/10.1007/978-3-642-33492-4_11
7. Fournier-Viger, P., Cheng, C., Cheng, Z.X., Lin, J.C.W., Selmaoui-Folcher, N.: Mining significant trend sequences in dynamic attributed graphs. Knowl. Based Syst. **182**(15), 1–25 (2019)
8. Fournier-Viger, P., et al.: A survey of pattern mining in dynamic graphs. WIREs Data Mining Knowl. Discov. e1372. https://doi.org/10.1002/widm.1372
9. Jin, R., McCallen, S., Almaas, E.: Trend motif: a graph mining approach for analysis of dynamic complex networks. In: Proceedings of the 7th IEEE International Conference on Data Mining, pp. 541–546. IEEE (2007)
10. Kaytoue-Uberall, M., Pitarch, Y., Plantevit, M., Robardet, C.: Triggering patterns of topology changes in dynamic graphs. In: 2014 IEEE/ACM International Conference on Advances in Social Networks Analysis and Mining, pp. 158–165 (2014)
11. Lenca, P., Vaillant, B., Meyer, P., Lallich, S.: Association rule interestingness measures: experimental and theoretical studies. In: Guillet, F.J., Hamilton, H.J. (eds.) Quality Measures in Data Mining. SCI, vol. 43, pp. 51–76. Springer, Heidelberg (2007). https://doi.org/10.1007/978-3-540-44918-8_3
12. Leung, C.W., Lim, E., Lo, D., Weng, J.: Mining interesting link formation rules in social networks. In: Proceedings of the 19th ACM Conference on Information and Knowledge Management, pp. 209–218 (2010)
13. Ozaki, T., Etoh, M.: Correlation and contrast link formation patterns in a time evolving graph. In: Proceedings of the Workshops of 11th IEEE International Conference on Data Mining, pp. 1147–1154 (2011)

14. Scharwächter, E., Müller, E., Donges, J.F., Hassani, M., Seidl, T.: Detecting change processes in dynamic networks by frequent graph evolution rule mining. In: Proceedings of the 16th IEEE International Conference on Data Mining, pp. 1191–1196 (2016)
15. Yan, X., Han, J.: gSpan: graph-based substructure pattern mining. In: Proceedings of the 2002 IEEE International Conference on Data Mining, pp. 721–724 (2002)

Sustainable Development Goal Relational Modelling: Introducing the SDG-CAP Methodology

Yassir Alharbi[1,3(✉)], Frans Coenen[1], and Daniel Arribas-Bel[2]

[1] Department of Computer Science, The University of Liverpool,
Liverpool L69 3BX, UK
{yassir.alharbi,coenen}@liverpool.ac.uk
[2] Department of Geography and Planning, The University of Liverpool,
Liverpool L69 3BX, UK
d.arribas-bel@liverpool.ac.uk
[3] Almahd College, Taibah University, Medina, Saudi Arabia

Abstract. A mechanism for predicting whether individual regions will meet there UN Sustainability for Development Goals (SDGs) is presented which takes into consideration the potential relationships between time series associated with individual SDGs, unlike previous work where an independence assumption was made. The challenge is in identifying the existence of relationships and then using these relationships to make SDG attainment predictions. To this end the SDG Correlation/Causal Attainment Prediction (SDG-CAP) methodology is presented. Five alternative mechanisms for determining time series relationships are considered together with three prediction mechanisms. The results demonstrate that by considering the relationships between time series, by combining a number of popular causal and correlation identification mechanisms, more accurate SDG forecast predictions can be made.

Keywords: Time series correlation and causality · Missing values · Hierarchical classification · Time series forecasting · Sustainable Development Goals

1 Introduction

Time series forecasting is a significant task undertaken across many domains [2,5,24]. The basic idea, given a previously unseen time series, is to predict the next point or points in the series. This is usually conducted using single-variate time series, although in some cases multi-variate time series are considered [5,24]. Given a short time series this is a particular challenge [13]. One application domain where this is the case is in the context of the data published with respect to the United Nations (UN) Sustainability for Development Goals (SDGs) [26]. Where, at time of writing, data spanning only 19 years was available; in other words times series comprised of a maximum of only 19 points. The SDG short

© Springer Nature Switzerland AG 2020
M. Song et al. (Eds.): DaWaK 2020, LNCS 12393, pp. 183–196, 2020.
https://doi.org/10.1007/978-3-030-59065-9_15

time series challenge is compounded by the large number of missing values that are a feature of the data set, meaning that many time series comprise fewer than 19 points. The aim here is to use the available short time series data to forecast whether a particular geographic region will meet the UN SDGs or not.

In [1] a SDG Attainment Prediction (SDG-AP) methodology was presented founded on the idea of a taxonomic hierarchy and designed to answer the question *"will geographic region x meet goal y by time t"*. The solution was conceptualised as a bottom-up hierarchical Boolean ("yes/no") classification problem. Each node within the taxonomic hierarchy had a Boolean classifier associated with it. The classifiers associated with the leaf nodes were built using the time series available within the UN SDG data set. The remaining nodes in the tree were associated with simple Boolean functions that took input from their child nodes. However, the leaf node classifiers were built assuming that each goal was independent of any other goals. This is clearly not the case. For example, the "No Poverty" and "Quality Education" SDGs are clearly related. Similarly, the time series associated with the goal "Clean Water and Sanitation" in (say) the geographic region "Egypt" are clearly related to the time series associated with the same goal in similar regions.

The hypothesis presented in this paper is that better SDG attainment prediction accuracy can be obtained by considering the possible relationships between SDG time series. Thus, with reference to [1], instead of building each leaf node classifier according to the relevant time series data (a one-to-one correspondence), it is proposed in this paper that it might be better if the time series data sets used to build the classifiers were more comprehensive, in other words, founded on a set of co-related time series. The challenge is then how to identify these related time series.

Given the above, this paper proposes the SDG Correlation/Causal Attainment Prediction (SDG-CAP) methodology designed to address the disadvantages associated with the work presented in [1], although the work in [1] provides an excellent forecasting benchmark. The main challenge is determining which time series are influenced by which other time series. This can be done by hand given a domain expert and sufficient time resource. However, automating the process is clearly much more desirable. The work presented in this paper provides a potential solution to this problem with a focus on time series within the same geographic region, as opposed to the same time series across different geographic areas (the latter is an item for future work). In the context of the proposed SDG-CAP methodology, this paper makes three contributions:

1. An investigation into mechanisms whereby relationships between short time series can be discovered.
2. A comparative investigation of missing value imputation methods.
3. The usage of multi-variate time series forecasting given known relationships across short time series.

Five mechanism are considered whereby relationships between time series can be discovered: (i) Granger Causality [10], (ii) Temporal Causal Discovery Framework (TCDF) [20], (iii) Least Absolute Shrinkage Selector Operator (LASSO)

[29], (iv) Pearson Correlation [4] and (v) a combination of all four. The effectiveness of the proposed mechanism is considered by comparing the forecast results produced with those given in [1] using Root Mean Square Error (RMSE) [14] as the comparater metric and a number of forecasting mechanisms.

The rest of the paper organised as follows. In the following section, Sect. 2, a brief literature review of the previous work underpinning the work presented in this paper is given. The SDG application domain and the SDG time series data set is described in Sect. 3. The proposed SDG-CAP methodology is then described in Sect. 4 and the evaluation of the proposed methodology in Sect. 5. The paper concludes with a summary of the main findings, and a number of proposed direction for future research, in Sect. 6.

2   Literature Review

In this section, a review of existing work directed at discovering relationships between time series is presented. A relationship between two-time series can be expressed either in terms of causality [3] or in terms of correlation [4]. Causality implies that a change in one variable results in a change in the other in either a positive or a negative manner. An alternative phrase for causality is "strong relationship". Correlation implies that the values associated with two variables change in a positive or negative manner with respect to one another [4]. Correlation can be viewed as a specialisation of causality, implying that a causal relationship signals the presence of correlation; however, the reverse statement does not hold. Each is discussed in further detail in the following two sub-sections, Subsects. 2.1 and 2.2, with respect to the specific mechanisms investigated in this paper. Five mechanisms are considered in total, two causality mechanisms, two correlation mechanisms and a combined mechanism. The first four were selected because they are frequently referenced in the literature. Collectively we refer to these mechanisms as *filtration* methods [34] because they are used to filter time series data (specifically SDG time series) so as to determine which time series are related in some way. This section then goes on, Subsect. 2.3, to consider relevant previous work directed at time series forecasting

2.1   Causality

As noted above, two causality mechanisms are considered in this paper: Granger Causality and the Temporal Causal Discovery Framework (TCDF). Granger causality is the most frequently cited mechanism for establishing causality found in the literature [17,19,21,22]. Granger Causality was introduced in the late 60s [10] and is fundamentally a statistical test of the hypothesis that an independent time series x can be used to forecast a dependent time series y. Granger causality is determined as defined by Eq. 1 using the value of time series X "past lags", and the value of time series y past lags plus a residual error e. Granger Causality has been used previously to determine the relationship between pairs of values in SDG time series as reported in [7]. However, the study was only able to find

20,000 pairs of values in the SDG data that featured causality, out of a total of 127,429 time series. It should be noted that the study only considered time series with ten or more observations, ignoring time series with a proportionally high number of missing values; this may be considered to be a limitation of this study.

$$y_t = a_1 X_{t-1} + b_1 Y_{t-1} + e \tag{1}$$

The TCDF is a more recent mechanism than Granger Causality [20]. It is a deep learning framework, founded on the use of Attention-based Convolutional Neural Networks, to discover non-linear causal relationships between time series. TCDF can find "confound delays" where the past time series can trigger a change in not only the next temporal step but in a number of future steps. TCDF is considered to be the current state of the art mechanism for causality discovery in time series because it outperforms many previously proposed mechanisms, including Granger Causality. One major limitation of TCDF, at least in the context of SDG time series, is that it does not perform well on short time series.

2.2 Correlation

Two correlation mechanism are considered in this paper: Pearson Correlation and the Least Absolute Shrinkage Selector Operator (LASSO). Pearson Correlation is one of the most frequently used correlation tests [4]. The Pearson Correlation coefficient is a number between +1 and −1 and shows how two variables are linearly related. It has been used in many studies to determine the nature of the linearity between variables [6,23,32]. The basic formula for Pearson is given in Eq. 2 where n is the number of observations, y_i is a value in time series Y, and x_i is a value in time series X.

$$r_{xy} = \frac{n \sum x_i y_i - \sum x_i \sum y_i}{\sqrt{n \sum x_i^2 - \left(\sum x_i\right)^2} \sqrt{n \sum y_i^2 - \left(\sum y_i\right)^2}} \tag{2}$$

Lasso [29] is a regression analysis method frequently used when respect to high dimensionality time series data; data featuring many variables, some of which may not be relevant. It is another widely used method [8,18,25,28]. LASSO reduces the dimensionality by penalising variances to zero, which will remove irrelevant variables from the model. From inspection of Eq. 3 it can be seen that the first part is the normal regression equation. The second part is a penalty applied to individual coefficients. If λ is equal to 0, then the function becomes a normal regression. However, if λ is not 0 coefficients are penalised.

$$\sum_{i=1}^{n} \left(y_i - \sum_j x_{ij} \beta_j \right)^2 + \lambda \sum_{j=1}^{p} |\beta_j| \tag{3}$$

2.3 Time Series Forecasting

Three time series forecasting mechanisms are considered in this paper: (i) Fbprophet, (ii) Multivariate Long short-term memory (LSTM) and (iii) Univariate LSTM. Fbprophet is an additive model proposed by Facebook [27]. The model decompose a time series y into three main parts, trend (g), seasonality (s) and holidays (h), plus an error term e, as shown in Eq. 4. For the SDG time series only g is relevant. Fbprophet was used in [1] to forecast SDGs attainment and is thus used for comparison purposes later in this paper.

$$y(t) = g(t) + s(t) + h(t) + \epsilon_t \tag{4}$$

While linear models such as ARMA and ARIMA [9] have been widely adopted in, and associated with, time series forecasting; non-linear models, inspired by neural networks, such as LSTM, have received a lot of attention in the past few years. LSTM were first introduced in 1997 in [12], and have been widely adopted ever since, especially in domains such as weather predictions [24] and stock market predictions [5]. With respect to evaluation presented later in this paper both single variate and multivariate LSTM are considered.

3 The United Nations' Sustainable Development Goal Agenda

Table 1. The eight 2000 Millennium Development Goals (MDGs)

1	To eradicate extreme poverty and hunger
2	To achieve universal primary education
3	To promote gender equality and empower women
4	To reduce child mortality
5	To improve maternal health
6	To combat HIV/AIDS, malaria, and other diseases
7	To ensure environmental sustainability
8	To develop a global partnership for development

In 2000 the United Nations (UN) announced its vision for a set of eight development goals, listed in Table 1, that all member states would seek to achieve [31]. These were referred to, for obvious reasons, as the Millennium Development Goals (MDGs). In 2015, the UN extended the initial eight MDGs into seventeen Sustainable Development Goals (SDGs), listed in Table 2, to be achieved by 2030 [26,30]. Each SDG has a number of sub-goals and sub-sub-goals associated with it; each linked to an attainment threshold of some kind. For example for SDG 1, "No Poverty", which comprises six sub-goals, the extreme poverty threshold is defined as living on less than 1.25 USD a day. In this paper we indicate SDG sub-goals using the notation $g\_s_1\_s_2\_...$, where g is the goal number, s_1 is the sub-goal number, s_2 is the sub-sub-goal number, and so on. For example SDG 2_22 indicates sub-goal 22 of SDG 2. The UN has made available the MDG/SDG data collated so far.[1]

Table 2. The seventeen 2005 Sustainable Development Goals (SDGs)

1	No poverty
2	Zero hunger
3	Good health and well-being
4	Quality education
5	Gender equality
6	Clean water and sanitation
7	Affordable and clean energy
8	Decent work and economic growth
9	Industry, innovation and infrastructure
10	Reduced inequality
11	Sustainable cities and communities
12	Responsible consumption and production
13	Climate action
14	Life below water
15	Life on land
16	Peace and justice strong institutions
17	Partnerships to achieve the goal

In Alharbi et al. [1] the complete set of SDGs and associated sub- and sub-sub-goals was conceptualised as a taxonomic hierarchy, as shown in Fig. 1. In the figure the root node represents the complete set of SDGs, the next level the seventeen individual SDGs, then the sub-goals referred to as "targets", the sub-sub-gaols referred to as "indicators" and so on. The same taxonomy is used with respect to the work presented in this paper.

The UN SDG data set comprises a single (very large) table with the columns representing a range of numerical and categorical attributes, and the rows representing single observations coupled with SDG sub-goals and sub-sub-goals. Each row is date stamped. The data set features 283 different geographical regions, and for each region there are, as of October 2019, up to 801 different time series [7]. The maximum length of a time series was 19 points, covering 19 year's of observations, although a time series featuring a full 19 observations is unusual; there were many missing values. In some cases, data from earlier years was

---

[1] https://unstats.un.org/SDGs/indicators/database/.

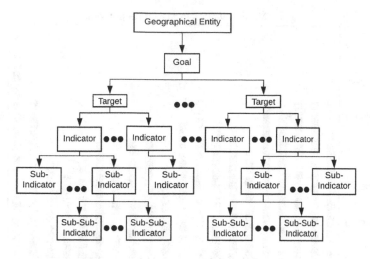

Fig. 1. The SDGs taxonomy proposed [1]

also included. In the context of the research presented in this paper, only data form the year 2000 onward was considered; 127,429 time series in total. By applying time series analysis to the data, trends can be identified for prediction/forecasting purposes [1].

The number of missing values in the SDG data set presented a particular challenge (see Fig. 2). The total theoretical number of observations (time series points) in the data was 2,548,580, while the actual number was 1,062,119; in other words, the data featured 1,486,461 missing values (58.3% of the total). Most of these missing values were missing in what can only be described as a random manner, but in other cases, the missing data could be explained because observations were only made following a five-year cycle.

4   The SDG Correlated/Causal Attainment Prediction Methodology

A schematic of the proposed SDG Correlated/Causal Attainment Prediction (SDG-CAP) Methodology is presented in Fig. 3. The input is the collection of SDG time series associated with a geographic region of interest. The output is a attainment prediction model. The input data is preprocessed in three steps: (i) Flatning, (ii) Imputing and (iii) Rescaling. During flatning [33] the input time time series were reshaped so that every record comprised a tuple of the form: $\langle Country, Goal, Target, Indicator, CategoricalIdentifiers, \{v_{2000}, v_{2001}, \ldots, v_{2019}\}\rangle$, where v_i is a value for the year i, and the categorical identifiers are things like gender and/or age which may be relevant to a particular goal. It was noted earlier that the SDG data collection features many missing values. For the purposes of the work presented in this paper, any time series with less than five values was removed during the flatning stage. As a consequence,

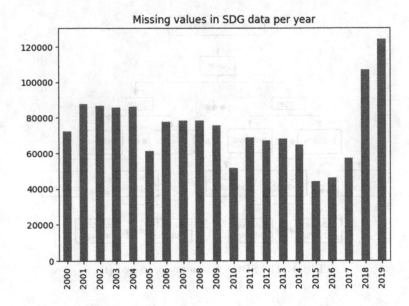

Fig. 2. Number of missing values in the SDG data set per year.

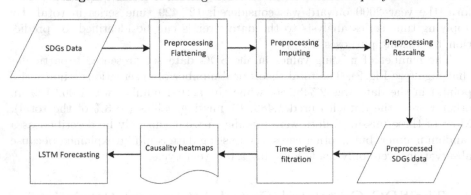

Fig. 3. Schematic of the SDG causality/correlation attainment predict (SDG-CAP) methodology

the total number of time series to be considered was reduced from 127,429 to 80,936. However, the remaining time series still featured up to thirteen missing values. The next step in the preprocessing was therefore to impute missing values. Experiments were conducted using four different imputation methods: (i) Linear, (ii) Krogh, (iii) Spline and (iv) Pchip [11,15,16]. The aim was to identify the most appropriate imputation method. The experiments were conducted using complete time series only from the Egypt sub_goal 3_2 time series. A random deletion of the data was applied to simulate the missing values situation, but with a ground truth in that the missing values were known. The four different candidate imputations algorithms were then applied. Root Mean Square Error

(RMSE) measurement was used to ascertain the performance of the different imputation methods. The results are presented in Table 3 with respect to Egypt sub-goal 3_2 time series. From the table, it can be seen that the worst average performance was associated with the Krogh method, while the Spline method produced the best average performance. Thus the Spline method was chosen to be incorporated into the proposed SDG-CAP approach. The final preprocessing step was to rescale the time series data so that it was referenced to a uniform scale. The reason for this is that the values in the various time series are referenced too many different numeric ranges, for example population counts in the millions against observed values in single digits.

Table 3. RMSE comparison of imputation methods used to generate missing values in the SDG data (best results in bold font)

SDG3.2.	Algorithm			
	Linear	Krogh	Spline	Pchip
1	0.212	3938.998	0.536	**0.168**
2	3.952	14421.321	1.959	**1.864**
3	0.047	**0.018**	0.047	0.031
4	**0.000**	102.356	4.089	**0.000**
5	0.251	37.856	0.250	**0.054**
6	**0.861**	2687.759	1.330	1.125
7	0.559	9.548	**0.374**	0.731
8	0.042	0.727	0.042	**0.017**
9	1.820	70.773	2.596	**1.250**
10	6.924	1005.504	**1.456**	28.018
11	5.707	14196.115	**2.320**	20.260
12	0.036	0.025	0.095	**0.020**
13	0.032	0.175	0.032	**0.015**
14	**0.256**	13.235	**0.256**	0.299
15	0.063	0.148	0.064	**0.017**
16	2.167	21.497	2.167	**1.175**
Ave. error	1.433	2281.629	**1.101**	3.440
Stand. dev.	2.198	4830.316	**1.223**	8.223

Once a "clean" data set had been generated the next step was to identify relationships within the data using an appropriate filtration method. As noted earlier experiments were conducted, reported on in the following evaluation section, using five different filtration mechanisms. Regardless of which filtration method is used, the outcome was presented as a heat map. An example fragment of a heat map generated using LASSO, and the geographic area Egypt, is given in Fig. 4. The darker the colour the greater the LASSO R^2 value. The leading diagonal represents SDG comparisons with themselves; hence, as expected, these are highly correlated. The heat map was then used to collate time series for the purpose of prediction model generation, by using the top 5 highest R^2 values. In other words the number of selected time series with respect to each goal was limited to a maximum of the top five most-related. These groups of time series were then used as the input to a Multivariate LSTM to predict future values, which in turn could be used for attainment prediction.

Time Series	SDG 1_12	SDG 1_13	SDG 1_15	SDG 1_16	SDG 1_17	SDG 1_20	SDG 1_22	SDG 1_25	SDG 1_26	SDG 1_27	SDG 1_28	SDG 1_30	SDG 1_31	SDG 1_32	SDG 1_34
SDG 1_12	1.000	0.410	0.328	0.154	0.267	0.372	0.640	0.877	0.746	0.738	0.744	0.745	0.744	0.746	0.877
SDG 1_13	0.410	1.000	0.354	0.598	0.395	0.132	0.509	0.400	0.520	0.520	0.520	0.520	0.520	0.520	0.400
SDG 1_15	0.328	0.354	1.000	0.000	0.037	0.021	0.167	0.448	0.228	0.222	0.227	0.227	0.226	0.228	0.444
SDG 1_16	0.154	0.598	0.000	1.000	0.649	0.288	0.493	0.116	0.428	0.436	0.430	0.429	0.430	0.428	0.117
SDG 1_17	0.267	0.395	0.037	0.649	1.000	0.165	0.739	0.218	0.651	0.663	0.654	0.653	0.656	0.652	0.219
SDG 1_20	0.372	0.132	0.021	0.288	0.165	1.000	0.353	0.290	0.372	0.371	0.372	0.372	0.372	0.372	0.294
SDG 1_22	0.640	0.509	0.167	0.493	0.739	0.353	1.000	0.602	0.890	0.894	0.891	0.891	0.892	0.891	0.603
SDG 1_25	0.877	0.400	0.448	0.116	0.218	0.290	0.602	1.000	0.722	0.712	0.720	0.720	0.719	0.722	0.976
SDG 1_26	0.746	0.520	0.228	0.428	0.651	0.372	0.890	0.722	1.000	0.928	0.928	0.928	0.928	0.928	0.723
SDG 1_27	0.738	0.520	0.222	0.436	0.663	0.371	0.894	0.712	0.928	1.000	0.928	0.928	0.929	0.928	0.713
SDG 1_28	0.744	0.520	0.227	0.430	0.654	0.372	0.891	0.720	0.928	0.928	1.000	0.928	0.928	0.928	0.721
SDG 1_30	0.745	0.520	0.227	0.429	0.653	0.372	0.891	0.720	0.928	0.928	0.928	1.000	0.928	0.928	0.722
SDG 1_31	0.744	0.520	0.226	0.430	0.656	0.372	0.892	0.719	0.928	0.929	0.928	0.928	1.000	0.928	0.720
SDG 1_32	0.746	0.520	0.228	0.428	0.652	0.372	0.891	0.722	0.928	0.928	0.928	0.928	0.928	1.000	0.723
SDG 1_34	0.877	0.400	0.444	0.117	0.219	0.294	0.603	0.976	0.723	0.713	0.721	0.722	0.720	0.723	1.000

Fig. 4. A fragment of the heat map produced using LASSO analysis and the geographic area Egypt

5   Evaluations

For the evaluation of the proposed SDG-CAT methodology the five different filtration mechanism listed earlier were used. Namely two causality mechanisms (Granger Causality and TCDF), two correlation mechanisms (LASSO and Pearson) and a combination of all four. For the last method the individual results were combined. The evaluation was conducted using the geographic area Egypt. Inspection of the time series for this region, 335 of them, indicated that in many cases there was no data for the years 2018 and 2019; hence seventeen point time series were used covering the time period 2001 to 2017. Some examples of discovered relationships between time series, identified using the combined method, are given in Fig. 5. To give one detailed illustration, Table 4 gives the individual relationship scores, using all five mechanisms, for SDG 17_56.

Recall that earlier in this paper it was hypothesised that by combining related time series better predictions could be made compared to results presented in [1] where an independence assumption was made. To measure this the SDG-CAT methodology was run with time series for 2001 to 2013, and predictions made for 2014 to 2017. The results given in [1] were generated for the same geographic region, Egypt, using Fbprophet. For the multivariate time series LSTM were used, single variate LSTM were also applied to the cleaned data for comparison purposes. RMSE was used as the comparison metric. For the multivariate forecasting, as noted above, the input was limited to the top five most-related time

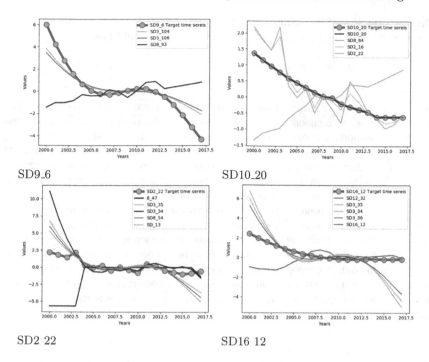

SD9_6   SD10_20

SD2 22   SD16 12

Fig. 5. Examples of related time series with respect to particular target SDGs using the combined method

Table 4. Example time series relationship scores, generated using a range of filtration mechanisms, for SDG 17_56 Fixed Internet broadband subscriptions

SDG 17_56	Lasso	Granger causality	Pearsons correleations	TCDF	SDG-CAP	SDGs code
SDG 8_13	0.263	0.614	0.529	2	3.407	Unemployment rate, by sex, age and persons with disabilities
SDG 16_43	0.008	0.0719	0.019	2	2.099	Proportion of voting rights of developing countries
SDG 9_5	0.000	0.941	0.000	1	1.941	Facilitate sustainable and resilient infrastructure development
SDG 3_35	0.094	0.637	1.114	0	1.845	Adults (15–24) newly infected with HIV
SDG 3_34	0.083	0.659	0.888	0	1.631	Adults (15–49) newly infected with HIV

series. The results are presented in Table 5, with best results highlighted in bold font. The method presented in [1] is described as the SDG-AP (SDG Attainment Prediction) method. From the table it can be seen that the combination method produced the best result. All the relation identification mechanisms, coupled with multivariate LSTM, produced better results than the Fbprophet

Table 5. Example RMSE results produced using SDG-CAP with a range of filtration methods, SDG-AP and Univariate LSTM (best results in bold font)

SDG	SDG-CAP, multivariate LSTM					SDG-AP Fbprophet	Univaritae LSTM
	Lasso	Grainger	Correlation	TCDF	Combined		
2_22	0.0000052	0.0052015	0.0000002	**0.0000002**	0.0000005	0.3231084	1.03190567
3_39	0.0000085	**0.0000001**	**0.0000001**	**0.0000001**	**0.0000001**	0.3180739	0.30534206
6_17	**0.0000002**	0.0000013	0.0000410	0.0000016	0.0000376	0.0420172	0.06473296
8_8	0.0000085	0.0000007	**0.0000006**	0.0000042	0.0000023	0.5924453	4.12603573
9_6	0.0002040	0.0008483	0.0000004	**0.0000002**	**0.0000002**	0.2308795	0.15737508
10_20	0.0000292	0.0000069	0.0047152	**0.0000001**	0.0000002	0.1747101	0.13596105
11_27	0.0000009	0.0000005	0.0000006	**0.0000003**	0.0000008	4.6060315	6.69974063
12_4	0.0000601	0.0000611	0.0000002	**0.0000001**	0.0001074	0.4021510	0.68321411
12_28	0.0000002	0.0000106	**0.0000001**	0.0004241	**0.0000001**	0.5756070	0.33681492
14_4	0.0000622	0.0000002	0.0000178	**0.0000001**	**0.0000001**	0.4025397	0.03858285
15_21	**0.0000003**	0.0022758	0.0000004	0.0085000	0.0000010	1.2691464	1.59389898
16_12	0.0000571	**0.0000001**	0.0000004	0.0000281	0.0000006	0.3846588	0.07288927
17_56	0.0000001	0.0000337	**0.0000001**	0.0000002	**0.0000001**	0.5947819	1.86160687
Ave. RMSE	0.0000336	0.0006493	0.0003675	0.0006892	**0.0000116**	0.7627808	1.31600770
Stand. dev.	0.0000545	0.0014538	0.0012551	0.0022575	**0.0000293**	1.1456063	1.9764099

results from [1] and univariate LSTM. It is interesting to note, however, that Fbprophet produced better predictions than when using univariate LSTM. It can also be observed, overall, that the proposed SDG-CAP methodology is well able to handle short time series.

6   Conclusion

In this paper the SDG-CAP methodology has been presented for predicting the attainment of SDGs with respect to specific geographic regions. The hypothesis that the paper sought to address was that better SDG attainment prediction could be obtained if the prediction was conducted using co-related time series rather than individual time series as in the case of previous work. The central challenge was how best to identify such co-related time series; a challenge compounded by the short length of SDG time series and the presence of many missing values in the UN SDG data set. Five different filtration mechanisms were considered, together with four different data imputation methods. The best filtration method was found to be a combination of the four others, and the best data imputation method was found to be Spline. Multivariate LSTM were used to conduct the forecasting. To test the hypothesis the proposed methodology was compared with the SDG-AP methodology from the literature and univariate LSTM forecasting. It was found that the hypothesis was correct, better SDG attainment prediction could be obtained using the SDG-CAP methodology which took into consideration co-related time series. It was also demonstrated that the proposed approach was well able to handle short time series. For future research, the intention is firstly to incorporate the proposed SDG-CAP methodology into a hierarchical bottom-up time series forecasting approach of the form presented in [1]. Secondly the intention is to consider co-related time series across geographic regions, not just within a single geographic region as in the case of this paper, bearing in mind the economic and geographical differences between different regions.

References

1. Alharbi, Y., Arribas-Be, D., Coenen, F.: Sustainable development goal attainment prediction: a hierarchical framework using time series modelling. In: KDIR (2019)
2. Athanasopoulos, G., Ahmed, R.A., Hyndman, R.J.: Hierarchical forecasts for Australian domestic tourism. Int. J. Forecast. **25**(1), 146–166 (2009)
3. Ben-gong, Z., Weibo, L., Yazhou, S., Xiaoping, L., Luonan, C.: Detecting causality from short time-series data based on prediction of topologically equivalent attractors. BMC Syst. Biol. **11**, 141–150 (2017)
4. Benesty J., Chen J., Huang Y., Cohen I.: Pearson correlation coefficient. In: Noise Reduction in Speech Processing. Springer Topics in Signal Processing, vol 2, pp. 1–4. Springer, Heidelberg. https://doi.org/10.1007/978-3-642-00296-0_5
5. Chen, K., Zhou, Y., Dai, F.: A LSTM-based method for stock returns prediction: a case study of China stock market. In: 2015 IEEE International Conference on Big Data (Big Data), pp. 2823–2824. IEEE (2015)
6. Hema Divya, K., Rama Devi, V.: A study on predictors of GDP: early signals. Procedia Econ. Finan. **11**, 375–382 (2014)
7. Dörgő, G., Sebestyén, V., Abonyi, J.: Evaluating the interconnectedness of the sustainable development goals based on the causality analysis of sustainability indicators. Sustainability **10**(10), 3766 (2018)
8. Epprecht, C., et al.: Comparing variable selection techniques for linear regression: Lasso and autometrics. Centre d'économie de la Sorbonne (2013)
9. De Gooijer, J.G., Hyndman, R.J.: 25 years of time series forecasting. Int. J. Forecast. **22**(3), 443–473 (2006)
10. Granger, C.W.J.: Investigating causal relations by econometric models and cross-spectral methods. Econometrica J. Econ. Soc. **37**, 424–438 (1969)
11. Hall, C.A., Weston Meyer, W.: Optimal error bounds for cubic spline interpolation. J. Approx. Theor. **16**(2), 105–122 (1976)
12. Hochreiter, S., Schmidhuber, J.: Long short-term memory. Neural Comput. **9**(8), 1735–1780 (1997)
13. Hyndman, R.J., Athanasopoulos, G.: Forecasting: Principles and Practice. OTexts (May 2018)
14. Hyndman, R.J., Koehler, A.B.: Another look at measures of forecast accuracy. Int. J. Forecast. **22**, 679–688 (2006)
15. Junninen, H., Niska, H., Tuppurainen, K., Ruuskanen, J., Kolehmainen, M.: Methods for imputation of missing values in air quality data sets. Atmos. Environ. **38**(18), 2895–2907 (2004)
16. Krogh, F.T.: Efficient algorithms for polynomial interpolation and numerical differentiation. Math. Comput. **24**(109), 185–190 (1970)
17. Lean, H.H., Smyth, R.: Multivariate Granger causality between electricity generation, exports, prices and GDP in Malaysia. Energy **35**(9), 3640–3648 (2010)

18. Li, J., Chen, W.: Forecasting macroeconomic time series: LASSO-based approaches and their forecast combinations with dynamic factor models. Int. J. Forecast. **30**(4), 996–1015 (2014)
19. Narayan, P.K., Smyth, R.: Multivariate Granger causality between electricity consumption, exports and GDP: evidence from a panel of Middle Eastern countries. Energy Policy **37**(1), 229–236 (2009)
20. Nauta, M., Bucur, D., Seifert, C.: Causal discovery with attention-based convolutional neural networks. Mach. Learn. Knowl. Extr. **1**(1), 312–340 (2019)
21. Wankeun, O., Lee, K.: Causal relationship between energy consumption and GDP revisited: the case of Korea 1970–1999. Energy Econ. **26**(1), 51–59 (2004)
22. Pao, H.-T., Tsai, C.-M.: Multivariate Granger causality between CO2 emissions, energy consumption, FDI (foreign direct investment) and GDP (gross domestic product): evidence from a panel of BRIC (Brazil, Russian Federation, India, and China) countries. Energy **36**(1), 685–693 (2011)
23. Pérez-Rodríguez, J.V., Ledesma-Rodríguez, F., Santana-Gallego, M.: Testing dependence between GDP and tourism's growth rates. Tour. Manage. **48**, 268–282 (2015)
24. Qing, X., Niu, Y.: Hourly day-ahead solar irradiance prediction using weather forecasts by LSTM. Energy **148**, 461–468 (2018)
25. Roy, S.S., Mittal, D., Basu, A., Abraham, A.: Stock market forecasting using LASSO linear regression model. In: Abraham, A., Krömer, P., Snasel, V. (eds.) Afro-European Conference for Industrial Advancement. AISC, vol. 334, pp. 371–381. Springer, Cham (2015). https://doi.org/10.1007/978-3-319-13572-4_31
26. Sapkota, S.: E-Handbook on Sustainable Development Goals. United Nations (2019)
27. Taylor, S.J., Letham, B.: Forecasting at scale. Am. Stat. **72**, 37–45 (2017)
28. Tian, S., Yan, Y., Guo, H.: Variable selection and corporate bankruptcy forecasts. J. Bank. Finan. **52**, 89–100 (2015)
29. Tibshirani, R.: Regression shrinkage and selection via the Lasso. J. Roy. Stat. Soc.: Ser. B (Methodol.) **58**(1), 267–288 (1996)
30. UN: Transforming our World: the 2030 Agenda for Sustainable Development. Working papers, eSocialSciences (2015)
31. United Nations Development programme. Millennium Development Goals (2007)
32. Vinkler, P.: Correlation between the structure of scientific research, scientometric indicators and GDP in EU and non-EU countries. Scientometrics **74**(2), 237–254 (2007)
33. Wang, E., Cook, D., Hyndman, R.J.: A new tidy data structure to support exploration and modeling of temporal data. arXiv e-prints arXiv:1901.10257 (January 2019)
34. Zhang, X., Hu, Y., Xie, K., Wang, S., Ngai, E.W.T., Liu, M.: A causal feature selection algorithm for stock prediction modeling. Neurocomputing **142**, 48–59 (2014)

Mining Frequent Seasonal Gradual Patterns

Jerry Lonlac[✉], Arnaud Doniec, Marin Lujak, and Stephane Lecoeuche

Digital Science CERI, IMT Lille Douai, University of Lille, 59500 Douai, France
{jerry.lonlac,arnaud.doniec,marin.lujak,
stephane.lecoeuche}@imt-lille-douai.fr

Abstract. Gradual patterns that capture co-variation of complex attributes in the form "when X increases/decreases, Y increases/decreases" play an important role in many real world applications where huge volumes of complex numerical data must be handled. More recently, they have received attention from the data mining community for exploring temporal data and methods have been defined to automatically extract gradual patterns from temporal data. However, to the best of our knowledge, no method has been proposed to extract gradual patterns that always appear at the identical time intervals in the sequences of temporal data, despite the knowledge that such patterns may bring for certain applications such as e-commerce. This paper proposes to extract co-variations of periodically repeating attributes from the sequences of temporal data that we call *seasonal gradual patterns*. We discuss the specific features of these patterns and propose an approach for their extraction by exploiting a motif mining algorithm in a sequence, and justify its applicability to the gradual case. Illustrative results obtained from a real world data set are described and show the interest for such patterns.

Keywords: Data mining · Gradual patterns · Temporality · Seasonality

1 Introduction

Due to the abundance of data collection devices and sensors, numerical data are ubiquitous and produced in increasing quantities. They are produced in many domains including e-commerce, biology, medicine, ecology, telecommunications, and system supervision. In recent years, the analysis of numerical data has received attention from the data mining community and methods have been defined for dealing with such data. These methods have allowed to automatically extract different kinds of knowledge from numerical data expressed under form of patterns such as quantitative itemset/association rules [12] and interval patterns [4,7]. More recently, gradual patterns that model frequent co-variations between numerical attributes, such as "the more experience, the higher the salary, and the lower the free time" aroused great interest in a multitude of areas. For example, in medicine, gradual patterns make it possible to capture the correlations

© Springer Nature Switzerland AG 2020
M. Song et al. (Eds.): DaWaK 2020, LNCS 12393, pp. 197–207, 2020.
https://doi.org/10.1007/978-3-030-59065-9_16

between memory and feeling points from the *Diagnostic and statistical manual of mental disorders*; in financial markets, where one would like to discover co-evolution between financial indicators, or in marketing for analyzing client databases. Several works have addressed gradual patterns mining and different algorithms have been designed for discovering gradual patterns from numerical data (e.g., [2,3,5]). Most of these algorithms use classical data mining techniques to extract gradual patterns. However, they are not relevant for extracting gradual patterns in certain application domains where numerical data present particular forms (e.g., temporal, stream, or relational data). So, some recent works have instead focused on extracting variants of gradual patterns on the numerical data supplied with specific constraints for expressing another kind of knowledge; for instance, the relational gradual pattern concept that enables to examine the correlations between attributes from a graduality point of view in multi-relational data [10]. Recently, in [8], the authors proposed an approach to extract gradual patterns in temporal data with an application on paleoecological databases to grasp functional groupings of coevolution of paleoecological indicators that model the evolution of the biodiversity over time. Although this approach deals with temporally annotated numerical data, it can be only used on the data constituted as a single valued sequence.

According to the requirements linked to data structures, new methods are needed to extract the forms of gradual patterns expressing typical knowledge to the data context. Each gradual pattern extracted is provided with a subsequence set of objects, called extension, supporting it. (Possibly numerous) extensions associated to gradual patterns are often useful in several application domains for deriving new and relevant knowledge to the expert. To this end, a Sequential Pattern Mining based approach for efficient extraction of frequent gradual patterns with their corresponding sequence of tuples was proposed in [6]. In [9], it was shown on geographical data that the analysis of different sequences of objects associated to the gradual patterns allows to identify how an object participates in the associations between attribute variations. When considering the databases made with many ordered value sequences, state of the art gradual pattern mining algorithms do not allow extracting another kind of knowledge that is typical of sequential data.

This paper proposes to extract *seasonal gradual patterns* [8] associated to the same sub-sequence of objects in all value sequences, vital in the e-commerce domain where it is very important to understand seasonal phenomena. The knowledge brought by such patterns can be used in logistics for decision marking in, e.g., inventory and supply chain management. Our approach can be seen as extending gradual patterns in the temporal context via the seasonality notion such that we include the repetitive temporal correlations between attributes. We transform the seasonal gradual patterns mining problem into the problem of enumerating all motifs with a wildcard symbol in a tuple sequences database and then exploit MaxMotif [1] algorithm on the obtained tuple sequences database to extract the frequent seasonal gradual patterns.

2   Preliminary Definitions

The problem of mining gradual patterns consists in mining attribute co-variations in a numerical dataset of the form *"the more/less X, . . . , the more/less Y"*. We assume herein that we are given a database Δ containing a set of objects $\mathcal{T}$ that defines a relation on an attribute set $\mathcal{I}$ with numerical values. Let $t[i]$ denote the value of attribute i over object t for all $t \in \mathcal{T}$. In Table 1, we give an illustrative example of a numerical database built over the set of attributes $\mathcal{I} = \{age, salary, cars, loans\}$. We consider each attribute twice: once to indicate its increasing ($\uparrow$ variation symbol) and once to indicate its decreasing ($\downarrow$). In the following, we denote "$t[i] \uparrow t'[i]$" (respectively "$t[i] \downarrow t'[i]$") to mean that the value of attribute i increases (respectively decreases) from t to t'.

A **gradual item** is defined under the form i^*, where i is an attribute of $\mathcal{I}$ and $* \in \{\uparrow, \downarrow\}$. A **gradual pattern** is a non-empty set of gradual items denoted by $(i_1^{*1}, \ldots, i_k^{*k})$. Considering the database Δ_1, $age^{\uparrow}$ is a gradual item and $g_1 = (age^{\uparrow}, salary^{\uparrow})$ is a gradual pattern meaning that *"the higher the age, the higher the salary"*. Moreover, the support of a gradual pattern is the extent to which a gradual pattern is present in a given database. Several support definitions (e.g., [2,5,8]) show that gradual patterns can follow different semantics. We adopt the definition of the support of a gradual pattern in [8] respecting the temporal order as the proportion of couples of consecutive tuples supporting the gradual pattern. To define this support, we introduce the following definitions:

Definition 1 (Gradual tuple motif). *Let $g = (i_1^{*1}, \ldots, i_k^{*k})$ be a gradual itemset and $M = t_1 t_2 \ldots t_n$ be a motif of consecutive tuples. M is gradual with respect to g if for all p such that $1 \leq p \leq k$ and for all j such that $1 \leq j < n$, $t_j[i_p] *_p t_{j+1}[i_p]$ holds.*

Considering the database of Table 1, $M_1 = t_1 t_2 t_3$ is a gradual tuple motif with respect to g_1. There may be several gradual tuple motifs respecting g.

Definition 2 (Maximal gradual tuple motif). *Let $g = (i_1^{*1}, \ldots, i_k^{*k})$ be a gradual itemset and M a gradual tuple motif respecting g. M is maximal if for any motif M' respecting g, $M \not\subset M'$.*

When considering the database Δ_1 and the gradual pattern g_1. $M_2 = t_6 t_7 t_8 t_9$ is not maximal with respect to g_1 because $M_3 = t_5 t_6 t_7 t_8 t_9$ is gradual with respect to g_1 and contains M_2. M_3 is a maximal gradual tuple motif with respect to g_1.

Definition 3 (Cover). *Let g be a gradual itemset of a database Δ. We define $Cover(g, \Delta)$ as the set of maximal gradual tuple motifs in respect to g in Δ.*

Considering again the database of Table 1 and the previous gradual itemset g_1, $Cover(g_1, \Delta_1) = \{t_1 t_2 t_3, t_5 t_6 t_7 t_8 t_9\}$.

Table 1. Database Δ_1

tid	age	salary	cars	loans
t1	22	1000	2	4
t2	24	1200	3	3
t3	28	1850	2	5
t4	20	1250	4	2
t5	18	1100	4	2
t6	35	2200	4	2
t7	38	3200	1	1
t8	44	3400	3	6
t9	52	3800	3	3
t10	41	5000	2	7

Table 2. Customer purchases database: Δ_2

Sid	purchase_timestamp	age (a)	freight_value (f)	payment_installments (pi)	payment_value (pv)
S^1	d1	22	8.72	2	18.12
	d2	24	22.76	3	141.46
	d3	28	19.22	4	179.12
	d4	20	17.20	1	72.20
	d5	18	8.72	1	28.62
	d6	35	27.36	3	175.26
	d7	38	16.05	4	65.95
	d8	44	15.17	4	75.16
S^2	d1	32	16.05	3	35.95
	d2	34	19.77	4	161.42
	d3	36	30.53	5	159.06
	d4	40	16.13	5	114.13
	d5	25	14.23	2	50.13
	d6	23	12.805	2	32.70
	d7	20	13.11	1	54.36
	d8	41	14.05	4	46.45
S^3	d1	28	77.45	3	1376.45
	d2	33	15.10	4	43.09
	d3	38	11.85	6	29.75
	d4	35	16.97	5	62.15
	d5	38	8.96	4	118.86
	d6	44	8.71	5	88.90
	d7	52	7.78	6	17.28
	d8	41	57.58	4	187.57

Definition 4 (Gradual tuple motif sequence). *Let g be a gradual itemset of a database Δ and $\overset{\circ}{f}$ be a function such that $\overset{\circ}{f}(M_1,\ldots,M_n) = M_1 \circ \ldots \circ M_n$ where $M_j(1 \leq j \leq n)$ is a gradual tuple motif. Then we define the gradual tuple motif sequence of g in Δ noted M_g^Δ as $M_g^\Delta = \overset{\circ}{f}(Cover(g,\Delta))$.*

A gradual tuple motif sequence is just a concatenation of gradual tuple motifs. Referring back to the example from Table 1, we have $M_{g_1}^{\Delta_1} = t_1 t_2 t_3 \circ t_5 t_6 t_7 t_8 t_9$.

3   Problem Statement

Temporal Data Sequences. Our approach finds its application on a numerical database Δ constituted of temporal data sequences. More precisely, the database Δ consists of object sequences $S = \langle S^1, \ldots, S^n \rangle$ described by the set of numerical attributes $\mathcal{I} = \{i_1, \ldots, i_k\}$, with $S^j = \{d_1, \ldots, d_l\}$, a set of periods considered. Table 2 is an example of temporal data sequences which gives information about customer purchases for a e-commerce website on three purchase cycles (sequences) S^1, S^2, S^3. Each sequence contains the data for eight dates $(d_1, \ldots, d_8)$. Without loss of generality, we assume that there are no other purchase dates between two consecutive dates and that the purchases are made continuously between two consecutive cycles.

Seasonal Gradual Patterns. In the case of a single object sequence, a gradual pattern corresponds to the one extracted by [8]. However, in seasonal gradual pattern context, we seek for the gradual patterns respected by the same gradual tuple motifs. To address this issue, we propose the definition of seasonal gradual patterns in which the notion of seasonality is introduced. Let us consider the temporal data sequence of Table 2. These data are extracted from a dataset regarding customer orders made at multiples marketplaces. The goal is to extract frequent co-variations between attribute values that occur frequently in identical periods, e.g. seasonal gradual patterns. We want to extract these patterns with the gradual tuple motifs associated that will represent the seasonality of each pattern. To illustrate our approach, we start by introducing some definitions.

Definition 5. *Let Δ be a temporal data sequence over a set of numerical attributes $\mathcal{I} = \{i_1, \ldots, i_k\}$, and of tuple sequences $S = \langle S^1, \ldots, S^n \rangle$. Given gradual item i^* with $i \in \mathcal{I}$, we define M_{i^*} as $M_{i^*} = \overset{\circ}{f}(M_{i^*}^{S^1} \ldots M_{i^*}^{S^n})$. M_{i^*} is the sequence formed of gradual tuple motifs that respect gradual item i^*.*

Referring back to the example from Table 2, we have: $M_{age\uparrow}^{S^1} = d_1 d_2 d_3 \circ d_5 d_6 d_7 d_8$, $M_{age\uparrow}^{S^2} = d_1 d_2 d_3 d_4 \circ d_7 d_8$, $M_{age\uparrow}^{S^3} = d_1 d_2 d_3 \circ d_4 d_5 d_6 d_7$. Then $M_{age\uparrow} = d_1 d_2 d_3 \circ d_5 d_6 d_7 d_8 \circ d_1 d_2 d_3 d_4 \circ d_7 d_8 \circ d_1 d_2 d_3 \circ d_4 d_5 d_6 d_7$. Note that for a given gradual item i^* corresponds to a unique gradual tuple motif sequence M_{i^*}. Let us now give some basic definitions and notations necessary to introduce our approach.

Let M_{i^*} be a motif sequence of gradual tuples. We denote by $\mathcal{O} = \{1 \ldots |M_{i^*}|\}$ the set of positions of the tuples in M_{i^*}.

Definition 6 (Inclusion). *A gradual tuple motif $M = t_1 \ldots t_m$ appears in a gradual tuple motif sequence $M_g = s_1 \ldots s_n$ at the position $l \in \mathcal{O}$ denoted $M \subseteq_l M_g$, if $\forall j \in \{1 \ldots m\}, t_j = s_{l+j-1}$ and $t_j \neq \circ$ (where $\circ$ is the wildcard symbol). We note by $\mathcal{L}_{M_g}(M) = \{l \in \mathcal{O} | M \subseteq_l M_g\}$ the support of M in M_g. We say that $M \subseteq M_g$ iff $\exists l \in \mathcal{O}$ such that $M \subseteq_l M_g$.*

Definition 7 (Frequent gradual tuple motif). *Let M_g be a gradual tuple motif sequence and M gradual tuple motif. Given a positive number $\theta \geq 1$, called quorum, we say that M is frequent in M_g when $|\mathcal{L}_{M_g}(M)| \geq \theta$.*

Henceforth, given a gradual tuple motif sequence M_g, the set of all frequent maximal gradual tuple motifs of M_g for the quorum θ is denoted by $\mathcal{E}^{\theta}_{M_g}$. We now consider a new kind of items that we call *seasonal gradual items*.

Definition 8 (Seasonal gradual item). *A seasonal gradual item with respect to a support threshold θ is defined under form $i^{(*,m)}$ in which i is an attribute of the given temporal data sequence, $* \in \{\uparrow, \downarrow\}$ and $m \in \mathcal{E}^{\theta}_{M_{i*}}$.*

If we consider the temporal data sequence of Table 2, $age^{(\uparrow, d_1 d_2 d_3)}$ is a seasonal gradual item with respect to $\theta = 3$ expressing that the values of the attribute age are increasing more frequently on the period "$d_1 d_2 d_3$". $age^{(\uparrow, d_5 d_6 d_7)}$ is not a seasonal gradual item with respect to $\theta = 3$ as the support of $d_5 d_6 d_7$ in $M_{age\uparrow}$ is equal to 2 (observed on S^1 and S^3, not on S^2).

Definition 9 (Seasonal gradual itemset). *A seasonal gradual itemset (pattern) $g = \{i_1^{(*_1, m)}, \dots, i_k^{(*_k, m)}\}$ is a non-empty set of seasonal gradual items, with $m \in \mathcal{E}^{\theta}_{M_g}$ and θ a support threshold.*

By considering the data of Table 2, $\{age^{(\uparrow, d_1 d_2 d_3)}, p\_i^{(\uparrow, d_1 d_2 d_3)}\}$ is a seasonal gradual pattern meaning that "an increase of *age* comes along with an increase of *payment_installments* more frequently on the period "$d_1 d_2 d_3$".

Definition 10 (Frequent seasonal gradual patterns mining problem). *Let Δ be a temporal data sequence and θ a minimum support threshold. The problem of mining seasonal gradual patterns is to find the set of all frequent seasonal gradual patterns of Δ with respect to θ.*

In the classical patterns mining framework, the problem of enumerating all motifs possibly interspersed with a wildcard symbol in a sequence of items [1,11] is related to the frequent seasonal gradual patterns mining problem. In fact, for a gradual item i^*, mining all frequent maximal gradual tuple motifs of M_{i*} corresponds to the problem of enumerating all maximal frequent motifs with a wildcard symbol in a sequence of tuples.

Table 3. Tuple sequences database $\Gamma(\Delta_2)$ obtained from database Δ_2

Gradual items	Tuple sequences
$a^{\uparrow}$	$d_1 d_2 d_3 \circ d_5 d_6 d_7 d_8 \circ d_1 d_2 d_3 d_4 \circ d_7 d_8 \circ d_1 d_2 d_3 \circ d_4 d_5 d_6 d_7$
$a^{\downarrow}$	$d_3 d_4 d_5 \circ d_8 d_1 \circ d_4 d_5 d_6 d_7 \circ d_8 d_1 \circ d_3 d_4 \circ d_7 d_8$
$f^{\uparrow}$	$d_1 d_2 \circ d_5 d_6 \circ d_8 d_1 d_2 d_3 \circ d_6 d_7 d_8 d_1 \circ d_3 d_4 \circ d_7 d_8$
$f^{\downarrow}$	$d_2 d_3 d_4 d_5 \circ d_6 d_7 d_8 \circ d_3 d_4 \circ d_5 d_6 \circ d_1 d_2 d_3 \circ d_4 d_5 d_6 d_7$
$pi^{\uparrow}$	$d_1 d_2 d_3 \circ d_4 d_5 d_6 d_7 d_8 \circ d_1 d_2 d_3 d_4 \circ d_5 d_6 \circ d_7 d_8 \circ d_1 d_2 d_3 \circ d_5 d_6 d_7$
$pi^{\downarrow}$	$d_3 d_4 d_5 \circ d_7 d_8 d_1 \circ d_3 d_4 d_5 d_6 d_7 \circ d_8 d_1 \circ d_3 d_4 d_5 \circ d_7 d_8$
$pv^{\uparrow}$	$d_1 d_2 d_3 \circ d_5 d_6 \circ d_7 d_8 \circ d_1 d_2 \circ d_6 d_7 \circ d_8 d_1 \circ d_3 d_4 d_5 \circ d_7 d_8$
$pv^{\downarrow}$	$d_3 d_4 d_5 \circ d_6 d_7 \circ d_8 d_1 \circ d_2 d_3 d_4 d_5 d_6 \circ d_7 d_8 \circ d_1 d_2 d_3 \circ d_5 d_6 d_7$

4   Extracting Seasonal Gradual Patterns

This section describes how to extract seasonal gradual patterns from a temporal data sequence. We first transform the frequent seasonal gradual patterns mining problem into the problem of enumerating all motifs with a wildcard symbol in a tuple sequences database by using the following definition.

Definition 11. *Let Δ be a temporal data sequence over a set of numerical attributes $\mathcal{I} = \{i_1, \ldots, i_k\}$. We define $\Gamma(\Delta)$ the tuple sequences database associated to Δ as $\Gamma(\Delta) = \{(i_1^{\uparrow}, M_{i_1^{\uparrow}}), (i_1^{\downarrow}, M_{i_1^{\downarrow}}), \ldots, (i_k^{\uparrow}, M_{i_k^{\uparrow}}), (i_k^{\downarrow}, M_{i_k^{\downarrow}})\}$.*

The tuple sequences database associated to database Δ_2 is given by Table 3. Proposition 1 illustrates the mapping between the set of seasonal gradual items of Δ_2 and the maximal motifs of $\Gamma(\Delta_2)$.

Proposition 1. *Let Δ be a temporal data sequence and θ a support threshold (quorum). $g = \{i_1^{(*_1, m)}, \ldots, i_k^{(*_k, m)}\}$ is a seasonal gradual pattern of Δ iff $\forall 1 \leq p \leq k$, $|\mathcal{L}_{M_{i_p^{*_p}}}(m)| \geq \theta$ with $Cover(m, \Gamma(\Delta)) = g$. Moreover $Cover(g, \Delta)$ is the set of maximal tuple motifs m of $\Gamma(\Delta)$ with $Cover(m, \Gamma(\Delta)) = g$.*

Definition 12 (Seasonal gradual pattern support computation). *Let Δ be a temporal data sequence and $g = \{i_1^{(*_1, m)}, \ldots, i_k^{(*_k, m)}\}$ be a seasonal gradual pattern of Δ. The support of g can be defined as follows:*

$$Supp(g, \Delta) = \left(min\{|\mathcal{L}_{M_{i_p^{*_p}}}(m)|, 1 \leq p \leq k\} \times |m|\right)/|\Delta|. \tag{1}$$

Given a user-defined threshold θ and a seasonal gradual pattern g, we say that g is frequent if its support is greater than or equal to θ. The support definition of seasonal gradual pattern satisfies the classical anti-monotony property.

Proposition 2. *Let M be a maximal gradual tuple motif of $\Gamma(\Delta)$ then $g = Cover(M, \Gamma(\Delta))$ is a seasonal gradual pattern in Δ, with:*

$$Supp(g, \Delta) \geq \left(min\{|\mathcal{L}_{M_{i_p^{*_p}}}(M)|, 1 \leq p \leq k\} \times |M|\right)/|\Delta| \tag{2}$$

The originality of seasonal gradual patterns as opposed to classical gradual patterns is that they allow to also discover seasonality inside the data in terms of graduality. After reducing the frequent seasonal gradual patterns mining problem from numerical database to a maximal motif mining problem as illustrated by Table 3, we use *MaxMotif* algorithm [1] on each gradual tuple motif sequence to extract the frequent gradual tuple motifs for given a user-defined threshold. *MaxMotif* algorithm is a polynomial space and polynomial delay algorithm for maximal pattern discovery of the class of motifs with wildcard or joker symbol. It is considered as the most effective specialized approach for enumerating motifs in a sequence. In our approach, we only consider patterns with solid characters, without wildcard symbol. The wildcard symbol for our approach is the character introduced to build gradual tuple motif sequences from gradual tuple motifs as given by Definition 4 (we consider the character 'o' as wildcard symbol for our study). The complexity of our proposed approach depends on the complexity of *MaxMotif* algorithm and the polynomial-time complexity to reduce seasonal gradual patterns mining problem to a maximal motif mining problem.

5   Experimental Results

Seasonal gradual patterns are well adapted to capture some common co-variations repeated with identical periods on attributes in the ordered data set; an example is temporal data, i.e. data produced with a temporal order on the objects, often in e-commerce domain. In order to illustrate the proposed method and show its importance, a first experimental study has been conducted on a real-world data set of customer purchases taken from the *Brazilian E-Commerce Public Data*.[1] This data set contains 99441 transactions of customer purchases on 19 attributes, with an attribute "order_date" on which transactions are ordered. The attribute "order_date" contains different values (different days) which will represent items of the tuple sequences database and other numerical attributes. For our experiments, we retrieve the order days from the "order_date" attribute and consider them as temporal variables $(d_1, \ldots, d_m)$. The used data set contains 0.56% of missing data, we removed all transactions with missing data and obtained a data set with 99000 transactions.

The experiments were carried out on a 2.8 GHz Intel Core i7 CPU, 32 GB memory with 8 cores. We focus on the variation of the number of frequent seasonal gradual patterns according to the minimum support ($MinSupp$) value, and the computation time required for discovering these patterns. We also show interesting knowledge brought by such patterns in the e-commerce domain.

Figure 1 left shows the variation of the number of frequent seasonal gradual patterns according to the minimum support. The number of patterns decreases when the minimum support increases; the number of extracted patterns is even less than 100 for a support threshold less than 0.25, which is easily exploitable by the user. Figure 1 right shows the computation time

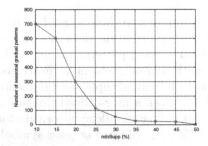
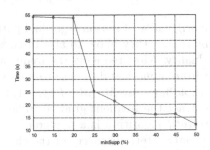

Fig. 1. Performances for the Brazilian E-Commerce Public Data set

---

[1] https://www.kaggle.com/anshumoudgil/olist-a-brazilian-e-commerce/report.

evolution taken by our approach for discovering seasonal gradual patterns according to the minimum support. We observe a decrease of computation time when the support threshold decreases. Figure 1 indicates that the number of seasonal gradual patterns is usually small and does not require much time for their extraction, which facilitates their practical exploitation. We found from e-commerce data set some interesting seasonal gradual patterns. We extracted the pattern $\{price^{(\uparrow,d_{21}d_{22}d_{23}d_{24}d_{25})}, freight\_value^{(\downarrow,d_{21}d_{22}d_{23}d_{24}d_{25})},$ $payment\_value^{(\uparrow,d_{21}d_{22}d_{23}d_{24}d_{25})}\}$, which means that *the higher the price, the lower is the freight value and the higher is the payment value frequently on the temporal sequence* $\langle d_{21}d_{22}d_{23}d_{24}d_{25}\rangle$. This trend of co-variation between the price of products and freight value is also revealed in pattern $\{Delivery\_delay^{(\uparrow,d_{18}d_{19}d_{20}d_{21})}, freight\_value^{(\downarrow,d_{18}d_{19}d_{20}d_{21})}, price^{(\uparrow,d_{18}d_{19}d_{20}d_{21})}\}$ with another attribute on the period $\langle d_{18}d_{19}d_{20}d_{21}\rangle$. These patterns could be useful to recommend and to manage business strategies. We have also conducted a second experiment on a real-world data set taken from the UCI Machine Learning Repository[2] which is the Stock Exchange data, in order to find out interesting knowledge (e.g. interesting seasons to invest) and give potentially useful suggestions for people who intend to invest. This data set is collected from imkb.gov.tr and finance.yahoo.com and is organized with regard to working days in Istanbul Stock Exchange. The lines of the data set represent returns of Istanbul Stock Exchange (*ISE*), with seven other international index; Standard & poorâ€^{TM}S 500 return index (SP), Stock market return index of Germany (*DAX*), Stock market return index of UK (*FTSE*), Stock market return index of Japan (*NIKKEI*), Stock market return index of Brazil (*BOVESPA*), MSCI European index (*MSCE_EU*), MSCI emerging markets index (*MSCI_EM*) with regard to working days from June 5, 2009 to February 22, 2011. The first column stands for the date from June 5, 2009 to February 22, 2011 and all next columns stand for Istanbul Stock Exchange with other international index. This data set is therefore suitable to our study framework, there is a temporal constraint on the data as the data lines are ordered over the years, each year is ordered over the months and each month over the days. It contains 536 lines and 9 attributes which are Stock market return index. The different days constitute the temporal variables $(d_1, \ldots, d_m)$. Table 4 shows the number of seasonal gradual patterns (*#Seasonal_GP*) and the number of seasonality (*#Seasonality*) found in this data set with our approach with respect to a minimum support threshold. We also report the number of gradual patterns extracted with the approach proposed by [8] (*#Temporal_GP*). We compare our proposed approach with the one proposed by [8] as this approach extracts gradual patterns whose sequences of corresponding objects respect the temporal order, but does not focus on seasonal ones and consider the entire data set as a single sequence of temporal data.

The number of seasonal gradual patterns is still less than the number of extracted temporal gradual patterns by the approach in [8] when varying the support threshold (Table 4). The number of seasonality is greater than the number of seasonal gradual patterns as a seasonal pattern can be associated with more than

---

[2] https://archive.ics.uci.edu/ml/datasets.php.

Table 4. Number of seasonal gradual patterns vs number of temporal gradual patterns

$minSupp$	#Temporal_GP	#Seasonal_GP (#Seasonality)
0.01	7873	48 (96)
0.015	6572	36 (68)
0.02	5507	28 (54)
0.03	4012	19 (34)
0.04	3238	16 (31)
0.05	2740	15 (17)
0.06	2361	13 (13)
0.065	2206	1 (1)

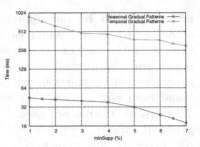

Fig. 2. Time vs support

one seasonality. Our proposed approach extracts a reasonable quantity of seasonal gradual patterns with their associated seasonality what is easy to manage for a domain expert. In addition, the approach in [8] does not provide the extensions associated to each gradual pattern while the seasonality associated to each seasonal gradual pattern can allow a better interpretation and explanation of graduality. Figure 2 shows the computational time taken by our approach and the approach in [8] when varying the support, with a logarithmic scale for time. Our approach exhibits a better speedup as it extracts fewer patterns than the approach in [8]. Interesting frequent seasonal gradual patterns with their seasonality found in the data of returns of Stock Exchange are as follows. We found the pattern $\{DAX^{(\uparrow,14...16)}, FTSE^{(\uparrow,14...16)}, MSCE\_EU^{(\uparrow,14...16)}\}$, i.e., the Stock market return index of Germany (DAX) increases gradually together with the Stock market return index of UK (FTSE) and the MSCI European index (MSCE_EU) more frequently between the 14th and 16th of each month.

6   Conclusions and Future Work

This paper proposes the seasonal gradual pattern concept which enables us to extract seasonal correlations between attributes from a graduality point of view in a temporal data sequence. Our approach formulates, in the temporal context, a seasonal gradual patterns mining problem as a problem of finding repeated patterns (frequent pattern) in a sequence with wildcards and exploit existing algorithms for enumeration of maximal motifs in a sequence. We also proposed a definition of the associated support measure at a seasonal gradual pattern to efficiently mine frequent patterns in temporal data sequence context. The experimental evaluation on the e-commerce real world data shows the feasibility of our approach and its practical importance. In the future work, we will enrich the experimental study and check the applicability of the approach to other temporal data, e.g., data on the flow of product stocks. Seasonal gradual patterns extracted from such data will allow data experts to detect seasonal co-variations between quantity of products for better management of the supply chain.

References

1. Arimura, H., Uno, T.: An efficient polynomial space and polynomial delay algorithm for enumeration of maximal motifs in a sequence. J. Comb. Optim. **13**(3), 243–262 (2007)
2. Di-Jorio, L., Laurent, A., Teisseire, M.: Mining frequent gradual itemsets from large databases. In: Adams, N.M., Robardet, C., Siebes, A., Boulicaut, J.-F. (eds.) IDA 2009. LNCS, vol. 5772, pp. 297–308. Springer, Heidelberg (2009). https://doi. org/10.1007/978-3-642-03915-7_26
3. Do, T.D.T., Termier, A., Laurent, A., Negrevergne, B., Omidvar-Tehrani, B., Amer-Yahia, S.: PGLCM: efficient parallel mining of closed frequent gradual itemsets. Knowl. Inf. Syst. **43**(3), 497–527 (2014). https://doi.org/10.1007/s10115-014-0749-8
4. Gasmi, G., Yahia, S.B., Nguifo, E.M., Bouker, S.: Extraction of association rules based on literalsets. In: Song, I.Y., Eder, J., Nguyen, T.M. (eds.) DaWaK 2007. LNCS, vol. 4654, pp. 293–302. Springer, Heidelberg (2007). https://doi.org/10. 1007/978-3-540-74553-2_27
5. Hüllermeier, E.: Association rules for expressing gradual dependencies. In: Elomaa, T., Mannila, H., Toivonen, H. (eds.) PKDD 2002. LNCS, vol. 2431, pp. 200–211. Springer, Heidelberg (2002). https://doi.org/10.1007/3-540-45681-3_17
6. Jabbour, S., Lonlac, J., Saïs, L.: Mining gradual itemsets using sequential pattern mining. In: FUZZ-IEEE, pp. 138–143 (2019)
7. Kaytoue, M., Kuznetsov, S.O., Napoli, A.: Revisiting numerical pattern mining with formal concept analysis. In: IJCAI, pp. 1342–1347 (2011)
8. Lonlac, J., Miras, Y., Beauger, A., Mazenod, V., Peiry, J.L., Mephu, E.: An approach for extracting frequent (closed) gradual patterns under temporal constraint. In: FUZZ-IEEE, pp. 878–885 (2018)
9. Ngo, T., Georgescu, V., Laurent, A., Libourel, T., Mercier, G.: Mining spatial gradual patterns: application to measurement of potentially avoidable hospitalizations. In: Tjoa, A.M., Bellatreche, L., Biffl, S., van Leeuwen, J., Wiedermann, J. (eds.) SOFSEM 2018. LNCS, vol. 10706, pp. 596–608. Springer, Cham (2018). https:// doi.org/10.1007/978-3-319-73117-9_42
10. Phan, N., Ienco, D., Malerba, D., Poncelet, P., Teisseire, M.: Mining multi-relational gradual patterns. In: SDM, pp. 846–854 (2015)
11. Pisanti, N., Crochemore, M., Grossi, R., Sagot, M.: Bases of motifs for generating repeated patterns with wild cards. IEEE/ACM Trans. Comput. Biol. Bioinform. **2**(1), 40–50 (2005)
12. Salleb-Aouissi, A., Vrain, C., Nortet, C.: Quantminer: a genetic algorithm for mining quantitative association rules. In: IJCAI, pp. 1035–1040 (2007)

Derivative, Regression and Time Series Analysis in SARS-CoV-2

Pedro Furtado$^{(\boxtimes)}$

Universidade de Coimbra, Coimbra, Portugal
pnf@dei.uc.pt

Abstract. The Covid-19 pandemic and the need of confinement have had a very significant impact on people's lives all over the world. Everybody is looking at curves and how those curves evolve to try to understand how their country has been and will be affected in the near future. Thanks to open data and data science tools, we can analyze the evolution of key factors. Derivatives, polynomial regression and time series analysis can be used to capture trends. In this paper we explore and evaluate the use of such techniques, concluding regarding their merits and limitations for the Covid-19 data series. We conclude that polynomial regression on derivative totals, with degree 2 or 3 achieved the lowest average errors (median 5.5 to 6%) over 20 countries, while PROPHET and ARIMA may excel in larger series.

Keywords: Time series analysis · Regression · Data analysis

1 Introduction

All through history, humanity has been hit by pandemics periodically, and there were already at least three significant global outbreak events only in the current century. Nevertheless, the one hitting the world in 2019 was the most serious in the first two decades of the century. In fact, the world health organization (WHO) alerted the world several times that "it was only a matter of time until a dangerous pandemic would ravage the world". The Corona virus 2019 disease (Covid-19), which hit China first and quickly expanded to all the world in 2019/2020, is an infectious disease caused by the "severe acute respiratory syndrome coronavirus 2" (SARS-CoV-2) virus. The threat posed by this virus and the fact that there was no prior immunization, no medicines and no vaccination available at the time, has resulted in a quick spreading and a considerable death toll, especially among oldest people. Authorities had to command social distancing, confinement of people to their homes and entire cities, regions and countries entered severe lockdowns in an effort to delay the spread of the virus and to avoid overburdening underequipped hospital's intensive care units (IUCs). Shops, schools and factories were closed, some countries declared various degrees of state of emergency to deal with the problem more effectively, the damage to economy was huge.

Both epidemiologists and common people became familiarized with the infamous curves of total and active cases, deaths and others, which depict the evolution of cases

© Springer Nature Switzerland AG 2020
M. Song et al. (Eds.): DaWaK 2020, LNCS 12393, pp. 208–220, 2020.
https://doi.org/10.1007/978-3-030-59065-9_17

in each category as time goes by. Epidemiologists have for long studied the growth rates and typical curves of a pandemic. The most famous initial model that gave rise to most modern epidemiology simulation models was SIR [10], which stands for Suspect-Infected-Recovered, and its workings is simple to understand. Given an initial population of N individuals, the model simulates the rate of transition between the three states (S, I and R). The curves described by SIR and related models are approximate estimations, depend on the setting of parameters, such as the incubation period, the contact rate within the population, the mean infectious period, social distancing factors, population and the population density. Besides epidemiology models, which depend on population-related parameters that need to be adjusted, it is also worth considering, as complementary means, the possibility of applying derivatives, regression and time series analysis directly, to rapidly plot past and possible near future trends. One example of technique is to apply polynomial regression with least squares optimization to fit polynomial coefficients to the curve, then estimating also into the near future. It should be noted that no method is sufficiently accurate if conditions change abruptly, such as when a lockdown is decided suddenly, but at least these complementary techniques give hints into possible evolutions in the near future. One possible simple application of these curve fitting options is an add-on to the graphing dashboards that allows users to superimpose and try more than one degree on a polynomial regression on a certain chart depicting curves.

In this paper we describe and apply the techniques to the curves of Covid-19 over a set of 20 countries to evaluate how well they fit to the near future curve. A set of techniques, pre-processing and transformations can be applied (e.g. polynomial degree, first derivative or logarithm).

The paper is structured as follows: Sect. 2 contains related work. Section 3 discusses the Covid-19 curves and preprocessing techniques. Section 4 discusses curve fitting techniques we developed to use with Covid-19. Section 5 contains experimental work to evaluate the feasibility of the techniques and Sect. 6 concludes.

2   Related Work

There are a few most frequently used curve fitting algorithms in the literature. Polynomial regression [1] is a type of regression analysis where the relationship between the independent variable x and the dependent variable y is modelled as an nth degree polynomial in x. Polynomial regression models are usually fit using least squares optimization [2]. The least-squares method minimizes the variance of the unbiased estimators of the coefficients. Another well-known technique for time series analysis is the Autoregressive Integrated Moving Average Model (ARIMA) [3, 4]. ARIMA models can apply an initial differencing step one or more times to eliminate non-stationarity, with AR meaning regression of the variable on its prior values, MA moving average, and I (for "integration") one or more replacements of the values with the difference between the values and the previous values. The purpose of each of these features is to make the model fit the data as closely as possible. Prophet [5] is Facebook's own proposal for time series analysis. At its core, the Prophet procedure is an additive regression model using a piecewise linear or logistic growth curve trend. Prophet automatically detects changes in trends, by selecting changepoints from the data, as part of its curve fitting process. Both ARIMA and Prophet are designed to also handle seasonality. In time series models a curve is typically decomposed into components such as trend, seasonality and residuals (seasonality is not relevant in Covid-19 series). In a recent work [6] we compared the prediction accuracies of ARIMA and Prophet for analysis of Telecom data. The results have shown that, after a fine tuning of ARIMA parameters, it provided more accurate results than Prophet for the Telecom data, although it required configuration and fine-tuning.

The discipline of Epidemiology and its models were already established long ago. Works in models for infectious diseases are reviewed in [7], and [8, 9] are other textbooks on the subject. The dynamics of an epidemic can be modelled as a set of differential equations, and one of the most famous initial models is SIR, by Kermack and McKendrick [10]. The mnemonic SIR stands for Susceptible (S), Infectious (I) and Recovered (R), while SEIR adds an Exposed (E) state. Given the three possible states (S, I and R), they are organized sequentially (S -> I -> R) such that individuals transition between them and the differential equations describe the change in the stock of each state per unit of time. Naturally, the sum of changes of S, I and R is 0, since the individuals transition between states (one more individual in one state corresponds to one less in the previous state). Between S and I the transition rate is βI, where β is the average number of contacts per person per time, multiplied by the probability of disease transmission in a contact between a susceptible and an infectious subject. Between I and R the transition rate is γ (number of recovered or dead during one time unit, divided by the total number of infected on that same time interval). If the duration of the infection is denoted by D, then $\gamma = 1/D$, since an individual experiences one recovery in D units of time. It is assumed that the permanence of each single subject in the epidemic states is a random variable with exponential distribution. With these differential equations it is possible to simulate the dynamics of a specific epidemic. References [11] and [12] are examples of works on mathematical modeling of Covid-19. While we have also been working with SIR-related models, in this paper we restrict our comparative analysis to the curve fitting and time series analysis approaches, which can be seen as complementary to help plot the past and near future trends. SIR, on the other hand, requires deduction of parameters such as the contact rate between persons and social distancing rate, and serves a what-if-analysis based on assumptions regarding those parameters.

3   Covid-19 Catastrophe Curves and Preprocessing

Figure 1 is a typical set of Covid-19 curves corresponding to a few countries, depicting the number of actives (number of persons identified as having covid-19, note that 80% of cases are asymptomatic and the true number of infections may be around 5 times more). Note that China had its outbreak considerably before the remaining countries. The first pre-processing step takes care of aligning curves by start of outbreak. Some countries have a lot more cases and faster growth, due to the population size and other factors such as traveling.

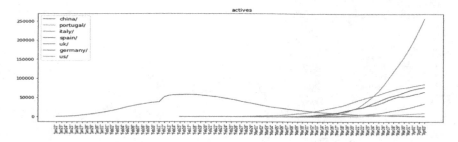

Fig. 1. Number of people infected (actives)

3.1 Alignment and Per Million Curves

Alignment refers to considering day one of each curve as the day when the number of cases reaches a certain threshold, then aligning all curves on their day one. After aligning on day one of each country based on total number of cases reaching 50, Fig. 2 shows most countries evolving in a steeper or smoother growing curve initially, then some of them already decreasing the rate of growth of new cases. At the time, US had the most daily cases and growth (a), but Spain, Portugal and Italy came first if analyzed per million of affected population (b).

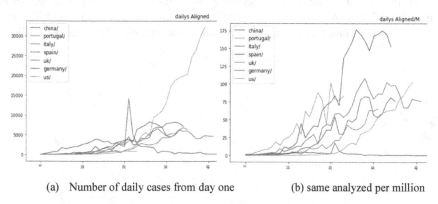

(a)   Number of daily cases from day one   (b) same analyzed per million

Fig. 2. New daily cases aligned and per million

3.2 Derivatives and Derivatives Relative to Value

Given social distancing and no other extraordinary events, the rate of change of daily cases is expected to decrease at a steady rate, and it is useful to analyze derivatives to see this. Figure 3(a) shows the evolution of totals from day one, while Fig. 3(b) shows that the rate of increase of totals is decreasing steadily.

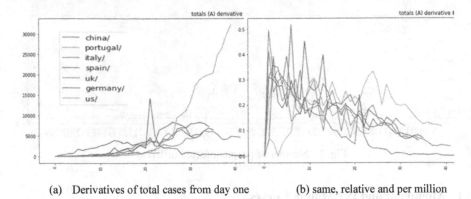

(a)   Derivatives of total cases from day one   (b) same, relative and per million

Fig. 3. Derivatives of totals (absolute and relative)

3.3 Moving Averages and Logs

In spite of the global trend, the curves in Fig. 3 have some high local variations. This reflects for instance the fact that the number of new daily cases has fluctuations related to testing procedures, possible lack of testing kits, reporting delays, new local outbreaks and many other factors. This variation can easily be smoothed by applying moving averages. Figure 4(a) is the result of applying two consecutive moving averages (MA) to Fig. 3(b) (1st MA over 3 days, 2nd over 5), smoothing the result. Figure 4(b) shows another example of preprocessing, the logarithm of the number of actives per million.

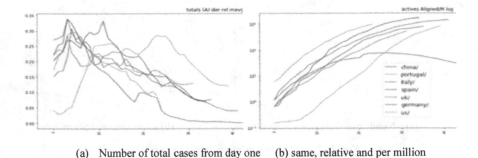

(a)   Number of total cases from day one   (b) same, relative and per million

Fig. 4. Smoothed and logarithmic

3.4 Importance of Analysis of Rate of Growth or Derivative

The evolution of the rate of change (derivative) of new daily cases captures an important tendency related to the slowing of the exponential growth rate much before the number of new daily cases starts to decrease itself. Also importantly, we can correlate these changes with public policies. Figures 5 and 6 show the variation of daily cases relative to the number of cases for Italy (Fig. 5) and for Germany (Fig. 6), and they also show the day when some of the measures were taken in those countries. From these figures we can see two main things: the rate of growth of new cases started declining very early; this was due to government-imposed social distancing and lockdown measures (significant events are shown on the curves), but also probably due to people voluntarily distancing themselves from others due to fear.

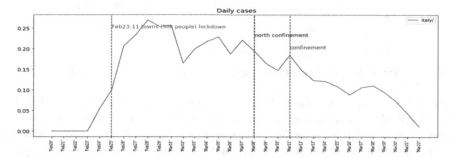

Fig. 5. Variation of daily cases relative to nr. of cases, Italy

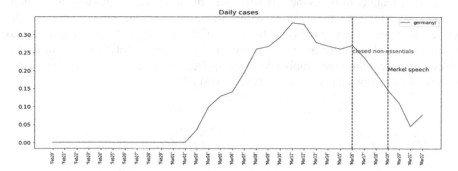

Fig. 6. Variation in daily cases relative to nr. of cases, Germany

4 Curve Fitting Techniques and Transformations

In this paper we study three main curve fitting techniques that are polynomial regression, ARIMA and PROPHET. Figure 7 shows an example of applying polynomial regression of degree 6 to the curve of daily cases in Italy. Polynomial regression uses least squares to fit the a_i coefficients of Eq. (1) so that it will be capable of fitting the curve as well as possible. The resulting polynomial can then be used also to estimate the near future trend.

$$a_0 x^n + a_1 x^{n-1} + \ldots + a_n \tag{1}$$

ARIMA and PROPHET are well-known time series analysis techniques. Figures 8 and 9 are examples showing the result of forecasting the variation of daily cases in USA

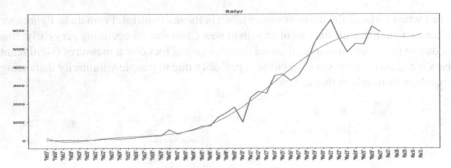

Fig. 7. Output of polynomial regression degree 6, daily cases in Italy

using ARIMA (Fig. 8), and the number of new daily cases in Portugal using Prophet (Fig. 9). ARIMA can apply transformations to obtain stationarity prior to fitting, and parameters p, d, q help configure those transformations [3, 4, 6]. A non-seasonal ARIMA model is classified as an "ARIMA(p, d, q)" model, where p is the number of autoregressive terms, d is the number of nonseasonal differences needed for stationarity, and q is the number of lagged forecast errors in the prediction equation. This way parameter d indicates the number of times the series has been differentiated to approximate stationarity in time, p indicates the order of the Autoregressive component and represents the delayed time period, and q indicates the order of the moving average component and represents the delayed forecast errors. For more details, please refer to [3, 4, 6]. In our current implementation we simply coded the application to test AIC [6] of the various possible combinations and choose the best (lowest AIC).

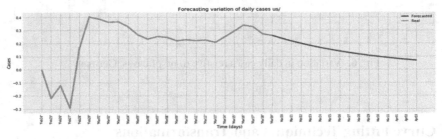

Fig. 8. ARIMA forecasting for USA (blue curve) (Color figure online)

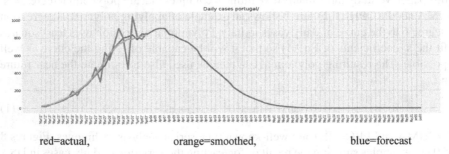

red=actual,   orange=smoothed,   blue=forecast

Fig. 9. Prophet forecasting for Portugal (blue curve) (Color figure online)

Transformation prior to curve fitting concerns calculating either a derivative (in discrete terms it is equivalent to the difference between consecutive days or groups of days), a logarithm, a logistic function or other function, with the objective of obtaining a more uniform series that is easier to fit well. As we have discussed before, techniques such as ARIMA already transform and decompose the series. In the case of polynomial regression with least squares optimization, we added the needed code to both transform and "inverse transform" to restore the original curve from the forecasted curve.

5 Experiments

We created an experimental setup based on python that collects all information regarding a set of more than 50 countries online from publicly available websites (e.g. WHO, world-o-meter, others). After automatic collection of all the data concerning the pandemics evolution curves (including numbers of new daily cases, evolution of total number of cases, number of active cases), all the datasets were aligned on the day when total cases reach 50. Then the 20 countries with more cases as-of-the-last-recorded-day was chosen. Our setup includes the following:

- **Countries:** us, spain, italy, germany, france, iran, uk, turkey, switzerland, belgium, netherlands, canada, austria, portugal, south-korea, brazil, israel, sweden, australia, norway, ireland. We also use China in 2nd experiment;
- **Datasets used:** totals and dailys;
- **Techniques:** Polynomial regression (POL), ARIMA and Prophet;
- **Transformations:** None (-), derivative (DER) Logarithm (LOG)
- **Polynomial degrees:** 1,2,3,4

Our first experiment compares the quality of the techniques and variations forecasting 15 new days in curves of 20 countries. The last 15 days are removed from the curve, the approaches run and finally the error is evaluated regarding the forecast of the 15 days that were missing for the model building phase. The error metric is mean relative error (MRE), given by $(\text{sum}(e_i)/y_i)$, where y_i is the real value for day i and $e_i = y_i\text{-}y'_i$, where y'_i is the forecasted value for day i. (note: we obtained error metrics RMSE, MAE, but the relative error eases comparison between countries and overall). The standard deviation (stdev) is the standard deviation of MRE of the different countries. For the second experiment we took a longest series (China, since it had 73 days of curve data) and compared the polynomial regressors, ARIMA and Prophet as we increase the days to forecast (20,30,40,50,55,60 days). Once again, the "new" forecasted days evaluated were of course absent from the model building step.

Note that if we were to evaluate the part of the curve that was used to train the models, the error would be small. Figure 10 ("the gold standard") shows the MRE for 20 countries considering the same curve for training and evaluation. Prophet and ARIMA were perfect (errors below 2.5%), POL 3 (polynomial of degree 3) had errors below 10% and POL DER 3 (polynomial on derivative data) had higher errors, between 5% and 25%. This shows that the sophistication of ARIMA and Prophet pays off in this case.

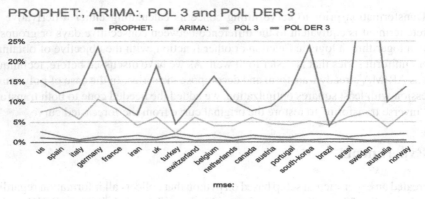

Fig. 10. 15-days forecast error for POL deg 3 over 20 countries

5.1 Comparison Over 20 Countries

Table 1 shows the results of experiment 1, which fitted truncated curves of 20 countries and measured average and median mean relative error for forecasting 15 days ahead. Besides testing POL, PROPHET and ARIMA, we also experimented with the pre-transformations DER (derivative) and LOG (logarithm).

Table 1. Average and median 15 days forecast error for each approach over 20 countries

type	Dataset	Transform	Degree	Avg MRE	Median MRE	Stddev
POL	totals	–	1	49.4%	50.3%	14.4%
POL	totals	–	2	21.6%	20.0%	12.6%
POL	totals	–	3	30.4%	26.8%	24.0%
POL	totals	–	4	67.7%	47.0%	89.5%
POL	totals	LOG	2	69.0%	36.9%	69.3%
POL	totals	LOG	3	85.9%	54.2%	75.8%
POL	totals	DER	2	9.4%	**5.4%**	19.0%
POL	totals	DER	3	11.0%	**6.0%**	17.9%
POL	totals	DER	4	15.0%	8.8%	18.0%
PROPHET	totals	–	–	58.0%	63.0%	18.1%
ARIMA	totals	–	–	37.9%	36.1%	17.0%
PROPHET	dailys	DER	–	67.7%	42.8%	89.9%
ARIMA	dailys	DER	–	64.1%	36.0%	94.0%

First of all, the results or Table 1 show that the daily dataset (versus totals) or the LOG (versus none or derivative DER) were not useful (worst errors). Table 1 also shows that polynomial regression over derivative data achieved the lowest errors overall (5.4

to 6% median MRE). Next comes polynomial regression without derivative (20 to 27%) and ARIMA coming only after those (36%). Note also that the standard deviations are not small, since we are dealing with very different curves of 20 countries.

Figure 11 shows MRE details of POL DER deg 3 for each of the 20 countries (USA, which had 89% MRE, is not shown in the chart since showing it would hide the differences between the other countries).

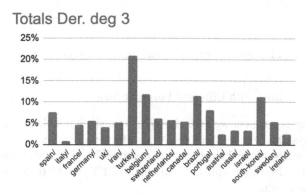

Fig. 11. 15 days forecast error for POL deg 3 over 20 countries

Next it is important to determine if these results are correlated somehow with the number of days of each series or with the average number of total cases over all days of each country. Figure 12 shows, for the best PROPHET, ARIMA and POL, the error versus the number of days the data series had (each circle represents a single country), and Fig. 13 shows the error versus the average number of total cases of each series. In Fig. 12 we do not find a definitive correlation between the number of days of the series and the error, but we do find that, in general, the errors of PROPHET and ARIMA vary more than POL. Similar conclusions apply to Fig. 13, where we also observe that all techniques had errors below 30% for average total cases between 15000 and 35000.

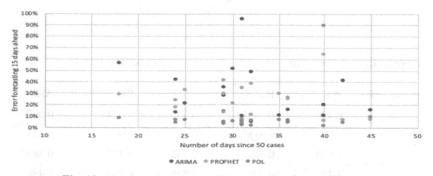

Fig. 12. Number of days since 50 cases versus forecasting error

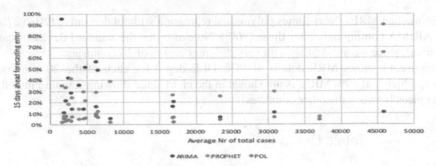

Fig. 13. Forecasting error versus average total nr. of cases

5.2 Forecasting China with Different Forecast Sizes

For the following experiment we have chosen China, since it is the longest series in all countries (73 days), and experiment forecasting different numbers of days using each of the tested approaches. Table 2 shows the results for POL (POLn(d) means polynomial regression over the derivative with degree n), PROPHET and ARIMA, and Fig. 14 is an illustration of the results.

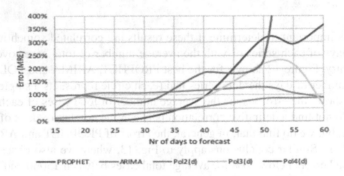

Fig. 14. MRE versus number of days to forecast (China)

Table 2. Error (MAE) using regression polynomials, prophet and ARIMA on China

Days to forecast	POL2(d)	POL3(d)	POL4(d)	PROPHET	ARIMA
15	0.450	0.780	0.980	0.044	0.097
20	1.038	0.915	0.987	0.029	0.145
30	1.088	0.855	0.742	0.132	0.283
40	1.191	0.939	1.858	0.817	0.498
50	1.306	2.198	2.399	2.541	0.812
60	0.910	0.592	29.619	2.752	0.849

It is interesting to see, from these results, that ARIMA was the most regular approach, with very good fit for forecasts of up to 30 days, then loosing quality slowly as the number of days to forecast increases. PROPHET was the best and almost perfect approach up to 30 days, but then exploded in error. Since, as we increase the number of days to forecast we are simultaneously reducing the number of days to build the forecasting model, this probably indicate that PROPHET needs a lot of prior data to optimize its fit well. POL with degree 2 had high error rate (around 100%), but that error was more or less stable, while POL degree 4 went off-scale and POL degree 3 also had very bad results for 50 and 55 days. This may indicate that the higher the degree of the polynomial, the higher the probability that it bounces off-scale. More generically, these results with China seem to indicate that, for longer series, ARIMA and PROPHET become more competent than POL. This makes sense intuitively, since ARIMA and PROPHET decompose the curve into components and model those, therefore they are much more sophisticated approaches than POL that are able to capture more detail if the series are longer/more complex. The problem facing those sophisticated techniques with the epidemiology curves is that we want to see trends and forecasts while things are happening and we still have only a few days or weeks of up-to-today information. For those cases, POL with the derivative seems more adequate.

6   Conclusions

In this paper we have studied the use of curve fitting and time series approaches to fit Covid-19 curves and to forecast few days ahead. Our main objective was to compare the techniques in order to understand their value for this objective. The data series were preprocessed and the techniques were tested against 20 countries. We concluded that polynomial regression (POL) with degree 3 over derivative data (DER) achieved the best quality on the typical series as-of 20 to 45 days from the outbreak in the country. However, we also concluded based on analysis of a larger series (China, which is the only much longer series) that both ARIMA and PROPHET were much better in that case, raising the possibility that they work better for longer series, related to their capacity to capture how components evolve. Note however that we want to capture the trends in real time, in times when the curves are still relatively short. As part of our current and future work we have also been testing application of the SIR epidemiological model with automatic curve fitting, therefore we will also compare it in future publications.

References

1. Fan, J.: Local Polynomial Modelling and Its Applications: From Linear Regression to Nonlinear Regression. Monographs on Statistics and Applied Probability. Chapman & Hall/CRC, Boca Raton (1996). ISBN 978-0-412-98321-4
2. Gergonne, J.D.: [1815] The application of the method of least squares to the interpolation of sequences. Historia Mathematica (Translated by Ralph St. John and S. M. Stigler from the 1815 French ed. 1(4): 439–447 (1974). https://doi.org/10.1016/0315-0860(74)90034-2
3. Box, G., Jenkins, G.M., Reinsel, G.C.: Time Series Analysis: Forecasting and Control, 3rd ed. Prentice-Hall (1994). ISBN 0130607746

4. Brockwell, P.J., Davis, R.A.: Time Series: Theory and Methods (2nd ed.), p. 273. Springer, New York (2009). https://doi.org/10.1007/978-1-4899-0004-3, ISBN 9781441903198
5. Prophet Forecasting at scale. https://facebook.github.io/prophet/. Accessed 16 Apr 2019
6. Pinho, A., Costa, R., Silva, H., Furtado, P.: Comparing time series prediction approaches for telecom analysis. In: Valenzuela, O., Rojas, F., Pomares, H., Rojas, I. (eds.) ITISE 2018. CS, pp. 331–345. Springer, Cham (2019). https://doi.org/10.1007/978-3-030-26036-1_23
7. Hethcote, H.: The mathematics of infectious diseases. SIAM Rev. **42**(4), 599–653 (2000). Bibcode:2000SIAMR..42..599H. https://doi.org/10.1137/s0036144500371907
8. Bailey, N.T.J.: The Mathematical Theory of Infectious Diseases and its Applications (2nd ed.). Griffin, London (1975). ISBN 0-85264-231-8
9. Anderson, R.M. (ed.): Population Dynamics of Infectious Diseases: Theory and Applications. Chapman and Hall, London-New York (1982). ISBN 0-412-21610-8
10. Kermack, W.O., McKendrick, A.G.: A Contribution to the Mathematical Theory of Epidemics. Proceedings of the Royal Society A. **115**(772), 700–721 (1927). Bibcode:1927RSPSA.115..700K. https://doi.org/10.1098/rspa.1927.0118
11. Prem, K., et al.: The effect of control strategies to reduce social mixing on outcomes of the COVID-19 epidemic in Wuhan, China: a modelling study. The Lancet Public Health (2020)
12. Kucharski, A.J., et al.: Early dynamics of transmission and control of COVID-19: a mathematical modelling study. The lancet infectious diseases

Machine Learning and Deep Learning

Building a Competitive Associative Classifier

Nitakshi Sood[✉] and Osmar Zaiane[✉] [ID]

Alberta Machine Intelligence Institute, University of Alberta,
Edmonton T6G2R3, Canada
{nitakshi,zaiane}@ualberta.ca

Abstract. With the huge success of deep learning, other machine learning paradigms have had to take back seat. Yet other models, particularly rule-based, are more readable and explainable and can even be competitive when labelled data is not abundant. However, most of the existing rule-based classifiers suffer from the production of a large number of classification rules, affecting the model readability. This hampers the classification accuracy as noisy rules might not add any useful information for classification and also lead to longer classification time. In this study, we propose SigD2 which uses a novel, two-stage pruning strategy which prunes most of the noisy, redundant and uninteresting rules and makes the classification model more accurate and readable. To make SigDirect more competitive with the most prevalent but uninterpretable machine learning-based classifiers like neural networks and support vector machines, we propose bagging and boosting on the ensemble of the SigDirect classifier. The results of the proposed algorithms are quite promising and we are able to obtain a minimal set of statistically significant rules for classification without jeopardizing the classification accuracy. We use 15 UCI datasets and compare our approach with eight existing systems. The SigD2 and boosted SigDirect (ACboost) ensemble model outperform various state-of-the-art classifiers not only in terms of classification accuracy but also in terms of the number of rules.

1 Introduction

Associative classifiers combine the concept of association rule mining and classification to build a classification model. In an associative classifier, for a rule in the form $X \rightarrow Y$, we choose the consequent(Y) of the rule to be the class label and the antecedent set(X) is a set of attribute-value pairs for the associated class label. In the literature, various associative classifiers have been proposed till now namely, CBA [11], CMAR [10], CPAR [14] etc. Although these classifiers are easily understandable, flexible and do not assume independence among the attributes, they require prior knowledge for choosing appropriate parameter values (support and confidence). Furthermore, the rules generated may include noisy and meaningless rules, which might hinder the classification. A rule is said to be noisy if it does not add any new information for prediction and instead

© Springer Nature Switzerland AG 2020
M. Song et al. (Eds.): DaWaK 2020, LNCS 12393, pp. 223–234, 2020.
https://doi.org/10.1007/978-3-030-59065-9_18

misleads the classification model. In other terms, a noisy rule would participate more often in misclassifications than in correct classifications. The authors in [9] proposed SigDirect, an associative classifier which mines statistically significant rules without the need for the support and confidence values. However, in this paper, we propose SigD2 where we introduce a more effective two stage pruning strategy to obtain a more accurate classification model. The proposed method reduces the number of rules to be used for classification without compromising on the prediction performance. In fact, the performance is improved. Most of the prevalent supervised classification techniques like Artificial Neural Networks (ANN), Support Vector Machines (SVM) etc, although provide very high classification accuracy, they act as a black box. The models produced by such classifiers are not straight forwardly explainable. However, the proposed associative classifier makes the model more explainable by producing only a minimal set of classification association rules (CARs). The proposed technique finds its immense usage in various health-care related applications, where the explanation of proposed models along with the classification accuracy are highly significant. In health-care, incorrect predictions may have catastrophic effect, so doctors find it hard to trust AI unless they can validate the obtained results. Furthermore, we also propose ACboost, which uses an ensemble of classification models obtained from the weak version of SigDirect, for boosting. Our goal is to strengthen the classifier using less number of rules for prediction. Since, SigDirect is a strong learner and produces already a lesser number of rules for prediction, we form a weak version of SigDirect called wSigDirect, by further reducing the number of rules to be used for classification as explained later in Sect. 3. We also propose ACbag which is defined as bagging on an ensemble of wSigDirect classifiers. With the use of this strategy of combining weak learners, the goal is to decrease the variance in the prediction and improve the classification performance henceforth. It was found that for most of the datasets ACboost performs better than SigD2, ACbag, SVM, or ANN; ANN which performs similarly to deep neural network (DNN) on these reasonably sized datasets. The main aim of this study is to make associative classifiers more competitive and to highlight their significance as opposed to the other machine learning based classifiers like neural networks which do not produce explainable predictions. Our contribution in this study is as follows:

- We propose SigD2, an associative classifier, which uses an effective two stage pruning strategy for pruning the rules to be used for classification. Using the proposed approach, the number of rules used for classification are reduced notably, without compromising on the classification performance.
- We propose ACbag, an ensemble based classifier founded on wSigDirect.
- We also propose ACboost, which is boosting the wSigDirect classifier, to improve the classification accuracy with an explainable base model. Therefore, making SigDirect more competitive for classification tasks.

The rest of the paper is organized as follows: Sect. 2 gives a literature review about some previously proposed associative classifiers, Sect. 3 explains the methodologies we have adapted in SigD2, ACbag and ACboost, Sect. 4 shows the evaluation results of our proposed classifier on UCI datasets and lastly, Sect. 5 gives the conclusion of the work and directions about future investigations.

2 Related Work

In this section, we briefly describe some related work on associative classification. Stemming from association rule mining, associative classifiers have been extensively studied in the last two decades. Liu et al. first proposed the classification based on association (CBA) technique in [11] and showed that the association rule mining techniques could be applicable to classification tasks. CBA uses the Apriori algorithm to generate CARs and database coverage for pruning the noisy rules. It uses the highest ranked matching rules as the heuristic for classification. Inspired by the idea of CBA, many authors came up with more efficient versions of associative classifiers. CPAR proposed by Yin and Han uses a dynamic programming based greedy strategy that generates association rules from the training dataset [14]. It prevents repeated calculation in rule generation and also selects best k rules in prediction. The associative classifiers have the ability to provide a readable classification model. The study done by Zaiane et al. in [15] focuses on the significance of obtaining a minimal set of CAR's without jeopardising the performance of the classifier. They propose a pruning strategy to reduce the number of rules in order to build an effective classification model without seriously compromising on the classification accuracy. The authors also propose heuristics to select rules which obtain high accuracy on the plot of correct/incorrect classification for each rule on the training set for effective rule pruning combined with the database coverage technique based on the given dataset. Tuning values for support and confidence parameters is an arduous task as it varies with the change in dataset. Li and Zaïane in [9] overcome this limitation by proposing SigDirect that tunes only one parameter that is the p-value, which computes the statistical significance of rules using Fisher's exact test. The authors proposed an instance centric rule pruning strategy for pruning the non statistically significant rules. Although SigDirect has proved to be quite competitive in terms of prediction, there are still noisy rules that can compromise the accuracy. Furthermore, ensemble models are widely used for enhancing the accuracy of the classification models using a combination of weak learners. The SAMME algorithm proposed by Hastie et al. in [8] is a multi-class extension of the binary Adaboost algorithm [7].

3 Methodology

In this section, we introduce the details about the proposed effective pruning technique as used in SigD2. Further, we extend our work to perform bagging and boosting over the ensemble of wSigDirect associative classifier.

3.1 SigD2

The aim of an associative classifier is to find knowledge from data in the form of association rules associating conjunctions of attribute-value pairs with class labels, and then use these rules for prediction. SigD2 processes the learning of rules in rule generation and rule pruning phases. It further uses these rules for prediction in the classification phase.

Rule Generation Phase: In this phase, we use the same approach proposed by Li and Zaïane for SigDirect in [9]. SigD2 also generates statistically significant CARs using the p-value from Fisher's exact test, of the rule in the form $X \to c_k$. The complete explanation of the generation process can be found in [9].

Algorithm 1: Algorithm for Two-Stage Pruning Strategy used in SigD2

Input: T: Pruning transaction database, **R**: Initial rule list from rule generation phase, **R$_{mid}$**: Rule list being formed after pruning the insignificant rules from R, **conf_threshold**: Confidence threshold value.

Result: R$_{new}$: Classification association rules to be used for prediction

while *rules exist in R* **do**

    Sort the rules in R in descending order of their confidence values

    Select the rule r_i with highest confidence from R and add to the R$_{mid}$

    if *conf(r_i) < conf_threshold* **then**

        | break

    Find all applicable instances in T that match the antecedent of rule r_i

    if *r_i correctly classifies a pruning instance in T* **then**

        Mark r_i as a candidate rule in the classifier

        Remove all instances in T covered by r_i

    Update the confidence values, based on the remaining transactions

    Remove the rule r_i from the R

end

for *each instance t in the original transaction database T* **do**

    Scan the CARs from R$_{mid}$ to find the matching CAR r_i, with highest confidence value

    if *$r_i \notin R_{new}$* **then**

        R$_{new}$.add(r_i)

        r_i.count=1

    else

        r_i.count+=1

    end

end

Rule Pruning Phase: The rule generation phase may produce many CARs which are noisy and would not only slow down the process of classification but also lead to incorrect classification. Originally, SigDirect only performs instance based rule pruning on generated rules. It was observed that, although the previous strategy produces globally best CARs, the rules were still noisy and could be further reduced. So the question is, how can we prune more rules without actually jeopardising the accuracy of the associative classifier?

We propose a two stage strategy for pruning, wherein we randomly divide the training set into train set and prune set in the ratio of 2:1. The rules are generated in the rule generation phase using the train set. However, for pruning, only the prune set is used. We sort the CARs in descending order according to confidence values. The proposed pruning process, consists of matching the CAR with highest confidence and scanning over all the transactions in the pruning dataset to see if they match. If the rule applies correctly on the transactions, it is marked and is selected to be used for classification and subsequently the matching transactions are removed from the pruning set. We re-calculate the confidence values of the remaining rules, each time using the remaining transactions in the pruning set and arrange them in the descending order. This process is repeated until either the rules or transactions have been covered or until the confidence threshold is reached. It is assumed that for a rule, if the confidence value in each iteration is less than the threshold, then that rule can be pruned as it is not able to cover at least few instances in the prune set. After this step, we obtain the rules which might be useful for classification. However, we still need to find the globally best CARs. So, further we apply the instance based pruning step as proposed in SigDirect [9]. For every instance in the pruning transaction database, the complete set of CARs generated from the previous step are scanned. The aim here is to find the matching CARs with the highest confidence value, such that, the class label of the rule and the transaction matches and the antecedent of the rule is the subset of the transaction. Furthermore, the count of how many times the rule has been selected in the pruning instances is maintained. This is later used in order to perform weighted classification using the number of times the CAR was selected in the pruning phase. Using the proposed approach only high quality rules with high confidence values are kept. This pruning strategy also avoids over-fitting on the data.

Classification Phase: After the pruning phase, the minimal set of statistically significant rules is obtained. Further we make predictions on the new instances from the test set. For a given new instance, the classification process would search the subset of the CARs that match the new instance in order to predict its class label. The three heuristics used for classification are such that, for all the matching CARs, each class's group should be ordered on the basis of sum of ln(p-value), sum of confidence value and the sum of ln(p-value).confidence. Explanation of the classification process can be found in [9]. Furthermore, we can also use two stage classification as proposed by Sood et al. in [13], to learn with a NN in a second phase to predict the classification rules to use.

3.2   Bagging and Boosting on wSigDirect

In this section, we perform bagging and boosting on the weak version of SigDirect, we call wSigDirect. While SigDirect is already a strong learner, we chose it over CBA as it gives a smaller number of rules. But we need to make it weaker to be used for ACbag and ACboost. We do this by further reducing the number of rules to be used for classification. The strategy for rule generation and rule pruning stays similar to that of the original SigDirect. However, for all the association rules obtained from the pruning phase for classification, we divide these rules as per the class label. Further, we chose the top η rules on the basis of highest confidence values from each class label group. The classification model thus obtained is called weak as it does not involve all the significant rules. We perform bagging and boosting on the ensemble model of wSigDirect over different trained datasets for prediction.

Bagging: ACbag is motivated by the approach proposed in [1]. The weak classifiers are learnt in parallel by picking instances randomly with replacement from the training data. Each wSigDirect model is learnt independent of each other. In bootstrap sampling, every observation has equal probability of appearing in the training dataset. Finally, we perform a majority voting over the results of the weak learners and predict the class label for each testing sample. Since, the base models are explainable, the ACbag can explain the responses of each learner, and the explanation of the ensemble would be the set of rules that were voted on by the ensemble. Furthermore, it was observed that the results obtained after performing bagging on wSigDirect are very comparable or slightly better than those achieved by bagging on the original SigDirect.

Boosting: Boosting is a process of improving the performance of a weak learning algorithm. It is done under the assumption that, the performance of the weak learner is at least slightly better than random guessing on different observations. In this phase, we propose ACboost which iteratively calls wSigDirect. This weak learner is converted to a strong learner either by weighted average of the predictions from weak learners or by considering prediction with majority voting. Given a training set, with features and class labels, we initialize the weights of our samples as one divided by the number of training instances. For the number of weak learners to be used sequentially, we train the first base learner using wSigDirect and obtain the misclassification error of the model. Further, the weight of the classifier is calculated based on its performance on the training data. Finally, the weight of each sample is updated, such that samples that were correctly classified are given less weights whereas the samples which were incorrectly predicted are given more weights. This would force the learner to pay more attention towards the incorrect predictions done by the previous learner. The iteration is continued till the maximum number of estimators (pre-set number of weak learners) are reached or a low training error is achieved. Finally, the prediction is done by using the weights of each classifier calculated previously to perform weighted prediction. This sequential learning of models helps in reducing the training error. We have used the methodology proposed for multi-class classification in SAMME algorithm [8], an extension of adaboost, which adds up a log term to the weight of the classifier making the boosting algorithm applicable for both two-class and multi-class classification tasks. Furthermore, since the rules produced by the base classifier are explainable therefore, there is a possibility of interpretation of results.

4   Experimental Results

We evaluate our SigD2 associative classifier on 15 UCI datasets [6]. We discretize the datasets as proposed in [2], so the classification accuracy might be marginally different from the previously reported results. We report the results after performing the average over 10 fold cross validation on each dataset. We use 90% of the total data as the train set and further divide the train set into train set and prune set in the ratio of 2:1.

Table 1. Comparison of classification accuracy of SigD2 with other rule-based classifiers

Datasets	#cls	#rec	C4.5	CBA	CMAR	CPAR	RIPPER	SigDirect	SigD2
Adult	2	48842	78.8	**84.2**	81.3	77.3	**84.1**	**84.1**	83.59
Anneal	6	898	76.7	94.5	90.7	95.1	**98.32**	96.99	**97.21**
Breast	2	699	91.5	**94.1**	89.9	93	**95.42**	91.7	92.7
Flare	9	1389	82.1	84.2	**84.3**	63.9	72.13	**84.23**	**84.3**
Glass	7	214	65.9	68.4	**71.1**	64.9	68.69	**70.56**	69.17
Heart	5	303	**61.5**	57.8	56.2	53.8	53.97	58.49	**59.81**
Hepatitis	2	155	84.1	42.2	79.6	75.5	78.06	**85.83**	86
Horse	2	368	70.9	78.8	82.3	81.2	**84.23**	81.23	**85.03**
Iris	3	150	91.3	93.3	94	94.7	**95.33**	94	**96**
Led7	10	3200	**73.9**	73.1	73.2	71.3	69.15	73.78	**73.81**
Mushroom	2	8124	92.5	46.5	**100**	98.5	100	100	100
PageBlocks	5	5473	92	90.9	90.1	**92.5**	96.83	91.21	92.18
Pima	2	768	70.5	74.6	74.4	74	66.36	**75.25**	**74.86**
Wine	3	178	71.7	49.6	92.7	88.2	91.57	**92.71**	**93.2**
Zoo	7	101	91	40.7	**93**	**94.1**	87.12	91	89.18
Average			79.62	71.52	83.52	81.2	82.75	**84.73**	**85.13**

Note- #cls indicates number of class labels and #rec indicate the number of records in dataset.

4.1   Classification Accuracy

We compare the performance of the proposed classifiers on 15 UCI datasets, with other rule-based classifiers like CBA, CMAR, CPAR, RIPPER, C4.5 and the original SigDirect, in terms of classification accuracy and number of classification rules in the final model. Further, we also compare ACboost with ANN and SVM in Table 2. We use the best parameters as stated by the authors in original respective papers as well as stated in [9]. In CBA and CMAR the parameters are tuned such that the minimum confidence values is set to be 50%, minimum value of support is set as 1%, the maximum number of CARs are limited to 80,000 and the size of number of antecedent items are limited to 6. The best parameters for RIPPER [3] are taken from [14]. The best parameters as stated in [9] are used

Table 2. Comparison of classification accuracy of ACboost with ACbag, SigD2, SigDirect, ANN and SVM

Datasets	SVM	ANN	DNN	SigDirect	SigD2	ACbag	ACboost
Adult	75.8	75.66	**85.35**	84.1	83.59	84.74	**85.23**
Anneal	85	93.964	**97.6**	96.99	97.21	**97.43**	97.31
Breast	95.7	**96.83**	**96.48**	91.7	92.7	93.86	92.62
Flare	73.8	**84.61**	70.3	84.23	84.3	84.31	**85.35**
Glass	68.6	70.148	66.9	70.56	69.17	**72.01**	**76.96**
Heart	55.4	56.72	55.6	58.49	59.81	**61.33**	**63.74**
Hepatitis	79.3	82.89	83.07	85.83	**86**	85.18	**90.89**
Horse	72.5	81.321	80.9	81.23	85.03	**85.3**	**85.7**
Iris	94.6	**98.09**	95.8	94	96	94.66	**97.33**
Led7	73.6	69.64	68.63	73.78	73.81	**74.84**	**75.21**
Mushroom	**99.8**	100	100	100	100	100	100
PageBlocks	91.2	**95.42**	95.08	91.21	**92.18**	91.24	92.13
Pima	74	**75.95**	75.15	75.25	74.86	75.53	**75.55**
Wine	94.9	91.662	**97.62**	92.71	93.2	94.04	**98.85**
Zoo	92.2	93.192	89.94	91	89.18	**94.28**	**98.9**
Average	81.76	84.406	83.89	84.738	85.136	**85.91**	**87.71**

for CPAR, C4.5 [12], SVM [4] and SigDirect, in order to have a fair comparison. For SigD2, we have performed a sensitivity analysis on the confidence threshold and it was found that threshold value lower than 30% or higher than 50%, does not lead to best results for all the considered datasets. Hence, we chose to vary the confidence threshold in the range of 30–50% depending on the dataset. For ANN, we use a shallow network with one hidden layer. The number of nodes in the hidden layer are set as the average of number of input and output nodes. The architecture may vary slightly with dataset, but we use ReLU (Rectified Linear Units) or sigmoid functions for activation and around 200 training epochs with a learning rate of 0.1. For ACboost and ACbag, the value of η is tuned in the range of 5–15 for every dataset. The number of estimators are varied in the range of 15–100 for each fold in every dataset and we report the best results. The value for parameters η and the number of estimators have been concluded after performing a sensitivity analysis on each of them. Table 1 shows that SigD2 performs quite well as compared to other rule-based and associative classifiers. The average performance over 15 datasets of SigD2 is better than all the other rule-based classifiers. Although, the difference between SigDirect and SigD2 on the basis of classification accuracy is marginal, when we compare the number of rules, we show that SigD2 outperforms SigDirect. In order to have a fair comparison, among different algorithms on various datasets, we analyse how many times did an algorithm win and how many times it was a runner up as

Table 3. SigD2 compared with other algorithms based on number of rules

Datasets	C4.5	CBA	CMAR	CPAR	SigDirect	SigD2	Difference with average # of rules
Adult	1176.5	691.8	2982.5	84.6	91.2	53.62	951.7 (94.67%)
Anneal	17	27.3	208.4	25.2	41.7	29.2	34.72 (54.31%)
Breast	8.8	13.5	69.4	6	10.9	7	14.72 (67.65%)
Flare	54.4	115.1	347.1	48.1	75.8	25.7	102.4 (79.93%)
Glass	14.8	63.7	274.5	34.8	55.6	23.1	65.58 (73.9%)
Heart	23.9	78.4	464.2	44	80.2	27.7	110.44 (77.3%)
Hepatitis	8.1	2.3	165.7	14.3	33.3	16	28.74 (64.23%)
Horse	25.6	116.4	499.9	19	90.4	41.5	108.76 (72.38%)
Iris	8.4	12.3	63.4	7.4	6.2	4.8	14.74 (75.43%)
Led7	63.2	71.2	206.3	31.7	104.3	54.4	40.94 (42.94%)
Mushroom	121.2	2	102.6	11.1	106.4	48.9	19.76 (28.77%)
PageBlocks	16.3	7.6	80.6	29.9	31.1	13.2	19.9 (60.12%)
Pima	24.4	43.2	203.3	21.7	36.6	11.3	54.54 (82.83%)
Wine	12.8	4.7	122.7	15.2	29.3	16.3	20.64 (55.87%)
Zoo	5.3	2	35	16.9	16.2	9	6.08 (40.31%)

shown in Table 4. The proposed pruning strategy is found to give quite promising results as compared to the other rule-based and associative classifiers. SigD2 outperforms RIPPER on 10 out of 15 datasets. Furthermore, Table 2 shows that ACboost outperforms all the classifiers including SigDirect, SigD2, ANN and SVM. We have also tried to compare our approach with DNN with 5 hidden layers. Since most of the considered datasets are not big enough to be used for DNN, the results might not be conclusive.

4.2   Number of Rules

The main advantage of the associative classifiers over the other machine learning supervised classifiers is its ability to build a model which is human readable. Noisy, redundant and uninteresting rules lead to longer classification time, reduce the performance of the classifier and also make it tedious for humans to analyse the model. Ideally, we want to achieve maximum accuracy with a minimum possible set of rules. Table 3 shows the comparison among different classifiers on the basis of number of rules generated. The two stage pruning technique is found to give a minimum number of rules without compromising the classification performance. Table 5 clearly shows that out of 15 datasets, on average SigD2 outperforms most of the contenders for at least 10 datasets with some ties in few cases as well. CBA is found to have less rules for some datasets but it is unable to provide a high accuracy in such cases. Our proposed strategy outperforms

CMAR on all datasets, the original SigDirect on all but one dataset and CPAR, C4.5 on 8 datasets. The number of rules is found to be appropriate enough to provide information about the classification model without compromising on the performance. In Table 3, we take the difference of the average of number of rules over all the other classifiers and the proposed classifier in the last column. It is found that the difference is substantial which essentially shows the significance of the proposed pruning strategy. We also compute the percentage decrease of the number of rules on average in Table 3. Furthermore, SigD2 is found to outperform RIPPER in terms of accuracy for most of the datasets, however, RIPPER obtains less rules comparatively. This is majorly because RIPPER greedily modifies the generated rules using the Minimum Discription Length (MDL) principle. RIPPER produces a kind of superset of rules covering all information required for classification in the form of intervals. This indicates that there is potential for further improvements. Furthermore, ACboost is said to be explainable as the base model called wSigDirect produces meaningful and readable rules. The ensemble model helps in determining the attributes which are of most indicative to determine a class. Consider the example of mushroom dataset, the rule produced will be in the format -: (habitat = leaves) and (cap-color = white) → (class = poisonous), where feature name 'habitat' has value 'leaves' and feature name 'cap-color' has value equal to 'white'. This rule along with other similar rules can be further used in the classification phase to determine whether a mushroom is poisonous or not. Similarly for ACbag, the readable rules from the base classifiers can help in interpreting the results.

4.3   Statistical Analysis

For better understanding the performance over various datasets, we use Demsar's method [5] to perform statistical tests in order to compare different algorithms over different datasets. We perform non parametric Friedman's test for comparing the contenders with the proposed approaches. The Friedman's test on

Table 4. Best and runner-up counts comparison from (a) Table 1 and (b) Table 2 on the basis of classification accuracy

(a)			(b)		
Classifiers	Best	Runner-up	Classifiers	Best	Runner-up
C4.5	2	0	SVM	0	1
RIPPER	5	2	ANN	4	1
CBA	1	1	DNN	3	2
CMAR	3	1	SigDirect	1	0
CPAR	1	2	SigD2	1	2
SigDirect	2	5	ACboost	9	3
SigD2	6	4	ACbag	1	6

algorithms in Table 1 and Table 2 gave significant results as the p-value obtained is less than alpha (=0.05), which shows that at least one of the samples is significantly different from other samples. Furthermore, we also perform Wilcoxon's signed-ranks test which is another non-parametric statistical hypothesis test to compare the performances of proposed algorithms and the contenders in a pairwise manner. The results in Table 5 show that, SigD2 is significantly better than C4.5, CBA, CMAR, CPAR and SVM. However, the performance when compared with the original SigDirect seems to be quite similar and the p-value comes out to be greater than 0.05. We assume that, although there might not be difference in terms of classification accuracy, however, the new pruning strategy of SigD2 is more substantial and promising as it has reduced the number of rules to a small number as compared to the original SigDirect. The results from ACboost are found to be statistically significant than those of SigD2, ANN, DNN and SVM as p-value is less than the significance level of 0.05. Thus, the results obtained in this section highlight the significance of the explainable models over the ones that are hard to interpret (ANN, DNN & SVM). SigD2 and ACboost are almost at par with other strong learners like neural network in terms of classification accuracy along with its ability to be interpreted using a limited number of rules.

Table 5. Statistical analysis of Table 1 and Table 2

Classifiers	Wins	Losses	Ties	p-value	Classifiers	Wins	Losses	Ties	p-value
SigD2 vs C4.5*	12	3	0	0.005	ACbag vs SigD2*	11	3	1	0.064
SigD2 vs RIPPER	10	4	1	0.074	ACbag vs SVM*	12	3	0	0.005
SigD2 vs CBA*	13	2	0	0.005	ACbag vs ANN	9	5	1	0.140
SigD2 vs CMAR*	11	2	2	0.033	ACbag vs DNN	8	6	1	0.140
SigD2 vs CPAR*	12	3	0	0.008	ACboost vs SigD2*	12	2	1	0.002
SigD2 vs SigDirect	10	4	1	0.272	ACboost vs SVM*	14	1	0	0.002
SigD2 vs SVM*	12	3	0	0.041	ACboost vs ANN*	10	4	1	0.016
SigD2 vs ANN	7	7	1	0.510	ACboost vs DNN*	10	4	1	0.022
SigD2 vs DNN	7	7	1	0.510					

(*) indicates statistically significant results with a p-value of 0.05.

5   Conclusion and Future Work

In this paper, we present a competitive associative classifier, which builds a rule-based model that is explainable, readable and minimalist. The classifier initially performs a rule generation step followed by a two phase rule pruning step to obtain the classification rules. The proposed rule pruning strategy reduces the rule set to a significantly small number. The proposed approaches are at par with the other supervised classifiers like ANN and SVM, which do not provide interpretable classification models. Furthermore, ACboost algorithm uses an ensemble of wSigDirect, to build a strong learner that boosts the prediction performance. The results obtained are very encouraging; we intend to use our proposed approach on various health-care related applications where explanation of prediction is required. Furthermore, since SigD2 produces human readable rules, we would like to study the possibility of injecting human expert knowledge to the obtained rules in order to further improve the prediction performance.

References

1. Breiman, L.: Bagging predictors. Mach. Learn. **24**(2), 123–140 (1996). https://doi.org/10.1023/A:1018054314350
2. Coenen, F.: The LUCS-KDD software library (2004). http://cgi.csc.liv.ac.uk/~frans/KDD/Software/
3. Cohen, W.: Fast effective rule induction. In: International Conference on Machine Learning, pp. 115–123. Elsevier (1995)
4. Cortes, C., Vapnik, V.: Support-vector networks. Mach. Learn. **20**(3), 273–297 (1995). https://doi.org/10.1007/BF00994018
5. Demšar, J.: Statistical comparisons of classifiers over multiple data sets. J. Mach. Learn. Res. **7**, 1–30 (2006)
6. Dua, D., Graff, C.: UCI machine learning repository (2017). http://archive.ics.uci.edu/ml
7. Freund, Y., Schapire, R.E.: Experiments with a new boosting algorithm. In: International Conference on Machine Learning, vol. 96, pp. 148–156 (1996)
8. Hastie, T., Rosset, S., Zhu, J., Zou, H.: Multi-class adaboost. Stat. Interface **2**(3), 349–360 (2009)
9. Li, J., Zaiane, O.R.: Exploiting statistically significant dependent rules for associative classification. Intell. Data Anal. **21**(5), 1155–1172 (2017)
10. Li, W., Han, J. and Pei, J.: CMAR: accurate and efficient classification based on multiple class-association rules. In: International Conference on Data Mining, pp. 369–376 (2001)
11. Liu, B., Hsu, W., Ma, Y.: Integrating classification and association rule mining. In: International Conference on Knowledge Discovery and Data Mining (1998)
12. Quinlan, J.R.: C4.5: programs for machine learning. Mach. Learn. **16**(3), 235–240 (1994)
13. Sood, N., Bindra, L., Zaiane, O.: Bi-level associative classifier using automatic learning on rules. In: International Conference on Database and Expert Systems Applications (2020)
14. Yin, X., Han, J.: CPAR: classification based on predictive association rules. In: SIAM International Conference on Data Mining, pp. 331–335 (2003)
15. Zaïane, O.R., Antonie, M.L.: On pruning and tuning rules for associative classifiers. In: International Conference on Knowledge-Based and Intelligent Information and Engineering Systems, pp. 966–973 (2005)

Contrastive Explanations for a Deep Learning Model on Time-Series Data

Jokin Labaien[1]([📧]) [ID], Ekhi Zugasti[2] [ID], and Xabier De Carlos[1] [ID]

[1] Ikerlan Technology Research Centre,
Basque Research and Technology Alliance (BRTA),
P° J.M. Arizmediarrieta, 2, 20500 Arrasate-Mondragón, Spain
{jlabaien,xdecarlos}@ikerlan.es
[2] Data Analysis and Cybersecurity Group, Mondragon University,
20500 Arrasate-Mondragón, Spain
ezugasti@mondragon.edu

Abstract. In the last decade, with the irruption of Deep Learning (DL), artificial intelligence has risen a step concerning previous years. Although Deep Learning models have gained strength in many fields like image classification, speech recognition, time-series anomaly detection, etc. these models are often difficult to understand because of their lack of interpretability. In recent years an effort has been made to understand DL models, creating a new research area called Explainable Artificial Intelligence (XAI). Most of the research in XAI has been done for image data, and little research has been done in the time-series data field. In this paper, a model-agnostic method called Contrastive Explanation Method (CEM) is used for interpreting a DL model for time-series classification. Even though CEM has been validated in tabular data and image data, the obtained experimental results show that CEM is also suitable for interpreting deep learning models that work with time-series data.

Keywords: Contrastive explanations · Time-series · Deep learning · Artificial intelligence

1 Introduction

Nowadays, many systems are monitored by multiple sensors, which provide data on how the system is evolving, and consequently research on temporal data has increased in recent years. DL algorithms are becoming really powerful, also for time-series data, in which the *Long Short-Term Memory (LSTM)* networks [9] are a key part of many state-of-the-art architectures. LSTMs are capable of preserving information from long term dependencies, and have proven to be very effective in processing temporal data [12].

Even though DL has gained strength, DL models are often considered blackboxes due to the lack of interpretability. Due to this problem, a new research area has been created, called *Explainable Artificial Intelligence (XAI)*, which is

© Springer Nature Switzerland AG 2020
M. Song et al. (Eds.): DaWaK 2020, LNCS 12393, pp. 235–244, 2020.
https://doi.org/10.1007/978-3-030-59065-9_19

focused on DL model interpretation. A lot of work has been done in recent years on interpretation issues, as many techniques have been proposed to facilitate the understanding of DL models [1,2], such as LRP [3], SHAP [10], LIME [11], Integrated Gradients [14], CEM [6], etc. These methods have been applied especially to image data [13,15], and more research is needed for time-series data [7,8].

CEM [6] is a perturbation-based method that provides local explanations. Although CEM offers two ways to interpret a model, either using *pertinent negatives (PN)* or *pertinent positives (PP)*, in this paper, PNs are used. Unlike other methods, the idea behind this paper is that applying CEM to time series data can allow us to give explanations such as "this time series is classified as class y because a particular point or group of points have value v (PP) when they should have value w (PN)". The authors apply CEM to a time series classification problem, concluding that this kind of explanation is viable in time series data.

This article is structured as follows. Section 2 provides the theoretical background of the DL methods used in the experiment and it briefly explains the CEM method. Section 3 describes the methodology used in the experiments. Section 4 describes the dataset used, the experimental framework and the hyperparameters of the models. Section 5 discusses the experimental results. Finally, in Sect. 6 the conclusions and future works are exposed.

2   Background

2.1   Long Short-Term Memory Networks

Long Short-Term Memory (LSTM) [9] networks are a variation of the standard *Recurrent Neural Networks (RNN)*. Traditional RNNs have shown to be useful in many problems, but they suffer from the vanishing gradient and exploding gradient problem, which leads to failing to detect long term dependencies in practice. To overcome this problem, LSTMs include some cells in their internals that control how to maintain the information in memory for long periods of time.

LSTMs, like all the RNNs, have the form of a chain of repeating modules, in which the knowledge is transferred through time, from one module to another. Each module of an LSTM is called "unit", and each "unit" is composed of four neural networks, which interact with each other to process the input data.

One of the keys of the success of the LSTMs is the cell state ($\mathbf{C}_t$). The function of the cell state is to transfer relative information throughout the entire sequence chain. As it is shown in Fig. 1, the cell state passes from one unit to another with some minor linear interactions, facilitating the learning of long-term dependencies. Moreover, each LSTM unit has its own hidden state ($\mathbf{h}$), that manages the internal state of the unit. The cell state information is updated by three gates: forget gate ($\mathbf{f}_t$), input gate ($\mathbf{i}_t$) and output gate ($\mathbf{o}_t$). The forget gate decides what information of the cell state to keep each time, forgetting the unnecessary information. The input gate $\mathbf{i}_t$ decides which values of the cell state have to be updated, and these values are updated by adding the new information stored in the candidate vector $\tilde{C}_t$ and forgetting the information decided to forget

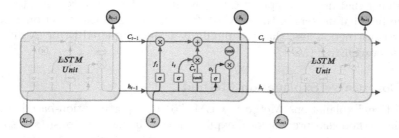

Fig. 1. A visualization of an LSTM cell.

by the forget gate $\mathbf{f}_t$. Finally, it has to be decided what is going to be the output of the unit, and the output gate $\mathbf{o}_t$ and the hidden state $\mathbf{h}_t$ are created. The whole process is summarized in Eq. (1).

$$
\begin{aligned}
f_t &= \sigma\left(W_f \cdot [h_{t-1}, x_t] + b_f\right) \\
i_t &= \sigma\left(W_i \cdot [h_{t-1}, x_t] + b_i\right) \\
\tilde{C}_t &= \tanh\left(W_C \cdot [h_{t-1}, x_t] + b_C\right) \\
C_t &= f_t * C_{t-1} + i_t * \tilde{C}_t \\
o_t &= \sigma\left(W_o [h_{t-1}, x_t] + b_o\right) \\
h_t &= o_t * \tanh\left(C_t\right)
\end{aligned}
\tag{1}
$$

$\mathbf{W}_x, b_x$ being the weights and the biases of each gate respectively, $x \in \{f, i, C, o\}$.

2.2 Autoencoders

Autoencoders (AE) [4] are neural networks trained unsupervisedly to reconstruct the input data. The AEs consist of two neural networks: an *encoder* and a *decoder*. The AEs can be either multilayer perceptrons, convolutional neural networks, recurrent neural networks, etc.

In Fig. 2 the structure of an AE is shown. The encoder can be defined as a function $: \mathbf{x} \in \mathbb{R}^n \to \mathbf{z} \in \mathbb{R}^d$, where $d < n$, that tries to compress the data of the input layer into a lower dimensional latent vector, containing the most important features of it. On the other hand, the decoder can be defined as a function $g : \mathbf{z} \in \mathbb{R}^d \to \tilde{\mathbf{x}} \in \mathbb{R}^n$ that takes the compressed latent vector of the input and it decompresses into features that

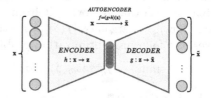

Fig. 2. A general structure of an AE.

closely matches the original input data. So, summarizing, an AE can be seen as a function f that maps an input $\mathbf{x} \in \mathbb{R}^n$ into its reconstruction $\tilde{\mathbf{x}} \in \mathbb{R}^n$, trying to find the best parameters of the network for minimizing a loss function $\mathcal{L}(\mathbf{x}, \tilde{\mathbf{x}})$, called reconstruction loss, that commonly is a Mean Squared Error (MSE) or a Mean Average Error (MAE).

2.3   Contrastive Explanation Method

Contrastive Explanations Method (CEM) [6] is a perturbation-based model-agnostic method that provide local explanations. The method consists of solving two different optimization problems, one for finding *Pertinent Negatives (PN)* and the other for finding *Pertinent Positives (PP)*.

Finding Pertinent Negatives. Let x_0 be an input of a black-box model f, $f(x_0)$ the prediction given and y_0 its corresponding class. Let $AE(\cdot)$ be an autoencoder trained for reconstructing an input. Denoting $\mathcal{X}/x_0$ to the space of missing parts with respect to x_0, finding pertinent negatives consist of finding an interpretable minimal perturbation $\delta \in \mathcal{X}/x_0$ such that $\arg\max_i [f(x_0)]_i \neq \arg\max_i [f(x_0 + \delta)]_i$. For finding pertinent negatives, the authors propose solving this optimization problem:

$$\min_{\delta \in \mathcal{X}/x_0} c \cdot f_\kappa^{\text{neg}}(x_0, \delta) + \beta\|\delta\|_1 + \|\delta\|_2^2 + \gamma \|x_0 + \delta - AE(x_0 + \delta)\|_2^2 \quad (2)$$

where $c, \beta, \gamma \geq 0$ are regularization parameters. The second and the third terms, $\beta\|\delta\|_1$ and $\|\delta\|_2^2$ respectively, are jointly called the elastic net regularizer and they are used for efficient feature selection in high-dimensional learning spaces. The third term $\gamma \|x_0 + \delta - AE(x_0 + \delta)\|_2^2$ ensures that the modified input $x_0 + \delta$ is close to the data manifold. The first term $f_\kappa^{\text{neg}}(x_0, \delta)$ is defined in this way:

$$f_\kappa^{\text{neg}}(x_0, \delta) = \max\left\{ [f(x_0 + \delta)]_{y_0} - \max_{i \neq y_0} [f(x_0 + \delta)]_i, -\kappa \right\} \quad (3)$$

where $[f(x_0 + \delta)]_i$ is the score given by the model f to the i-th class prediction. Introducing $f_\kappa^{\text{neg}}(x_0, \delta)$ to the Eq. 2, ensures $x_0 + \delta$ to be predicted as a different class than y_0. The parameter $\kappa \geq 0$ is a confidence parameter to control the separation between $[f(x_0 + \delta)]_{y_0}$ and $\max_{i \neq y_0} [f(x_0 + \delta)]_i$.

Finding Pertinent Positives. For finding pertinent positives, let $\mathcal{X} \cap x_0$ be the space of existing components of x_0 and let $\delta \in \mathcal{X} \cap x_0$ be an interpretable perturbation such that removing it from x_0 the prediction is still the same, i.e $\arg\max_i [f(x_0)]_i = \arg\max_i [f(\delta)]_i$. To this end, similar to finding pertinent negatives, the following optimization problem needs to be solved:

$$\min_{\delta \in \mathcal{X} \cap x_0} c \cdot f_\kappa^{\text{neg}}(x_0, \delta) + \beta\|\delta\|_1 + \|\delta\|_2^2 + \gamma \|\delta - AE(\delta)\|_2^2 \quad (4)$$

where the first term $f_\kappa^{\text{neg}}(x_0, \delta)$ is defined in this way:

$$f_\kappa^{\text{neg}}(x_0, \delta) = \max\left\{ \max_{i \neq y_0} [f(\delta)]_i - [f(\delta)]_{y_0}, -\kappa \right\} \quad (5)$$

To solve the optimization problems (2) and (4), a projected fast iterative shrinkage-thresholding algorithm, called FISTA [5], is used.

3   Methodology

In this paper a model proposed for a multiclass time-series classification problem is interpreted using CEM. As described in the previous section, the CEM method consist of solving the optimization problems of Eqs. (2) and (4). Thus, first of all, a classification model f has to be proposed and an AE needs to be defined for ensuring that the changed input is close to the data manifold. Therefore, in this section the proposed classification model and the AE are exposed and the way that in which CEM is used is described.

3.1   Classification Model

The model proposed for the classification part is a combination of an LSTM and a Fully Connected Layer (FCN). The LSTM is used for processing the data and the FCN is used for classifying it [16]. Figure 3 shows an outline of the model architecture. Firstly, the input of the model is processed by the LSTM layer in time-steps. In this way, in each time-step, the LSTM uses what it has learned before in addition to the current input to update the current hidden state. The last hidden state ($\mathbf{h}_n$) of the network is the input of the FCN. The activations $\mathbf{a}$ of the FCN are computed as follows

$$\mathbf{a} = \mathbf{W}_{fc} \cdot \mathbf{h}_n^T + b_{fc} \tag{6}$$

where $\mathbf{W}_{fc}$ and b_{fc} are the weights and the biases learned during training process, and $\mathbf{h}_n^T$ denotes the transpose of the last hidden state. After the activations are calculated, a *softmax* function is applied, returning the target as a probability vector $\hat{y}$, in which each value $\hat{y}_i \in \hat{y}$ is computed as follows

$$\hat{y}_i = \frac{e^{a_i}}{\sum_j e^{a_j}} \tag{7}$$

and denotes the probability that the input belongs to class i. Afterwards, the index of the maximum probability value is taken as the class predicted by the model. In training time, the weights of the model are adjusted by minimizing the *Categorical Crossentropy Loss (CCE)* in batches.

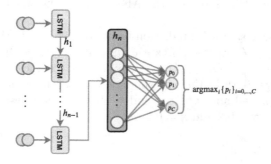

Fig. 3. Proposed classification model.

3.2   Autoencoders

As seen in Eq. (2) and (4), the optimization problems include a term regarding an AE. This term ensures that the modified input is close to the data manifold. The architecture proposed for the AE is based on LSTMs, since they have demonstrated to work well when processing time-series data, and FCNs. The proposed AE can be seen in Fig. 4. First, the input data is processed with the LSTM. Then, the last hidden state of the LSTM has the information of the whole input and it is encoded into a lower-dimensional vector by the FCN. Then, the encoded vector is repeated to feed the decoder, which is another LSTM. Finally, the hidden states of the decoder are connected to an FCN layer, that converts the hidden states of the encoder into arrays with the same dimension as the inputs, using a sigmoid activation function. In this case, the weights of the model are adjusted for minimizing the *Mean Squared Error (MSE)*.

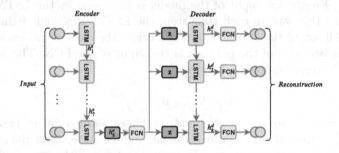

Fig. 4. Proposed LSTM-FCN AE.

3.3   Contrastive Explanations Method

As stated above, in this paper CEM PNs are studied. In this scenario, the x_0 of Eq. (2) is a multivariate time-series $\mathbf{x}$, and the δ denotes the PN that makes the predicted class to change (i.e. $\arg\max_i [f(\mathbf{x})]_i \neq \arg\max_i [f(\mathbf{x} + \delta)]_i$), being f the classification model. Moreover, the AE of Eq. (3) denotes the AE proposed above.

Since the changed sample's prediction has to be different to the original class, i.e $\arg\max_i [f(\mathbf{x})]_i \neq \arg\max_i [f(\mathbf{x} + \delta)]_i$, $\max_{i \neq y} [f(\mathbf{x} + \delta)] > [f(\mathbf{x} + \delta)]_y$. Therefore, $[f(\mathbf{x} + \delta)]_y - \max_{i \neq y} [f(\mathbf{x} + \delta)]_i \in [-1, 0)$, and thus, κ has to be chosen in the range $[0, 1]$. In the experiments, a set of different γ and κ parameters have been proved and it is concluded that the best results for this case study are given by $\gamma = 0.2$ and $\kappa = 0.5$.

4   Experimental Framework

4.1   PenDigits Dataset Description

In this work, a public time-series dataset, named PenDigits, is used. The PenDigits dataset $\mathcal{D}$ is a handwritten digit classification dataset. Each data sample $X_i \in \mathcal{D}$ is a 2-dimensional multivariate time-series, denoted as $X_i = \{\mathbf{x}_1^{(i)}, \mathbf{x}_2^{(i)}\}$, where $\mathbf{x}_1^{(i)} \in \mathbb{R}^8$ denotes the trajectory of the pen across the coordinate x of a digital screen and $\mathbf{x}_2^{(i)}$ denotes the trajectory of the pen across the coordinate y. Each sample is labeled with a single class label, representing the digit drawn. In Fig. 5 a sample of the dataset is showed.

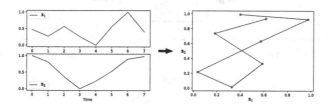

Fig. 5. A sample of PenDigits dataset.

The dataset was crated by 44 writers and it is divided in two sets: training set and testing set. The training test is composed by 7.494 different samples and the testing set is composed by 3.498 different samples.

4.2   Framework and Hyperparameters

The experiments are run on an Nvidia-Docker container that uses ubuntu 18.04. The models were implemented using the Keras library of Tensorflow. The Tensorflow version used in this case is TensorFlow 2.1.0. The optimization of both models was performed using Adam. The models have been trained in minibatches of 32 samples. The training process has stopped at epoch 163 for the classification model and at epoch 134 for the AE, because EarlyStopping has been used. Moreover, the learning rate at the beginning has been set to 0.1 and has been decreased every epoch using exponential decay. For training the models an NVIDIA TITAN V GPU has been used, with a memory of 12 GB, in an Intel i7-6850K 3.6 Ghz machine with 32 GB of DDR4 RAM.

Each of the models used in this work has different hyperparameters. For the model used for classification, the LSTM layer has 64 units and the FCN has 10 units and softmax activation function. For the AE, the encoder and the decoder LSTMs have 16 units, the FCN of the encoder encodes the last hidden state of the first LSTM into a 4-dimensional vector, therefore, the encoder's FCN uses 4 units. Since the AE has to reconstruct the input data, the last FCNs have 15 units and a sigmoid activation function.

5   Experimental Results

In this work, PenDigits dataset has been used, since it is a simple time-series classification dataset and it is easily interpretable for anyone. Although the main objective of this work is not to propose a classification model, the model used achieves 98.11% of accuracy and a micro-average F1 score of 0.979 in validation data. On the other hand, the proposed AEs is valid to reconstruct the data, since the MSE for validation data is 0.0064.

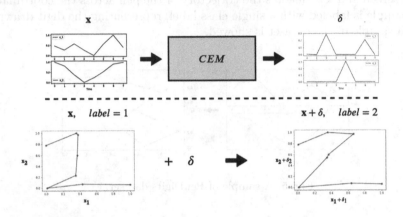

Fig. 6. Process used for giving explanations using CEM.

In Fig. 6 the process used for giving the explanations is illustrated. As shown in the figure, an input **x** representing a one is used to obtain its pertinent negatives δ by optimizing Eq. 2. The pertinent negatives δ represent the changes that need to be made in the input **x** for the model to classify it as another class. In this example, it can be seen that changing the position among the x axis of the third and seventh points and changing the position among the y axis of the sixth point, **x** changes from a one to a two.

In this paper, CEM method has been applied to a variety of digits, for example in Fig. 7 the explanations given to 3 samples are illustrated. In the first case, a "1" is changed to a "2" by simply moving the third point from the center to

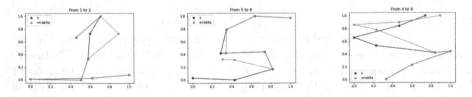

Fig. 7. The original samples (green), **x**, versus the changed ones (red), **x** + δ. (Color figure online)

the right, to simulate the curved shape of the "2". In the second case a "5" is converted to a "6" by making three small changes. In this second case, the most significant changes are found in the last two points, and by moving them, CEM has created the rounded shape of the bottom of a "6". In the third case a "4" has been changed to a "9" by changing the first four points. It can be seen that the changes have been done for simulating the rounded shape of top of a "9". We have tested the CEM method for 150 samples and in general the modifications are made with sense, causing the label of the input to change. Moreover, the relationship between the label of class x and the label of $x + \delta$ is similar in all the samples. In Table 1 the percentages of the changes between the class of the original samples and the changed ones are given. It can be seen that, for example, generally the digit "4" is related to the digit "9", and the changes are done for changing from one to another, and this happens also for all other classes. For example, the digit "2" is converted into a "1" in the 80% of the cases, the changes in digit "7" make it "1" in 54.55% of the cases, the digit "8" changes into a "5" in the 50% of the cases, etc.

Table 1. % of changes from x's class to $x + \delta$'s class.

$x \to x + \delta$	0	1	2	3	4	5	6	7	8	9
0	0	0	0	0	41.67	0	0	0	50	8.33
1	0	0	25	0	0	12.5	0	25	37.5	0
2	0	80	0	0	0	0	0	0	20	0
3	0	21.43	0	0	0	28.57	0	50	0	0
4	14.29	7.14	0	7.14	0	0	0	14.29	7.14	50
5	0	15.38	15.38	7.7	7.7	0	7.7	0	15.38	30.76
6	23.1	7.7	7.7	0	0	7.7	0	0	53.8	0
7	0	54.55	18.18	0	0	0	0	0	27.27	0
8	11.1	16.67	0	0	0	50	0	0	0	22.22
9	0	16.66	0	0	16.66	16.66	0	0	50	0

6   Conclusions

In this work, CEM has been validated in a time-series classification use case. Previously, as far as it is known, CEM has not been used in time-series data, and in this work, it is shown that it can be effectively used in these scenarios to create meaningful explanations. The pertinent negatives given by CEM offers a different way to understand the model's decisions, and unlike other XAI methods such as SHAP, LIME, LRP, etc., that their explanations are based on feature importance, the pertinent negatives explanations provide information of what should be changed in the input to be classified as other class. Looking at the results, it can be seen that the CEM method is also useful to find relationships between different classes, giving an intuition of which class is closer to another.

Although this is a work in progress, in which CEM is validated for a simple classification problem, the idea in the future is to validate for anomaly detection in a sensorized industrial scenario, since it can provide information about what should be changed for not occurring an anomaly, and this can be useful for fixing it.

References

1. Adadi, A., Berrada, M.: Peeking inside the black-box: a survey on explainable artificial intelligence (XAI). IEEE Access **6**, 52138–52160 (2018)
2. Arrieta, A.B., et al.: Explainable artificial intelligence (XAI): concepts, taxonomies, opportunities and challenges toward responsible AI. Inf. Fusion **58**, 82–115 (2020)
3. Bach, S., Binder, A., Montavon, G., Klauschen, F., Müller, K.R., Samek, W.: On pixel-wise explanations for non-linear classifier decisions by layer-wise relevance propagation. PloS One **10**(7), e0130140 (2015)
4. Ballard, D.H.: Modular learning in neural networks. In: AAAI, pp. 279–284 (1987)
5. Beck, A., Teboulle, M.: A fast iterative shrinkage-thresholding algorithm for linear inverse problems. SIAM J. Imaging Sci. **2**(1), 183–202 (2009)
6. Dhurandhar, A., et al.: Explanations based on the missing: towards contrastive explanations with pertinent negatives. In: Advances in Neural Information Processing Systems, pp. 592–603 (2018)
7. Giurgiu, I., Schumann, A.: Additive explanations for anomalies detected from multivariate temporal data. In: Proceedings of the 28th ACM International Conference on Information and Knowledge Management, pp. 2245–2248 (2019)
8. Guillemé, M., Masson, V., Rozé, L., Termier, A.: Agnostic local explanation for time series classification. In: 2019 IEEE 31st International Conference on Tools with Artificial Intelligence (ICTAI), pp. 432–439. IEEE (2019)
9. Hochreiter, S., Schmidhuber, J.: Long short-term memory. Neural Comput. **9**(8), 1735–1780 (1997)
10. Lundberg, S.M., Lee, S.I.: A unified approach to interpreting model predictions. In: Advances in Neural Information Processing Systems, pp. 4765–4774 (2017)
11. Ribeiro, M.T., Singh, S., Guestrin, C.: Why should i trust you?: Explaining the predictions of any classifier. In: Proceedings of the 22nd ACM SIGKDD International Conference on Knowledge Discovery and Data Mining, pp. 1135–1144. ACM (2016)
12. Sagheer, A., Kotb, M.: Time series forecasting of petroleum production using deep LSTM recurrent networks. Neurocomputing **323**, 203–213 (2019)
13. Selvaraju, R.R., Cogswell, M., Das, A., Vedantam, R., Parikh, D., Batra, D.: Grad-CAM: visual explanations from deep networks via gradient-based localization. In: Proceedings of the IEEE International Conference on Computer Vision, pp. 618–626 (2017)
14. Sundararajan, M., Taly, A., Yan, Q.: Axiomatic attribution for deep networks. In: Proceedings of the 34th International Conference on Machine Learning-Volume 70, pp. 3319–3328. JMLR. org (2017)
15. Van Looveren, A., Klaise, J.: Interpretable counterfactual explanations guided by prototypes. arXiv preprint arXiv:1907.02584 (2019)
16. Zhao, J., Deng, F., Cai, Y., Chen, J.: Long short-term memory-fully connected (LSTM-FC) neural network for PM2. 5 concentration prediction. Chemosphere **220**, 486–492 (2019)

Cyberbullying Detection in Social Networks Using Deep Learning Based Models

Maral Dadvar[(✉)] and Kai Eckert

Web-Based Information Systems and Services, Stuttgart Media University, Nebelstrasse 8, 70569 Stuttgart, Germany
{dadvar,eckert}@hdm-stuttgart.de

Abstract. Cyberbullying is a disturbing online misbehaviour with troubling consequences. It appears in different forms, and in most of the social networks, it is in textual format. Automatic detection of such incidents requires intelligent systems. Most of the existing studies have approached this problem with conventional machine learning models and the majority of the developed models in these studies are adaptable to a single social network at a time. Recently deep learning based models have been used for similar objectives, claiming that they can overcome the limitations of the conventional models, and improve the detection performance. In this paper, we investigated the findings of a recent literature in this regard and validated their findings using the same datasets as they did. We further expanded the work by applying the developed methods on a new dataset. We aimed to further investigate the performance of the models in new social media platforms. Our findings show that the deep learning based models outperform the machine learning models previously applied to the same dataset. We believe that the deep learning based models can also benefit from integrating other sources of information and looking into the impact of profile information of the users in social networks.

Keywords: Deep learning · Online bullying · Neural networks · Social networks · Transfer learning · YouTube

1   Introduction

With the emergence of Web 2.0 there has been a substantial impact on social communication, and relationships. Besides all the benefits that it might bring them, the online presence of adolescents also make them vulnerable to threats and social misbehaviours such as cyberbullying. Studies show that about 18% of the children in Europe have been involved in cyberbullying[1]. Cyberbullying needs to be understood and addressed from different perspectives. Automatic detection and prevention of these incidents can substantially help to tackle this problem. There are already tools developed which can flag a bullying incident and programs which try to provide support to the victims. There are also many research conducted on automatic detection and prevention of cyberbullying,

---

[1] EU COST Action IS0801 on Cyberbullying (https://sites.google.com/site/costis0801/).

© Springer Nature Switzerland AG 2020
M. Song et al. (Eds.): DaWaK 2020, LNCS 12393, pp. 245–255, 2020.
https://doi.org/10.1007/978-3-030-59065-9_20

which we will address in more details in the next section, but this problem is still far from resolved. Most of the existing studies [1–3] have used conventional Machine Learning (ML) models to detect cyberbullying incidents. Recently Deep Neural Network Based (DNN) models have also been applied for detection of cyberbullying [4, 5]. In [5], authors have used DNN models for detection of cyberbullying and have expanded their models across multiple social media platforms. Based on their reported results, their models outperform traditional ML models, and authors have stated that they have applied transfer learning which means their developed models for detection of cyberbullying can be adapted and used on other datasets.

In this contribution, we begin by reproducing and validating the [5] proposed models and their results on the three datasets, Formspring [6], Twitter [7] and Wikipedia [8], which have been used by the authors. Cyberbullying takes place in almost all of the online social networks; therefore, developing a detection model which is adaptable and transferable to different social networks is of great value. We expand our work by re-implementing the models on a new dataset. For this purpose, we have used a YouTube dataset which has been extensively used in cyberbullying studies [1, 9]. The ultimate aim was to investigate the interoperability and the performance of the reproduced models on new datasets, to see how adaptable they are to different social media platforms and to what extent models trained on a dataset (i.e., social network) can be transferred to another one. This provides a base to compare the outcome of DNN models with the conventional ML models. In the remainder of this paper, we reported the reproduced experimental setup, datasets and findings (Sect. 2), we investigated the adaptability of the methods on the YouTube dataset (Sect. 3), and in Sect. 4 we discussed our findings, compared our results with previous attempts on the same dataset, and pointed out potential future works.

2 Reproduced Experimental Setup

In this study, we have first reproduced the experiments conducted in [5] on the datasets used by the authors namely, Formspring [6], Wikipedia [8], and Twitter [7]. We have used the same models and experimental setup for our implementations. In this section, we have briefly introduced the datasets and explained the models and other experiment components. For further details please see the reference literature.

2.1 Datasets

In this study three datasets are used; Formspring (a Q&A forum), Wikipedia talk pages (collaborative knowledge repository) and Twitter (microblogging platform). All these datasets are manually labelled and publicly available. One problem that all these datasets share, is that the datasets are skewed, and there is a class imbalance, i.e., the number of posts labelled as bullying is significantly less than the neutral ones. This causes the classification results to be biased towards non-bullying posts. Therefore as it will be explained in more details in the next section, we oversampled the bullying class in the datasets. Furthermore, the size of the posts in terms of number of words differs across datasets. This can affect the number of distinct words encountered in each dataset.

Therefore, long posts (measured based on the number of words) are truncated to the size of post ranked at 95% in that dataset.

Wikipedia. A talk page in Wikipedia is where the discussions among those who have contributed to the editing of a Wikipedia page are maintained. This dataset includes more than 10,000 discussion comments from English Wikipedia' talk pages. All comments were manually annotated by ten persons. In total 13,590 comments were labelled as a personal attack.

Formspring. This is a question-answering platform. The dataset includes 12,000 pairs of questions-answers which were manually annotated by three persons. In total 825 pairs was annotated as cyberbullying by at least two persons.

Twitter. From this microblogging platform, 16,000 tweets were collected and manually annotated. The tweets were collected by search of terms which refer to religious, sexual, gender, and ethnic minorities. In total 3117 were labelled as sexist and 1937 were labelled as racist. The remaining tweets were labelled as neither.

2.2 Models and Methods

In this section the four DDN models that we experimented for cyberbullying detection are described. We also have experimented with three methods for initializing word embeddings, which will be briefly explained in follow.

Deep Neural Network Based Models. In this study four different DNN models were used for detection of cyberbullying: Convolutional Neural Network (CNN), Long Short-Term Memory (LSTM), Bidirectional LSTM (BLSTM) and BLSTM with attention. These models respectively vary in complexity in their neural architecture. CNNs are mostly used for image and text classification [10] as well as sentiment classification [11]. LSTM networks are used for learning long-term dependencies. Their internal memory makes these networks useful for text classification [12, 13]. Bidirectional LSTMs, increase the input information to the network by encoding information in both forward and backward direction. BLSTM with attention, gives more direct dependence between the state of the model at different points in time [14].

All the models have identical layers except for the neural architecture layer which is unique to each model. The embedding layer, which will be explained in more details in following, processes a fixed length sequence of words. There are two dropout layers which are used to avoid overfitting, once before (with dropout rates of 0.25) and one after (with dropout rates of 0.5) the neural architecture layer. Then there is the fully connected layer which is a dense output layer with the number of neurons equal to the number of classes. The last layer is the softmax layer that provides softmax activation. All the models are trained using backpropagation with Adam optimizer and categorical cross-entropy loss function. All the reference codes can be found in the author's GitHub repository[2].

---

[2] https://github.com/sweta20/Detecting-Cyberbullying-Across-SMPs.

Initial Word Embedding. Word embedding is the process of representing each word as real value vector. The embedding layer of our models processes a fixed length sequence of words. In this study three methods are used for initializing word embeddings: random, GloVe [15] and SSWE [16]. Using initial words embeddings during the training can improve the model to learn task specific word embeddings. Task specific word embeddings can differentiate the style of cyberbullying among different online platform as well as topics. The GloVe vectors mostly improve the performance of the models over the random vector initialization. However, in GloVe method only the syntactic context of the word in considered and the sentiment conveyed by the text is ignored. This problem is overcome in the SSWE method by incorporating the text sentiment as one of the parameters for word embedding generation. In this study different dimension size for word embeddings are experimented. Since there was no significant difference in the result of dimensions from 30 to 200, the results of the dimension size 50 are reported.

2.3 Workflow and Results

We started our experiments by implementing the DDN based models using Keras Python package[3]. The datasets went through the pre-processing steps such as stop-words and punctuations removal. The performance of the models were evaluated using five-fold cross-validation and precision, recall and *F1*-score evaluation metrics were used to report the performance. In order to overcome the problem caused by the imbalance in the datasets, the number of bullying class in the datasets were oversampled and the bullying posts were tripled in the training data. To illustrate the effect of oversampling, the BLSTM with attention model was used with three word embedding methods, once on the original datasets and once on the oversampled datasets (see Table 1a).

Table 1a. Performance evaluation of the BLSTM with attention models, with three word embeddings on the original and the oversamples datasets. F: Formspring, T: Twitter, W: Wikipedia, +: Oversampled

Dataset	Label	Precision			Recall			*F1*-score		
		Random	Glove	SSWE	Random	Glove	SSWE	Random	Glove	SSWE
F	Bully	0.37	0.60	0.50	0.34	0.43	0.43	0.35	0.50	0.46
F+	Bully	0.91	0.88	0.86	0.98	0.95	0.92	0.94	0.91	0.89
T	Racism	0.81	0.84	0.82	0.71	0.69	0.75	0.76	0.76	0.78
T+	Racism	0.95	0.95	0.96	0.99	0.99	0.99	0.97	0.97	0.97
T	Sexism	0.73	0.75	0.71	0.71	0.85	0.77	0.72	0.79	0.74
T+	Sexism	0.95	0.94	0.94	0.99	0.99	0.99	0.97	0.96	0.97
W	Attack	0.80	0.76	0.81	0.68	0.74	0.65	0.74	0.75	0.72
W+	Attack	0.94	0.93	0.92	0.99	0.98	0.98	0.96	0.96	0.95

---

[3] https://keras.io/.

The oversampling has significantly (Mann-Whitney U test, P < 0.001) improved the performance of the models in all the datasets, especially those with a smaller number of bullying posts in their training data such as Formspring. Initial word embeddings affect the data representation for the models which use them during the training to learn task specific word embeddings. Comparing the performance of the reference and the reproduced models shows that the majority of the reproduced results were within the standard deviation of the reference results (Table 1b). The highest inconsistencies were observed in the recall values of original Twitter dataset with GloVe and SSWE word embeddings. In Table 2a we have reported the F1-scores of different initial word embeddings on two DDN models; CNN as the simplest model, and BLSTM with attention as the most complex model.

As results show, the performance of the models was influenced by different initial word embeddings. Using Random initial word embeddings outperformed the SSWE and GloVe in original datasets. However, in oversampled datasets, the initial word embeddings did not show a significant effect on cyberbullying detection. We noticed that the inconsistencies among the reference and reproduced $F1$-scores mostly occurred in CNN model on Twitter dataset (Table 2b). The performance of all four DNN models while using SSWE as the initial word embeddings is summarized in Table 3a. Same as the reference work, we also noticed that the LSTM were outperformed by other models, and the performance gaps in the other three models were quite small. Following the above mentioned inconsistencies, we further observed that the main difference between the reproduced and reference results are due to the differences in recall values (Table 3b).

Table 1b. Difference in performance of the reference and the reproduced BLSTM with attention models, with three word embeddings on the original and the oversamples datasets. Negative values indicate higher performance of the reproduced models. F: Formspring, T: Twitter, W: Wikipedia, +: Oversampled

Dataset	Label	Precision			Recall			F1-score		
		Random	Glove	SSWE	Random	Glove	SSWE	Random	Glove	SSWE
F	Bully	0.15	-0.04	0.13	0.06	0.06	-0.05	0.09	0.01	0.01
F$^+$	Bully	-0.07	-0.03	0.04	0.00	0.02	-0.01	-0.04	-0.01	0.02
T	Racism	-0.14	-0.10	-0.06	0.02	0.07	0.02	-0.06	-0.01	-0.02
T$^+$	Racism	-0.01	-0.05	-0.06	-0.01	-0.04	-0.03	-0.01	-0.04	-0.04
T	Sexism	-0.08	0.11	0.12	-0.07	-0.33	-0.30	-0.07	-0.14	-0.15
T$^+$	Sexism	-0.07	0.01	-0.06	-0.02	-0.08	-0.07	-0.04	-0.05	-0.07
W	Attack	-0.03	0.05	0.01	0.06	-0.07	0.03	0.02	-0.01	0.02
W$^+$	Attack	-0.13	-0.07	-0.05	-0.08	-0.09	-0.12	-0.08	-0.08	-0.08

3 Application and Evaluation of the Methods on a New Dataset

In this section we investigated the adaptability and performance of the reproduced methods on a new social media platform and dataset; YouTube. We investigate how the DNN models would perform in this dataset in comparison to the previous ML models used on this dataset for detection of cyberbullying.

3.1 YouTube Dataset

YouTube is one of the most popular user-generated content video platforms and prone to misbehaviours such as cyberbullying. In this study we use a YouTube dataset which has been created by [1]. This dataset was developed by searching for topics sensitive to cyberbullying, such as, gender and race. From the retrieved videos, the comments of the users as well as their publicly available profile information were extracted. The final dataset consists of about 54,000 comments from 3,858 distinct users. The comments were manually annotated by 2 persons. In total about 6,500 of the comments were labelled as bullying.

Table 2a. Comparison of the $F1-$scores for CNN and BLSTM with attention models with three word embedding methods on the original and the oversamples datasets. F: Formspring, T: Twitter, W: Wikipedia, +: Oversampled

Dataset	Label	Random		GloVe		SSWE	
		CNN	BLSTM attention	CNN	BLSTM attention	CNN	BLSTM attention
F	Bully	0.41	0.35	0.33	0.5	0.27	0.46
F$^+$	Bully	0.89	0.94	0.86	0.91	0.74	0.89
T	Racism	0.77	0.76	0.68	0.76	0.66	0.78
T$^+$	Racism	0.90	0.97	0.90	0.97	0.86	0.97
T	Sexism	0.58	0.72	0.46	0.79	0.48	0.74
T$^+$	Sexism	0.79	0.97	0.80	0.96	0.73	0.97
W	Attack	0.71	0.74	0.72	0.75	0.67	0.72
W$^+$	Attack	0.87	0.96	0.84	0.96	0.87	0.95

3.2 Workflow and Results

We used the same experimental settings as explained in Sect. 2 for the new dataset. We continued our experiments by implementing the DDN based models. The YouTube dataset also suffers from the class imbalance and the number of bullying posts is significantly smaller than the neutral ones. Therefore we oversampled the bullying posts of the dataset and their number was tripled. Table 4 shows the performance of the BLSTM with attention model using the three initial word embeddings in both the original and

Table 2b. Difference in the $F1$-scores of the reference and the reproduced CNN and BLSTM with attention models with three word embedding methods on the original and the oversamples datasets. Negative values indicate higher performance of the reproduced models.

Dataset	Label	Random			GloVe			SSWE		
		CNN	BLSTM attention		CNN	BLSTM attention		CNN	BLSTM attention	
F	Bully	-0.11	0.09		0.01	0.01		0.07	0.01	
F⁺	Bully	0.02	-0.04		0.07	-0.01		0.17	0.02	
T	Racism	-0.09	-0.06		0.05	-0.01		0.04	-0.02	
T⁺	Racism	0.00	-0.01		0.05	-0.04		0.07	-0.04	
T	Sexism	0.01	-0.07		0.15	-0.14		0.15	-0.15	
T⁺	Sexism	0.14	-0.04		0.13	-0.05		0.19	-0.07	
W	Attack	0.01	0.02		0.00	-0.01		0.07	0.02	
W⁺	Attack	-0.04	-0.08		0.05	-0.08		0.01	-0.08	

the oversampled dataset. We also used different dimension sizes for word embeddings, from 25 to 200. Here we have reported the average of all the experimented demission sizes for each word embedding.

Table 3a. Performance comparison of the various DNN models with SSWE as the initial word embeddings – reproduced. F: Formspring, T: Twitter, W: Wikipedia, +: Oversampled

Dataset	Label	Precision				Recall				F1-score			
		CNN	LSTM	BLSTM	BLSTM attention	CNN	LSTM	BLSTM	BLSTM attention	CNN	LSTM	BLSTM	BLSTM attention
F+	Bully	0.94	0.78	0.79	0.86	0.61	0.93	0.94	0.92	0.74	0.85	0.76	0.89
T+	Racism	0.97	0.96	0.97	0.96	0.77	0.92	0.99	0.99	0.86	0.94	0.98	0.97
	Sexism	0.94	0.89	0.95	0.94	0.60	0.96	0.99	0.99	0.73	0.92	0.97	0.97
W+	Attack	0.93	0.90	0.94	0.93	0.82	0.91	0.98	0.98	0.87	0.91	0.96	0.96

As the results show, oversampling of the dataset significantly (Mann-Whitney U test, $P < 0.001$) improved the performance of the models in all three word embeddings. Overall, the SSWE has the highest $F1$-score and precision while Random embeddings resulted in the highest recall. The performance measures of all the DNN based models using SSWE initial word embedding is presented in Table 5. The LSTM model had the lowest performance in comparison to other models, mainly due to near zero recall. While BLSTM has the highest $F1$-score and recall, BLSTM with attention also performed quite similar with slightly higher precision in the cost of a lower recall.

Table 3b. Difference in the performance of the reference and the reproduced DNN models with SSWE as the initial word embeddings. Negative values indicate higher performance of the reproduced models. F: Formspring, T: Twitter, W: Wikipedia, +: Oversampled

Dataset	Label	Precision				Recall				F1-score			
		CNN	LSTM	BLSTM	BLSTM attention	CNN	LSTM	BLSTM	BLSTM attention	CNN	LSTM	BLSTM	BLSTM attention
F+	Bully	-0.01	0.13	0.12	0.04	0.29	-0.08	-0.13	-0.01	0.17	0.03	0.1	0.02
T+	Racism	-0.04	-0.05	-0.05	-0.06	0.17	-0.12	-0.04	-0.03	0.07	-0.09	-0.05	-0.04
	Sexism	-0.02	-0.05	-0.07	-0.06	0.32	-0.03	-0.05	-0.07	0.19	-0.04	-0.05	-0.07
W+	Attack	-0,01	-0.20	-0.04	-0.06	0.01	-0.37	-0.17	-0.12	0.01	-0.30	-0.11	-0.09

Table 4. Performance evaluation of the BLSTM with attention models, with three word embedding methods on the YouTube original dataset and the oversamples dataset. Y: YouTube, +: Oversampled

Dataset	Label	Precision			Recall			F1-score		
		Random	Glove	SSWE	Random	Glove	SSWE	Random	Glove	SSWE
Y	Bully	0.41	0.47	0.19	0.18	0.29	0.11	0.22	0.35	0.12
Y+	Bully	0.93	0.89	0.96	0.91	0.84	0.88	0.92	0.86	0.92

Table 5. Performance comparison of the various DNN models with SSWE as the initial word embeddings – YouTube Data. Y: YouTube, +: Oversampled

Dataset	Label	Precision				Recall				F1-score			
		CNN	LSTM	BLSTM	BLSTM attention	CNN	LSTM	BLSTM	BLSTM attention	CNN	LSTM	BLSTM	BLSTM attention
Y+	Bully	0.88	0.86	0.94	0.96	0.7	0.08	0.93	0.88	0.78	0.14	0.93	0.92

3.3 Transfer Learning

Transfer learning is the process of using a model which has been trained on one task for another related task. Following [5] we also implemented the transfer learning procedure to evaluate to what extent the DNN models trained on a social network, here Twitter, Formspring, and Wiki, can successfully detect cyberbullying posts in another social

Table 6. Performance comparison of the three transfer learning approaches using BLSTM with attention. F: Formspring, T: Twitter, W: Wikipedia, Y: YouTube, +: Oversampled

Train Dataset	Approaches	Test Y		
		Precision	Recall	*F1*-score
F+	Complete	0.74	0.19	0.30
	Feature Level	0.82	0.50	0.62
	Model Level	0.73	0.80	0.76
T+	Complete	0.46	0.09	0.15
	Feature Level	0.89	0.52	0.66
	Model Level	0.83	0.99	0.90
W+	Complete	0.68	0.14	0.23
	Feature Level	0.81	0.67	0.74
	Model Level	0.99	0.96	0.97

network, i.e., YouTube. For this purpose we used the BLSTM with attention model and experimented with three different approaches.

Complete Transfer Learning. In this approach, a model trained on one dataset is directly used in other datasets without any extra training. As the results in Table 6 show, the recalls are quite low but varying in all three datasets. This can indicate that the nature of cyberbullying is different in these different datasets. However, the complete transfer learning approach shows that bullying nature in YouTube is more similar to Formspring (*F1*-score = 0.30) and then to Wikipedia (*F1*-score = 0.23) in comparison to Twitter (*F1*-score = 0.15). This might be due to the similarity of the nature of these social networks. YouTube, Formspring and Wikipedia all have longer posts and are task oriented, while Twitter has short posts and is more general purpose.

Feature Level Transfer Learning. In this approach, a model is trained on one dataset and only learned word embeddings are transferred to another dataset for training a new model. The evaluation metrics of the transferred models show improvements (Table 6) in both precision and recall for all the datasets. This improvement compared to previous leading approach, indicates the importance of learned word embeddings and their impact cyberbullying detection. As illustrated in the table, Wikipedia has the highest performance with *F1*-score = 0.74.

Model Level Transfer Learning. In this approach, a model is trained on one dataset and learned word embeddings, as well as network weights, are transferred to another dataset for training a new model. The improvement of results in this learning approach (Table 6) was not significant compared to the feature level learning approach. This indicates that the transfer of network weights is not as essential to cyberbullying detection as the learned word embeddings.

4   Conclusion and Future Work

In this study, we successfully reproduced the reference literature [5] for detection of cyberbullying incidents in social media platforms using DNN based models. The source codes and materials were mostly well organized and accessible. However, there were some details and settings that were not clearly stated. These might have been the reason for some of the inconsistencies in our results. We further expanded our work by using a new social media dataset, YouTube, to investigate the adaptability and transferability of the models to the new dataset and also to compare the performance of the DNN models against the conventional ML models which were used in previous studies on the YouTube dataset for cyberbullying detection. Often, the datasets for cyberbullying detection contains very few posts marked as bullying. This imbalance problem can be partly compensated by oversampling the bullying posts. However, the effects of such prevalence on the performance of models need to be further assessed. Our study shows that the DNN models were adaptable and transferable to the new dataset. DNN based models coupled with transfer learning outperformed all the previous results for the detection of cyberbullying in this YouTube dataset using ML models. In [17, 18] authors have used context-based features such as the users' profile information and personal demographics to train the ML models which has resulted in F1-score = 0.64. In [1] the discrimination capacity of the detection methods were improved to 0.76 by incorporating expert knowledge. We believe that the DNN models can also benefit from integrating other sources of information and as the future work we recommend to look into the impact of profile information of the social media users and to investigate the improvement of the models by considering the above mentioned sources of information.

References

1. Dadvar, M., Trieschnigg, D., de Jong, F.: Experts and machines against bullies: a hybrid approach to detect cyberbullies. In: Sokolova, M., van Beek, P. (eds.) AI 2014. LNCS (LNAI), vol. 8436, pp. 275–281. Springer, Cham (2014). https://doi.org/10.1007/978-3-319-06483-3_25
2. Dinakar, K., Reichart, R., Lieberman, H.: Modeling the Detection of Textual Cyberbullying, pp. 11–17. Association for the Advancement of Artificial Intelligence (2011)
3. Dadvar, M., de Jong, F.: Improved cyberbullying detection through personal profiles. In: International Conference on Information and Knowledge Management, Proceedings on Conference on Cyberbullying (2012)
4. Zhang, X., et al.: Cyberbullying detection with a pronunciation based convolutional neural network. In: 2016 15th IEEE International Conference on Machine Learning and Applications (ICMLA), pp. 740–745 (2016)
5. Agrawal, S., Awekar, A.: Deep learning for detecting cyberbullying across multiple social media platforms. In: Pasi, G., Piwowarski, B., Azzopardi, L., Hanbury, A. (eds.) ECIR 2018. LNCS, vol. 10772, pp. 141–153. Springer, Cham (2018). https://doi.org/10.1007/978-3-319-76941-7_11
6. Reynolds, K., Kontostathis, A., Edwards, L.: Using machine learning to detect cyberbullying. In: Proceedings of the 10th International Conference on Machine Learning and Applications, ICMLA 2011, vol. 2, pp. 241–244 (December 2011)

7. Waseem, Z., Hovy, D.: Hateful symbols or hateful people? Predictive features for hate speech detection on Twitter. In: Proceedings of the NAACL Student Research Workshop, pp. 88–93 (2016)
8. Wulczyn, E., Thain, N., Dixon, L.: Ex machina: personal attacks seen at scale. In: Proceedings of the 26th International Conference on World Wide Web, WWW 2017, pp. 1391–1399 (2016)
9. Dadvar, M.: Experts and Machines United Against Cyberbullying. University of Twente, Enschede, The Netherlands (2014)
10. Chen, T., Xu, R., He, Y., Wang, X.: Improving sentiment analysis via sentence type classification using BiLSTM-CRF and CNN. Exp. Syst. Appl. **72**, 221–230 (2017)
11. Kim, Y.: Convolutional Neural Networks for Sentence Classification. arxiv.org (2014)
12. Zhou, C., Sun, C., Liu, Z., Lau, F.C.M.: A C-LSTM neural network for text classification. Adv. Neural Inf. Process. Syst., 649–657 (2015)
13. Johnson, R., Zhang, T.: Supervised and semi-supervised text categorization using LSTM for region embeddings (2016)
14. Zhou, P., et al.: Attention-based bidirectional long short-term memory networks for relation classification. In: Proceedings of the 54th Annual Meeting of the Association for Computational Linguistics (Volume 2: Short Papers), pp. 207–212 (2016)
15. Pennington, J., Socher, R., Manning, C.: Glove: global vectors for word representation. In: Proceedings of the 2014 Conference on Empirical Methods in Natural Language Processing (EMNLP), pp. 1532–1543 (2014)
16. Tang, D., Wei, F., Yang, N., Zhou, M., Liu, T., Qin, B.: Learning sentiment-specific word embedding. In: ACL, pp. 1555–1565 (2014)
17. Dadvar, M., Ordelman, R., De Jong, F., Trieschnigg, D.: Improved cyberbullying detection using gender information. In: Dutch-Belgian Information Retrieval Workshop, DIR 2012, pp. 23–26 (2012)
18. Dadvar, M., Trieschnigg, D., Ordelman, R., de Jong, F.: Improving cyberbullying detection with user context. In: Serdyukov, P., et al. (eds.) ECIR 2013. LNCS, vol. 7814, pp. 693–696. Springer, Heidelberg (2013). https://doi.org/10.1007/978-3-642-36973-5_62

Predicting Customer Churn for Insurance Data

Michael Scriney[⊠], Dongyun Nie, and Mark Roantree

Insight Centre for Data Analytics, School of Computing, Dublin City University,
Dublin, Ireland
{michael.scriney,dongyun.nie,mark.roantree}@dcu.ie

Abstract. Most organisations employ customer relationship management systems to provide a strategic advantage over their competitors. One aspect of this is applying a *customer lifetime value* to each client which effectively forms a fine-grained ranking of every customer in their database. This is used to focus marketing and sales budgets and, in turn, generate a more optimised and targeted spend. The problem is that it requires a full customer history for every client and this rarely exists. In effect, there is a large gap between the available information in application databases and the types of datasets required to calculate customer lifetime values. This gap prevents any meaningful calculation of customer lifetime values. In this research, we present an approach to generating some of the missing parameters for CLV calculations. This requires a specialised form of data warehouse architecture and a flexible prediction and validation methodology for imputing missing data.

1 Introduction

One of the major goals of Customer Relationship Management is to maximise the *Customer Lifetime Value* (CLV) for the purpose of supporting long term business investment [8]. CLV is a measure that focuses on predicting the net profit that can accrue from the *future* relationship with customers [4]. This metric can be calculated by recording the behaviours of the customer over the longer term and thus, help to build a customised business strategy. It has been a popular research topic, addressed by researchers in different ways, for example, formulaic CLV [11] and Probability Model CLV [15]. One of the core elements in CLV models [5] and the calculation of CLV scores is customer *retention* or its opposite, customer *churn*. In the business sector, customer churn is commonly used not only to support CLV predictions, but to maximise customer profitability by establishing resource allocation decisions for marketing, sales, and customer interaction. As a result of the benefits that churn analysis provides, this topic has become popular for industrial research in recent years. Some of business based research focuses on statistical efforts, often required for CLV calculations [17]. Information technology based research generally experiments with data mining

Research funded by Science Foundation Ireland Grant SFI/12/RC/2289_P2.

M. Song et al. (Eds.): DaWaK 2020, LNCS 12393, pp. 256–265, 2020.
https://doi.org/10.1007/978-3-030-59065-9_21

techniques [7] to try to generate the variables needed for CLV scores. In the telecom sector, churn analysis research has been shown to require a specific set of variables [18] for effective results.

1.1 Problem Statement

One of the issues with CLV research and the generation of variables such as *churn* is the highly theoretical nature and focus of this area of research. There has been little research on deriving necessary attributes from real world datasets which require activities such as the construction, transformation and enrichment of datasets to make them suitable for existing CLV calculations. Researchers in [2] highlighted the variables that are required as input to CLV calculations. Here, a is the acquisition rate; A is the acquisition cost per customer; d is the yearly discount rate; m is the net income of a transaction; R is the retention cost per customer per year; and r is the yearly retention rate.

On the surface, it appears as if the generation of CLV scores for all customers is a straightforward process but in reality, many of these variables are not easily extracted from enterprise databases. From [2], m and d can be deduced using feature extraction and a detailed clustering process but all others will generally require some form of imputation after a segmentation process. Customer *segmentation* is regarded as a natural process to help companies to classify customers and plan market investment strategies such as direct sales. As such, it has been widely adopted by industry planners or in data warehousing similar efforts include fragmentation of the data and queries [13]. Moreover, it plays a critical role in the development of the company's position by combining product differentiation and marketing segmentation to provide resources, objectives and competences to the company.

1.2 Contribution and Paper Structure

In previous work [10], we presented a methodology for constructing a unified client record, as calculating customer lifetime values (CLV) is not possible without a complete client history. In this paper, we extend this work as we employ a suite of machine learning algorithms to derive the retention rate r for all customers.

The challenge is due to the fact that no single model has been shown to provide the best accuracy. Our approach begins by process of feature extraction from the unified customer dataset and using these variables, derive the retention rate, r, suitable for CLV calculations. We then perform customer churn prediction using ten experimental configurations in order to determine the best method for calculating r. In this way, we provide an understanding of which methods deliver accurate churn predictions for individual customers. A robust validation mechanism uses a number of metrics by which to determine those models that perform best.

Paper Structure. The paper is structured as follows: in Sect. 2, we discuss related research in predicting customer churn; Sect. 3 describes the steps necessary to construct the dataset used as input for the ten models; in Sect. 4, we present our results, evaluation and discussion; and finally, in Sect. 5 we present our conclusions.

2   Related Research

In [6], the authors introduce a hybrid approach for calculating customer churn by combining decision trees and neural networks. The method was then evaluated using supermarket data. Similar to our work a significant amount of prepossessing of the data is required. However, the authors did not provide a comparison of the hybrid approach to other models. The authors in [1] analyse insurance data using logistic regression with a generalised additive model (GAM). This research uses data from the insurance sector but here, the researchers benefited from more fine-grained data, which provided a month-by-month view of the data. As a result, the authors did not see the need to provide a comparison between the GAM model and other classification algorithms. In [3], the authors present a means of predicting customer churn for motor insurance. They compare four methods used to calculate churn: decision trees, neural networks, logistic regression and support vector machines. In terms of accuracy across models, the authors neural network approach had a similar accuracy to ours ($\sim$88%). However, the authors' dataset focused specifically on motor insurance. Additionally, our evaluation compares ten different classification methods. In [16], the authors propose a one-class support vector machine which can be used to under sample data. The efficacy of the approach was evaluated using five classification methods on a motor insurance fraud dataset with a credit card churn dataset. The five methods employed were: decision trees, support vector machines, logistic regression, probabilistic neural networks and a group method for data handling. Similar to the authors research, we employ decision trees, support vector machines and neural networks for our evaluation. However, the authors' insurance dataset focused on fraud detection within motor insurance while our approach attempts to calculate customer churn across multiple insurance types. The authors in [19] combine deep and shallow modelling to predict customer churn on insurance data. Similar to our approach, their evaluation compared the performance of their method with several classification algorithms using a similar set of metrics. However, the authors used a large dataset consisting solely of life insurance policies whereas our dataset contains several policy types. This difference is crucial as it results in different sets of dimensions, motivating the need for different methods to be applied. In [12], the authors evaluate the *staying power* of various models of churn prediction for two domains: insurance and internet service providers. The insurance dataset comprises life insurance churn data and four predictive method were used: logit models and decision trees both with and without bagging. The authors found the decision tree method with bagging to show the best performance. In our research we employ a wider range of prediction algorithms to provide a greater comparison of churn prediction methods.

In summary, there are more commonly used when predicting churn for insurance data: decision trees, support vector machines and logistic regression models. However, recent research examined the efficacy of various neural networks. Factors such as granularity, size, available features (and the types of each feature) have a significant impact when determining which model performs best.

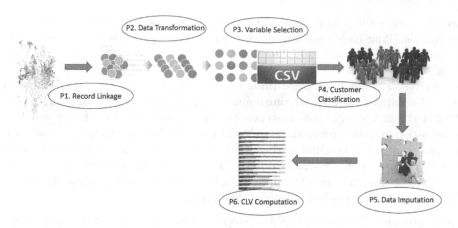

Fig. 1. ETL pipeline architecture

3   Data Transformations

In this section, we provide a brief outline of the Extract Transform Load (ETL) architecture but focus on those components which are novel to our architecture and crucial to imputing retention data. The dataset used in this work originated from our collaborator in the insurance sector. In this sector, transactions focused on selling policies and not on building customer profiles and thus, the Extract component in our architecture acquired approx. 500,000 insurance policies.

3.1   System Architecture

An ETL pipeline comprises a series of components extracting data from input sources, transforming the data to match the system's data model, and loading into a data mart (data cube) for reporting and analysis. Our approach, shown in Fig. 1, is a specialised form of ETL [14], due to the specific requirements of the task (customer lifetime value) and the nature of the data. In particular, this work began with a dataset that was policy-focused and not customer-focused. In effect, it was not suited to analysis by customer. Thus, the first step involved a process known as record linkage where, upon acquisition, data was pivoted to be customer-focused, where a customer record contained 1 or more policies. This work was presented in [10] and, while it provided a more holistic customer record, the data was not suited to the imputation algorithms necessary to impute the missing CLV variables. In addition, the dataset was still unclassified in terms of customer types (good, bad, average).

3.2   Churn Analysis Data Transformation

In this paper, we focus on components P2 and P5 from Fig. 1. The data used is initially based on two large imports: **detail** and **aggregate**. Detail provides a *policy centric* view year-on-year, recording the type, current and renewal premium for each policy. `Aggregate` is an aggregation of a unified customer record, detailing high level information on customers who hold policies generated during earlier work [10]. The large data imports are combined with other data sources within the warehouse to provide a dataset suitable for predicting *customer churn*. There are three processes involved in the transformation (P2) of a dataset suitable for churn analysis: `Aggregation`, `Augmentation` and `Preparation`. `Aggregation` constructs the initial per-policy view which provides information on policy renewals. `Augmentation` adds features to this dataset such as customer information and pricing. These two processes can be equated to the E and T processes within a standard `ETL` (Extract, Transform, Load) architecture. The final process `Preparation` provides a final transformation of the dataset so that is it ready for machine learning algorithms.

Aggregation. The goal of the first step is to construct a policy centric view containing those policies that may or may not been renewed. This involves a RollUp operation on the `detail` view to create an aggregated view containing the policy identifier (`policy_id`), the number of years for which the policy is held (`years_held`) and whether or not the policy was renewed (`renewed`). In total, the dataset used for our work contains 443,893 unique policies, of which 300,646 were not renewed with the remaining 143,247 renewed by the customer.

Augmentation. The next step is `augmentation` where views within the warehouse are integrated with the policy-centric aggregation. In total, seven additional views are integrated: policy prices, family policy holders, latest renewal premium, insurance type, location, payment method and gender. **Policy Prices** include the average premium and the standard deviation for premium, which can indicate the amount of variation in year-on-year premium prices. **Family Policy Holders** is the number of family members per customer who also hold policies with the company. **Latest Renewal Premium** is the latest premium for a given policy. **Insurance Type** is the type of insurance, which has four possible values: `Private Motor`, `Commercial Motor`, `Home` and `Travel`. **Location** is the county the customer resides in. **Payment Method** indicates if the premium is paid either in full or monthly. Finally, **Gender** relates to the gender of the policy holder. The result is a dataset with fourteen dimensions including a class label of *Renewed* or *Not Renewed* as seen in Table 1 where: `Name` is the name of the feature; `Description` briefly describes the feature and `Type` indicates if *Categorical* or *Continuous*. For our evaluation, the dimensions representing unique identifiers (`pid` and `cid`) were not used.

Preparation. There are four steps in the preparation phase: *cleaning, sampling, encoding* and *splitting*. In this dataset, just 27 records were removed leaving a dataset with 443,866 rows. Determining whether or not a policy is renewed is, in effect, a classification problem. The class labels for each policy are `Renewed` or `Not Renewed`. As is common with real world data, our dataset has a class imbalance where 300,621 records are labelled `"Renewed"` and the remaining 143,245 records are labelled `"Not Renewed"`. This class imbalance can

Table 1. Post-integration dataset features

Name	Description	Type
pid	The policy identifier	Categorical
cid	The policy holder identifier	Categorical
years	The number of years the policy was held for	Continuous
avg_total	The average premium since first purchase	Continuous
std_total	The standard deviation of the premium	Continuous
family	The number of family members of the policy holder who also hold policies	Continuous
renew_p	The current renewal premium price	Continuous
total_p	The current premium price	Continuous
pol_type	The policy type (e.g. Home, Car, Travel ...)	Categorical
pay_type	The payment type, either Partial (pays monthly) or Full (payment in full on purchase)	Categorical
gender	The gender of the policy holder	Categorical
county	The county of the policy holder	Categorical
province	The province of the policy holder	Categorical
Class	Value: Renewed or Not Renewed	Categorical

greatly affect classification results and three methods are generally employed to resolve this: undersampling, oversampling and synthetic sampling. As we have a large number of records for the minority Renewed class, *undersampling* was the method selected to address this issue. Using this method, 143,245 records with the class label Not Renewed were randomly chosen so that both classes had the cardinality. The downside to this approach is that some of the Not Renewed data could have increased the effectiveness our analysis. This is addressed in our conclusions. After undersampling, the dataset comprised 286,490 records, with an equal distribution of the classes renewed and not renewed (143,245 records each). The encoding step transforms categorical dimensions so they are ready for machine learning algorithms. The dimensions encoded were insurance_type, payment_method and county. The final step splits the data into training and testing sets using the 80/20 configuration.

4   Algorithm Selection and Validation

Due to the characteristics of insurance data and the fact that research into customer lifetime value is quite theoretical in nature, it was decided to use a range of statistical methods and try to determine what works best. In this section, we begin by presenting the set of algorithms used to impute the retention value (churn), then proceed to discuss the evaluation strategy and results and finally, we present a discussion on the results.

Algorithm Selection. The process of determining customer churn in any domain is generally a classification problem with two classes: `Renewed` and `Not Renewed`. The classification methods we employed were: Bernoulli Naive Bayes; Multinomial Naive Bayes; two types of support vector machines; two decision trees; and a series of artificial neural network (ANN) configurations. Support Vector Machines are used regularly in classification. For our experiments we used one Linear Support Vector machine to provide a baseline to our other methods. Two experimental configurations using Naive Bayes were employed, one using a Bernoulli model and another using a multinomial model which has been shown to have increased performance on binary data in some instances [9]. For both models, 100 different alpha values were used on each, ranging from 0.0 to 1 in degrees of 0.01. Two decision trees using the CART (Classification and Regression) algorithm were employed, the first using `entropy` as the splitting measure and the second using Gini impurity. For both approaches, a decision tree was created for each level of depth until the maximum depth was reached and at each depth, test data was used to obtain the accuracy of the tree. Artificial Neural Networks (ANNs) have seen extensive use in predicting customer churn due to their ability to model interactions between features that may otherwise go unnoticed. For our experiments, 20 different configurations of ANNs were constructed with various configurations of hyperparameters.

Evaluation Metrics. We now describe the evaluation metrics used to compare the different prediction models. The measures `TP`, `TN`, `FP` and `FN` are *true positive*, *true negative*, *false positive* and *false negative* respectively. The metrics are: Accuracy, Precision, Recall, Specificity and F_1 score. Standard accuracy (percentage of correct classifications) is insufficient in evaluating a classifier but provides a useful baseline. The precision, recall and specificity metrics provide more information as to the actual performance of a classifier *within* classes. All model configurations will be validated using all 5 metrics.

Results and Discussion. We begin this section with an overview of the 4 different algorithms in isolation, reporting on their relative performances. We then take a comparative view across all algorithms, using different configurations for the more complex models. Unsurprisingly the Linear SVM show a weak performance with an accuracy of 0.754 and an F_1 score of 0.76. However, this model was always intended as a baseline for our evaluation of other models. For both Naive model types, 100 different alpha values were used, ranging from 0.0 to 1 in degrees of 0.01. Interestingly, these changes had no effect on the accuracy score across model configurations. For the algorithm which incorporated entropy, the best performing tree had a depth of 11 with an accuracy of 88.82%. For the Gini-tree, the best performing depth was also 11 and with a very similar accuracy of 88.72%. The results of the top 5 performing configurations can be seen in Table 2, where `id` is the experimental id; `epoch` is the number of epochs; `hlayer` is the number of hidden layers; `hnode` is the number of hidden nodes; `tr_ac` is the accuracy of the training data; `tr_l` is the loss of the training data; `te_ac` is the accuracy on the test data; and finally, `te_l` is the loss on the test data. For all 5 configurations, a dropout rate of 0.02 was used. From Table 2, experiment 5 is the best performing with an accuracy of 0.888 on the test dataset. This model consisted of one hidden layer with 31 hidden nodes with a dropout rate of 0.2%. There were other models with increased training accuracy tr_ac but are not shown as they have a lower te_ac than 88.6% which is generally an indication of over fitting.

Table 2. Configuration of the top five performing ANNs

id	epoch	hlayer	hnode	tr_ac	tr_l	te_ac	te_l
5	50	1	31	0.892	0.251	0.889	0.259
12	50	2	56	0.893	0.25	0.884	0.265
15	37	2	56	0.889	0.26	0.885	0.268
17	37	2	66	0.892	0.252	0.887	0.266
18	37	2	36	0.891	0.257	0.886	0.263

Discussion. Table 3 provides a comparison across all experimental model and parameter configurations. Method is the classification algorithm and configuration used; acc is the overall accuracy; err is the overall error; pre is the precision; rec is recall; spe is specificity; and F_1 is the F_1 score. Overall, most models performed well with 7 of the experiments achieving an accuracy > 0.88, with 6 of those having an F_1 score > 0.89. Interestingly, the difference between the two decision tree methods (Entropy & Gini split) was so small (> 5 decimal places) that they effectively performed the same. The worst performing method was the multinomial Naive Bayes with an accuracy of 0.69 and an F_1 score of 0.678. In terms of accuracy, the best performing model was ANN-5 with an accuracy of 0.889. This configuration also achieved the highest F_1 score with 0.893. On the other hand, both decision tree methods have higher precision (0.938 vs 0.920) and specificity (0.931 vs 0.914) scores. However, ANN-5 had a higher recall rate (0.867 vs 0.851). Between these three high performing configurations, ANN-5 had the highest number of true negatives (24487) while both decision tree methods had a higher number of true positives (26766 and 26767). By examining the NB-Bernoulli model results, there is a clear requirement for more in-depth statistics than accuracy alone. This method has an overall accuracy of 0.776 but there is a difference between the measures for recall and specificity (0.717 and 0.879 respectively), indicating that this method is better at predicting negative classifications over positive ones. If we examine the ANN configurations, while ANN-5 has the highest overall accuracy and F_1 score, other methods show a higher value for specificity (the highest being ANN-17 with 0.929). However, ANN-5 shows the highest value for recall out of all neural network configurations indicating that it performs best when predicting positives classes. A high recall value necessitates a low *false negative* rate. Out of all methods employed ANN-5 has the lowest rate of fn, with $4,070$ records being classified incorrectly. The question of which model and configuration to use depends ultimately on the classification most important to businesses. From our findings, a decision tree classifier is recommended for organisations that wish to obtain the highest number of correct *negative* classes, while ANN-5 should be used if the goal is to correctly identify the highest number of *positive* classes. As the ultimate goal of our research is to impute `retention` for its use in CLV calculations, this current step sought to obtain the highest number of correct negative classes so the method DT - Gini is selected for CLV calculations.

Table 3. Comparison of classification methods

Method	acc	pre	rec	spe	F_1	tp	tn	fp	fn
NB-Bernoulli	0.776	0.911	0.717	0.879	0.802	25999	18477	2551	10271
NB-Multinomal	0.691	0.651	0.706	0.679	0.678	18594	21023	9956	7725
DT-Entropy	**0.887**	**0.938**	**0.851**	**0.931**	**0.892**	**26766**	**24048**	**1784**	**4700**
DT-Gini	**0.887**	**0.938**	**0.851**	**0.931**	**0.892**	**26767**	**24055**	**1783**	**4693**
SVM-Linear	0.754	0.779	0.742	0.769	0.760	22234	20997	6316	7751
ANN-5	**0.889**	**0.920**	**0.867**	**0.914**	**0.893**	**26449**	**24478**	**2301**	**4070**
ANN-12	0.884	0.930	0.852	0.922	0.889	26730	23917	2020	4631
ANN-15	0.885	0.924	0.858	0.917	0.890	26578	24133	2172	4415
ANN-17	0.887	0.937	0.853	0.929	0.893	26934	23893	1816	4655
ANN-18	0.886	0.919	0.863	0.912	0.890	26412	24370	2338	4178

5   Conclusions and Future Work

In this paper, we presented an approach to generating one of the key parameters for CLV calculations: retention, a process that requires a specialised form of ETL architecture and a degree of flexibility in selection of models used to impute retention. Our evaluation showed that an artificial neural network provided the highest accuracy and F_1 score followed closely by two decision tree algorithms. While no single model or model configuration achieved the highest score across all evaluation metrics, our approach identified the best model configuration depending on the user's prediction requirements. Our current work remains focused on the identification and selection of best model configuration. Recall that our under sampling method randomly chose a recordset that *may* exclude instance data suited to the predictions of retention. To address this, we are re-running all experiments using different datasets to determine if further improvements can be found in our results. Given the high scores achieved by the neural network models, we are also examining hyperparameter tuning to explore other avenues to improve the prediction accuracy.

References

1. Günther, C.C., et al.: Modelling and predicting customer churn from an insurance company. Scand. Actuar. J. **2014**(1), 58–71 (2014)

2. Berger, P.D., Nasr, N.I.: Customer lifetime value: marketing models and applications. J. Interact. Market. **12**(1), 17–30 (1998)
3. Bolancé, C., Guillen, M., Padilla-Barreto, A.E.: Predicting probability of customer churn in insurance. In: León, R., Muñoz-Torres, M., Moneva, J. (eds.) MS 2016. LNBIP, vol. 254, pp. 82–91. Springer, Cham (2016). https://doi.org/10.1007/978-3-319-40506-3_9
4. Di Benedetto, C.A., Kim, K.H.: Customer equity and value management of global brands: bridging theory and practice from financial and marketing perspectives. J. Bus. Res. **69**(9), 3721–3724 (2016)
5. Gupta, S.: Modeling customer lifetime value. J. Serv. Res. **9**(2), 139–155 (2006)
6. Hu, X., Yang, Y., Chen, L., Zhu, S.: Research on a customer churn combination prediction model based on decision tree and neural network. In: 5th International Conference on Cloud Computing and Big Data Analytics (ICCCBDA), pp. 129–132 (2020)
7. Lemmens, A., Croux, C.: Bagging and boosting classification trees to predict churn. J. Market. Res. **43**(2), 276–286 (2006)
8. Ling, R., Yen, D.C.: Customer relationship management: an analysis framework and implementation strategies. J. Comput. Inf. Syst. **41**(3), 82–97 (2001)
9. Metsis, V., Androutsopoulos, I., Paliouras, G.: Spam filtering with naive Bayes-which naive Bayes? In: CEAS, Mountain View, CA, vol. 17, pp. 28–69 (2006)
10. Nie, D., Roantree, M.: Detecting multi-relationship links in sparse datasets. In: ICEIS 2019, vol. 1, pp. 149–157. SciTePress (2019). https://doi.org/10.5220/0007696901490157
11. Reinartz, W.J., Kumar, V.: On the profitability of long-life customers in a non-contractual setting: an empirical investigation and implications for marketing. J. Market. **64**(4), 17–35 (2000)
12. Risselada, H., Verhoef, P.C., Bijmolt, T.H.: Staying power of churn prediction models. J. Interact. Market. **24**(3), 198–208 (2010)
13. Roantree, M., Liu, J.: A heuristic approach to selecting views for materialization. Softw. Pract. Exp. **44**(10), 1157–1179 (2014)
14. Scriney, M., McCarthy, S., McCarren, A., Cappellari, P., Roantree, M.: Automating data mart construction from semi-structured data sources. Comput. J. **62**(3), 394–413 (2019)
15. Sohrabi, B., Khanlari, A.: Customer lifetime value (CLV) measurement based on RFM model. Iran. Account. Auditing Rev. **14**(47), 7–20 (2007)
16. Sundarkumar, G.G., Ravi, V., Siddeshwar, V.: One-class support vector machine based undersampling: application to churn prediction and insurance fraud detection. In: 2015 IEEE International Conference on Computational Intelligence and Computing Research (ICCIC), pp. 1–7. IEEE (2015)
17. Tamaddoni, A., Stakhovych, S., Ewing, M.: The impact of personalised incentives on the profitability of customer retention campaigns. J. Market. Manage. **33**(5), 1–21 (2017)
18. Ullah, I., Raza, B., Malik, A.K., Imran, M., Islam, S.U., Kim, S.W.: A churn prediction model using random forest: analysis of machine learning techniques for churn prediction and factor identification in telecom sector. IEEE Access **7**, 60134–60149 (2019)
19. Zhang, R., Li, W., Tan, W., Mo, T.: Deep and shallow model for insurance churn prediction service. In: 2017 IEEE International Conference on Services Computing (SCC), pp. 346–353. IEEE (2017)

3. Berry, M.J.A., Linoff, G.S.: Data mining techniques: for marketing, sales, and customer support. J. Inf. Sci. Manag. 12(1), 14–80 (1997)

4. Bolancé, C., Guillen, M., Padilla-Barreto, A.E.: Predicting probability of customer churn in insurance. In: Leon, R., Kacprzyk, J., Gil-Aluja, J. (eds.) Soft Computing Applications. AISC, vol. 894, pp. 82–91. Springer, Cham (2019). https://doi.org/10.1007/978-3-319-19704-3_7

5. De Bock, K.W., Van den Poel, D.: Reconciling performance and interpretability in customer churn prediction using ensemble learning based on generalized additive models. Expert Syst. Appl. 39(8), 6816–6826 (2012)

6. Chandar, M., Laha, A., Krishna, P.: Modeling churn behavior of bank customers using predictive data mining techniques. In: National Conference on Soft Computing Techniques for Engineering Applications (SCT-2006)

7. Coussement, K., Van den Poel, D.: Churn prediction in subscription services: an application of support vector machines while comparing two parameter-selection techniques. Expert Syst. Appl. 34(1), 313–327 (2008)

8. Mena, C.G., De Caigny, A., Coussement, K., De Bock, K.W., Lessmann, S.: Churn prediction with sequential data and deep neural networks. A comparative analysis (2019)

9. Verbeke, W., Dejaeger, K., Martens, D., Hur, J., Baesens, B.: New insights into churn prediction in the telecommunication sector: a profit driven data mining approach. Eur. J. Oper. Res. 218(1), 211–229 (2012)

10. Shirazi, F., Mohammadi, M.: A big data analytics model for customer churn prediction in the retiree segment. Int. J. Inf. Manag. 48, 238–253 (2019)

11. Gür Ali, Ö., Aritürk, U.: Dynamic churn prediction framework with more effective use of rare event data: the case of private banking. Expert Syst. Appl. 41(17), 7889–7903 (2014)

12. Buckinx, W., Van den Poel, D.: Customer base analysis: partial defection of behaviourally loyal clients in a non-contractual FMCG retail setting. Eur. J. Oper. Res. 164(1), 252–268 (2005)

13. Lemmens, A., Croux, C.: Bagging and boosting classification trees to predict churn. J. Mark. Res. 43(2), 276–286 (2006)

Supervised Learning

Scalable Machine Learning on Popular Analytic Languages with Parallel Data Summarization

Sikder Tahsin Al-Amin and Carlos Ordonez(⊠)

Department of Computer Science, University of Houston,
Houston, TX 77204, USA
carlos@central.uh.edu

Abstract. Machine learning requires scalable processing. An important acceleration mechanism is data summarization, which is accurate for many models and whose summary requires a small amount of RAM. In this paper, we generalize a data summarization matrix to produce one or multiple summaries, which benefits a broader class of models, compared to previous work. Our solution works well in popular languages, like R and Python, on a shared-nothing architecture, the standard in big data analytics. We introduce an algorithm which computes machine learning models in three phases: Phase 0 pre-processes and transfers the data set to the parallel processing nodes; Phase 1 computes one or multiple data summaries in parallel and Phase 2 computes a model in one machine based on such data set summaries. A key innovation is evaluating a demanding vector-vector outer product in C++ code, in a simple function call from a high-level programming language. We show Phase 1 is fully parallel, requiring a simple barrier synchronization at the end. Phase 2 is a sequential bottleneck, but contributes very little to overall time. We present an experimental evaluation with a prototype in the R language, with our summarization algorithm programmed in C++. We first show R is faster and simpler than competing big data analytic systems computing the same models, including Spark (using MLlib, calling Scala functions) and a parallel DBMS (computing data summaries with SQL queries calling UDFs). We then show our parallel solution becomes better than single-node processing as data set size grows.

1 Introduction

Machine learning is essential to big data analytics [1,10,20]. With higher data volume and varied data types, many new machine learning models and algorithms aiming at scalable applications [5,6]. Popular big data systems like parallel DBMS (e.g. Vertica, Teradata) and Hadoop systems (e.g. Spark, HadoopDB, Cassandra) offer ample storage and parallel processing of popular machine learning algorithms but the processing time can be slower. Besides, they do not have efficient native support for matrix-form data and out-of-box sophisticated mathematical computations. Nowadays, with the advancement of cloud technology

© Springer Nature Switzerland AG 2020
M. Song et al. (Eds.): DaWaK 2020, LNCS 12393, pp. 269–284, 2020.
https://doi.org/10.1007/978-3-030-59065-9_22

(e.g. AWS, Azure, Google Cloud), data can be stored in a single machine or a large cluster. Analysts can distribute the data set in the cloud and analyze it instead of avoiding the complex set up process of parallel systems. However, cloud systems are costly (costs vary depending on services), and using the cloud for simple analysis may not be beneficial (i.e., may not be cost-effective). On the other hand, mathematical systems like Python, R provide comprehensive libraries for machine learning and statistical computation. Analysts can install them easily and analyze small data sets locally in their machine.But those systems are not designed to scale to large data sets and the single machine is challenging to analyze the large data sets [10].

Within big data, data summarization has received much attention [5,12,15] among the machine learning practitioners. Summarization in parallel DBMS is losing ground as SQL queries are not a good choice for analytics and UDFs are not portable. Hadoop systems like Spark [21], is a better choice but they are slow for a few processing nodes, has scalability limitations, and even slower than DBMS in case of summarization [15]. With these motivations in mind, here, we present a data summarization algorithm that works in a parallel cluster, does not require a complex set up of parallel systems (e.g. DBMS, Hadoop), is solvable with popular analytic languages (e.g. Python, R) and is faster than the existing popular parallel systems. Exploiting the summarization, we can compute a wide variety of machine learning models and statistics on the data set either in a single machine or in parallel [5,15].

Our contributions include the following: (1) We present a new three-phase generalized summarization algorithm that works in a parallel cluster (or a remote cluster in the cloud). (2) We improve and optimize the summarization algorithm for classification/clustering problems initially proposed in [5]. (3) We improve and optimize the technique to read the data set from disks in blocks. (4) We study the trade-offs to compute data summarization in a parallel cluster and a single machine. Analysts can have a better understanding which is a common problem nowadays. In our work, we used R as our choice of analytic language combined with C++ to develop our algorithms, but it can be applied to other analytic platforms like Python. With the dedicated physical memory, R or Python itself cannot scale to deal with data sets larger than the proportion of memory allocated and is forced to crash. Also, we used a local parallel cluster to perform the experiments but our research applies to both local parallel cluster and a remote cluster in the cloud. Experimental evaluation shows our generalized summarization algorithm works efficiently in a parallel cluster, scalable and much faster than Spark and a parallel DBMS. This article is a significant extension and deeper study of [15], where the Gamma summarization matrix was initially proposed.

This is the outline for the rest of the article. Section 2 introduces the definitions used throughout the paper. Section 3 presents our theoretical research contributions where we present our new algorithm to compute summarization in a parallel cluster. Section 4 presents an extensive experimental evaluation. We discuss closely related work in Sect. 5. Conclusions and directions for future work are discussed in Sect. 6.

Table 1. Basic symbols and their description

Symbol	Description	Symbol	Description
X	Data set	d	Number of attributes/columns in X
X_I	Partitioned data set	Γ	Gamma Summarization Matrix
$\mathbf{X}$	Augmented X with Y	Γ^k	k-Gamma Summarization Matrices
Y	Dependent Variable	Θ	Machine learning model
Z	Augmented X with 1s and Y	p	Number of processing nodes
n	Number of records/rows in X	b	Blocks to read data

2 Definitions

2.1 Mathematical Definitions

We start by defining the input matrix X which is a set of n *column* vectors. All the models take a $d \times n$ matrix X as input. Let the input data set be defined as $X = \{x_1, ..., x_n\}$ with n points, where each point x_i is a vector in $\mathbf{R}^d$. Intuitively, X is a wide rectangular matrix. X is augmented with a $(d+1)$th dimension containing an output variable Y, making X a $(d+1) \times n$ matrix and we call it $\mathbf{X}$. We use $i = 1 \ldots n$ and $j = 1 \ldots d$ as matrix subscripts. We augment $\mathbf{X}$ with an extra row of n 1s and call that as matrix Z with a $(d+2) \times n$ dimension (Table 1).

We use Θ to represent a machine learning model or a statistical property in a general manner. Thus Θ can be any model like: LR, PCA, NB, KM or any statistical property like: Covariance or Correlation matrix. For each ML model Θ can be defined as, $\Theta = \{list\ of\ matrices/vectors\}$. For LR: $\Theta = \beta$, the vector or regression coefficients; for PCA: $\Theta = U, D$, where U are the eigen vectors and D contains the squared eigenvalues obtained from SVD; for NB: $\Theta = \{W, C, R\}$, where W is the vector of k class priors, C is a set of k mean vectors and R are k diagonal matrices with standard deviations; and for KM: $\Theta = \{W, C, R\}$, where W is a vector of k (number of clusters) weights, C is a set of k centroid vectors and R is a set of k variance matrices.

2.2 Parallel Cluster Architecture

We are using p processing nodes in parallel. Each node has its CPU and memory (shared-nothing architecture) and it cannot directly access another node storage. Therefore, all processing nodes communicate with each other transferring data. And, data is stored on disk, not in virtual memory.

3   Theory and Algorithm

First, we give an overview of the original summarization matrix introduced in
[15] for DBMS. Here, we make several improvements. We propose a new three-
phased generalized algorithm that computes summarization in a parallel cluster.
Also, we improve and optimize the k-summarization matrices algorithm which
was introduced in [5] (as Diagonal Gamma Matrix). Next, we discuss how we can
integrate the parallel algorithm into an analytic language. Finally, we analyze
the time and space complexity of our algorithm.

3.1   Gamma Summarization Matrix and ML Model Computation

Here, we review the Gamma summarization matrix (Γ) [5,15] and computation
of several ML models (Θ) exploiting Γ. The main algorithm had two steps:

1. Phase 1: Compute summarization matrix: one matrix Γ or k matrices Γ^k.
2. Phase 2: Compute model Θ based on Gamma matrix (matrices).

Phase 1: Matrix Γ (Gamma), is a fundamental matrix that contains a complete,
accurate, and sufficient summary. If we consider X as the input data set, n
counts the total number of points in the dataset, L is the linear sum of x_i, and
Q is the sum of vector outer products of x_i, then from [15], the Gamma (Γ) is
defined below in Eq. 1. We first define n, L, Q as: $n = |X|$, $L = \sum_{i=1}^{n} x_i$, and
$Q = XX^T = \sum_{i=1}^{n} x_i \cdot x_i^T$. Now, the Gamma ($\Gamma$) matrix:

$$\Gamma = \begin{bmatrix} n & L^T & 1^T \cdot Y^T \\ L & Q & XY^T \\ Y \cdot 1 & YX^T & YY^T \end{bmatrix} = \begin{bmatrix} n & \sum x_i^T & \sum y_i \\ \sum x_i & \sum x_i x_i^T & \sum x_i y_i \\ \sum y_i & \sum y_i x_i^T & \sum y_i^2 \end{bmatrix} \tag{1}$$

X is defined as a $d \times n$ matrix, and Z is defined as a $(d+2) \times n$ matrix as
mentioned in Sect. 2. From [15], we can easily understand that Γ matrix can be
computed in the two ways: (1) matrix-matrix multiplication i.e., ZZ^T (2) sum
of vector outer products i.e., $\sum_i z_i \cdot z_i^T$ So, in short, the Gamma computation
can be defined as: $\Gamma = ZZ^T = \sum_{i=1}^{n} z_i \cdot z_i^T$

Now, from [5], k-Gamma (Γ^k) is given in Eq. 2. The major difference between
the two forms of Gamma is, we do not require parameters off the diagonal in
Γ^k as in Γ. So, we need only a few parameters out of the whole Γ, namely,
n, L, L^T, Q. That is, we require only a few sub-matrices from Γ. Also, in Γ, the
Q is computed completely whereas in Γ^k, the Q is diagonal. So, we can also call
this a Diagonal-Gamma matrix.

$$\Gamma^k = \begin{bmatrix} n & L^T & 0 \\ L & Q & 0 \\ 0 & 0 & 0 \end{bmatrix}, where\ Q = \begin{bmatrix} Q_{11} & 0 & 0 .... & 0 \\ 0 & Q_{22} & 0....... & 0 \\ 0 & 0 & Q_{33}..... & 0 \\ 0 & 0 & 0........ & Q_{dd} \end{bmatrix} \tag{2}$$

Phase 2: Both Γ and Γ^k provide summarization for a different set of machine learning models (Θ). For Linear Regression (LR) and Principal Component Analysis (PCA), we need one full Γ assuming element off-diagonal is not zero. And for Naïve Bayes (NB) and k-means (KM), k-Gamma matrices are needed where k is the number of classes/clusters. We briefly discuss how to compute each model (Θ) below. The details of the model computation are discussed in [5].

LR: We can get the column vector of regression coefficients ($\hat{\beta}$), from the above mentioned Γ, with: $\hat{\beta} = Q^{-1}(\mathbf{X}Y^T)$

PCA: There are two parameters, namely the set of orthogonal vectors U, and the diagonal matrix (D^2) which contains the squared eigen values. We compute ρ, the correlation matrix as $\rho = UD^2U^T = (UD^2U^T)^T$. Then we compute PCA from the ρ by solving Singular Value Decomposition (SVD) on it. Also, we express ρ in terms of sufficient statistics as: $\rho_{ab} = \frac{(nQ_{ab}-L_aL_b)}{(\sqrt{nQ_{aa}-L_a^2}\sqrt{nQ_{bb}-L_b^2})}$

NB: Here, we need the k-Gamma matrix. We focus on $k = 2$ classes for NB. We compute N_g, L_g, Q_g as discussed in Phase 1 for each class. The output is three model parameters: mean (C), variance (R), and the prior probabilities (W). We can compute these parameters from the Γ^k matrix for each class label with the following statistical relations. Here, $N_g = |X_g|$ and we take the diagonal of $L \cdot L^T$ and Q, which can be manipulated as a 1-dimensional array instead of a 2D array.

$$W_g = \frac{N_g}{n}; \ C_g = \frac{L_g}{N_g}; \ R_g = \frac{Q_g}{N_g} - diag\frac{[L_gL_g^T]}{N_g^2} \tag{3}$$

KM: Similar to NB, we introduce similar model parameters N_j, L_j, Q_j (where $j = 1,..,k$) as the subset of X which belong to cluster k, the total number of points per cluster ($|X_j|$), the sum of points in a cluster ($\sum_{\forall x_i \in X_j} x_i$) and the sum of squared points in each cluster ($\sum_{\forall x_i \in X_j} x_i x_i^t$) respectively. From these statistics, we compute C_j, R_j, W_j as similar to NB presented in Eq. 3. Then, the algorithm iterates executing two steps starting from random initialization until cluster centroids become stable. Step 1 determines the closest cluster for each point (using Euclidean distance) and adds the point to it. And Step 2 updates all the centroids C_k by computing the mean vector of points belonging to cluster k. The cluster weights W_k and diagonal covariance matrices R_k are also updated based on the new centroids.

3.2 Parallel Algorithm to Compute Multiple Data Summaries

Here, we present our main contributions. Our generalized computation of summarization matrix in the parallel cluster using p processing nodes is shown in Fig. 1. We propose a new 3 phase algorithm to compute Γ (or Γ^k) in the parallel cluster and how ML models (Θ) can be computed exploiting it.

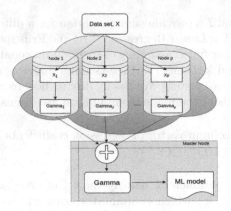

Fig. 1. Computation of Gamma matrix in a parallel cluster.

1. Phase 0: Pre-process the data set. Transfer data to the processing nodes (p nodes).
2. Phase 1: Compute summarization matrix in parallel across p nodes: Γ or Γ^k. This phase will return p partial (local) summarization matrices (Γ_I or Γ_I^k, $I = 1, 2, ..., p$).
3. Phase 2: Add partial summarization matrices to get final Γ or Γ^k on the master node. Compute model Θ based on Γ or Γ^k.

Phase 0: Data set X is moved to the p processing nodes. Nowadays, data can reside either in the parallel cluster, cloud (remote cluster), or in a large local machine. Also, the number of processing nodes may vary. In any case, data must be transferred into the processing nodes. We split the data set X into p processing nodes. There are several partitioning strategies available but we used the row-based partitioning (horizontal partitioning). As Γ is a $d \times d$ matrix, we need all the d columns in each node. If we choose column-based (vertical partitioning) or block-based partitioning, it is possible that the Γ in different nodes may end up having different sizes. A good way to select the data set size in each partition (row-based) is n/p. So, each node in the parallel cluster has the same number of rows except for the p-th node.

Phase 1: We compute Γ on each node locally. We optimize the technique to read data in blocks so that it can handle very large files. For each node, the partitioned data set (X_I) is read into $b = 1...b$ blocks of same size (m) where $m < |X_I|$. The block size depends on the number of records (n_I) in X_I. As discussed in [14], we define the block size as $\log n_I$. As $\log n_I \ll n_I$, even if n_I is very large, each block will easily fit in the main memory. Processing data one block at a time has many benefits. It is the key to being able to scale the computations without increasing memory requirements. External memory (or out-of-core) algorithms do not require that all of the data be in RAM at one time. Data is processed one block at a time, with intermediate results updated for each block. When all the data is processed, we get the final result. Here, we read each block (b) into the main memory and compute Gamma for that block ($\Gamma(b)$). This partial Gamma is added to the Gamma computed up to the previous block ($b-1$). We iterate this process until no blocks are left and get the Gamma (Γ_I) for that node. As each node has all the d columns, the size of each Γ_I will be $d \times d$.

Optimization of k-Gamma Matrix: Similarly, for k-Gamma matrices (Γ^k) we perform the same procedure as mentioned above. First, we partition the data set, then compute partial k-Gamma (Γ_I^k) in each node locally. We study the algorithm further and made an improvement to compute Γ^k from [5]. As discussed previously, for k-Gamma, we only need n, L and $diag(Q)$. Here both L and $diag(Q)$ can be represented as a single vector and we do not need to store Q as a matrix. Hence, Γ^k can be represented as a single matrix of size $d \times 2k$ where each Gamma is represented in two columns (L and Q). We still need to store the value of n in a row, which makes the Γ^k as $(d+1) \times 2k$. Hence, we are using minimal memory to store Γ^k even if the value of k is very large. This is a major improvement from the previous version where one Gamma Matrix was stored per class/cluster in the main memory. Also, we have to access only one matrix which is faster than accessing from a list of matrices in any programming language. Computing Γ_I on each node can be shown in Algorithm 1. Computing Γ_I^k will be similar to Algorithm 1.

Data: Partitioned Data Set ($X_I, I = 1, 2..p$) from Phase 0
Result: Γ_I
Read X_I into $b = 1, 2, ..., b$ blocks;
while *next(b)* **do**
 | read(b) ;
 | $\Gamma_b = $ Gamma(b) ;
 | $\Gamma_I = \Gamma_b + \Gamma_I$;
end
return Γ_I
Algorithm 1: Sequential Gamma computation on each node (Phase 1)

Phase 2: After all the Γ_Is ($\Gamma_1, \Gamma_2, ..., \Gamma_p$) are computed in each node locally, we need to combine them and get the final Γ. In Phase 2, at first, all the partial Γ_Is are sent to a master node to perform the addition (sequential) or we can perform it in a hierarchical binary tree manner. Hierarchical processing performs the addition in multiple levels (bottom-up) until we get the final addition at the top level. On the other hand, in sequential processing, all the partial Γ_I are transferred to the main memory of the master node. The partial Γ_Is are sent in a compressed format. So, we decompress it on the master node. Now, to get the final Gamma matrix (Γ), we just need to perform a simple matrix-addition operation of all the partial Γ_Is. That is, we compute $\Gamma = \Gamma_1 + \Gamma_2 + ... + \Gamma_p$. Similarly, the final Γ^k will be $\Gamma^k = \Gamma_1^k + \Gamma_2^k + ... + \Gamma_p^k$. Now, using this Γ or

Γ^k, we compute the machine learning models (Θ) at the end of Phase 2. Model (Θ) computations are discussed in Sect. 3.1.

3.3   Integrating the Parallel Algorithm into an Analytic Language

We will discuss how we integrated our algorithm, into the R language, using the Rcpp [7] library. R, a dynamic language, provides a wide variety of statistical and graphical techniques, and is highly extensible. However, our solution is applicable to any other programming language which provides an API to call C++ code. Specifically, our solution can easily work in Python, launching k Python Gamma processes in parallel. On the other hand, SQL queries are slow, UDFs are not portable, Spark not easy to debug and Java is slower than C++. So, analytic languages like Python and R are more popular among analysts nowadays.

Key insight: Phase 1 must work in C++ (or C). The sum of vector outer products must be computed block by block in C++, not in the host language. Computing $z_i * z_i^T$ in a loop in R or any other analytic language is slow: usually one-row-at-a-time. Computing $Z * Z^T$ with traditional matrix multiplication is slow due to Z^T materialization, even in RAM. We used Rcpp, an R add-on package that facilitates extending R with C++ functions to compute Phase 1. Rcpp can be used to accelerate computation by replacing an R function with its C++ equivalent function. In Rcpp, only the reference gets passed to the other side but not the actual value when we pass the values. So, memory consumption is very efficient and the run time is the same. In addition to Rcpp, we used the RCurl [11] package to communicate over the network.

Model computation in Phase 2 can be efficiently done calling existing R (or other analytic languages) functions. While Phase 1 is basically exploiting C++, Phase 2 uses the analytic language "as is". It would be too difficult and error-prone to reprogram all the ML models. Instead, our solution requires just changing certain steps in each numerical method, rewriting their equations based on the data summaries (1 or k). Our experiments will show model computation takes less than one second in every case, even for high d models.

As an extra benefit, our solution gives flexibility to the analyst to compute data summaries in a parallel cluster (local or cloud), but explore many statistics matrices and models locally. That is, the analysts can enjoy analytics "for free" without the overhead and price to use the cloud. Moreover, our parallel solution is simple, more general and we did not need any complicated library like "Revolution R" [17] that requires Windows operating system or "pbdR" [16] that provides high-level interfaces to MPI requires a complex set up process.

3.4   Time and Space Complexity Analysis

For parallel computation in the cluster, let p be the number of processing nodes under a shared-nothing architecture. We assume $d \ll n$ and $p \ll n$. From [15], the time complexity for computing the full Gamma in a single machine is $O(d^2 n)$. As we are computing Γ in blocks per node, the time complexity is proportional to block size. Let, m be the number of records in each block and b be the total

Table 2. Base data sets description

Data set	d	n	Description	Models applied
YearPredictionMSD	90	515K	Predict if there is rain or not	LR, PCA
CreditCard	30	285K	Predict if there is raise in credit line	NB, KM

number of blocks per processing nodes and each block size is fixed. Then, for each block time complexity of computing Γ will be $O(d^2b)$. For a total of m blocks, it will be $O(md^2b)$. When all the blocks are read, $mb = n$. In our case of parallel computation, as each $X_I \epsilon X$ is hashed to p processing nodes, the time complexity will be $O(d^2n/p)$ per processing nodes. Computing Γ in total of b blocks of fixed size m will make the time complexity $O(md^2b/p)$. In case of k-Gamma matrix, we only compute L and diagonal of Q of the whole Gamma matrix. So, for Γ^k, it will be $O(mdb/p)$ in each processing nodes.

In case of transferring all the partial Γ, if we transfer to the master node all at once: $O(d^2)$, for sequential transfer: $O(d^2p)$, for hierarchical binary tree fashion: $O(d^2p + log_2(p)d^2)$. We take advantage of Gamma to accelerate computing the machine learning models. So, the time complexity of this part does not depend on n and is $\Omega(d^3)$.

In case of space complexity and memory analysis, our algorithm uses very little RAM. In each node, space required by Γ in main memory is $O(d^2)$. And it is $O(kd)$ for Γ^k, where k is the number of classes/clusters. As Γ or Γ^k does not depend on n, the space required by each processing node in the parallel cluster will be same as computing it in a single node ($O(d^2)$ and $O(kd)$ respectively). Also, as we are adding the new Γ with the previous one for each block, the space does not depend on the number of blocks.

4 Experimental Evaluation

We present an experimental evaluation in this section. First, we introduce the systems, input data sets, and our choice of programming languages. We compare our proposed algorithm with Spark running in parallel clusters and a parallel DBMS to make sure our algorithm is competitive with other parallel systems. We also compare processing in parallel cluster vs single machine. All the time measurements were taken five times and we report the average excluding the maximum and minimum value.

4.1 Experimental Setup

Hardware and Software: We performed our experiments using our 8-node parallel cluster each with Pentium(R) Quadcore CPU running at 1.60 GHz, 8 GB

RAM, and 1 TB disk space. For single machine, we conducted our experiments on a machine with Intel Pentium(R) Quadcore CPU running at 1.60 GHz, 8 GB RAM, 1 TB disk, and Linux Ubuntu 14.04 operating system. We developed our algorithms using standard R and C++. For parallel comparison, we used Spark-MLlib and programmed the models using Scala. And we used Vertica as a parallel DBMS.

Data Sets: Computing machine learning models on raw data is not practical. Also, it has hard to obtain public data sets to compute all the models. Therefore, we had to use common data sets available and replicate them to mimic large data sets. We used two data sets as our base data sets: YearPredictionMSD and CreditCard data set, summarized in Table 2, obtained from the UCI machine learning repository. We include the information about the models which utilize these data sets. We sampled and replicated the data sets to get varying n (data set size) and d (dimensionality), without altering its statistical properties. We replicate them in random order. The columns of the data sets were replicated to get $d = (5, 10, 20, 40)$ and rows were replicated to get $n = (100K, 1M, 10M, 100M)$. In both cases, we chose d randomly from the original data set.

Table 3. Time (in Seconds) to compute the ML models in our solution ($p = 8$ nodes) with Γ and in Spark ($p = 8$ nodes) (M = Millions)

Θ (Data set)	n	d	Our solution (p=8) Phase 0	Phase 1	Phase 2	Total	Spark (p=8) Partition	Compute Θ	Total
LR	1M	10	9	3	9	21	7	41	48
(Year-	10M	10	23	20	9	52	17	286	303
Prediction)	100M	10	317	209	9	535	161	1780	1941
PCA	1M	10	9	3	9	21	7	15	22
(Year-	10M	10	23	20	9	52	17	46	63
Prediction)	100M	10	317	209	9	535	161	277	438
NB	1M	10	11	4	9	24	7	Crash	Crash
(credit-	10M	10	28	27	9	64	25	Crash	Crash
card)	100M	10	335	243	9	587	231	Crash	Crash
KM	1M	10	11	4	9	24	7	64	71
(credit-	10M	10	28	27	9	64	25	392	417
card)	100M	10	335	243	9	587	231	Stop	Stop

4.2   Comparison with Hadoop Parallel Big Data Systems: Spark

We compare the ML models in parallel nodes ($p = 8$) with Spark, a data processing engine developed to provide faster and easy-to-use analytics than Hadoop MapReduce. We partition the data set using HDFS and then run the algorithm in Spark-MLlib. We used the available functions in MLlib, Spark's scalable machine learning library to run the ML models. We emphasize that we used the recommended settings and parameters as given in the library documentation. Here, we are taking the data sets with a higher n ($n = 1M, 10M, 100M$) and medium d ($d = 10$) to demonstrate how large data sets perform on both.

Table 3 presents the time to compute the ML models in the parallel cluster with R and in Spark. For each entry, we round it up to the nearest integer value. The 'Phase 0' column is the time to split the data set X and transfer X_Is to the processing nodes. We used the standard and fastest UNIX commands available to perform this operation. The 'Phase 1' column shows the maximum time to compute Γ_Is among p machines. We report the maximum time because the parallel execution cannot be faster than the slowest machine. The 'Phase 2' column shows the total time to send the partial Gamma matrices (Γ_I) to the master node in a compressed format, decompress them on the master node, add them to get the final Gamma (Γ) and compute the model (Θ) based on Γ. This time is almost similar regardless of the value of n and d. The reason is that Γ is $d \times d$ which is very small. Moreover, Γ is sent in a compressed format over the network. In the receiving end (master node), we take advantage of R run time. The decompression, addition of the Γ_Is, all these operations are very fast in R (<1 sec). So, from transferring Γ_Is to get the final Γ, it is almost a constant time (~ 8 sec). On the other hand, the ML model computation (Θ) also happens in R run time, very fast, and takes a fraction of a second (~ 1 sec). Hence, for 'Phase 2', we put a constant time 9 s for each entry. In the Spark part of Table 3, the 'Partition' column is the time to load the data set in HDFS and we report the time to compute the models in Spark-MLlib in 'Compute Θ' column.

Despite HDFS being faster to partition the data sets (Table 3), the total time is much faster in our method for most cases. HDFS is faster in partitioning because we are splitting and transferring the data set sequentially over the network. A parallel partition that sends blocks in parallel is already implemented efficiently in DBMS and is beyond the scope of this paper. In case of Linear Regression (LR), the Spark-MLlib trains and outputs the coefficients and intercept as the model. We load the data set and fit the data set to get the model. Spark's performance is slow when fit is called and we can see that our Γ is almost $10X$ faster. For PCA, the Spark-MLlib uses a similar algorithm as Γ. For a large X, it computes $X^T.X$ by computing the outer product of each row of the matrix by itself, then adding all the results up. This is the Q from our Γ which is manipulated in the main memory by each worker node. Still, Spark is slightly slower for computing the PCA model than our method in all cases. For Naïve Bayes (NB)model, Spark-MLlib implements multinominal Naïve Bayes which takes an RDD labeled point and an optional smoothing parameter as input and outputs the model. The major drawback of this model is, having negative values in the data set crashes the model which has happened for Creditcard data set here. The Spark crashed showing "illegalArgumentException" as the model requires non-negative values. As for k-means, the MLlib implementation includes a parallelized variant of k-means++ [2] which generates a k-means model. The distributed version of the algorithm is roughly $O(k)$, so this suffers a slower start with a large k. It is also expensive when the model is trained. We put "Stop" because Spark could not finish the computation in 30 mins.

4.3   Comparison with a Parallel DBMS:

We compare our solution with a parallel columnar DBMS (Vertica) running on p processing nodes. As columnar DBMSs store data by columns and not by rows, it is much faster than a row DBMS [13]. We adapted the solution presented in [15] using UDFs and SQL queries which is the current best solution to compute the Gamma summarization matrix in a parallel array DBMS. As there is no prior solution of k-Gamma matrix in a DBMS, here we only compare our solution with the Gamma matrix. We already know that the ML model (Θ) computation is very fast ($\sim$1 sec) in the main memory exploiting Γ. So, we only report the time to compute the Γ using p processing nodes.

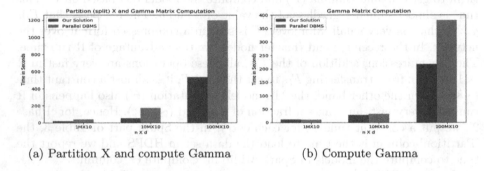

(a) Partition X and compute Gamma   (b) Compute Gamma

Fig. 2. Time (in Sec) comparison for Γ on $p = 8$ nodes: our solution vs parallel DBMS for varying n and d (M = millions)

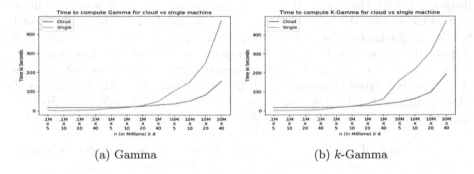

(a) Gamma   (b) k-Gamma

Fig. 3. Time comparison for Γ and Γ^k in parallel cluster ($p = 8$ nodes) and single machine ($p = 1$ node) for varying n and d.

Figure 2 shows the comparison to compute Γ between our solution and the parallel columnar DBMS. We compute Γ for varying n ($1M, 10M, 100M$) and $d = 10$. Figure 2a shows the comparison when we split the data set into p processing nodes and compute Γ and Fig 2b shows the comparison to just compute

Γ using p machines (data set is already partitioned and loaded into DBMS). We show both plots to give the parallel DBMS a fair chance because it is often assumed that data is already stored in the DBMS. We use standard SQL queries to COPY (Partition) the data set in all machines. As partitioning in DBMS is slow, we can see that parallel DBMS performs much slower than our solution for all n when it has to partition the data first. Our solution also performs better for Γ computation as n grows (Fig. 2b). Moreover, DBMS solutions using UDF are not portable and they require a lot of memory to scale-up.

4.4   Understanding Trade-Offs: Parallel Cluster and Single Machine

We compute the Γ and Γ^k on a parallel cluster and single machine to understand the trade-offs between them. For both cases, we used our optimized version of the algorithms. Γ is computed on YearPredictionMSD data set to compute models like LR and PCA, and Γ^k is computed on the CreditCard data set to compute NB and KM models. The total time to compute the Γ and Γ^k for parallel cluster and the single machine can be plotted in Fig. 3. We can see that single machine performs better when n and d is low ($\leq 1M \times 10$) in both cases. The reason is, the parallel cluster is spending much time in partitioning the data set and transferring the partial Γ_I (or Γ_I^k) matrices. Parallel cluster seems to be more faster from $n = 1M$ and $d = 20$. When n is very high ($n = 10M$ or more), the parallel cluster is at least $2X$ to $4X$ faster than the local machine. The reason is, a single machine cannot scale as data size grows due to limited memory. However, the model computation part utilizing Γ or Γ^k is almost same for both. So, the parallel cluster is the obvious choice when it comes to summarizing very large data sets.

5   Related Works

Summarization of scalable machine learning algorithms was done in a parallel manner in [15]. However, this work was developed for a parallel array DBMS and did not work for classification or clustering models. In this paper, we removed the use of DBMS completely which was the main focus on [15]. We adapted the algorithm, generalized, and implemented such a way that it can work in a parallel cluster efficiently. Moreover, we introduced k-Gamma matrices that can compute models like NB and KM which are significantly different from [15]. We also made use of reading data in blocks to read an infinite amount of input data. Similar to our proposed k-Gamma matrix, the summaries of [22] and [4] represent a (constrained) diagonal version of Γ because dimension independence is assumed (i.e. cross-products, covariances, correlations are ignored) and there is a separate vector to capture L. From a computational perspective, our Γ computation boils down to one matrix multiplication, whereas those algorithms work is aggregations. Also, our summarization is more general and it helps to compute more complex models like LR, PCA, NB, and KM that could not be solved with older summaries. Parallel processing for data summarization has received moderate attention. [12] highlights the following techniques: sampling, incremental aggregation, matrix factorization, and similarity joins. Research has developed fast algorithms based mostly on sampling, data summarization, and gradient descent [8], generally working in a sequential manner (data mining). Stochastic (incremental) gradient descent (SGD) [9] is a popular approach, useful when there is a convex function to optimize (like least-squares in LR). As for drawbacks, SGD is naturally sequential (difficult to process in parallel), it obtains an approximate solution and it is difficult to adapt to non-convex functions (e.g. clustering).

From a "systems" angle, R combined with C++ did not exist and nobody thought we could insert efficient C++ code for a very common computation on parallel machines. However, R has been used for parallel computing on computer clusters, on multi-core systems, and in grid computing. There are many available packages in R for parallel computing and they are reviewed and compared in [18] based on development, usability, acceptance, and performance. There is a large body of work on computing machine learning models in Hadoop "Big Data" systems, before with MapReduce [3] and currently with Spark [21]. On the other hand, computing models with parallel DBMSs have received less attention [9,19] because they are considered cumbersome and more difficult to program. This article is a significant step forward and is fundamentally different from [5] which worked only on a single machine. We introduced a new generalized algorithm to compute Γ in a parallel cluster. Also, we improved the k-Gamma algorithm where k summarization matrices (each $d \times d$) were needed in [5] to compute NB and KM models. The improved algorithm needs only one matrix ($d + 1 \times 2k$). Also, [5] cannot scale to big data as it was done in a local machine. Experimental results prove that our new solution does not have any limitation: neither main memory nor CPU power available.

6   Conclusions

We presented an improved 3-phase algorithm to compute ML models. Specifically, we added a pre-processing phase, to partition and distribute the data set. Also, parallel processing is fully automated and we now cover a wide spectrum of unsupervised and supervised ML models. We introduced a general, parallel, summarization algorithm that can work across multiple programming languages and platforms. We then studied how to integrate our parallel algorithm into the R language, a popular language in ML and statistics. We justified why C++ code is required and so we focused on optimizing summarization, with specialized C++ functions for a fundamental vector outer product, returning one or multiple Gamma matrices (Γ^k). We showed the actual model computation, fortunately, can be done with existing R functions, eliminating the need to reprogram them. An experimental evaluation shows our solution is either faster or more scalable than Spark. On the other hand, our solution is remarkably faster than a previous prototype programmed with SQL queries and UDFs, the best previous solution based on the same approach.

Our research opens many possibilities for future work. We will tackle other ML models, including HMMs, LDA, and SVMs. We plan to compare tradeoffs when integrating our algorithm with Python, another popular language with significantly different syntax and evaluation compared to R. Even though processing in one machine is slower than a parallel cluster, we intend to study how to accelerate computation with multicore CPUs and GPUs in a single box. We would like to encode our result summarization matrix in a general format that can be consumed by any language or system. It should be feasible to detect intermediate computations in analytic source code, where our summarization matrix or matrices may accelerate or simplify processing.

References

1. Al-Jarrah, O.Y., Yoo, P.D., Muhaidat, S., Karagiannidis, G.K., Taha, K.: Efficient machine learning for big data: a review. Big Data Res. **2**(3), 87–93 (2015)
2. Arthur, D., Vassilvitskii, S.: k-means++: the advantages of careful seeding. In: Proceedings of the Eighteenth Annual ACM-SIAM Symposium on Discrete Algorithms, SODA, pp. 1027–1035 (2007)
3. Behm, A., et al.: ASTERIX: towards a scalable, semistructured data platform for evolving-world models. Distrib. Parallel Databases (DAPD) **29**(3), 185–216 (2011). https://doi.org/10.1007/s10619-011-7082-y
4. Bradley, P., Fayyad, U., Reina, C.: Scaling clustering algorithms to large databases. In: Proceedings of the ACM KDD Conference, pp. 9–15 (1998)
5. Chebolu, S.U.S., Ordonez, C., Al-Amin, S.T.: Scalable machine learning in the R language using a summarization matrix. In: Hartmann, S., Küng, J., Chakravarthy, S., Anderst-Kotsis, G., Tjoa, A.M., Khalil, I. (eds.) DEXA 2019. LNCS, vol. 11707, pp. 247–262. Springer, Cham (2019). https://doi.org/10.1007/978-3-030-27618-8_19
6. Dean, J., et al.: Large scale distributed deep networks. In: Proceedings of the Advances in Neural Information Processing Systems, pp. 1232–1240 (2012)
7. Eddelbuettel, D.: Seamless R and C++ Integration with Rcpp. Springer, New York (2013). https://doi.org/10.1007/978-1-4614-6868-4
8. Gemulla, R., Nijkamp, E., Haas, P., Sismanis, Y.: Large-scale matrix factorization with distributed stochastic gradient descent. In: Proceedings of the KDD, pp. 69–77 (2011)
9. Hellerstein, J., et al.: The MADlib analytics library or MAD skills, the SQL. Proc. VLDB **5**(12), 1700–1711 (2012)
10. Hu, H., Wen, Y., Chua, T., Li, X.: Toward scalable systems for big data analytics: a technology tutorial. IEEE Access **2**, 652–687 (2014)
11. Lang, D.T., Lang, M.D.T.: Package 'RCurl' (2012)
12. Li, F., Nath, S.: Scalable data summarization on big data. Distrib. Parallel Databases **32**(3), 313–314 (2014). https://doi.org/10.1007/s10619-014-7145-y
13. Ordonez, C., Cabrera, W., Gurram, A.: Comparing columnar, row and array DBMSS to process recursive queries on graphs. Inf. Systems **63**, 66–79 (2016)
14. Ordonez, C., Omiecinski, E.: Accelerating EM clustering to find high-quality solutions. Knowl. Inf. Syst. **7**(2), 135–157 (2004). https://doi.org/10.1007/s10115-003-0141-6

15. Ordonez, C., Zhang, Y., Cabrera, W.: The Gamma matrix to summarize dense and sparse data sets for big data analytics. IEEE Trans. Knowl. Data Eng. (TKDE) **28**(7), 1906–1918 (2016)
16. Ostrouchov, G., Chen, W.C., Schmidt, D., Patel, P.: Programming with big data in R (2012). http://r-pbd.org/
17. Rickert, J.: Big data analysis with revolution R enterprise. Revolution Analytics (2011)
18. Schmidberger, M., Morgan, M., Eddelbuettel, D., Yu, H., Tierney, L., Mansmann, U.: State-of-the-art in parallel computing with R. J. Stat. Softw. **47** (2009)
19. Stonebraker, M., et al.: MapReduce and parallel DBMSs: friends or foes? Commun. ACM **53**(1), 64–71 (2010)
20. Xing, E.P., et al.: Petuum: a new platform for distributed machine learning on big data. IEEE Trans. Big Data **1**(2), 49–67 (2015)
21. Zaharia, M., Chowdhury, M., Franklin, M., Shenker, S., Stoica, I.: Spark: cluster computing with working sets. In: HotCloud USENIX Workshop (2010)
22. Zhang, T., Ramakrishnan, R., Livny, M.: BIRCH: an efficient data clustering method for very large databases. In: Proceedings of the ACM SIGMOD Conference, pp. 103–114 (1996)

Which Bills Are Lobbied? Predicting and Interpreting Lobbying Activity in the US

Ivan Slobozhan[1], Peter Ormosi[2(✉)], and Rajesh Sharma[1]

[1] Institute of Computer Science, University of Tartu, Tartu, Estonia
ivan.slobozhan@gmail.com, rajesh.sharma@ut.ee
[2] Norwich Business School, University of East Anglia, Norwich, UK
P.Ormosi@uea.ac.uk

Abstract. Using lobbying data from OpenSecrets.org, we offer several experiments applying machine learning techniques to predict if a piece of legislation (US bill) has been subjected to lobbying activities or not. We also investigate the influence of the intensity of the lobbying activity on how discernible a lobbied bill is from one that was not subject to lobbying. We compare the performance of a number of different models (logistic regression, random forest, CNN and LSTM) and text embedding representations (BOW, TF-IDF, GloVe, Law2Vec). We report results of above 0.85% ROC AUC scores, and 78% accuracy. Model performance significantly improves (95% ROC AUC, and 88% accuracy) when bills with higher lobbying intensity are looked at. We also propose a method that could be used for unlabelled data. Through this we show that there is a considerably large number of previously unlabelled US bills where our predictions suggest that some lobbying activity took place. We believe our method could potentially contribute to the enforcement of the US Lobbying Disclosure Act (LDA) by indicating the bills that were likely to have been affected by lobbying but were not filed as such.

Keywords: Lobbying · Rent seeking · Text classification · US bills

1 Introduction

Lobbying consumes a significant amount of resources, which surpasses the money spent for example on campaign contributions. OpenSecrets.org reports that lobbying expenditure reached around $3.55 billion in 2010 (although it has started declining slowly since then, dropping to $3.24 billion by 2013). US lobbying regulations ensure that much of the lobbying activities are disclosed to the public. As a result, there is ample information on the particulars of lobbying activities, and the access to this large amount of data has spurred numerous empirical works on lobbying [6].

We thank the Center for Responsive Politics (OpenSecrets.org) for making their lobbying data available.

© Springer Nature Switzerland AG 2020
M. Song et al. (Eds.): DaWaK 2020, LNCS 12393, pp. 285–300, 2020.
https://doi.org/10.1007/978-3-030-59065-9_23

The main contribution of this paper is a novel way to gauge whether a piece of legislation was lobbied or not. For this, we start on the premise that lobbying changes the text of legislation in a way that makes them discernible from non-lobbied legislation. Take *rent seeking* for example. When businesses compete they earn normal profit as a result of the competitive process in the market. An obvious way to increase profits is to either collude, or monopolise the market, both of which would be blocked by antitrust agencies. The easiest way for companies to achieve super-normal profit is by lobbying governments to introduce laws and regulations that ensure that they are sheltered from competition. The economics literature calls this phenomenon rent seeking, referring to the objective of lobbying businesses to appropriate this *rent* (i.e. super-normal profit). Rent seeking is hugely harmful for society, firstly because large amounts of resources are spent on a non-productive activity (lobbying), but also because the resulting markets are less competitive, meaning higher prices and therefore reduced welfare for consumers. We posit that if these legislative provisions, offering preferential treatment to certain interest groups, are similar across the various pieces of legislation, then the text of lobbied legislation should be discernible from non-lobbied ones.

For this we rely on a database of lobbying activity in the US, and experiment with a number of text classification methods. In this respect our work diverges from previous works that apply text classification to expedite and improve the handling of large amounts of legal documents. By training a model to distinguish between lobbied and non-lobbied bills, our main objective is to improve legal analysis by discovering classification rules that had been unknown to human analysts.

This is important for multiple reasons. First of all, records on whether a bill had been lobbied may be incomplete. A classification algorithm could help ascertain if unlabelled bills have been lobbied or not. Second, although the US system is more transparent, the same is not true in jurisdictions where lobbying regulations are relatively new. For example, in the European Union there is very little information on the laws that are targeted by lobbyists. Using a model trained on US law we could investigate the use of transfer learning together with a much smaller sample of hand-labelled EU data to work on a model fitted to EU laws. Finally, our fitted model can also be informative for gauging the amount of rent seeking in the economy. Although not all lobbying activities should be considered as rent seeking, lobbying facilitates rent seeking - in a similar logic as in [13]. Moreover, [15] estimated that lobbying activity accounts for around 2/3 of all rent seeking related welfare loss, with the figure being higher in more concentrated, and lower in less concentrated industries.

As another contribution, the paper also tests the impact of more intensive lobbying. From the economics and finance literature we know that stakeholders with the largest expected profits from favourable policies and regulations are most likely to lobby most intensively [12]. For this reason we expected more intensive lobbying associated with more discernible (for the algorithm) features when compared to non-lobbied legislation.

Using standard natural language processing (NLP) tools, we train a number of different models to classify bills into lobbied and non-lobbied groups. In particular, we used logistic regression, random forest and neural networks models. In our first, simple experiments, we achieve above 0.85 AUC and accuracy of 78%. As a next step we show that lobbying intensity improves model performance, up to 0.95 AUC and 88% of accuracy implying that intensively lobbied bills are more different from non-lobbied ones (following our assumption that these are more likely to be subject to rent-seeking).

We also propose a method that could be used for unlabelled data (legislative bills, where we do not have any information about lobbying). Through this we show that there is a considerably large number of previously unlabelled US bills where our predictions suggest that some lobbying activity took place. This is more likely to be in certain areas, such as energy and healthcare. We believe our method could potentially contribute to the enforcement of the US Lobbying Disclosure Act (LDA) by indicating the bills that were likely to have been affected by lobbying but were not filed as such.

The rest of the paper is organised as follows. The next Section describes the literature review in this domain. In Sect. 3, we introduce the dataset, and Sect. 4 describes the results of our analysis. Finally, we conclude in Sect. 6 with some future directions.

2   Related Works

In general, there is an increasing amount of literature that applies NLP in the legal domain [5]. Some of these focus more on solutions to automate summarising legal texts, such as court rulings [7] or [11], applying SVM and naive Bayes classification of individual sentences to Bag of Words, TF-IDF, and dense features in order to improve summary precision.

A subset of these applied NLP works in law draws on text classification methods. For example, [2] use text classification methods (TF-IDF for feature extraction and SVM for text classification) in order to classify which domain a legal text belongs to. In another paper, [14] propose a semi-supervised learning method to classify legal texts. In this model the first step is the unsupervised learning of text region embedding, which is then fed into a supervised CNN.

Finally, a large number of NLP applications in law focus on prediction. [18] set out to predict various aspects of patent litigation, with mixed results. Other works focus on the prediction of court rulings, such as the European Court of Human Rights (ECRH) decisions by [1], or French Supreme Court rulings by [17].

There is a well-established body of literature on lobbying, and it is beyond the remits of this paper to provide an overview of these. In a systematic review of the relevant empirical works, [6] takes account of the main strands of empirical papers and the challenges to empirical research on lobbying. It also discusses the advantages, disadvantages, and effective use of the main types of data available. Nevertheless, none of these reviewed works used methods similar to ours.

The closest we can relate our paper to previous literature is in the area looking at the impact of lobbying on the specific bills they are targeting. [9] found a direct association between lobbying activities and bill outcomes, and that public attention reduces the effects of lobbying efforts, suggesting that lobbying is most effective when focused on less salient issues. In another paper, [19] looks at the difference between bills that were lobbied ex post and those lobbied before they were passed. Finally, in [10] the authors look at the determinants of interest group lobbying on particular bills after the bills have been passed, and identifies the areas where lobbying focusing on the implementation (rather than the formation) of legislation is more likely.

3   Dataset

The data was downloaded from the Center for Responsive Politics. The dataset contains detailed information on a large number of lobbying instances. For the purposes of this paper our focus is on the legislative bills that were lobbied. At the time of downloading the data (Dec 2018) the data contained information on lobbying activities related to 54,713 US bills. Table 1 shows the breakdown of these bills by bill type - most of them are House of Representative Bills or Senate Bills.

Table 1. Lobbied legislative bills by bill type

Bill type	n
House Concurrent Resolution (H.Con.Res)	334
House Joint Resolution (H.J.Res)	348
House of Representatives Bill (H.R.)	31879
House Resolution (H.Res)	1290
Senate Bill (S.)	19938
Senate Concurrent Resolution (S.Con.Res)	150
Senate Joint Resolution (S.J.Res)	177
Senate Resolution (S.Res)	597

We downloaded all bills available in text format from the US Congress' website.[1] We then marked out the bills that had been lobbied, and then matched it with a similar sample (n = 48,411) of other bills where we had no evidence that there was any lobbying and thus, we assumed that there was no lobbying in these cases.[2] This resulted in a total sample of 103,243 labelled bills (54,377 lobbied, 48,530 non-lobbied). Table 2 shows the breakdown of the sample into subject areas.

---

[1] An example of a House Bill is given here: https://www.congress.gov/bill/114th-congress/house-bill/3791/text.

[2] In the US, lobbying activities (above a certain threshold) need to be disclosed, and non-compliance can result in a pecuniary sanction (fine) or, in some cases up to 5 years imprisonment. In Sect. 5 we revisit this assumption.

Table 2. Number of bills by subject area and lobbying activity

Subject	Not lobbied	Lobbied
Agriculture and Food	675	1130
Animals	206	322
Armed Forces and National Security	3001	4067
Arts, Culture, Religion	304	58
Civil Rights and Liberties, Minority Issues	507	382
Commemorations	3934	414
Commerce	756	1411
Congress	3928	849
Crime and Law Enforcement	1949	2622
Economics and Public Finance	716	975
Education	1824	2474
Emergency Management	546	799
Energy	716	1847
Environmental Protection	692	1452
Families	370	259
Finance and Financial Sector	723	2086
Foreign Trade and International Finance	3657	3567
Government Operations and Politics	2719	2664
Health	3364	6943
Housing and Community Development	405	806
Immigration	836	1245
International Affairs	4107	2008
Labor and Employment	786	1355
Law	558	673
Native Americans	549	653
Private Legislation	838	203
Public Lands and Natural Resources	2728	2883
Science, Technology, Communications	595	1205
Social Sciences and History	64	18
Social Welfare	726	771
Sports and Recreation	420	93
Taxation	3485	5679
Transportation and Public Works	1120	2114
Water Resources Development	607	644

We also tested how much lobbying-intensity affected classification performance. The reason we thought this was important, was that lobbying activities are largely heterogeneous. For example, some lobbying activities might not lead to changes in the text of the legislation. Intuitively, less intensive lobbying is less likely to lead to any changes in legislative provisions. Also, some lobbying can be benign, and more likely to make only small changes to a given piece of legislation. On the other hand, for lobbying driven by rent seeking the same is probably not true. We posit that businesses with more to gain from lobbying (rent seeking) are more likely to lobby intensively, and therefore lobbying intensity is more likely to be correlated with having provisions in a bill that make these lobbied bills different from non-lobbied ones. To test this, we introduce the information we had on lobbying intensity into the way we labelled our data.

In Table 3 we show the number of bills associated with different levels of lobbying intensity. Around a half of the bills in our sample were not lobbied, roughly another quarter of them were lobbied between 1–10 times, and the rest even more frequently.

For our analysis we created different labels to reflect lobbying intensity. Let *lobbied* denotes the number of times a bill was lobbied, then, we created three versions of the datasets using following logic:

$$D_1 = \begin{cases} 1 & \text{if } lobbied \geq 1 \\ 0 & \text{if } lobbied = 0 \end{cases} \tag{1}$$

$$D_2 = \begin{cases} 1 & \text{if } lobbied \geq 10 \\ 0 & \text{if } lobbied = 0 \end{cases} \tag{2}$$

$$D_3 = \begin{cases} 1 & \text{if } lobbied \geq 50 \\ 0 & \text{if } lobbied = 0 \end{cases} \tag{3}$$

Table 3. Number of bills exposed to different levels of lobbying intensity

Number of times lobbied	Number of bills
(0.0]	48530
(1.0, 5.0]	18511
(5.0, 10.0]	7338
(10.0, 50.0]	14924
(50.0, 100.0]	5072
(100.0, 200.0]	3836
(200.0, 500.0]	3003
(500.0, 1000.0]	1136
(1000.0,]	893

We used these labels to create three balanced 'datasets', with D_1 mapping out dataset 1 and so on. The respective sample sizes of datasets for label D_1, D_2 and D_3, are 103, 243, 57,728 (28,864 lobbied and non-lobbied respectively), and 27,880 bills (13,940 lobbied and non-lobbied respectively).

4   Evaluation

In this section, we present the results of our evaluation. First, we describe the algorithms (Sect. 4.1), next, the metrics we used for evaluating our approach (Sect. 4.2), then, the overall approach for text pre-processing, feature generation, and hyperparameter tuning is discussed (Sect. 4.3) and finally, we present the results (Sect. 4.4).

4.1   Problem Modeling and Algorithms

We modeled the problem as a binary classification task. Our objective was to classify a given document into one of the two categories, that is, if the document has been lobbied or not. To solve this task, we used three types of algorithms: logistic regression, random forests, [3] and neural networks, more specifically, using recurrent neural networks (LSTM). We also experiment with various feature extraction algorithms such as bag of words (BOW), term frequency-inverse document frequency (TF-IDF), word embeddings for neural networks, and a domain specific Law2Vec embedding, which we chose, given our task relates to legal documents. [4] The primary motivation behind the selected machine learning algorithms is to experiment with approaches considered conventional (such as logistic regression and random forests), and compare them with deep learning models (LSTM, CNN) that are good in capturing sequential patterns in the data. To make our findings useful for the legal domain, we needed to offer interpretable results. For this reason it was important for us to investigate, for example, how well an interpretable model (like the logistic regression) compares to black-box networks for our classification tasks and how different feature extractions and word-encoding approaches contribute to the performance results.

4.2   Metrics

We checked the performance of our three algorithms using two main classification metrics: accuracy (ACC) and area under a receiver operating characteristic curve (AUC ROC).

1. **Accuracy:** is defined as a ratio of correctly classified observations to the number of all observations. The perfect binary classifier will have 100% accuracy, and random binary classifier has 50% of accuracy on a balanced dataset.
2. **AUC ROC:** is equal to the probability that a classifier will rank a randomly chosen positive observation higher than a randomly chosen negative one. AUC ROC is calculated by plotting true positive rate against the false-positive rate at different thresholds. True positive rate is the proportion of actual positives that are identified correctly, and the false-positive rate is the ratio between the false positives and the total actual negative cases. After that the area of this curve is calculated to get AUC ROC. The perfect binary classifier will have AUC ROC equal to 1, and in a random binary classifier ROC AUC equals to 0.5.

4.3   Approach

Our pipeline consists of the following three steps.

1. **Data Cleaning:** We applied conventional text pre-processing steps to our raw documents (the text of bills). In particular, we lowercase the text, deleted numbers, English stopwords, law stopwords, special characters and punctuation from the text. After that, for each word, we perform lemmatisation. For the logistic and random forest, we did not truncate or pad the sentences. However, due to computational issues in using the LSTM model, we set a max size for the sentence to be the average sentence length after the first part of our pre-processing pipeline. After that, we truncated all the sentences which were above the mean length. Those sentences that are below the defined length are padded with special tokens.
2. **Feature creation:** Next, we transformed the preprocessed text into a set of features that can be fitted into a machine learning model. For logistic regression and random forest we used TF-IDF on bag of n-grams and bag of words approach for text representation with a dictionary size set to 25000. For the neural network, we used 300 dimensional GloVe word embeddings, [16] and Law2Vec 200 dimensional embeddings.
3. **Hyperparameter tuning:** Finally, we hypertuned the model using algorithm-specific parameters on the validation dataset, where we tried to find parameters that maximize AUC ROC. For example, we searched for the best value of n for the models trained using TF-IDF on a bag of n-grams. In particular, for logistic regression, we grid searched the best parameters for regularization strength, and penalty type. In case of random forest, we experimented with a larger set of hyperparameters such as maximum tree depth, splitting criteria, minimum samples per split, and minimum leaf size. For neural networks, we experimented only with different optimization algorithms and the number of recurrent layers.

After the best parameters have been determined, we then used the validation dataset to find the threshold that maximizes the accuracy. Finally, we ran our experiments on a test set and reported the accuracy using the best threshold we found on the validation dataset.

4.4   Results

We perform our experiments using three different versions of the dataset, which aims to capture lobbying intensity through different labeling, as explained in Sect. 3. We denoted these as Labelling 1, 2, and 3. The corresponding results are reported in Table 4. In each of these three versions of the dataset, we split the data into train, validation, and test sets with proportions of 72% for train, 8% for validation, and 20% for test, respectively.

It appears that the best performing model and feature sets are logistic regressions with TF-IDF, and LSTM with GloVe embeddings. In many text classification applications neural networks with word embeddings work better than other models [8], especially when researchers have access to a large corpus of text data. We observe this in our case as well, especially if one looks at Table 4. Regarding the word embedding representations, we TF-IDF provides the best AUC ROC and accuracy on the test sample. Interestingly, Law2Vec is slightly outperformed by both GloVe and TF-IDF.

The performance of the logistic model stands out. This would suggest that in our binary classification problem the classes (lobbied - non-lobbied) are linearly separable. On the other hand, the performance of deep learning models did not exceed the logistic regression, which is likely to be down to the relatively small size of our sample. In the most informative model that compares high-intensity lobbied bills with non-lobbied bills (Labelling 3), we have 13,217 lobbied and 14,915 non-lobbied bills. This is small, especially given that our median bill length is 4790 words (the mean is 10413), so each observation contains a very large number of features. It is likely that there are complex non-linear relationships between these features and the classes, but to fully explore this complexity we would need much larger samples. Another possible reason is that the logistic regression model, compared to neural network do not need sophisticated and time consuming hyperparameter tuning. Due to computation limitations we are not able to explore a large set of possible hyperparameters for the neural network models. On the other hand, it is true that the good performance of the logistic model also suggests that there are clear features (such as the frequency of specific n-grams) in these bills, which form a linear relationship with our two classes. This is crucial in our application (text classification in Law), where interpretability is very important for users. In Sect. 4.5 we provide an introduction to these key features.

Comparison of the three sets of results clearly indicates that the prediction improves as we re-define our label in terms of lobbying intensity. In the first experiment (top section of Table 4) we compare bills that were not lobbied, with bills that were lobbied, irrespective of the number of times. This provides the worst results. This is in line with intuition: it is likely that bills that were lobbied only once are not hugely different from those that were not lobbied at all (for example, the lobbying might have been for a benign, minor correction of the text, or the lobbying might have not successfully changed the text of the legislation at all).

For Labelling 2 (middle section of Table 4) and 3 (bottom section of Table 4) the results show improvement. In these experiments we compared bills that were not lobbied with bills that were lobbied intensively, at least 10, and at least 50 times respectively. The results suggest that the difference between the text of lobbied and non-lobbied bills becomes more discernible where there is more intensive lobbying. Put differently, a bill that was not lobbied is more similar to a bill that was lobbied only once, than to a bill that was lobbied, say, 20 times.

Table 4. Classification results - results for our three labels

Model	Validation		Test	
	AUC ROC	ACC.	AUC ROC	ACC.
Labelling 1				
Logistic regression (TF-IDF)	0.8566	77.51%	0.8609	78.19%
Logistic regression (BOW)	0.8233	74.58%	0.8253	74.72%
Random forest (TF-IDF)	0.8451	76.23%	0.8498	76.72%
LSTM (GloVe 300d. embeddings)	0.8658	78.12%	0.8652	78.31%
LSTM (Law2Vec 200d. embeddings)	0.8514	77.24%	0.8503	77.21%
CNN (GloVe 300d. embeddings)	0.8520	77.14%	0.8550	77.68%
CNN (Law2Vec 200d. embeddings)	0.8529	76.71%	0.8501	76.71%
Labelling 2				
Logistic regression (TF-IDF)	0.9318	85.95%	0.9321	85.73%
Logistic regression (BOW)	0.8337	82.20%	0.8920	81.19%
Random forest (TF-IDF)	0.9169	83.83%	0.9179	83.39%
LSTM (GloVe 300d. embeddings)	0.9334	86.14%	0.9300	85.61%
LSTM (Law2Vec 200d. embeddings)	0.9204	84.35%	0.9222	84.25%
CNN (GloVe 300d. embeddings)	0.9251	84.95%	0.9280	85.16%
CNN (Law2Vec 200d. embeddings)	0.9240	84.98%	0.9257	84.87%
Labelling 3				
Logistic regression (TF-IDF)	0.9557	88.79%	0.9548	88.79%
Logistic regression (BOW)	0.9129	84.54%	0.9128	84.16%
Random forest (TF-IDF)	0.9431	86.69%	0.9430	85.80%
LSTM (GloVe 300d. embeddings)	0.9505	89.38%	0.9447	87.86%
LSTM (Law2Vec 200d. embeddings)	0.9406	86.91%	0.9393	86.37%
CNN (GloVe 300d. embeddings)	0.9519	88.70%	0.9487	88.00%
CNN (Law2Vec 200d. embeddings)	0.9450	87.14%	0.9459	87.05%

4.5 Interpretation of the Most Important Features

In this subsection, we make an attempt to explain which features played the most important role in generating our results. The good performance of the logistic model means that we have a better chance to interpret what features are driving our classification algorithm.

We extracted the most important features using the logistic regression model with TF-IDF algorithm on a bag of unigrams and bigrams, trained on the dataset with Labelling 3 (as this labelling gave us the best performance). Among the most important features we can find *congress appropriation*, which refers to appropriation bills – i.e. bills that decide on how to allocate federal funds to various specific federal government departments, agencies and programs. Increased lobbying activity of these bills that directly decide on how to spend money are not surprising.

Scanning through the 100 most important features, one also finds a list of senator names: *Cartwright, Polis, Roe, Murphy, Reed, Kelly*. It is likely that bills introduced by these Senators received more lobbying than bills introduced by others, which is why we pick up their names among the top features.

The top feature list also contains a number of terms that are typically associated with legislation that limit competition in one way or another. Terms like *exception, reauthorization, protection, prevent, copyright, patent*, are possible signs of the regulatory protection of some market players, or the creation of regulatory monopolies through patents or copyrights.

Finally, one can also see patterns of the sectors and topics where more lobbying happens, such as finance: *insurance, health saving, credit union, share agreement, flood insurance, saving, tax freedom*; public health: *abortion, care assistance, overdose, smoker, cancer screening*; infrastructure: *infrastructure, building code, federal land*; or associated with socially controversial topics: *abortion, marriage, partnership, ammunition, gender identity*.

Looking at each subject more specifically can lead us to more fine-tuned feature importance discussions. For lack of space we cannot discuss all of these, but we provide some examples. Looking at bills on Foreign Trade and International Finance, Fig. 1 shows *preference, protection, credit, subsidy*, and *extension* among the positive features (indicating higher probability of lobbying). This is not surprising, these terms are typically associated with various trade barriers, one of the prime manifestations of successful rent seeking lobbying by US-based producers. Other features, such as *combination* and *partnership* are signs of export/import partnership, which are often the subject of trade-related rent seeking activities. Of course, finding import, export, or currency (words that are inherent in trade related documents) among the important features shows that our selection of stopwords would have to be further fine-tuned to each subject area specifically.

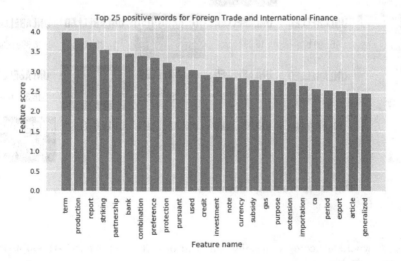

Fig. 1. Most important positive words for Foreign Trade and International Finance

5 Application to Unlabelled Data

As mentioned earlier, one of the limitations of using the OpenSecrects.org data is that it only labels the bills that were lobbied, making the implicit assumption that all unlabelled bills were not lobbied. As explained above, in the US, lobbying activities are required to be disclosed, violations of which can lead to severe penalties. Nevertheless, there has been over 14,000 such violations since 1995,[3] which would suggest that non-compliance is a non-trivial problem. Our proposed approach below offers a way to verify if those bills that are not entered in the OpenSecrets.org database have been subject to similar lobbying activities as those that are listed by OpenSecrets.org.

In our experiment, we downloaded all available bills from the US Congress' website (254,806 bills). As very old bills could have had different wordings, and short bills are likely to have limited amount of information for our analysis, we constrained this sample to bills after 1990, and bills that were at least 2000 word long, which left us with a sample of 81,998 bills. From the lobbied bills we only used the ones where there was intensive lobbying (50 instances or more), i.e. where we were most certain to find distinctive features due to the lobbying (13,940 bills).

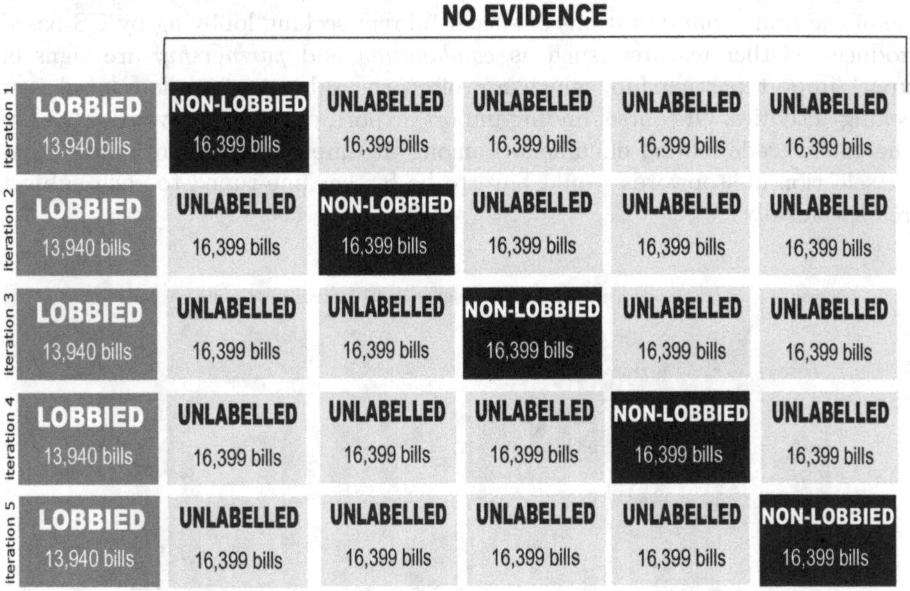

NO EVIDENCE

iteration 1 LOBBIED 13,940 bills	NON-LOBBIED 16,399 bills	UNLABELLED 16,399 bills	UNLABELLED 16,399 bills	UNLABELLED 16,399 bills	UNLABELLED 16,399 bills
iteration 2 LOBBIED 13,940 bills	UNLABELLED 16,399 bills	NON-LOBBIED 16,399 bills	UNLABELLED 16,399 bills	UNLABELLED 16,399 bills	UNLABELLED 16,399 bills
iteration 3 LOBBIED 13,940 bills	UNLABELLED 16,399 bills	UNLABELLED 16,399 bills	NON-LOBBIED 16,399 bills	UNLABELLED 16,399 bills	UNLABELLED 16,399 bills
iteration 4 LOBBIED 13,940 bills	UNLABELLED 16,399 bills	UNLABELLED 16,399 bills	UNLABELLED 16,399 bills	NON-LOBBIED 16,399 bills	UNLABELLED 16,399 bills
iteration 5 LOBBIED 13,940 bills	UNLABELLED 16,399 bills	UNLABELLED 16,399 bills	UNLABELLED 16,399 bills	UNLABELLED 16,399 bills	NON-LOBBIED 16,399 bills

Fig. 2. Extracting information from non-labelled data

---

[3] https://www.hklaw.com/en/insights/publications/2017/11/what-is-the-lobbying-disclosure-act-lda.

First, to estimate a model that predicts lobbying in a bill, we took our 13,940 lobbied bills (labelled as lobbied), and used cross-validation to take 5 rotated samples (each consisting of $81,998/5 = 16,399$ bills) from the unlabelled bills and labelled them as non-lobbied. This cross-validation exercise is shown on Fig. 2. Then we estimated our model (using a logistic model given its relatively good performance and speed) and deployed it on the remaining 'unlabelled' sample to predict the probability that a given unlabelled bill was lobbied. We then moved on to the next iteration, where we used the same lobbied sample, but another 16,399 unlabelled bills were selected and labelled as non-lobbied. Then we estimated our model for this new set of labelled bills, and deployed it on the remaining sample, and so on. For each unlabelled bill and for each iteration, we stored the estimated probability that it was lobbied. The five batches in our iterations gave us 4 predictions for each unlabelled bill. We then took the average of these 4 predictions as a probability that an unlabelled bill was directly or indirectly affected by lobbying activity.

Figure 3 plots these average probabilities over time (calendar quarter of the release of the bill). This shows an increasing trend in the percentage of unlabelled bills being affected by lobbying, indicating, that for more recent bills, almost half had at least a 50% probability that they were affected by lobbying, and almost 10% of unlabelled bills were predicted to have been lobbied with over 90% probability.

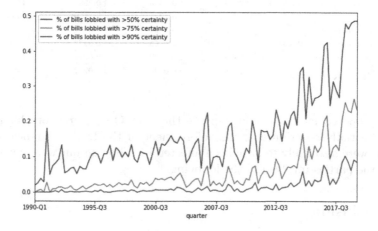

Fig. 3. Proportion of non-labelled bills with evidence of lobbying

Finally, Table 5 presents the proportion of unlabelled bills where we predicted a high probability of lobbying activity, broken down to subject areas. To preserve space we only report 10 subject areas with the highest probability. It shows that in subjects such as *Energy, Finance and Financial Sector, Science and Technology,* and *Health* around 5% of the unlabelled bills were affected by lobbying with more than 90% probability. To give an example, the GREENER

Fuels Act (S.2519 and H.R.5212) was most likely to have been lobbied but was not recorded as such on OpenSecrets.org at the time of us accessing the data (Dec 2018). It is possible that there is a lag in recording lobbied bills, but even if this is the case, and if these bills were later added to the lobbied list, it would confirm that our model made the right prediction.

The above findings can imply two things. In the US all lobbying activity has to be reported but our findings suggest that there are bills that have not been filed under the Lobbying Disclosure Act (LDA), but carry the hallmarks of lobbied bills. First, these bills could have been indirectly affected by lobbying (i.e. were not lobbied but the legislator designed them in a way that made them similar to lobbied bills). There is also a possibility that not all bill-specific lobbying activity is reported, and the OpenSecrets.org data is incomplete.

Table 5. The proportion of unlabelled bills with evidence of lobbying by subject area (top 10 highest probability subjects)

Subject	Lobbied with >50% probability	Lobbied with >75% probability	Lobbied with >90% probability	Total number of unlabelled bills
Energy	0.4144	0.1799	0.0674	1262
Finance and Financial Sector	0.3737	0.1698	0.0554	1678
Commerce	0.3302	0.1101	0.0259	1508
Emergency Management	0.3052	0.1381	0.0442	724
Science, Technology, Communications	0.2989	0.1346	0.0503	1114
Health	0.2850	0.1221	0.0420	6453
Labor and Employment	0.2576	0.0761	0.0172	1747
Transportation and Public Works	0.2437	0.0865	0.0177	2208
Environmental Protection	0.2309	0.0939	0.0271	1884
Immigration	0.2261	0.0745	0.0232	1464

Our proposed method could improve the data OpenSecrets.org holds, and could potentially contribute to the enforcement of the LDA by indicating the bills that were also likely to have been affected by lobbying but were not filed as such by the parties involved in the lobbying.

6   Conclusion

Many times the automation of handling large amounts of legal documents comes from the desire to improve work efficiency by substituting out human handling of cases. We believe our paper belongs in a different group. Even humans with the highest level of domain specific expertise on lobbying, legislation, and rent seeking would struggle to mark out those bills that had been targeted by lobbying. We propose the training of an algorithm to find patterns that distinguish lobbied bills from non-lobbied ones.

For the legal field to learn from this exercise, our future work will focus on a more detailed analysis of what factors are important in the distinction between the two types of bills. For this we would also like to perform more exhaustive experiments, looking at how our results change with time, with subject area, or with the identity of the lobbying organisation - all of which is available in our dataset - affects our results. Because our linear models perform well, it has the appeal to make it interpretable, which is important for social science applications.

Moreover, we would also like to experiment with transfer learning (domain adaptation) and examine if our model, together with a small sample of labelled data from another English-speaking jurisdiction, can be used to predict lobbying activity in countries where such data is less easily available than in the US.

Acknowledgement. This work is supported by H2020 SoBigData++.

References

1. Aletras, N., Tsarapatsanis, D., Preoţiuc-Pietro, D., Lampos, V.: Predicting judicial decisions of the European court of human rights: a natural language processing perspective. PeerJ Comput. Sci. **2**, e93 (2016)
2. Boella, G., Di Caro, L., Humphreys, L.: Using classification to support legal knowledge engineers in the Eunomos legal document management system. In: Fifth International Workshop on Juris-Informatics (JURISIN) (2011)
3. Breiman, L.: Random forests. Mach. Learn. **45**(1), 5–32 (2001). https://doi.org/10.1023/A:1010933404324
4. Chalkidis, I., Kampas, D.: Deep learning in law: early adaptation and legal word embeddings trained on large corpora. Artif. Intell. Law **27**(2), 171–198 (2018). https://doi.org/10.1007/s10506-018-9238-9
5. Dale, R.: Law and word order: NLP in legal tech. Nat. Lang. Eng. **25**(1), 211–217 (2019)
6. De Figueiredo, J.M., Richter, B.K.: Advancing the empirical research on lobbying. Ann. Rev. Polit. Sci. **17**, 163–185 (2014)
7. Farzindar, A., Lapalme, G.: Legal text summarization by exploration of the thematic structure and argumentative roles. In: Text Summarization Branches Out, pp. 27–34 (2004)
8. Goldberg, Y.: Neural network methods for natural language processing. Synth. Lect. Hum. Lang. Technol. **10**(1), 1–309 (2017)
9. Grasse, N., Heidbreder, B.: The influence of lobbying activity in state legislatures: evidence from Wisconsin. Legislative Stud. Q. **36**(4), 567–589 (2011)
10. Grossmann, M., Pyle, K.: Lobbying and congressional bill advancement. Int. Groups Adv. **2**(1), 91–111 (2013). https://doi.org/10.1057/iga.2012.18
11. Hachey, B., Grover, C.: Extractive summarisation of legal texts. Artif. Intell. Law **14**(4), 305–345 (2006). https://doi.org/10.1007/s10506-007-9039-z
12. Hill, M.D., Kelly, G.W., Lockhart, G.B., Van Ness, R.A.: Determinants and effects of corporate lobbying. Financial Manag. **42**(4), 931–957 (2013)
13. Laband, D.N., Sophocleus, J.P.: The social cost of rent-seeking: first estimates. Public Choice **58**(3), 269–275 (1988). https://doi.org/10.1007/BF00155672
14. Li, P., Zhao, F., Li, Y., Zhu, Z.: Law text classification using semi-supervised convolutional neural networks. In: 2018 Chinese Control and Decision Conference (CCDC), pp. 309–313. IEEE (2018)

15. Lopez, R.A., Pagoulatos, E.: Rent seeking and the welfare cost of trade barriers. Public Choice **79**(1–2), 149–160 (1994). https://doi.org/10.1007/BF01047924

16. Pennington, J., Socher, R., Manning, C.D.: Glove: global vectors for word representation. In: EMNLP (2014)

17. Sulea, O.-M., Zampieri, M., Vela, M., Van Genabith, J.: Predicting the law area and decisions of French supreme court cases. arXiv preprint arXiv:1708.01681 (2017)

18. Wongchaisuwat, P., Klabjan, D., McGinnis, J.O.: Predicting litigation likelihood and time to litigation for patents. In: Proceedings of the 16th Edition of the International Conference on Artificial Intelligence and Law, pp. 257–260. ACM (2017)

19. You, H.Y.: Ex post lobbying. J. Polit. **79**(4), 1162–1176 (2017)

FIBS: A Generic Framework for Classifying Interval-Based Temporal Sequences

S. Mohammad Mirbagheri[✉] and Howard J. Hamilton

Department of Computer Science, University of Regina, Regina, Canada
{mirbaghs,Howard.Hamilton}@uregina.ca

Abstract. We study the problem of classifying interval-based temporal sequences (IBTSs). Since common classification algorithms cannot be directly applied to IBTSs, the main challenge is to define a set of features that effectively represents the data such that classifiers can be applied. Most prior work utilizes frequent pattern mining to define a feature set based on discovered patterns. However, frequent pattern mining is computationally expensive and often discovers many irrelevant patterns. To address this shortcoming, we propose the FIBS framework for classifying IBTSs. FIBS extracts features relevant to classification from IBTSs based on relative frequency and temporal relations. To avoid selecting irrelevant features, a filter-based selection strategy is incorporated into FIBS. Our empirical evaluation on eight real-world datasets demonstrates the effectiveness of our methods in practice. The results provide evidence that FIBS effectively represents IBTSs for classification algorithms, which contributes to similar or significantly better accuracy compared to state-of-the-art competitors. It also suggests that the feature selection strategy is beneficial to FIBS's performance.

Keywords: Interval-based events · Temporal interval sequences · Feature-based classification framework

1 Introduction

Interval-based temporal sequence (IBTS) data are collected from application domains in which events persist over intervals of time of varying lengths. Such domains include medicine [1–3], sensor networks [4], sign languages [5], and motion capture [6]. Applications that need to deal with this type of data are common in industrial, commercial, government, and health sectors. For example, some companies offer multiple service packages to customers that persist over varying periods of time and may be held concurrently. The sequence of packages that a customer holds can be represented as an IBTS.

This research was supported by funding from ISM Canada and the Natural Sciences and Engineering Research Council of Canada.

M. Song et al. (Eds.): DaWaK 2020, LNCS 12393, pp. 301–315, 2020.
https://doi.org/10.1007/978-3-030-59065-9_24

IBTSs can be obtained either directly from the applications or indirectly by data transformation. In particular, temporal abstraction of a univariate or multivariate time series may yield such data. Segmentation or aggregation of a time series into a succinct symbolic representation is called *temporal abstraction* (TA) [3]. TA transforms a numerical time series to a symbolic time series. This high-level qualitative form of data provides a description of the raw time series data that is suitable for a human decision-maker (beacause it helps them to understand the data better) or for data mining. TA may be based on knowledge-based abstraction performed by a domain expert. An alternative is data-driven abstraction utilizing temporal discretization. Common unsupervised discretization methods are Equal Width, Symbolic Aggregate Approximation (SAX) [7], and Persist [8]. Depending on the application scenario, symbolic time series may be categorized as point-based or as interval-based. Point-based data reflect scenarios in which events happen instantaneously or events are considered to have equal time intervals. Duration has no impact on extracting patterns for this type. Interval-based data, which is the focus of this study, reflect scenarios where events have unequal time intervals; here, duration plays an important role. Figure 1 depicts the process of obtaining interval-based temporal sequences.

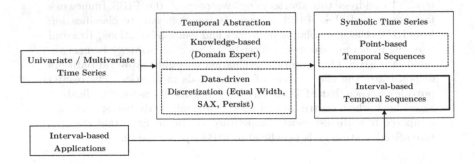

Fig. 1. Process of obtaining interval-based temporal sequences

Classifying IBTSs is a relatively new research area. Although classification is an important machine learning task and has achieved great success in a wide range of applications (fields), the classification of IBTSs has not received much attention. A dataset of IBTSs contains longitudinal data where instances are described by a series of event intervals over time rather than features with a single value. Such dataset does not match the format required by standard classification algorithms to build predictive models. Standard classification methods for multivariate time series (e.g., Hidden Markov Models [9] and recurrent neural networks), time series similarity measures (e.g., Euclidean distance and Dynamic Time Warping (DTW) [10]), and time series feature extraction methods (e.g., discrete Fourier transform, discrete wavelet transform and singular value decomposition) cannot be directly applied to such temporal data.

In this paper, we formalize the problem of classification of IBTSs based on feature-based classifiers and propose a new framework to solve this problem. The major contributions of this work are as follows:

- We propose a generic framework named FIBS for classifying IBTSs. It represents IBTSs by extracting features relevant to classification from IBTSs based on relative frequency and temporal relations.
- To avoid selecting irrelevant features, we propose a heuristic filter-based feature selection strategy. FIBS utilizes this strategy to reduce the feature space and improve the classification accuracy.
- We report on an experimental evaluation that shows the proposed framework is able to represent IBTSs effectively and classifying them efficiently.

The rest of the paper is organized as follows. Related work is presented in Sect. 2. Section 3 provides preliminaries and the problem statement. Section 4 presents the details of the FIBS framework and the feature selection strategy. Experimental results on real datasets and evaluation are given in Section 5. Section 6 presents conclusions.

2   Related Work

To date, only a few approaches to IBTS classification can be found in the literature. Most of them are domain-specific and based on frequent pattern mining techniques. Patel et al. [2] proposed the first work in the area of IBTS classification. They developed a method that first mines all frequent temporal patterns in an unsupervised setting and then uses some of these patterns as features for classification. They used Information Gain, a measure of discriminative power, as the selection criterion. After features are extracted, common classification techniques, such as decision trees or Support Vector Machines (SVM), are used to predict the classifications for unseen IBTSs.

Extracting features from frequent temporal patterns presents some challenges. Firstly, a well-known limitation of frequent pattern mining algorithms is that they extract too many frequent patterns, many of which are redundant or uninformative. Several attempts have been made to address this limitation by discovering frequent temporal patterns in a supervised setting [11,12]. For example, Batal et al. [11] proposed the Minimal Temporal Patterns (MPTP) framework to filter out non-predictive and spurious temporal patterns to define a set of features for classifying Electronic Health Record (EHR) data. Secondly, discovering frequent patterns is computationally expensive. Lastly, classification based on features extracted from frequent patterns does not guarantee better performance than other methods.

In contrast to the approaches based on frequent pattern mining, a few studies offer similarity-based approaches to IBTS classification. A robust similarity (or distance) measure allows machine learning tasks such as similarity search, clustering and classification to be performed. Towards this direction, Kostakis et al. [13] proposed two methods for comparing IBTSs. The first method, called the *DTW-based* method, maps each IBTS to a set of vectors where one vector is created for each start- or end-point of any event-interval. The distances between the vectors are then computed using DTW. The second method, called *Artemis*, measures the similarity between two IBTSs based on the temporal relations that are shared between events. To do so, the IBTSs are mapped into a bipartite graph and the Hungarian algorithm is employed. Kotsifakos et al. [14] proposed the Interval-Based Sequence Matching (*IBSM*) method where each time point is represented by a binary vector that indicates which events are active at that particular time point. The distances between the vectors are then computed by Euclidean distance. In all three methods, IBTSs are classified by the k-NN classification algorithm and it was shown that IBSM outperforms the two other methods [14] with respect to both classification accuracy and runtime. Although the reported results are promising, such classifiers still suffer from major limitations. While Artemis ignores the duration of the event intervals, DWT-based and IBSM ignore the temporal relations between event intervals.

A feature-based framework for IBTS classification, called *STIFE*, was recently proposed by Bornemann et al. [15]. STIFE extracts features using a combination of basic statistical metrics, shapelet [16] discovery and selection, and distance-based approaches. Then, a random forest is constructed using the extracted features to perform classification. It was shown that such a random forest achieves similar or better classification accuracy than k-NN using IBSM.

3   Problem Statement

We adapt definitions given in earlier research [5] and describe the problem statement formally.

Definition 1 (*Event interval*). Let $\Sigma = \{A, B, ...\}$ denote a finite alphabet. A triple $e = (l, t_b, t_f)$ is called an event interval, where $l \in \Sigma$ is the event label and $t_b, t_f \in \mathbb{N}$, ($t_b < t_f$) are the beginning and finishing times, respectively. We also use $e.x$ to denote element x of event interval e, e.g. $e.t_b$ is the beginning time of event interval e. The duration of event interval e is $d(e) = t_f - t_b$.

Definition 2 (*E-sequence*). An event-interval sequence or e-sequence $s = \langle e_1, e_2, ..., e_m \rangle$ is a list of m event intervals placed in ascending order based on their beginning times. If event intervals have equal beginning times, then they are ordered lexicographically by their labels. Multiple occurrences of an event are allowed in an e-sequence if they do not happen concurrently. The duration of an e-sequence s is $d(s) = max\{e_1.t_f, e_2.t_f, ..., e_m.t_f\} - min\{e_1.t_b, e_2.t_b, ..., e_m.t_b\}$.

Definition 3 (*E-sequence dataset*). An e-sequence dataset D is a set of n e-sequences $\{s_1, ..., s_n\}$, where each e-sequence s_i is associated with an unique identifier i.

Table 1 depicts an e-sequence dataset consisting of four e-sequences with identifiers 1 to 4.

Table 1. Example of an e-sequence dataset

Id	Event Label	Beginning Time	Finishing Time	Event Sequence
1	A	8	28	A
	B	18	21	B
	C	24	28	C
	E	25	27	E
2	A	1	14	A
	C	6	14	C
	E	8	11	E
	F	8	11	F
3	A	6	22	A
	B	6	14	B
	C	14	20	C
	E	16	18	E
4	A	4	24	A
	B	5	10	B
	D	5	12	D
	C	16	22	C
	E	18	20	E

Problem Statement. Given an e-sequence dataset D, where each e-sequence is associated with a class label, the problem is to construct a representation of D such that common feature-based classifiers are able to classify previously unseen e-sequences similar to those in D.

4   The FIBS Framework

In this section, we introduce the FIBS framework for classifying e-sequence datasets. Many classification algorithms require data to be in a format reminiscent of a table, where rows represent instances (e-sequences) and columns represent features (attributes). Since an e-sequence dataset does not follow this format, we utilize FIBS to construct feature-based representations to enable standard classification algorithms to build predictive models.

A *feature-based representation* of a dataset has three components: a class label set, a feature set, and data instances. We first give a general definition of a feature-based representation based on these components [17].

Definition 4 (*Feature-based representation*). A feature-based representation $K = (C, F, X)$ is defined as follows. Let $C = \{c_1, c_2, ..., c_k\}$ be a set of k

class labels, $F = \{f_1, f_2, ..., f_z\}$ be a set of z features (or attributes), $X = \{x_1, x_2, ..., x_n\}$ be a set of n instances, and let $y_i \in C$ denote the class label of instance $x_i \in X$.

In supervised settings, the set of class labels C of the classes to which e-sequences belong is already known. Therefore, in order to form the feature-based representation, FIBS extracts the feature set F and the instances X from dataset D. To define the F and X components, we consider two alternative formulations based on relative frequency and temporal relations among the events. These formulations are explained in the following subsections.

4.1   Relative Frequency

Definition 5 (*Relative frequency*). The relative frequency $R(s, l)$ of an event label $l \in \Sigma$ in an e-sequence $s \in D$, which is the duration-weighted frequency of the occurrences of l in s, is defined as the accumulated durations of all event intervals with event label l in s divided by the duration of s. Formally:

$$R(s, l) = \frac{1}{d(s)} \sum_{e \in s \,\wedge\, e.l = l} d(e) \tag{1}$$

Suppose that we want to specify a feature-based representation of an e-sequence dataset $D = \{s_1, s_2, ..., s_n\}$ using relative frequency. Let every unique event label $l \in \Sigma$ found in D be used as a feature, i.e., let $F = \Sigma$. Also let every e-sequence $s \in D$ be used as the basis for defining an instance $x \in X$. The feature-values of instance x are specified as a vector containing the relative frequencies of every event label $l \in \Sigma$ in s. Formally, $X = \{x_1, x_2, ..., x_n\} \in \mathbb{R}^{n \times |\Sigma|}$, $x_i = \langle R(s_i, l_1), R(s_i, l_2), ..., R(s_i, l_{|\Sigma|}) \rangle$.

Example 1. Consider the feature-based representation that is constructed based on the relative frequency of the event labels in the e-sequence dataset shown in Table 1. Let the class label set C be $\{+, -\}$ and the feature set F be $\{A, B, C, D, E, F\}$. Assume that the class label of each of s_1, s_3, and s_4 is $+$ and the class label of s_2 is $-$. Table 2 shows the resulting feature-based representation.

Table 2. Feature-based representation constructed based on relative frequency

A	B	C	D	E	F	Class
1.00	0.15	0.20	0	0.10	0	+
1.00	0	0.62	0	0.23	0.23	−
1.00	0.50	0.38	0	0.13	0	+
1.00	0.25	0.30	0.35	0.10	0	+

4.2   Temporal Relations

Thirteen possible temporal relations between pairs of intervals were nicely cate-gorized by Allen [18]. Table 3 illustrates Allen's temporal relations. Ignoring the "equals" relation, six of the relations are inverses of the other six. We emphasize seven temporal relations, namely, equals (q), before (b), meets (m), overlaps (o), contains (c), starts (s), and finished-by (f), which we call the *primary* temporal relations. Let set $U = T \cup I$ represents the thirteen temporal relation labels, where $T = \{q, b, m, o, c, s, f\}$ is the set of labels for the primary temporal relations and $I = \{t^{-1} \mid t \in T - \{q\}\}$ is the set of labels for the inverse temporal relations.

Table 3. Allen's temporal relations between two event intervals

Primary Temporal Relation	Inverse Temporal Relation	Pictorial Example
α equals β	β equals α	
α before β	β after α	
α meets β	β met-by α	
α overlaps β	β overlapped-by α	
α contains β	β during α	
α starts β	β startted-by α	
α finished-by β	β finishes α	

Exactly one of these relations holds between any ordered pair of event inter-vals. Some event labels may not occur in an e-sequence and some may occur mul-tiple times. For simplicity, we assume the first occurrence of an event label in an e-sequence is more important than the remainder of its occurrences. Therefore, when extracting temporal relations from an e-sequence, only the first occurrence is considered and the rest are ignored. With this assumption, there are at most $\binom{|\Sigma|}{2}$ possible pairs of event labels in a dataset.

Based on Definition 4, we now define a second feature-based representation, which relies on temporal relations. Let $F = \binom{\Sigma}{2}$ be the set of all 2-combinations of event labels from Σ. The feature-values of instance x_i are specified as a vector containing the labels corresponding to the temporal relations between every pair that occurs in an e-sequence s_i. In other words, $X = \{x_1, x_2, ..., x_n\} \in U^{n \times \binom{|\Sigma|}{2}}$, where an instance $x_i \in X$ represents an e-sequence s_i.

Example 2. Following Example 1, Table 4 shows the feature-based representation that is constructed based on the temporal relations between the pairs of event labels in the e-sequences given in Table 1. To increase readability, 0 is used instead of $\varnothing$ to indicate that no temporal relation exists between the pair.

Table 4. Feature-based representation constructed based on temporal relations

A, B	A, C	A, D	A, E	A, F	B, C	B, D	B, E	B, F	C, D	C, E	C, F	D, E	D, F	E, F	Class
c	f	0	c	0	b	0	b	0	0	c	0	0	0	0	+
0	f	0	c	c	0	0	0	0	0	c	c	0	0	q	−
s^{-1}	c	0	c	0	b	0	b	0	0	c	0	0	0	0	+
c	c	c	c	0	b	s	b	0	b^{-1}	c	0	b^{-1}	0	0	+

4.3   Feature Selection

Feature selection for classification tasks aims to select a subset of features that are highly discriminative and thus contribute substantially to increasing the performance of the classification. Features with less discriminative power are undesirable since they either have little impact on the accuracy of the classification or may even harm it. As well, reducing the number of features improves the efficiency of many algorithms.

Based on their relevance to the targeted classes, features are divided by John et al. [19] into three disjoint categories, namely, strongly relevant, weakly relevant, and irrelevant features. Suppose $f_i \in F$ and $\bar{f}_i = F - \{f_i\}$. Let $P(C \mid F)$ be the probability distribution of class labels in C given the values for the features in F. The categories of feature relevance can be formalized as follows [20].

Definition 6 (*Strong relevance*). A feature f_i is strongly relevant iff

$$P(C \mid f_i, \bar{f}_i) \neq P(C \mid \bar{f}_i) \tag{2}$$

Definition 7 (*Weak relevance*). A feature f_i is weakly relevant iff

$$\begin{aligned} P(C \mid f_i, \bar{f}_i) = P(C \mid \bar{f}_i) \text{ and} \\ \exists\, g_i \subset \bar{f}_i \text{ such that } P(C \mid f_i, g_i) \neq P(C \mid g_i) \end{aligned} \tag{3}$$

Corollary 1 (*Irrelevance*). A feature f_i is irrelevant iff

$$\forall\, g_i \subseteq \bar{f}_i, \quad P(C \mid f_i, g_i) = P(C \mid g_i) \tag{4}$$

Strong relevance indicates that a feature is indispensable and it cannot be removed without loss of prediction accuracy. Weak relevance implies that the feature can sometimes contribute to prediction accuracy. Features are relevant if they are either strongly or weakly relevant and are irrelevant otherwise. Irrelevant features are dispensable and can never contribute to prediction accuracy.

Feature selection is beneficial to the quality of the temporal relation representation, especially when there are many distinct event labels in the dataset. Although any feature selection method can be used to eliminate irrelevant features, some methods have advantages for particular representations. Filter-based selection methods are generally efficient because they assess the relevance of features by examining intrinsic properties of the data prior to applying any classification method. We propose a simple and efficient filter-based method to avoid producing irrelevant features for the temporal relation representation.

4.4   Filter-Based Feature Selection Strategy

In this section, we propose a filter-based strategy for feature reduction that can also be used in unsupervised settings. We apply this strategy to avoid producing irrelevant features for the temporal relation representation.

Theorem 1. *An event label l is an irrelevant feature of an e-sequence dataset D if its relative frequencies are equal in every e-sequence in dataset D.*

Proof. Suppose event label l occurs with equal relative frequencies in every e-sequence in dataset D. We construct a feature-based representation $K = (C, F, X)$ based on the relative frequencies of the event labels as previously described. Therefore, there exists a feature $f_i \in F$ that has the constant value of v for all instances $x \in X$. We have $P(C \mid f_i) = P(C)$. Therefore, $P(C \mid f_i, g_i) = P(C \mid g_i)$. According to Corollary 1, we conclude f_i is an irrelevant feature.   □

We provide a definition for *support* that is applicable to relative frequency. If we add up the relative frequencies of event label l in all e-sequences of dataset D and then normalize the sum, we obtain the support of l in D. Formally:

$$sup(D, l) = \frac{1}{n} \sum_{s \in D} R(s, l) \tag{5}$$

where n is the number of e-sequences in D.

The support of an event label can be used as the basis of dimensionality reduction during pre-processing for a classification task. One can identify and discard irrelevant features (event labels) based on their supports. We will now show how the support is used to avoid extracting irrelevant features by the following corollary, which is an immediate consequence of Theorem 1.

Corollary 2. *An event label l whose support in dataset D is 0 or 1 is an irrelevant feature.*

Proof. As with the proof of Theorem 1, assume we construct a feature-based representation K based on the relative frequency of the event labels. If $sup(l, D) = 0$ then, there exists a mapping feature $f_i \in F$ that has equal relative frequencies (values) of 0 for all instances $x \in X$. The same argument holds if $sup(l, D) = 1$. According to Theorem 1, we conclude f_i is an irrelevant feature.   □

In practice, situations where the support of a feature is exactly 0 or 1 do not often happen. Hence, we propose a heuristic strategy that discards probably irrelevant features based on a confidence interval defined with respect to an error threshold ϵ.

Heuristic Strategy: If $sup(D, l)$ is not in a confidence interval $[0 + \epsilon, 1 - \epsilon]$, then event label l is presumably an irrelevant feature in D and can be discarded.

4.5   Comparison to Representation Based on Frequent Patterns

In frequent pattern mining, the support of temporal pattern p in a dataset is the number of instances that contain p. A pattern is frequent if its support is no less than a predefined threshold set by user. Once frequent patterns are discovered, after computationally expensive operations, a subset of frequent patterns are selected as features. The representation contains binary values such that if a selected pattern occurs in an e-sequence the value of the corresponding feature is 1, and 0 otherwise. Example 3 illustrates a limitation of classification of IBTSs based on frequent pattern mining where frequent patterns are irrelevant to the class labels.

Example 3. Consider Table 1 and its feature-based representation constructed based on relative frequency, as shown in Example 1. In this example, the most frequent pattern is A, which has a support of 1. However, according to Corollary 2, A is an irrelevant feature and can be discarded for the purpose of classification. For this example, a better approach is to classify the e-sequences based on the presence or absence of F such that the occurrence of F in an e-sequence means the e-sequence belongs to the $-$ class and the absence of F means it belongs to the $+$ class.

In practice, the large number of frequent patterns affects the performance of the approach in both the pattern discovery step and the feature selection step. Obviously, mining patterns that are later found to be irrelevant, is useless and computationally costly.

5   Experiments

In our experiments, we evaluate the effectiveness of the FIBS framework on the task of classifying interval-based temporal sequences using the well-known random forest classification algorithm on eight real world datasets. We evaluate performance of FIBS using classifiers implemented in R version 3.6.1. The FIBS framework was also implemented in R. All experiments were conducted on a laptop computer with a 2.2 GHz Intel Core i5 CPU and 8GB memory. We obtain overall classification accuracy using 10-fold cross-validation. We also compare the results for FIBS against those for two well-known methods, STIFE [15] and IBSM [14]. In order to see the effect of the feature selection strategy, the FIBS framework was tested with it disabled (FIBS baseline) and with its error threshold ϵ set to various values.

5.1 Datasets

Eight real-world datasets from various application domains were used to evaluate the FIBS framework. Statistics concerning these datasets are summarized in Table 5. More details about the datasets are as follows:

- **ASL-BU** [5]. Event intervals correspond to facial or gestural expressions (e.g., head tilt right, rapid head shake, eyebrow raise, etc.) obtained from videos of American Sign Language expressions provided by Boston University. An e-sequence expresses an utterance using sign language that belongs to one of nine classes, such as wh-word, wh-question, verb, or noun.
- **ASL-BU2** [5]. ASL-BU2 is a newer version of the ASL-BU dataset with improvements in annotation such that new e-sequences and additional event labels have been introduced. As above, an e-sequence expresses an utterance.
- **Auslan2** [4]. The e-sequences in the Australian Sign Language dataset contain event intervals that represent words like girl or right.
- **Blocks** [4]. Each event interval corresponds to a visual primitive obtained from videos of a human hand stacking colored blocks and describes which blocks are touched as well as the actions of the hand (e.g., contacts blue, attached hand red, etc.). Each e-sequence represents one of eight scenarios, such as assembling a tower.
- **Context** [4]. Each event interval was derived from categorical and numeric data describing the context of a mobile device carried by a person in some situation (e.g., walking inside/outside, using elevator, etc.). Each e-sequence represents one of five scenarios, such as being on a street or at a meeting.
- **Hepatitis** [2]. Each event interval represents the result of medical tests (e.g., normal, below or above the normal range, etc.) during an interval. Each e-sequence corresponds to a series of tests over a period of 10 years that a patient who has either Hepatitis B or Hepatitis C undergoes.
- **Pioneer** [4]. Event intervals were derived from the Pioneer-1 dataset available in the UCI repository corresponding to the input provided by the robot sensors (e.g., wheels velocity, distance to object, sonar depth reading, gripper state, etc.). Each e-sequence in the dataset describes one of three scenarios: move, turn, or grip.
- **Skating** [4]. Each event interval describes muscle activity and leg positions of one of six professional In-Line Speed Skaters during controlled tests at seven different speeds on a treadmill. Each e-sequence represents a complete movement cycle, which identifies one of the skaters.

Table 5. Statistical information about datasets

Dataset	# e-sequences	# Event Intervals	e-sequence Size			$|\Sigma|$	# Classes
			min	max	avg		
ASL-BU	873	18, 250	4	41	18	216	9
ASL-BU2	1839	2, 447	4	93	23	254	7
Auslan2	200	2, 447	9	20	12	12	10
Blocks	210	1, 207	3	12	6	8	8
Context	240	19, 355	47	149	81	54	5
Hepatitis	498	53, 692	15	592	108	63	2
Pioneer	160	8, 949	36	89	56	92	3
Skating	530	23, 202	27	143	44	41	6

5.2 Performance Evaluation

We assess the classification accuracy of FIBS on the set of datasets given in Sect. 5.1, which is exactly the same set of datasets considered in work on IBSM and STIFE [14,15]. For a fair comparison and following [15], in each case, we apply the random forest algorithm using FIBS to perform classifications. We adopt the classification results of the IBSM and STIFE methods, as reported in Table 5 in [15].

Table 6 shows the mean classification accuracy on the datasets when using FIBS baseline, FIBS with the error threshold ϵ ranging from 0.01 to 0.03 (using the feature selection strategy defined in Sect. 4.4), STIFE, and IBSM. The best performance in each row is highlighted in bold.

Table 6. Mean classification accuracy of each framework on eight datasets. The last two rows indicate the mean and median results of each method across all datasets.

Dataset	FIBS_Baseline	FIBS_0.01	FIBS_0.02	FIBS_0.03	STIFE	IBSM
ASL-BU	**94.98**	89.95	90.68	88.46	91.75	89.29
ASL-BU2	**94.43**	92.39	92.67	93.61	87.49	76.92
Auslan2	40.50	41.00	41.00	41.00	**47.00**	37.50
Blocks	100	100	100	100	100	100
Context	97.83	98.76	98.34	98.34	**99.58**	96.25
HEPATITIS	84.54	**85.14**	83.55	83.94	82.13	77.52
Pioneer	**100**	**100**	**100**	**100**	98.12	95.00
Skating	96.73	97.93	98.31	**98.5**	96.98	96.79
Mean	**88.63**	88.15	88.07	87.98	87.88	83.66
Median	95.86	95.16	95.49	**95.98**	94.37	92.15

According to the Wilcoxon signed ranks tests applied across the results from the datasets given in Table 6, each of the FIBS models has significantly higher accuracy than IBSM at significance level 0.05 (not shown). Compared with the STIFE framework, each of the FIBS models outperforms on four datasets, loses on three datasets, and ties on Blocks dataset at 100%. The Wilcoxon signed ranks tests do not, however, confirm which method is significantly better. Overall, the results suggest that FIBS is a strong competitor in terms of accuracy.

5.3 Effect of Feature Selection

The same experiments to classify the datasets using the random forest algorithm, which were given in Sect. 5.2, were conducted to determine the computational cost of FIBS with and without the feature selection strategy. Figure 2 shows the number of features produced by the frameworks and the execution time of

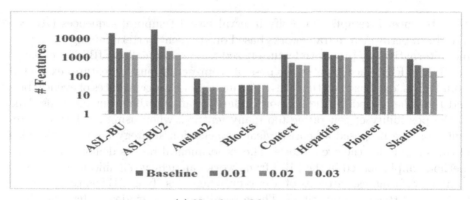

(a) Number of features

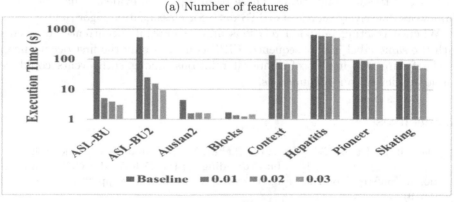

(b) Execution time (s)

Fig. 2. Effect of feature selection strategy on the eight datasets based on different error thresholds ϵ: (a) number of generated features on a log scale with base 10, (b) execution time (s) on a log scale with base 10.

applying the frameworks recorded on a log scale with base 10. The error threshold ϵ was varied from 0.00 (baseline) to 0.03 by 0.01.

As shown in Fig. 2a, applying the feature selection strategy reduces the number of features, and consequently decreases the execution time in all datasets (Fig. 2b). In particular, due to a significant reduction in the number of irrelevant features for ASL-BU and ASL-BU2, applying the FIBS framework with the strategy achieves over an order of magnitude speedup compared to FIBS without the strategy. As shown by the mean classification accuracy of the models in Table 6, applying the strategy also either improves the accuracy of the classification or does not have a significant adverse effect on it in all datasets. This result was confirmed by the Wilcoxon signed ranks tests at significance level 0.05 (not shown). Overall, the above results suggest that incorporating the feature selection strategy into FIBS is beneficial.

6   Conclusion

To date, most attempts to classify interval-based temporal sequences (IBTSs) have been performed in frameworks based on frequent pattern mining. As a simpler alternative, we propose a feature-based framework, called FIBS, for classifying IBTSs. FIBS incorporates two possible representations for features extracted from IBTSs, one based on the relative frequency of the occurrences of event labels and the other based on the temporal relations among the event intervals. Due to the possibility of generating too many features when using the latter representation, we proposed a heuristic feature selection strategy based on the idea of the support for the event labels. The experimental results demonstrated that methods implemented in the FIBS framework can achieve significantly better or similar performance in terms of accuracy when classifying IBTSs compared to the state-of-the-art competitors. These results provide evidence that the FIBS framework effectively represents IBTS data for classification algorithms.

When extracting temporal relations among multiple occurrences of events with the same label in an e-sequence, FIBS considers only the first occurrences. In the future, the impact of temporal relations among such events could be studied under various assumptions.

References

1. Sheetrit, E., Nissim, N., Klimov, D., Shahar, Y.: Temporal probabilistic profiles for sepsis prediction in the ICU. In: Proceedings of the 25th ACM SIGKDD International Conference on Knowledge Discovery & Data Mining, pp. 2961–2969. ACM (2019)
2. Patel, D., Hsu, W., Lee, M.L.: Mining relationships among interval-based events for classification. In: Proceedings of the 2008 ACM SIGMOD International Conference on Management of Data, SIGMOD 2008, pp. 393–404. ACM, New York (2008)
3. Moskovitch, R., Shahar, Y.: Medical temporal-knowledge discovery via temporal abstraction. In: AMIA Annual Symposium Proceedings, pp. 452–456. American Medical Informatics Association (2009)

4. Mörchen, F., Fradkin, D.: Robust mining of time intervals with semi-interval partial order patterns. In: Proceedings of the 2010 SIAM International Conference on Data Mining, pp. 315–326. SIAM (2010)
5. Papapetrou, P., Kollios, G., Sclaroff, S., Gunopulos, D.: Mining frequent arrangements of temporal intervals. Knowl. Inf. Syst. **21**(2), 133 (2009)
6. Liu, Y., Nie, L., Liu, L., Rosenblum, D.S.: From action to activity: sensor-based activity recognition. Neurocomputing **181**, 108–115 (2016)
7. Lin, J., Keogh, E., Wei, L., Lonardi, S.: Experiencing SAX: a novel symbolic representation of time series. Data Min. Knowl. Disc. **15**(2), 107–144 (2007)
8. Mörchen, F., Ultsch, A.: Optimizing time series discretization for knowledge discovery. In: Proceedings of the Eleventh ACM SIGKDD International Conference on Knowledge Discovery in Data Mining, pp. 660–665. ACM (2005)
9. Rabiner, L.R.: A tutorial on hidden Markov models and selected applications in speech recognition. Proc. IEEE **77**(2), 257–286 (1989)
10. Berndt, D.J., Clifford, J.: Using dynamic time warping to find patterns in time series. In: Workshop, K.D.D. (ed.) Seattle, pp. 359–370. AAAI Press, WA (1994)
11. Batal, I., Valizadegan, H., Cooper, G.F., Hauskrecht, M.: A temporal pattern mining approach for classifying electronic health record data. ACM Trans. Intell. Syste. Technol. (TIST) **4**(4), 63 (2013)
12. Moskovitch, R., Shahar, Y.: Classification-driven temporal discretization of multivariate time series. Data Min. Knowl. Disc. **29**(4), 871–913 (2014). https://doi.org/10.1007/s10618-014-0380-z
13. Kostakis, O., Papapetrou, P., Hollmén, J.: ARTEMIS: assessing the similarity of event-interval sequences. In: Gunopulos, D., Hofmann, T., Malerba, D., Vazirgiannis, M. (eds.) ECML PKDD 2011. LNCS (LNAI), vol. 6912, pp. 229–244. Springer, Heidelberg (2011). https://doi.org/10.1007/978-3-642-23783-6_15
14. Kotsifakos, A., Papapetrou, P., Athitsos, V.: IBSM: interval-based sequence matching. In: Proceedings of the 2013 SIAM International Conference on Data Mining, pp. 596–604. SIAM (2013)
15. Bornemann, L., Lecerf, J., Papapetrou, P.: STIFE: a framework for feature-based classification of sequences of temporal intervals. In: Calders, T., Ceci, M., Malerba, D. (eds.) DS 2016. LNCS (LNAI), vol. 9956, pp. 85–100. Springer, Cham (2016). https://doi.org/10.1007/978-3-319-46307-0_6
16. Ye, L., Keogh, E.: Time series shapelets: a new primitive for data mining. In: Proceedings of the 15th ACM SIGKDD International Conference on Knowledge Discovery and Data Mining, pp. 947–956. ACM (2009)
17. Tang, J., Alelyani, S., Liu, H.: Feature selection for classification: a review. Algorithms and applications, Data classification, p. 37 (2014)
18. Allen, J.F.: Maintaining knowledge about temporal intervals. Commun. ACM **26**(11), 832–843 (1983)
19. John, G.H., Kohavi, R., Pfleger, K.: Irrelevant features and the subset selection problem. In: Machine Learning Proceedings 1994, pp. 121–129. Elsevier (1994)
20. Yu, L., Liu, H.: Redundancy based feature selection for microarray data. In: Proceedings of the Tenth ACM SIGKDD International Conference on Knowledge Discovery and Data Mining, pp. 737–742. ACM (2004)

Multivariate Time Series Classification: A Relational Way

Dominique Gay[1(✉)], Alexis Bondu[2], Vincent Lemaire[3], Marc Boullé[3], and Fabrice Clérot[3]

[1] LIM-EA2525, Université de La Réunion, Saint-Denis, France
dominique.gay@univ-reunion.fr
[2] Orange Labs, Paris, France
alexis.bondu@orange.com
[3] Orange Labs, Lannion, France
{vincent.lemaire,marc.boulle,fabrice.clerot}@orange.com

Abstract. Multivariate Time Series Classification (MTSC) has attracted increasing research attention in the past years due to the wide range applications in e.g., action/activity recognition, EEG/ECG classification, etc. In this paper, we open a novel path to tackle with MTSC: a *relational* way. The multiple dimensions of MTS are represented in a relational data scheme, then a propositionalisation technique (based on classical aggregation/selection functions from the relational data field) is applied to build interpretable features from secondary tables to "flatten" the data. Finally, the MTS flattened data are classified using a selective Naïve Bayes classifier. Experimental validation on various benchmark data sets show the relevance of the suggested approach.

Keywords: Multivariate Time Series Classification · Feature selection · Bayesian modeling · Propositionalisation · Interpretable models

1 Introduction

Multivariate Time Series Classification (MTSC) arise from many application areas [1], e.g., human activity recognition, motion/gesture classification, ECG/EEG classification, audio spectra, handwriting, manufacturing classification, etc.

For an incoming d-dimensional MTS, $\tau = \langle X^1, X^2, \ldots, X^d \rangle$ where, for $i = 1..d$, $X^i = \langle (t_{1_i}, x_{1_i}), (t_{2_i}, x_{2_i}), \ldots, (t_{m_i}, x_{m_i}) \rangle$ are univariate time series (with $x_{k_i} \in \mathbb{R}$ the value of the X^i series at time t_{k_i}), the goal is to predict the value of a categorical target variable, say label, given a training set of labeled MTS.

While the literature for *univariate* TSC is substantial [3], existing approaches generally cannot be straightforwardly translated for MTSC problems. Besides recent deep learning based approaches [13–15], various effective methods have been suggested for MTSC: e.g., considering the reputation of Dynamic Time

© Springer Nature Switzerland AG 2020
M. Song et al. (Eds.): DaWaK 2020, LNCS 12393, pp. 316–330, 2020.
https://doi.org/10.1007/978-3-030-59065-9_25

Warping (DTW) Nearest Neighbor for the univariate case, two different general-izations for MTS have been tried [21]. With SMTS [5], Baydogan et al. proceed a two-step random forest approach for bag-of-words modeling then classifica-tion; subsequently they suggest LPS [6] which builds a bag-of-words representa-tion based on the leaves of regression trees trained on segments extracted from MTS; and thereafter, they also introduce AutoRegressive Forests (ARF [22]) for MTSC. Karlsson et al. [16] exploit tree ensembles over randomly selected shapelets (gRSF). Furthermore, Schäfer & Leser suggest WEASEL+MUSE [20] which extends WEASEL [19] to build discriminative features, based on symbolic Fourier approximation and bag-of-patterns, to feed a logistic regression model. They also led benchmark comparative experiments with the above representa-tive contenders on a well-known repository of 20 MTS data sets [4]. In terms of predictive performance, the results indicates that WEASEL+MUSE and a deep learning architecture, MLSTM-FCN [15], take the lead of the benchmark even if there is no statistically significant difference of performance with gRSF, SMTS, LPS and ARF methods.

In this paper, in order to tackle with MTSC, we open and explore a new path in which multivariate time series will be seen as multi-relational data.

As a motivating example, we consider the 4-class BasicMotions MTSC data set [1]. Basic Motions (standing, walking, running and playing badminton) are the classes of the problem and are described by 6-dimensional MTS collected through 3D accelerometer data, i.e., (x, y, z), and 3D gyroscope data, i.e., $(roll, pitch, yaw)$. In this con-text, considering the variable $v = min(DerivativeValue(pitch))$, i.e., the minimum value the derivative transform of the 5th dimension, and its discretization into four informa-tive intervals, the contingency table

Table 1. Context: 4-class BasicMotions data (40 series of length 100, over 6 dimen-sions – 3D from accelerometer (x, y, z) and 3D from gyroscope (roll, pitch, yaw). Class-contingency table for the discretiza-tion of the constructed variable $v = min(DerivativeValue(pitch))$, i.e., the mini-mum value of the derivative transform of the pitch dimension.

v	c_1	c_2	c_3	c_4
$v \leq -7.8$	10	0	0	0
$-7.8 < v \leq -2.2$	0	10	0	0
$-2.2 < v \leq -0.624$	0	0	0	10
$-0.624 < v$	0	0	10	0

(see Table 1) indicates a perfect discrimination of the four classes. A straight-forward interpretation highlights that the minimum value of the pitch speed is characteristic of the different class motions.

As far as we know, MTSC have not yet been approached from a relational data classification point of view. Our approach, called KMTS, brings a method-ological contribution to MTSC literature as it generalizes the underlying con-cepts of the above intuitive example to efficiently extract simple and inter-pretable features for MTSC, as follows: *(i)*, firstly, we transform the original MTS into multiple representations which are stored in secondary tables as in relational data scheme; *(ii)*, then, informative and robust descriptors are extracted from relational data, using a regularized Bayesian propositionalisation method; *(iii)*, thirdly, a selective Naïve Bayes classifier is trained on the obtained flattened data.

The rest of the paper successively presents the main concepts of our KMTS approach in Sect. 2, the experimental validation in Sect. 3 and opens future perspectives after concluding in Sect. 4.

2   MTSC via a Relational Way

Our approach, KMTS, is based on *(i)* the computation of multiple yet simple representations of time series, and their storage in a relational data scheme, *(ii)* a recently suggested approach for relational data classification [10] using feature construction through propositionalisation and, supervised feature selection and classification through a selective Naïve Bayes classifier [9]. In the following, we describe these two steps with a particular attention to make the paper self-contained.

2.1   Multiple Representations of MTS in Relational Schemes

Since [2], a consensus has emerged from the TSC community that transforming time series from the time domain to an alternative data space is one of the best catalyst for accuracy improvement. As recent methods [7,18] has proven to achieve top accuracy results on transformed univariate time series, we also generates six simple transformations of the dimensions of MTS commonly used in the literature in addition to the original representation:

- **Derivatives:** We use derivatives (D) and double derivatives (DD) of the original time series. These transformations allow us to represent the local evolution of the series *(i.e., increasing/decreasing, acceleration/deceleration).*
- **Cumulative sums:** We also use simple (S) and double (SS) cumulative Sums of the series, computed using the trapeze method. These transformations allow us to represent the global cumulated evolution of the series.
- **Auto-correlation:** The (ACF) transformation describes the correlation between values of the signal at different times and thus allows us to represent auto-correlation structures like repeating patterns in the time series. The transformation by auto-correlation is:

$$\tau_{i\rho} = <(t_1, \rho_1), ..., (t_m, \rho_m)> \quad \text{where} \quad \rho_k = \frac{\sum_{j=1}^{j=m-k}(x_j - \bar{x}).(x_{j+k} - \bar{x})}{m.s^2}$$

and where $\bar{x}$ and s^2 are the mean and variance of the original series.
- **Power Spectrum:** A time series can be decomposed in a linear combination of sines and cosines with various amplitudes and frequencies. This decomposition is known as the Fourier transform. The Power Spectrum (PS) is: $PS(\tau_i) = <(f_1, a_1), ..., (f_n, a_n)>$, where f_k represents the frequency domain, a_k the power of the signal and n the number of considered frequency values (by default $n = m$). This transformation is commonly used in signal processing and encodes the original series into the frequency domain.

In order to keep the whole procedure time-efficient, among the numerous representations existing in the literature, we picked some of thoses that can be computed with at most sub-quadratic time complexity: e.g., the fast Fourier transform allows to produce ACF and PS representation in $O(m \log m)$, where m stands for the series' length.

To gather the various computed representations, we investigate two different relational data schemes. In every case, the root table is made of two attributes (columns), the series ID and the class value. Depending on the scheme, secondary tables are designed as follows:

- one representation per secondary table (i.e. 7 tables). In this scheme, in Fig. 1, each table is described by the following attributes: the series' ID (linked to the one from the primary table), the "x-axis" (i.e. time or frequency for PS representation), plus one column for each dimension. We refer to this scheme as 7rep_7T.
- all-in-one scheme: only one secondary table containing all representations of all dimensions of the MTS, i.e., $7 \times d$ attributes plus the series ID and the x-axis. We refer to this scheme as 7rep_1T.

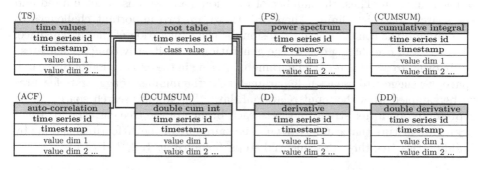

Fig. 1. Relational scheme, 7rep_7T, where each of the seven secondary tables holds a representation of the MTS.

2.2 KMTS: Interpretable Feature Selection and Classification

Feature Construction Through Propositionalisation - In order to build features from secondary tables, we use propositionalisation; that is the process of adding columns containing information extracted from secondary tables to the root table [17]. For the MTS case, propositionalisation may generate different aggregate features from various representations of the multiple dimensions. The introductive variable v, i.e., the *minimum of the derived time series in the fifth dimension* is an example of such aggregate feature. To avoid untractable search space, propositionalisation techniques usually exploit a restricted language for feature generation, i.e., using a finite set of construction rules. In our approach, a construction rule is similar to a function in a programming language. It is defined by its name, the list of its operands and its return value. The operands and the return value are typed. The operands can be a column of a table, the output of another rule *(i.e. another generated feature)*, or a constant coming from the training set.

Since the variables that define time series are numerical, and for interpretability purposes, we use a combination of:

- *(i)* historical and interpretable aggregate functions from relational data base domain dedicated to numerical variables, namely, *min, max, sum, count (distinct), median, mean, stdev.*
- *(ii)* a *Selection* function to allow restriction to intervals of timestamp/frequency and value variables in secondary tables.

Thus, another example of aggregate feature using the selection operator could be: *Max(Selection(derivative, 14 < timestamp < 69), ValueDim5)*, i.e., the maximum value of the derivative transform of dimension 5, in the time interval [14; 69]. Here, the *Max* function is applied on the output of another construction rule, the *Selection* exploited to identify a particular time period.

In this context, the search space for the features that can be generated consists of all possible function compositions, only limited by the type of operands of each function. Thus, the number of function compositions is not limited and the search space is infinite. Therefore, there are two important challenges to overcome: i) the combinatorial explosion for the exploration of the search space; ii) the risk of over-fitting due to the generation of arbitrarily complex features.

In order to avoid non-trivial parameter setting in the exploration of the search space, we suggest to use a single parameter K, the number of aggregate features to be sampled from the input relational data. The infinite search space can be represented by a tree structure where each branch of the tree corresponds to an aggregate feature that can be drawn. The sampling of the K features is done by building this tree through sequential steps *(denoted by 1, 2, 3, 4 in Fig. 2)*.

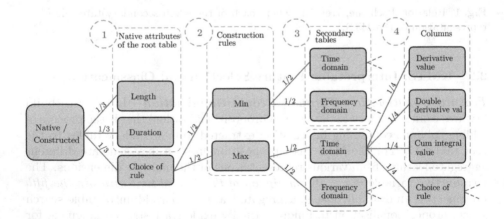

Fig. 2. Feature construction tree example for one dimension.

Due to space limitation, in Fig. 2, we only consider one dimension and 3 out of 6 representations in the *all-in-one* schema. The sequential steps for feature sampling are:

- (step 1) consists in choosing either a native feature belonging to the root table, or the generation of an additional feature. Here, we assume that the root table contains two native features that describe the length and the duration of the time series. An additional choice to generate an additional feature is represented by the node named *"Choice of rule"*.
- (step 2) consists in choosing the construction rule, here, the *Min* or *Max* functions. The other steps correspond to the operand choice of these two functions.
- (step 3) consists in choosing the secondary table
- (step 4) corresponds to the choice of the column on which to apply the current function. Once again, there is an additional choice that allows the algorithm to generate the input of the current function *(Min or Max)* by applying another construction rule.

While the width of the feature construction tree is finite because the set of the construction rules and the secondary tables are finite, by contrast, the depth of the tree is infinite due to the potentially infinite function compositions. In order to sample K features from such a tree, the drawing of features follows a particular prior distribution which is a Hierarchy of Multinomial Distributions with potentially Infinite Depth *(HMDID)* [10]. This HMDID distribution is represented in Fig. 2 by the probabilities assigned to the edges between the nodes of the tree. The algorithmic solution consists in iteratively moving a collection of tokens down the tree, according to the HMDID distribution. The number of tokens that move forward is finite, which means that the tree is only partially and progressively explored. Consequently, this algorithm can efficiently draw aggregate features with restrictions to the available computer memory.

Feature Selection Through Supervised Discretisation and Classification - After propositionalisation, aggregate features of the main table are not guaranteed to be class-informative. As all generated features are numerical due to the nature of aggregate functions, a supervised pre-processing step is led for filtering uninformative features and partition them into intervals, that is univariate discretisation.

In the Bayesian framework [8], supervised discretisation of a variable X is seen as a model selection problem and solved in Bayesian way through optimization algorithms. According the Maximum A Posteriori (MAP) approach, the best discretisation model M_X is the one that maximizes the probability of a discretisation model given the input data D, i.e., $P(M_X \mid D) \propto P(M_X) \times P(D \mid M_X)$. The prior $P(M_X)$ and the likelihood $P(D \mid M_X)$ are both computed with the parameters of a specific discretization which is uniquely identified by the number of intervals, the bound of the intervals and the class frequencies in each interval. Therefore, the prior exploits the hierarchy of parameters and is uniform at each stage of the hierarchy.

Switching to negative logarithm refers to information theory and defines our evaluation criterion, noted c (for cost in Eq. 1).

$$c(M_X) = -\log(P(M_X)) - \log(P(D \mid M_X)) = L(M_X) + L(D|M_X) \quad (1)$$

The prior part of the optimization criterion favors simple models with few intervals, and the likelihood part favors models that fit the data regardless of their complexity. In terms of information theory, this criterion is interpreted as coding lengths: the term $L(M_X)$ represents the number of bits used to describe the model and $L(D|M_X)$ represents the number of bits used to encode the target variable with the model, given the model M_X. Greedy bottom-up algorithms [8] allows to find the most probable model given the input data in $O(N \log N)$ time complexity, where N is the number of time series.

In order to avoid the construction of unnecessary complex features, we add a construction cost (related to the propositionalisation procedure) to the prior part of c, resulting in $c^*(M_X)$ (Eq. 2). Intuitively, the construction cost $L(X)$ is even more important when the considered aggregate feature X is complex. The added construction cost modifies the balance between the prior and likelihood terms by taking into count the complexity of the evaluated feature. The construction cost $L(X)$ is recursively defined due to the multiple function compositions. In Eq. 3, the term $log(K+1)$ describes the cost of choosing to generate a new feature in addition to the K native features (if any) of the root table. The term $log(R)$ describes the cost of choosing a particular construction rule among R possible rules. The recursive side appears with the term $\sum_{o \in \mathcal{R}} L(X_o)$ that describes the cost of constructing a new feature for each operand of the current construction rule $\mathcal{R}$. A natural trade-off appears: the more complex the feature is, the more it is penalized by the prior, and the higher the likelihood have to be compensated $L(X)$. Compression gain (CG) evaluates the MAP model M_X^* by comparing its coding length with the one of M_X^0 that includes a single interval (Eq. 2). Features with a negative CG are considered as uninformative.

$$c^*(M_X) = L(X) + L(M_X) + L(D|M_X) \quad \text{and} \quad CG = 1 - \frac{c^*(M_X^*)}{c^*(M_X^0)} \quad (2)$$

$$\text{where } L(X) = log(K+1) + log(R) + \sum_{o \in \mathcal{R}} L(X_o) \quad (3)$$

Thus, the cost criterion c^* is used to pre-process the informative aggregate features by training discretisation models. Then, all these univariate preprocessied models are gathered together and used to learn a Selective Naïve Bayes [9] (SNB). The SNB classifier aims to select the most informative subset of features by using a specifically designed compression-based criterion. This way, the whole KMTS procedure is regularized to avoid unnecessary complex features and models, thus avoiding over-fitting.

3   Experimental Validation

The experimental evaluation of our approach KMTS are performed to discuss the following questions:

Q_1 Concerning KMTS, how does the predictive performance evolve w.r.t. the number generated features and relational schemes? How many relevant features are selected? Are there preferred dimensions/representations for feature selection? And what about the time efficiency of the whole process?

Q_2 Are the performance of KMTS comparable with state-of-the-art MTSC methods?

Experimental Protocol and Data Sets - Most of the literature are based on M. Baydogan 20 data sets [4]. Recently, in 2018, pursuing the success of the largest univariate TSC repository, the UEA team also released a 30 MTSC repository [1] with some overlapping with Baydogan repository. Both repositories exhibit a large variety of MTSC application domains with various numbers of dimensions, classes and series' lengths. Predefined train/test sets are provided and we used it per se.

3.1   Accuracy Evolution w.r.t. the Number of Features

We study the evolution of accuracy w.r.t. K, the number of extracted features on the 30 data sets of UEA repository [1]. In Table 2, we report accuracy results of KMTS for increasing $K = 10, 100, 1000, 10000$ on original MTS, i.e., without transformations (notice that similar behaviors are observed when using the 7 representations). As expected, accuracy increases with K. While we can expect better accuracy from even more generated features (but with increasing computational time), a few more training MTS seem to also improve accuracy. This can be seen in the $10 - CV$ column (Table 2), where we report 10-folds cross-validation accuracy results. Indeed, when using 90% of available data for training, KMTS achieves better average results on 23/30 data sets (e.g., for Ering and Handwriting data). Another important observation is about the "stable-with-K" but poor accuracy results (for AtrialFibrillation, FaceDetection, FingerMovements, HandMovementDirection MotorImagery, SelfRegulationSCP2 and StandWalkJump data). For these data, KMTS found no class-informative attributes out of the 10000 generated, the major class is predicted, therefore the bad accuracies. Since KMTS is a regularized approach based on estimated per-class frequencies, data with (very) small training set size (AtrialFibrillation, StandWalkJump, ...) are a difficult task. For FaceDetection data, we may conjecture that KMTS has high bias, thus aggregate features are not the good way to tackle with. Notice that generalizations of DTW-NN also obtain poor accuracy results on these data sets [1].

Table 2. Accuracy results for KMTS with K, incremental number of extracted features on original data, all dimensions in a secondary table and using 7 representations in the two suggested schemes (1 secondary table for all dimensions and their representations vs 1 secondary table for each representation).

Data sets	Train	Test	Dim	Length	Classes	Original representation					7 representations	
						$K = 10$	$K = 100$	$K = 1000$	$K = 10000$	$K = 10000$ (10-CV)	7rep.1T	7rep.7T
ArticularyWordRecognition	275	300	9	144	25	0.2467	0.9500	0.9800	0.9833	0.9878±0.0137	0.9800	0.9767
AtrialFibrillation	15	15	2	640	3	0.3333	0.3333	0.3333	0.3333	0.3333±0.0000	0.3333	0.3333
BasicMotions	40	40	6	100	4	0.9750	1.0000	1.0000	1.0000	1.0000±0.0000	0.9250	1.0000
CharacterTrajectories	1422	1436	3	182	20	0.7946	0.9554	0.9735	0.9735	0.9811±0.0055	0.9708	0.9861
Cricket	108	72	6	1197	12	0.7639	0.9583	0.9583	0.9861	0.9833±0.0255	0.9583	0.9722
DuckDuckGeese	60	40	1345	270	5	0.2000	0.3000	0.4800	0.4600	0.5100±0.1640	0.3800	0.4600
EigenWorms	128	131	6	17984	5	0.5954	0.7481	0.8168	0.8550	0.8725±0.0670	0.8779	0.9237
Epilepsy	137	138	3	206	4	0.7681	0.9493	0.9710	0.9710	0.9855±0.0178	0.9783	0.9783
ERing	30	30	4	65	6	0.4370	0.5481	0.7111	0.7148	0.9733±0.0200	0.7926	0.8037
EthanolConcentration	261	263	3	1751	4	0.2510	0.3840	0.4411	0.4335	0.4444±0.0596	0.2814	0.4183
FaceDetection	5890	3524	144	62	2	0.5000	0.5000	0.4997	0.4900	0.5364±0.0114	0.5119	0.5000
FingerMovements	316	100	28	50	2	0.4900	0.4900	0.4900	0.4900	0.4951±0.0060	0.4900	0.4900
HandMovementDirection	320	147	10	400	4	0.2027	0.2027	0.2027	0.2027	0.2993±0.0062	0.2027	0.2027
Handwriting	150	850	3	152	26	0.0835	0.1600	0.2506	0.2941	0.5800±0.0366	0.3129	0.3094
Heartbeat	204	205	61	405	2	0.6439	0.7073	0.7220	0.7610	0.7677±0.0609	0.7220	0.7463
InsectWingbeat	30000	20000	200	78	10	0.2454	0.5664	0.6576	0.6618	0.6679±0.0062	0.4349	0.6645
JapaneseVowels	270	370	12	29	9	0.7000	0.9595	0.9541	0.9595	0.9703±0.0191	0.7811	0.9595
Libras	180	180	2	45	15	0.4500	0.7278	0.8167	0.8167	0.9000±0.0468	0.8944	0.9222
LSST	2459	2466	6	36	14	0.4700	0.5264	0.5446	0.5568	0.5614±0.0161	0.6269	0.5714
MotorImagery	278	100	64	3000	2	0.5000	0.5000	0.5000	0.5000	0.4973±0.0054	0.5000	0.5000
NATOPS	180	180	24	51	6	0.6000	0.7833	0.7667	0.9222	0.9389±0.0324	0.8444	0.8611
PEMS-SF	267	173	963	144	7	0.7688	0.9538	0.9769	0.9769	1.0000±0.0000	0.9884	0.9884
PenDigits	7494	3498	2	8	10	0.5560	0.8473	0.8988	0.9108	0.9562±0.0055	0.9551	0.9397
PhonemeSpectra	3315	3353	11	217	39	0.0820	0.0835	0.0892	0.0957	0.1113±0.0068	0.1712	0.1807
RacketSports	151	152	6	30	4	0.5066	0.7763	0.8224	0.8816	0.9106±0.0338	0.8026	0.8224
SelfRegulationSCP1	268	293	6	896	2	0.7850	0.8225	0.8055	0.8123	0.8271±0.0486	0.8191	0.9044
SelfRegulationSCP2	200	180	7	1152	2	0.5000	0.5000	0.5000	0.5000	0.5000±0.0000	0.5000	0.5000
SpokenArabicDigits	6599	2199	13	93	10	0.5730	0.8549	0.9541	0.9700	0.9779±0.0037	0.9741	0.9718
StandWalkJump	12	15	4	2500	3	0.3333	0.3333	0.3333	0.3333	0.2333±0.1528	0.3333	0.3333
UWaveGestureLibrary	120	320	3	315	8	0.2250	0.7750	0.8813	0.9000	0.9432±0.0384	0.8969	0.8750

3.2   About Relational Schemes

The two last columns of Table 2 reports accuracy results of KMTS for $K = 10000$ using the two suggested relational data schemes 7rep_1T and 7rep_7T. Considering Win-Tie-Loss versus original MTS data with $K = 10000$, 7rep_1T scores 11-6-13 and 7rep_7T scores 13-9-8. The scheme with seven representations stored in seven secondary tables take the advantage in terms of accuracy results and we focus on this scheme for the rest of the experiments. This also confirms the benefit of using additional simple representations of original times series to improve predictive performance.

3.3   Distribution of Selected Features, Representations and Dimensions

As KMTS select informative features to build a Naïve Bayes classifier, we study the distribution of informative and selected features for each data set in Fig. 3. For some data sets, no informative attribute is found and poor accuracy results are obtained as explained earlier. For most of the other data sets, more than 100 informative features are found except for Ering, DuckDuckGeese which contains a small number of training series. Furthermore, the number selected features (that are embarked in the SNB classifier) are generally an order of magnitude lesser than the number of informative ones.

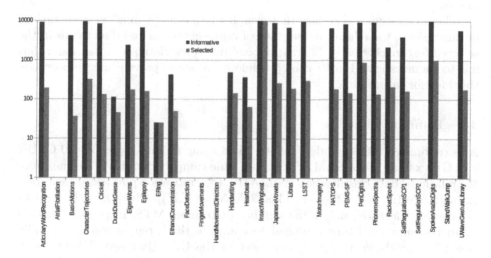

Fig. 3. Distribution of informative and selected features among the $K = 10000$ generated features, for each data set.

In Fig. 4, we study the relative distribution of the selected features into the seven representations for each data set. In most cases, all the seven representations are present in the selected features. A few exceptions stand: e.g., there is

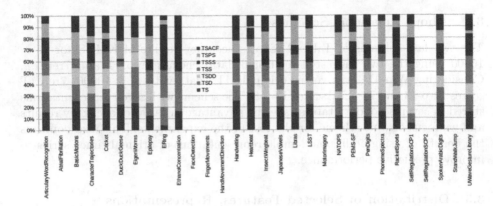

Fig. 4. Relative distribution of the seven representations among selected features in SNB for each data set.

no SS features for BasicMotions and EigenWorm data and relatively few PS features for HeartBeat and UWave data. Concerning the distribution of the selected features among the dimensions of MTS, we compute the percentage of dimensions not used in selected attributes: for most the data sets, all dimensions are present in the selected features, except for DuckDuckGeese (resp. Heartbeat and PEMS-SF) for which 95% (resp. 54% and 81%) of the available dimensions are unused.

These two studies also show that even if there is no "killing" representations or dimensions, the relative importance of representations and dimensions in the selected features is clearly different depending on the data set at hand and thus has to be investigated further for possible accuracy improvement; we postpone this idea for future work.

3.4   Running Time

All experiments are run under Ubuntu 18.04 using an Intel Core i5-6400 CPU@ 2.70 GHz x4 and 16 Go RAM. The overall time complexity of KMTS comes from the relational data classification method [10] (discretisation plus feature selection through selective Naïve Bayes) and is $\mathcal{O}(K.Nlog(K.N))$, where K is the number of generated features and N the number of training MTS. In practice, with a small computational time overhead to compute the 7 representations, KMTS is efficient as shown in Fig. 5. For most of the UEA data sets, KMTS (with $K = 10000$) runs in less than 100 s. For InsectWingbeat, the biggest data set with 50000 MTS, about 3 h are needed. In Fig. 6, we report the evolution of running time w.r.t. K for each data sets. As we observed earlier that increasing K leads to better accuracy, it is good to notice that it also means additional computational cost. For example, for InsectWingbeat, setting $K = 10^5$ to reach better accuracy will demand about $10^5 s$ of computation.

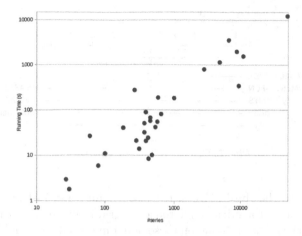

Fig. 5. Average running time results (10-cross-validation) vs. data set size (number of series) of KMTS on original representations for $K = 10000$ features on UEA repository data sets.

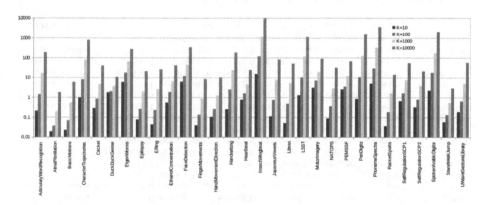

Fig. 6. Average running time results (10-CV) of KMTS on original representations for incremental K number of features on UEA repository data sets.

3.5 Predictive Performance Comparison with State-of-the-Art

In order to compare the predictive performance of KMTS with state-of-the-art MTSC methods, we use the Baydogan repository [4] that is composed of 20 data sets (6 of which are also in the UEA repository). KMTS with $K = 10000$ using 7rep_7T is compared with 9 contenders: WEASEL [19], SMTS [5], LPS [6], ARF [22], DTWi [21], ARK [11], gRSF [16], MLSTM-FCN [15] and MUSE. All results are taken from Schäfer & Leser MUSE paper [20]. Full results are reported in Table 3 and the critical difference diagram [12] stemming from Friedman test with post-hoc Nemenyi test is shown in Fig. 7.

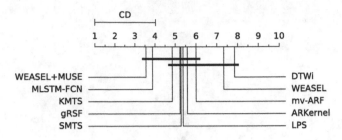

Fig. 7. Critical difference diagram

KMTS rises to the third place in terms of mean rank, just after MUSE and MLSTM-FCN. Since the critical difference diagram indicates that no significant difference of performance is found on these benchmark data sets, KMTS is among the best MTSC methods of the literature.

Table 3. Accuracy results comparison with state-of-the-art MTSC methods on Baydogan repository [4]. Results are reported from [20].

Data sets	WEASEL	SMTS	LPS	ARF	DTWi	ARK	gRSF	MLSTM-FCN	MUSE	KMTS
ArabicDigits	0.9455	0.9640	0.9710	0.9520	0.9080	0.9880	0.9750	0.9900	0.9918	0.9836
AUSLAN	0.7586	0.9470	0.7540	0.9340	0.7270	0.9180	0.9550	0.9500	0.9909	0.9607
CharTraj	0.9738	0.9920	0.9650	0.9280	0.9484	0.9000	0.9940	0.9900	0.9734	0.9949
CMUsubject16	0.9655	0.9970	1.0000	1.0000	0.9300	1.0000	1.0000	1.0000	1.0000	0.9655
DigitShapes	1.0000	1.0000	1.0000	1.0000	0.9375	1.0000	1.0000	1.0000	1.0000	1.0000
ECG	0.8500	0.8180	0.8200	0.7850	0.7900	0.8200	0.8800	0.8700	0.8800	0.8300
JapVowels	0.7892	0.9690	0.9510	0.9590	0.9622	0.9840	0.8000	1.0000	0.9757	0.9730
KickvsPunch	0.8000	0.8200	0.9000	0.9760	0.6000	0.9270	1.0000	0.9000	1.0000	0.6000
Libras	0.7280	0.9090	0.9030	0.9450	0.8880	0.9520	0.9110	0.9700	0.8944	0.9487
LP1	0.8000	0.8560	0.8620	0.8240	0.7600	0.8600	0.8400	0.8000	0.9400	0.9600
LP2	0.6330	0.7600	0.7040	0.6260	0.7000	0.6340	0.6670	0.8000	0.7333	0.5000
LP3	0.6670	0.7600	0.7200	0.7700	0.5666	0.5670	0.6330	0.7300	0.9000	0.7667
LP4	0.8670	0.8950	0.9100	0.9060	0.8667	0.9600	0.8667	0.8900	0.9600	0.8933
LP5	0.5900	0.6500	0.6900	0.6800	0.5400	0.4700	0.4500	0.6500	0.6900	0.6300
NetFlow	0.9326	0.9770	0.9680	-	0.9756	-	0.9140	0.9500	0.9382	0.9869
PenDigits	0.8338	0.9170	0.9080	0.9230	0.9270	0.9520	0.9320	0.9700	0.9128	0.8915
Shapes	1.0000	1.0000	1.0000	1.0000	1.0000	1.0000	1.0000	1.0000	1.0000	1.0000
UWave	0.7627	0.9410	0.9800	0.9520	0.9158	0.9040	0.9290	0.9700	0.9159	0.9531
Wafer	0.9911	0.9650	0.9620	0.9310	0.9743	0.9680	0.9920	0.9900	0.9967	0.9900
WalkvsRun	1.0000	1.0000	1.0000	1.0000	1.0000	1.0000	1.0000	1.0000	1.0000	1.0000
mean rank	7.3250	5.2750	5.3750	6.0000	7.8500	5.5750	5.2250	3.8750	3.5500	4.8500

4   Conclusion and Perspectives

Our methodological contribution, KMTS, explores a relational way for multivariate time series classification (MTSC). Storing multiple representations of MTS in relational data scheme and interpretable feature construction/selection are the key ideas of KMTS, which end up with efficient and effective classification of MTS. The whole process achieves very competitive accuracy results compared with recent state-of-the-art contenders on benchmark data sets. In addition, the suggested approach allows interpretable features to be extracted from the dimensions of MTS and their alternative representations, resulting in a very advantageous compromise between (i) computation time, (ii) accuracy results and (iii) features interpretability.

To achieve better accuracy results, KMTS could be improved in many ways: *(i)* the ending Bayesian classifier could be swapped for e.g., ensemble methods like random forests or xgboost; *(ii)* a closer look at the data domain where KMTS fails to find informative features, could help in finding the adequate representations and aggregate functions commonly used by domain experts in their respective domain; *(iii)* KMTS could also be wrapped in a feed forward/backward selection procedure to focus on the most informative dimensions and representations as suggested in [7].

References

1. Bagnall, A.J., et al.: The UEA multivariate time series classification archive, 2018. CoRR abs/1811.00075 (2018). http://timeseriesclassification.com
2. Bagnall, A.J., Davis, L.M., Hills, J., Lines, J.: Transformation based ensembles for time series classification. In: Proceedings of the Twelfth SIAM International Conference on Data Mining, (SDM 2012), Anaheim, California, USA, 26–28 April 2012, pp. 307–318 (2012)
3. Bagnall, A., Lines, J., Bostrom, A., Large, J., Keogh, E.: The great time series classification bake off: a review and experimental evaluation of recent algorithmic advances. Data Min. Knowl. Disc. **31**(3), 606–660 (2016). https://doi.org/10.1007/s10618-016-0483-9
4. Baydogan, M.G.: Multivariate time series classification data sets (2019). http://www.mustafabaydogan.com
5. Baydogan, M.G., Runger, G.: Learning a symbolic representation for multivariate time series classification. Data Min. Knowl. Disc. **29**(2), 400–422 (2014). https://doi.org/10.1007/s10618-014-0349-y
6. Baydogan, M.G., Runger, G.: Time series representation and similarity based on local autopatterns. Data Min. Knowl. Disc. **30**(2), 476–509 (2015). https://doi.org/10.1007/s10618-015-0425-y
7. Bondu, A., Gay, D., Lemaire, V., Boullé, M., Cervenka, E.: FEARS: a feature and representation selection approach for time series classification. In: Proceedings of The 11th Asian Conference on Machine Learning, ACML 2019, Nagoya, Japan, 17–19 November 2019, pp. 379–394 (2019)
8. Boullé, M.: MODL: a Bayes optimal discretization method for continuous attributes. Mach. Learn. **65**(1), 131–165 (2006)
9. Boullé, M.: Compression-based averaging of selective Naive Bayes classifiers. J. Mach. Learn. Res. **8**, 1659–1685 (2007)
10. Boullé, M., Charnay, C., Lachiche, N.: A scalable robust and automatic propositionalization approach for Bayesian classification of large mixed numerical and categorical data. Mach. Learn. **108**(2), 229–266 (2019)
11. Cuturi, M., Doucet, A.: Autoregressive kernels for time series. CoRR abs/1101.0673 (2011). https://arxiv.org/abs/1101.0673

12. Demšar, J.: Statistical comparisons of classifiers over multiple data sets. JMLR **7**, 1–30 (2006)
13. Ismail Fawaz, H., Forestier, G., Weber, J., Idoumghar, L., Muller, P.-A.: Deep learning for time series classification: a review. Data Min. Knowl. Disc. **33**(4), 917–963 (2019). https://doi.org/10.1007/s10618-019-00619-1
14. Hsu, E.-Y., Liu, C.-L., Tseng, V.S.: Multivariate time series early classification with interpretability using deep learning and attention mechanism. In: Yang, Q., Zhou, Z.-H., Gong, Z., Zhang, M.-L., Huang, S.-J. (eds.) PAKDD 2019. LNCS (LNAI), vol. 11441, pp. 541–553. Springer, Cham (2019). https://doi.org/10.1007/978-3-030-16142-2_42
15. Karim, F., Majumdar, S., Darabi, H., Harford, S.: Multivariate LSTM-FCNS for time series classification. Neural Netw. **116**, 237–245 (2019)
16. Karlsson, I., Papapetrou, P., Boström, H.: Generalized random shapelet forests. Data Min. Knowl. Disc. **30**(5), 1053–1085 (2016). https://doi.org/10.1007/s10618-016-0473-y
17. Lachiche, N.: Propositionalization. In: Sammut, C., Webb, G.I. (eds.) Encyclopedia of Machine Learning and Data Mining, pp. 1025–1031. Springer, Boston (2017). https://doi.org/10.1007/978-1-4899-7687-1_686
18. Lines, J., Taylor, S., Bagnall, A.J.: Time series classification with HIVE-COTE: the hierarchical vote collective of transformation-based ensembles. ACM Trans. Knowl. Disc. Data **12**(5), 52:1–52:35 (2018)
19. Schäfer, P., Leser, U.: Fast and accurate time series classification with WEASEL. In: Proceedings of the 2017 ACM on Conference on Information and Knowledge Management, CIKM 2017, Singapore, 06–10 November 2017, pp. 637–646 (2017)
20. Schäfer, P., Leser, U.: Multivariate time series classification with WEASEL+MUSE. CoRR abs/1711.11343 (2017). http://arxiv.org/abs/1711.11343
21. Shokoohi-Yekta, M., Wang, J., Keogh, E.J.: On the non-trivial generalization of dynamic time warping to the multi-dimensional case. In: Proceedings of the 2015 SIAM International Conference on Data Mining, Vancouver, BC, Canada, 30 April–2 May 2015, pp. 289–297 (2015)
22. Tuncel, K.S., Baydogan, M.G.: Autoregressive forests for multivariate time series modeling. Pattern Recogn. **73**, 202–215 (2018)

Unsupervised Learning

Behave or Be Detected! Identifying Outlier Sequences by Their Group Cohesion

Martha Tatusch[(✉)] [iD], Gerhard Klassen[iD], and Stefan Conrad[iD]

Heinrich Heine University, Universitätsstr. 1, 40225 Düsseldorf, Germany
{tatusch,klassen,stefan.conrad}@hhu.de

Abstract. Since the amount of sequentially recorded data is constantly increasing, the analysis of time series (TS), and especially the identification of anomalous points and subsequences, is nowadays an important field of research. Many approaches consider only a single TS, but in some cases multiple sequences need to be investigated. In 2019 we presented a new method to detect behavior-based outliers in TS which analyses relations of sequences to their peers. Therefore we clustered data points of TS per timestamp and calculated distances between the resulting clusters of different points in time. We realized this by evaluating the number of peers a TS is moving with. We defined a stability measure for time series and subsequences, which is used to detect the outliers. Originally we considered cluster splits but did not take merges into account. In this work we present two major modifications to our previous work, namely the introduction of the jaccard index as a distance measure for clusters and a weighting function, which enables behavior-based outlier detection in larger TS. We evaluate our modifications separately and in conjunction on two real and one artificial data set. The adjustments lead to well reasoned and sound results, which are robust regarding larger TS.

Keywords: Outlier detection · Time series analysis · Clustering

1 Introduction

With increasing understanding about the value of data and the rising amount of connected sensors in the world of the IoT, more data is recorded every day than ever before. This enables a time aware analysis of the accumulated data by regarding it as time series. The time-driven data view not only allows the extraction of trends and seasons but also an interpretation of behavior. This is especially the case when several time series are considered at the same time. In our paper [20] we introduced an outlier detection algorithm based on the relative behavior of time series. As this was a novel approach we were aware of some drawbacks and application specific requirements. In concrete we noticed that earlier clusters had a high impact and that a cluster split would not be treated the same way as a cluster merge. While the latter is an application

© Springer Nature Switzerland AG 2020
M. Song et al. (Eds.): DaWaK 2020, LNCS 12393, pp. 333–347, 2020.
https://doi.org/10.1007/978-3-030-59065-9_26

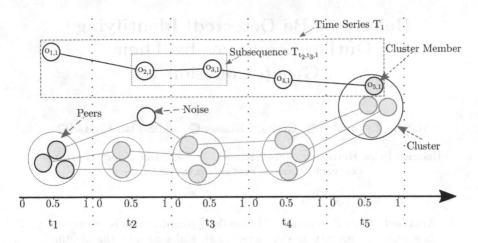

Fig. 1. Illustration of relevant terms regarding the time from t_1 to t_5.

dependent circumstance the first causes a high dependence on early points in time, which is not wanted in most cases. In order to overcome these drawbacks we now introduce a weighting function and a new way of calculating the cluster proportions of two clusters. For this purpose we make use of the jaccard index which led to good results in [12] as well. Both extensions are tested separately and in conjunction. We highlight the differences and allow the user to choose carefully between those extensions - depending on his application.

Our original approach focuses on data sets with multivariate time series with discrete values, same length and equivalent time steps. Those time series are clustered per point in time and anomalous subsequences are detected by analysing the behavior of those. The behavior is defined as the change of peers over time. This leads us to the *subsequence_score* which represents the stability of a subsequence over time. An illustration of the relevant terms can be seen in Fig. 1.

With a calculated *outlier_score* for every subsequence and a threshold parameter τ we managed to detect anomalous time series. The outlier score depends on the subsequence score of a subsequence and the best subsequence score of a subsequence in the according cluster. In our work we differentiate three different types of outliers: *anomalous subsequences*, *intuitive outliers* and *noise*.

Our approach is different to other proposals which use cluster algorithms, as those either cluster time series as a whole [9,11,17], extract feature sets first [22], or consider subsequences of a single time series only [4]. None of the presented methods consider the cohesion of a time series regarding its peers. Our algorithm also differs from approaches which do not take time into account like [2] or which only regard subsequences of single time series [5,15]. In contrary to those methods, we assume an information gain for one sequence from other sequences which have a semantic correlation.

In this paper we show once again, that we can identify an impact of other time series to one time series that is different to the granger causality [10] and that this influence can be used to detect anomalous subsequences. The adaptations of our original algorithm are well motivated and lead to different but sound results.

2 Related Work

Algorithms which detect outliers in time series are no novelty. There are actually various specialized approaches for different applications. Most methods deal with one time series only, while fewer ones regard multiple time series at the same time. There are different types of outliers, such as significantly deviating data points, uncommon subsequence patterns in periodic time series or changing points, which indicate that the further course of the sequence will change.

In many cases outliers of any type are identified with adapted autoregressive-moving-average (ARMA) models [3, 16]. Although these techniques are performing very well in most cases and factually are state-of-the-art, they lack the implementation of exterior information like other semantic correlated time series. There are also other methods which make use of decomposition techniques such as STL [6]. These methods work on time series which can be actually decomposed, but fail if this is not the case. Finally there are presented works which use dynamic time warping (DTW) [18] in order to detect anomalies.

There are also approaches which tackle the problem of finding outliers in multiple time series. Similar to our algorithm these methods are using peers of a time series to determine whether it is anomalous or not. The most recent works use Probabilistic Suffix Trees (PST) [19] or Random Block Coordinate Descents (RBCD) [23] in order to detect suspicious time series or subsequences. In contrary to our approach, in which the behavior of a time series is the central idea, the named methods analyse the deviation of one time series to the others. Our assumption that the change or the adherence of a time series to its peers is a crucial difference to all present methods. This behavior centered view is implemented by clustering time series per timestamp which is similar to identifying its peers per point in time. Then the movement of this time series relative to its peers is analysed. The result of this is described as a subsequence score, which also can be viewed as the stability over time of a time series regarding the adherence to its peers. The degree of change, also called transition, is an important factor to the subsequence score. It is also essential in cluster evolution methods such as [12], which try to match clusters of different time points. Works of this kind usually introduce a parameter which determines whether the dissimilarity of two clusters is too big to match. However, a match of clusters is a very subjective task and highly dependent on the used definitions. Further this is not necessary in order to detect outliers and thus not relevant for our work. The approach of Landauer et al. [14] uses an anomaly score, which is based on transitions of a single time series. This is different to our method, since we use the information of multiple time series.

The analysis of time series behavior like presented in this paper not only detects surprisingly deviating data points and subsequences with regard to a single time series, but also identifies new, behavior-based outliers. Our approach is also different from those which cluster whole time series, since such approaches do not consider the cluster transitions, which is an expressive feature on its own. The algorithm presented in this paper is able to detect anomalous subsequences, although they would have been assigned to one cluster in a subsequence clustering.

3   Fundamentals

Before introducing the method, some basic definitions regarding time series analysis used in the underlying paper [20] and this work are given, since they may vary in literature. An illustration of them can be seen in Fig. 1.

Definition 1 (Time Series). *A multivariate time series $T = o_{t_1}, ..., o_{t_n}$ is an ordered set of n real valued data points of arbitrary dimension. The data points are chronologically ordered by their time of recording, with t_1 and t_n indicating the first and the last timestamp, respectively.*

Definition 2 (Data Set). *A data set $D = T_1, ..., T_m$ is a set of m time series of same length and equivalent points in time. The set of data points of all time series at a timestamp t_i is denoted as O_{t_i}.*

Definition 3 (Subsequence). *A subsequence $T_{t_i,t_j,l} = o_{t_i,l}, ..., o_{t_j,l}$ with $j > i$ is an ordered set of successive real valued data points beginning at time t_i and ending at t_j from time series T_l.*

Definition 4 (Cluster). *A cluster $C_{t_i,j} \subseteq O_{t_i}$ at time t_i, with $j \in \{1, ..., q\}$ being a unique identifier (e.g. counter) and q being the number of clusters, is a set of similar data points, identified by a cluster algorithm or human. This means that all clusters have distinct labels regardless of time.*

Definition 5 (Cluster Member). *A data point $o_{t_i,l}$ from time series T_l at time t_i, that is assigned to a cluster $C_{t_i,j}$ is called a member of cluster $C_{t_i,j}$.*

Definition 6 (Noise). *A data point $o_{t_i,l}$ from time series T_l at time t_i is considered as noise, if it is not assigned to any cluster.*

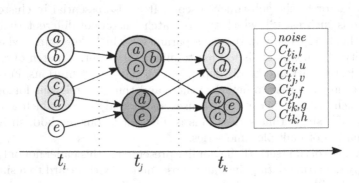

Fig. 2. Example for cluster transitions of time series $T_a, .., T_e$ over time.

Definition 7 (Clustering). *A clustering is the overall result of a clustering algorithm or the set of all clusters annotated by a human for all timestamps. In concrete it is the set* $\zeta = \{C_{t_1,1}, ..., C_{t_n,q}\} \cup Noise$.

An example for the above definitions can also be seen in Fig. 2. Five time series of a data set $D = T_a, T_b, T_c, T_d, T_e$ are clustered per timestamp for the time points t_i, t_j and t_k. The data points of a time series T_l are denoted by the identifier l for simplicity reasons. The shown clustering consists of six clusters. It can be described by the set $\zeta = \{C_{t_i,l}, C_{t_i,u}, C_{t_j,v}, C_{t_j,f}, C_{t_k,g}, C_{t_k,h}\} \cup \{o_{t_i,e}\}$. As $o_{t_i,e}$ is not assigned to any cluster in t_i, it is marked as noise for this timestamp. The data points $o_{t_i,a}, o_{t_i,b}$ of time series T_a and T_b in t_i are cluster members of the yellow cluster $C_{t_i,l}$.

4   Method

The cohesion of a sequence with its peers over time is described by the term *over-time stability*. Our approach is based on the assumption that unstable behavior over time indicates an irregularity. In order to rate the over-time stability of a sequence by means of a so called *subsequence_score*, the proportion of cluster members from earlier timestamps who migrated together into another cluster in later timestamps has to be calculated. For this reason, the *temporal cluster intersection* was introduced [20]:

$$\cap_t\{C_{t_i,a}, C_{t_j,b}\} = \{T_l \mid o_{t_i,l} \in C_{t_i,a} \wedge o_{t_j,l} \in C_{t_j,b}\}$$

with $C_{t_i,a}$ and $C_{t_j,b}$ being two clusters, $t_i, t_j \in \{t_1, ...t_n\}$ and $l \in \{1, ..., m\}$. The proportion p of two Clusters $C_{t_i,a}$ and $C_{t_j,b}$ with $t_i < t_j$ is then calculated by:

$$p(C_{t_i,a}, C_{t_j,b}) = \begin{cases} 0 & \text{if } C_{t_i,a} = \emptyset \\ \frac{|C_{t_i,a} \cap_t C_{t_j,b}|}{|C_{t_i,a}|} & \text{else} \end{cases}$$

As this proportion is asymmetric since it only describes the proportion of $C_{t_i,a}$ that is contained in $C_{t_j,b}$, a merge of clusters has no negative impact on the score. However, in some use cases it might be wanted to treat merges and splits equally, because a well-separated clustering is desired. With this calculation it is not possible to distinguish whether a time series has the best possible score because it always remains in its well-separated cluster or because its cluster only merged into other ones but never split off.

In order to punish merges and splits the same way, the jaccard index can be used to obtain the proportion. For this, we introduce the *temporal cluster union* of two clusters $C_{t_i,a}, C_{t_j,b}$:

$$\cup_t\{C_{t_i,a}, C_{t_j,b}\} = \{T_l \mid o_{t_i,l} \in C_{t_i,a} \vee o_{t_j,l} \in C_{t_j,b}\}$$

with $l \in \{1, ..., m\}$. Now the proportion $\hat{p}$ can be calculated by the jaccard index of two clusters:

$$\hat{p}(C_{t_i,a}, C_{t_j,b}) = \begin{cases} 0 & \text{if } C_{t_i,a} = \emptyset \wedge C_{t_j,b} = \emptyset \\ \frac{|C_{t_i,a} \cap_t C_{t_j,b}|}{|C_{t_i,a} \cup_t C_{t_j,b}|} & \text{else} \end{cases}$$

with $t_i < t_j$.

Regarding the example in Fig. 2, the proportion p of cluster $C_{t_i,l}$ and $C_{t_j,v}$ would be

$$p(C_{t_i,l}, C_{t_j,v}) = \frac{|C_{t_i,l} \cap_t C_{t_j,v}|}{|C_{t_i,l}|} = \frac{2}{2} = 1$$

and therefore ideal. In contrast to that, the proportion $\hat{p}$ would be

$$\hat{p}(C_{t_i,l}, C_{t_j,v}) = \frac{|C_{t_i,l} \cap_t C_{t_j,v}|}{|C_{t_i,l} \cup_t C_{t_j,v}|} = \frac{2}{3} = 0.\overline{6}$$

as the merge of cluster $C_{t_i,l}$ and $C_{t_i,u}$ lowers the score.

Using the proportion, each subsequence $T_{t_i,t_j,l}$ of time series l beginning at timestamp t_i and ending at t_j is rated by the following *subsequence_score* in [20]:

$$subsequence\_score(T_{t_i,t_j,l}) = \frac{1}{k} \cdot \sum_{v=i}^{j-1} p(cid(o_{t_v,l}), cid(o_{t_j,l}))$$

with $l \in \{1, ..., m\}$, $k \in [1, j-i]$ being the number of timestamps between t_i and t_j where the data point exists and *cid*, the cluster-identity function

$$cid(o_{t_i,l}) = \begin{cases} \emptyset & \text{if the data point is not assigned to any cluster} \\ C_{t_i,a} & \text{else} \end{cases}$$

returning the cluster which the data point has been assigned to in t_i. In words, it is the average proportion of the sequence's clusters it migrated with from t_i to t_j. Here, the impact of all preceding time points to the score is weighted equally. For longer sequences, this can lead to a tendency towards a worse rating, since slow changes in cluster membership might influence the rating quite considerably. Assuming that the nearer past is more meaningful than the more distant past, we formulate a weighting that can be used in the subsequence score.

Regarding a time interval $[t_1, t_k]$, the proportion at time t_i with $t_1 \leq t_i \leq t_k$ gets the weighting $\frac{2 \cdot i}{k(k+1)}$ resulting by the division of i with the Gauss's Formula

$$\frac{i}{\sum_{a=1}^{k} a} = \frac{i}{\frac{k(k+1)}{2}} = \frac{2 \cdot i}{k(k+1)}.$$

The weighting function can easily be adjusted for time intervals starting at time $t_s > t_1$. The subsequence score is then calculated as follows:

$$weighted\_subseq\_score(T_{t_i,t_j,l}) = \sum_{v=i}^{j-1} \frac{2 \cdot (v - i + 1)}{k(k+1)} p(cid(o_{t_v,l}), cid(o_{t_j,l}))$$

with $k \in [1, j - i]$ again being the number of timestamps between t_i and t_j where the data point exists. Since the sum of all weightings of a subsequence's timestamps is always 1, there is no need to normalize the score to an interval of $[0, 1]$ by averaging it.

In the example of Fig. 2, the score of time series T_a between time points t_i and t_k would be

$$subsequence\_score(T_{t_i,t_k,a}) = \frac{1}{2} \cdot (1.0 + 0.\overline{6}) = 0.8\overline{3}$$

whereby the rating with the weighted subsequence score would be

$$weighted\_subseq\_score(T_{t_i,t_k,a}) = (\frac{1}{3} \cdot 1.0 + \frac{2}{3} \cdot 0.\overline{6}) = 0.78$$

The second proportion which is smaller than 1 has thus more influence on the score now. The combination of the weighted subsequence score and the jaccard proportion $\hat{p}$ has the following result:

$$weighted\_jaccard\_score(T_{t_i,t_k,a}) = (\frac{1}{3} \cdot 0.\overline{6} + \frac{2}{3} \cdot 0.5) = 0.56$$

With the help of the subsequence's rating an outlier score can be calculated for each by determining the deviation of their stability from the best subsequence score of their cluster. Formally, the best score of a cluster $C_{t_j,a}$ for sequences starting at t_i and ending at t_j is given by

$$best\_score(t_i, C_{t_j,a}) = max(\{subsequence\_score(T_{t_i,t_j,l}) \mid cid(o_{t_j,l}) = C_{t_j,a}\}) \;.$$

A subsequence's outlier score is then described by

$$outlier\_score(T_{t_i,t_j,l}) = best\_score(t_i, cid(o_{t_j,l})) - subsequence\_score(T_{t_i,t_j,l}) \;.$$

The outlier score is therefore dependent on the over-time stability of the considered cluster's members. The smaller the best score is, the smaller is the highest possible outlier score. The detection of outlier sequences can be done by using a threshold τ [20]:

Definition 8 (Outlier). *Given a threshold* $\tau \in [0, 1]$, *a subsequence* $T_{t_i,t_j,l}$ *is called an outlier, if its probability of being an outlier is greater than or equal* τ. *That means, if*

$$outlier\_score(T_{t_i,t_j,l}) \geq \tau \;.$$

In addition to these outlier sequences, subsequences that consist entirely of noise data points from the clustering algorithm are identified as *intuitive outliers*. Sequences whose last data point is labeled as noise are not assigned to a cluster which the best score can be determined from, so they do not get an outlier score.

5 Experiments

In the following, several experiments on different (artificially generated and real world) data sets are performed in order to evaluate the effects of the modifications of this paper regarding the original method. In all cases the density-based clustering algorithm *DBSCAN* [8] was used for clustering. We will differentiate between the *original method* from [20], the *jaccard method* (where the proportion is calculated by the jaccard index), the *weighted method* (where the weighting is included in the subsequence score), and the *weighted jaccard method* (where all modifications are integrated). In all experiments the same parameter settings for ϵ, $mitPts$ and τ were used for the investigated methods in order to make the results comparable. Please note, that dependent on the method in some cases another parameter choice could have been beneficial.

5.1 Artificially Generated Data Set

For a targeted evaluation of the properties, at first an artificially generated data set with 40 timestamps is considered. The data set was generated so that initially four starting points (for four groups of time series) were selected. In addition, the maximum distance of the centroids of two successive time points and the number of members were chosen for each group. The centroids as well as the members' data points were then calculated randomly for each time point, whereby the distance of the members to the centroids could not exceed 0.03. After generating the normal data points, one completely random outlier sequence and three targeted outlier sequences were inserted. For the completely random sequence all data points were chosen randomly and the distance between two consecutive points was set to not being greater than 0.1. The remaining outlier sequences were generated as follows: The data points were always set with a

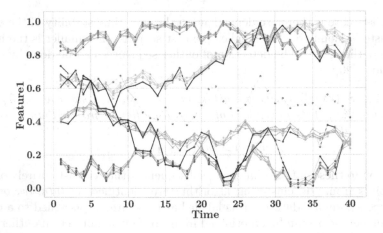

Fig. 3. Achieved results on the generated data set with $\epsilon = 0.025$, $minPts = 3$ and $\tau = 0.7$ by the original method. (Color figure online)

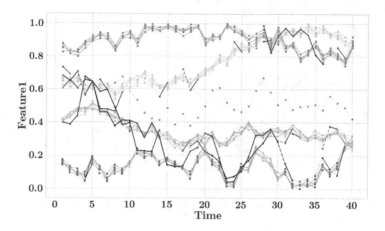

Fig. 4. Achieved results on the generated data set with $\epsilon = 0.025$, $minPts = 3$ and $\tau = 0.7$ by the weighted method. (Color figure online)

maximum distance of 0.06 to a centroid. The clusters were chosen randomly whereby the distance of the latest data point and the next centroid could not exceed 0.2. Additionally, the sequence always had to be allocated for at least 5 time points to the same cluster before choosing the next one. For all points, care was taken to ensure that they were between 0 and 1.

The time series data was clustered per timestamp with the parameter setting $\epsilon = 0.025$ and $minPts = 3$. All four methods were performed on the clustering with the threshold $\tau = 0.7$. The results are illustrated in the Figures Fig. 3, Fig. 4, Fig. 5 and Fig. 6. Red dots represent noise data points while other colors

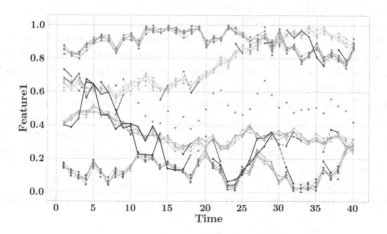

Fig. 5. Achieved results on the generated data set with $\epsilon = 0.025$, $minPts = 3$ and $\tau = 0.7$ by the jaccard method. (Color figure online)

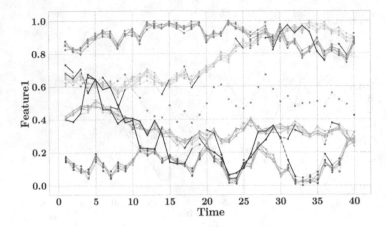

Fig. 6. Achieved results on the generated data set with $\epsilon = 0.025$, $minPts = 3$ and $\tau = 0.7$ by the weighted jaccard method. (Color figure online)

indicate the cluster membership. Black lines stand for outliers that are found with the outlier score and dashed lines represent intuitive outliers.

The original method (Fig. 3) detects all four outlier sequences and marks almost the whole time series as such. However, some parts of the outlier sequence in the yellow clusters (second from the top) are quite stable and therefore should not be detected as outliers in regard to their over-time stability. When considering the results of the weighted method (Fig. 4) one can see, that some smaller parts of the time series are marked as outliers. The most obvious example is the outlier sequence of the yellow clusters. This effect shows, that the intention of the weighting, that the more distant past has a lower impact on the score than the nearer past, is therefore satisfied. The jaccard method (Fig. 5) leads to a more sparsely detection, as well. This can be explained by the fact that due to some merges (for example in the yellow clusters) the best subsequence score of the clusters is decreased and consequently the highest outlier score is decreased, too. The effect of the lower best score can also be seen between the timestamps 29 and 35. In contrast to the weighted method, the "M" shape is not marked completely. The combination of both modifications is illustrated in Fig. 6. Since the nearer past is weighted more strongly here, the merge of the blue and yellow clusters at time point 26 has not as much influence on the best score. Therefore the "M" shape is detected as outlier. However, there are some differences in regard to the results of the weighted method. Overall fewer outlier sequences are found. An example can be seen in the first time stamps. This behavior is reasoned as the jaccard index lowers the best possible score in the clusters.

5.2 Airline On-Time Performance Data Set

This data set holds 29 features like the scheduled and actual departure time for flights reported by certified U.S. air carriers. In total it contains 3.5 million

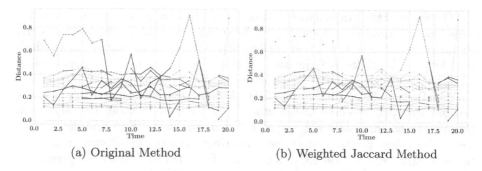

(a) Original Method   (b) Weighted Jaccard Method

Fig. 7. Achieved results on the Airline On-Time Performance Data Set with $\epsilon = 0.03$, $minPts = 3$ and $\tau = 0.5$.

records with each representing a flight. Originally this data set is provided by the U.S. Department of Transportation's Bureau of Transportation Statistics [7]. In order to make the data set suitable for our approach we interpreted the feature set of every airline as a sequence. Further we made these time series equidistant by calculating the average of their features for every day. Finally we normalized the data set with the min-max normalization and clustered it per timestamp.

In this experiment we compare the original method [20] with the modified approach presented in this paper. Both modifications are applied and the result is illustrated in Fig. 7b. The first noticeable difference to the original [20] approach in Fig. 7a is the lower amount of marked outliers. This can be explained with both adjustments: First of all, the introduced jaccard index leads to overall lower subsequence scores, thus the best score of a cluster is lower and therefore the outlier score is lower. Second, the weighting function allows time series to change their peers over time if it is done consequently. This means that time series are not considered to be suspicious if they made a stable change, which is to expect when regarding larger time series. Actually the original approach cannot handle the amount of points in time and tends to become more sensitive with rising amount of time stamps. In contrary, the adjusted version performs more robust and can handle more timestamps better.

On the second sight, one might notice that the adjusted method detects slightly different outliers than the original approach (e.g. the two upper outliers between timestamp 17.5 and 20.0). However, those differences in this example are too small to be reasoned with a specific modification.

5.3   GlobalEconomy Data Set

The GlobalEconomy data set is obtained from the website theglobaleconomy.com [1]. It holds over 300 indicators for different features for 200 countries over more than 60 years. For illustration reasons we chose 20 countries and two features, namely the education spendings and the unemployment rate. Please note, that the amount of countries can vary per timestamp, because there are missing values in the data set.

The result of the original method and the modified approach presented in this paper, can be seen in Fig. 8 and Fig. 9. The colors represent the detected clusters, circles represent behavior-based outliers and red font is indicating noise which was detected by DBSCAN. In case a country is detected as a behavior-based outlier and as noise by DBSCAN it is represented as a circle with red font. The abbreviations are according to ISO 3166. At first glance it is noticeable that our original approach detected more outliers than the new method. Let us explain this by the example of Kyrgyzstan (KGZ) in the years 2010 and 2011: KGZ leaves the yellow cluster and at the same time joins the green cluster in 2011. In our original calculation KGZ is punished for this transition by applying the old cluster proportion function. At the same time the subsequence score of the Marshall Islands (ISL) is not influenced in 2011, because it was not assigned to a cluster in 2010. Thus the outlier score of Kyrgyzstan is negatively influenced. In the weighted jaccard method Kyrgyzstan is not detected as an outlier, because the Marshall Islands are punished for the merge with Kyrgyzstan in 2011. This leads to a lower *best_score* and at the same time to a lower *outlier_score* of Kyrgyzstan. In summary, Kyrgyzstan is not detected as an outlier, because the Marshall Islands are now punished for merging.

An example of finding new outliers is Honduras (HND) in the years from 2013 to 2015. The old technique did not identify Honduras as an outlier in the years 2014 and 2015, while the modified method does. Again this has to do with the low subsequence score of the Marshal Islands in 2014, but this time the cluster proportion of the original approach is punishing the Marshal Islands for splitting from its peers in the previous years. However, this is not the only reason Honduras is not marked as an outlier. It actually benefits from rejoining the yellow cluster in 2015, although the yellow cluster contains more than twice

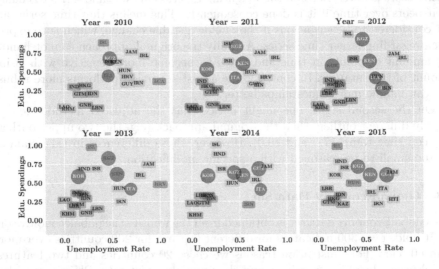

Fig. 8. Achieved results on the GlobalEconomy Data Set with $\epsilon = 0.18$, $minPts = 2$ and $\tau = 0.4$ by the original method. (Color figure online)

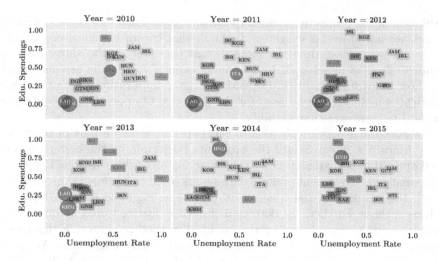

Fig. 9. Achieved results on the GlobalEconomy Data Set with $\epsilon = 0.18$, $minPts = 2$ and $\tau = 0.4$ by the weighted jaccard method. (Color figure online)

the amount of countries now. In concrete that means, that the comparison of the years of 2013 and 2015 was influencing the subsequence score of Honduras in a positive way. The weighted jaccard approach takes the new constellation of the yellow cluster into account. In contrary to the original method, the comparison of the years 2013 and 2015 is not beneficial to its subsequence score. Further more the merge with the Marshall Islands in 2014 is punished by the jaccard index.

Another interesting observation is, that the jaccard index now enables the identification of outlier clusters. In Fig. 9 one can observe, that Laos (LAO) and Cambodia (KHM) form a cluster in the years from 2010 to 2011. The merge to the big blue cluster in 2012 has a fairly high influence on their subsequence scores so that they are detected as outliers in 2013. Although the two countries are more stable in the subsequence from 2012 to 2013, they have not stabilized to the level of their peers in the blue cluster. This finally happens in the year of 2014.

6   Conclusion and Future Work

The analysis of time series data – especially the identification of conspicuous sequences – is an important field in data mining. So far, there are only a few approaches for the detection of outliers in multiple time series. In [20] we presented an outlier detection algorithm which analyses the behavior of groups of time series by clustering the data per timestamp using an arbitrary clustering algorithm. As this was a novel approach, there were still some handicaps and application dependent properties. In this paper, we focused on two of these and proposed the following solutions: First, we presented another technique for the calculation of the proportion, which treats merges and splits of clusters equally. Second, we introduced a weighting function that causes a higher impact of a sequence's nearer past than the more distant one. Our results show, that the intended effects were achieved by our modifications. All results are meaningful and show individual qualities. Dependent on the application, one of the four investigated methods can be used for the detection of anomalous subsequences in regard to their over-time stability.

However, the aspects dealt with in this paper were only a part of the procedure's difficulties. There is still the problem of determining the best parameter τ and optimal hyperparameters for the clustering algorithms such as DBSCAN. Additionally, the treatment of noise data points could be improved. As proposed in [20], the inclusion of the time series' deviations might lead to an advanced analysis of those. Further, the detection of outlier clusters would be interesting. Partly they are already found by the modified method presented in this paper. Finally, the procedure could be adjusted to handle fuzzy clusterings. With the help of over-time stability measures for hard [21] and fuzzy clusterings [13] a good basis for the outlier detection can be provided.

Acknowledgement. We would like to thank the Jürgen Manchot Foundation, which supported this work by financing the AI research group *Decision-making with the help of Artificial Intelligence* at Heinrich Heine University Düsseldorf.

References

1. Global economy, world economy. https://www.theglobaleconomy.com/
2. Ahmad, S., Lavin, A., Purdy, S., Agha, Z.: Unsupervised real-time anomaly detection for streaming data. Neurocomputing **262**, 134–147 (2017)
3. Ahmar, A.S., et al.: Modeling data containing outliers using ARIMA additive outlier (ARIMA-AO). In: Journal of Physics: Conference Series, vol. 954 (2018)
4. Banerjee, A., Ghosh, J.: Clickstream clustering using weighted longest common subsequences. In: Proceedings of the Web Mining Workshop at the 1st SIAM Conference on Data Mining, pp. 33–40 (2001)
5. Cheng, H., Tan, P.N., Potter, C., Klooster, S.: Detection and characterization of anomalies in multivariate time series. In: Proceedings of the 2009 SIAM International Conference on Data Mining, pp. 413–424 (2009)
6. Cleveland, R.B., Cleveland, W.S., McRae, J.E., Terpenning, I.: STL: a seasonal-trend decomposition procedure based on loess (with discussion). J. Off. Stat. **6**, 3–73 (1990)
7. Computing, S., Graphics, S.: Airline on-time performance. http://stat-computing.org/dataexpo/2009/the-data.html. Accessed 15 July 2019
8. Ester, M., Kriegel, H.P., Sander, J., Xu, X.: A density-based algorithm for discovering clusters a density-based algorithm for discovering clusters in large spatial databases with noise. In: Proceedings of the Second International Conference on Knowledge Discovery and Data Mining, pp. 226–231 (1996)
9. Ferreira, L.N., Zhao, L.: Time series clustering via community detection in networks. Inf. Sci. **326**, 227–242 (2016)
10. Granger, C.W.J.: Investigating causal relations by econometric models and cross-spectral methods. Econometrica **37**(3), 424 (1969)

11. Huang, X., Ye, Y., Xiong, L., Lau, R.Y., Jiang, N., Wang, S.: Time series k-means: a new k-means type smooth subspace clustering for time series data. Inf. Sci. **367–368**, 1–13 (2016)

12. Kalnis, P., Mamoulis, N., Bakiras, S.: On discovering moving clusters in spatio-temporal data. In: Bauzer Medeiros, C., Egenhofer, M.J., Bertino, E. (eds.) SSTD 2005. LNCS, vol. 3633, pp. 364–381. Springer, Heidelberg (2005). https://doi.org/10.1007/11535331_21

13. Klassen, G., Tatusch, M., Himmelspach, L., Conrad, S.: Fuzzy clustering stability evaluation of time series. In: Lesot, M.-J., et al. (eds.) IPMU 2020. CCIS, vol. 1237, pp. 680–692. Springer, Cham (2020). https://doi.org/10.1007/978-3-030-50146-4_50

14. Landauer, M., Wurzenberger, M., Skopik, F., Settanni, G., Filzmoser, P.: Time series analysis: unsupervised anomaly detection beyond outlier detection. In: Su, C., Kikuchi, H. (eds.) ISPEC 2018. LNCS, vol. 11125, pp. 19–36. Springer, Cham (2018). https://doi.org/10.1007/978-3-319-99807-7_2

15. Malhotra, P., Vig, L., Shroff, G.M., Agarwal, P.: Long short term memory networks for anomaly detection in time series. In: ESANN (2015)

16. Munir, M., Siddiqui, S.A., Chattha, M.A., Dengel, A., Ahmed, S.: FuSEAD: unsupervised anomaly detection in streaming sensors data by fusing statistical and deep learning models. Sensors **19**(11), 2451 (2019)

17. Paparrizos, J., Gravano, L.: k-shape: Efficient and accurate clustering of time series. In: Proceedings of the 2015 ACM SIGMOD International Conference on Management of Data, pp. 1855–1870 (2015)

18. Salvador, S., Chan, P.: Toward accurate dynamic time warping in linear time and space. Intell. Data Anal. **11**(5), 561–580 (2007)

19. Sun, P., Chawla, S., Arunasalam, B.: Mining for outliers in sequential databases. In: ICDM, pp. 94–106 (2006)

20. Tatusch, M., Klassen, G., Bravidor, M., Conrad, S.: Show me your friends and i'll tell you who you are. finding anomalous time series by conspicuous cluster transitions. In: Data Mining. AusDM 2019. Communications in Computer and Information Science, vol. 1127, pp. 91–103 (2019)

21. Tatusch, M., Klassen, G., Bravidor, M., Conrad, S.: How is your team spirit? cluster over-time stability evaluation (forthcoming). In: Machine Learning and Data Mining in Pattern Recognition, 16th International Conference on Machine Learning and Data Mining, MLDM (2020)

22. Truong, C.D., Anh, D.T.: A novel clustering-based method for time series motif discovery under time warping measure. Int. J. Data Sci. Anal. **4**(2), 113–126 (2017). https://doi.org/10.1007/s41060-017-0060-3

23. Zhou, Y., Zou, H., Arghandeh, R., Gu, W., Spanos, C.J.: Non-parametric outliers detection in multiple time series a case study: power grid data analysis. In: AAAI (2018)

Detecting Anomalies in Production Quality Data Using a Method Based on the Chi-Square Test Statistic

Michael Mayr[✉][iD] and Johannes Himmelbauer[✉][iD]

Software Competence Center Hagenberg, Softwarepark 21, 4232 Hagenberg, Austria
{michael.mayr,johannes.himmelbauer}@scch.at
https://www.scch.at/

Abstract. This paper describes the capability of the *Chi-Square test statistic* at detecting outliers in production-quality data. The goal is automated detection and evaluation of statistical anomalies for a large number of time series in the production-quality context. The investigated time series are the temporal course of sensor failure rates in relation to particular aspects (e.g. type of failure, information about products, the production process, or measuring sites). By means of an industrial use case, we show why in this setting our chosen approach is superior to standard methods for statistical outlier detection.

Keywords: Unsupervised outlier detection · Statistical time series modeling · Chi-Square Test Statistic · Numerical analysis

1 Introduction and Motivation

The industry is part of an economy that produces material goods where the production process is highly automatized. In industrial manufacturing, the usage of sensors, and therefore the amount of produced data is increasing continuously. This trend is part of the Industry 4.0 revolution and enables a huge source for complex sensor data [12]. The explosion of the available data, which is generated at all levels of the production process, enables companies to increase product quality, flexibility, and productivity [4]. When a generating process (e.g. sensor measurements) behaves unusual, it generally results in the creation of an anomaly. Therefore, an anomaly often contains useful information about the abnormal characteristics of the system itself and the entities that impact the data generation process. By recognizing these unusual characteristics, it is possible to gain useful application-specific insights [1].

Nowadays, most companies also collect information related to the quality of the production. Production-quality data usually originates from testing the output of the production process, either manually or automatically by the use

Supported by Software Competence Center Hagenberg (SCCH).

of test sensors. In discrete manufacturing, the data typically consists of different test results where each test either passes or fails (e.g. a sensor may test electric conductivity, optical imbalances or various other relevant factors). In the ideal setting, every piece produced is fully tested and its results are stored in a production-quality database. In that case, the investigated production-quality time series are the temporal course of sensor failure rates in relation to particular aspects (e.g. type of failure, information about products, or measuring sites). This type of data can provide useful insights into the general state of the production process. The motivation of the work presented in this paper is mainly rooted in an industrial use case that we worked on in collaboration with one of our company partners. There the main aim is to go towards a highly automated monitoring tool of the achieved production-quality. An important task in this context is the automatic detection of relevant, suddenly occurring anomalies (i.e. a sudden significant increase of a failure rate).

The intuition of a statistical outlier detection approach is that standard data follows a generating mechanism, for example, a statistical process. Statistical methods either assume a known underlying distribution of the observations or at least statistical estimations of unknown distribution parameters [10]. These methods classify data points as abnormal data if the point deviates (strongly) from the model assumptions. Outlier detection is a well-known problem and is researched in many different domains like intrusion detection and fraud detection [11]. The different domains may share the same base or slightly altered algorithms for identifying anomalies. The priorities, however, may be different. For our industrial use case of monitoring production-quality data, we will show the advantage of considering additionally to the failure rates themselves also the underlying absolute amount of produced sensors for the evaluation of outliers. It will be the key to achieve the (by the company's experts) desired results in a far better way than with available standard unsupervised outlier detection techniques (*local outlier factor (LOF)* [14], *agglomerative hierarchical clustering (AHC)* [13] and *Grubbs* [7]).

2 Background

This section describes and visualizes production-quality data and its hierarchical structure. Furthermore, the distribution assumption is stated and discussed.

2.1 Production Quality Data

At our industrial partner, the production process consists of several components and work steps. Production-quality data originates from various sensors in the automatized production process. These sensors perform different tests (e.g. electric conductivity tests, optical imbalance tests) in different stages of the production process. A test may pass or fail. The production-quality time series are the temporal course of sensor failure rates in relation to particular aspects (e.g. type of failure, information about products, production characteristics, or measuring sites). By visualising the failure rates of these tests concerning different aspects, one gains insight into the quality of the production process. There are several dimensions which might be interesting in the context of quality control, like *products, sensor test positions*, or *machine operators*. Each of them enables the company to gain different insights into the production-quality. Some aspects identify flaws in the production process of specific products, whereas others give insight into test sensor reliability and possible faulty test sites. Section 2.1 shows the variables used in this paper to describe production-quality data. The time dimension is denoted as T and contains several equally granular time intervals t, e.g. years, months or weeks. In the following, o_t refers to the observation size, i.e. the number of product pieces that were tested within the according time interval t, always with respect to a given analytical and type-of-failure dimension (see Sect. 2.1). The corresponding failure rate y_t is given by the proportion of observed failure tests in relation to the total number of tests o_t. It is important to note that with the use of an analytical dimension, the observation size changes, as one limits the area of interest.

Notation	Interval	Description
$Y = \{y_t : t \in T\}$	$\{y_t \in \mathbb{R} \mid 0 \leq y_t \leq 1\}$	% failure rate per time interval t, i,e, $\frac{yabs_t}{o_t}$
$O = \{o_t : t \in T\}$	$\{o_t \in \mathbb{N} \mid 0 < o_t < \infty\}$	absolute number of tests per time interval t

Furthermore, a production-quality time series is represented as a single graph in this paper. The failure rate y_t is plotted as a line chart with the y-axis on the left side, whereas the observation size o_t is plotted as a histogram, with the y-axis on the right side. The time t on the x-axis is the same for both variables. Figure 1 shows an example representation of a real-world production-quality time series with an underlying hierarchy problem (see. Sect. 2.1).

Data Hierarchy. The real-world production-quality data is stored in different *OLAP cubes*. A *OLAP cube* is stored as a multi-dimensional array of data [9] and consists of measurement values (e.g. failure rates) which are categorized by dimensions (e.g. date, type-of-failure, test positions). An important characteristic is the aspect of hierarchy, where the elements of a dimension may be organized as a set of parent-child relationships [16], e.g. year - month - day, failure group - failure type - failure. In the context of production-quality, one can gain high-level insights into the quality of the production process by analyzing the failure rates of a specific type of failure over some time. For a more detailed, lower levelled, quality diagnosis, one may add another dimension, e.g. products or test positions. One can denote the type-of-failure dimension as higher-levelled dimension and the analytical dimension, which restricts the area of interest, as the lower-levelled dimension. In this paper, we tackle two different problems when detecting outliers in this hierarchically structured data:

- **Hierarchy Problem 1:** In the existence of an outlier with respect to a certain member of a lower-levelled dimension (e.g. a defective test sensor at a certain test position leads to a very high failure rate for the corresponding test position) this outlier will also be propagated to the higher-levelled dimension. For the task of automatically monitoring the production-quality data, it would be of interest to solely detect the outlier in the problem source dimension, i.e. the lower-levelled dimension.
- **Hierarchy Problem 2:** In the existence of an outlier with respect to a certain higher-levelled dimension, this outlier will also be propagated to the lower-levelled dimension as the data of the higher-levelled dimension is simply split up. Imagine an anomalous value in a specific type-of-failure dimension, e.g. electrical conductivity failure rate. If one wants to investigate, whether the anomalous value originates from, e.g. a faulty test connector on a testing grid, one may analyze the chosen type-of-failure dimension against the dimension of sensor test positions on the testing grid. However, if the anomalies cause is not related to those positions, the anomaly is split up and propagated into the absolute number of test positions, as only the area of interest changes; i.e. the observation size. Figure 1 shows a real-world production-quality data sample, concerning this hierarchy problem. The first chart shows the aggregated failure rates and observation sizes for a specific type-of-failure over the span of a year with a weekly time granularity. The second chart has the same data basis as the chart above, however, the aggregated failure rates and observation sizes for the specific type-of-failure are put into relation with the sensor test positions on a testing grid.

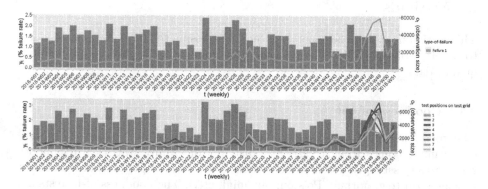

Fig. 1. A visual representation of production-quality data. In both figures y_t is represented as a line chart with the y-axis on the left side, whereas o_t is represented as a histogram, with the y-axis on the right side. These figures specifically address the hierarchy problem 2, where an anomaly propagates from a higher-levelled dimension to the lower-levelled dimension (see Sect. 2.1).

Distribution Assumption. The binomial distribution is able to model the behaviour of production-quality data if following conditions apply [15]:

- There is a fixed number of sensor tests.
- Each sensor test result is independent.
- Each sensor test represents one of two test results, namely failure and non-failure.
- The probability of a failure p is the same for each test.

Given the fact, that $yabs_t$ (absolute amount of test failures) in a group of o_t observations with failure probability p follows a binomial distribution with mean $\mu = o_t * p$ and variance $\sigma^2 = o_t * p * (1 - p)$, then one may derive distribution characteristics of the sample proportion $\hat{p}$ [15]. In production-quality data, o_t is sufficiently large enough to assume that the distributions of $yabs_t$ and the sample proportion $\hat{p}$ are approximately normal. μ and σ^2 of $yabs_t$ are $o_t * p$ and $o_t * p * (1-p)$ and the same as μ and σ^2 of the binomial distribution $Binom(o_t, p)$. In this paper, it is assumed that all o_t Bernoulli experiments follow the same failure probability p, $yabs_t \sim Binom(o_t, p)$, with the assumption that each test does not influence the outcome of another test. This statistical assumption is the basis for the proposed method in this paper. Section 4.5 provides insight into the viability of the assumption. Furthermore, the statistical *Grubbs* test, which is based on the assumption of data normality, is used for statistical evaluation of the proposed method. This distribution assumption is also used in Sect. 4, where synthetic production-quality time series are generated based on the binomial distribution.

3   Methods

This section describes the general concept of assessing the fit of statistical models to a set of observations. Furthermore, this concept is applied to production-quality data.

3.1   Goodness of Fit

The goodness-of-fit tests assess whether it is reasonable to assume that a random sample comes from a particular distribution. Many statistical techniques rely on the assumption that observations come from a population that has a specific form (e.g. normal, Poisson, binomial, etc.). The goodness-of-fit tests are a form of hypothesis testing where the **H0** specifies that the data follows a specific distribution and the alternative hypothesis states that the data does not follow a specific distribution [3]. In the case of outlier detection in production-quality data, the *Chi-Square Goodness of Fit* [6] comes in handy. The *Chi-Square Goodness of Fit* tests whether a data sample comes from a population with a specified binomial distribution. This method determines how well the theoretical binomial distribution fits the empirical distribution. This test applies to any univariate distribution for which the cumulative distribution function can be calculated [2]. The test determines whether there is a significant difference between the expected and observed frequency in k data categories. In the case of *production-quality data* there are two categories, namely failure and non-failure of sensor tests, thus $k = 2$. By using the *Chi-Square Test Statistic* one can include the underlying observation size, which strongly influences the importance of the quality measure, in the statistical model.

The formula used for *Chi-Square Goodness of Fit* defines as

$$\chi^2 = \sum_{i=1}^{k}(O_i - E_i)^2/E_i \tag{1}$$

where χ^2 is the *Chi-Square* test value, O_i is the observed frequency for category i and E_i the expected frequency calculated by $E_i = N \times (F(L_u) - F(L_l))$, where F is the cumulative distribution function concerning the tested distribution, L_u and L_l are the upper and lower bound for category i. N denotes the amount of samples. The test statistic follows approximately a *Chi-Square distribution* with $df = k - x$, where k denotes the number of categories and x the number of estimated population parameters. In case of production-quality data, $k = 2$ and $x = 1$ as the binomial distribution probability is estimated. The hypothesis gets rejected if $\chi^2 > \chi^2_{1-\alpha,\,k-x}$, where $\chi^2_{1-\alpha,\,k-x}$ is the *Chi-Square* critical value with $k - x$ degrees of freedom and significance level α [3].

3.2 Statistical Outlier Detection in Production Quality Data

This section describes the appliance of the above-explained *Chi-Square Goodness of Fit* test in the context of production-quality data. The following sections describe the general appliance procedure and the implicit advantages of this statistical approach.

Outlier Detection with Goodness of Fit. The described *Chi-Square Goodness of Fit* test (see Sect. 3.1) also applies to production-quality data, if the assumptions stated in Sect. 2.1 hold. The general idea is to test whether $yabs_t$ follows an estimated failure probability that is considered normal. As $\bar{X} = \hat{\mu} = n\hat{p}$, Eq. 2 estimates the mean failure probability $\hat{p}$ from a production-quality reference time series which is considered normal. $yabs_t = y_t \times o_t$ is the absolute amount of failed tests at time t. As normal behaviour in production-quality data is rare, and "normality" may vary weekly, regularly updating and adjusting the reference time-series to the normality definition is recommended.

$$\hat{p} = \frac{\sum_{t=1}^{T}(yabs_t)}{\sum_{t=1}^{T}(o_t)} \tag{2}$$

One can compare the data points individually against the mean sample probability by defining for each production-quality data point the observed amount of failure and non-failure, i.e. $O_t(F) = yabs_t$ and $O_t(NF) = o_t - yabs_t$, where

F denotes "failure" and NF "non-failure". The expected amount of failure and non-failure are stated as $E_t(F) = o_t \times \hat{p}$ and $E_t(NF) = o_t \times (1 - \hat{p})$. The null hypothesis and the alternative are stated as:

- **H0**: *The proportions of failure $O_t(F)$ and non-failure $O_t(NF)$ follow the proportions that were estimated with $\hat{p}$ from the reference set, formally $O_t(F) \leq E_t(F) \wedge O_t(NF) \geq E_t(NF)$ as negative outliers are ignored.*

- **H1**: *At least one of the proportions of the null hypothesis is false, formally $O_t(F) > E_t(F) \vee O_t(NF) < E_t(NF)$.*

This means the **H0** states that the analyzed production-quality data point has the same or a smaller failure probability p compared to the estimated $\hat{p}$ from the reference set. The alternative states that the data point follows a higher failure probability than $\hat{p}$. With this in mind, one can define the *Chi-Square Goodness of Fit* test statistic on production-quality data as

$$\chi_t^2 = \frac{(O_t(F) - E_t(F))^2}{E_t(F)} + \frac{(O_t(NF) - E_t(NF))^2}{E_t(NF)} \tag{3}$$

Because $\chi_t^2 \sim Chisq(df = 1)$ one can calculate the corresponding p-values from the *Chi-Square* distribution with $df = 1$. Due to the high amount of observed tests in real-world data, one can set the confidence interval for rejecting the null hypothesis quite low; e.g. $\alpha = 0.001$. If the null hypothesis is rejected, a score value $S(t)$, which states the outlyingness of an anomalous data point, is calculated by using the resulting p-value of the test. The term $(\log_{10}(\alpha) + 1)$ performs a shift of the scoring function to the interval $[1, \infty[$.

$$S(t) = \begin{cases} 0, & \text{if } \chi_t^2 > \alpha. \\ \left|\log_{10}\left(\chi_t^2\right)\right| + (\log_{10}(\alpha) + 1), & \text{otherwise.} \end{cases} \tag{4}$$

Outlier Trigger Detection in Hierarchical Data. With the *Chi-Square Goodness of Fit* test, one can identify trigger dimensions in production-quality data, as this test statistic includes the underlying observation size. The two problems stated in Sect. 2.1 can be statistically solved by the proposed method. Anomalies in the causing dimension will have a higher statistically validated score $S(t)$ than its repercussions. In Sect. 4.4 an experiment of the proposed method is performed as a proof-of-concept on synthetic generated data and then applied to real-world data in Sect. 4.5.

4   Results

The purpose of this section is to evaluate the proposed method compared to established ones. In the first part, the design of experiments is presented. It includes the selection of relevant performance metrics and data sets, as well as the formalization of the overall experimentation process. In the second part of the section, selected outlier detection methods are tested and compared according to the previously defined procedures. The experiments are evaluated on synthetic as well as real-world data.

4.1   Synthetic Data Sets

Since the real-world production-quality data does not contain any labels, it is more difficult to validate the results. Therefore, some basic synthetic data sets are generated. These are used to check whether the used algorithms are able to detect some typical anomalies one expects to find in real-world data. This is, of course, not a real validation or test for the algorithms. It can, however, help to answer the research questions. It may show flaws that might be missed if one only works with unlabeled real-world data. First, the details of the synthetic data are discussed. After an explanation of the experiment setup, a conclusion concerning the results using the synthetic data is given.

Data Generation. First, the length of the production-quality time series that will be generated is defined. Synthetic data with length $T = 20, 50, 100, 200, 400$ is generated and evaluated. For each data point o_t Bernoulli trails are computed. Bernoulli trials are sequences of independent dichotomous trials, each with probability p of success, where the sample space consists of two possible outcomes (failure and non-failure) [19]. The binomial distribution $Binom(o_t, p_{basis})$ arises from a sequence of o_t independent Bernoulli trials, each with probability p_{basis} of success. The idea is to generate T data points which follow a binomial distribution $yabs_t \sim Binom(o_t, p_{basis})$ where $yabs_t$ denotes the number of failures in o_t Bernoulli experiments with a failure probability of p_{basis}. The value of o_t is calculated randomly in a preset boundary. As the properties of o_t change in terms of size and variance in real-world data, different boundaries are tested. Many different p_{basis} values (e.g., 0.01, 0.05, 0.1, etc.) are used for data generation, as real-world data follows greatly different probabilities for each analyzed time series.

Outlier Generation. In each generated production-quality time series 10% outliers are injected. The time t where the outlier occurs is calculated randomly. The new value at t is defined as $yabs_t \sim Binom(o_t, p_{basis} \times p_{incr})$ where p_{incr} denotes the probability increase and p_{basis} the original failure probability. Different p_{incr} values are evaluated by defining the p_{incr} by a specific percentage of p_{basis}. In this thesis the increase of the outlier probability is defined as 1%, 10%, 50% and 100% of p_{basis}.

4.2   Real World Production-Quality Sets

Real-world data has no labels indicating outliers. Manual labelling of outliers is necessary. The labelling process is based on domain expertise. For this purpose, various time series in different hierarchy levels and different dimensions are selected. The anomalies are manually marked in each time series by domain knowledge experts.

4.3   Performance Metrics

Outlier detection can be seen as a special case of (binary) classification problem on data with extremely unbalanced classes. Meaning that the well-known metrics based on the confusion matrices are usable also in the context of outlier detection. The confusion matrix is a 2×2 matrix specifying TP, FP, TN and FN, where TP (true-positives) is the number of correctly labelled anomalous data points by the detection algorithm. FP (false-positives) is the number of normal data points that are incorrectly labelled as anomalous. FN (false negative) is the number of anomalous data points incorrectly labelled as normal, and TN (true negative) is the number of normal data points correctly labelled as normal. Given the large expected disproportion between anomalous and normal data points the true-positive rate ($TPR = \frac{TP}{TP+FN}$) and false-positive rate ($FPR = \frac{FP}{FP+TN}$) are suitable metrics [17].

Area Under Curve (AUC). Most anomaly detectors require a definition of some threshold value that significantly impacts the resulting TPR and FPR. Extensive information about the properties of an anomaly detection system can be gained by observing the changes in its behaviour (relation between TPR and FPR) while modifying the threshold value. This observation can be formalized by plotting the receiver-operator characteristics curve (ROC) and calculating the area under this curve (AUC) [5]. The ROC curve can be obtained by plotting the FPR on the X-axis vs the TPR on the Y-axis and the corresponding AUC value can be calculated by applying the trapezoidal rule. Each point of the curve represents the performance of the detector using a specific detection threshold [17]. The higher the AUC, the better the detector. The AUC does not provide insight into the specific threshold, however, the optimal threshold settings for the used detection methods can be tailored to the contextual needs by minimizing e.g. the FPR while maximizing the TPR [17].

4.4   Experiments on Synthetic Data

In the following sections, different experiments are performed on synthetic data. After describing the experiments, the results are discussed.

Experiment 1 - Constant vs Varying Observations. The goal of this experiment is to provide insight into the performance of the algorithm when O is constant versus O is varying. It is expected, that with constant O, all used algorithms perform well. As with varying O, the algorithm based on the *Chi-Square Goodness of Fit* test, is expected to perform substantially better than the other methods. In Table 1, the parameters, and their testing values are shown. A grid evaluation is performed, meaning that every possible parameter combination is used. With the defined parameter space in Table 1, a total of 64 parameter combinations are tested. For each parameter combination the algorithm runs $n = 100$. In every run, a new random production-quality time series is generated with respect to the current parameter combination. The used test parameters represent real-world data characteristics. The p_{basis} probability is used as time series construction and can be assumed as normal behaviour. By adding outlier at random positions with $p_{outlier} > p_{basis}$ one can test different scales of outliers.

Table 1. The parameter grid values which are tested in the experiment. The different test values approximate common characteristics of real world production-quality data.

Variable				
O	[20000, 80000]	[1000, 10000]	[1000, 1000000]	[45000, 55000]
p_{basis}	0.01	0.05	0.1	0.3
$p_{outlier}$	$p_{basis} \times 1.01$	$p_{basis} \times 1.1$	$p_{basis} \times 1.5$	$p_{basis} \times 2$

Figure 2 shows the aggregated results of the grid evaluation. The $\overline{AUC}$ value represents the mean of the AUC values produced by the different experiments with different parameter combinations. The data is grouped by *Method* and *Observation Type*. The mean of the grid evaluation is taken for each grouping. The results mirror the expectations. With constant observation size, all algorithms produce a high AUC value. Surprisingly LOF does not perform as well as its competitors, despite testing the LOF algorithm with different k values in each run. In case of varying observation size, the detection based on the *Chi-Square Goodness of Fit* test, outperforms every other algorithm by a significant amount. This is expected, as it includes O in the test statistic. Table 4 shows the performance of the algorithms concerning the different observation size boundaries. This table shows that with increasing the variance in O, the algorithms that do not include O in the calculation, start to perform worse than our proposed method. Constant O is uncommon in real-world conditions. Thus, a varying observation size for the following experiments is assumed. Table 3 shows the effects of certain percentage increases in p_{base}. As one can see in the results, a 1% increase of p_{base} is hardly detected by any outlier detection algorithm. With a 10% increase from p_{base}, the results of the algorithm get better. The *Chi-Square Goodness of Fit* test already outperforms the other methods. A further increase of the factor shows the superiority of the *Chi-Square Goodness of Fit* test.

Table 2. Shows the $\overline{AUC}$ score for each method concerning constant or varying O.

ID	Method	Observations Type	$\overline{AUC}$
1	LOF	const	0.7520108
2	Clust	const	0.8936892
3	Chi	const	0.8655743
4	Grubbs	const	0.9007381
5	LOF	vary	0.7185458
6	Clust	vary	0.7496863
7	Chi	vary	0.8674208
8	Grubbs	vary	0.7654686

Table 3. Shows the $\overline{AUC}$ score for each method concerning the factor of increase in p_{base} for outliers.

ID	Method	Outlier Incr. Factor	$\overline{AUC}$
1	LOF	1.01	0.5017837
2	Clust	1.01	0.5214262
3	Chi	1.01	0.5558262
4	Grubbs	1.01	0.5230366
5	LOF	1.10	0.5987464
6	Clust	1.10	0.6550681
7	Chi	1.10	0.9151572
8	Grubbs	1.10	0.6840349
9	LOF	1.50	0.8385810
10	Clust	1.50	0.8729595
11	Chi	1.50	0.9987019
12	Grubbs	1.50	0.8929315
13	LOF	2.00	0.9350718
14	Clust	2.00	0.9492912
15	Chi	2.00	0.9999981
16	Grubbs	2.00	0.9618713

Table 4. Shows the $\overline{AUC}$ score for each method with different test observation sizes.

ID	Method	Observation Size	$\overline{AUC}$
5	LOF	[20000–80000]	0.6439594
6	Clust	[20000–80000]	0.6699002
7	Chi	[20000–80000]	0.8856340
8	Grubbs	[20000–80000]	0.6863387
13	LOF	[5000–10000]	0.7116211
14	Clust	[5000–10000]	0.7433979
15	Chi	[5000–10000]	0.8314794
16	Grubbs	[5000–10000]	0.7609412
17	LOF	[45000–55000]	0.8000567
18	Clust	[45000–55000]	0.8357606
19	Chi	[45000–55000]	0.8851492
20	Grubbs	[45000–55000]	0.8491258
21	LOF	[5000–100000]	0.6103557
22	Clust	[5000–100000]	0.6243626
23	Chi	[5000–100000]	0.8422442
24	Grubbs	[5000–100000]	0.634325

Experiment 2 - Detecting Outlier Triggers. The goal of this experiment is to provide insight into the performance of the algorithm when operating on hierarchical data structures. As described in Sect. 2.1, there are two hierarchical problems to evaluate. Concerning **Hierarchy Problem 1**, outliers occurring in lower-levelled dimensions must deviate heavily from the data to have an impact on parent dimensions. The results in Table 3 show very high $\overline{AUC}$ values for each tested method in case of high probability outliers (100% increase of p_{basis}). Most traditional outlier detection algorithms are able to find such huge outliers,

Table 5. The parameter grid values which are tested in the hierarchy experiment. The different test values try to approximate common hierarchy characteristics and behaviour of real world production-quality data.

Variable			
$p_{outlier}$	$p_{basis} \times 1.1$	$p_{basis} \times 1.5$	$p_{basis} \times 2$
n_{groups}	2	10	20

Table 6. The experiment shows the algorithms capabilities of solving the **Hierarchy Problem 2** (see Sect. 2.1), where *% Succ.* denotes the percentage of successful top-level detections across the grid-search and *Abs. Succ.* denotes the corresponding successful detection counts.

ID	Method	% Succ.	Abs. Succ.
1	LOF	0.077	69
2	Chi	1	900
3	Clust	0.129	116
4	Grubbs	0.057	51

however, only the *Chi-Square Goodness of Fit* test is able to statistically validate the root cause by including the observation size. Concerning **Hierarchy Problem 2**, where a restricting dimension binds O (e.g., test n sensor positions on a test grid). For this problem, an experiment is performed, where 100 production-quality time series with constant O are generated. The generated time series are injected with various outliers (see Table 5). After that, each time series is partitioned into n time series with only $\frac{O}{n}$ observations per data point. This happens by sampling $yabs_t$ experiments from o_t. The randomly sampled $yabs_t$ Bernoulli trails are partitioned into n groups and the failed experiments are counted for each group. The different anomaly detection algorithms are used on the top-level, as well as on the second level of the hierarchy. The detector results are subsetted to match points of interests (outlier injection indices). A ground-truth is constructed which states, that the detector score (concerning the injected outlier) in the top-level, must be greater than the ones in the partitions. As well as in the previous experiment, a grid evaluation is performed (see Table 5). The mean of the successful detection percentages (see Table 6) of different parameter combinations is calculated. In this grid-search a constant observation size is assumed; i.e. $O_t = 100000$. Furthermore, the failure probability p_{basis} fluctuates around 0.05 by a standard deviation of 1%; i.e. $\mu = 0.05$ and $\sigma = 0.005$. The actual success percentages and absolute counts of detecting the outlier in the top-level are given in Table 6. For each parameter combination in the grid-search, 100 runs are tested, leading to an overall of 900 evaluations per detector. As expected, the *Chi-Square Goodness of Fit* test shows its superiority in the context of production-quality data.

4.5   Experiments on Real World Production-Quality Data

In the following section, an experiment is performed on real-world production-quality data. After describing the experiment, the results are discussed.

Experiment 3 - Performance Evaluation on Real-World Data. The goal of this experiment is to provide insight into the performance of the algorithms when applied to real-world data. It is expected that all used algorithms perform approximately as good as on the synthetic data. Nevertheless, the detector, based on the *Chi-Square Goodness of Fit* test, is expected to perform significantly better than the other detectors. For this test, 40 time series in different hierarchy levels and different dimensions are selected. The outliers are manually marked in each time series by domain knowledge experts. The lengths of the time series vary between 10 and 60, as domain experts mostly analyzed the production-quality data on a weekly time granularity. All in all, 163 data points label as outliers and 2064 data points label as normal behaviour. The algorithms loop the different time series, each time testing the time series with the different detection methods. The following shows the AUC results of the detection methods when applied to real-world production-quality data (Table 7):

Table 7. The experiment shows the method's capabilities in real-world data.

ID	Method	AUC
1	LOF	0.787
2	Chi	0.993
3	Clust	0.769
4	Grubbs	0.980

Surprisingly, the *Grubbs* test performs better than expected on real-world production-quality data. A possible explanation can be found when looking at the results in the synthetic data evaluation. In Table 4 one can see, that all other methods perform well when the variance of the observation size is small. Further data analysis has shown, that the randomly sampled and manually marked time series do not represent as heavy fluctuation in O as tested in the synthetic data section. Another explanation could be, that the marked outliers which are significant for the domain experts, can mostly be detected by any of the detection algorithms. Synthetic data is also generated with 1% outliers, which were hardly detected by any of the anomaly detectors, leading to a damping of the AUC. The expertly marked outliers in real-world data, often deviate strongly from the surrounding data, leading to better performance on every detection algorithm.

Experiment 4 - Finding Trigger Dimension in Real-World Data. The following experiment showcases trigger dimension identification in real-world data. It is expected, that the experiments conducted in Sect. 4.4 reflects in real-world conditions. The following chart is based on the production-quality time series described in Sect. 1. As expected, the *Chi-Square Goodness of Fit* method is able to correctly identify the top-level as trigger dimension (Fig. 2).

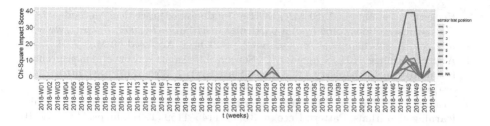

Fig. 2. This chart shows the calculated production-quality impact scores (see Sect. 3.2) of the top-level (a specific type-of-failure represented as *NA*) and of the second-level (the sensor test positions on a testing grid from 1 to 8) as described in Fig. 1.

5   Conclusion

In this section, the results of the paper are summarized and potential future research is suggested. As a basis of this paper, an assumption that production-quality data can be reasonably approximated by a binomial distribution with a specific failure probability is stated. An outlier detection method based on the *Chi-Square Goodness of Fit* test statistic [8] is proposed, which is based on the distribution assumption mentioned above. This proposed statistical method can pinpoint outlier trigger dimensions in the hierarchically structured production-quality time series, due to the characteristic of the goodness-of-fit test. To test the viability of the proposed method and thus the validity of the distribution assumption, standard unsupervised outlier detection techniques like *LOF* [14], *AHC* [18] and *Grubbs* [7]) are implemented. Several conducted experiments prove the superiority of the proposed method in comparison to mentioned standard techniques in the context of anomaly detection in production-quality data. The results presented in Sect. 4.5 show that the proposed method model real-world production-quality anomalies well while minimizing false-positive and false-negative test results in comparison to standard techniques. Furthermore, the results in Sect. 4.4 show the superiority of the proposed outlier detection technique in comparison to the standard outlier detection algorithms, concerning fluctuation of the underlying observation size. Standard techniques perform as well as the proposed technique, when observation size is constant, however, perform substantially worse when observation size is varying. By including the underlying observation size in the test statistic (see Sect. 3.2), anomalies can be rated based on their impact on production-quality, as well as anomaly trigger dimensions can be identified (see Sect. 4.4, Sect. 4.5).

References

1. Aggarwal, C.C.: Outlier analysis. In: Data Mining, pp. 237–263. Springer, Cham (2015). https://doi.org/10.1007/978-3-319-14142-8_8
2. Heckert, A., et al.: NIST/SEMATECH e-Handbook of Statistical Methods - 1.3.5.15. Chi-Square Goodness-of-Fit Test (2003). https://www.itl.nist.gov/div898/handbook/eda/section3/eda35f.htm. Accessed 09 May 2019

3. Heckert, A., et al.: NIST/SEMATECH e-Handbook of Statistical Methods - 7.2.1. Do the observations come from a particular distribution? (2003). https://www.itl.nist.gov/div898/handbook/prc/section2/prc21.htm. Accessed 09 May 2019
4. Andreas Schütze, N.H., Schneider, T.: Sensors 4.0 - smart sensors and measurement technology enable industry 4.0. J. Sens. Sens. Syst. **7**, 359–371 (2018). https://doi.org/10.5194/jsss-7-359-2018
5. Bradley, A.P.: The use of the area under the roc curve in the evaluation of machine learning algorithms. Pattern Recogn. **30**(7), 1145–1159 (1997). https://doi.org/10.1016/S0031-3203(96)00142-2, http://www.sciencedirect.com/science/article/pii/S0031320396001422
6. Cochran, W.G.: The χ^2 test of goodness of fit. Ann. Math. Stat. **23**(3), 315–345 (1952). https://doi.org/10.1214/aoms/1177729380
7. E. Grubbs, F.: Procedure for detecting outlying observations in samples. Technometrics **11**, 1–21 (1974). https://doi.org/10.1080/00401706.1969.10490657
8. Karl Pearson, F.R.S.: X. on the criterion that a given system of deviations from the probable in the case of a correlated system of variables is such that it can be reasonably supposed to have arisen from random sampling. London Edinburgh Dublin Philos. Mag. J. Sci. **50**(302), 157–175 (1900). https://doi.org/10.1080/14786440009463897
9. Gray, J., Bosworth, A., Lyaman, A., Pirahesh, H.: Data cube: a relational aggregation operator generalizing group-by, cross-tab, and sub-totals. In: Proceedings of the Twelfth International Conference on Data Engineering. pp. 152–159, February 1996. https://doi.org/10.1109/ICDE.1996.492099
10. Kriegel, H.-P., Kröger, P., Zimek, A.: Outlier detection techniques. In: Tutorial, 16th ACM SIGKDD Conference on Knowledge Discovery and Data Mining (2010), conference presentation at http://www.dbs.ifi.lmu.de/~zimek/publications/KDD2010/kdd10-outlier-tutorial.pdf
11. Hodge, V.J., Austin, J.: A survey of outlier detection methodologies. Artif. Intell. Rev. **22**(2), 85–88 (2004). https://doi.org/10.1007/s10462-004-4304-y
12. Lasi, H., Fettke, P., Kemper, H.G., Feld, T., Hoffmann, M.: Industry 4.0. Bus. Inf. Syst. Eng. **6**(4), 239–242 (2014). https://doi.org/10.1007/s12599-014-0334-4
13. Torgo, L.: Resource-bounded fraud detection. In: Neves, J., Santos, M.F., Machado, J.M. (eds.) EPIA 2007. LNCS (LNAI), vol. 4874, pp. 449–460. Springer, Heidelberg (2007). https://doi.org/10.1007/978-3-540-77002-2_38
14. Breunig, M.M., Kriegel, H.-P., Ng, R.T., Sander, J.: LOF: identifying density-based local outliers. In: Proceedings of the 2000 ACM SIGMOD International Conference on Management of Data, SIGMOD 2000, pp. 93–104. Association for Computing Machinery, New York (2000). https://doi.org/10.1145/342009.335388
15. Michelle Lacey: The Binomial Distribution. http://www.stat.yale.edu/Courses/1997-98/101/binom.htm (1997). Accessed 05 May 2019
16. Olap Council: OLAP and OLAP Server Definitions (1995). http://www.olapcouncil.org/research/glossaryly.htm. Accessed 10 May 2019
17. Tharwat, A.: Classification assessment methods. Appl. Comput. Inform. (2018). https://doi.org/10.1016/j.aci.2018.08.003. http://www.sciencedirect.com/science/article/pii/S2210832718301546

18. Torgo, L.: Data Mining with R, Learning with Case Studies. Chapman and Hall/CRC (2010). http://www.dcc.fc.up.pt/~ltorgo/DataMiningWithR

19. Wu, Q., Vos, P.: Chapter 6 - inference and prediction. In: Gudivada, V.N., Rao, C. (eds.) Computational Analysis and Understanding of Natural Languages: Principles, Methods and Applications, Handbook of Statistics, vol. 38, pp. 114–115. Elsevier (2018). https://doi.org/10.1016/bs.host.2018.06.004, http://www.sciencedirect.com/science/article/pii/S0169716118300099

Learning from Past Observations: Meta-Learning for Efficient Clustering Analyses

Manuel Fritz[✉], Dennis Tschechlov, and Holger Schwarz

University of Stuttgart, Universitätsstraße 38, 70569 Stuttgart, Germany
{manuel.fritz,dennis.tschechlov,holger.schwarz}@ipvs.uni-stuttgart.de

Abstract. Many clustering algorithms require the number of clusters as input parameter prior to execution. Since the "best" number of clusters is most often unknown in advance, analysts typically execute clustering algorithms multiple times with varying parameters and subsequently choose the most promising result. Several methods for an automated estimation of suitable parameters have been proposed. Similar to the procedure of an analyst, these estimation methods draw on repetitive executions of a clustering algorithm with varying parameters. However, when working with voluminous datasets, each single execution tends to be very time-consuming. Especially in today's Big Data era, such a repetitive execution of a clustering algorithm is not feasible for an efficient exploration. We propose a novel and efficient approach to accelerate estimations for the number of clusters in datasets. Our approach relies on the idea of meta-learning and terminates each execution of the clustering algorithm as soon as an expected qualitative demand is met. We show that this new approach is generally applicable, i.e., it can be used with existing estimation methods. Our comprehensive evaluation reveals that our approach is able to speed up the estimation of the number of clusters by an order of magnitude, while still achieving accurate estimates.

Keywords: Data mining · Clustering · Meta-learning

1 Introduction

Clustering is a fundamental primitive for exploratory tasks. Manifold application domains rely on clustering techniques, such as computer vision, information access and retrieval, or business purposes, e.g, for grouping customers, for workforce management and for planning tasks [18].

Jain identified three main purposes of clustering techniques [18]: (1) Assessing the structure of the data, i.e., to exploit clustering to gain better insights into data, to generate hypotheses or to detect anomalies. (2) Grouping entities, so that previously unseen entities can be assigned to a specific cluster. (3) Compressing data, i.e., to create a summarization of data. Especially on voluminous datasets, clustering has a particular exploratory power to fulfill these

© Springer Nature Switzerland AG 2020
M. Song et al. (Eds.): DaWaK 2020, LNCS 12393, pp. 364–379, 2020.
https://doi.org/10.1007/978-3-030-59065-9_28

main purposes. In order to achieve valuable clustering results, an analyst has to select proper parameters. For the most commonly used family of clustering algorithms, k-center clustering algorithms [33], this is the expected number of clusters k. However, for an arbitrary, previously unseen dataset, choosing promising parameters is a tremendous pitfall. Wrong parameters can lead to wrong assessments, groupings or compressings of the data, and thus significantly reduce the exploratory power of clustering results. Especially novice analysts, without an in-depth domain knowledge, require further support for finding solid parameters.

Such an assistance is provided by estimation methods that automatically provide the number of clusters in datasets [4–6, 8, 17, 24, 25, 29, 30]. These methods execute a clustering algorithm several times with varying parameters. Subsequently, they provide the most promising parameters. However, each execution of a clustering algorithm is a long-running task, since numerous iterations within the algorithm are performed. Approaches to limit the number of iterations to a fixed threshold (and thus reducing the runtime) can lead to bad clustering results. It is not clear how to set such a threshold in order to avoid a significant loss of quality. These problems become even more severe, when analyzing large datasets in today's Big Data era, since they require usually even more iterations until a satisfying result is achieved.

In our work, we propose a generic approach to accelerate estimation methods. This new approach draws on meta-learning to dynamically limit the number of iterations in each execution of the clustering algorithm. Instead of setting a fixed threshold for the number of iterations, we aim to learn the quality progress throughout iterations of a clustering algorithm on previously clustered datasets [13]. To the best of our knowledge, existing meta-learning approaches for clustering solely focus on the algorithm selection [3, 32], yet no previous work draws on meta-learning approaches to accelerate the execution of clustering algorithms and analyzes the effects of this acceleration on estimation methods.

Our contributions include the following:

- We analyze existing estimation methods and identify major commonalities. These commonalities are important as they allow to apply our new approach on top of all these estimation methods.
- We propose a generic approach to accelerate estimation methods and show how it exploits meta-learning.
- In our comprehensive evaluation on a distributed Apache Spark cluster, we show that our approach significantly outperforms the conventional executions of estimation methods in terms of runtime. At the same time, our approach provides very similar estimates for the number of clusters. Thus, the proposed approach is a strong fit for analyzing large datasets.

The remainder of this paper is structured as follows: We present related work in Sect. 2. We describe the generic procedure of estimation methods in Sect. 3 and discuss how we exploit meta-learning for our new approach to accelerate these estimation methods. In Sect. 4, we summarize the results of a comprehensive evaluation of our approach on a distributed Apache Spark cluster. Finally, we conclude this work in Sect. 5.

2   Related Work

Exploratory data analysis aims to support analysts in finding suitable algorithms and parameters for analytical tasks [31]. In general, a distinction is made between supervised and unsupervised learning. For supervised learning, automated methods to find suitable algorithms and parameters are emerging in the area of automated machine learning (AutoML) [11]. These methods draw on ground-truth labels, such as class labels, which are already available in the training data. The underlying hyperparameter optimization techniques [27] can exploit these labels and therefore automatically come up with a solid result.

For unsupervised learning, no ground-truth labels are contained in the dataset. Hence, it is undefined what a correct solution looks like, which means that this information must be obtained either from the analyst or from additional evaluation criteria. As a consequence, AutoML approaches and hyperparameter optimization techniques are not well-studied for unsupervised learning.

A commonly used unsupervised learning technique is clustering, especially k-center clustering [33]. Here, analysts have to define certain parameters in advance, where the number of clusters k to be generated is of most interest. The quality of this choice can only be revealed after the execution of the clustering algorithm. Therefore, the exploration of large parameter search spaces is a time-consuming process. To automate this process, numerous methods to estimate the number of clusters have been proposed [4–6,8,17,24,25,29,30]. They typically proceed in an iterative manner by (1) identifying which parameter to execute next on which subset of the data, (2) executing the clustering algorithm, and subsequently (3) evaluating each result according to a specific metric. Hence, the total runtime for estimating the number of clusters is the sum of several executions of the clustering algorithm plus the runtime of the estimation method, i.e., for defining the execution settings and evaluating the result. Prior work either focuses on (a) accelerating clustering algorithms, (b) applying meta-learning to clustering algorithms, or on (c) improving estimation methods, but does not analyze the combinations and effects on the respective others. We present related work in all three areas.

2.1   Accelerating Clustering Algorithms

All k-center clustering algorithms proceed in an iterative manner, i.e., the same sequence of steps is repeated until a given convergence criterion is met. In each iteration, the entities are assigned to the closest centroid, which is the center of a cluster. Subsequently, the center is moved to a better position in order to minimize the variance of each cluster. k-center clustering algorithms typically converge, when no entities can be assigned to a closer centroid.

Previous examinations [13,22] show that a reduction of runtime can be achieved by reducing the number of iterations of the clustering algorithm. Mexicano et al. focus on the displacement of the centroids after each iteration [22]. They assume that the maximal centroid displacement happens in the first iteration. Hence, they propose to stop the clustering algorithm once the centroid displacement is less than 5% of the maximum centroid displacement and thereby neglect explicitly setting a maximum number of iterations. However, they did not address in detail why the coefficient is set to 5% and how their approach correlates to the final clustering quality.

A reduction of the runtime for k-center clustering algorithms can also be reached in three other ways: (a) by improving the selection of the initial centroids [2,15], (b) by making distance calculations more efficient [9,19], and (c) by performing the calculations on a distributed system, e.g., on Hadoop or Spark [12,14]. Note, that our novel approach can be combined with all of these improvements to achieve additional speed-ups.

2.2 Meta-Learning for Clustering Analyses

Nowadays, there is no commonly accepted definition of meta-learning. Vilalta and Drissi describe meta-learning as a study on how an algorithm "can increase in efficiency through experience" with the goal of the algorithm to adapt to the domain or task [32]. In an offline phase, so-called meta-knowledge is collected by performing several executions of a clustering algorithm and measuring relevant properties. In the subsequent online phase, this meta-knowledge is exploited in order to enhance algorithms on previously unseen datasets. Meta-knowledge can have several forms, i.e., there is no definition or limitation of this knowledge [16]. Also, there are several possibilities how to exploit this meta-knowledge for an enhancement of the algorithms, i.e., to achieve faster or more accurate results.

In the context of clustering analysis, meta-learning can be used to predict a clustering algorithm based on the clustering results on similar datasets [7,10,23,28]. These approaches rely on meta-features as instantiation of meta-knowledge. Meta-features are specific dataset characteristics, such as the number of entities, the number of dimensions, mean values etc. They are extracted in an offline phase from numerous datasets together with the results of various clustering algorithms. In the subsequent online phase, a previously unseen dataset is considered. The dataset that is most similar to this unseen dataset is identified via its meta-features and the best-performing clustering algorithm is applied. The difference in the works are the used (a) meta-features, (b) clustering algorithms, (c) quality measures for measuring the performance of clustering results, and the (d) overall meta-learning approach. Furthermore, related work in this area solely focuses on the selection of a clustering algorithm and thereby completely neglects its parameters, which were set to fixed values in these works.

2.3 Estimation Methods

Estimation methods require a prior definition of the search space $\mathcal{R}$. Within this search space, these methods aim to estimate the number of clusters k. To this end, we can divide related work into two groups: Estimation methods are either (a) exhaustive, meaning they perform an exhaustive search in the search space $\mathcal{R}$, or (b) non-exhaustive, i.e., they do not perform an exhaustive search. We will present commonly used methods within both categories.

Exhaustive Estimation Methods. Exhaustive estimation methods proceed by evaluating each single clustering result in the search space $\mathcal{R}$ and subsequently choose the one with the best quality measure.

Various clustering validity measures can be used to evaluate the clustering results [4–6,8,25,29]. These measures assess the internal quality of a clustering result, i.e., compactness, separation, or arbitrary combinations thereof. Regarding the compactness, the sum of squared errors (SSE) is a fundamental validity measure. It measures the squared distance from each entity to its centroid. The silhouette coefficient [25] focuses on the separation. It measures the distance to the closest centroid and thereby states, whether an entity should be assigned to another cluster. The Calinski-Harabasz Index [4], Coggins-Jain Index [5], Davies-Bouldin Index [6] and Dunn Index [8] address different combinations of compactness and separation.

Another area of clustering validity measures arose from information theory, e.g., the Akaike Information Criterion (AIC) [1] or the Bayesian Information Criterion (BIC) [26]. They consist of two terms: The first term measures the fitness of the model, whereas the second term is a penalty regarding the number of parameters in a model. The goal of the latter is to avoid overfitting in terms of a too high value for k. This penalty term is larger for BIC than for AIC. Sugar and James proposed the so-called jump method [29]. This method proceeds by calculating the distortion of the resulting clusters. Subsequently, a rate distortion function is applied, which allows to compare clustering results.

Non-exhaustive Estimation Methods. The idea of non-exhaustive estimation methods is to perform an ascending (or descending) search in $\mathcal{R}$. The search strategies stop, as soon as the clustering results for subsequent values for k barely differ according to a certain metric.

Estimation methods following the ascending non-exhaustive search principle are the gap statistic [30], G-Means [17] or X-Means [24]. The gap statistic relies on the notion of a standard error of clustering results to avoid an exhaustive search. On the other hand, G-Means and X-Means proceed in a hierarchical way, by splitting clustering results into smaller clusterings until further splits provide no better results according to a certain metric or $max(\mathcal{R})$ is met.

To the best of our knowledge, none of the mentioned related work addresses how estimation methods can be accelerated in a generic way, i.e., by applying meta-learning from previous executions of a clustering algorithm and how this approach affects the overall exploration process.

3   Efficiently Estimating the Number of Clusters

In this section, we demonstrate commonalities across existing estimation methods and generalize these commonalities. Furthermore, we introduce our generic approach to accelerate estimation methods and explain how it can be employed with existing estimation methods. Our approach draws on meta-learning, which exploits characteristics of previously conducted clustering explorations.

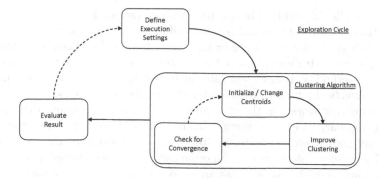

Fig. 1. Exploration to estimate the number of clusters.

3.1 Generic Method to Estimate the Number of Clusters

We analyzed prevalent estimation methods and identified several commonalities. Figure 1 emphasizes the general procedure of all estimation methods.

All estimation methods firstly define the execution settings, i.e., the subset of the input dataset and the parameter k of the clustering algorithm. Thereafter, the clustering algorithm is executed, which comprises the following steps: (1) determine the position of the centroids, (2) improve the clustering by (re-) assigning entities to the closest centroid, and (3) check for convergence. Several clustering iterations are performed until a convergence criterion is achieved, e.g., until no entities change assignments to a closer centroid anymore. After the clustering algorithm is executed, the result is evaluated according to the estimation method and its used metric. This process is repeated with varying parameters or on varying subsets of the data until the estimation method no longer provides further execution settings. Finally, the estimated number of clusters in the input dataset is determined according to the specific estimation method (cf. Sect. 2.3).

All examined estimation methods draw on a repetitive execution of the clustering algorithm. Typically, several iterations of the clustering algorithm are performed and each iteration may become very time-consuming due to many distance calculations between entities and centroids.

3.2 Termination of k-center Clustering Algorithms

Given the importance of the number of clustering iterations, the question arises when to terminate the algorithm. Macqueen and Lloyd proposed to perform k-Means, a frequently used instantiation of a k-center clustering algorithm, until the centroids do not change their position anymore [20,21]. However, when considering many entities or dimensions, numerous iterations have to be performed until the algorithm finally converges.

An easy approach to reduce the runtime of the clustering algorithm is to allow a fixed number of iterations which should be conducted. However, it is challenging to choose a promising value for this threshold: Too few iterations lead to a insufficient result, whereas too many iterations lead to a high runtime. Besides that, a generic threshold is not feasible, because of too many influencing factors, such as the feature space or data distribution. Furthermore, when considering the repetitive execution of the clustering algorithm as part of a certain estimation method, it is not clear how such a fixed threshold for the clustering iterations affects the final estimation for the number of clusters.

We draw our work on the our previously proposed quality-driven early-stopping approach [13]. This meta-learning approach aims to learn the typical progress of quality during clustering iterations and formalizes this as an regression. Subsequently, this regression function can be exploited in order to terminate the clustering algorithm as soon as an expected quality of the clustering result is achieved. Hence, this approach does not terminate the clustering algorithm based on a fixed number of iterations, but after the clustering approximates a specific qualitative demand. However, it has not been assessed before (a) how to use this approach in an exploratory setting, i.e., in combination with estimation methods, and (b) how it affects the runtime and accuracy of these methods.

3.3   Our Approach

Our approach aims to accelerate estimation methods by applying meta-learning in order to terminate the clustering algorithm once a specific qualitative demand is met. We draw on our previous work [13] in order to contrast the changerate of clustering validity measures θ between two subsequent clustering iterations i to the expected quality of a clustering. This is necessary, since values of clustering validity measures may be unbounded and provide solely a relative insight into clustering results. On the other hand, the final clustering result is only available at the very end, when no entity changes membership anymore. Hence, our previously proposed meta-learning approach aims to contrast unbounded clustering validity measures to the expected current clustering quality (in percent) compared to the final result.

To this end, we distinguish between two phases: In an offline phase, a clustering algorithm is executed on several datasets and with different parameters, similar to an exploratory process conducted by analysts. However, in each iteration of the clustering algorithm, we measure clustering validity measures (cf. Sect. 2.3). In [13], we showed that the corresponding overhead caused by most clustering validity measures is negligible. Thus, the results of the offline phase are a cheap by-product of previous executions of a clustering algorithm, e.g., of previous exploratory clustering analyses. Subsequently, we investigate the relationship between the recorded clustering validity measures with the resulting quality of the clustering and subsequently formalize this relationship with a regression function r. In the online phase, we exploit r on previously unseen datasets. This regression can be used to terminate the clustering algorithm after a certain quality is expected to be achieved by measuring the clustering validity measure. Hence, the task of the analyst is to provide a qualitative demand q of the clustering approximation. We showed that considerable runtime savings are possible, while still meeting the qualitative demand. Furthermore, we unveiled

---

Algorithm 1: Method for estimating the number of clusters

Input: $\mathcal{D}$: dataset, k_{min}: lower estimation bound, k_{max}: upper estimation bound, em:
  estimation method, r: regression function for early stopping, q: qualitative demand
Output: $k_{estimate}$: estimated number of clusters in $\mathcal{D}$ according to em

1   $\mathcal{K} \leftarrow \{\}$;
2   **repeat**
      /* define execution settings   */
3       $\mathcal{D'} \leftarrow$ subset of $\mathcal{D}$ according to em;
4       $k_{test} \leftarrow$ select $k_{test} \in [k_{min}, k_{max}]$ according to em;
      /* perform clustering algorithm   */
5       $i \leftarrow 0$;
6   **repeat**
7            $\mathcal{C} \leftarrow$ perform clustering iteration with k_{test} on $\mathcal{D'}$;
8   **if** $i > 0$ **then**
9            $\mid$ $\underline{cvm_{i-1} \leftarrow cvm_i}$;
10          $\underline{cvm_i \leftarrow \text{calculate clustering validity measure}}$;
11   **if** $i > 0$ **then**
12          $\mid$ $\underline{\theta = |(cvm_{i-1} - cvm_i)/cvm_{i-1}|}$;
13          $i \leftarrow i + 1$;
14   **until** $i > 1$ *and* $r(q) \geq \theta$;
      /* evaluate result   */
15       $m \leftarrow$ calculate metric for $\mathcal{C}$ according to em;
16       $\mathcal{K} \leftarrow \mathcal{K} \cup \{(k_{test}, m)\}$;
17 **until** em *provides no further execution settings to test*;
18 $k_{estimate} \leftarrow$ estimated number of clusters from $\mathcal{K}$ according to em;

---

that the separation (sum of distances between the centroids) as clustering validity measure leads to the best results in terms of accuracy of the demanded quality and least runtime overhead in each iteration.

Algorithm 1 outlines how the meta-learning approach can be integrated into existing estimation methods for the number of clusters in datasets. Changes in contrast to the regular execution of estimation methods are underlined. As described in Sect. 3.1, the approach works as follows: (1) Defining the execution settings (lines 3–4), (2) performing the clustering algorithm (lines 5–14), and (3) evaluating the result of the clustering (lines 15–16). Finally, the estimation is made (line 18). During the execution of the clustering algorithm, it is necessary to calculate the clustering validity measure in each iteration to derive the change rate θ (lines 8–12) and subsequently to check for convergence (line 14), i.e., check if θ meets the predicted threshold from the qualitative demand of $r(q)$.

3.4   Discussion of Generality

The proposed approach in Algorithm 1 is generally applicable for various estimation methods and k-center clustering algorithms. On the one hand, estimation methods can exploit our approach, because they follow a common procedure as discussed in Sect. 3.1. Furthermore, they repeatedly execute the clustering algorithm. Thereby, for each execution of the clustering algorithm, the quality can be approximated by applying meta-learning. On the other hand, our approach also preserves generality for k-center clustering algorithms, such as k-Means, k-Medians or Gaussian Mixture Models. These algorithms proceed similarly (cf. Fig. 1) and aim to minimize their specific notion of variance from entities to the

Table 1. Experimental datasets

	Dataset	Entities	Attributes
I	Heterogeneity Activity Recognition	33,741,500	5
II	HIGGS	11,000,000	28
III	HEPMASS	10,500,000	28
IV	Gas sensor array under dynamic gas mixtures	8,386,765	19
V	SUSY	5,000,000	18
VI	KDD Cup 1999 Data	4,898,431	33
VII	US Census Data (1990)	2,458,285	68
VIII	Individual household electric power consumption	2,049,280	7
IX	Poker Hand	1,025,010	10
X	Skin Segmentation	245,057	3

Table 2. Estimation methods

Abbr.	Name	Parameters
AIC	Akaike Information Criterion [1]	
BIC	Bayesian Information Criterion [26]	
CHI	Calinski-Harabasz Index [4]	
CJI	Coggins-Jain Index [5]	
DBI	Davies-Bouldin Index [6]	
DUI	Dunn Index [8]	
JUM	Jump Method [29]	$Y = r/2$
SIL	Silhouette coefficient [25]	
GAP	Gap Statistic [30]	$b = 5$
GME	G-Means [17]	$\alpha = 0.0001$
XAI	X-Means (AIC) [24]	
XBI	X-Means (BIC) [24]	

closest centroid throughout several clustering iterations. Hence, our approach addresses the convergence of k-center clustering algorithms in an exploratory setting, i.e., during the execution of estimation methods.

4   Evaluation

As shown in the previous section, our approach is generic and can be applied on top of several estimation methods. Yet, it is unclear how our approach affects estimation methods, i.e., if significant runtime savings can be achieved while still achieving promising estimates for the number of clusters. Therefore, our comprehensive evaluation addresses the feasibility of the proposed approach.

Firstly, we evaluate the runtime performance of the new approach. Secondly, we investigate how the estimates of our approach differ from a conventional execution, i.e., without meta-learning, by addressing 12 commonly used estimation methods for the number of clusters in datasets. Before we present the results of our comprehensive evaluation, we explain the experimental setup.

4.1   Experimental Setup

We evaluated our approach on 10 different datasets using 12 estimation methods and 3 clustering methods. We repeated each experiment 3 times and focus on median values. We do not store any values throughout these 3 runs, i.e., perform each run from scratch. This results in more than 1,000 ($= 10 * 12 * 3$) different runs. In the following, we present the different variations in more detail.

Datasets. Table 1 shows the datasets from the UCI machine learning repository[1] that we used for the evaluation. They differ in size, number of entities, number

---
[1] https://archive.ics.uci.edu/ml/datasets.html.

of attributes, origin and context. In order to use k-center clustering algorithms, we removed any non-numeric attributes as well as class labels, timestamps and missing values, if existent.

Estimation Methods. As our approach is generally applicable for various estimation methods, we implemented it using all estimation methods introduced in Sect. 2.3. Table 2 summarizes the estimation methods and their abbreviation used throughout the evaluation. Furthermore, the parameters for the estimation methods are shown, if required. We kept the variables and proposed values provided by the corresponding authors, where required and available.

For all estimation methods, we set the search space to $R = [2; 25]$, since the used datasets mostly originate from classification tasks and have a similar number of classes. The ground truth for the number of clusters is out of scope for this evaluation, since we focus on the differences to a conventional execution of estimation methods. If an estimation method failed to provide an estimation within a predefined time budget of 30 min, we stopped the execution and mark the corresponding estimation as failed. The runtime for the repetitive execution of the clustering algorithm is out of scope for the time budget.

Clustering Methods. Since k-Means is one of the most commonly used k-center clustering algorithm [33], we draw our evaluation on this algorithm. Note however, that our observations can be transferred to other k-center clustering algorithms, since they proceed similarly. We based our experiments on the Apache Spark implementation of k-Means.

For the baseline (BASE), we rely on the convergence criterion of the implementation of k-Means in Spark, i.e., our proposed meta-learning approach is not applied. This implementation additionally requires to specify the maximum number of iterations, which we set to 100 for our experiments.

To implement our meta-learning approach, we used the regression function r from our previous work, which was built on the same datasets [13]. This function is formally denoted in Eq. 1, where q denotes the qualitative demand.

$$r(q) = (6.16\mathrm{e}{-}05)q^2 - (3.61\mathrm{e}{-}03)q - 2.37\mathrm{e}{-}01 \qquad (1)$$

For our experiments, we set the qualitative demand of the meta-learning approach to 90% (MTL-90) and 99% (MTL-99). Hence, the respective thresholds for the convergence of the clustering algorithm were set based on the regression curve. We focus on these values, because we thoroughly evaluated the meta-learning approach for 90% in our previous work. The assumption for using a qualitative demand of 99% is that this would yield a result very close to the final clustering result. However, it is not clear (a) how big the runtime savings for such approximations are and (b) how different the results are compared to MTL-90 and the baseline. Furthermore, we use the separation clustering validity measure in each iteration of the clustering algorithm, since we achieved the best results with it in our previous work.

Infrastructure. We conducted all of our experiments on a distributed Apache Spark cluster, which consists of one master node and six worker nodes.

The master node has a 12-core CPU with 2.10 GHz each and 192 GB RAM. Each worker has a 12-core CPU with 2.10 GHz each and 160 GB RAM. Each node in this cluster operates on Ubuntu 18.04. We installed OpenJDK 8u191, Scala 2.11.12 and used Apache Hadoop 3.2.0 as well as Apache Spark 2.4.0.

We cached the dataset after loading it to memory and repartitioned it to 60 partitions. Throughout the experiment, we did not cache any other values in order to achieve comparable statements regarding the overall runtime.

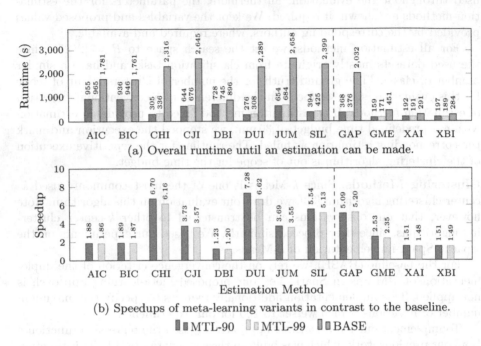

(a) Overall runtime until an estimation can be made.

(b) Speedups of meta-learning variants in contrast to the baseline.

▮▮MTL-90   ▯▯MTL-99   ▯▮BASE

Fig. 2. Runtime comparison of MTL-90, MTL-99 and BASE averaged over all datasets. The dashed line depicts the separation of exhaustive estimation methods (left) and non-exhaustive estimation methods (right).

4.2   Runtime Evaluation

Fig. 2 depicts the runtime comparison for all estimation methods averaged over all datasets. Figure 2a depicts the overall runtime until an estimation can be made per each k-Means execution method, whereas Fig. 2b shows the speedups of MTL-90 and MTL-99 in contrast to the baseline.

It can be seen that all estimation methods benefit from our meta-learning approach in terms of the overall runtime. Especially exhaustive methods benefit more from our approach, since the clustering algorithm is executed more often on the whole dataset in contrast to non-exhaustive methods. Also, GAP highly benefits from the meta-learning approach, since it repeatedly executes k-Means on large synthetically created datasets (cf. Sect. 2.3). GME, XAI and XBI benefit to a smaller extent, since they perform k-Means on smaller subsets of the data in each step.

Figure 2b unveils that speedups between 1.23 and 7.28 (MTL-90) and 1.20 and 6.62 (MTL-99) can be achieved. For certain datasets and estimation methods, we even obtain higher speedups of a factor of more than 17.

The main reason for the reduction of the overall runtime per estimation method can be found in the individual reduction of the runtime for each execution of the clustering algorithm. Therefore, we investigate the number of k-Means iterations for exhaustive estimation methods, since they benefit most from our approach. Figure 3 summarizes these iterations for all k-Means execution methods and datasets. These values are aggregated over the whole search space $\mathcal{R}$. Thus, they provide insights into how many iterations of the clustering algorithm are performed within a complete exploration process.

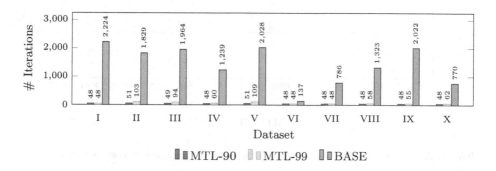

Fig. 3. Number of iterations performed in $\mathcal{R}$ until convergence.

Figure 3 shows that many iterations are required until the clustering algorithm terminates for the baseline BASE. While some datasets require more than 2,000 iterations, others draw on few hundred iterations. This confirms our assumption that finding a fixed threshold for the number of iterations until a clustering algorithm found promising results is challenging, since the achieved quality at a certain iteration of a clustering algorithm highly depends on data characteristics.

On the other hand, MTL-90 and MTL-99 require only very few iterations. In order to perform k-Means for the whole search space $\mathcal{R}$, most often much less than 100 iterations are performed, which explains the tremendous speedups from above. This underlines that our meta-learning approach doesn't rely on a fixed number of iterations, but rather addresses the clustering quality. Furthermore, due to the fewer clustering iterations and a negligible overhead of our approach, we conclude that our approach also leads to less resource consumption, such as CPU or RAM, throughout the whole exploration process.

4.3 Accuracy Evaluation

Since cluster analysis is an unsupervised learning task, the ground truth, i.e., the correct number of clusters is not known in advance for an arbitrary dataset. Hence, we evaluate the predictions of our approach compared to the baseline for each estimation method. To this end, we address the deviation of the meta-learning variants to the baseline BASE, i.e., without applying meta-learning. Formally, we denote this as $\Delta k = k_{MTL} - k_{BASE}$, where k_{MTL} and k_{BASE} depict the estimated values for k according to MTL-90, MTL-99 and BASE, respectively. This formalization enables us to investigate if our meta-learning approach tends to over- or underestimate the number of clusters compared to the baseline, i.e., a conventional execution of k-Means.

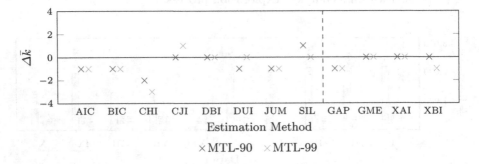

Fig. 4. Accuracy comparison between early stopping variants in contrast to BASE.

Figure 4 summarizes the results, where $\Delta \bar{k}$ denotes the averaged values of Δk over all 10 datasets. In general, the results show that only minor deviations are achieved. The values for $\Delta \bar{k}$ range between -3 and $+1$. As this range offers only little space for improvements, the results between MTL-90 and MTL-99 barely differ. For a few estimation methods, i.e., CHI, CJI and XBI, the estimates provide higher deviations for MTL-99 than for MTL-90. We assume that the randomness in the initialization step of k-Means leads to these minor deviations.

Furthermore, the proposed meta-learning approach tends to underestimate the number of clusters more often than to overestimate it. However, as $\Delta k = -3$ is the highest underestimation, we regard it as acceptable in regards to the significant runtime savings as previously shown.

We further argue that with these minor deviations and huge runtime savings, an analyst can manually search for probably even better parameters in a much smaller search space. Hence, we emphasize that the proposed meta-learning approach is of paramount interest for analysts and exploratory clustering analyses.

5 Conclusion

In this work, we introduce a novel approach to accelerate estimation methods, which is generally applicable for existing estimation methods and k-center clustering algorithms. We base our work on a prior work that exploits meta-learning in order to reduce the runtime of k-center clustering algorithms tremendously by trading-off the resulting clustering quality to a certain degree.

In our comprehensive evaluation, we showed that our approach significantly outperforms the conventional execution of several existing estimation methods in terms of runtime, while still providing very accurate estimates. Therefore, our approach is a strong fit for analyzing large datasets, since each conventional execution of a clustering algorithm is a long-running task. Especially novice analysts can benefit from our meta-learning approach, as they typically define large parameter search spaces, where each single execution of a k-center clustering algorithm is costly to perform.

In future work, we want to address how the proposed meta-learning approach can be transferred to other families of clustering algorithms and their parameter estimation methods as well.

Acknowledgements. This research was partially funded by the Ministry of Science of Baden-Württemberg, Germany, for the Doctoral Program 'Services Computing'. Some work presented in this paper was performed in the project 'INTERACT' as part of the Software Campus program, which is funded by the German Federal Ministry of Education and Research (BMBF) under Grant No.: 01IS17051.

References

1. Akaike, H.: A new look at the statistical model identification. IEEE Trans. Autom. Control **19**(6), 716–723 (1974)
2. Bahmani, B., Moseley, B., Vattani, A., Kumar, R., Vassilvitskii, S.: Scalable K-Means++. Proc. VLDB Endow. **5**(7), 622–633 (2012)
3. Brazdil, P., Carrier, C.G., Soares, C., Vilalta, R.: Metalearning: Applications to Data Mining. Springer Science & Business Media, Berlin (2008)
4. Caliński, T., Harabasz, J.: A dendrite method for cluster analysis. Commun. Stat. **3**(1), 1–27 (1974)
5. Coggins, J.M., Jain, A.K.: A spatial filtering approach to texture analysis. Pattern Recogn. Lett. **3**(3), 195–203 (1985)
6. Davies, D.L., Bouldin, D.W.: A cluster separation measure. IEEE Trans. Pattern Anal. Mach. Intell. PAMI-1(2), 224–227 (1979)
7. De Souto, M.C.P., Prudêncio, R.B.C., Soares, R.G.F., De Araujo, D.S.A., Costa, I.G., Ludermir, T.B., Schliep, A.: Ranking and selecting clustering algorithms using a meta-learning approach. In: Proceedings of the International Joint Conference on Neural Networks, pp. 3729–3735 (2008)
8. Dunn, J.C.: Well-separated clusters and optimal fuzzy partitions. J. Cybern. **4**(1), 95–104 (1974)
9. Elkan, C.: Using the triangle inequality to accelerate k-means. In: Proceedings of the Twentieth International Conference on Machine Learning, pp. 147–153 (2003)
10. Ferrari, D.G., de Castro, L.N.: Clustering Algorithm Recommendation: A Meta-learning Approach. In: Panigrahi, B.K., Das, S., Suganthan, P.N., Nanda, P.K. (eds.) SEMCCO 2012. LNCS, vol. 7677, pp. 143–150. Springer, Heidelberg (2012). https://doi.org/10.1007/978-3-642-35380-2_18

11. Feurer, M., Klein, A., Eggensperger, K., Springenberg, J., Blum, M., Hutter, F.: Efficient and robust automated machine learning. In: Advances in Neural Information Processing Systems (2015)
12. Fritz, M., Albrecht, S., Ziekow, H., Strüker, J.: Benchmarking big data technologies for energy procurement efficiency. In: Proceedings of the 23rd America's Conference on Information Systems (AMCIS 2017) (2017)
13. Fritz, M., Behringer, M., Schwarz, H.: Quality-driven early stopping for explorative cluster analysis for big data. SICS Softw.-Intensive Cyber-Phys. Syst. **34**, 1–12 (2019). https://doi.org/10.1007/s00450-019-00401-0
14. Fritz, M., Muazzen, O., Behringer, M., Schwarz, H.: ASAP-DM: A framework for automatic selection of analytic platforms for data mining. Softw.-Intensive Cyber-Phys. Syst. **35**, 1–13 (2019)
15. Fritz, M., Schwarz, H.: Initializing k-Means Efficiently: Benefits for Exploratory Cluster Analysis. In: Panetto, H., Debruyne, C., Hepp, M., Lewis, D., Ardagna, C.A., Meersman, R. (eds.) OTM 2019. LNCS, vol. 11877, pp. 146–163. Springer, Cham (2019). https://doi.org/10.1007/978-3-030-33246-4_9
16. Giraud-Carrier, C., Vilalta, R., Brazdil, P.: Introduction to the special issue on meta-learning. Mach. Learn. **54**(3), 187–193 (2004)
17. Hamerly, G., Elkan, C.: Learning the k in kmeans. Adv. Neural Inf. Process. Syst. (NIPS) **17**, 1–8 (2004)
18. Jain, A.K.: Data clustering: 50 years beyond K-means. Pattern Recogn. Lett. **31**(8), 651–666 (2010)
19. Kanungo, T., Mount, D., Netanyahu, N., Piatko, C., Silverman, R., Wu, A.: An efficient k-means clustering algorithm: analysis and implementation. IEEE Trans. Pattern Anal. Mach. Intell. **24**(7), 881–892 (2002)
20. Lloyd, S.P.: Least squares quantization in PCM. IEEE Trans. Inf. Theory **28**(2), 129–137 (1982)
21. Macqueen, J.B.: Some methods for classification and analysis of multivariate observations. Proc. Fifth Berkeley Symp. Math. Stat. Prob. **1**, 281–297 (1967)
22. Mexicano, A., Rodríguez, R., Cervantes, S., Montes, P., Jiménez, M., Almanza, N., Abrego, A.: The early stop heuristic: A new convergence criterion for K-means. In: AIP Conference Proceedings, vol. 1738 (2016)
23. Nascimento, A.C.A., Prudêncio, R.B.C., de Souto, M.C.P., Costa, I.G.: Mining rules for the automatic selection process of clustering methods applied to cancer gene expression data. In: Alippi, C., Polycarpou, M., Panayiotou, C., Ellinas, G. (eds.) ICANN 2009. LNCS, vol. 5769, pp. 20–29. Springer, Heidelberg (2009). https://doi.org/10.1007/978-3-642-04277-5_3
24. Pelleg, D., Moore, A.: X-means: Extending K-means with efficient estimation of the number of clusters. In: Proceedings of the 17th International Conference on Machine Learning, pp. 727–734 (2000)
25. Rousseeuw, P.J.: Silhouettes: A graphical aid to the interpretation and validation of cluster analysis. J. Comput. Appl. Math. **20**(C), 53–65 (1987)
26. Schwarz, G.: Estimating the dimension of a model. Ann. Stat. **6**, 461–464 (1978)
27. Snoek, J., Larochelle, H., Adams, R.P.: Practical Bayesian optimization of machine learning algorithms. Adv. Neural Inf. Process. Syst. **4**, 2951–2959 (2012)
28. Soares, R.G.F., Ludermir, T.B., De Carvalho, F.A.T.: An analysis of meta-learning techniques for ranking clustering algorithms applied to artificial data. In: Alippi, C., Polycarpou, M., Panayiotou, C., Ellinas, G. (eds.) ICANN 2009. LNCS, vol. 5768, pp. 131–140. Springer, Heidelberg (2009). https://doi.org/10.1007/978-3-642-04274-4_14

29. Sugar, C.A., James, G.M.: Finding the number of clusters in a dataset: An information-theoretic approach. J. Am. Stat. Assoc. **98**(463), 750–763 (2003)
30. Tibshirani, R., Walther, G., Hastie, T.: Estimating the number of clusters in a data set via the gap statistic. J. R. Stat. Soc. Ser. B Stat. Methodol. **63**(2), 411–423 (2001)
31. Tukey, J.W.: Exploratory Data Analysis. Pearson Addison Wesley, Reading (1977)
32. Vilalta, R., Drissi, Y.: A perspective view and survey of meta-learning. Artif. Intell. Rev. **18**(2), 77–95 (2002)
33. Wu, X., et al.: Top 10 algorithms in data mining. Knowl. Inf. Syst. **14**(1), 1–37 (2008)

Parallel K-Prototypes Clustering with High Efficiency and Accuracy

Hiba Jridi[(✉)], Mohamed Aymen Ben HajKacem, and Nadia Essoussi

LARODEC, Institut Supérieur de Gestion de Tunis, Université de Tunis,
41 Avenue de la Liberté, Cité Bouchoucha, 2000 Le Bardo, Tunisia
jridi_hiba@hotmail.com, medaymen.hajkacem@gmail.com,
nadia.essoussi@isg.rnu.tn

Abstract. Big data is often characterized by a huge volume and mixed types of data including numeric and categorical. The k-prototypes is one of the best-known clustering methods for mixed data. Despite this, it is not suitable to deal with huge volume of data. Several methods have attempted to solve the efficiency problem of the k-prototypes using parallel frameworks. However, none of the existing clustering methods for mixed data, satisfy both accuracy and efficiency. To deal with this issue, we propose a novel parallel k-prototypes clustering method that improves both efficiency and accuracy. The proposed method is based on integrating a parallel approach through Spark framework and implementing a new centers initialization strategy using sampling. Experiments were performed on simulated and real datasets show that the proposed method is scalable and improves both the efficiency and accuracy of the existing k-prototypes methods.

Keywords: Parallel clustering · K-prototypes · Mixed data · Large data · Centers initialization · Spark

1 Introduction

Nowadays, large volumes of data are being collected from different sources and there is a high demand for methods and tools that can efficiently analyse such volumes of data referred to as Big data. Big data is often characterized by four Vs [12]: *Volume* which refers the huge amounts of data generated instantly, ascending from tera-bytes to peta-bytes and on to zeta-bytes. *Variety* indicates the different formats and types of data such as numerical, categorical and textual. *Velocity* refers to the speed of the incoming and updated data, and *Value* represents the hidden valuable information [10].

Clustering is an important technique in machine learning, which has been used to organize data into groups of similar data points called clusters [18]. Many clustering methods have been proposed in the literature, which can be grouped into five main categories such as hierarchical, density-based, grid-based, model-based and partitioning. These clustering methods were used in several

© Springer Nature Switzerland AG 2020
M. Song et al. (Eds.): DaWaK 2020, LNCS 12393, pp. 380–395, 2020.
https://doi.org/10.1007/978-3-030-59065-9_29

applications such as topic detection [8], customer segmentation [2], document clustering [4,9] and image organization [29].

Unfortunately, traditional clustering methods are not suitable for clustering huge amounts of mixed data. This is explained by the high computational cost of these methods which require unrealistic time to build the grouping [16]. For example, k-prototypes, one of the best-known clustering methods for mixed data, does not scale with large volume of data. Recently, several methods have attempted to solve the efficiency problem of the k-prototypes, by distributing clustering process using parallel frameworks [13–15,21]. However, all such studies have improved efficiency at the expense of accuracy since they are sensitive to the initialization cluster centers which may lead to local optimum solutions.

To deal with these issues, we propose in this work a new **Parallel K-Prototypes** clustering method with high Efficiency an Accuracy method for large mixed data referred to as **PKP**. PKP is a k-prototypes based method that supports both accuracy and efficiency by respectively integrating a parallel approach through Spark framework and implementing a new centers initialization strategy using sampling. The proposed method consists of two phases namely *parallel center initialization* and *parallel data clustering*. The first phase is dedicated to generating initial cluster centers from the input data using sampling. The second phase is devoted to clustering the input data by applying k-prototypes algorithm.

The rest of this paper is organized as follows: Sect. 2 discusses related works which propose to deal with large and mixed data. Then, Sect. 3 presents the k-prototypes method, MapReduce and Spark frameworks. After that, Sect. 4 describes the proposed PKP method while Sect. 5 presents experiments that we have performed to evaluate the performance of the proposed method. Finally, Sect. 6 presents conclusion and future works.

2   Related Works

One of the most fundamental challenges for Big data is how to deal with the increasingly available amounts of data. Although, traditional clustering methods cannot be adopted for such overwhelming volumes, several clustering methods based on parallel frameworks have been designed in the literature to deal with large data [3,26,33]. The parallelization can be done using different frameworks such as Message Passing Interface (MPI) [22,28], MapReduce [5] or Graphics Processing Unit (GPU) [11,25]. MapReduce has become a popular framework for parallelizing algorithms thanks to its features such as fault-tolerance and load balancing [5]. Despite the efficiency of the above methods to deal with large data, they can not support the mixed types of data and are limited to only numeric attributes.

To deal with mixed data, several clustering methods were designed in the literature [1,17,19,23]. K-prototypes [17] is one of the most widely-used clustering methods for mixed data because of its efficacy. Several methods have attempted to solve the efficiency problem of the k-prototypes, by distributing clustering process using parallel frameworks [16] such as k-prototypes using MapReduce framework [21], Spark based k-prototypes [13] and Accelerated version of MapReduce-based k-prototypes [15]. However, all such methods have improved efficiency at the expense of accuracy since they are sensitive to the initialization cluster centers which may lead to local optimum solution.

In order to deal with the initialization of cluster centers, various methods were proposed in the literature [20,25,34]. For instance, Forgy [7] has proposed a strategy to assign each data object to one of the k random clusters and then, the centers of initial clusters are updated. Other works have been focused on meta-heuristic methods [34] as they are less sensitive to cluster initialization. Most of optimization clustering algorithms are not appropriate for large mixed data because they require unrealistic time to build the grouping. Overall, none of the existing clustering methods for mixed data, satisfies both accuracy and efficiency. For this, we propose a novel parallel k-prototypes method for large mixed data with high efficiency and accuracy.

3   Background

This section first presents the k-prototypes method, then presents the MapReduce framework followed by the Spark framework.

3.1   K-Prototypes Method

Given a mixed dataset $X = \{x_1 \ldots x_n\}$ containing n data objects, described by m_r numeric attributes and m_t categorical attributes, the aim of k-prototypes [17] is to find k clusters by minimizing the following cost function:

$$J = \sum_{i=1}^{n} \sum_{j=1}^{k} u_{ij} d(x_i, c_j), \tag{1}$$

where $u_{ij} \in \{0,1\}$ is an element of the partition matrix U_{n*k} indicating the membership of data object i in cluster j, $c_j \in C = \{c_1 \ldots c_k\}$ is the center of the cluster j and $d(x_i, c_j)$ is the dissimilarity measure which is defined as follows:

$$d(x_i, c_j) = \sum_{r=1}^{m_r} \sqrt{(x_{ir} - c_{jr})^2} + \sum_{t=1}^{m_t} \delta(x_{it}, c_{jt}), \tag{2}$$

where x_{ir} represents the value of numeric attribute r and x_{it} represents the value of categorical attribute t for data object i. c_{jr} represents the mean of numeric attribute r, which is defined as follows:

$$c_{jr} = \frac{\sum_{i=1}^{|c_j|} x_{ir}}{|c_j|}, \tag{3}$$

where $|c_j|$ the number of data objects assigned to cluster j. c_{jt} represents the most common value (mode) for categorical attributes t and cluster j, which can be defined as follows:

$$c_{jt} = a_t^h, \tag{4}$$

where

$$f(a_t^h) \geq f(a_t^z), \quad \forall z, \quad 1 \leq z \leq m_c, \tag{5}$$

where $a_t^z \in \{a_t^1 \ldots a_t^{m_c}\}$ is the categorical value z and m_c is the number of categories of categorical attribute t. $f(a_t^z) = |\{x_{it} = a_t^z | p_{ij} = 1\}|$ is the frequency count of attribute value a_t^z. For categorical attributes, $\delta(p, q) = 0$ when $p = q$ and $\delta(p, q) = 1$ when $p \neq q$. The main algorithm of k-prototypes method is described by Algorithm 1.

Algorithm 1: The main algorithm of the k-prototypes method

Input: X: Data set, k: number of clusters
Output: Cluster centers
1. Select randomly k initial cluster centers from X.
2. Assign each data point in X to the closest center by computing distances using Eq. (2).
3. Update the cluster centers using Eqs. (3) and (4).
4. If the new cluster centers and the previous ones are the same, then terminate; otherwise, return to Step 2.

3.2   MapReduce Framework

MapReduce is a powerful parallel programming framework for processing large scale data which is characterized by its programming simplicity, fault tolerance and linear scalability [5]. MapReduce consists of two principle phases namely map and reduce. Each phase has $<Key, Value>$ pairs as input and output stored in an associated distributed file system. The map phase executes a map function to transform input $<Key, Value>$ pairs into intermediate $<Key', Value'>$ pairs. Then, the intermediate $<Key', Value'>$ pairs are executed using a reduce function to merge the produced list into a single $<Key'', Value''>$ pair. However, MapReduce suffers from a significant problem with iterative algorithms [27]. Hence, many of I/O operations occur during each iteration and this decelerates the running time. Several frameworks have been proposed for extending the MapReduce framework to support iterations such as Twister [6], Spark [32] and Phoenix [31]. Among these frameworks, Spark is the most powerful tool for data processing because of its distributed in-memory computational engine.

3.3 Spark Framework

Spark is a parallel framework for large scale data processing designed to solve the MapReduce limitations. It is introduced to run with Hadoop, specially by reading data from HDFS. Spark uses a special structure of data named Resilient Distributed Dataset (RDD) which presents a read only collection of objects partitioned across a cluster of machines that form the main core of Apache Spark and recoverable in case of loss in one of the partitions. Also, RDDs can be persisted, reused and cached in memory to decrease I/O disk operations. Besides, it provides two types of functions which can be performed in an RDD namely, transformations and actions. The transformations are used to apply a function to RDDs and return new RDDs. Map, ReduceBykey, MapPartition and Sample are examples of transformations. The actions, such as filter and count, are used to return a value or write the result of the computation in an external storage.

4 Parallel K-Prototypes Method with High Efficiency and Accuracy for Large Mixed Data (PKP)

This section first presents the proposed method, then an illustrative example followed by the complexity analysis.

4.1 Proposed Method

In order to build the grouping of large scale mixed data, we propose a novel accurate and efficient Parallel K-Prototypes method which we call PKP. The proposed method consists into two MapReduce jobs namely centers initialization and data clustering (shown in Fig. 1). The first MapReduce job is devoted to generating initial cluster centers from the input dataset using random sampling. The second MapReduce job is concerned with the clustering of the input dataset using k-prototypes.

Centers Initialization MapReduce Job: In the first MapReduce job, we pick up a fixed size data-sample from the input dataset using random sampling. To do so, this job first loads the input dataset from HDFS into an RDD object with m chunks by calling *textFile* function. Then, each chunk is processed in the map phase to produce an intermediate set of centers. Then, the reduce phase collects the intermediate centers and extracts the final cluster centers which will be used as initial centers in the data clustering MapReduce job.

Map Phase: During this phase, a *sample()* function is first used to generate a random sample of size α without replacement from each chunk. Then, the *mapPartitionToPair()* function is applied on each chunk to run the k-prototypes on the sample data to obtain k intermediate centers. Finally, each chunk emits its generated intermediate centers associated with its quality value in terms of Squared Error measure (SSE) as $<Key, Value>$ pairs to the reduce phase.

Reduce Phase: During this phase, the *ReduceByKey()* function is used to collect the set of $(k.m)$ intermediate centers and selects k centers having the minimal value of SSE since the least value can lead to good clustering quality results. Finally, the selected cluster centers are sent to the data clustering MapReduce job in order to build the grouping of the entire dataset.

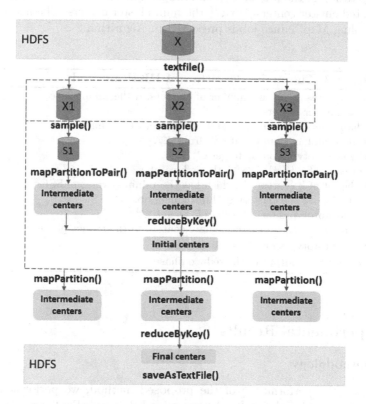

Fig. 1. Data flow of PKP method

Data Clustering MapReduce Job: Once the initial cluster centers are extracted from the previous job, the data clustering MapReduce job is performed to get the final cluster centers from the dataset.

Map Phase: During the map phase, a *mapPartition()* function is used to run the k-prototypes on each RDD in order to generate the intermediate cluster centers. Then, the intermediate cluster centers are emitted to a single reduce phase to generate the final centers.

Reduce Phase: Given the intermediate cluster centers, we consider each center as data object. Then, the reduce phase executes the k-prototypes on them and returns the final centers as the output. In our implementation, we use the

ReduceByKey() function. Finally, the cluster centers will be stored in HDFS using *saveAsTextFile()* function.

Let $X = \{X_1 \ldots X_m\}$ the input dataset where X_p is the portion of X associated to RDD p. Let $S = \{S_1 \ldots S_m\}$ the data-sample where S_p the data-sample extracted from X_p. Let C_p^1 and C_p^2 the set of k intermediate centers extracted from map task p in the first and second MapReduce job respectively. Let C^* the best selected cluster centers. Let C^f the final cluster centers. The main steps of data sampling MapReduce job is presented in Algorithm 2 .

Algorithm 2: The main algorithm of PKP method

Input: X: dataset, K: the number of clusters, α:the sample size
Output: Cluster centers

1 Load data from the input dataset X and generate m chunks.
2 Generate a random sample data S_p from X_p.
3 Run the k-prototypes on S_p to get C_p^1.
4 Emit m pairs of $<SSE, C_p^1>$ to the reduce phase.
5 Select the set of k centers C^* which has the minimal value of SSE.
6 Emit $<1, C^*>$ to the clustering MapReduce job.
7 Run the k-prototypes on X_p using C^* to get C_p^2.
8 Emit m pairs $<1, C_p^2>$ of intermediate centers to the reduce phase
9 Run the k-prototypes on all C_p^2 to get C^f .
10 Emit $<1, C^f>$ as output of the reduce phase.

---

5 Experimental Results

5.1 Methodology

To evaluate the performance of the proposed method, we performed experiments on both real and simulated large mixed datasets. First, we compare the performance of the proposed method versus the following existing methods: conventional k-prototypes (KP), forgy k-prototypes (F-KP), MapReduce-based k-prototypes (MR-KP) and Spark-based k-prototypes (S-KP). Then, we study the impact of sample size on the performance. Finally, we evaluate the Spark performance by analyzing the scalability of the proposed method.

5.2 Environment and Datasets

The experiments were performed on a cluster of 4 machines where each machine has 1-core 2.30 GHz CPU E5400 and 4 GB of memory. The experiments were executed using Apache Spark version 2.4.1, Apache Hadoop 2.6.0 and Windows 18.04. We conducted the experiments on the following real and simulated datasets.

- Simulated dataset (SD): Four mixed large datasets with ranging from 1 million to 4 million data objects. Each object is characterized by 5 numeric and 5 categorical attributes. A gaussian distribution is used to generate the numeric values where the mean is 350 and the sigma is 100. The categorical values are generated using the data generator developed in Institut Pasteur Project Plateform.[1] We refer the following notations SD1, SD2, SD3 and SD4 to denote a simulated dataset containing 1, 2, 3 and 4 million data objects respectively.
- Poker Hand dataset (Poker): is a real dataset used to detect hand situation in Poker hand playing in which 5 playing cards are picked up from a standard set of 52 cards. It is obtained from UCI machine learning repository.[2] Poker dataset contains 1 million observations where each observation is described by 5 numeric attributes and 5 categorical attributes.
- KDD Cup dataset (KDD): is a real dataset used to detect connection attacks simulated in a military network environment. It is obtained from UCI machine learning repository.[3] KDD dataset contained 5 million connections where each connection is described by 33 numeric and 3 categorical attributes (Table 1).

Table 1. Summary of datasets

Dataset	Number of objects	Attributes	Domain
SD1	1.000.000	5 numeric, 5 categorical	Simulated
SD2	2.000.000	5 numeric, 5 categorical	Simulated
SD3	3.000.000	5 numeric, 5 categorical	Simulated
SD4	4.000.000	5 numeric, 5 categorical	Simulated
Poker	1.000.000	5 numeric, 5 categorical	Gaming
KDD	5.000.000	33 numeric, 3 categorical	Intrusion detection

5.3   Evaluation Measures

To evaluate the quality of PKP, we use Sum of the Squared Error (SSE) [30], defined as given in Eq. (6). It is one of the widely-used partitional clustering measures that aims to evaluate the compactness of the obtained cluster centers by calculating the squared distance between each data object and the cluster center to which it belongs.

$$SSE = \sum_{i=1}^{n} \sum_{j=1}^{k} d(x_i, c_j) \tag{6}$$

---

[1] https://projets.pasteur.fr/projects/rap-r/wiki/Synthetic_Data_Generation.
[2] http://archive.ics.uci.edu/ml/datasets/Poker.
[3] https://archive.ics.uci.edu/ml/datasets/KDD+Cup+1999+Data.

where x_i is the data object, c_j represents the cluster center, n the number of data objects and k the number of clusters.

To assess the ability of parallel implementation to scale when we increase the number of machines and the dataset size, we use Speedup, Scaleup and Sizeup measures [24].

The Speedup measures the ability of the designed parallel method to scale well when the number of machines increases and the size of data is fixed. This measure is defined as follows:

$$Speedup = \frac{T_1}{T_m} \qquad (7)$$

where T_1 and T_m represent the execution time using a single machine and m machines respectively.

The Scaleup measure is used to evaluate the performance of the parallel method when increasing both the number of machines and the size of data. This measure is defined as follows:

$$Scaleup = \frac{T_s}{T_{m*s}} \qquad (8)$$

where T_s is the execution time when using a single machine to process data of size s and T_{m*s} is the execution time when using m number of machines for processing dataset of size s.

The Sizeup measures the ability of the designed parallel method to scale well when we increase the dataset size and the number of machines is fixed. This measure is defined as follows:

$$Sizeup = \frac{T_{s'}}{T_s} \qquad (9)$$

where $T_{s'}$ and T_s represent the execution time on a single machine of the dataset size s' and s respectively.

5.4   Comparison of PKP Performance Versus Existing Methods

We evaluate in this section the efficiency and accuracy of the proposed method on simulated and real datasets compared to existing methods. For each dataset, we tried three different cluster numbers 10, 50 and 100 and the sample size is set to 40% of the input dataset. We fixed the number of iterations to 20 for KP, F-KP, MR-KP and S-KP while for PKP we fixed it to 10 iterations for the centers initialization MapReduce job and 10 iterations for the data clustering MapReduce job. The obtained results are reported in Table 2.

Concerning the efficiency results, PKP is the best and S-KP is the next best as illustrated in Table 2. PKP outperformed S-KP and MR-KP by up to 2 and 10 times respectively. PKP and S-KP were much faster than MR-KP because of the advantage of in-memory computations of Spark framework when processing large scale data.

Concerning the accuracy results, PKP achieved the lowest SSE values as shown in Table 2. This is explained by the proposed initialization strategy that selects the best choice of initial centers from the input dataset. The results of PKP and S-KP improved as k increased since the number of clusters affects the clustering process.

Table 2. Comparison of PKP with existing methods on simulated and real datasets

Dataset	Method	k = 10		k = 50		k = 100	
		Time (s)	SSE (E7)	Time (s)	SSE (E7)	Time (s)	SSE (E7)
SD1	KP	41.34	263.79	87.83	55.27	150.17	35.77
	F-KP	52.49	273.75	139.37	52.07	254.32	36.95
	MR-KP	12.33	263.79	23.27	55.27	38.24	35.77
	S-KP	8.07	287.14	6.14	57.66	5.41	38.41
	PKP	**1.95**	**259.83**	**3.64**	**52.08**	**5.92**	**35.35**
SD2	KP	101.24	518.46	207.79	106.73	375.82	70.68
	F-KP	207.21	549.73	636.62	107.61	873.65	70.67
	MR-KP	24.47	518.46	59.70	106.73	93.11	70.68
	S-KP	5.62	520.35	6.43	107.12	8.83	70.69
	PKP	**3.27**	**517.76**	**4.67**	**103.03**	**6.91**	**69.93**
SD3	KP	351.13	791.33	471.08	159.08	543.28	107.84
	F-KP	520.95	791.69	878.06	160.83	532.23	108.24
	MR-KP	90.47	791.33	119.24	159.08	139.08	107.84
	S-KP	61.48	805.43	50.12	171.23	45.40	107.91
	PKP	**9.99**	**784.35**	**5.28**	**157.84**	**3.77**	**106.27**
SD4	KP	629.35	1035.30	968.89	1029.60	1154.69	986.21
	F-KP	995.12	1233.91	1254.23	1029.92	1547.3	1005.33
	MR-KP	163.69	1035.30	240.33	1029.60	287.33	986.21
	S-KP	40.70	1044.64	78.3	1029.90	94.6	997.81
	PKP	**16.31**	**1034.97**	**35.63**	**1028.53**	**40.61**	**980.20**
Poker	KP	38.04	1.00	61.56	0.62	120.51	0.43
	F-KP	69.01	1.01	103.43	0.84	139.36	0.44
	MR-KP	12.99	1.00	17.94	0.62	33.27	0.43
	S-KP	8.67	0.96	5.84	0.85	7.14	0.46
	PKP	**2.84**	**0.94**	**3.46**	**0.61**	**4.41**	**0.41**
KDD	KP	922.18	1040.66	1249.01	812.58	1669.42	787.81
	F-KP	1021.32	1146.86	1434.96	825.76	1933.01	804.25
	MR-KP	228.68	1040.66	311.14	812.58	419.87	787.81
	S-KP	57.94	1044.89	70.13	865.57	97.13	830.03
	PKP	**37.18**	**1040.32**	**41.36**	**807.57**	**68.22**	**730.53**

5.5 Evaluation of the Impact of the Sample Size on the Performance of EA-KP Method

Fig. 2 shows the impact of the sample size on the accuracy and efficiency results when k is set to 50. As shown in Fig. 2, for SD1, when the sample size is small (30%), the running time is increased by up to 50%, while the SSE value is reduced by up to 2%. The improvement of the efficiency was not beneficial because of the loss quality. On the other hand, when the sample size is large (70%), the SSE value is improved by as low as 1% while the running time is increased by up to 1%. The improvement of the accuracy was marginal, considering that the

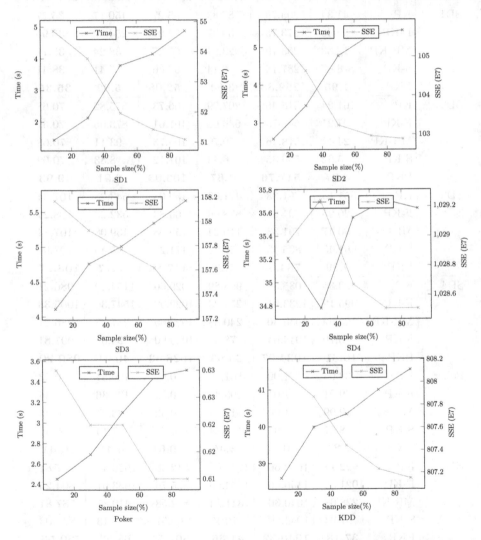

Fig. 2. Impact of sample size on the performance of EA-KP method for simulated and real datasets

added time was substantial. Overall, we can conclude that the best sample size provides a good trade-off between accuracy and efficiency.

5.6   Scalability Analysis

The speedup measure aims to maintain a constant dataset size and increase the number of machines from 1 to 4. The perfect parallel method demonstrates linear speedup: a system with m times the number of machines yields a speedup of m. Figure 3 illustrates the speedup results of SD1, SD2, SD3 and SD4 datasets and shows that when the size of the data set increases, the speedup of PKP becomes approximately linear, especially when the data set is large such as 3 million and 4 million data objects. Therefore, we can conclude that when the dataset size increases the speedup becomes nearly linear.

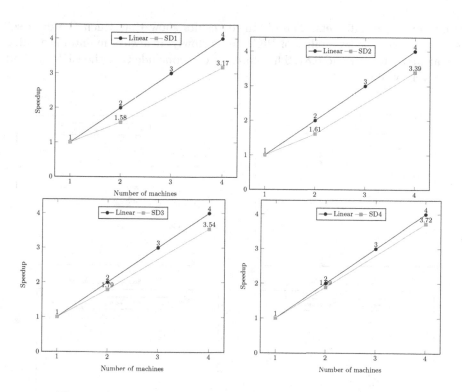

Fig. 3. The evaluation of speedup results on simulated datasets

The scaleup analysis evaluates the ability of the designed algorithm to maintain the same execution time when increasing the dataset size and the number of machines simultaneously. The perfect parallel method provides scaleup values very close or equal to 1. The datasets size of 1 million, 2 million and 4 million are processed on 1, 2 and 4 machines respectively. Figure 4 shows the scaleup

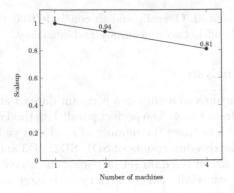

Fig. 4. The evaluation of scaleup results on simulated datasets

results on these data sets. The obtained results show that when the data set becomes larger the scalability of PKP drops slowly. It always maintains a value of scaleup between 1 and 0.81. Therefore, we can conclude that the PKP method scales very well.

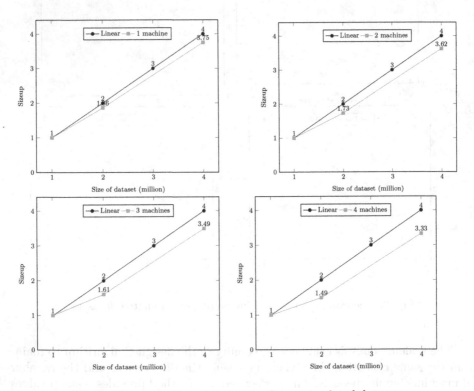

Fig. 5. The evaluation of sizeup results on simulated datasets

The sizeup analysis aims to evaluate the behavior of PKP by holding the number of machines and increasing the dataset size. To measure the performance of sizeup, we have fixed the number of machines to 1, 2, 3 and 4 respectively. Figure 5 shows the sizeup results on different machines. The obtained results show, when the number of machines is small such as 1 and 2 that the sizeup results are approximately the same. However, when we increase the number of machines, the value of sizeup on 3 or 4 machines decreases significantly compared to that of 1 or 2 machines on the same datasets. Therefore, we can conclude that PKP method has a very good sizeup performance.

6   Conclusion

In this work, we have proposed a new parallel k-prototypes clustering method with high efficiency and accuracy for large mixed data. The proposed method is designed to support both accuracy and efficiency by respectively integrating a parallel approach through Spark framework and implementing a new centers initialization strategy using sampling. Experiments on huge simulated and real datasets have shown the efficiency and accuracy of the proposed method compared to existing ones. In spite of the improvement offered by the proposed method PKP, some enhancement might be sought in future works. An exciting direction for future work is to analytically investigate the minimum sample size required to produce similar clustering results as the conventional k-prototypes method. Another promising work is to combine some automatic clustering methods such as Bayesian Information Criterion (BIC) for enabling PKP to detect the number of clusters automatically.

References

1. Ahmad, A., Dey, L.: A k-mean clustering algorithm for mixed numeric and categorical data. Data Knowl. Eng. **63**(2), 503–527 (2007)
2. Alkhayrat, M., Aljnidi, M., Aljoumaa, K.: A comparative dimensionality reduction study in telecom customer segmentation using deep learning and PCA. J. Big Data **7**(1), 9 (2020)
3. Ben HajKacem, M.A., Ben N'Cir, C.E., Essoussi, N.: Stimr k-means: an efficient clustering method for big data. Int. J. Pattern Recogn. Artif. Intell. **33**, 1950013 (2019)
4. Ben N'Cir, C.E., Essoussi, N.: Using sequences of words for non-disjoint grouping of documents. Int. J. Pattern Recogn. Artif. Intell. **29**(03), 1550013 (2015)
5. Dean, J., Ghemawat, S.: MapReduce: simplified data processing on large clusters. Commun. ACM **51**(1), 107–113 (2008)
6. Ekanayake, J., et al.: Twister: a runtime for iterative MapReduce. In: Proceedings of the 19th ACM International Symposium on High Performance Distributed Computing, pp. 810–818. ACM (2010)
7. Forgy, E.W.: Cluster analysis of multivariate data: efficiency versus interpretability of classifications. Biometrics **21**, 768–769 (1965)

8. Fraj, M., HajKacem, M.A.B., Essoussi, N.: A novel tweets clustering method using word embeddings. In: 2018 IEEE/ACS 15th International Conference on Computer Systems and Applications (AICCSA), pp. 1–7. IEEE (2018)

9. Fraj, M., Ben Hajkacem, M.A., Essoussi, N.: Ensemble method for multi-view text clustering. In: Nguyen, N.T., Chbeir, R., Exposito, E., Aniorté, P., Trawiński, B. (eds.) ICCCI 2019. LNCS (LNAI), vol. 11683, pp. 219–231. Springer, Cham (2019). https://doi.org/10.1007/978-3-030-28377-3_18

10. Gandomi, A., Haider, M.: Beyond the hype: Big Data concepts, methods, and analytics. Int. J. Inf. Manage. 35(2), 137–144 (2015)

11. Gmys, J., Mezmaz, M., Melab, N., Tuyttens, D.: A GPU-based branch-and-bound algorithm using integer-vector-matrix data structure. Parallel Comput. 59, 119–139 (2016)

12. Gorodetsky, V.: Big Data: opportunities, challenges and solutions. In: Ermolayev, V., Mayr, H., Nikitchenko, M., Spivakovsky, A., Zholtkevych, G. (eds.). CCIS, vol. 469, pp. 3–22Springer, Cham (2014). https://doi.org/10.1007/978-3-319-13206-8_1

13. HajKacem, M.A.B., N'Cir, C.E.B., Essoussi, N.: KP-S: a spark-based design of the k-prototypes clustering for big data. In: 2017 IEEE/ACS 14th International Conference on Computer Systems and Applications (AICCSA), pp. 557–563. IEEE (2017)

14. Ben HajKacem, M.A., Ben N'cir, C.-E., Essoussi, N.: Scalable random sampling k-prototypes using spark. In: Ordonez, C., Bellatreche, L. (eds.) DaWaK 2018. LNCS, vol. 11031, pp. 317–326. Springer, Cham (2018). https://doi.org/10.1007/978-3-319-98539-8_24

15. HajKacem, M.A.B., Nćir, C.E.B., Essoussi, N.: One-pass mapreduce-based clustering method for mixed large scale data. J. Intell. Inf. Syst. 52(3), 619–636 (2019)

16. HajKacem, M.A.B., N'cir, C.-E.B., Essoussi, N.: Overview of scalable partitional methods for Big Data clustering. In: Nasraoui, O., Ben N'cir, C.-E. (eds.) Clustering Methods for Big Data Analytics. USL, pp. 1–23. Springer, Cham (2019). https://doi.org/10.1007/978-3-319-97864-2_1

17. Huang, Z.: Extensions to the k-means algorithm for clustering large data sets with categorical values. Data Min. Knowl. Disc. 2(3), 283–304 (1998)

18. Jain, A.K.: Data clustering: 50 years beyond k-means. Pattern Recogn. Lett. 31(8), 651–666 (2010)

19. Ji, J., Bai, T., Zhou, C., Ma, C., Wang, Z.: An improved k-prototypes clustering algorithm for mixed numeric and categorical data. Neurocomputing 120, 590–596 (2013)

20. Ji, J., Pang, W., Zheng, Y., Wang, Z., Ma, Z., Zhang, L.: A novel cluster center initialization method for the k-prototypes algorithms using centrality and distance. Appl. Math. Inf. Sci. 9(6), 2933 (2015)

21. Kacem, M.A.B.H., N'cir, C.E.B., Essoussi, N.: Mapreduce-based k-prototypes clustering method for big data. In: 2015 IEEE International Conference on Data Scienceand Advanced Analytics (DSAA), pp. 1–7. IEEE (2015)

22. Kang, Q., Träff, J.L., Al-Bahrani, R., Agrawal, A., Choudhary, A.N., Liao, W.K.: Scalable algorithms for MPI intergroup allgather and allgatherv. Parallel Comput. 85, 220–230 (2019)

23. Li, C., Biswas, G.: Unsupervised learning with mixed numeric and nominal data. IEEE Trans. Knowl. Data Eng. 4, 673–690 (2002)

24. Luke, E.A.: Defining and measuring scalability. In: Proceedings of Scalable Parallel Libraries Conference, pp. 183–186. IEEE (1993)

25. Owens, J.D., Houston, M., Luebke, D., Green, S., Stone, J.E., Phillips, J.C.: GPU computing. Proc. IEEE 96, 879–899 (2008)

26. Shahrivari, S., Jalili, S.: Single-pass and linear-time k-means clustering based on mapreduce. Inf. Syst. **60**, 1–12 (2016)
27. Singh, D., Reddy, C.K.: A survey on platforms for big data analytics. J. Big Data **2**(1), 1–20 (2014). https://doi.org/10.1186/s40537-014-0008-6
28. Snir, M., Gropp, W., Otto, S., Huss-Lederman, S., Dongarra, J., Walker, D.: MPI-the Complete Reference: The MPI Core, vol. 1. MIT Press, Cambridge (1998)
29. Wang, X., Wang, X., Wilkes, D.M.: An efficient image segmentation algorithm for object recognition using spectral clustering. In: Machine Learning-Based Natural Scene Recognition for Mobile Robot Localization in An Unknown Environment, pp. 215–234. Springer, Singapore (2020). https://doi.org/10.1007/978-981-13-9217-7_11
30. Xu, R., Wunsch, D.C.: Clustering algorithms in biomedical research: a review. IEEE Rev. Biomed. Eng. **3**, 120–154 (2010)
31. Yoo, R.M., Romano, A., Kozyrakis, C.: Phoenix rebirth: scalable MapReduce on a large-scale shared-memory system. In: 2009 IEEE International Symposium on Workload Characterization (IISWC), pp. 198–207. IEEE (2009)
32. Zaharia, M., Chowdhury, M., Franklin, M.J., Shenker, S., Stoica, I.: Spark: cluster computing with working sets. HotCloud **10**(10), 95 (2010)
33. Zhao, W., Ma, H., He, Q.: Parallel *K*-means clustering based on MapReduce. In: Jaatun, M.G., Zhao, G., Rong, C. (eds.) CloudCom 2009. LNCS, vol. 5931, pp. 674–679. Springer, Heidelberg (2009). https://doi.org/10.1007/978-3-642-10665-1_71
34. Zheng, Z., Gong, M., Ma, J., Jiao, L., Wu, Q.: Unsupervised evolutionary clustering algorithm for mixed type data. In: IEEE Congress on Evolutionary Computation, pp. 1–8. IEEE (2010)

Self-Organizing Map for Multi-view Text Clustering

Maha Fraj[✉], Mohamed Aymen Ben Hajkacem, and Nadia Essoussi

Université de Tunis, Institut Supérieur de Gestion, LARODEC,
2000 Le Bardo, Tunisia
maha.fraj.m@gmail.com, medaymen.hajkacem@gmail.com,
nadia.essoussi@isg.rnu.tn

Abstract. Text document clustering represents a key task in machine learning, which partitions a specific documents' collection into clusters of related documents. To this end, a pre-processing step is carried to represent text in a structured form. However, text depicts several aspects, which a single representation cannot capture. Therefore, multi-view clustering present an efficient solution to exploit and integrate the information captured from different representations or views. However, the existing methods are limited to represent views using terms frequencies based representations which lead to losing valuable information and fails to capture the semantic aspect of text. To deal with these issues, we propose a new method for multi-view text clustering that exploits different representations of text. The proposed method explores the use of Self-Organizing Map to the problem of unsupervised clustering of texts by taking into account simultaneously several views, that are obtained from textual data. Experiments are performed to demonstrate the improvement of clustering results compared to the existing methods.

Keywords: Text clustering · Multi-view · Self-Organizing Map

1 Introduction

Text clustering aims to organize a collection of documents into several clusters, such that documents in the same cluster are as similar as possible, whereas those in different clusters are as dissimilar as possible [1]. This technique has been widely applied to many fields such as information retrieval [24], topic detection [2] and social networks analysis [20]. Several clustering methods were proposed in the literature [9,15] which can be categorized into hierarchical, partitional and neural network based. Among these categories, Self-Organizing Map (SOM) [10] is very popular unsupervised neural network for the analysis of high-dimensional patterns in machine learning applications [21]. SOM is designed to implement a nonlinear projection of high dimensional space onto a low-dimensional space called map. The nodes on the map correspond to clusters of the input samples and can be visualized. Compared to other text clustering methods, SOM allows visualizing the similarity between documents within the low-dimensional map.

© Springer Nature Switzerland AG 2020
M. Song et al. (Eds.): DaWaK 2020, LNCS 12393, pp. 396–408, 2020.
https://doi.org/10.1007/978-3-030-59065-9_30

On the other hands, text clustering mainly consists of two phases: the first pre-processing phase which formats the textual data into a structured form by using a representation model, while the second phase which consists in running a clustering algorithm to partition the data samples into distinct groups of documents related to the same topics. The pre-processing is a fundamental phase, in which the representation scheme helps identify the hidden pattern that might improve the clustering results. To this end, multiple text representation models have been proposed in the literature, such as the Vector Space Model [19], topic models [4] and more recently word embeddings [16]. However, in the absence of an optimal representation model for text, tackling such data becomes challenging for clustering algorithms. Moreover, text depicts multiple facets, that a single representation fails to capture. More precisely, the different facets of text usually correspond to different features spaces i.e. representations, each of which contains a piece of information that is not captured or explicitly represented by the other features. This issue is formally referred to as multi-view learning, such that each view corresponds to a feature space. So, multi-view text clustering refers to clustering textual data with multiple representations by integrating the information held in each view, in order to improve the clustering results. Several multi-view clustering methods were proposed in the literature [3,11,12,14,25]. For example, Bickel et al. [3] proposed multi-view versions of K-means and EM methods where the clustering algorithm is alternately applied on two conditionally independent views, and the results are bootstrapped. Hussain et al. [8] proposed a multi-view document clustering which applies individual clustering on each view, then aggregates different ensemble techniques: Cluster Based Similarity Matrix, Affinity Matrix and Pair-wise Dissimilarity Matrix to obtain a final consensus clustering. Although the existing methods have admittedly shown efficient performance over textual data sets, they only consider a single representation i.e. the terms frequencies, across natural splits of data. Moreover, multiples views certainly provides different perspectives for the same data, however the abundant amount of information raises the high dimensionality issue and integrating such information is challenging.

To deal with these issues, we propose in this paper a new multi-view text clustering method which exploits different text representation models to capture and integrate information from each view and maintain both syntactic and semantic aspects of text. Moreover, the proposed method uses the Self-Organizing Map to not only overcome the issue of high dimensionality by mapping the different views onto a low-dimensional space, but also to represent the intrinsic structure of the multi-view data by preserving the topology of each view.

The remainder of this paper is organized as follows: Sect. 2 reviews related work to subspace based methods for multi-view clustering. The proposed multi-view approach for text clustering is presented in Sect. 3. The experimental results are discussed in Sect. 4. Conclusions are given in Sect. 5.

2   Related Work

The multi-view subspace clustering methods first seek a common lower dimensional subspace that represents the intrinsic structure of the multi-view data then run and then applies a clustering algorithm to obtain the partitions. In [7] the subspace learning is formulated as a convex joint optimization problem. A low-rank linear projection is performed in [6] to uncover shared information and minimize the semantic gap across views. The proposed algorithm CoKmLDA in [28] first applies K-means on each view to obtain cluster assignments, the Linear Discriminant Analysis (LDA) is then used to project each view into a lower dimensional subspace. Using the clustering results from other views to impose a similar structure for all subspaces. The final cluster labels for all samples obtained from each subspace have to be consistent across all views. In [22], sparse subspace matrices are constructed from each view then a spectral clustering algorithm is performed. Other approaches were based on Non-negative Matrix Factorization (NMF). The idea is to find a common latent factor among multi-view data through low rank factor matrices. Liu et al. [14] proposed multiNMF which regularizes the coefficient matrices towards a common consensus. Recently, Nie et al. [17] introduced MLAN, a graph-based model that learns a local manifold structure and performs clustering simultaneously. [30] proposed a multi-manifold regularized NMF where the main contribution is to preserve the geometrical structure of the multi-view data through consensus manifold and consensus coefficient matrix. The approach in [26] adopted semi-NMF, a variant of NMF and followed a deep learning strategy. Newly approaches were proposed to tackle incomplete multi-viw data [23, 27].

3   Self-Organizing Map for Multi-view Text Clustering

The proposed multi-view method is based on different representation models of text. When documents are clustered based on the traditional Vector Space Model, and the tf-idf scheme in particular which only considers the occurrence of a word in a document, identifying semantically related documents becomes hard. Consequently, our method intends to enrich the pre-processing step by incorporating other representation schemes such that each representation corresponds to a view that captures a particular aspect of the text. Hence, each document will have three distinct vector representations. The views are then presented as parallel layers, and mapped onto a low-dimensional subspace using SOM architecture in order to uncover a latent structure. Finally, we run a clustering algorithm to obtain distinct documents clusters. The overall process is illustrated in Fig. 1.

3.1   Document Representation

Vector Space Model (VSM) is the most commonly used method for text representation [19]. The VSM is an algebraic model in which documents and terms

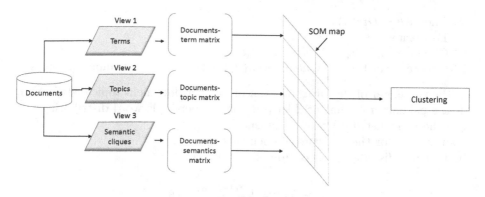

Fig. 1. SOM for multi-view text clustering

are represented as vectors in a multidimensional space and can be represented as a term-document matrix in which the values correspond to the Term Frequency-Inverse Document Frequency (tf-idf) weights [18]. *TF-IDF* is a weighting method that is used to score the importance of a word in a document based on the number of times it occurs in the document itself and in the entire collection of documents. The tf-idf weight is calculated through two values:

The *Term Frequency (TF)* measures how frequently a term appears in a document as follows:

$$tf_{(t,d)} = \frac{\text{Number of times term t appears in a document } d}{\text{Total number of terms in the document } d} \tag{1}$$

The *Inverse Document Frequency (IDF)* measures the relevance of a term in the whole collection of documents, terms that are rare overall in the data set are considered more important.

$$idf_{(t)} = \log(\frac{\text{Total number of documents}}{\text{number of documents containing term t}}) \tag{2}$$

The intuition behind the TF-IDF weighting measure is that the importance of a word should increase proportionally to the number of times that word appears in a document. Words such as "is", "the", "a" are very common in the English language and tend to appear more often than other words but they carry no meaning in them, therefore their values are offset by their idf weights.

As a result, the total tf-idf weight is calculated as follows:

$$tf - idf(t,d) = tf_{(t,d)} * idf_{(t)} \tag{3}$$

Latent Dirichlet Allocation Model (LDA). The Latent Dirichlet Allocation model (LDA) is a probabilistic model that identify the underlying topics in a corpus of documents [4]. LDA assumes that a document is represented by topic distributions, whereas a topic is provided by word distributions given by the following a probabilistic process:

    * Choose $\theta \sim Dir(\alpha)$
      For each word w:
    * Choose a topic $z_n \sim Multinomial(\theta)$
    * Choose a word $w_n \sim Multinomial(\beta_k)$, where k is the number of topics.

α is the parameter of the Dirichlet prior on the per-document topic distribution. β is the parameter of the Dirichlet prior on the per-topic word distribution. θ_m is the topic distribution of document d_m
z_v is the topic for the vth word of document d_m.
The Dirichlet distribution is computed as follows:

$$p(\theta|\alpha) = \frac{\Gamma(\sum_{i=1}^{k} \alpha_i)}{\prod_{i=1}^{k} \Gamma(\alpha_i)} \theta_1^{\alpha_1 - 1} \cdots \theta_k^{\alpha_k - 1} \tag{4}$$

The LDA model is used along with Gibbs sampling [5] to discover topics represented by a documents-topic matrix.

The Skip-gram model is a neural network that produces word embeddings, while retaining both semantic and syntactic information of words [16]. The vector representation is learned through the adjustment of the network weights, such that words that appear in the same context have similar vector representation. In order to obtain the vector representation for each document, a new feature space is built using the Skip-gram words representation. To this end, words are clustered by applying the K-means algorithm with the cosine distance. The obtained semantic cliques i.e. the clusters of words correspond to the new features from which a document-semantics matrix is built. The entries of this matrix are tf-idf weights of the semantic cliques, such that:

$$w_{ij} = \frac{tf_{ij} \times idf_i}{\sum_{t \in d_j} tf_{ij} \times idf_i} \tag{5}$$

where w_{ij} is the weight of the semantic clique S_i in the document d_j, tf_{ij} is the frequency of S_i in d_j that is the sum of the tf weights of terms t belonging to clique S_i and document d_j as expressed by (6), idf_i is the idf weighting of S_i which is the sum of the idf weights of words w in S_i (7). The denominator is for normalization.

$$tf_{ij} = \sum_{l=1} tf(t_l \in S_i, d_j), \, i \in \{1,..,K\}; \, j \in \{1,..,N\} \tag{6}$$

$$idf_i = \sum_{l=1} idf(t_l \in S_i) \quad i \in \{1,\cdots,K\} \tag{7}$$

3.2 SOM for Multi-view Clustering

After the generation of views in three different feature space, each document is represented by three vectors: traditional representation with tf-idf, topical vector with LDA, and vector based on semantic cliques with Skip-gram. These vectors constitute the inputs to the SOM neural network, such that each view is an input layer. We first recall the basic concepts of SOM, then we adapt the SOM architecture for multi-view document clustering.

3.2.1   Basic Concepts of SOM

Self-organizing map is an unsupervised neural network model also know as Kohonen network, that projects high dimensional input vectors of data onto a low-dimensional sapce [10]. The obtained feature space is a topological map that enables the partitioning of the input data into similar groups. Generally, SOM consists of two layers: the input layer contains the input vector as represented in their original space, and the output layer consists of the nodes of the map. Moreover, each node i.e. neuron on the map corresponds to a set of inputs. The learning algorithm of SOM is as follows:

1. *Initialization:* Start with random values for initial weights w_i
2. *Matching*: Determine the winning neuron c, at a time index t according to the smallest Euclidean distance

$$c = \arg \min_i ||x_j - w_i||, \ i = 1, 2, \cdots, M \tag{8}$$

   where x_j is an input vector, M is the number of neurons.
3. *Weights Updating*: Adjust the weights of the winning neuron and its neighbors, such that:

$$w_i(t + 1) = w_i(t) + \epsilon(t) \times h_{ci}(t) \times (x_j(t) - w_i(t)) \tag{9}$$

$$h_{ci} = \exp\left(-\frac{||r_c - ri||^2}{2\sigma^2(t)}\right) \tag{10}$$

   where $h_c i$ is the neighborhood kernel function, $\epsilon(t) \in [0, 1]$ is the learning rate and $\sigma(t)$ defines the width of the kernel, both value decrease monotonically at each time index, r_c and r_i are the position vectors of nodes c and i on the map.

3.2.2   Multi-view SOM

In order to adapt the SOM for multi-view clustering, the three obtained views are used as input layers instead of one single layer. To this end, each view is a separate layer that corresponds to a feature space: VSM, LDA, and Skip-gram, hence each document is represented with three numeric vectors x_1, x_2, and x_3. Each input layer correspond to an output layer consisting of a two-dimensional topological map as shown in Fig. 2. The weight vectors are randomly initialized and updated after computing the wining neuron. More precisely, for each corresponding input and output layers, distances between input vectors and weight vectors to find the best matching neuron i.e. the neuron defined by the smallest Euclidean distance. Lastly, in order to assign a document to a final output node, an overall distance is then calculated such that:

$$D = \sum_i D_i(x_i, n_i), \ i = 1, 2, 3 \tag{11}$$

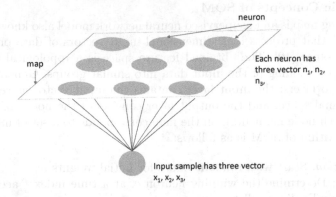

neuron

map

Each neuron has three vector $n_1, n_2, n_3,$

Input sample has three vector $x_1, x_2, x_3,$

Fig. 2. The mapping of a multi-view document

After the training step of SOM, the output map consists of clusters such that a cluster can correspond to one neuron or a set of neurons that belongs to the same class. Hence, the positions of the neurons in the map are important, neighboring neurons have similar vector representations and indicate a particular pattern of the data. Moreover, the topological map can be exploited to determine the properties of the data, such that similar documents are represented by neurons located in neighboring regions of the map. The training algorithm of this step is given in Algorithm 1.

Algorithm 1. Multi-view SOM

1: **input**: multi-view representations of documents
2: **output**: Topological map of clustered documents
3: For each view $i \in \{1, 2, 3\}$
4: Repeat
5: Initialize random weights w
6: Determine winning node using Eq8
7: Update weights of winning neuron and its neighbors using Eq9 and Eq10
8: until max iteration
9: End For
10: Calculate overall distance using Eq11
11: Assign document sample to the neuron with the smallest distance

---

3.2.3 Clustering

Although the SOM provides clusters of documents given by the neurons on the map, the number of output neurons is however more important than the desired number of clusters. A neuron on the map is associated to a single document or to a set of documents, thus a neuron on the map may represent a cluster, while other neurons are "empty" and have no documents assigned to them. Therefore, in order to have multiple neurons representing a cluster, a clustering algorithm is applied in a second level. The output neurons on the map are grouped into a number of distinct regions corresponding to the desired number of clusters. Consequently, each input document is assigned to a cluster according to their nearest output neuron. This process is illustrated in Fig. 3.

Given that neighboring neurons have similar vector representation and distant neurons on the map are considered unrelated, a distance matrix can be calculated and used for agglomerative hierarchical clustering.

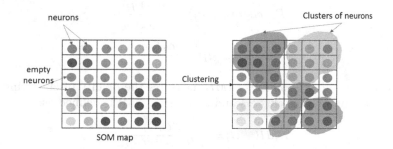

Fig. 3. Clustering of the SOM

4   Experimental Results

In order to evaluate the performance of the proposed method, we conduct several experiments on different data sets with regards to three evaluation measures. First, we carry out a comparison with the equivalent single view methods. Second, our method is evaluated against two existing methods for multi-view clustering.

4.1 Data Sets Description

Four well known data sets for text mining are used for experiments. The *Reuters R8* data sets is a subset of Reuters data set with 2189 documents belonging to 8 classes. The *20 Newsgroups* consists of 2828 news articles distributed on 20 classes. The *WebKB* data set is a collection of 4168 web pages collected from computer science departments, belonging to 4 classes (student, faculty, project, course). The *BBC Sport* consists of 737 documents from the BBC Sport website corresponding to sports news articles belonging to 5 areas: football, rugby, tennis, athletics and cricket. Before applying the clustering algorithms, a preprocessing step is performed on the data sets including stop words removal. Stop words removal consists in eliminating common words that appear frequently, and offer no additional semantic value.

4.2   Evaluation Measures

To measure the quality of the clustering and compare it with existing methods, three evaluation measures are utilized: the F-measure [13], the Normalized Mutual Information (NMI) [29], and Purity [17]. Given a set of clusters $C = \{c_1, c_2, \ldots, c_k\}$ and the gold standard classes $G = \{g_1, g_2, \ldots, g_j\}$:

   F-measure is a trade-off between *Precision* and *Recall* such that:

$$F - measure(c_k, g_j) = 2 * \frac{Precision(c_k, g_j) \times Recall(c_k, g_j)}{Precision(c_k, g_j) + Recall(c_k, g_j)} \tag{12}$$

$$Precision(c_k, g_j) = \frac{|c_k \cap g_j|}{|c_k|} \tag{13}$$

$$Recall(c_k, g_j) = \frac{|c_k \cap g_j|}{|g_j|} \tag{14}$$

Normalized Mutual Information (NMI) measures the quality of clustering with regards to the number of clusters and their sizes. NMI is defined as:

$$NMI(C, G) = \frac{I(C, G)}{[E(C) + E(G)]/2} \tag{15}$$

where I is the mutual information and $E(C)$ is entropy.

$$I(C, G) = \sum_k \sum_j \frac{|c_k \cap g_j|}{N} \log \frac{N|c_k \cap g_j|}{|c_k||g_j|} \tag{16}$$

$$E(C) = - \sum_k \frac{|s_k|}{N} \log \frac{|s_k|}{N} \tag{17}$$

Purity: measures the number of correctly assigned documents, where each cluster is assigned to the dominant class in that cluster. The larger the number of clusters is, the higher is the Purity. Unlike NMI, Purity cannot trade off the quality of the clustering against the number of clusters

$$Purity(C, G) = \frac{1}{N} \sum_k \max_j |c_k \cap g_j| \tag{18}$$

For all measures, the values range from 0 to 1, such that values closer to 0 represent poor quality.

4.3 Experimental Results

For the training, SOM requires predefining the size and structure of the network, the neighborhood function, and the learning rate. These parameters are generally selected experimentally.

For the first comparison, the proposed method is evaluated against the single view based clustering. Each view correspond to a single text representation model which are the VSM, the LDA model, and the Skip-gram model. We use classic SOM for all single view methods.

Given the results in Table 1, we notice that the best results were scored for the bbc sports data, with F-measure, NMI, Purity of 0.797, 0.658 and 0.734 respectively, this could be related to the size of the data set. The lowest results were scored for the 20 Newsgroupes, this data set contains the most number of classes. However, the LDA method socored the highest NMI and Purity for the Reuters Data with 0.485 and 0.642 respectively. Furthermore, the results show variation of performance of the single view based methods with regard to each data set. The Skip-gram model outperformed the other single view methods on three data sets: 20 Newsgroups, WebKB, and BBC Sports, while VSM gave better results than LDA on the BBC Sports. This shows that each view presents different data patterns.

Table 1. Comparison of clustering results with single view methods

		F-measure	NMI	Purity
Reuters	VSM	0.622	0.342	0.553
	LDA	0.688	**0.485**	**0.642**
	Skip-gram	0.642	0.456	0.562
	Proposed method	**0.709**	**0.464**	**0.606**
20 Newsgroup	VSM	0.217	0.161	0.184
	LDA	0.285	0.204	0.213
	Skip-gram	0.374	0.368	0.328
	Proposed method	**0.445**	**0.446**	**0.382**
webKB	VSM	0.438	0.120	0.390
	LDA	0.542	0.187	0.519
	Skip-gram	0.556	0.153	0.512
	Proposed method	**0.618**	**0.255**	**0.597**
BBC Sport	VSM	0.662	0.440	0.635
	LDA	0.580	0.329	0.554
	Skip-gram	0.777	0.655	0.730
	Proposed method	**0.797**	**0.658**	**0.734**

To further evaluate the proposed method, we compare it against two other multi-view clustering methods: the Multi-view K-means (MVKM) prposed in [3]

and the Multi-view via ensemble method (MVEM) in [8]. The results in Table 2 are averaged on 50 iterations for each method. The proposed approach outperformed the other two methods. The MVKM is based on the tf-idf representation and co-training of K-means, while the MVEM is based on ensemble techniques to aggregate individual clustering obtained from each view. The results shows that taking into account different representations and preserving the topology of each view can improve the clustering results in comparison to other multi-view clustering methods.

Table 2. Comparison of clustering results with multi-view methods

		F-measure	NMI	Purity
Reuters	MVEM	0.490	0.337	0.493
	MVKM	0.648	0.428	0.541
	Proposed method	**0.709**	**0.464**	**0.606**
20 Newsgroup	MVEM	0.380	0.305	0.300
	MVKM	0.431	0.380	0.373
	Proposed method	**0.445**	**0.446**	**0.382**
webKB	MVEM	0.542	0.268	0.448
	MVKM	0.564	0.321	0.460
	Proposed method	**0.618**	**0.255**	**0.597**
BBC Sport	MVEM	0.719	0.617	0.653
	MVKM	0.693	0.546	0.633
	Proposed method	**0.797**	**0.658**	**0.734**

5   Conclusion

In this paper, we have proposed a novel method for multi-view text clustering. Different from existing works, our method explores the use of three representation models i.e. VSM, LDA, Skip-gram to generate different views that respectively capture syntactic, topical, and semantic aspect of text. Moreover, we exploit the SOM to handle the issue of high dimensionality by mapping the different views onto a low-dimensional space. Furthermore, SOM helps maintain the topological properties of each view while uncovering the intrinsic structure of the multi-view data to improve the clustering results. The conducted experimentation shows that, in comparison to single view based clustering, using multiple views improves the clustering quality. The experiments also show that the proposed method yields better results compared to other multi-view clustering methods.

References

1. Aggarwal, C.C., Zhai, C.: Mining Text Data. Springer, Boston (2012). https://doi.org/10.1007/978-1-4614-3223-4
2. Allan, J.: Topic Detection and Tracking: Event-Based Information Organization, vol. 12. Springer, Boston (2012). https://doi.org/10.1007/978-1-4615-0933-2
3. Bickel, S., Scheffer, T.: Multi-view clustering. In: ICDM, vol. 4, pp. 19–26 (2004)
4. Blei, D.M., Ng, A.Y., Jordan, M.I.: Latent Dirichlet allocation. J. Mach. Learn. Res. **3**, 993–1022 (2003)
5. Bolstad, W.M.: Understanding Computational Bayesian Statistics, vol. 644. Wiley, Hoboken (2010)
6. Ding, Z., Fu, Y.: Low-rank common subspace for multi-view learning. In: 2014 IEEE International Conference on Data Mining, pp. 110–119. IEEE (2014)
7. Guo, Y.: Convex subspace representation learning from multi-view data. In: AAAI, vol. 1, p. 2 (2013)
8. Hussain, S.F., Mushtaq, M., Halim, Z.: Multi-view document clustering via ensemble method. J. Intell. Inf. Syst. **43**(1), 81–99 (2014). https://doi.org/10.1007/s10844-014-0307-6
9. Johnson, S.C.: Hierarchical clustering schemes. Psychometrika **32**(3), 241–254 (1967)
10. Kohonen, T.: The self-organizing map. Proc. IEEE **78**(9), 1464–1480 (1990)
11. Kumar, A., Daumé, H.: A co-training approach for multi-view spectral clustering. In: Proceedings of the 28th International Conference on Machine Learning (ICML 2011), pp. 393–400 (2011)
12. Kumar, V., Minz, S.: Multi-view ensemble learning: an optimal feature set partitioning for high-dimensional data classification. Knowl. Inf. Syst. **49**(1), 1–59 (2015). https://doi.org/10.1007/s10115-015-0875-y
13. Larsen, B., Aone, C.: Fast and effective text mining using linear-time document clustering. In: Proceedings of the Fifth ACM SIGKDD International Conference on Knowledge Discovery and Data Mining, pp. 16–22. Citeseer (1999)
14. Liu, J., Wang, C., Gao, J., Han, J.: Multi-view clustering via joint nonnegative matrix factorization. In: Proceedings of the 2013 SIAM International Conference on Data Mining, pp. 252–260. SIAM (2013)
15. MacQueen, J., et al.: Some methods for classification and analysis of multivariate observations. In: Proceedings of the Fifth Berkeley Symposium on Mathematical Statistics and Probability, Oakland, CA, USA, vol. 1, pp. 281–297 (1967)
16. Mikolov, T., Chen, K., Corrado, G., Dean, J.: Efficient estimation of word representations in vector space. arXiv preprint arXiv:1301.3781 (2013)
17. Nie, F., Cai, G., Li, X.: Multi-view clustering and semi-supervised classification with adaptive neighbours. In: AAAI, pp. 2408–2414 (2017)
18. Salton, G., Buckley, C.: Term-weighting approaches in automatic text retrieval. Inf. Process. Manag. **24**(5), 513–523 (1988)
19. Salton, G., Wong, A., Yang, C.S.: A vector space model for automatic indexing. Commun. ACM **18**(11), 613–620 (1975)
20. Serrat, O.: Social network analysis. In: Knowledge Solutions, pp. 39–43. Springer, Singapore (2017). https://doi.org/10.1007/978-981-10-0983-9_9
21. Shieh, S.L., Liao, I.E.: A new approach for data clustering and visualization using self-organizing maps. Expert Syst. Appl. **39**(15), 11924–11933 (2012)
22. Yin, Q., Wu, S., He, R., Wang, L.: Multi-view clustering via pairwise sparse subspace representation. Neurocomputing **156**, 12–21 (2015)

23. Yin, Q., Wu, S., Wang, L.: Unified subspace learning for incomplete and unlabeled multi-view data. Pattern Recogn. **67**, 313–327 (2017)
24. Zhai, C., Massung, S.: Text data management and analysis: a practical introduction to information retrieval and text mining. In: Association for Computing Machinery and Morgan & Claypool (2016)
25. Zhang, G.Y., Wang, C.D., Huang, D., Zheng, W.S., Zhou, Y.R.: Tw-co-k-means: two-level weighted collaborative k-means for multi-view clustering. Knowl.-Based Syst. **150**, 127–138 (2018)
26. Zhao, H., Ding, Z., Fu, Y.: Multi-view clustering via deep matrix factorization. In: AAAI, pp. 2921–2927 (2017)
27. Zhao, L., Chen, Z., Yang, Y., Wang, Z.J., Leung, V.C.: Incomplete multi-view clustering via deep semantic mapping. Neurocomputing **275**, 1053–1062 (2018)
28. Zhao, X., Evans, N., Dugelay, J.L.: A subspace co-training framework for multi-view clustering. Pattern Recogn. Lett. **41**, 73–82 (2014)
29. Zhuang, F., Karypis, G., Ning, X., He, Q., Shi, Z.: Multi-view learning via probabilistic latent semantic analysis. Inf. Sci. **199**, 20–30 (2012)
30. Zong, L., Zhang, X., Zhao, L., Yu, H., Zhao, Q.: Multi-view clustering via multi-manifold regularized non-negative matrix factorization. Neural Networks **88**, 74–89 (2017)

Author Index

Printed in the United States
By Bookmasters